D0206315

THE
Zionist
Ideology

GIDEON SHIMONI

BRANDEIS UNIVERSITY PRESS

Published by University Press of New England

Hanover and London

Brandeis University Press
Published by University Press of New England, Hanover, NH 03755
© 1995 by the Trustees of Brandeis University
All rights reserved
Printed in the United States of America   5 4 3 2 1

Published with the support of the Jacob and Libby
Goodman Institute for the Study of Zionism.

The photographs in this volume are reproduced with the
kind permission of the Central Zionist Archives, Jerusalem.

Library of Congress Cataloging-in-Publication Data

Shimoni, Gideon.
    The Zionist ideology / Gideon Shimoni.
        p.   cm.   —   (The Tauber Institute for the Study of European
Jewry series ; 21)
    Includes bibliographical references and index.
    ISBN 0–87451–703–6
    1. Zionism—History.   I. Title.   II. Series.
DS149.S497354 1995
320.5'4'095694—dc20
                                                                        94-35265

∞

The Tauber Institute for the Study of European Jewry Series

Jehuda Reinharz, General Editor

The Tauber Institute for the Study of European Jewry, established by a gift to Brandeis University from Dr. Laszlo N. Tauber, is dedicated to the memory of the victims of Nazi persecutions between 1933 and 1945. The Institute seeks to study the history and culture of European Jewry in the modern period. The Institute has a special interest in studying the causes, nature, and consequences of the European Jewish catastrophe within the contexts of modern European diplomatic, intellectual, political, and social history.

The Jacob and Libby Goodman Institute for the Study of Zionism was founded through a gift to Brandeis University by Mrs. Libby Goodman and is organized under the auspices of the Tauber Institute. The Goodman Institute seeks to promote an understanding of the historical and ideological development of the Zionist movement through an exploration of the seminal issues in the history of Zionism and the State of Israel.

for my father
MORDECHAI

and in memory of my mother
RACHEL

Contents

PART THREE Fundamental Issues

Illustrations follow page 166

Preface

The history of Zionism is far from being a virgin field of research and writing. A plethora of fine studies on diverse aspects of Zionist history has issued from the work of scholars since the establishment of Israel, mostly in Israel itself but also in the United States. To attempt here a listing of the contributors to the field to whom my own work is indebted would be a futile exercise as well as tedious for the reader. Specifically on the ideological aspects of Zionism, all scholars are indebted to the late Ben Halpern's profound study *The Idea of the Jewish State*, whose first edition was published in 1961, and also to Arthur Hertzberg's *The Zionist Idea*, first published in 1959. Hertzberg's discerning selection of source abstracts has enduring value for all who teach on the history of Zionism. Shlomo Avineri's elegant and perceptive *The Making of Modern Zionism* has likewise become a staple text. On these foundations, but incorporating the cumulative advances in research of recent years, the present study seeks to explain the origins of the Zionist ideology and to explicate, as comprehensively as is possible in a single volume, the variegation and development of that ideology from its beginnings until the establishment of the State of Israel.

My use of the term "ideology" as an action-oriented set of ideas is more precisely defined in this book's first chapter. In essence, I have set out to survey and analyze the articulated expressions of what Zionists said they believed. Of course, for historians, this cannot by any means be the whole story (if ever the "whole" story is possible). Are there not disparities between what the ideologists said and what they really believed, not to speak of contradictions between what they said they believed and actually did? Then there is the ultimate question— what is primary: the idea or the material reality? Does the ideology give rise to the praxis or is it merely a reflection of the praxis?

The present study does not pretend to answer such questions, except perhaps on certain particular points where the sheer weight of evidence at this stage of our knowledge is compelling. Taking account of the evolving historical context in which Zionist ideology was articulated, I have primarily sought to clarify the fundamental propositions and contentions that constituted its consensual common denominators and to delineate the contours of variance that generated the dynamics of dissensus in the Zionist movement.

To this end, a serviceable distinction that I have adopted (with acknowledgment to Martin Seliger) is that between the fundamental and the operative dimensions of ideology. The fundamental, as I employ the term, is the permanent propositions that inhere in the action-oriented system of ideas constituting an ideology and determine its final goals; the operative is the varying and fluctuating rationalizations or ideational reflections of strategy and tactics that serve the fundamental ideas. Although it is not always possible to separate these two dimensions, I have attempted throughout to highlight the fundamental more than the operative.

Two self-evident premises concerning the nature of the Zionist ideology underlie its treatment in this study. One is that, whatever else Zionism may have been, it also was a phenomenon belonging to the genre of nationalism. The other premise is that Zionism was of the "utopian" type (in the sense employed by Karl Mannheim), that is to say, an ideology that sought not to preserve and justify an existing reality but rather to change it and attain something envisioned but not yet existing. Accordingly, to facilitate comparative analysis of the variegated versions or subideologies of Zionism, I have sought to examine them analytically in three dimensions: diagnosis of a given problematic reality, vision of the desired transformed or new reality, and means advocated for attainment of that envisioned reality.

The book is divided into three parts. The first attempts to identify the social carriers of those ideas that came to constitute the Jewish national ideology in its Zionist form. After thus attempting to account for the social origins of the ideology, it then focuses more specifically on those ideas that possibly mark its beginnings. Part Two examines the inner process of variegation undergone by the Zionist ideology in its mature form. Within the context of the Zionist movement's history, it surveys the emergence and fundamental ideas of General Zionism, National-Religious Zionism, Labor Zionism in all its variety, and Revisionist Zionism. Part Three of the book then selects two fundamental themes that cut laterally across these horizontal divisions, raising crucial issues that remain unresolved to this very day. First are the implications of Zionist ideology for the secularized identity of modern Jews. The second is the critical ideological issue of right to the land that Jews traditionally call Eretz Israel. Here the focus is on the fundamental ideological dimension of the Zionist claim to national self-determination and self-fulfillment in the face of the contrary national claim of those now known as the Palestinians, an issue that goes to the root of the tragic conflict between Arab and Jew to this very day.

Being a study of articulated ideas and formulations, its sources are primarily the published writings of the major ideologues of Zionist history. These are available in overwhelming abundance, not only in a vast array of newspapers, periodicals, pamphlets, and autobiographies but more particularly in a plenitude of "collected writings of . . ." Indeed, a Zionist tradition appears to exist that obliges the followers or associates of almost every party or factional leader, from the top echelons down to secondary and tertiary ranks, if not lower, to issue volumes of such collected speeches and writings. There can be few nationalisms richer than Zionism in this genre of writing.

For access to these myriad sources I owe a great debt of gratitude to a number of libraries and archives. Above all, I wish to thank the Jewish National and University Library at the Hebrew University of Jerusalem. I have found it to be a prodigious treasure house for sources of the type that made this book possible. Its librarians rendered to me every service and assistance a researcher could wish for. In particular I wish to thank Mr. Shlomo Goldberg, head of the Circulation Department. I also wish to thank the director and workers of the Central Zionist Archives in Jerusalem. In this book's area of inquiry its holdings overlap considerably with those of the Jewish National and University Library. Whatever was not readily available in the one was invariably accessible in the other, and with the same helpful courtesy in both. My thanks are also due to the staff of the Jabotinsky Institute in Tel Aviv and the Rabbi Kook Institute in Jerusalem.

In transliterating from the Hebrew sources I have tried to provide the English reader with as plain a phonetic equivalent as possible without using complex diacritical marks or making some of the finer distinctions, such as those between *aleph* and *ayin* or *tav* and *tet*. A hyphen has been used to separate the article from the noun (e.g., *ha-irgun*). Although *kh* has been used for the Hebrew *khaf* to distinguish it from the guttural *het*, the letter *h* serves for both *het* and *heh*. Readers unfamiliar with Hebrew therefore should be aware that *h* should sometimes be pronounced as the English *h* and at other times as the *ch* in "loch" or in the German "ach." Names of persons and organizations have been transliterated according to the same principles except where a different usage is highly familiar—for instance, Borochov, Chaim Weizmann, and Zionei Zion. The synonomous place names Palestine, Eretz Israel, and Zion have been used interchangeably in accordance with the appropriate cultural-political context. The unique quality of the Hebrew term *Ha-aretz* (meaning Eretz Israel) has been indicated by "The Land."

Special appreciation is reserved for Professor Yitzhak Warszawski, who, some six years ago, while responsible for the "Zionist Library" of the World Zionist Organization, urged me to undertake this enterprise and found the funds that facilitated the initial stage of research. The interest and encouragement of Dr. Zalman Abramov likewise sustained me in this endeavor. At a later stage I benefited from a grant by the Hebrew University's Ben Eli (Honig) Fund, for which I am grateful. I wish to express my deep appreciation to a former student and present colleague, Jonathan Kaplan, who not only rendered me valuable research assistance in the early stages of this project but guided and sustained me through all the tribulations of a novice thrust into the confusing but now indispensable world of the personal computer. I also wish to thank David Mendelsson, another former student who assisted me at some stages of my preparation of the manuscript.

Thanks are due, too, to Jehuda Reinharz of Brandeis University, who encouraged me and waited patiently for the manuscript, to Sylvia Fuks Fried of that university's Tauber Institute, and to the editors at the University Press of New England for seeing to the publication of this book with proficiency and care. I am grateful to the University of Washington's Jewish Studies Program for inviting me to be the Stroum Visiting Professor in 1993–1994. I could not have wished for a more friendly and warm environment in which to put the finishing touches to this work.

A number of academic colleagues gave me the benefit of their expertise and comments after reading various parts and drafts of the manuscript. They are, at the Hebrew University, Shmuel Almog, Jonathan Frankel, Yosef Heller, Israel Kolatt, and Michael Silber; Anthony D. Smith of the University of London in the London School of Economics; Yosef Gorny of Tel Aviv University; Arye Fishman of Bar Ilan University; Yosef Salmon of Ben-Gurion University of the Negev; and David Shaari of Jerusalem. Their comments helped me to avoid many errors. I am deeply grateful for their collegial assistance. Of course, they bear no responsibility for the errors and faults that doubtless remain.

But my deepest gratitude of all goes out to my wife, Toni, who was in many ways my partner in the writing of this book.

Jerusalem, 1994   *G.S.*

PART ONE

Origins of the Zionist Ideology

CHAPTER ONE

Social Origins of Jewish Nationalism

I N T H E H I S T O R Y of the Jews the phenomenon of Zionism and the
establishment of the State of Israel to which it gave rise are truly
epoch-making. Few, if any, historians would disagree with this statement.
Not only has Zionism radically transformed the political status, the socioeconomic profile, and the psychological self-image of the Jews, but in myriad ways
it has influenced the life of every community, religious movement, and
organization in contemporary Jewish life.

Now that the State of Israel exists and its gates are open to any Jew who needs
or wishes to enter, has Zionism fulfilled its purpose? Addressing this question is
not the prerogative solely of historians. Contemporary and future generations of
Jews, both in Israel and in the Jewish Diaspora, will determine the answer. It is
the historian, however, who is best equipped to elucidate what the intentions of
the Zionists were in the first place. This is a composite task that requires the
unraveling of many layers of thought, activity, and interaction. The present
study focuses on one such layer—the ideology of Zionism; ideology in the sense
of a coherent, action-oriented set of ideas that provides those who subscribe to
it with a comprehensive cognitive map of their position and purposes.[1] In
simpler terms, this is an inquiry into the ideas formulated and articulated by
those who led or otherwise influenced the adherents of the Zionist movement.

Dispersed over many different countries and exposed to diverse social and
political environments, the formulators of these ideas were impelled to seek a
variety of ideological syntheses. Kaleidoscopic combinations, which included
strains of liberalism and authoritarianism, socialism and religious faith, created
a rich and highly variegated spectrum of versions or subideologies of Zionism.
The present inquiry will attempt a survey of these composite formulations. First,
however, it will explore their origins. It will seek to identify the class or type of
person whose ideas germinated and developed into the Zionist ideology in its
mature form. In the ensuing chapters some of the personalities whose thought
will engage our attention—Theodor Herzl, David Ben-Gurion, and Vladimir
(Ze'ev) Jabotinsky, for example—were political leaders of note; others—for

example, Asher Ginzberg (Ahad Ha'am), Aharon David Gordon, and Martin Buber—played minor roles in the political and organizational fields but expounded ideological formulations that influenced the movement or gave expression to profound issues that inhered in Zionism and endure unto this very day. Two such issues call for particular scrutiny: the ideological implications of Zionism for secularized Jewish identity and the ideological justification of Jewish right to national self-determination in Palestine.

Ethnicity and Nationalism

A distinguishing mark of the ideas constituting the Zionist ideology is the proposition that the Jews are, actually or potentially, a nation. Accordingly, in consonance with the assumptions of the broader genus of ideology known as nationalism, the various formulations of Zionist ideology analyze the condition of the Jews, attempt to identify its defects, and postulate a solution.

Of course, attempts to define the terms "nation" and "nationalism" are legion, and it is highly doubtful if specialists in this thorny field can ever reach full agreement. These difficulties led Hugh Seton-Watson to say: "I am driven to the conclusion that no 'scientific definition' of a nation can be devised; yet the phenomenon has existed and exists. All that I can find to say is that a nation exists when a significant number of people in a community consider themselves to form a nation, or behave as if they formed one."[2] However, for the present purpose of indicating some propositions, which are widely agreed to be constitutive of nationalist ideologies and have a direct bearing on Zionist ideology, it will suffice to mention two.

First, as a "state of mind," nationalist ideology ascribes to the collectivity called a nation a high place in the hierarchy of the individual's values. Identification with the nation is regarded as essential for his freedom, well-being, and self-realization. It follows that in a nationalist state of mind the attributes of ethnicity become highly ranked values. Consciousness of common origin is the core attribute, and it is usually compounded by a combination of other commonalities, such as language, religion, and territory.[3]

Second, as a political phenomenon, nationalist ideology aspires to self-determination for the putative nation, and under optimal conditions this requires the nation to be coextensive with the state. As Ernest Gellner concisely states: "Nationalism is primarily a political principle which holds that the political and national unit should be congruent."[4]

In the interest of conceptual clarity I would contend that it is advisable to identify the first proposition, where it stands on its own, with "ethnicism." Although "nationalism" proper subsumes such "ethnicism," it goes beyond it insofar as it involves also the second proposition. "Cultural nationalism" may further be distinguished from unqualified "nationalism" by virtue of its noninsistence upon congruence of the ethnic unit with a *territorial* political entity of its own. The usage to be adopted here therefore distinguishes between (1) ethnicity: the mere presence of ethnic attributes, such as consciousness of common origin (whether mythic or actual), common language, religion, and territory (or at least association with a territory); (2) ethnicism: the conversion of such attributes of ethnicity into highly ranked values (whereas ethnicity may be other-defined, ethnicism must be self-defined; it is a state of mind of positively valued self-awareness); and (3) nationalism: ethnicism transformed by the principle that the ethnic unit, generally now called "the nation," and the polity should be congruent, a principle the full satisfaction of which requires political independence within the ethnic unit's own territory. Where the nationalist aspiration is limited to forms of autonomy for the ethnic unit not necessarily requiring territorial-ethnic congruence, the appropriate term is "cultural nationalism." One must, of course, allow for cases where an evolved or imposed territorial polity creates the conditions for coalescence of more than one ethnic entity as a "nation."

Notwithstanding the conformance of Zionist ideology to nationalist doctrine in general, there is a tendency to emphasize the uniqueness of Zionism, mainly because, on the eve of the era of emergent nationalisms, the Jews did not inhabit a territory of their own but were dispersed among many other nations and states. Therefore, whereas nationalism generally involved a struggle for liberation from foreign rule or for territorial secession from a larger political unit, the Jewish case required a return to a former territorial homeland. Another characteristic often regarded as unique was the lack of a single vernacular language. Although Hebrew never ceased being the main language of "high" Jewish culture, which meant mainly rabbinical discourse, by the eighteenth century the vernacular used by Jews was divided between Yiddish, Ladino, and the languages of a variety of countries in which Jews were domiciled.[5]

However, this apparent uniqueness results from an overly narrow typological perspective on nationalisms. The more sophisticated and comprehensive the typology of nationalisms one applies, the less unique Zionism appears to be. Thus, Hugh Seton-Watson identified the Jews as one of a number of "diaspora nations" that developed a nationalism of their own. This category includes the overseas Indians and Chinese, who formed large new national communities in lands outside their original continental homelands, and the Greeks and Armenians, Lebanese and Volga Tartars, who, each in a somewhat different manner, formed diasporas numerically more or less balanced with the populations of their original homelands.[6] The more ramified typology suggested by Anthony D. Smith places Zionism in a similar company of nationalisms, those of the Armenians, the Greeks, the overseas Indians and Chinese, and the African-American nationalism associated with Marcus Garvey. In Smith's comprehensive typology these constitute a pre-independence, ethnic diaspora type; that is to say, a type that emerges out of a preexistent diasporic *ethnie*—the French word for ethnic community or cultural unit, which Smith prefers to use and defines as "a named human population possessing a myth of common descent, common historical memories, elements of shared culture, an association with a particular territory, and a sense of solidarity."[7]

Within such a comparative typological context, the distinctiveness of Zionism is evident, but there is little that is unique. Parallels may readily be found for almost all of the apparently unique features of Zionism. These range from the important roles played by the sacral myth of being chosen for a special destiny and the drive to return to the ancient homeland, to the complex, contradiction-riddled interaction between religious and secular motifs and the resort to historicist invocation (and sometimes invention) of a usable past. Above all, the Armenian case bears the greatest similarity to that of the Jews, although a significant difference is worthy of note: the Armenians always retained a territorial homeland of compact Armenian population, and a far smaller proportion of the Armenians were in diaspora.[8]

Recognition that Zionism is unique only in the sense that each and every nationalism is unique, although also sharing fundamental commonalities that can be typologically compared, opens up the way to understanding the origins of Zionism within the context of a more general theory that accounts for the origin of nationalism. In this regard, there is wide (although not universal) agreement among the specialists that nationalisms—and by the same token, nationalist ideologies—are properly identifiable only from the latter part of the eighteenth century onward.[9] This contradicts the way nationalist ideologists invariably depict their own nationalism, as an immanent force inhering from time immemorial in their nation, only waiting to be awakened and launched toward fulfillment of its destiny.

Most theories that attempt to account for the birth of nationalism regard it as a product of the transformation from predominantly rural and agricultural, traditionalist European society to modern urban and industrial society—this complex transformation is what is generally connoted by the term "modernization"—but they differ over identification of the crucial factors involved. Marxist interpretations, of course, emphasize changes in the means of production and regard nationalist ideology as no more than a reflection of the class interests of the capitalists. Other theories shift the emphasis to cultural factors. Ernest Gellner's is an important example of such a theory.[10] He argues that nationalism is "the result of the distinctive structural requirements of industrial society," a society whose productive system is based on cumulative science and technology and requires mobile, "viable and usable human beings." This calls for universal literacy in a homogenized culture; a standardized, unifying linguistic medium; and an all-embracing educational system that can provide both generic and specific training. Hence, the structural logic and dynamic of growth-oriented industrial society makes it necessary and unavoidable for state and culture to become congruous. This underlying reality produces nationalist ideology, which provides the necessary societal transformation with justification and rationale. In performing this function, it uses elements of preexisting group identity to cultivate the population's consciousness of being a nation; and if such elements are lacking, it sometimes simply "invents" the nation.

In contrast with Gellner's theory, Elie Kedourie has argued that nationalism is by no means a necessary consequence of industrial society.[11] Nationalist ideology is an artificial invention of a segment of the intelligentsia, initially in European society and thereafter all over the world. The ideologists of nationalism create and mold the nation, rather than vice versa; it is they who insist on imposing homogeneity and the idea of being a nation upon a pliable population. (The implication of Kedourie's interpretation is that it would be well for societies to do without the influence of the nationalist ideologists, whereas it follows from Gellner's approach that society really has no choice in the matter.)

Benedict Anderson has added an evocative dimension to this subject, one that may be applied in refinement of both Gellner's and Kedourie's theories. He argues that "nation-ness, as well as nationalism, are cultural artifacts of a particular kind"; the nation is "an imagined political community." In accord with Gellner he holds that the capacity to "imagine" the nation "was the spontaneous distillation of a complex 'crossing' of discrete historical forces" (those elucidated by Gellner, it may be argued, even though Anderson places particular emphasis upon the new mode of communication created by "print-capitalism"). Compatibly with Kedourie, Anderson further contends that, once created, the capacity to imagine being a nation "became 'modular,' capable of being transplanted, with varying degrees of self-consciousness, to a great variety of social terrains."[12]

Whatever may be the analytical merits of theories that emphasize the causal role of "modernization" as the generator of nationalisms, they have limited explanatory value for the Jewish case. This limitation results from the diasporic and subordinate-minority situation of the Jews prior to and during the era of rising nationalisms, a situation that distanced the Jewish collectivity from the primary circumstances that generated the nationalisms of Europe. What the theories we have mentioned above render explicable in regard to the Jews is the disintegration of their autonomy as a corporative community living according to its own laws and cultural norms, the granting to them of civic rights, and their propulsion toward acculturation and assimilation with the majority. Where these theories of nationalism fall short of explanatory adequacy is precisely in regard to the genesis of a Jewish nationalism that was the very antithesis of the trends they explain. Zionism aspired to a level of collective

Jewish autonomy higher even than had existed before the era of nationalisms and advocated a reversal of the thrust toward assimilation.

This is not to say that modernist theories are devoid of contributions to the explanation of Zionism's genesis. Gellner recognizes the Jewish case as what he calls a diaspora nationalism, "a distinctive, very conspicuous and important sub-species of nationalism."[13] But Gellner's theory places inordinate emphasis on the pressure exerted upon the Jewish minority by the modernizing state's "interest in depriving the minority of its economic monopolies." He argues that the former interest in protecting the minority—all the better to exploit it—is displaced by the modernizing state's need to propel the majority population "in the direction which was once open only to a minority and stigmatized group." The state also buys off discontent in the wider population by dispossessing and persecuting the minority. Consequently, the alternative that faces the minority is either to assimilate or to "endeavour to shed both its specialization and its minority status, and create a state of its own." Of course, in the case of the Jews, being a diaspora nationalism, this requires the acquisition of a territory, and, states Gellner, "the most famous and dramatic case of a successful diaspora nationalism is Israel."

Although there is some validity in this explanation, it is one-dimensional. It takes account only of the reactive aspect in the genesis of Zionism, reaction to economic displacement and social hostility (antisemitism). As the historical record to be traced in this chapter will show, an explanation must also take account of continuities in the collective ethnic consciousness and solidarity of the Jews, within each state and across the boundaries of states. While assimilation was still progressing most promisingly, and also quite independently of antisemitism when it later arose, not only religious traditionalists but also part of the Jewish intelligentsia decried the humiliating self-negation that assimilation exacted and rose to the defense of Jewish cultural distinctiveness. As will be shown, the genesis of Jewish nationalism is traceable to their ethnically self-affirming sentiments and views, which antedated the appearance of anti-semitism as a major factor. Even if we grant the European states' differential treatment and displacement of the Jews, we know that the most obvious option taken up was emigration to the New World. Gellner's approach fails to explain adequately why a segment nevertheless chose a Jewish national solution and why only the Land of Israel proved sufficiently motivating for a sustained national movement.

In this respect, Kedourie's approach, which rejects the premise that industrial society necessarily requires cultural homogenization, may be more adequate for the explanation of Zionism. The causal significance it attributes to the ideological inventiveness of the intelligentsia and the scope it implicitly leaves for the role of irrational but powerful myths, nurtured by the ethnoreligious collectivity, offer possibilities of coping with some of the questions left unanswered by more deterministic theories of nationalism. Yet Kedourie too is overly one-dimensional. He leaves us with little other than the element of mimesis, the imitation by Jewish intelligentsia of the artificially created nationalist ideologies prevalent in Europe.

An instructive example of the nonapplicability of important elements in the explanatory framework provided by Gellner is the revival of the Hebrew language. The linguistic transformation attendant upon the development of most European nationalisms involved the displacement of the universal language of high culture (Latin) by the various vernacular languages of low culture, a process propelled by the development of print technology. But the case of Hebrew patently fails to conform to that model, for it was Hebrew that had perennially remained the language of the rabbinical and literary "high" culture of Jewry everywhere. It was the language of a variegated literature and was used for communal records, letters and contracts throughout the period of dispersion. On the other hand, hybrid vernaculars, notably Yiddish (and also Ladino, Judeo-Arabic, and Kurdish Aramaic, among others), had become the "low" cultural vernacular of Jews except where Jewish language had been almost totally displaced by the vernaculars of the surrounding gentile population.

In the case of Zionism, therefore, it was the "high" language, revived and modernized, that replaced the "low" language of Jewish discourse used for all communicative purposes, not the converse. Moreover, the causal relationship appears to have been the converse of that indicated by those theories that identify modernized linguistic transformation as a cause of nationalist ideology. As we shall show, the Hebrew revival began as a concomitant of those elements in the *haskala*, or Jewish Enlightenment movement of the late eighteenth and nineteenth centuries, that reflected the perseverance of Jewish ethnic consciousness, notwithstanding their being part of the *haskala*'s general orientation toward full participation in the modernizing state and integration with the majority culture. This happened initially in central Europe and with greater and more lasting momentum in eastern Europe. However, the *haskala* writers in eastern Europe did not yet suggest speaking Hebrew as a language of ordinary communication. In the final analysis, it was the full-blooded Zionist national ideology, exemplified above all by Eliezer Ben-Yehuda, that revitalized and transformed Hebrew from "high" sacral language to modern vernacular, and it did so with great tenacity and by swimming against the stream. In sum, at least insofar as the Jewish case is concerned, it was ethnic consciousness leading to increasingly self-affirming nationalist ideology that generated literary transformation, rather than the converse.[14]

The Jewish case is so patently one in which a preexisting ethnic identity was of paramount importance that only an account of the genesis of nationalism that recognizes the great significance of preexisting ethnic ties holds promise for the explanation of Zionism's emergence. Such an approach has been cogently advanced by Anthony D. Smith. Although cognizant of the importance of modernization, Smith argues forcefully that it is no more than "a catalyst and amplifier of existing forces." He does not find that it has the weight and causal power attributed to it by Gellner.[15]

Smith describes his own standpoint as one intermediate to that of "modernist" theories, like those of Gellner and Anderson, and "perennialist" theories that emphasize the primordial attributes underlying ethnic-national identity and therefore claim that nations are perennial units of the human historical experience and hence not exclusively the creation of modernity.[16] Smith argues for the near-ubiquity in every historical period, not of nations but of ethnic collectivities (for which, as we have already noted, he prefers to use the French term *ethnie*).[17] He takes full cognizance of the impersonal forces of modernization in facilitating or propelling the transformation of such *ethnie* into nations but equally attaches significance to the ethnic heritages that precede modernization and persist alongside it. He thus seeks to understand the rise of contemporary nations in the context of their ethnic background and formulates a typology that takes account of "ethnic nationalisms" as a major type.

According to Smith, "[e]thnic nationalisms start from a pre-existent homogeneous entity, a recognizable cultural unit." Their initial concern, therefore, is to ensure the survival of the group's cultural identity. That generally entails ensuring the political survival of the group, which in turn leads to the aspiration to create a state as a means to those ends. The emergence of such ethnic nationalisms is located in the broad process of transformation from what Smith terms "possessive polity" to "scientific state," a process starting in the scientific states of western Europe, notably England and France, and continuing with endeavors at emulation by the imperial frameworks of central-eastern Europe. The "possessive" polity is one in which the population is the personal possession of its rulers, as, for example, in Tudor England or Bourbon France. The scientific state seeks to homogenize the population within its boundaries, linguistically and otherwise. It is "a powerful solvent of the traditional order," which erodes the authority of traditional religion, works for the privatization of religion, and "challenges the cosmic image of the religious *Weltanschauung*."[18] Yet, given the ethnic heterogeneity encompassed by the original imperial frameworks of Europe and the fact that homogenization of the population is a process that takes time and has to overcome difficulties, there remain "sociological minorities" possessed of a distinctive culture within the larger political unit.

According to Smith's account, the emergence of nationalist ideology within such "sociological minorities," of which the Jews are a case in point, may be located within this context and, more specifically, within the processes affecting their intelligentsias. Intelligentsia is defined broadly to include, but not to be equated with, "intellectuals." It is not a class in the usual sense since it derives from members of various social classes. Rather, it is a stratum of persons "who apply and disseminate ideas, not only create and analyze them." Thus, "their differentiating characteristic is exposure to higher education in some form," and "they usually aspire to professional positions in society or to public affairs"; typically, they are journalists, lawyers, academics, teachers, and doctors.[19] Smith contends—in accord on this point with both Gellner and Kedourie—that the intelligentsia is the most relevant group in exploring the emergence of nationalism, although not necessarily in its subsequent diffusion. The nationalist ideology of minorities like the Jews is born of the problematic situation of the intelligentsia as an elite socialized in, and in some sense alienated from a double frame of reference—the traditional religion, on the one hand, and the modernizing state on the other.

Smith identifies three broad options or currents of response to the dilemma of this intelligentsia. The first is "assimilationist," characterized as "the aspiration to merge into a common humanity." The second is "traditionalist" (elsewhere he calls this "neo-traditionalist"), which means a retreat into religious traditionalism. The third, and the most formative for nationalism, is what Smith terms "reformist." Since both the ethnic-religious tradition and the modern, culturally homogenizing state are compelling frames of reference for the reformist, he searches for a serviceable synthesis between tradition and modernity. This leads to religious reform and reinterpretation based on some putative "essence" of the tradition, which some reformists—the more secularized ones—come to identify with the "national spirit" of the ethnic community rather than with the religion. They tend to become what Smith calls "revivalist reformists" who seek to slough off those elements of the ethnic community's religious tradition that are considered archaic or unworthy and who call for a thorough cultural revival in accord with modernity.[20]

In this way, the dilemma of the reformist section of the intelligentsia points in the direction of a potentially nationalist solution. However, this solution does not necessarily materialize until the reformists are joined by the assimilationist section of the intelligentsia, which is generally better equipped to take the lead in a national movement. This happens if and when the assimilationists become disillusioned with their messianic-like faith in a common humanity. But, Smith emphasizes, it is not the disappointed assimilationist so much as the searching reformist who is the principal generator of nationalism. Smith sums up with the following proposition: "Nationalism is born among the intelligentsia, when the 'messianic' assimilationists try to realize their former vision by adopting the ethnicity solution of the defensive reforming 'revivalists.'" This fusion produces "the ideological spark of the nationalist movement."[21]

Jewish Ethnicity and Modernity

That the Jews were a clearly defined social unit with distinctive ethnic and religious attributes (answering par excellence to the description of what Smith calls an *ethnie*) for many hundreds of years before the era of nationalisms set in is a truism that does not call for elaboration here.[22] It is the impact of modernity, mediated by the culturally homogenizing state that we must consider if we are to explain the genesis of the particular ethnic nationalism that came to be known as Zionism. More particularly germane are the evolving ideological orientations of a stratum of Jewish intelligentsia produced by modernity.

The most fundamental and far-reaching effect upon the Jewish *ethnie* exerted by the modernizing process of state formation in Europe was its extension— however erratically, ambivalently, and controversially—of the civic rights of citizenship to the Jews. This was, above all, a function of the logic inhering in the modernizing state as interpreted by authorities who were in some degree influenced by liberal ideas stemming from the European Enlightenment. (Those who upheld clericalist and reactionary ideas usually put up a fight against Jewish emancipation.) There were sporadic overtures in this direction in the second half of the eighteenth century, notably the double-edged legislation of Austro-Hungarian emperor Joseph II of the 1780s, which interfered with Jewish customs in order to enforce greater integration.[23] Also, access of Jews to citizenship rights became implicit in the Constitution of the United States of America of 1789. But the turning point toward emancipation for the Jews was the grant of equal citizenship to the Jewish subjects of revolutionary France by the National Assembly in 1791. In its wake, notwithstanding heated public controversy and many reverses, the legal or civic emancipation of the Jews in all the states of western and central Europe was virtually completed by the 1870s.

The Jewish ethnic-religious collectivity, or *ethnie*, as a whole was certainly weakened by the processes of civic emancipation, intellectual "enlightenment" (the term used to describe the absorption of spheres of knowledge mostly associated with university education), and integration, however incomplete and defective, into the social structures of the various states of Europe. As a rule, the effect was not only a dismantling of the largely autonomous, corporative frameworks in which Jewry had carried on its life for centuries but also interference with the former unity of the Jewish *ethnie*. Within two or three generations at the most, a new type emerged—the French or German or Italian Jew, each possessed of a different composite of identity and each divided from the other as never before by state boundaries, geographical, linguistic, and to some extent also nationalist-ideological. The communal institutions of each Jewish community also underwent a metamorphosis. Since the civic status of the individual Jew now placed him in a direct relationship with the state, rather than in one mediated by a corporative Jewish community, communal institutions became increasingly voluntaristic and decreasingly comprehensive in their compass of the Jewish population in each country.

Notwithstanding these effects of the modernizing European states, it is widely agreed by historians that all of this by no means meant the demise of the diasporic Jewish ethnic-religious collectivity; rather, it amounted in sum only to a transformation of that collectivity, its singularity abiding with hardly less salience than in former times. Tracing the lines of transformation, its continuities and discontinuities, and explaining the phenomenon as a whole is a mammoth task of enormous complexity.[24] Here, we may no more than indicate some of the profounder factors involved. One constellation of such factors has to do with the atavistic tenacity of negative cultural stereotypes rooted in European Christian culture's inveterate legacy of Jew hatred. Deeply ingrained prejudices, so far from disappearing under conditions of civic emancipation, were exacerbated by these conditions.[25] Indeed, the transmutations of traditionalist Christian Jew hatred—first, into a secularized hostility generated within the European Enlightenment and thereafter into racist antisemitism—were, by the mid-twentieth century, to prove infinitely more catastrophic for the Jews than anything previously experienced in their millennial history of persecution.

Another factor of note was the failure of Jews to undergo the occupational diversification generally expected by the advocates of Jewish emancipation. Even though the opening of prospects for economic mobility was energetically taken up by Jews, and with prodigious success, it followed lines no less singular than the Jewish occupations of the past and, indeed, more conducive to hostility. Thus, in Germany the upward occupational mobility of Jews tended to take place selectively only in those sectors of the economy structurally linked to their previous occupations. Moneylenders and peddlers became financial and commercial entrepreneurs, and tailors moved into textile manufacture, but Jews did not enter into agriculture or heavy industry. In a secondary stage of development the offspring of middle-class Jews became inordinately salient in certain professions such as medicine and law. In sum, their upward mobility merely resulted in new forms of occupational concentration and self-segregation. Fed by the cultural heritage of Jew hatred, many a Gentile perceived the prodigiously successful upward economic mobility of the Jews as a presumptuous provocation.[26]

Inveterate cultural-religious continuities and traits of the Jews, in dynamic interaction with the Jews' treatment by the social environment, form the converse side of the explanation for the durability of the Jewish ethnoreligious collectivity. Even in Germany, where the acculturation and integration of the Jews proceeded apace in the course of the nineteenth century, they soon came to constitute a rather distinct subculture.[27] Among the factors contributing to this phenomenon of transformation without dissolution of pronounced ethnic distinctiveness, mention must be made of the perennial migrations of Jews resulting from the uneven progress of the emancipatory process in the various states of Europe, as well as from variations in economic conditions. This continual movement of Jews from areas of still prevalent traditionalism in the east of Europe (*Ostjuden*) to Germany and the West reinforced the latter's residual traditionalist Jewish elements and raised the level of ethnic consciousness. Correspondingly, it exacerbated the hostility toward Jews harbored by elements in the majority society.

A primary concomitant of this fundamental transformation was the increasing exposure of Jews to the homogenizing educational influences—linguistic, cultural, and intellectual—of the evolving states in which Jews were now citizens. This stimulated an inner Jewish intellectual effervescence that came to be known as the *haskala* (*Aufklärung* in German, Enlightenment in English). Emanating mainly from Berlin at the turn of the eighteenth century, the *haskala* was a Jewish mode of the European intellectual trend known as the Enlightenment of the seventeenth and eighteenth centuries, which elevated the criteria of universal human reason above those transmitted by traditionalist religion as arbiters of true knowledge and morality. The main ideological underpinning of the Jewish version of Enlightenment, seminally formulated by Moses Mendelssohn (1729–1786), was the claim that Judaism was inherently and eminently compatible with those new criteria of reason. *Haskala* assumed a variety of operative forms, the common basis of which was acquisition of such Enlightenment-induced knowledge (another, rather less accurate description would be "secular knowledge") and its application to the Jewish cultural heritage. Access to such knowledge was dependent upon literary facility in European languages (preeminently German in the eighteenth and nineteenth centuries) and was acquired through exposure to university education or autodidactically, generally mediated by social contact with gentile intelligentsia. The common denominator of the program of action advocated by *maskilim* (votaries of the *haskala*) was dissemination among fellow Jews of such forms of knowledge, which required prior acquisition of the linguistic prerequisites. One pioneering step in this direction was Moses Mendelssohn's translation of the Bible into German, accomplished in the early 1780s. The *maskilim* called, first and foremost, for reform of the education to which Jews were exposed within their own community and encouragement of further acquisition of education outside it. Beyond this basic desideratum of change, the *maskilim* advanced, with various emphases and intensity, a program of reforms. These included advocacy of occupational diversification for Jews; changes in Jewish life-styles, such as dress and manners; and, most significantly, reforms in Jewish liturgy and rituals—all aimed at greater compatibility with the modernizing social norms of the state.

As noted earlier, the defining characteristics associated with the term "intelligentsia" include exposure to higher education and engagement in the formulation or dissemination of intellectual ideas and in public affairs. Hence, it should be evident that, at least with reference to the early stages of the transformation of Jewry, the terms "*maskilim*" and "intelligentsia" are virtually coterminous. This small but widening stratum of Jewish intelligentsia was marked by varying degrees of detachment from Jewish religious traditionalism. It was expressed in a wide spectrum of ideological orientations, ranging from the polarity of cosmopolitan alienation from all Jewish religious traditionalism, through reformist formulations of the religious tradition, and on to the other polarity of neotraditional reformulations. The term "neoorthodoxy" properly describes the latter, whereas "orthodoxy" is most properly reserved for the rigid and self-isolating type of traditionalism that crystallized in defensive reaction to modernity in the course of the nineteenth century.[28]

Undoubtedly, the main thrust, common to the entire ideological spectrum, was toward integration into the societal structures of the majority—economic, cultural, political, and also nationalist. Only the religious structures of the host society were excluded as magnets for integration, except for those Jews who opted for conversion.[29] This involved a concerted effort to efface any residual attributes of Judaism that could be considered national and therefore inconsonant with the spirit of Clermont-Tonnerre's famous dictum in the French National Assembly: "To the Jews as individuals—everything; to the Jews as a nation—nothing." Such ideological orientation toward integration into the societal tissue of the state found its most profound expression in the emergence of a reformed Judaism, primarily in Germany, Hungary, and the United States.

The overall impact of the *haskala* and of the incipient Jewish intelligentsia, who were its social bearers, upon the Jews as an *ethnie* was an ambiguous complex in which intentions and effects were not entirely congruous. Its effects were at one and the same time disintegrative and integrative, self-dissolving and self-restoring. *Haskala* served in some ways as a conduit for diffusion of Enlightenment-induced knowledge and attitudes, the better to facilitate Jewish assimilation, and in other ways as a vehicle for modernizing the Jewish collectivity in order to rehabilitate and foster it. Already in the early stage of the Berlin *haskala* at the turn of the eighteenth and nineteenth centuries, this ambiguity was evident in the distinction roughly discernible between the German-medium *maskilim*, most of whom reconceptualized Judaism purely as a religion and were bent on eradication of any and every national residue, and by contrast the Hebrew-medium *maskilim*, most (but not all) of whom evinced a comprehensive sense of Jewish solidarity and a principled affirmation of ethnic particularities such as the Hebrew language, the preservation of the memory of the ancient temple, and the upholding of the Jewish messianic vision of the future. The latter belief had a distinctly ethnicist core since it involved the end of exile and the restoration of the Jews to the Land of Israel at least as preliminary to the universal end of time. But most *maskilim* followed Moses Mendels-sohn in treating this belief as a remote ultimate vision serving a purely liturgical purpose and having no bearing whatsoever upon the absolute loyalty of Jews to the state.[30] Although in the research literature on the *haskala* these particularities are sometimes labeled "national," this is an anachronistic usage, even if excusable as a convenience.[31] The terms "ethnicity" and "ethnicism," as we have defined them, are more adequate, although they too are no more than retrospective analytical constructs.

Whether intentionally or not, the use of the Hebrew language for the larger part of the Berlin *haskala*'s literary output, notably in the periodical *Ha-me'assef,* released it from its purely traditional rabbinical confines and set it on a path of revival as a serviceable secular literary medium. Willy-nilly, this had an ethnically self-affirming effect even though, it should be noted, the distance between that and Hebrew as a spoken vernacular was still vast. Also double-edged in effect were the *haskala*'s emphasis upon the biblical past and its initiation of the enterprise of reconstructing the history and cultural heritage of the Jews, which flowered in the Verein für Cultur und Wissenschaft der Juden (the Society for the Culture and Science of the Jews, founded by a group of *maskil* scholars in 1819), as well as its aspiration to heal the Jews of their anomalous socioeconomic characteristics. While proposing such self-respecting measures of modernization, the sights of the *maskilim* remained set upon facilitating integration within the majority society. However, the advantage of historical hindsight enables us to perceive that these innovations provided some of the prerequisites for notions of national revival when they began to be voiced sporadically in the course of the nineteenth century. The most notable of these prerequisites were the literary revival of Hebrew, the romantic evocation of interest in the Bible, and the active advocacy of socioeconomic productivization.

What can be said of the *haskala*'s ambiguous impact upon the cohesion of the Jews as an *ethnie* applied also to the development of a reformed Judaism. Initially, religious reforms were introduced mainly by laymen in a number of congregations in the states of Germany and limited to changes calculated to foster decorum in Jewish ritual, such as introduction of German into the liturgy as well as for the sermon and also use of instrumental music. But by the 1830s a new generation of reformers, who combined *haskala* with rabbinical training, was beginning to displace Hebrew and eliminate prayers and beliefs that smacked of "national" notions, such as those expressing longings for Zion and belief that messianic redemption from exile would bring about return to an independent existence in Zion. To be sure, messianic redemption itself was retained as a central concept, but it was converted into a universal vision mirroring the ideals of the Enlightenment.

In 1845, at a conference of rabbis in Frankfurt—the second of its kind—seeking a consensus on principles of reform, Rabbi Zacharias Frankel (1801–1875), a major

Wissenschaft scholar, who later (in 1854) became head of the Jüdisch-Theologisches Seminar at Breslau, objected vigorously to these tendencies on the basis of "positive historical" principles. These principles may be said to have expressed the integrative impulses immanent in the *haskala*. They were rooted in a conception of Judaism not as abstract ethical monotheism nor as commanding law but rather as organically evolving historical experience. According to this view, authentic, intrinsic elements of that experience, such as the Hebrew language and the relationship to Zion, were inviolable.

As the guideline for legitimate reform and its limits in Judaism, Frankel invoked a talmudic principle (tractate Avoda Zara, 3b) that "that which was adopted by the entire community of Israel and was accepted by the people and became part of its life could not be changed by any authority."[32] Frankel recognized that developmental changes had always taken place in Judaism and should continue, but he argued that they must emanate from the people: "the will of the entire community must decide"; it must not be treated as "mere clay to be molded by the will of theologians and scholars." Scholars might apply critical historical inquiry into Judaism to seek out authentic patterns and pointers to change but they must enjoy the popular confidence of the community of Israel, which remained the ultimate arbiter of reform.

The assumptions of Frankel's "positive historical Judaism" were probably influenced by contemporary intellectual currents of romanticism that counter-balanced the Enlightenment's elevation of abstract reason with their emphasis on sentiment and on organic, historically evolved attachments. In particular, the displacement of the theory of natural law by the historical school of jurisprudence developed by Friedrich K. von Savigny (1779–1861) appears to have influenced the "positive historical" approach of Frankel.[33] The *historische Rechtschule*, to which Savigny belonged, viewed the law in historical perspective as the expression of the *Volksgeist*, or evolving organic essence of the people's life.

The problems of determining the exact nature of the spirit or essence of a people and its collective will need not concern us here. It is the manifestation of a romantic-historical affirmation of ethnic attributes such as the Hebrew language and the relationship to Zion that is germane to our survey of the paradoxical impact of intellectual modernization upon the Jewish *ethnie*. In this context, sight must not be lost of the fact that Frankel and his associates of the positive-historical school of thought were part and parcel of the predominant ideological thrust of the *haskala* toward integration into the social and national life of the state (or at any rate of the bourgeois class of that state). To label Frankel and his associates Jewish nationalists would be to empty the term of real meaning. Their intention was to advance the emancipation and integration of the Jews, and they differed from other reformers only on the question of what was the proper synthesis between the Jewish ethnoreligious tradition and the norms of the modernizing state, which *maskilim* viewed through the prism of their primary frame of reference—the German bourgeoisie. If the pitfalls of anachronism are to be avoided, the most that can be said is that their approach had the effect of containing the ethnically disintegrative function of the *haskala* and of attendant religious reforms and thereby may be analytically recognized as a factor of Jewish ethnic reinforcement in the nineteenth century.

The historiography and historical reflection of Heinrich Graetz was a kindred manifestation of the same factor.[34] Born into a traditionalist Jewish family in Posen, under German rule, he began to acquire secular learning autodidactically and for a time came under the influence of Rabbi Samson Raphael Hirsch, the leading figure of neoorthodoxy (i.e., that strain of orthodoxy that welcomed emancipation and accepted exposure to Enlightenment learning yet remained strictly observant and opposed to reform). However, he eventually associated himself closely with the positive-historical Judaism of Zacharias Frankel, who asked Graetz to join the faculty of the Jewish Theological Seminary in Breslau in 1854. It was there that he produced most of his monumental history of the Jews, which appeared in eleven volumes from 1853 to 1876 and was in due course translated into a number of languages.

One may perhaps best gain an appreciation of Graetz's significance for the ethnic consciousness of the nineteenth-century Jewish intelligentsia by considering what historical awareness and image of the Jewish entity it was apt to create in the mind of the reader. It was, above all, an image of continuous vitality, quite the opposite of petrification following supersession by universal Christianity as was the conventional wisdom of gentile learning. In this respect, it should be noted that Graetz was in accord with the intellectual defense of and apologia for Judaism conducted even by religious reformers like Abraham Geiger (1810–1874). However, unlike the latter, Graetz's history depicted Judaism not merely as a religion or community of faith. It demonstrated an intrinsic national-political dimension of Judaism "rooted in the firm soil of national life" that contrasted with the character of Christianity as a religion of personal salvation. Furthermore, Judaism was always future-oriented, looking forward, through all vicissitudes, to an ultimate redemption that was connected particularistically with the Land of Israel as well as universally with all of mankind.

In Graetz's writings one may find such statements as "The Torah, the nation of Israel and the Holy Land stand, one might say, in a mystical relationship to each other; they are inseparably united by an invisible bond."[35] Graetz also wrote the following:

The history of the post-Talmudic era, therefore, still possesses a national character [*einen nationalen Character*]. It is by no means the mere history of a religion or of a church. Its object is not simply the course of development of a doctrine, but also that of an independent people, which, though it possesses no soil, fatherland, geographical boundaries, or state organism, replaced these concrete conditions with spiritual powers. Though scattered over the civilized portions of the earth and attached to the land of their hosts, the members of the Jewish race did not cease to feel themselves a single people in their religious conviction, historical memory, customs and hopes. As the history of an ethnic group [*eines Volksstammes*], therefore, Jewish history is far removed from being a mere history of literature or of scholars which it is branded by those given to ignorance and partiality.[36]

In a blend of empirical research, bearing marks of Leopold Ranke's influence, with an underlying Hegelian philosophy of history, Graetz's reconstruction of the Jewish past conveys the dialectical evolution of the dual essence or idea of Judaism—its God-idea and its national-political idea. In Graetz's interpretation, the God-idea expressed itself in Jewish history not as an abstraction of ethical monotheism but in standards of morality characterizing the Jews—family morality, mutual responsibility, social justice and charity. It is a story of the constantly fluctuating fusion and separation of the elements of religion and polity in Judaism inspired throughout by the survival-conducive belief in their final synthesis through the ultimate redemption in Zion. Unlike the extreme reformists he did not convert the force majeure of dispersion into a virtue, *galut* (exile) into the very mission of the Jews. An ultimate synthesis or unity of the God-idea and the national-political idea by a restored Jewish independence in Zion was not discounted.

Hence, Graetz could welcome the first unmistakably nationalist exposition of secular character by a Jew, calling for return to Jewish independence in Zion—Moses Hess's *Rome and Jerusalem*—when it appeared in 1862. But in the context of our present discussion, it is highly instructive that, in welcoming Hess's exposition, Graetz was very much the exception amid the contemporary Jewish intelligentsia, most of whom either ignored or ridiculed Hess. Although Graetz's historiography was fast becoming the most widely diffused work of its kind, only by indirect inference was it compatible with Hess's explicit nationalism. Its perceived overt implications were part and parcel of the ideological affirmation of emancipation and integration prevalent in the Jewish intelligentsia. To the question of whether Hess's exposition was already a full expression of the Zionist form of Jewish nationalism we shall need to return later. As for Graetz's intellectual enterprise, in sum one cannot say more than that it was an intellectual reinforcement of the ethnic cement that continued to bind Jewish identity. It was an expression of ethnicism, not yet Jewish nationalism.

The positive-historical school was an intellectual trend occupying a place within the central arena of Jewish communal life. On the sidelines of that arena there was another ethnically affirmative phenomenon among Jews for whom Jewish observances and precepts had ceased to be normatively binding and who had moved away from communal frameworks or in some cases had been born on the periphery, sometimes the offspring of mixed marriages or apostate parents.

Joseph Salvador (1796–1873), born in Montpellier in the south of France, is a striking illustration of this phenomenon.[37] A descendant of Marranos on his father's side, with a Catholic mother, and growing up in the period following Jewish emancipation in France, he was able to acquire a secular education that included the university and qualification as a medical doctor. Salvador therefore had hardly any Jewish background and by the strict letter of the Jewish legal code (the *halakha*), was not even a Jew. Yet he identified himself as a Jew. In a work published in 1860, he explained that his motivation to study the ancient history of the Jews was first stimulated in 1819, while he was still a medical student, when he was shocked at hearing that anti-Jewish riots had broken out in Germany, this in the new age of liberty and tolerance.

The massive enterprise of research and writing into which Salvador was drawn was animated throughout by a drive to reveal not only the greatness of Jewish antiquity but also proudly to stake out its claim into the future. The intellectual context in which Salvador functioned was different from but in many respects parallel to that of the Jewish Enlightenment in Germany and its offshoots in the Wissenschaft des Judentums, as well as in the religious reformers' transmutation of traditionalist messianic beliefs into a universal mission of dispersion. Like them, Salvador found the essence of Judaism in the biblical rather than the postbiblical period, and like Mendelssohn himself, Salvador found greater congruity between the Mosaic faith and the Enlightenment's rational principles than between the latter and Christianity. However, his intellectual enterprise ran at a tangent from that of the *haskala*. He functioned as one already assimilated into the intellectual milieu of liberal and enlightened but still deeply Christian religious thought. Sharing in this milieu's conviction that religion had yet to fulfill its indispensable role for the social and moral betterment of mankind, the gravamen of Salvador's message was that Judaism, so far from being superseded and displaced, still had a unique and critically important destiny.

With tendentious hindsight some early historians of Zionism, notably Nahum Sokolow, fancied that in Salvador they had discovered one of the earliest Jewish nationalists—indeed a precursor of Zionism. In a manner reminiscent of their microscopic scanning of Benedict de Spinoza's thought, much was made of some isolated statements relating positively to the question of whether the "ancient republic of the Hebrews" might not one day be reestablished. "Why not?" Salvador had answered; there was no reason that the Christian nations should not one day recognize the important contribution Judaism still was destined to make for the benefit of all mankind and declare: "Children of Israel, whom we have oppressed and slandered for so long, we offer you with joy the corner of the earth inhabited by your ancestors."[38]

To nominate Joseph Salvador as a proto-Zionist or even as a Jewish nationalist in a general sense is, however, to misinterpret the very essence of his stance. His messianic conception was wholly compatible, by his lights, with emancipated Jewry continuing as a religion in Diaspora. The ultimate stage of messianic consummation—which he held to be very imminent, not deferred beyond the horizons of history—was to be universal and in effect de-Judaized. Jerusalem was to be restored not for particularist Jewish national independence but, much as the Christian Jansenists thought, as the new Rome, center of a new universal religion, a fusion based on the pristine Mosaic essence underlying both Judaism and Christianity. Salvador epitomized an emancipated intellectual reaffirmation of self-esteem and pride in Judaism, carried on the wings of an apologetic denial that the Jews' values and destiny had been wholly superseded by those of Christianity. His importance in the context of our examination of the impact of modernity upon Jewish ethnic cohesion is as an illustration of an occasional boomerang effect: reappropriation of a sense of ethnic pride and solidarity by Jews already emancipated and integrated but never wholly so.

This was not a commonplace phenomenon; only a few extraordinary individuals exemplified it in the mid-nineteenth century. Perhaps the most idiosyncratic of all was Benjamin Disraeli, who, although baptized in childhood, was at pains to glorify the Jewish heritage by his own inimitable lights. Ferdinand Lassalle as a young man, before he became a famous Socialist leader in Germany, also evinced a similar, fleeting, romantic tendency. The most significant example of all (and one that in some ways paralleled that of Salvador) was Moses Hess, to whose ideas we shall return in the next chapter, when we consider certain proto-Zionist manifestations of the mid-nineteenth century. As we shall see, however, the most salient of these manifestations emanated less from the secularized intelligentsia than from some innovative religious traditionalists, most notably Rabbis Yehuda Alkalai and Zvi Hirsch Kalischer.

While taking note of these ethnicist tendencies in Europe during the heyday of emancipation, it is important to maintain a balanced perspective. They formed the middle ground between the inertia of traditionalism and the thrust of the Enlightenment intelligentsia, whether secularized, devotees of reformed religion, or neoorthodox. That dominant thrust was best represented by the response of Rabbi Adolf Jellinek (1821–1893), the chief rabbi in Vienna in 1882, when Leo Pinsker exposed to him his fully fledged nationalist proposals for "autoemancipation" through return to a Jewish territorial home. Jellinek rejected them out of hand. He told Pinsker that his views were shortsighted and that he exaggerated the importance of antisemitism. "We feel at home in Europe," he said, "and we consider ourselves Germans, French, English, Magyars, Italians, to the marrow of our bones. . . . We have lost the sense of Hebrew nationality."[39]

The Modernizing Intelligentsia in Eastern Europe

If it may be said that the aggregate effect of modernity was more to transform than to efface the ethnic distinctiveness of the Jews in west-central Europe, this holds, a fortiori, for eastern Europe. Throughout the nineteenth century and into the twentieth, the Jews in czarist Russia (and similarly, though less important in quantitative terms, in Romania and the Austro-Hungarian empire) continued to constitute a well-defined *ethnie*. This is not to say that the czarist empire was exempt from the process of modernization involving the increase of bureaucratic controls and cultural homogeneity and the sloughing off of corporative structures. However, not only was the general process retarded in comparison with the states of western Europe, but in regard to the Jews it failed to carry with it a corresponding civic emancipation.

Although Jewish communal autonomy was undermined by the czarist government's abolition of the *kahal* (the officially recognized corporative community organization) in 1844, its residual quasi-political functions persisted even up to 1917.[40] Moreover, the Jews retained their own vernacular. In the census of 1897, no less than 98 percent of the Jews declared Yiddish as their spoken language. In addition, Hebrew continued to serve richly for "high" cultural expression, both in the traditional sphere of rabbinic learning and in the innovative literary creativity of the *haskala*. A literature and newspapers and journals in Hebrew and Yiddish enjoyed a distribution in tens of thousands at the turn of the century. In a sense, the Pale of Settlement, comprising fifteen provinces and Congress Poland (with its ten provinces) in the west and south of the Russian empire, provided something approximating, however inadequately, a territorial basis for the Jewish *ethnie*. At the end of the nineteenth century the Jews were close to eleven percent of the total population within that strip of territory. In some provinces (e.g., Grodno and Minsk) this percentage was as high as fifteen percent. In many shtetls (townlets) they were a majority. All told, they made up between a third and a half of the major cities of the Pale. Jews had their own educational institutions (the *hadorim, talmudei torah*, and yeshivas) parallel to that of other ethnic communities and of the developing—but backward by Western standards—Russian school system. According to estimates published in 1904 by the Jewish Colonization Association (ICA), there were about 370,000 children in Jewish schools as opposed to only 60,000 Jewish children in Russian schools and Jewish Russian-language schools.[41]

Much the same Jewish ethnic attributes continued to exist well into the twentieth century. Of course, the new dispensation of states after the First World War greatly diversified the conditions of Jewish existence throughout eastern Europe and accelerated acculturation into each state's dominant language and culture, thereby weakening, overall, the bonds of the Jewish *ethnie*. Nevertheless, the complex multiethnic configuration of the new states, in combination with their unstable political culture and with the weighty heritage of hostility toward the Jews, conspired to preserve the essential attributes that made the Jews a distinctive ethnic community, not only within the boundaries of each new state, with varying intensity, but even in a sense transcending state boundaries.

Independent Poland may be said to have contained the dynamic core of the Jewish diasporic *ethnie* in the twentieth century. According to the Polish census of 1921, there were 2,853,318 Jews in Poland, constituting 10.5 percent of the total population, and 70 percent declared that they belonged to the "Jewish nationality." By 1931 the Jewish population had risen to 3,113,933 although their percentage of the total population dropped to 9.8. Of these no less than 2,489,084 still declared Yiddish as their mother tongue. Another 243,500 indicated Hebrew as their mother tongue, but this may be regarded as largely demonstrative of their Zionist sentiment rather than reflective of the real situation. Polish was thus the mother tongue of only some 12 percent of all Jews in Poland in 1931.[42]

In Russia the beginnings of the *haskala* phenomenon were very much an extension of the Mendelssohnian *haskala*, reaching the Pale of Settlement largely by route of Austrian-ruled Galicia, where German cultural influence was strong and the regime of Joseph II actively promoted elements of the *haskala* program. The seminal figure of the *haskala* in Russia, Yitzhak Ber Levinsohn (1788–1860), whose main work, *Te-uda be-Israel* (Mission in Israel), appeared in 1828, was very influenced by the Mendelssohnian model and advocated much the same program of reforms in relation to Jewish education and occupational diversification. Yet Levinsohn's emphases already reflected the very considerable difference between the social and cultural environments of the German states and czarist Russia. Above all, the difference lay in the relative absence within the immediate Pale of Settlement social environment of a reference group bearing the enlightened intellectual attributes that the *maskil* aspired to acquire and with whom he might seek to be socially integrated. (There were exceptions, such as Warsaw, which did have a Polish social reference group possessed of such attributes.) Consequently, until the mid-nineteenth century at least, the "European" higher learning that *maskilim* in czarist Russia aspired to acquire and disseminate was, to all intents and purposes, that of German higher culture. German, rather than the languages of the indigenous populations of the Pale of Settlement, such as Polish and Lithuanian, was the medium of instruction in several schools founded by *maskilim* in the 1820s and 1830s. German-Jewish practices of religious reform did not, however, penetrate deeply into Russian Jewry. This was another important factor in the greater preservation of Jewish ethnic distinctiveness there than in the West.

The same difference between the enlightened reference group of Berlin society and the alienating social context of the majority ethnic populations in the Pale of Settlement goes far toward explaining the failure of religious reform to issue in a widespread movement in Russia. To this must be added the further alienating effect of coercive czarist interference with and attempted manipulation of the rabbinate. Its scheme, first instigated in 1935, to create a Russian-speaking Crown rabbinate endowed with exclusive governmental recognition failed to produce a new religious leadership enjoying the respect of the Jewish public as well as governmental approbation. There were, to be sure, fervent advocates of religious reform among the *maskilim* in Russia, notably Joachim Hayim Tarnopol (1810–1900), Leon Mandelstamm (1819–1899), and Moshe Leib Lilienblum (1843–1910), but even they were constrained by the realities of Jewish life in the Pale to confine their proposals mainly to changes in the synagogue service and ritual law deemed necessary on practical grounds. They did not seek to undermine the authority of the *halakha* nor to engage in theological reinterpretation. Nor did they, moreover, try to diminish the role of Hebrew nor remove expressions of hope for return to Zion in the liturgy. In short, their approach was close to that of Zacharias Frankel and the conservative wing of the religious reformers in Germany.[43]

Overall in eastern Europe a far more bitter resistance to manifestations of *haskala* was put up by the massive and deeply entrenched forces of Jewish traditionalism. Consequently, the early *maskilim* in Russia were a smaller, weaker, and more intimidated social stratum than in the West, and they tended to gravitate around a small number of wealthy Jewish merchants whose privileged status—after 1855 they had the right to live outside the Pale of Settlement, and they enjoyed their own channels of communication with the czarist government—provided some independence from normative community controls.

In 1863 a group of such wealthy, privileged Jews, headed by Joseph Yossel Guenzburg, founded in St. Petersburg the Society for the Dissemination of Enlightenment. This marked a shift in orientation away from German and toward the Russian language and culture. The society's object was "to spread the knowledge of the Russian language among the Jews, to publish and assist others in publishing, in Russian as well as in Hebrew, useful works and journals, to aid in carrying out the purposes of the society, and, further, to assist the young in devoting themselves to the pursuit of science and knowledge."[44] Writers and scholars such as Avraham Dov Lebensohn, Avraham Mapu, Yehuda Leib Gordon (who became secretary of the society in 1872), Lev Levanda, and Yehuda Leib (Leo) Pinsker joined the society.

From the beginning, differences arose over the question of whether Hebrew or Russian was to have priority in the work of the society. Leon Rosenthal, one of its founders (and later the author of a two-volume history of the society), was an advocate of Hebrew and of an approach respectful of the tradition. The "russifiers" were strongest in the Odessa branch and included Ossip Rabinowitz, who had founded the Russian-language paper *Razsvet* in 1860, and—indicative of his remoteness at this stage from a Jewish nationalist position—Yehuda Leib Pinsker.

Among the activities of the society were publishing primers for teaching Russian and, in the 1870s, a collection on the views of the Talmud sages, with a Hebrew text and a Russian translation, as well as provision of subventions for translation of Hebrew prayer books into Russian. Grants were made to authors of Hebrew books on mathematics and the natural sciences, and the Hebrew periodicals *Ha-tzefirah* and *Ha-melitz* were supported. Assistance was also provided for Jewish students in Russian institutions of higher education.

As in the West, the potential implications of the *haskala* were ambiguous; they were integrative as well as disintegrative of the Jewish ethnic collectivity. There also were great regional differences.[45] However, the sheer demographic mass of Jewry in the East and the continued vitality and pervasiveness of its religious traditionalism, compounded by the absence of a magnetic cultural reference group in the immediate social environment, weighed the balance of the eastern *haskala* in favor of its integrative effects. All in all, the *haskala* functioned more as a modernizing transformer of the Jewish *ethnie* than it did as a conduit for integration into the czarist state, more as an ethnic cement than as an ethnic solvent. The clearest expression of this was the *haskala*'s remarkable role in the development of the Hebrew language into a serviceable and versatile literary medium as well as its role in providing a secularized ideological underpinning (and for some, an alternative) for the deeply rooted ethnoreligious consciousness of Jewry in eastern Europe. This ideological underpinning may be said to have been ethnicist (or in other words, conducive to a nationalist state of mind) because it elevated the attributes of Jewish ethnicity to highly ranked values. This ideological tendency emanating from the eastern European *haskala* found its clearest expressions in the views of David Gordon (1831–1886) in the 1860s and in those of Peretz Smolenskin (1842–1885) in the 1870s, the former representing an intermediate mode of identity between traditionalism and *haskala* and the latter a clearly secularized mode.

David Gordon retained the religiosity imbibed in a traditionalist home and in a Vilna yeshiva, although also acquiring some secular learning. After spending some time in England, he returned to eastern Europe and in 1858 became assistant editor (and in 1880 editor) of the Hebrew weekly *Ha-magid*, published in Lyck, East Prussia, close to the Russian border. In the columns of that paper he consistently expressed views that conflated support for attempts at Jewish resettlement of Eretz Israel (which, as we shall see in the next chapter, were being propagated mainly by a small number of traditionalist rabbis, notably Zvi Hirsch Kalischer) with an ethnicism influenced by secular concepts of the Enlightenment intelligentsia. Indeed, to him is attributed coinage of the Hebrew term *leumi* (national). Without rejecting the path of emancipation and civic integration wherever Jews were domiciled, he deplored any abandonment of Jewish religious and "national" distinctiveness. By his lights, "the mission" of the Jew was "to progress in civic life and in acquisition of secular learning" while at the same time "standing guard as firmly as a rock over all principal religious matters that are bound up and intertwined with Jewish national life in the chain of its history in days past and its hopes for days yet to come." In this way, he argued, Jews would not only "prepare themselves and become deserving of equal civic rights in the lands of their dispersion" but also "pave the way to our redemption, to the return to our Holy Land, to becoming one nation again in The Land as of old."[46]

A more secularized ethnicism, born of the *haskala*, issued from the pen of another Hebrew periodical editor, Peretz Smolenskin. His biography was typical of the *maskilim*. Born in a shtetl in the northeast of the Pale of Settlement, his boyhood was spent in the yeshiva of Shklov, where he had showed signs of intellectual rebelliousness. There followed some years of wandering and earning a livelihood with difficulty as a teacher of sorts until he gravitated to Odessa, the most modern of Russian cities and a center of Enlightenment influence. There Smolenskin spent his early twenties autodidactically acquiring *haskala* knowledge and beginning to develop his talents as a writer. These came to full fruition when, having moved to Vienna, he founded in 1868 the journal *Ha-shahar* (The dawn).

From 1881 until his death in 1885, Smolenskin was a forceful advocate of Eretz Israel–oriented Jewish nationalism. However, in the present context our concern is with the earlier position he articulated, especially in a series of writings that appeared in *Ha-shahar* between 1875 and 1877. At that time Smolenskin declared emphatically that the Jews were a nation, denying, at the same time, that a territory was a necessity for nationhood. "Nation is not distinguishable from nation by the fact that the blood of its forefathers flows in its veins," he wrote, "but rather in commonalities shared by members of a society, manners, aspirations, temperaments, qualities, beliefs, laws of living, historical development . . . and in all these respects there is no people in the world as deserving of the name nation [*am*] as Israel, and no informed inquirer would say that the epithet nation is dependent upon a state or upon a territory. Germans living in Rome are Germans, Italians in Austria are Italians, and Jews wherever they are are Jews."[47] Smolenskin described the Jews as an archetypal people, a spiritual people, (*am ha-ruah*) whose bonds were not (or no longer were) territorial but rather matters of brotherhood (*ahva*) and national feeling (*ha-regesh ha-leumi*) and a common historically experienced literature and culture rooted in the Torah (Bible) and the Hebrew language. In short, by his lights, cultural attributes were the defining factors of the Jewish nation.

The distinguishing marks of the Smolenskin school of *haskala* were, first, elevation of ethnic attributes, such as the common language, literary texts, and historical experiences, to the level of commanding values; and second, fervent opposition to assimilationist ideas or tendencies of any sort. Smolenskin was particularly acerbic on this score, regarding such tendencies as nothing short of betrayal; he not only launched unbridled attacks on the reformers of Judaism in the West but even cast blame on Moses Mendelssohn, who antedated these developments. Third, the common religion was considered a part of this broader framework of ethnic or national attributes rather than vice versa. The approach was thus secular, departing from the traditionalist Jewish self-understanding. In terms of the definitions employed in our present discussion, Smolenskin's ideological tradition might be said to have represented a transition from "ethnicism" to "cultural nationalism." It fell short of being nationalism in an unqualified sense insofar as it never insisted on independence through coextensiveness of the ethnic collective and a territorial polity.

This became a rich tradition of thought that later branched off into two of the profoundest versions of nationalist ideology in eastern European Jewry— those of Asher Ginzberg (Ahad Ha'am, 1856–1927) and Simon Dubnow (1860–1941), the former the exponent of what came to be known as cultural Zionism; the latter, of Jewish diaspora nationalism. After 1881, on the controversial question of where to direct Jewish emigration, Smolenskin adopted a position strongly in favor of Eretz Israel. This would make Ahad Ha'am a closer successor of his tradition of thought, but the continuities between his "spiritual nation" concept and Dubnow's nationalist ideology are no less striking.

The *haskala* generated a Jewish intelligentsia in Russia, of which Peretz Smolenskin was an important example. But there were tributaries other than the *haskala* to the formation of that intelligentsia, and its components formulated ideological positions other than that of Smolenskin. By the 1880s a combination of imposed governmental measures and economic and occupational motivations had produced a small but growing stratum of secular, partly russified Jews; that is to say, Jews who spoke Russian, conducted much of their social activity in Russian, and even engaged in literary activity in Russian.[48]

Governmental pressures aimed at assimilating the Jews into Russian society had issued, in the reign of Nicholas I, in creation of a special network of government schools for Jews; studies were conducted initially in German, but the curriculum also included Russian language, history, and geography taught in a patriotic Russian spirit. In the 1860s the Russian language displaced German. Although the development of these schools was retarded owing to the uncooperativeness of the Jewish population, they nevertheless represented the first breach in the wall of traditionalist Jewish education and did play some role in the russification process. Much the same may be said of the two rabbinical seminaries set up by the state, one in Vilna and the other in Zhitomir, aiming to produce russified modern rabbis and teachers for the schools. Later, in the early 1870s, even highly traditionalist families were motivated to submit their sons to a russifying education in government schools in order to spare them from full military service (a law of 1874 made four years of military service compulsory for all citizens of the state, but only one year was required for graduates of secondary schools).

These pressures were compounded by the aspirations of Jews to improve their

economic and occupational prospects. Their expanding involvement in entre-
preneurial economic activity in fields such as government liquor monopoly
concessions, sugar, and timber brought with it greater exposure to russification,
at least in respect of increasing proficiency in the Russian language. In 1859,
Jewish merchants of the First Guild were permitted to live outside the Pale of
Settlement, a right that was extended in 1865 to qualified artisans. Moreover, a
law of 1861 permitted residence outside the Pale to any Jew who had graduated
from secondary school. In the years that followed, a broader interpretation of
this law included occupations connected with medical services, such as
pharmacists and their assistants, male nurses, midwives, and the like. Out of this
economic mobility there emerged a small Jewish bourgeoisie of considerable
wealth—such as the families of Guenzburg, Poliakov, Zak, and Brodsky, mostly
resident outside the Pale of Settlement—who took a lead in prodding the Jewish
population as a whole toward greater acculturation and integration into Russian
society.

These processes brought about a significant increase in attendance at Russian
governmental schools. In the decade from 1870 to 1880 the number of Jewish
students in the Gymnasiums grew fourfold. In 1880, nearly eight thousand were
in these schools, constituting 11.5 percent of the total of Gymnasium students in
the Pale of Settlement. Also, the number of Jewish students in universities rose
steadily. In 1864 there were only 129, constituting 3.4 percent of the total in the
Pale. By 1886 this had risen to 1,858, constituting 14.3 percent of the total.

The cumulative effect of these developments was the emergence of a
second-generation reservoir for the Jewish intelligentsia, functioning in the
Russian language rather than in Hebrew and therefore producing a second type
of intelligentsia, different in orientation from the more autodidactic, Hebrew-
medium *maskilim*. The size of this reservoir is difficult to determine with
accuracy, probably a little over 1 percent of the 5,125,000 Jews in Russia
according to the 1897 census.[49] However, it is evident that by the 1870s a few
thousands of the Jewish intelligentsia had found in the Russian intelligentsia a
proximate social reference group.

The Russian intelligentsia was a social factor very peculiar to nineteenth-
century Russia and made a very distinctive mark on its development.[50] One
ideological stream was that of the Slavophiles, who sought to conserve the
organic uniqueness of Russia and recoiled from westernization. They looked to
the revival of Russia's putative past glory, when harmonious unity reigned
between the people, its church, its aristocracy, and its czar. Hostility toward the
Jews inhered in this ideological orientation. The revolutionary Narodnik movement found inspiration in the common Russian peasantry and its putatively
natural communalism, which presaged, in its eyes, Russia's unique path to a
Socialist society of equality and brotherhood without the necessity of passing
through a westernizing capitalist stage. In the 1870s many young Jews were attracted

to this movement, but the attitude toward them was inherently ambiguous and proved unsympathetic, if not openly hostile, in response to the pogroms of the 1880s. It was the liberal, westernizing stream of ideology within the Russian intelligentsia that proved relatively the most receptive to the participation of Jews, although it too was characterized by ambiguity on the Jewish question. If the Narodniks tended to associate Jews with the evils of capitalism and the forces oppressing the pure Russian folk, the liberal westernizers predicated the acceptability of Jews upon their shedding all Jewish particularism.

By the 1870s numbers of Jews had become involved in political activities of the Russian intelligentsia, whether of the Narodnik type or the liberal, westernizing type. Concurrently, some of the *maskil* type of Jewish intelligentsia, whose cultural activity focused on Hebrew, had begun to assume leadership roles within the Russian Jewish community itself. Outstanding examples of this type were Lev Levanda, Avraham Ber Gottleber, Yehuda Leib Gordon, and Moshe Leib Lilienblum. The fragmented state of the Jewish community's authority structure—in itself largely the result of the homogenizing state's intervention over the past century—facilitated the emergence of these *maskilim* as a third political force, vying with both the broader stratum of traditionalist rabbis (itself fragmented) and the small elite of wealthy bourgeois notables such as the Guenzburgs and Poliakovs.[51]

Emergence of Eretz Israel–Oriented Nationalism

There is general agreement among historians as to the immediate circumstances that gave birth to an Eretz Israel–oriented Jewish nationalist movement.[52] It took place in the Russian Empire (and, at about the same time but more marginally in significance, in Romania) in the wake of the convulsive wave of pogroms that swept over the southern parts of the Pale of Settlement in 1881 and continued sporadically until 1884. Given the nationalist potential within the Jewish *ethnie* of eastern Europe to which we have already alluded, it is arguable that such a nationalist movement might sooner or later have emerged irrespective of the events of the early 1880s in Russia. Be that as it may, there can be no doubt that those events constituted a crisis that dramatically precipitated matters and unleashed the *ethnie*'s immanent nationalist potential.

A number of processes, all predating 1881, now converged to have this effect. One was the frenetic urge to emigration that spread like wildfire through the Pale of Settlement and brought thousands of refugees and would-be emigrants to the border between Russia and Austrian Galicia, Brody in particular. Conflating this were the exaggerated hopes kindled by the concern of Western Jewish philanthropic organizations—the Alliance Israélite Universelle of Paris, followed by Anglo-Jewry's Mansion House Fund, Baron Maurice de Hirsch's proposals, and parallel efforts by the Hebrew Emigrant Aid Society in the United States. As soon became evident, the immediate facilitation of mass emigration was beyond the capacity—and perhaps even the will—of these Western Jewish agencies. However, the confluence of the spontaneous emigration urge with hopes and proposals relying on Western philanthropic intervention stimulated an ideological controversy of unprecedented intensity over the Jewish problem in general and the emigration question in particular.

About August 1881 a widespread public debate on emigration burst out, reflected in the Russian Jewish press of the time. The controversy revolved around two questions: Should emigration be encouraged and should it be left to flow to the "new world" of America or directed as far as possible to Eretz Israel? In either case, should it not be channeled on national rather than purely individual lines by creating collective settlement projects? The traditionalist rabbis generally rejected emigration as a major option out of concern lest it lead to the disintegration of traditionalist observance and authority in the more permissive New World. More significantly, the lines of division fell between the established oligarchy of notables such as Baron Guenzburg and the Poliakov brothers in St. Petersburg, on the one side, and a cross section of the Hebrew-medium and Russian-medium intelligentsia on the other side. Remaining faithful to their deal of emancipation in Russia, the notables took a stand against active encouragement and organization of emigration out of concern lest it provoke charges of disloyalty to Russia. In contrast, Moshe Leib Lilienblum (1843–1910), formerly an outspoken advocate of religious reforms to fit the Jews for civic rights and the spirit of the age, spoke for many of the intelligentsia whose faith in progress toward equal civic rights was shattered by the events of 1881 when he argued fervently that the situation was intolerable; Jew hatred was rife because the Jew remained an alien everywhere in his dispersion, and the only answer was to return to Eretz Israel "to which we have an historic right which was not lost when we lost rule of the country, any more than the peoples of the Balkans lost their rights to their lands."[53]

Within the popular school of thought that advocated not only emigration but also that it be channeled along collective national lines, debate raged over the destination of preference, Eretz Israel or America. Young idealists were to be found on both sides. The Am Olam (Eternal People) group formed on the basis of a leftist ideological preference for the concentrated establishment of collective Jewish settlements in America, with a view to the attainment of some kind of regional autonomy. The smaller Bilu group, to whom we shall return later in this chapter, formulated the first pioneering ideology of a cadre destined for Eretz Israel. Ideologically, both were milestone developments; in practice little came of either. Am Olam created a number of settlements, the most notable of which was New Odessa in Oregon, but both the movement and its settlements proved to be ephemeral.[54]

This emigration debate served, in turn, to accelerate another incipient process in Russian Jewry, the transformation of Jewish political behavior from the old pattern of paternalistic intercession by an elite to a new mode of politics based explicitly on the principle of self-help and expressed in mass organization of "the people." Whereas the participants in the emigration debate came from all three categories of leadership in Russian Jewry—the broad stratum of traditionalist rabbis, the small coterie of wealthy and privileged notables, and the rising but thin stratum of intelligentsia—the new popular-based style of political action was the creation of the latter alone. Stepping into a political void created by the disruption of rapport between the Jewish notables and the post–Alexander II czarist government and by the reluctance of those notables to advocate emigration as a solution for the problems of Russian Jewry, the intelligentsia burst through to the forefront of the Jewish public arena.

Within this context a factor of profound significance dramatically strengthened the hand of that segment of the *maskil* intelligentsia, long in germination but still minor in influence until that time, that advocated a self-affirming nationalist orientation for Jewry. That factor was the shock of disillusionment that shattered the belief in the progress of liberalism in Russia, a belief that had underlain the confidence of the majority of the Jewish intelligentsia that in Russia, as elsewhere in Europe, Jews were advancing toward attainment of equal civic rights and could become integrated into Russian society.

The extent of czarist government responsibility for and condonation of the 1880s pogroms is still a somewhat moot point but not so the crucial fact that a considerable segment of the Jewish intelligentsia—high school youths, university students, literati, and professionals—were shaken to the core and disillusioned by the almost universal condonation of the pogroms, explicit or implicit, not only on the Right and in government circles but even throughout the progressive, revolutionary spectrum in Russia. The refrain was ubiquitously unsympathetic to the Jews: the pogroms, even if deplored as breaches of public order, were interpreted as an inevitable reaction of the Christian population to the "tribal exclusiveness," "religious fanaticism," and "exploitation" of the Jews, as the governmental authority put it even as it established local commissions of inquiry into the question in August 1881. Alternatively, the pogroms were regarded as the suffering, enraged Ukrainian peasants' retribution for the Jew who "takes the land, the woods, the taverns from out of your hands . . . curses you, cheats you, drinks your blood," as one notorious statement of the Narodnaia Volia populist revolutionaries had it at about the same time.[55] Disillusioned by these manifestations of hostility to the Jews right across the political board, many of the young Jewish intelligentsia abandoned their former faith in the forces of progress in Russia and turned back toward the Jewish ethnic community, some even reappearing repentantly in the synagogues at the mourning prayers conducted for victims of the pogroms.

This phenomenal turnabout of those who had believed in a program of emancipation and integration into the host state and society reached its most dramatic proportions in the wake of the pogroms in Russia. But it had happened before that time (in Eliezer Ben-Yehuda, the pioneer of Hebrew as a modern vernacular, for example, in the 1870s), and it continued to occur thereafter in western Europe (Theodor Herzl and Max Nordau, founding leaders of the Zionist Organization, were the most famous examples) and throughout the course of Zionism's later development.

In Russia of the 1880s, this dramatic development was grist for the mill of those *maskil* literati, like Peretz Smolenskin, who had long inveighed against all forms of assimilation and advocated Jewish self-affirmation. At the same time, these advocates too were propelled toward more radical conceptions. Whereas Smolenskin, for example, had based his program on cultural-linguistic dimensions held to be viable within the Russian state, he now turned toward the emigration option, with Eretz Israel as the decidedly preferred destination. This double shift in orientation—of formerly integration-oriented members of the intelligentsia as well as of others who were already nationalist-oriented— converged with deeply rooted traditionalist ideas and efforts concerned with Jewish settlement in Eretz Israel, a convergence that dispelled some of the antagonisms between traditionalists and the *maskil* intelligentsia. A basis for common endeavor thus existed that was to have the most far-reaching effect in facilitating the growth of an Eretz Israel–oriented nationalist movement. It also had the effect of counterbalancing the purely rational and pragmatic contemplation of *any* territory as a potential national refuge for Jewish emigration (an ideological orientation and program that later came to be known as territorialism), since Eretz Israel was inherent in traditionalist Jewish self-understanding.

This was the vortex of political and intellectual activity out of which there began to emerge an organized following for an explicitly enunciated Eretz Israel–oriented nationalist ideology. At first the groups or associations that mushroomed were but loosely interrelated. Hovevei Zion (Lovers of Zion) was the name by which some of these groups went. (In Vilna, for example, the name chosen was the different but synonymous Ohavei Zion.) It was, in all, a weak organizational framework with as yet inchoate ideological parameters, but it already incorporated some sharply defined ideological formulations, the foremost of which was a booklet written by Leo (Yehuda Leib) Pinsker and first published anonymously in Berlin in 1882 in the German language, titled *Autoemanzipation: Mahnruf an seiner Stammegenossen von einem russischen Juden* (Autoemancipation: An appeal to his compatriots by a Russian Jew).[56]

In retrospect, it would not be exaggerated to say that Pinsker's *Autoemancipation* became for the ideology of Zionism what Marx and Engels's *Communist*

Manifesto was for that of socialism. It bears so distinguished a comparison by virtue of its pathos and its incisive, crystal-clear exposition rather than as the trigger that set off the movement; for Hovevei Zion associations were already in existence when the pamphlet saw publication in September 1882, and even then it appeared in Berlin, in German, addressed at least as much to Western as to Eastern Jewry. Owing to government censorship, only an incomplete Hebrew translation appeared in consecutive issues of *Ha-magid* in late 1882 and early 1883, and a Yiddish translation appeared only in 1884. Nor should *Autoemancipation* be considered a summation of contemporary Hibbat Zion ideology as a whole. Quite apart from the fact that it was written from a purely secular vantage point and therefore did not reflect the traditionalist elements of Hibbat Zion, it also did not adequately comprehend the deep, ethnically rooted quest for religiocultural reformulation that characterized the Smolenskin–Ahad Ha'am tradition of thought. Hence, it was not bound to the mythic imperative of Eretz Israel and could rationally contemplate a solution in any practicably suitable territory. What Pinsker's *Autoemancipation* did reflect, and superbly so, was the ideological reformulation of the now disillusioned members of the liberal, largely russianized Jewish intelligentsia. For the core and crux of its exposition was the outright rejection of that intelligentsia's normative ideological proposition, namely, that the preferential option for Jews everywhere was the attainment of civic rights (emancipation) and their integration into the host society of the state in which they were domiciled. Pinsker now argued that this proposition was demonstrably false because in reality it was impossible to realize the option it posited.

Pinsker offered a searching diagnosis of the Jewish problem, according to which the ultimate defect lay in the Jew's condition of national homelessness. "The essence of the problem," he averred, "lies in the fact that, in the midst of the nations among whom the Jews reside, they form a distinctive element which cannot be assimilated, which cannot readily be digested by any nation." This was not just a manifestation of the universal dislike of all people for foreigners. The aversion or, conversely, the hospitality that met the foreigner in a strange land could be repaid in equal coin in his home country; but the Jew, wrote Pinsker, "can make no such return; consequently he can make no claim to hospitality."

Since the Jew is nowhere at home, nowhere regarded as a native, he remains an alien everywhere. That he himself and his forefathers as well are born in the country does not alter this fact in the least. In the great majority of cases, he is treated as stepchild, as a Cinderella; in the most favorable cases he is regarded as an adopted child whose rights may be questioned; *never* is he considered a legitimate child of the fatherland.

The specifics of Pinsker's attempt to explain the mental mechanism or process by which this condition of homelessness engendered a universal hatred of the Jews bear the marks of concepts drawn from his medical training in an era of prevalent scientific positivism that attributed much to instinct and heredity. Pinsker asserted that neither civic emancipation itself nor the most fervent endeavors to be integrated were capable of eradicating or overcoming the immutable obstacle of Jew hatred, which he termed Judeophobia.

Among the living nations of the earth the Jews occupy the position of a nation long since dead. . . . The world saw in this people the uncanny form of one of the dead walking among the living. The ghostlike apparition of a people . . . without land or other bond of union, no longer alive and yet moving about among the living. . . . Fear of the Jewish ghost has been handed down and strengthened for generations and centuries.

According to Pinsker this pathological fear of an alien entity with the appearance of a ghostly apparition was what "led to a prejudice which, in its turn, in connection with other forces"—he discussed in particular the factor of economic rivalry and jealousy—"paved the way for Judeophobia." As a "psychic aberration" transmitted for two thousand years, it had become virtually "hereditary" and "incurable." "He must be blind indeed," declared Pinsker with bitter irony, "who will assert that the Jews are not *the Chosen People*, the people chosen for universal hatred."

Having thus diagnosed the problem and identified the core defect in the Jewish condition—namely, homelessness—Pinsker drew the important conclusion that "we should not persuade ourselves that humanity and enlightenment will ever be radical remedies for the malady of our people." Instead, a way had to be found of so adjusting the relations of the Jews to other nations that there would never be any further basis for the Jewish question. "The proper, the only remedy would be the creation of a Jewish nationality, of a people living upon its own soil, the auto-emancipation of the Jews; their emancipation as a nation among nations by the acquisition of a home of their own." The means toward that solution had a prerequisite: the regaining of that self-respect and human dignity of which the persecuted and despised Jews had been robbed. Pinsker waxed eloquent on this motif:

What a pitiful figure do we cut! We do not count as a nation among the other nations, and we have no voice in the council of the peoples, even in affairs which concern us. Our fatherland is the other man's country; our unity—dispersion, our solidarity—the general hostility to us, our weapon—humility, our defense—flight, our individuality—adaptability, our future—tomorrow. What a contemptible role for a people which once had its Maccabees!

Self-help, that is to say, autoemancipation, was the fundamental instrumentality posited by Pinsker for attainment of national restoration. Hillel's saying, "If I am not for myself, who will be for me? And if not now, when?" formed the motto of his pamphlet. As for the specific plan of action, it must be noted that Pinsker was prompted to write his pamphlet as a direct appeal to Jews at large only after he had met with a disappointing response from various Western

Jewish leaders (notably Dr. Adolf Jellinek, chief rabbi of Vienna) whom he had visited in mid-1882 in an effort to gain their support. However, it is clear from his later correspondence that he continued to hold that the active involvement of Western Jewish notables was vital and to yearn for the appearance of a great leader, a Moses, from that quarter.[57] Indeed, it was only with reluctance that he became the chosen leader of Hibbat Zion, and he never felt himself to be truly adequate to the task. In *Autoemancipation* he recognized that the Hibbat Zion societies already in existence provided a nucleus and a beginning, but he urged them to unify and to convoke a "national congress," which in turn would form a "directorate." That body's foremost task would be to seek an accessible and suitable territory as a haven and refuge for Jews and then to mobilize "an associated body of capitalists" who would help with the systematic purchase of the land and settlement of "several million Jews" in the course of time. Eretz Israel was desirable—"Perhaps the Holy Land will again become ours. If so, all the better," he wrote—but he dispassionately cautioned that this ought not to be regarded as a sine qua non. "The goal of our present endeavors must be not the 'Holy Land' but a land of our own," he wrote. "Thither we shall take with us the most sacred possessions which we have saved from the shipwreck of our former fatherland, the *God-idea* and the *Bible*. It is these which have made our old fatherland the Holy Land and not Jerusalem or the Jordan."

Among the largely disparate groups constituting the still inchoate Eretz Israel–oriented nationalist movement there also emerged one that enunciated an intense ideological platform on thoroughly secular premises (in part Socialist as well), postulating the ultimate attainment of Jewish national sovereignty in Eretz Israel and committing its followers to personal ascent to Zion and dedication to that purpose. This was the small group of high school youth and university students formed in Kharkov in 1881 under the name Bilu, acronym for *Beit Ya'akov lekhu ve-nelkha* ("O House of Jacob come ye and let us go" [Isa. 2:5]).[58]

The Biluim were a phenomenon of small dimensions and meager attainments in practice. But they were moved by the lofty aspirations of an avant-garde nationalist ideology, and in the imaginations of later generations of Zionist youth an aura of heroic myth came to attach itself to them. The core of the first group in Kharkov consisted of a handful of students at the veterinary institute of Kharkov University, and they were striking examples of those young people who underwent a sudden ideological about-face in the wake of the 1881 pogroms—from identification with progressive liberal and revolutionary ideas current in the university milieu to reaffirmation of their Jewish identity in a nationalist spirit. In so doing, they transferred to the Jewish *ethnie* ideas of "going to the people" and intense personal commitment imbibed from the Russian populist context.

The founding group in Kharkov published an appeal to the Jewish youth that appeared in *Ha-melitz* on May 16, 1882, in which it contended that all of the purported enlightened progress of the nineteenth century had brought nothing but scorn and humiliation to the Jews. "We are aliens here and we shall be aliens there [in the West]." The only path to salvation was "the path to Zion, Zion, Zion! the land of our forefathers, Eretz Israel." The undersigned declared that they were willing and ready to devote all their youthful vigor to the great task of national restoration in Zion. A later ideological formulation of the Bilu stated that their aim was "to redeem and endeavor to restore [the people of] Israel to the land bequeathed by their forefathers . . . to carry the national flag and to instil it in the heart of every person bearing the name of Hebrew . . . to spread among the Jews of Eretz Israel productive work . . . by the sweat of their brows and the labor of their hands . . . without seeking the help of others."[59]

The fervently nationalist motivation of the founding Biluim is evident in a private letter from one of their number, Ze'ev Dubnow (to his brother the historian Simon Dubnow), in which he declared that their ultimate purposes were "to take possession in due course of Palestine and to restore to the Jews the political independence of which they now have been deprived for two thousand years." They would do this through "the establishment of colonies of farmers and artisans in Eretz Israel" in an endeavor "to place all of the land and its productivity in the hands of the Jews." He added that it would also be necessary to teach the future young generations the use of arms. "Then there will come that glorious day whose advent was prophesied by Isaiah," when the Jews, "with arms in their hands, if necessary, will publicly proclaim themselves masters of their ancient homeland."[60]

The Biluim aspired to become a countrywide and even worldwide movement, serving as the youthful avant garde of Jewish national revival. They dreamed of the imminent *aliya* of some four thousand members who would become the exemplars of colonization on a communal basis. To this end, they initially set out to obtain the permission of the Ottoman authorities in Constantinople for the establishment of settlements in Eretz Israel. According to the program that the few Biluim who reached Eretz Israel presented to Baron de Rothschild's agents in November 1883 (and that the Baron promptly rejected), the projected Bilu colonies were to be devoid of private property and subject to severe discipline in compliance with their elected leaders, and the Biluim were not to marry for three years so that they might give their undivided service to the national cause. But in the final analysis it is clear that their purposes were predominantly nationalist and only marginally Socialist.[61]

In fact, the record of the Biluim's attainments is dismal. Their membership in Russia never reached more than about five hundred in some twenty-five associations, which disbanded within a few years, and their efforts to gain from the Ottoman authorities a *firman* (license) permitting settlement in Eretz Israel came to naught. It was precisely the Ottomans' concern to avoid the formation of yet another national group aspiring to independence that prompted them, in

April 1882, to ban altogether the entry of Russian, Rumanian, and Bulgarian Jews into the area of Eretz Israel (the rest of the Ottoman Empire remained open to Jews). In all, only about sixty Biluim actually reached Eretz Israel at different times; many left the country, and only fifteen settled permanently in various colonies: six in Rishon Le-Zion and seven in Gadera, the latter (established in December 1884) becoming the only settlement wholly founded by Biluim and the eighth established since 1882.

At the first conference of Hovevei Zion associations (including representatives from Romania and some other countries), held at Kattowitz in 1884, Pinsker was elected president, and Lilienblum was chosen secretary. Yet by no means could Pinsker's initial ideological formulation in *Autoemancipation* or even the views aired by Lilienblum be regarded as binding for the entire range of Hovevei Zion groups. As for the Bilu, their boldly idealistic ideas were quite out of the ordinary. Indeed, the inchoate character of the movement was evident in the fact that it was not until 1887, at a conference held at Druskieniki, that the collective name Hibbat Zion was adopted by the disparate groups. Even then, the movement's ideological character, although identifiably nationalist and oriented on Eretz Israel, remained poorly defined beyond the core idea of fostering settlement in Eretz Israel with a view to the gradual restoration there of elements of Jewish national existence. Moreover, Hibbat Zion's development was hampered by the repressive czarist regime's withholding of legal sanction until as late as 1890, when its central committee in Odessa was granted such sanction as the ostensible Society for the Support of Jewish Farmers and Artisans in Syria and Palestine. The total membership of Hibbat Zion as a movement in Russia is difficult to assess. At a rough estimate it probably rose to a peak of some fourteen thousand active, dues-paying members by the end of 1885 in over one hundred associations and then fluctuated and declined to about eight or ten thousand by 1895.[62] On this foundation, the Zionist organization developed in Russia after Theodor Herzl founded it worldwide in 1897. During Herzl's presidency, from 1897 until his death in 1904, the movement in Russia reached a peak of roughly fifty-six thousand, with an estimated active core of some eight thousand.[63]

The Role of the Intelligentsia

There can be no doubt that the leadership of Hibbat Zion and its ideological pace-setters were drawn primarily from the Jewish intelligentsia, of both the Hebrew *maskil* and the partly russianized types whose emergence we have traced. It should be noted, however, that the lines of distinction between intelligentsia and middle class were blurred. In a society in which the path to intellectual literary and publicist activity characteristic of the intelligentsia was often autodidactic and where such intellectual activity seldom could provide a livelihood, the Jewish intelligentsia lived off a variety of middle-class and professional occupations. Typically, Leo Pinsker was a physician; Menahem Ussishkin, secretary of the Hovevei Zion association in Moscow, was an engineer; and Ahad Ha'am (Asher Ginzberg), probably the foremost thinker in the early Zionist movement, had a position in the Wissotzky tea company. When, in October 1883, Pinsker initiated the formation of a central committee in Odessa whose task was to coordinate and unite all the disparate Hovevei Zion associations in Russia, he compiled a list of thirty-four invitees, which is extant. It may serve as an indication of the anticipated leadership of Hibbat Zion in Odessa, very much the capital city of the Jewish intelligentsia and also of Hibbat Zion. At least twenty-three of the invitees were middle-class, mostly wealthy by the standards of the time. They included some members of the Brodsky industrialist family, three bankers, a factory owner, a miller, a stockbroker, and a number of merchants. Another six were professionals (excluding Pinsker and Lilienblum): three physicians, one pharmacist, one attorney, and one notary. However, there were acknowledged *maskilim* among both the middle-class and professional categories.[64]

This stratum of intelligentsia, intertwined with professional and commercial middle-class persons, continued to lead the Eretz Israel–oriented nationalist movement in its political Zionist stage after Theodor Herzl's founding of the Zionist Organization in 1897. A detailed analysis of the occupations of participants in the first Zionist congress held in Basel in 1897 has shown that of 246 identifiable participants (the occupations of 27 of these being unknown) from 20 countries, 60 had upper-middle-class business occupations (53 businessmen, 3 industrialists and 4 financiers), and 141 had professional occupations, including 38 students, 21 writers, 9 editors, 13 journalists, and a variety of physicians, engineers, dentists, and chemists.[65]

In the Russian branch of the Zionist movement (still the grass-roots base of the entire movement) in the period 1897 to 1904, of fourteen elected delegates who served on the Greater Actions Committee of the Zionist Organization, only two, both of whom were rabbis, did not have a higher secular education of some sort. They included five doctors, five engineers, and a lawyer.[66] This middle-class-cum-intelligentsia leadership stratum of eastern European Zionism shared a common Jewish identity profile. Typically, they came from homes in which the level of ritual observance had already been modified by some *haskala* influences, and in many cases they had passed from a traditionalist elementary education in the *heder* (religious schoolroom) to a secondary education in the Gymnasium (Russian secondary school) rather than in the yeshiva (religious academy for talmudic study). The mass following of Hibbat Zion and early Zionism in eastern Europe was, however, much more traditionalist and lower middle class than the leadership. Small-scale traders and artisans were far more typical of rank-and-file Zionist membership than were the growing numbers of factory and other employed workers. The latter tended to veer away from Zionism toward a working-class organization that promised immediate economic improvements. They were to swell the ranks of the Socialist Jewish Algemeyner Arbeter Bund (popularly designated the Bund) after it was launched in 1897. Only later, in the first decade of the twentieth century, did a segment of the Jewish working class begin to form its own Socialist synthesis with Zionism in a variety of rather fluid groupings, the most durable of which was called Poalei Zion. To this development we shall return in a later context.

The evidence is abundant that much the same identity and social profile continued to be typical of Zionists in the eastern European region that formed independent Poland after the First World War.[67] In western and central Europe the middle-class social base of Zionism and, in particular, the role of the intelligentsia in the emergence and spread of the movement was, if anything, even more marked than in the East. The first Eretz Israel—oriented nationalist formations in the West were composed almost entirely of émigré students from the Russian Pale of Settlement or Galicia. Such was the Kadima (Progress) society of students in Vienna formed in 1883, although its founding father and leading spirit, Nathan Birnbaum (1864–1937), was a first-generation Viennese. A kindred group was the Russisch-Jüdischer Wissenschaftlicher Verein (Russian-Jewish Scientific Society) in Berlin, formed by émigré students, some of whom were destined for important roles in the Zionist movement. They included Leo Motzkin, Shmaryahu Levin, Nahman Syrkin, Victor Jacobson, and Chaim Weizmann.

Although at least one of the members of this *Verein* was born and educated in Germany (Heinrich Loewe, a historian) and it touched a fringe of the larger student body of Jews "native" to Germany, the genesis of German Jewry's "indigenous" Zionist organization, the Zionistische Vereinigung für Deutschland (ZVfD), took an independent and distinctive course of its own. It was the creation of a part of the Jewish intelligentsia whose nurseries were the students' fraternities at German universities. Unlike the Jewish intelligentsia of Russia, who were still rooted in a full-blown *ethnie* marked off by its own language, cultural differentiae, and civic disabilities, the Jewish intelligentsia of Germany were acculturated in the German language and culture and civically undifferentiated, at any rate formally and theoretically, from other Germans. This produced an ambience very different from that in which the eastern European Hibbat Zion emerged. German Zionism emerged out of social units that answered the need for *Gemeinschaft* (i.e., an intimate social and cultural support system) felt by the Jewish student intelligentsia, who, notwithstanding their studied acculturation, were not fully accepted by their gentile social and cultural reference groups. Hence, the first Jewish nationalist frameworks to emerge in German Jewry were not only student groups but ones that copied the character of German student fraternities of the time.[68] At a later stage, another social form was adopted, on the initiative of the same type of Jewish student, which once again assumed an intimate, identity-serving character following on gentile German patterns—the Jewish youth movement Blau-Weiss, modeled on the German Wandervogel. This too proved to be a nursery for Zionism, although not exclusively so.

Almost all of the front-rank leaders of the ZVfD up to the First World War were university-educated, mostly in law.[69] These included Max Bodenheimer (1865–1940), Arthur Hantke (1874–1955), Felix Rosenblueth (1887–1978), Kurt Blumenfeld (1884–1963), and Siegfried Moses (1887–1974), all of whom at some stage or other also occupied important positions in the world Zionist Organization. Particularly noteworthy are several personalities whose academic training equipped them for important advisory, planning, and administrative roles in the world movement. One was Arthur Ruppin (1876–1943), who, in addition to his legal training, published pioneering sociological-demographic studies of the Jews. After making a study of Jewish settlements in Palestine on behalf of the Zionist executive, in 1908 he was appointed director of the important Palestine Office of the Zionist Organization set up in Jaffa. Franz Oppenheimer, a professor in the fields of sociology and economics at the University of Frankfurt from 1919 to 1929, was another social scientist who made a distinctive contribution. His ideas concerning planned cooperative settlements influenced the development of Zionist settlement in Palestine after 1909. Richard Lichtheim (1885–1963), holder of a degree in economics, served as diplomatic representative of the Zionist Organization in Constantinople before the First World War and later headed its organization department in London. Yet another academic of note was Otto Warburg (1859–1938), a botanist who was president of the world Zionist Organization from 1911 until 1920.

The biographies of many of these German-Jewish intelligentsia provide illustrations of the phenomenon of the returning intelligentsia, of "conversion" from belief in integration with the majority society to Jewish national self-affirmation. Such conversion also had the added significance of movement from the periphery of Jewish communal life to a position rivaling that of the established conventional leadership of Jewish communities. An example was the first president of the ZVfD (he served from 1897 to 1910), Max Bodenheimer, who described the transformation that he underwent when he was a young lawyer thus:

The Zionist idea was the result of a sudden inspiration. It was like a light that suddenly broke forth within me. . . . Whereas shortly before I had wrestled with the decision to abandon Judaism and seek refuge from Jew-hatred in new surroundings where my origin was unknown, I was now filled with a holy zeal to serve the cause of my people. Perhaps it came from the fact that I suddenly recognized the futility of such an assimilation for the people as a whole, perhaps also because my feeling of honor resisted such a flight from the community into which I had been born.[70]

Of course, the supreme exemplar of this phenomenon was Theodor Herzl (1860–1904), the founder of the Zionist Organization. Born in Budapest, Hungary, and domiciled in Vienna, where he became a prominent journalist and feuilletonist, he was what might be termed highly German/European-acculturated. To the Zionist congress that Herzl convened for the first time in 1897 he spoke in the name of "that part of Jewry which is modern and cultured, which has outgrown the ghetto" and had "returned home, as it were."[71] The same might be said of the second great figurehead of political Zionism, Max Nordau (1849–1923). Also born in Hungary, he was a writer, journalist, and social critic of note who, like Herzl, belonged to that section of the German/European-acculturated intelligentsia that turned from the trajectory of integration into the majority society to advocacy of Jewish nationalism. We shall examine the implications of their conversions for Zionist ideology in a later chapter.

The case of Colonel Albert Edward Williamson Goldsmid (1846–1903) in England was one of the most dramatic—also the most idiosyncratic—of all conversions to Jewish national affirmation from a postacculturated position. (In Goldsmid's case "postassimilated" would not be an exaggerated description.)[72] In the course of a distinguished military career in the British army, in which he rose to the rank of lieutenant colonel and to the post of chief of staff of the Sixth Division in the Anglo-Boer War, Goldsmid visited Palestine in 1883 and was inspired to return to the Judaism his parents had abandoned. He became one of the founders of Hovevei Zion in England and its leader and later cooperated with Herzl in adopting the political Zionist program and forming the English Zionist Federation in 1898.

To note the primary role of the intelligentsia in the early leadership of Zionism and, in particular, the important phenomenon of return of highly acculturated intelligentsia from the periphery of Jewish life to leadership roles in Zionism is not to say that this pattern engulfed the entire stratum of intelligentsia. Far from it. Even in Russia, real as was the disillusionment with the prospects for liberal emancipation in the wake of the 1880s pogroms, it did not deflect more than a part of the Jewish intelligentsia from doggedly persisting in that course. For example, the periodical *Voskhod*, the main mouthpiece of the liberal Jewish intelligentsia, still allied with the wealthy notables, remained inhospitable to the new Jewish nationalist program.[73] At the turn of the century a variety of ideological orientations interacted within the Jewish intelligentsia. The range included identification with Russian revolutionary forces, the Socialist Bund, and a variety of Jewish nationalist ideology, articulated most eloquently by the historian Simon Dubnow, that advocated national-cultural autonomy within the Diaspora.

The Role of Religious Traditionalists

Note must also be taken of the very important fact that from the outset the formation and growth of Hibbat Zion owed much to a stratum of traditionalist rabbis who participated in it or lent it their moral support. This was an immanent outgrowth of preexisting traditionalist ideas and schemes for Jewish settlement in Eretz Israel, traceable primarily to a loosely coordinated association that was active in the early 1860s. It was known as Hevrat Yishuv Eretz Israel (Society for Settlement of Eretz Israel), or the Colonisationsverein für Palästina and was centered in Frankfurt an Oder. In the next chapter we shall return to consider the ideas of its key participants, notably Rabbi Zvi Hirsch Kalischer. For the present it must be noted that this strain of traditionalist thought broke with quietist resignation to the condition of *galut* (exile). The hermeneutical innovations of Rabbi Kalischer and his like-minded associates had rendered the idea of volitional settlement in Eretz Israel, interpreted as human action "from below," compatible with ultimately divine intervention "from above." They avidly advocated resettlement of Zion by productively engaged, religiously observant Jews. Although by 1865 the Society for Settlement of Eretz Israel had become defunct, the energetic activities of Kalischer and his associates had set in train a strain of traditionalist thought and activity, comprising both messianic and practical motifs, which continued to find expression in traditionalist circles and in Hebrew periodicals, notably *Ha-magid*, which was published in Lyck, East Prussia, but enjoyed a readership in the Russian Pale of Settlement.[74]

This traditionalist strain of thought was in large part a defensive religious-cum-ethnicist reaction to Reform Judaism's jettisoning of return to Zion and restoration of the Temple ritual as essential ingredients of the messianic vision. Vigorous rejection of Reform Judaism and ardent advocacy of the resettlement of Eretz Israel by productive Jews were the planks of a platform of ideas common to otherwise diverse persons, ranging from the utopian-socialist prodigal son of Jewry, Moses Hess, to the essentially traditionalist Rabbi Kalischer, who contemplated the restoration of the sacrificial ritual as part and parcel of his resettlement program.

Kalischer described himself as belonging to an intermediate generation of "remnant [*seridim*] rabbis in Germany who are in awe of the word of God, and in whose hearts there burns the love of all that is holy."[75] By this he seems to have meant rabbis in central Europe who remained faithful to the core traditionalist ambience still prevalent in the Russian Pale of Settlement and were appalled by the development of Reform Judaism but who also were cognizant of changes in European society such as the burgeoning of nationalist movements and the advance of civic emancipation. Kalischer, as we shall later show, sought a way to harness some of the effects of these developments in order to facilitate resettlement of Zion as a quickening stage toward divine redemption.

Throughout the 1860s and 1870s the idea of a "resettled Eretz Israel" (*eretz noshevet,* in Kalischer's words) enjoyed the support of various rabbis and religiously observant Jews who equally deplored Reform Judaism's deethnicizing tendencies but were far more receptive to Enlightenment influences than was Kalischer. They included a number of personalities who, while upholding religious observance, were in major respects *maskilim.* They might be described as religiously conservative *maskilim.* Their prototype was David Gordon of *Ha-magid,* to whom we referred earlier. Another was Saul Pinhas Rabinowitz (1845–1910; known by the nom de plume "Shefer") of Warsaw who wrote for *Ha-tzefira* in the late 1870s and translated Graetz's *History of the Jews* into Hebrew. Yet another example was Samuel Joseph Fuenn (1818–1890), editor of the periodical *Ha-carmel* published in Vilna, which reflected a traditionalism tinged by moderate Enlightenment influences. Particularly important was Yehiel Michel Pines (1842–1912), who synthesized an essentially traditionalist understanding of Jewish self-definition with wide-ranging *maskil* awareness. In 1878 he settled in Jerusalem, having been appointed director of the Moses Montefiore Testimonial Fund (Mazkeret Moshe), which fostered the productivization of the Jewish population. By the late 1860s, Pines had reacted to central European Reform Judaism by vigorously reaffirming the attachment to Zion. He embraced an ethnicism akin to that of the eastern European *maskilim* and devoid of the messianic emphases of Kalischer. Yet he retained the traditionalist conception that the Jews are a people only by virtue of their religion.[76]

A number of those personalities who had been associated with the idea of resettling Eretz Israel during Kalischer's lifetime joined Hibbat Zion from its inception in the early 1880s. They ranged across the spectrum from thoroughly traditionalist rabbis like Israel Joshua Trunk of Kutnow, Poland (1820–1893), or ones barely tinged by *haskala* ideas like David Friedman of Karlin (1828–1917) through to articulate synthesizers of *haskala* and religious observance like David Gordon. The two most active rabbinic personalities in Hibbat Zion, Shmuel Mohilewer (1824–1898) and Mordecai Eliasberg (1817–1899), were not of preeminent stature, but they gained support from a few of the most eminent rabbinical authorities of the age, notably Naftali Zvi Yehuda Berlin (*Ha-natziv*) of Volozhin (1817–1893) and even, albeit hesitatingly, the famous Elhanan Spektor of Kovno (1817–1896).

Our delineation of the categories of rabbis who joined Hibbat Zion would not be complete without mentioning a small number for whom *haskala* values so outweighed the traditionalist that they might well be classed as nonorthodox rabbis. Some were even practitioners of religious reforms, but only moderate ones, compatible with a strongly ethnicist spirit akin to that of the positive-historical approach developed by Zacharias Frankel in Breslau. Indeed, this type came to be associated with the semisecret order called Bnei Moshe, founded in 1889, whose guiding spirit was the preeminent ideologue of secular cultural Zionism, Asher Ginzberg (known by his pen name, Ahad Ha'am). They included Zvi Malter (1864–1925) and David Neumark (1866–1924) and also Moses Gaster (1856–1939), who became *haham* (head rabbi) of the London Sephardi community, as well as Marcus Ehrenpreis (1869–1951), Armand Kaminka (1866–1950), and Marcus Braude (1869–1949), who officiated as "modern," that is to say, moderately Reform rabbis in eastern European congregations.[77]

Yet the majority of traditionalist rabbinical authorities and all of the important Hasidic leaders (*admorim*) withheld their support from Hibbat Zion from the outset or, after vacillating in the 1880s, incrementally withdrew from Hibbat Zion thereafter.[78] It is noteworthy that their objections were not in the first instance theological in nature. It was mainly to the perceived secularizing influence of Jewish nationalism and its undermining of traditionalist norms and rabbinical authority that they objected. It is instructive that some important rabbis who withheld or withdrew their support from Hibbat Zion, such as Joseph Baer Soloveitchik (1820–1892) of Brisk and Eliezer Gordon (1840–1910), head of the Telz Yeshiva, were willing to support settlement in Eretz Israel provided that it was wholly under traditionalist control. They entertained the notion of establishing an entirely independent traditionalist Hibbat Zion.[79] Had the rabbis been capable of launching and sustaining such an enterprise on their own, it is entirely conceivable that no halakhic or homiletical considerations would have presented insurmountable obstacles. It seems, however, that the rabbis doubted their own capability to contend with the worldly diplomacy and secular methods required for such an enterprise. As even Mohilewer, who proved his activism within Hibbat Zion, admitted, "Obviously persons who devote all their days to Torah study and worship, and know naught outside the walls of the house of study, are not capable of conducting efforts [*la-asot hishtadlut*] by natural means for our redemption." This task was up to "the worldly wise, the ministers of state, the wealthy, those fit to come into the courts of kings."[80] Hence, rabbis like Mohilewer felt obliged to cooperate with the *maskilim* while endeavoring to influence the nationalist settlement movement from within.[81]

In all, this traditionalist accretion had a formative influence on Hibbat Zion, although varying from one association to another. Two of the most important, those of Odessa and Warsaw, were dominated by the intelligentsia. Vilna had an association of mixed traditionalist and *maskil* composition, whereas, to give another example, Bialystok's heavily traditionalist composition included Rabbi Shmuel Mohilewer himself, who in 1893 founded an office called Mizrahi (acronym for *merkaz ruhani*, meaning spiritual center) to propagate the cause countrywide among traditionalist Jews. Not only did traditionalists have a founding stake in the social composition of the Hibbat Zion associations, but (the bold organizational strokes painted by ideologues like Lilienblum and Pinsker notwithstanding) the whole pattern of *aliya* (ascent) and settlement in Eretz Israel, the religious profile of the new *yishuv* (Jewish sector of Palestine) and also its financial support system in the 1880s and 1890s was very much in line with traditionalist precedents. Hibbat Zion did not produce any overall system of financial backing for concerted settlement of Eretz Israel. Mostly piecemeal, disjointed settlement activity emanated from local associations in Romania and Russia. The unfulfilled hopes of Rabbis Alkalai and Kalischer that great Jewish philanthropists would support Jewish resettlement in Eretz Israel were at last realized, after 1883, when Baron Edmond de Rothschild of Paris became the major sponsor of settlement activity. However, from the ideological perspective of purely nationalist self-help propounded in Pinsker's *Autoemancipation* or by the Biluim, this proved to be an ironical development, since the baron's motivations and ideological orientation were of a very different order. Although he broke with the traditionalist precedent of providing philanthropic support only for the old *yishuv* population, his generous but authoritarian maintenance of the new *yishuv* settlers was predicated upon a nonnationalist conception of the *yishuv* as no more than a productive and healthy complement to the advancing emancipation of Jews throughout the Diaspora.[82]

The traditionalist rabbis of Hibbat Zion did not submit supinely to the secularized intelligentsia's initiative and control. Mohilewer aspired to a swing in the balance that would give a controlling influence to the religiously observant Jews. After the exacerbation of tension with secularist *maskilim* in 1888–89 over the question of observing the sabbatical year (*shemita*) in Eretz Israel and after the resignation of the aging and ailing Pinsker in mid-1889, Mohilewer made a bid for the leadership of Hibbat Zion. He was only partly successful, gaining control of funds and propaganda but only as one of a collective leadership that replaced Pinsker. This gain too was short-lived because the terms of the Russian government's grant of legal sanction to Hibbat Zion in 1890 disallowed any countrywide organization and recognized only a committee of Odessan residents to be known as the Society for Support of Jewish Farmers and Artisans in Syria and Palestine. This placed the balance of control squarely in the hands of the *maskil* intelligentsia, who were the dominant factor in Odessa. Thereafter, in the course of the 1890s, a number of traditionalist rabbis and their following began to abandon Hibbat Zion, and organized traditionalist opposition began to manifest itself.

As we shall see in a later chapter of this work, the relationship between secularists and traditionalists in Zionism was a perennial source of dissonance and remains unresolved to this very day. Yet the advantages that accrued from this confluence of secular and religious tributaries were profoundly significant. All of the other popularly based new political movements that emerged in modern Jewish life (such as the Socialist Jewish Bund, founded in 1897, and the orthodox association, Agudat Israel, founded in 1912) appealed only to segments of Jewry, by class or by mode of identity on the religious-secular divide. Zionist ideology alone drew upon the mythic force of the Jewish *ethnie* as a whole, looking, Janus-faced, backward to the ethnic past, which was inseparable from religion, as well as forward to a modernized ethnic future in the shape of a nation in its own state. In dialectical terms, it purported to form a synthesis out of the thesis of traditionalism and the antithesis of enlightened modernism.[83]

Genesis of Jewish Nationalism

Although the ideological and organizational innovations of Theodor Herzl are yet to be considered, we have surveyed a sufficient period of emergent Jewish nationalism and identified enough of its social foundations to venture a summing up of the process in the light of the explanatory theory that served as the launching pad for our survey, that of Anthony D. Smith.

To recapitulate, Smith takes the position that ethnicity is both the source of a major category of nationalisms and a basic resource of nationalisms in general. Nationalisms are best understood neither as historically perennial manifestations of primordial human traits nor as the new and necessary outcome of processes associated in one way or another with modernization. Nationalist minorities in particular are in essence transformations of preexisting ethnic entities (*ethnies*). The transformation is generated, quickened, or precipitated by processes associated with modernization (hence, nationalism is certainly a "modern" phenomenon), but nationalisms are not the creation ex nihilo, or necessary outcome, of modernization. Nor are they merely the artificial creations of intellectual inventiveness. Certainly, the intelligentsia are the formative social factor in generating nationalist awareness and formulating nationalist ideology, but they assume this role by virtue of their roots in the preexisting *ethnie*. More precisely, that segment of the intelligentsia that comes to formulate the core of nationalist ideology is driven to it by the inner logic of its search for a workable synthesis between its deeply rooted and ongoing ethnic consciousness and the environmental transformations wrought by modernity.

Whether or not this explanatory framework holds for all known nationalisms of minority groups in Europe and for nationalism in Africa and Asia is a vastly complex question far beyond our scope. In the case of the Jews, however, the emergence of Zionism, which proved to be their most enduring and successful form of nationalism, certainly bears out the validity of this approach in all essentials.[84] The crucially formative factor in the emergence of a Jewish nationalist ideology was the dilemma experienced by a segment of the Jewish intelligentsia, itself a new stratum of Jews spawned by the modernization process that transformed the societal environment of European Jewries from the late eighteenth century onward.

A variegated spectrum of options appeared to be open to that intelligentsia. In roughly schematic terms, they may be divided, as Smith notes, into three tendencies: assimilationist, reformist, and neotraditionalist.

Those who evinced the reformist tendency experienced dilemmas of dual social affinity and cultural identity that launched them on a quest for a way successfully to integrate into the modernizing state to which they were subject without jettisoning the Jewish *ethnie*. But a more microscopic focus on the Jewish case reveals further differentiation into two categories of such reformist intelligentsia, each reducible in turn to two more. These two subcategories of reformists might be labeled "integrationist" and "ethnicist." Both advocated reform (a better word here might be "transformation") of the Jewish *ethnie* to fit it for modernity. The integrationists mostly believed they had found the way in religious reforms that sloughed off Judaism's potentially national attributes, reducing it to a religious denomination and hence an entity compatible with the denominations of Christianity. But the ethnicists withdrew from this trajectory at stages they deemed to be self-negating and therefore injurious to their still ethnic-conditioned sense of human dignity. The inner logic of their quest drove them toward formulation of an ethnicist, potentially nationalist option. This was then reinforced by the social environment's closure of alternative options, the latter factor in turn explicable in terms of a complex syndrome of residual religious and cultural animosities to Jews reformulated, largely in reaction to Jewish emancipation, as racist antisemitism and exacerbated by abrasive socioeconomic interactions. In the next chapter we shall consider a few clearly nationalist ideological formulations that made isolated appearances in the mid-nineteenth century, notably that of Moses Hess. But as we have seen in the present chapter, the mainstream ideological antecedent of Jewish nationalism in Europe is better described as an ethnicism, that is to say, the heightened valuation and active promotion of ethnic attributes. These included the Hebrew language, Jewish historical memory, and the ethnic-religious myth of Jewish destiny linked to Zion. Overall, this ethnicism was but a variation of the Jewish intelligentsia's prevalent consensus favoring the aspiration toward equal civic rights and integration.

The ethnicists might in turn be subdivided into two strains differentiated largely by geographical location. One strain was the historicist school of religious reform in west-central Europe, epitomized by Rabbi Zacharias Frankel and the historian Heinrich Graetz, who detached themselves from the trajectory of religious reform at the point where it abandoned such historically sanctified national attributes as the Hebrew language and the longing for return to Zion. Since emancipation and integration still underlay their ideological program, these intellectuals remained fixed at a prenationalist stage of ethnic self-affirmation (ethnicism). To be sure, an isolated eruption of unmistakable nationalist ideology did occur—Moses Hess's *Rome and Jerusalem* of 1862. Hess was one of a few cases of nineteenth-century European Jewish intellectuals (Joseph Salvador in a certain sense was another) who had opted quite successfully for integration into particular strata of the majority society but who, on largely idiosyncratic intellectual grounds still faithful to universalist ideas, had rebounded to strong ethnic self-affirmation. In Hess's case the rebound was so powerful that he leapt the gulf to nationalism. Yet, as we shall later show, this was an isolated and inconsequential phenomenon; it calls for accounting as a *historical* event but falls short of being of *historic* import.

The second strain of ethnicists was present in the relatively well preserved Jewish ethnic communities of eastern Europe, especially that of czarist Russia and among its pockets of émigrés in the West. These were the Hebraized *maskilim*, whose development we traced in this chapter. The prototype of this ideological strain was the secularized Peretz Smolenskin, but it included a variety of nuances from that of the religiously observant *maskil* David Gordon to that of Eliezer Ben-Yehuda, who as early as the 1870s rebounded from an integrationist identification with the Russian populist revolutionary cause to a fervently nationalist position. These eastern European "ethnicists" were the seminal formulators of a nascent nationalist ideology. It was forged out of their quest for a workable synthesis of the secular values and knowledge they chose to absorb from modernity and the distinctive Jewish ethnic cultural values to which they continued to be bound and which they strove to revitalize. Their contemptuous rejection of the central European model of religious reformism and their resolute efforts to revive Hebrew as a functional cultural medium were the hallmarks of their ideological bent. Ethnicism of this strain might just as well be labeled cultural nationalism. Thus far, the two strains of ethnicists.

Also reformist but more outward in orientation and more prevalent in the emerging nineteenth-century Jewish intelligentsia were what might be termed the integrationists. These were upholders of the liberal belief that the inexorable march of progress would bring civic emancipation to Jews everywhere and lead to their successful integration into the societal environment of each and every modern state. They too may be differentiated into two further strains. The first occupied leadership roles in the modernizing institutions of the Jewish communities. It encompassed individual adherents of religious reform and of orthodox religious observance alike, from leaders such as Adolphe Crémieux of the Alliance Israélite Universelle in Paris and Moses Montefiore of the Board of Deputies of British Jews in London to the wealthy Baron Guenzburg and the *maskil* poet Yehuda Leib Gordon of the Society for the Dissemination of Enlightenment in Russia. The second strain of integrationists was characterized by noninvolvement in the institutional leadership of the Jewish communities. These were well-acculturated intelligentsia types already steeped in the European languages and literatures of their particular social reference groups but only peripherally connected with the institutions, religious or philanthropic-inter-cessionist, of Jewish communities. They were advocates of integration into the civic and national fabric of the various states in which Jews were situated but not necessarily of total disappearance of the Jews as a denominational entity. Theodor Herzl and Max Nordau personified this type before they adopted a Jewish nationalist position in the 1890s.[85]

The noninstitutionally involved integrationist type to which Herzl initially belonged must be distinguished from the advocates of assimilationism proper for whom the Jewish entity, whether as religion or as ethnicity, was entirely dispensable and who aspired (in Anthony Smith's words) to "merge into a common humanity." Famous examples that come to mind are Leon Trotsky, Pavel Akselrod, and Lev Martov in Russia. This type of Jewish intelligentsia remained fixed on its course despite such reactionary setbacks as the 1880s pogroms and the failure of the 1905 revolution in Russia. There were, to be sure, cases of dramatic return from universalist causes to identification with the Jewish community. But these were exceptions. As a rule, that part of the Jewish intelligentsia, in Russia no less than elsewhere in Europe, that was inspired by cosmopolitan visions of a common humanity, usually of Socialist hue, remained outside Jewish nationalism and, indeed, came to be Zionism's most uncompro-mising and tenacious ideological antagonist.

Hence, at this point a correction, at least terminological if not typological, of Smith's theoretical account is called for. At least in the Jewish case it was not, as he suggests, the assimilationists who became disappointed with their vision and turned to the nationalist solution of the reformists. Rather, it was from the other subtype of reformists, which I have termed the integrationists, that there were repeated defections. Included among these defectors were Eliezer Ben-Yehuda in the 1870s, Moshe Leib Lilienblum and Leo Pinsker in 1881, and Theodor Herzl, Max Nordau, Max Bodenheimer, and many others thereafter. It was they who constituted the major part of the phenomenal turnabout that, after 1881, ignited the spark of Jewish nationalism when they converged with the core of a Jewish ethnicism or cultural nationalism promoted by veterans such as Peretz Smolen-skin and younger ideologues such as Asher Ginzberg (Ahad Ha'am), who had never strayed from their ingrained ethnicism.

In this distinction, too, there lies the key to defining and delimiting the often-debated role of antisemitism in the emergence of Zionism.[86] There can be no doubt that it was a major causal factor but not in regard to the progenitors and formative core of Jewish nationalism, the ethnicists. Their ideological formulations, although cognizant of antisemitism, were first and foremost an immanent expression of profound identity dilemmas that made them seek reform of the Jewish *ethnie* in accord with modernity but without sacrificing it to the homogenizing state. This propelled them toward formulation of a cultural-nationalist ideology. For the integrationists, on the other hand, anti-semitism and related factors of blocked social and economic mobility were certainly crucial. Their change of ideological direction was caused or precipitated by the implications of antisemitism, if not by direct personal exposure to it. In sum, it may therefore be said that antisemitism may be regarded as a critical causal factor in the "ignition" of Zionism as a movement but is inadequate as a causal explanation of Zionism's genesis.

Last but not least, an empirically grounded account of the genesis of Zionism calls for another modification of Smith's theoretical framework; it relates to the role of religious traditionalism.[87] A striking case of the "neotraditionalist" intelligentsia in Smith's meaning of the term was that of Nathan Birnbaum (1864–1937). A *maskil* of distinguished intellect who was variously a Zionist, a Socialist, and a Yiddishist, he concluded his intellectual odyssey, after 1914, as an advocate of withdrawal into the protective shell of orthodox religion.[88] However, Birnbaum's was an exceptional case. As a rule, the traditionalist category of intelligentsia, by definition, can mean only those members of the traditionalist intellectual stratum—in other words, essentially the rabbinate—who had also acquired some secular higher education or who were at least exposed to and autodidactically influenced by some degree of rational, scientific Enlightenment literature. In nineteenth-century western and central Europe there was, as we have noted, a stratum of such traditionalists. But despite their acerbic rejection of religious reform, they upheld the same integrationist ideological orientation as did the religious reformers. Indeed, the prototype of such a neotraditionalist intelligentsia, Samson Raphael Hirsch in Germany, would have no truck whatsoever with the traditionalist calls for a return to Zion aired by Rabbi Kalischer in the 1860s. Hirsch reformulated traditionalism in a manner he considered compatible with integration into German society, a reformulation that came to be known as neoorthodoxy and that proved to be distinctly inhospitable to Zionism.

As we have seen, however, one may discern a category of other rabbis who aligned themselves with Hibbat Zion and afterward with the Zionist Organi-zation. They drew upon a tradition of thought and homiletical interpretation that had been advocating Jewish resettlement of Eretz Israel since the mid-nineteenth century (albeit with almost no success). Although premodern messianic motivations were central to this tradition, their reformulation, making natural human action a legitimate stage on the path to divine redemption, reflected the response to modernity of a variety of rabbinical types. They ranged from Rabbi Moses Gaster in London, who, like Hirsch, combined higher education with religious orthodoxy, to Rabbi Mohilewer in Russia, who was ready to accommodate only a modicum of modernity. Mohilewer represented a traditionalist conceptual corridor, with its own universe of discourse, that converged with that of the ethnicists. Moreover, plain nonintelligentsia traditionalist Jews constituted a large part of the following of Hibbat Zion and indeed their rabbinic leaders aspired to control of the movement. Even after the defection of many rabbis in the 1890s and thereafter, traditionalist Jews formed a significant part of the following of the world Zionist Organization inaugurated by Theodor Herzl.

In sum, the formative progenitors of the Eretz Israel–oriented nationalist movement that later came to be known as Zionism were the category of Jewish intelligentisia that we have labeled ethnicists—particularly their eastern European strain, which had evinced a cultural-nationalist ideology even before the phenomenal turning point of the early 1880s in Russia. If Anthony Smith's emphasis on the critical role of returning "assimilationists" is borne out by empirical evidence relating to other nationalisms, then we have here a distinguishing mark of the Jewish case. Be that as it may, the ignition spark, as it were, of the Jewish nationalist movement was the turnabout not of dyed-in-the-wool cosmopolitan assimilationists but of a significant number of the second subtype of reformists, the integrationists (to be sure, often semantically misnamed assimilationists), first in eastern Europe and afterward in the West, and their conjunction with the inverately ethnicist core of the intelligentsia in eastern Europe and their émigré offshoots in the West. Yet the capacity of this movement to gain a popular following of significant mass was due largely to a third, contemporaneous conjunction—with a segment of the traditionalist rabbis who resiliently reformulated connections with Eretz Israel that inhered profoundly in the religious traditions of the Jewish *ethnie*.

CHAPTER TWO

Ideological Precursors of Zionism

The Methodological Problem

I N T H E C O U R S E of our broad-canvas account of the social origins of the Eretz Israel–oriented nationalism that developed into Zionism, reference has been made to mid-nineteenth-century manifestations of what appeared to be strikingly similar ideas, notably those of Moses Hess (1812–1875) and of Rabbis Yehuda Hai Alkalai (1798–1878) and Zvi Hirsch Kalischer (1795–1874). This raises the question of whether the precise origin of the Zionist ideology may be traced back to the ideas formulated by such persons, thereby antedating the emergence in the 1880s of a recognizable Jewish national movement. Daunting methodological difficulties have long beset attempts to answer this question. What is required, in the first instance, is agreement on the definition of that which is connoted by the term "the Zionist idea." But how can this be attained, given the developmental nature of the ideology and its variability over time and place?

One methodological solution that suggests itself is to seek out the common denominators of the Eretz Israel–oriented nationalist ideology in its recognizably well-formed manifestation, from the emergence of Hibbat Zion in the 1880s until, and including, the founding of the Zionist organization in 1897. These denominators may then be used as a yardstick by which to measure the degree of similarity exhibited by earlier ideological manifestations. Following this procedure, it may be suggested that the common denominator of Zionist ideology comprises four major propositions, relating to (1) definition of the nature of the Jews as a social entity, (2) diagnosis of the perceived problematic situation of this entity, (3) advocacy of a solution, and (4) proposals of means for attaining that solution.

The first, defining the nature of the Jews as a social entity, posits *that the Jews are a distinctive entity possessing attributes associated with the modern concept of nation, as well as attributes associated with religion.* On this point, it is germane to recall Benedict Anderson's illuminating observation that the modern "nation" is, in the final analysis, a cultural artifact, an "imagined community" of a particular kind.[1] It is doubtful whether the way traditionalist Jews understood themselves was comfortably compatible with an "imagining" of the Jews as a nation in the sense common to modern European nationalisms. The traditionalist conceptual corridor to consciousness of being a nation passed through religious "imaginings" of unique chosenness and divine providence. In his daily prayers, the Jew thanked God for "not making us like all the nations"; the attributes contemporary social science identifies as ethnicity were subsumed by the Jewish belief system, and the Jews being in any sense a nation was comprehended as a dependent implication of that belief system or religion. Nor were the immutable ties of traditionalist Jews with Eretz Israel and their anticipation of ultimate restoration to it dependent on the imagining of being a nation; they too inhered fundamentally in their messianic belief, religious precepts, and ritual practices. Hence, those who clung to traditionalist Jewish self-understanding well into the era of nationalism accommodated the concept of nationalism only with difficulty.

Thus, even Yehiel Michel Pines (1842–1913), who uniquely combined Enlightenment learning and religious traditionalism and who settled in Eretz Israel in 1878, reacted sharply to secular Zionism in the 1890s, arguing that "Israel is not a natural nation in origin, for its peoplehood [*amamuto*] from the beginning was not born naturally, that is to say, as a result of a common race and territory, but rather out of the Torah and the covenant of faith. . . . The Jewish people is different from all the nations and cannot be defined in terms of 'natural nationalism' [*leumiyut tivit*], which you [secular nationalists] wish to attribute to it against its will." In a statement that today sounds almost as if it anticipated Anderson's definition of the nation as an imagined community, Pines argued: "'Nationalism' is a concept, that is to say, a thought-image [*tziyur shel mahshava*]. Every thought-image that has no basis in reality is nothing but a false image. What basis is there in reality for the thought-image of Jewish nationality other than the subsuming of the people by its Torah and faith?"[2]

The prerequisite for traditionalist Jewish imagining of nation and nationalism was some exposure to the modern secular context of the term. It makes sense to speak of nationalism in regard to traditionalist Jews only if it can be shown that its adherents were able to imagine the Jewish nation as a framework broader than its religion—at least, for all practical purposes, during an interim phase between present realities and ultimate divine redemption—and, hence, also as a framework in which cooperation with secularized Jews was conceivable and palatable. In this sense, it is arguable that Yehiel Michel Pines qualifies for definition as a Jewish nationalist, since the logic of his argumentation against a "normal" national interpretation of the Jewish entity was, in fact, predicated upon his Enlightenment-induced capacity to imagine the nation in secular terms in the first place. Certainly, he differed in this regard from those of his contemporaries who remained wholly blinkered by the unadulterated traditionalist self-understanding of the Jewish entity. Yet it remains an instructive fact that even Pines could not, in the final analysis, come to terms with the normal (i.e., predominantly secular) nationalist ideology of its leadership.[3]

The second proposition, diagnosing the perceived problematic situation of the Jewish entity, posits *that its situation under conditions of dispersion is critically defective.* It is important to note, however, that stated baldly thus, this proposition inhered deeply in traditionalist Judaism's millennial grappling with the twin concepts of *galut* (exile) and *geula* (redemption). Although a variety of explanations for the state of being in exile vied with each other (*galut* as punishment, as a form of trial, as a manifestation of cosmic disorder and so on)[4] throughout Jewish history, there could be no doubt that *galut* was by definition a defective condition and that traditionalist Judaism looked forward to the ultimate advent of its conceptual opposite, *geula.* It was only with the emergence of Reform Judaism in the nineteenth century that this cardinal aspect of the Jewish belief system was disrupted. Reform Judaism tended to eliminate territorial Zion from its concept of redemption, reinterpreting that concept in universalistic terms.

In this respect, what was entirely novel about the diagnosis of the condition of *galut* that characterized Zionist ideology from the time of Hibbat Zion was the conceptual matrix in which it transformed that diagnosis into a new social force. Whereas the traditional conceptual matrix was essentially messianic, the crucial motifs of the Zionist ideology were worldly. To be sure, there was in Judaism a venerable, if minority, tradition of interpretation that has been dubbed "active messianism."[5] Contrary to the "passive messianism" that generally prevailed, it posited the need for natural, human action, but—it must be emphasized—only as a stage in the process of ultimately divine redemption. It was therefore but a variety of the messianic conceptual matrix. By contrast, the Zionist ideology focused on the actual problems of Jewish existence rather than on the cosmic dispensation of God; on the relationship between Gentiles and Jews rather than on the relationship between God and His chosen people.[6] More specifically, the Zionist ideology vigorously contradicted the notion that civic emancipation of the Jews in their diasporic condition was satisfactory as a solution. On the contrary it contended that emancipation exacerbated the defective condition of the Jewish dispersion. It advocated national self-emancipation through mundane actions such as settlement and political activity rather than mystical explorations into the manifestations of God's will as revealed in Judaism's sacred texts. It called for self-help, not acts of piety and penitence, even if these motivated actual ascent to Zion, as they might have for "active messianists."

Yet it cannot be said that the traditionalist following of Hibbat Zion and, thereafter, the orthodox religious wing of the Zionist organization ever abandoned the messianic motif. Rather, by dint of homiletical reinterpretation, it rendered that motif subordinate to worldly motifs, thereby facilitating cooperation with secularized Zionists. Hence, it would be apt to describe the conceptual matrix of Zionism as transmessianic, that is to say, transcending the messianic motif yet not necessarily dispensing with it. A more adequate formulation of the above-mentioned second proposition of Zionist ideology might therefore be as follows: *the situation of the Jewish entity under conditions of dispersion is critically defective in a worldly sense.* This did not, however, necessarily preclude the belief that it was also defective in a messianic sense.

The third proposition related to the advocated solution. Still rather inchoate in the phase between the emergence of Hibbat Zion in the early 1880s and the program set out by Theodor Herzl in his *Der Judenstaat* of 1896, it ranged from the limited conception of gradual *ingathering and settlement of Jews in Eretz Israel under conditions of religious and cultural autonomy* to the more radical aspiration for a *sovereign Jewish state and the gathering therein of a major part of the Jewish people.* Moreover, it still wavered somewhat between insistence upon Eretz Israel and contemplation of any suitable territory.

The fourth and last proposition related to the means proposed for attainment of the desired solution. Although there were differences in emphasis and priorities, the common principle was that of Jewish self-help, and the means included *the revival of national self-respect, morale, and culture; settlement in Eretz Israel; and diplomatic activity to facilitate such settlement.* In Herzl's political Zionist program the last meant obtaining an internationally recognized charter that might lead to the attainment of a state for the Jews.

Of course, these propositions represent an analytical extrapolation rather than any actual formulation articulated by Zionists. But they may serve as a yardstick by which to measure the similarity of what have been termed "proto-Zionist" ideas formulated prior to the emergence of the recognizable Jewish national movement that came to be known as Zionism.

Moses Hess

No exponent of proto-Zionist ideas has been more exhaustively researched than Moses Hess and no proto-Zionist tract more celebrated than his *Rome and Jerusalem*, which appeared in 1862.[7] Although the book is excessively discursive and, taken in conjunction with his other writings, reveals a less than systematic thinker and many inconsistencies, there can be no doubt that it qualifies as an eloquent expression of Jewish nationalist ideology and foreshadows all of the postulates extrapolated above.

The example of other nationalisms, especially that of the Italians, is explicit in the title chosen by Hess: *Rome and Jerusalem: The Last National Question.*

With unmistakable nationalist rhetoric he speaks of "the regeneration of the Jewish nation," "the political rebirth of our people," and "the restoration of a Jewish state." It is Hess's premise that "in religion" the Jewish people "conserved its nationality," that is to say that the Jews are a nation, and their religion is an expression of their *Volksgeist* rather than vice versa. Indeed, this premise provides the basis for one of Hess's leitmotifs: whereas Christianity, being a religion of personal salvation is endangered by Enlightenment rationalism, Judaism, being a national culture and not merely a religion, is not so endangered and has a future that holds out great promise for the redemption of mankind as a whole.

Also in regard to his diagnosis of Jewry's diasporic situation, Hess's *Rome and Jerusalem* is remarkable for its apparent prescience. In arguing that civic emancipation would not bring full acceptance of the Jew into gentile society, Hess presaged the central postulate common to Pinsker and Herzl, although less coherently and radically: "Wherefore the illusion? The European nations have always considered the existence of the Jews in their midst as an anomaly. We shall always remain strangers amongst the nations. They may tolerate us and even grant us emancipation, but they will never respect us as long as we place the principle *ubi bene ibi patria* above our own great national memories."[8]

Hess not only anticipated that emancipation in itself was no solution but also perceived the beginnings of a shift in the rationale of anti-Jewish hostility from a religious to a racist basis. It was of no avail for the Jew to estrange himself from Judaism or to reform his religion. "Even conversion itself does not relieve the Jew from the enormous pressure of German Jew-hatred. The German hates the Jewish race more than the religion; he objects less to the Jews' peculiar beliefs than to their peculiar noses."[9] Furthermore, his Socialist ideological background informed his diagnosis of the Jewish situation with emphases that anticipated later Socialist Zionism. Thus, he asserted that the Jews in exile "cannot devote themselves successfully to productive labor" and that "a common native soil is a primary condition, if there is to be introduced among the Jews better and more progressive relations between capital and labor."[10]

In proposing that the solution was to revive Jewish national consciousness and restore a Jewish state in Eretz Israel, Hess clearly foreshadowed the crux of Pinsker's *Autoemancipation* and Herzl's *Der Judenstaat*. Note must, however, be taken of a major conceptual difference: unlike their formulations, Hess's was infused with a pronounced messianic vision, albeit in nontraditionalist, universalized form. Yet at the same time, Hess did not envisage a total ingathering of the exiles; Jewish statehood was to supplement rather than totally displace continued diasporic emancipation.

As for the means to be adopted to attain the Jewish restoration, they did not get systematic attention in Hess's *Rome and Jerusalem*. Still, it is clear that he supported contemporary efforts to foster Jewish settlement in Eretz Israel. He praised the endeavors of Rabbi Zvi Hirsch Kalischer in this regard and identified with the Colonisationsverein für Palästina (Colonization Association for Palestine) with which Kalischer was closely associated. (We shall consider the activities and significance of this association later in this chapter.) Hess himself suggested practical measures, such as the founding of a public corporation to finance the restoration to Zion and the setting up of agricultural schools and cooperative settlements with public credits. But he set store mainly by diplomatic means. In the light of France's revolutionary role and emancipatory record in the past, as well as her interests in the disintegrating Ottoman empire, his hopes focused above all on that country: "France beloved friend, is the savior who will restore our people to its place in universal history."[11] In this vein he commended the proposals of Ernest Laharanne, who in his work *La Nouvelle question d'Orient* (1860) had called for reestablishment of a Jewish state in Palestine with French help as part of a new political dispensation within the Middle East. Hess envisaged that France, acting as international patron of the Jewish restoration, would gain a charter from the Ottomans facilitating Jewish resettlement of Eretz Israel.

In sum, Hess's *Rome and Jerusalem* already exhibited the essentials of all four propositions constituting the common denominator of mature Zionist ideology. Yet there is no evidence of significant causal sequence linking his ideas to those of Pinsker and Herzl some twenty and thirty years later. Neither showed particular awareness of Hess's ideas at the time they formulated their own views.[12] *Rome and Jerusalem* had failed to make a significant impression on Hess's contemporaries. As might be expected, the leading figure in reform Judaism, Abraham Geiger, gave it short shrift, as did Ludwig Philippson, editor of the important newspaper *Allgemeine Zeitung der Judentums*. It elicited a sympathetic response only from the few contemporary exponents of kindred, if less explicitly nationalist, Jewish ethnicism (as defined in the previous chapter), such as Heinrich Graetz, the historian, and David Gordon, the subeditor of *Ha-magid*. Not until 1888–1889 did a Hebrew translation appear in a series of issues of *Ha-magid*, and only ten years later, in 1899, did a new translation appear as a book.[13]

In the light of those known responses to Hess's *Rome and Jerusalem* and in the absence of evidence showing significant influence of his ideas on those who later founded an organized Jewish national movement, Hess exemplifies the "precursor" phenomenon, that is to say, the phenomenon of a person who expresses ideas that precede in time the emergence of social movements animated by much the same ideas. Yet, amazing as Hess's prefiguration of Zionist ideology may appear to be, it is not beyond the bounds of reasonable historical explanation within the framework of the general account of Zionism's social origins given in the first chapter of this book. For, as was noted there, Hess's ideas were but an extreme variant of Jewish ethnic self-affirmation manifested by part of the emerging intelligentsia (the ethnicists) of west-central Europe in the nineteenth century, the period of advancing, if highly flawed, emancipation for the Jews. Biographically, Hess was an early example of what became a common occurrence in the last quarter of the nineteenth century, the rebounding to Jewish ethnicism of Jewish intelligentsia who had earlier abandoned their traditionalist background and sought integration into particular social and intellectual circles of the emancipatory host society. We shall, accordingly, briefly trace this development in the life of Hess.

Hess's early upbringing was that of a traditionalist Jewish child in the Rhineland, but as a young man he left that background behind, studied at Bonn University for a time, and found his way prior to the 1848 revolutions to a group of Left Hegelians that included Karl Marx. Hess and Marx cooperated quite closely for a number of years, although Marx in due course scorned Hess's "unscientific," idealistic mode of socialism. In these years Hess traversed the path of integration into his chosen reference groups of the majority society. To be sure, more recent scholarship has revealed in Hess's career a constancy of Jewish self-awareness that coexisted alongside his idealistic socialism, rather than a total replacement of the one by the other. Nevertheless, it cannot be gainsaid that in the 1840s and 1850s Hess was inclined to advocate Jewish assimilation and doubted that Jews as a collectivity had any future universal contribution to make. This was especially evident in his second book, *The European Triarchy*, which appeared in 1841.[14] Indeed, in 1844, in an essay titled *Über das Geldwesen* (On money), he wrote highly disparagingly of the so-called money cult of Judaism underlying the capitalist ethos, although, to be sure, he directed even sharper barbs at Christianity's deepening of that degenerate ethos. He traced it back to the sacrificial blood cult in ancient Judaism. Karl Marx's better-known essay, "On the Jewish Question," bore a strong resemblance to that of Hess.[15]

Against this biographical background, Hess's *Rome and Jerusalem*, published in 1862, marks an apparently sudden transformation of his views, almost a penitent act of return to the Jewish roots of his childhood. He said as much in his opening passages:

After an estrangement of twenty years, I am back with my people. I have come to be one of them again, to participate in the celebration of the holy days, to share the memories and hopes of the nation. . . . A thought which I believed to be forever buried in my heart has been revived in me anew. It is the thought of my nationality which is inseparably connected with the ancestral heritage and the memories of the Holy Land, the Eternal City, the birthplace of the belief in the divine unity of life, as well as the hope in the future brotherhood of men.[16]

The close affinity between the ideological position that Hess now adopted and the position that was described in chapter 1 as "ethnicist" is evident, above all, in Hess's admiration for Graetz's historiography and in his deprecation of reformed Judaism. Hess was in frequent correspondence with Graetz. In *Rome and Jerusalem* he cited Graetz as an authority, and he translated parts of Graetz's work on the history of the Jews into French. Hess's affinity with the "positive historical" school of thought is confirmed, moreover, by the fact that, notwithstanding his innovatively explicit drawing out of its nationalist potential, even he did not escape entirely from the pervasive emancipationist ideological climate of his time. His advocacy of Jewish national restoration in Zion was not advanced as a total negation of emancipation in the Diaspora, for he was far from despairing of its promise. In describing the position he envisaged "after the restoration of the Jewish state," he commented: "For just as at the time of the return from the Babylonian exile not all the Jews settled in Palestine but the majority remained in the lands of the exile . . . so need we not look forward to a larger concentration of Jews at the future restoration." Immigration to the Jewish state was to be from eastern Europe and Arab lands, rather than from the West. "Even after the establishment of the Jewish State," he wrote, "the majority of the Jews who live at present in the civilized occidental countries will undoubtedly remain where they are." He argued that this enjoyment of civic rights was entirely compatible with Jewish racial (or ethnic) pride and cognizance of Jewish nationality. On this premise he condemned the "new" type of Jew, arguing that he "who denies the existence of Jewish nationality, is not only a deserter in the religious sense, but is also a traitor to his people, his race and even to his family."[17]

In essence, therefore, Hess's views in *Rome and Jerusalem* were an isolated manifestation of highly assertive ethnicism that arose alongside the mainstream current of ethnicism exemplified by Zacharias Frankel and Heinrich Graetz. Because of its call for considerable ethnic-territorial congruence as a goal, argued largely on secular grounds, Hess's ethnicism is indistinguishable from nationalism. He made the leap to nationalism and was the first to author a full ideological exposition. However, his ideological formulations belong to an intellectual milieu still very different from that which later produced a Jewish nationalist movement. They were a product of the particular social and intellectual reference group into which he had successfully integrated.

As one close study of Hess's intellectual and social milieu has shown, he reached the turning point from alienation to reidentification with Jewishness in the course of his involvement in the 1850s with a specific group of French Utopian Socialists.[18] Hess found a comfortable social and intellectual environment in this group. Unlike the young Hegelians with whom he had been associated earlier, these Utopian Socialists were not inclined to anti-Jewish views. However, they drew inspiration from Christian religious values in the formulation of their messianic-like vision for the future. Although they were not entirely negative in their assessment of Judaism's original contribution to those values, they regarded the teachings of Jesus and hence of Christianity as a higher stage in the advance toward a reformed world order of universal brotherhood. Hess was not unaffected by the note of dissonance evocative of the ancient

Jewish-Christian antagonism. In this context, his Jewish self-awareness was reawakened, and he reacted by raising the banner of Judaism and staking out a claim for the Jewish mission in history and its supreme significance for the ultimate universal vision. He developed the thesis that the path to the ultimate messianic social order of universal peace led from Moses and the prophets to Spinoza and thence to a Jewish national revival as the precondition for its realization.

Hess's mode of Jewish national affirmation was thus highly idiosyncratic in that it was activated by a form of Christian millenarian thought as mediated by the ideas of this rather peripheral group of French Utopian Socialists. Hence, too, all of the specific ideas of Hess that we have found to match the later postulates of mature Zionism were encompassed within a comprehensive conceptual framework of messianic character. It was, to be sure, a quasi-messianism, that is to say, a secularized messianism.[19] Hess did not expect the coming of an incarnate divine redeemer or believe in traditionalist Jewish eschatology. "The 'end of days', so often spoken of by the Prophets," he wrote, "is not to be understood to mean, as some misinterpret it, the end of the world, but it denotes the period when the development and education of humanity will reach their highest point." Yet, for Hess, "the socialist rabbi," as he was scornfully dubbed by the "scientific" Socialists, this quasi-messianism was no less meaningful than the traditionalist eschatology was for Rabbi Kalischer, whose views on Jewish restoration to Zion he quoted with approval. He anticipated that "pious Jews will join hands with the enlightened on the common ground of Jewish nationalism."[20] The essence of Hess's intellectual odyssey was a series of social and ideological attachments in search of a messianic end. The stations of that odyssey included his break from the traditionalist Judaism of his grandfather's home, his captivation by Spinoza's thought, his utopian socialism, his ambivalent attraction to the Christian ethos and search for a synthesis with that of Judaism, and his ultimate reaffirmation of Jewish national identity as the path to the final messianic self-redemption of humanity.[21]

Christian Ideas of Jewish Restoration

The particular brand of Christian ideas associated with Hess's Utopian Socialist compatriots could have a direct influence on his "proto-Zionist" thought because he internalized those ideas in the course of integrating into that particular social reference group. Most forms of Christian millenarianism were, however, nurtured within deeply religious Christian circles that, by definition, excluded Jews unless they converted. Christian millenarianism, therefore, could influence Jews only indirectly, by encouraging and assisting those Jewish efforts at resettlement of Zion that were perceived to be prerequisites for the ultimate Christian myth of mankind's redemption.

On the basis of such ideas, an abundance of Christian exponents of Jewish restoration to Zion appeared throughout the eighteenth and nineteenth centuries. One of the earliest examples was a Danish merchant, Oliger Paulli (1644–1714), who, in memoranda to various European monarchs, enthusiastically advocated the establishment of a Jewish monarchy in Palestine and in 1695 went to London in an abortive attempt to win over the support of William III for his schemes.

In the first half of the nineteenth century, England became the main nursery of projects for the restoration of the Jews to Palestine.[22] These drew upon a long tradition of chiliastic religious ideas going back to the pietistic Protestants of the mid-sixteenth century. Restorationism derived from an interpretation of certain biblical passages that foretold the second advent of Jesus Christ to establish a reign that would last for a millennium (one thousand years) and that involved the return of the Jews to Zion and their embrace of Christianity either before or after this second advent.

The interaction of such religious millenarian ideas with political policies and projects reached its zenith toward the mid-nineteenth century against the background of the "Eastern Question," that is to say, the precarious state of the Ottoman Empire, of which Palestine formed a part. This was a question of international politics that commanded the attention of the European powers, causing them to seek ways and means of disrupting or, alternatively, buttressing the Ottoman Empire—"the sick man of Europe." Within this context the archadvocate in Britain of Jewish restoration to Palestine was Anthony Ashley Cooper, later seventh earl of Shaftesbury (1801–1885), who was also a renowned philanthropist, social reformer, and, above all, evangelist. Another example was Colonel Charles Henry Churchill (grandson of the fifth duke of Marlborough), an officer on the staff of the allied army that had compelled Mehemet Ali to withdraw from Palestine. In 1841, Colonel Churchill presented Sir Moses Montefiore with a plan for Jewish resettlement of Palestine. A particularly notable later advocate of similar ideas was the one-time foreign service diplomat, journalist, and traveler Sir Laurence Oliphant (1829–1888), who devoted many years of advocacy and practical efforts to the restoration of the Jews to Palestine. In his book *The Land of Gilead* (1880) and in various negotiations he proposed that Jewish settlements be established east of the Jordan under the auspices of the Turks and with the support of France and Great Britain. Oliphant ultimately settled in Palestine (in the Druse village of Usafiya near Haifa), where he continued to assist the Jewish settlers in whatever ways he could.

Yet the projects and schemes advanced by Christian advocates of Jewish restoration to Zion failed to arouse a significant response from Jews at large. The ideals of emancipation and integration that dominated the aspirations of enlightened Jews did not sit well with restorationist enthusiasm. Moreover, restorationist purposes were extraneous and alien to the eschatological vision of Judaism because they saw Jewish restoration to Zion not as an end in itself but rather as a necessary stage or portent of the second advent of Christ and the end of days in Christian terms. The case of Lord Shaftesbury is highly instructive in this regard. Although he energetically marshaled his restorationist arguments before Palmerston in political terms, his underlying motivation was religious-millenarian. "I am forced to argue politically, financially, commercially; these considerations strike him home," he recorded in his diary in August 1840.[23] Shaftesbury was, after all, associated closely with the London Society for Promoting Christianity Among the Jews. It is also characteristic that his advocacy of restoration went hand in hand with reservations concerning the full civic emancipation of the Jews in England. In the midcentury debates on the Emancipation Bill, permitting Jews to enter Parliament without taking the usual oath "on the true faith of a Christian," Lord Shaftesbury was to be found among those speaking against it on the ground that waiver of the oath was a violation of religious principle.[24]

It is therefore hardly surprising that the conventional leadership of western European Jewish communities by and large politely evaded the proddings and projects of Christian restorationists. When Charles Henry Churchill addressed his appeal to Sir Moses Montefiore in 1841, submitting that Jews should "simultaneously throughout Europe" launch an intensive campaign for restoration under European protection and urging that "it is for the Jews to make a commencement," this was not taken up by the Board of Deputies of British Jews, of which Montefiore was president. The resolution passed at the meeting of the board on November 7, 1842, reads:

That the President be requested to reply to Colonel Churchill to the effect that this Board, being appointed for the fulfilment of special duties and deriving its pecuniary resources from the contributions to the several congregations it represents, is precluded from originating any measures for carrying out the benevolent views of Colonel Churchill respecting the Jews of Syria; that this Board is fully convinced that much good would arise from the realisation of Colonel Churchill's intentions, but is of the opinion that any measures in reference to this subject should emanate from the general body of the Jews throughout Europe, and that this Board doubts not that if the Jews of other countries entertain the propositions those of Great Britain would be ready and desirous to contribute towards it their most zealous support.[25]

The Board then filed away into oblivion Colonel Churchill's ardent proto-Zionist appeal. Montefiore's dedication to the Jewish population of Eretz Israel was already legendary throughout the Jewish world, but his objectives fell far short of those advocated by Christian restorationists or, for that matter, by contemporary Jewish advocates of resettlement in Eretz Israel. Some cross-fertilization of ideas did occur, however, between the latter and Christian restorationists. A striking example of this was Mordecai Manuel Noah (1785–1851), an American Jew of Sephardic origin, a journalist, author, and politician who also served as his country's consul in Tunis from 1813 to 1816.

Notwithstanding the many eccentricities and gyrations of Noah's career, he was widely regarded as one of the most prominent Jews in the United States toward the middle of the nineteenth century.[26] His ideas were, in essence, a Jewish, postemancipationist mirror image of Christian restorationism. The first expression of his ideas was between 1818 and 1825, at which time they assumed the form of a plan for establishing on Grand Island in the Niagara River a "city of refuge" to be named Ararat. He was to serve as a sort of ruler-"Judge" until such time as officials might be democratically elected. Adopting the dubious theory that the American Indians belonged to the Ten Lost Tribes of Israel, he invited them to join the Jewish immigration that he anticipated would populate Ararat. Dressed in resplendent garb, he went so far as to dedicate the new "state" in a ceremony at the local Episcopal church in Buffalo in 1825.

Viewed in the context of contemporary schemes for immigration from Europe and of communal-religious settlement projects such as those of the Mormons and the Transcendentalists' Brook Farm settlement in New England, Noah's project was not as bizarre as it might appear today. He justified Ararat as a training ground for acquiring the governmental skills that would facilitate the final Jewish restoration to Zion. In religious terms, it was a stage on the path to ultimate divine redemption. In secular terms it had something in common with what was later, in the twentieth century, to be dubbed "territorialism," that is to say, the search for any territory that could provide a viable refuge for persecuted Jews.

Undeterred by Ararat's utter failure, Noah turned in 1844 to the idea of Jewish restoration of Palestine as a "new Judea" under the protection of either Britain or the Great Powers in concert. Although invoking putative political interests too, his new scheme was designed above all to appeal to Christian restorationists. His exposition of the plan was presented before audiences composed mostly of New York Christians, many of whom had been exposed to restorationist ideas. In his discourse, Noah pandered to upholders of those ideas, saying that he "fully appreciated . . . the pious and benevolent objects of the Society for Evangelizing the Jews" but appealed to them to "unite in efforts to promote the restoration of Jews in their *unconverted state* [Noah's emphasis] relying on the fulfillment of the prophecies and the will of God for attaining the objects they have in view after the great advent shall have arrived."[27] In sum, Noah was a case of cross-fertilization of ideas with Christian restorationism.

Another instance of a significant relationship between a Christian restorationist and Jewish attempts to resettle Eretz Israel was that of Sir Laurence Oliphant. He conducted a correspondence with Peretz Smolenskin and employed as his secretary and interpreter Naphtali Herz Imber (author of the

Hatikva, which was to become Israel's national anthem). This mutual relationship was made possible partly because he repeatedly disavowed conversionist motivations[28] but was mainly owing to the fact that his restorationist diplomatic activities coincided with the emergence of the Hibbat Zion movement in the early 1880s and with the first nationalist-motivated wave of settlement in Palestine.

Having conducted spirited but abortive negotiations with the Turkish government in Constantinople in 1879, Oliphant's name became well known among eastern European Jewry, so when he traveled in eastern Europe in early 1882, in the wake of the Russian pogroms, he was met at railway stations on his route with enthusiastic petitions from crowds of Jews. In the frenetic search for avenues of emigration in general and hopes for Eretz Israel in particular, Russian Jews had formed exaggerated notions of Oliphant's importance. Back in Constantinople in mid-1882, Oliphant endeavored, again in vain, to help the small Bilu group carry out their plans. Undaunted by all his setbacks, he continued to encourage the efforts of Hibbat Zion and settled with his wife in Haifa in late 1882. Oliphant may thus be said to epitomize the role of encouragement played by Christian restorationists but also to illustrate its limited effectiveness.

There is ample evidence that Jewish advocates of resettlement in Eretz Israel certainly were aware of their Christian counterparts. For example, both Moses Hess and David Gordon cited them, particularly Ernest Laharanne's *La Nouvelle question d'Orient.* However, they invoked them only in an instrumental manner, to reinforce their own contentions rooted in Jewish concepts and motivations.[29] No doubt, the cumulative weight of Christian restorationist ideas, particularly those appealing to the political interests of European powers, contributed to the intellectual and political atmosphere that accorded a degree of credibility to various "proto-Zionist" proposals by Jews in the course of the nineteenth century. By the same token, they had a bearing on the history of Zionism as a movement, for they endowed some leading statesmen—Arthur James Balfour is the most famous example—with a predisposition favorable to Zionism. After the 1880s and particularly with Herzl's advent, the Zionist leadership willingly drew upon Christian protagonists as a valuable support and ally in its diplomatic efforts. Indeed, notable roles were performed by a number of Christians, ranging from the clergyman William H. Hechler, who aided Herzl's diplomatic efforts, to Baffy Dugdale, niece of Lord Balfour, who was an important aide to Chaim Weizmann in the 1930s and 1940s. But this was in the period when Zionist ideology and the Zionist Organization were already fully formed and functioning. Before the 1890s there was some cross-fertilization of ideas, but there does not appear to have been significant collaboration. It should here be noted, however, that this is a subject that still awaits definitive research. A summing up at this point calls for some caution. In our present state of knowledge, at any rate, a comprehensive historical explanation of the genesis of Zionist ideology can assign to the Christian restorationists no more than a peripheral role.

The Precursor Phenomenon

The historiographical difficulties attendant upon attempts to account for the considerable range of ideas bearing a similarity to Zionism expressed before 1880, by Christians as well as Jews, has led to the use, variously, of the synonymous terms "proto-Zionists," "precursors," "harbingers," and "forerunners" of Zionism (*mevasrei ha-tzionut*). The implication is that there is a hiatus of some sort between the earlier and the later phenomena, else there would be no need for recourse to such terms, and one could simply identify the earlier as the "beginning" of the phenomenon or its "first" manifestation.

Early Zionist historiography on this point lacked analytical clarity and was tinged by the "historicism" of Zionism itself, that is to say, by the attempt to press the past into the service of the ideology. Thus, Nahum Sokolow, whose *History of Zionism* (1919) was the first to appear,[30] was at pains to prove that Zionism had an impressive genealogy in Jewish history and that it was but the awakening of an ever immanent national spirit acknowledged by Jews and Gentiles alike. Although purporting to explore "the origin and development of the Zionist idea," he eclectically marshaled a myriad of ideas, some of which were only remotely akin to Zionism. They included Menasseh ben Israel's pleas in the seventeenth century for readmission of the Jews to Britain on the basis of biblical prophecies. These made dispersion of the Jews "to the ends of the earth" a necessary stage in their restoration to Zion, which in turn was the precondition for universal messianic redemption. Thus, one finds in Sokolow's work such anachronistic statements as "Menasseh was nothing if not a Zionist, if we look upon Zionism in the light of his time."[31]

The approach of Adolf Boehm, whose *Die Zionistische Bewegung* (The Zionist movement) first appeared in 1920, was more analytically discriminating; he separated out as *Vorläufer* (precursors) only the major Jewish and Christian advocates of some form of Jewish return to Zion or restoration of Zion to the Jews during the nineteenth century. Boehm thus gave prominence to Mordecai Manuel Noah. He also bracketed together Moses Montefiore, Rabbi Zvi Hirsch Kalischer, and the Alliance Israélite Universelle in its early period under the leadership of Adolphe Crémieux. To Moses Hess he attributed special significance, calling his *Rome and Jerusalem* "the first classic work of modern Zionism."[32] As Christian precursors he included Benjamin Disraeli; George Eliot, whose novel *Daniel Deronda* (1876) raised ideas of Jewish restoration to Zion; and English diplomats and soldiers such as Lord Palmerston, Colonels George Gawler and C. R. Conder, and Laurence Oliphant.

Later scholarship shunned tendentious attempts to display the rich genealogy of the Zionist idea and focused more analytically upon the secularization of thought as the prerequisite for anything that could pass as Zionism. A seminal article in Hebrew by Dov Weinryb, published in 1937, thus argued that the beginnings of the Zionist idea could be found only in those ideas and proposals that were essentially secular, that is to say, down-to-earth and realistic rather than predicated upon divine intervention. Weinryb defined the idea of Zionism thus: "The establishment of a safe refuge, a national home, a territorial center, Jewish state etc. by means of systematic human action without awaiting the action of supernatural and rationally inscrutable forces—that is to say the intention of Zionism is secular, by the hand of man and not by the divine hand."[33]

Weinryb did not, however, subject the various precursors to close examination with the litmus test of secularism. Instead, he contended that the historian should seek to account for the genesis of Zionism by analyzing the socioeconomic factors that caused Zionism to emerge; his task was to uncover the moral and spiritual needs, problems, and aspirations of the Jews that caused the Jewish nationalist answer to be formulated. He went on to examine these under such heads as the need and desire for productivization, the urge to emigrate, the influence of European nationalisms, and the desire to revitalize the Hebrew language.

Ben Zion Dinaburg (later Dinur) ostensibly applied the same criterion (i.e., the secular impulse) in his copiously documented studies.[34] However, what Dinur came up with was an account of the genesis of the Zionist idea that skirted Christian ideas and invoked Jewish sources as far back as the eclipse of the Sabbatean messianic eruption of the seventeenth century. In these sources he discerned a shift from the passive messianism, which had been prevalent for centuries, to a new active messianism. The analytic basis for such far-reaching conclusions was so elastic an interpretation of the secular impulse as to include mere shifts of emphasis toward realistic self-exertion away from either of the alternative poles of totally deterministic quietism or Sabbatean false-messianic fervor. Dinur perceived the first such shift, marking "the beginning of a more realistic course of messianic activity," as early as the *aliya* (ascent to The Land) of Rabbi Yehuda He-hasid (Yehuda the Pious) at the head of his group of followers, reputed to have been as large as one thousand, in the year 1700.

According to Dinur's account, the convulsive messianic movement of Sabbatai Zevi in the seventeenth century, although bitterly disappointing in the end, had the long-term effect of cracking the wall of passivity in regard to the condition of *galut*. Notwithstanding the consequent withdrawal from messianic excitement, the Sabbatean convulsion left a residue of impatience with the *galut* that found expression in Rabbi Yehuda's "more realistic course of messianic activity," as Dinur put it. Collating a host of sources from that time onward— Dinur identified some fifteen major collective *aliyot* (ascents to Zion) in the eighteenth and nineteenth centuries—he discerned what he termed "ideological" changes related to the conception of exile and redemption. One was an innovative proposition that loss of the consciousness of exile and forgetting of Jerusalem were themselves the *cause* of the exile's perpetuation rather than its result. "*Galut* was not only a punishment for our sins it was the sin itself." Ascent to Eretz Israel was posited as the foremost corrective (*tikun*) for the sin of *galut*. Another ideological innovation was a renewed emphasis on the attachment to the Land of Israel, and a new "conception that activity aimed at resettling The Land was a necessary means towards preparing for and quickening the coming of divine redemption." A third emphasis, so contended Dinur, was ascription to the *tzadik* (Hasidic spiritual leader) of a special duty requiring that he purposefully lead the way to the natural act of ascent and settlement in The Land. These "ideological" innovations, Dinur argued, were evidence that *aliyot* like that of 1700 were not just the last residue of the Sabbatean phenomenon; rather, they "heralded a new chapter in the annals of the search for paths to redemption." Dinur went as far as to say that "the activating forces leading to the reconstitution of the State of Israel already inhered in these innovations."[35]

Today, most historians would agree that Ben Zion Dinur's fervent Zionist ideological convictions overly influenced his broad-canvas account of the genesis of Zionism.[36] It was an account that portrayed Zion as the pivot of a people of unbroken organic unity and Zionism as the natural unfolding of an immanent propulsion toward Zion. Neither Dinur's attribution of "realism" to specific *aliyot*, such as that of Rabbi Yehuda He-hasid, nor his general thesis that return to Eretz Israel played so pivotal a role in the exilic history of the Jewish people has been confirmed by later research. Yet it should be noted, to Dinur's credit, that his account did not rest solely on the putative changes within traditionalist Jewry that we have been discussing. His perspective was bifocal. It also scanned the process of emancipation and enlightenment within European Jewry and pointed to its ambiguous effects on Jewish national awareness. Although fully cognizant of the fact that the overwhelming ideological trend was away from national self-awareness, he highlighted the distinction between *maskilim* who were "on the bridge crossing to the wider world beyond" and others who remained "within the walls" of the Jewish people. The latter type, he said, "neither found it possible nor desirable 'to jump out of their skin.' For, also the 'new' was for them Jewish, thoroughly Jewish." They regarded enlightenment not as a means toward disintegration of the Jewish entity but rather as a corrective therapy for it. Dinur argued that in this stream of the *haskala* there already inhered the foundations of the national renaissance of the Jews. As our earlier survey of modernity's impact on the Jewish *ethnie* throughout Europe would suggest, Dinur's account of the genesis of Jewish nationalism was here on far firmer ground than was his thesis concerning changes in traditionalist concepts and acts of *aliya*.

To be sure, more recently a similar scholarly claim has been made concerning one specific collective *aliya*, that of disciples of the Gaon of Vilna between 1808 and 1847. It has been argued (by Arie Morgenstern) that this *aliya* was motivated by notions of messianic activism that abrogated the prevalent quietism of traditionalists; that the intention of the Gaon's disciples was to settle in The Land as directed by him out of a sense of imminent redemption, seeking to hasten its advent by their actions.[37] According to this account, it was only following the failure of the Messiah to appear in the year of expectation 5600 (1840), that the subcommunity formed by this wave of *aliya*, known as the *perushim* (seceders) underwent an extreme reversion to quietism manifested in pious devotion to religious study and spiritual improvement as the sole human means that could have a bearing upon the hastening of the redemption. One was to hold faith in a miraculous redemption; rebuilding of The Land could do nothing to hasten its coming. Henceforth, this became the dominant norm of the Ashkenazi "old *yishuv*," that is, the part of Palestine's traditionalist population that stemmed from Europe.[38] But this thesis has aroused much scholarly controversy. It is argued that ascription to the *perushim* of innovative, realistic activism as a stage in the redemptive process is without real foundation, that in fact it was first to last characterized by an elitist dedication to study and a quietistic holding of faith in divine redemption.[39]

It must be noted, however, that even if Dinur's earlier conclusions or Morgenstern's recent thesis were to be accepted, they would contribute but little to our search for the origins of the particular conceptual matrix and propositions that came to constitute the Zionist idea. Even if nineteenth century manifestations of what may be dubbed "active," in contrast to "passive" messianism can be demonstrated, and even if they called for resettlement of Eretz Israel, the fact remains that they did not transcend the confines of the messianic conceptual framework. Those to whom we may attribute adherence to "active messianism" did not detach themselves from the expectation of an imminent miraculous redemption; they merely introduced a component of human action into the process of expectation. Their motives and intentions did not issue from down-to-earth analysis of the actual problems of Jewish existence vis-à-vis the societal environment. The Jews' relationship with God rather than their relationship with the rest of mankind remained the conceptual matrix of their ideas.

The most analytically profound of all attempts to clarify the concept of "precursors" and its place in the genesis of Zionism was that of Jacob Katz.[40] Katz posited a sociological criterion, namely the "social fertility" of the idea. Since the subject of the history of Zionism is, after all, the process by which the aims of Zionism were realized through socially mobilized action, Katz argued that one should limit the phenomenon of precursors to those who not only aired similar ideas but also were able to mobilize social action toward realization of these ideas. This criterion eliminated most of the individuals, Jewish as well as Christian, who had been included in earlier historiographical accounts. Mostly, Katz pointed out, these persons were idiosyncratic individuals, quite out of touch with social reality. Katz regarded Mordecai Manuel Noah as an example of just such an utterly unrealistic eccentric. One may comment that even if he somewhat exaggerated Noah's detachment from reality, Katz's main point remains valid: only in its aspect of providing an emigration scheme to the United States with all its promising freedoms did Noah's Ararat engage some attention from the few European Jews of note with whom he established contact.[41] Even so, nothing came of Noah's unsolicited appointment of "commissioners" to organize mass migration from Europe to Ararat, including Rabbis Solomon Herschell and Raphael Meldola of London and Eduard Gans and Leopold Zunz in Berlin. Noah's later reversion to advocacy of a Jewish state in Palestine, expressed in his 1844 "Discourse on the Restoration of the Jews," lacked even the appeal of an emigration outlet to the United States. The fact is that neither Noah nor any of the entire panoply of Christian advocates of similar ideas were able to stimulate any action-directed social cohesion on the part of the Jews.

In regard to our search for the ideological origins of Zionism, the implication of Jacob Katz's criterion is that we shall be rewarded not by the discovery of those who first articulated some, or even all of the propositions of that ideology. Rather, we need to discover the first manifestation of social cohesion prompted by these propositions, that is to say, when those propositions found expression in some form of organized or coordinated and goal-directed action. If both the ideational propositions and the social action they generated were of much the same kind as the ideology whose origins we seek, and if, in addition, there is evidence of social continuity between them, then we may say that we have discovered the "beginning" of the ideology. If there is no evidence of continuity—that is to say, if there is an hiatus between the two manifestations under examination, then we are dealing with a phenomenological relationship rather than a causal or consequential sequence, and it becomes appropriate to call the earlier manifestation "precursors."

By this criterion, Katz concluded that although numerous persons, both Jewish and Christian, expressed ideas incorporating, in various combinations, propositions constitutive of later Zionist ideology in its mature form, only one congeries of such persons should be regarded as "precursors." These were the key persons associated with the Hevrat Yishuv Eretz Israel or Colonisationsverein für Palästina (Colonization Association for Palestine), which had a brief existence from 1860 to 1865.[42]

The most significant personality associated with this society was Rabbi Zvi Hirsch Kalischer, but its founder and guiding spirit was Haim Luria (1821–1878). Luria was a religious Jew who claimed descent from the famous sixteenth century kabbalist Rabbi Yitzhak Luria ("the Arie" of Safed). He worked as a teacher and as owner of a boardinghouse for Jewish children in Frankfurt an der Oder, and it was from there that he attempted to coordinate the activities of the Colonisationsverein. In this task it seems that he proved rather ineffectual and even aroused suspicions of mismanagement. Be that as it may, the ideological common denominator of the leading figures associated with this society was the idea of resettling Eretz Israel with productively employed Jews. This was to be done with down-to-earth, realistic plans and means, although Luria himself along with almost all of the persons associated with the society were religious Jews, not secularists. The aims and regulations of the society included the statement that it "wished to establish and nurture, with the help of God, in peace, a large colony of farmers and wine-growers in the Holy Land . . . the colonists will give a tithe of the produce of the earth to the poor and to the Torah scholars of Eretz Israel." Entitled to membership were persons who paid a fee of at least ten reichsthaler or who undertook to pay two reichsthaler per year for at least three years or persons of notable reputation whom the society invited to join. At its peak the society claimed a few hundred members and sympathizers throughout Europe, but such affiliation required little more than support for the idea of productive settlement on a very modest scale. Even if the germs of nationalist ideas are identifiable in the thinking of the society's core—a doubtful question to which we shall return—this was certainly not recognized at large. For example, Chief Rabbi Nathan Adler of London was a member, but neither he nor his son and successor, Hermann, were to approve of nationalist ideas in the 1880s and 1890s.

Branches that proved to be ephemeral were founded in Berlin, Breslau, and Leipzig. David Gordon of the Hebrew journal *Ha-magid* joined the society, as did Rabbis Alkalai and Kalischer and Josef Natonek, a younger rabbi in Hungary. When Luria apprised Moses Hess of the society's existence, he too joined.[43] Although diffusely and ineffectually, Luria and these key personalities propagated their ideas through articles in the Jewish press. They made approaches to the Alliance Israélite Universelle and Jewish philanthropists in an attempt to win over their support for land purchases and settlement in Eretz Israel. It was Luria who saw to the publication of Kalischer's major work, *Derishat Zion* (Seeking Zion) in 1862.

On the face of things, the ideas mooted and propagated by this circle of personalities, jointly and severally, bear a definite similarity to those advanced later by groups that embodied the mature Zionist ideology—certainly the Hibbat Zion groups that mushroomed in the 1880s if not the more politically oriented Zionist Organization founded by Theodor Herzl in 1897. Yet it is clear that the actual origins of Zionism as a movement cannot be ascribed to the actions of this congeries of persons. The Colonisationsverein had collapsed by 1865, and the sum total of the separate and collective endeavors of all the persons associated with it was minuscule. Apart from the creation of the first agricultural training school in Eretz Israel, Mikwe Israel, in 1871 (an act largely prompted by the efforts of Rabbis Alkalai, Kalischer, and Natonek), neither a consequential organizational instrument for a national movement nor even an advance in settlement of Eretz Israel were generated by the endeavors of these persons. But it remains germane to consider whether this loose congeries of persons, although clearly not giving birth to Zionism as a *movement*, did give birth to the *ideology* of Zionism. In order to establish this, the fact that at least a few of its moving spirits expressed a series of ideas similar to those constitutive of Zionist ideology is not sufficient. We also need to know whether the conceptual matrix of their ideas (that is to say, their underlying conceptions and intentions) was the same as that of fully fledged Zionist ideology, and if it was indeed the same, whether a consequential chain of influence links these ideas to those evinced from the 1880s onward. In regard to the modernist, if not the secularist, in this company, Moses Hess, we have already noted the absence of any consequential chain. But what of the religious traditionalists associated with the Colonisationsverein?

Traditionalist Precursors

Repeated mention has been made of two of the most salient and ardent of the early advocates of Jewish return to Zion: Yehuda Hai Alkalai (1798–1878) and Zvi Hirsch Kalischer (1795–1874). Since both were traditionalist rabbis, it is well to recall our earlier methodological-semantic observation that it makes sense to speak of such persons as nationalists only if it can be shown that they were able to "imagine" or conceptualize the Jewish nation as a framework more comprehensive than its religion, at least for all practical purposes and in an interim phase between present realities and ultimate divine redemption.

That Alkalai and Kalischer were impressed by the contemporary resurgence of small European nations around them is evident from some references to this in their writings. Alkalai mentions the example of the Serbs and other Balkan peoples and states that "the spirit of the time demands of all states that they establish themselves and uplift their languages, and demands likewise of us that we establish the house of our life and uplift and revive our sacred language."[44] Kalischer likewise pointed to the example of other European peoples:

Why is it that the people of Italy and of other states give up their lives for the land of their fathers; it should be all the more so for a land considered sacred by all of the world. . . . It is to the glory of the people of Israel to show for the land of their forefathers that love which is called national [in the source this appears as a non-Hebrew word, written in Hebrew characters—"nationale"]. Are we inferior to all other peoples, whose lives and possessions are considered as nought compared to the love of their land and people? Look to the example of the people of Italy, of Poland, of Hungary, who laid down their lives and gave up their silver and gold, but were uplifted for the sake of their inherited land. Yet shall we, the Children of Israel, whose inheritance is the most glorious of lands, acknowledged as holy by all the inhabitants of the world, be silent and like a lifeless person? We should be ashamed of ourselves. If all other peoples acted for the sake of their own honor, the more so should we act not only for the honor of our forefathers but also for the honor of God who chose Zion as His seat.[45]

However, apart from such references, the writings of Alkalai and Kalischer were thoroughly traditionalist and predominantly messianic in character. They consisted overwhelmingly of homiletical discourse (*drush*), whose rules of proof were tendentious selection of passages from Judaism's sacred texts.[46] Typical is the following example from Alkalai's work of 1843, *Minhat Yehuda* (The offering of Judah). Citing a biblical passage (Num. 10:36), "Return O Lord, unto the tens and thousands of the families of Israel," and a talmudic comment on this to the effect that "the Divine Presence can be felt only if there are at least two thousand and two tens of thousands of Israel together," Alkalai concluded: "First and foremost for the redemption of our souls we must cause at least twenty-two thousand to return to the Holy Land so that the Divine Presence may descend among us; afterward, He will grant us and all Israel further signs of his favor."[47]

Another of Alkalai's interpretations drew upon a theme of Jewish lore that divided the messianic redemption into two stages: first there will appear the Messiah, son of Joseph, who will reconquer Eretz Israel; thereafter, the Messiah, son of David, will appear miraculously to lead the Jewish people back to The Land. Alkalai argued that self-help and the use of natural means was called for in the first stage, and he identified the Messiah, son of Joseph, with the *asefa meusheret* (constituent assembly or assembly of notables), whose formation he urged. More significantly, Alkalai adopted a line of argument already used by another Sephardic rabbi, Yehuda Bibas of Corfu. Following Bibas, Alkalai distinguished between the ordinary obligations of individual repentance and the special obligation of "collective repentance upon which redemption is dependent," which meant return to The Land "to adorn the place of our Temple and to hold the Torah in the courtyards of the House of our God."[48]

Kalischer marshaled similar interpretations of sacred texts to prove that redemption will take place in stages, the first of which required natural means and self-help. In his main work on the subject of Jewish redemption, *Derishat Zion* (Seeking Zion), he cited a passage from the prophet Isaiah that predicted that the Children of Israel "shall be gathered one by one." This he adduced as proof that "all of Israel would not return from exile at one time, but you will be gathered one by one" (i.e., in stages). On the basis of such homiletical arguments he concluded:

The redemption of Israel, for which we long, is not to be imagined as a sudden miracle. The Almighty, blessed be His Name, will not suddenly descend from on high and command His people to go forth. He will not send the Messiah in a twinkling of an eye, to sound the great trumpet for the scattered of Israel and gather them into Jerusalem. He will not surround the Holy City with a wall of fire or cause the Holy Temple to descend from the heavens. The bliss and the miracles that were promised by His servants, the prophets, will certainly come to pass—everything will be fulfilled—but we will not run in terror and flight, for the redemption of Israel will come by slow degrees and the ray of deliverance will shine forth gradually.[49]

In another passage, Kalischer went on to ask: "Can we rationally [*mi-derekh ha-sekhel*] explain why the redemption will begin by natural human means, and why the Lord blessed be He, will not send his messiah, sanctified by His love, to His sacred people all at once in a revealed miracle?" To this question he answered:

Yes, we can. We know that all our worship of God is in the form of trials by which He tests us. When God created man and placed him in the Garden of Eden, He also planted the Tree of Knowledge and then commanded man not to eat of it. Why did he put the Tree in the Garden, if not as a trial? Why did He allow the Snake to enter the Garden, to tempt man if not to test whether man would observe God's command? When Israel went forth from Egypt, God again tested man's faith with hunger and thirst along the way. The laws given us in the Torah about unclean animals which are forbidden us as food are also a continuous trial—else why did the Almighty make them so tempting and succulent? . . . If the Almighty would suddenly appear, one day in the future, through undeniable miracles, this would be no trial. What straining of our faith would there be in the face of the miracles and wonders attending a clear heavenly command to go up and inherit the land and enjoy its fruit? Under such circumstances what fool would not go there, not because of his love of God, but for his own selfish sake? Only a natural beginning of the Redemption is a true test of those who initiate it.[50]

The crux of the historiographical problem regarding Alkalai's and Kalischer's place in the history of Zionism lies in evaluation of the relative weight to be ascribed to the mundane, realistic motifs in their writings and actions, on the one hand, and the traditionalist messianic motifs on the other. The few passages bespeaking exposure to the nationalism of the European nations, such as the one quoted above, have led some scholars to infer that the overwhelming preoccupation of Alkalai and Kalischer with homiletical discourse to prove that resettlement of Zion was a necessary stage toward messianic redemption was merely a rationale; that is to say, their underlying motivation was already nationalist but their universe of discourse was necessarily traditionalist.[51] In support of this view it is noted that both were situated in geopolitically borderline places between west-central and eastern Europe. Kalischer lived in Posen, a boundary area subject to the interacting influences of advancing emancipation in Germany on the one side and the retarded conditions of the Russian Pale of Settlement on the other. Alkalai lived in the Austro-Hungarian environment of seething national tensions and was also exposed to changes arising from the advance of civic emancipation. This interpretation is further strengthened by the fact that even in later periods the homiletical mode saturates the writings of rabbis associated with Zionism proper, including the two most important leaders of all, Rabbis Mohilewer and Reines. However, as the penetrating research of Jacob Katz has shown, historical understanding of the motivations and thought of both Kalischer and Alkalai (especially the former) tends to be marred by anachronistic reading of nationalism into their writings and deeds. Katz has argued that weighed in the balance of all that can be unraveled about the development of their ideas, it cannot be said that their few references to contemporary nationalism were anything but ancillary to their primary traditionalist-messianic motivations.

Revising Katz's seminal analysis, the leading second-generation scholar in this field, Yosef Salmon, finds in Kalischer "signs of a tendency to augment traditional messianic concepts with modern imperatives." Salmon points in particular to his 1864 commentary on the Passover *Hagada* (ritual text), in which he appears to shift the emphasis from the divine messianic climax to "becoming a free people in Eretz Israel."[52] Salmon's account renders Alkalai's and Kalischer's thought consonant with that of indisputably national-religious thought in Hibbat Zion, if not even later. Certainly, their formulation of the two-stage process of messianic redemption was repeatedly invoked by national-religious rabbis. Moreover, there is evidence that their ideas resonated sporadically into the 1870s, notwithstanding the Colonisationsverein's dissolution by 1865. An example is the regulations of the Society for Working and Redemption of The Land, established in Eretz Israel in 1876, which led to the attempt of traditionalist Jews to form a farming settlement called Petah Tikva.[53]

Examination of the ideas of Alkalai and Kalischer from the perspectives of the three dimensions of ideology postulated earlier in this chapter reveals that they approximate most to the postulates of fully fledged Zionism in regard to the dimension of means. However, they are at variance, in major respects, with the dimensions we labeled diagnosis of the problem and advocacy of a solution.

In regard to means, we have already mentioned that Alkalai, drawing homiletically upon the sacred sources of Judaism, advocated the establishment of a kind of constituent assembly of Jewish notables. He also urged that a tithe on income be imposed and that a fund and company be created to purchase land in Eretz Israel. Furthermore, he advocated teaching and use of the Hebrew language as a spoken language, the better to unify the Jewish people in preparation for the redemption. In his practical endeavors to fulfill these aspirations he corresponded with the famous philanthropist Moses Montefiore in England and the notable Adolph Crémieux in France. He traveled throughout Europe to propagate his ideas and ultimately settled in Eretz Israel, where he died in 1878.

Kalischer, who left a deeper impression on historical memory than did Alkalai, had in 1836 proposed to Baron Rothschild of Frankfurt that he purchase land in Eretz Israel, first and foremost the Holy Temple site so that the sacrificial cult might be reinstated there. In 1860 he convened a gathering of several central European rabbis in an attempt to found an association to foster settlement in Eretz Israel. His main work, *Derishat Zion,* appeared in 1862, by which time he had become a participant in the Colonisationsverein für Palästina, founded by Haim Luria at Frankfurt an der Oder. He too corresponded, made appeals, and traveled extensively to advance his ideas and was instrumental in persuading the Alliance Israélite Universelle to found the Mikwe Israel agricultural school near Jaffa in 1870. Kalischer too proposed schemes for raising funds, for engaging the financial support of wealthy Jewish notables like Montefiore and the Rothschilds, and for creating a company to finance and organize a program of land settlement.

There can be no doubt that all of this amounted to down-to-earth means of the same sort that Hibbat Zion later advocated and that in insisting upon realistic human action as a prerequisite for Divine Redemption, Alkalai and Kalischer were boldly innovative (although not unprecedentedly so) within the context of traditionalist discourse on Eretz Israel and messianic redemption. Also, it is reasonable to infer that they were responding to various changes in the social and political structure of their European environment, changes that we today identify by the term modernity. Above all, they were responding to the challenge of Reform Judaism. Theirs was a very distinctive intermediate response, between the two dominant orthodox responses of their time—namely, the integrationist neoorthodox response epitomized alternatively by Samson Raphael Hirsch of Frankfurt am Main and Azriel Hildesheimer of Pressburg and then Berlin and the isolationist ultraorthodox response epitomized by the Hatam Sofer (Rabbi Moses Sofer), or more precisely by his disciples, in Pressburg. What Kalischer, Alkalai, and their major associates in the Colonisationsverein were proposing was a third strategy of response to the impact of modernity and the attendant threat of Reform Judaism: the exploitation of emancipationist modernity itself in order to quicken the messianic redemption. The resettlement of Eretz Israel was to be the means to that end.[54]

Even after full allowance has been made for this distinctive response to modernity, it remains evident that the core problem Alkalai and Kalischer set out to resolve was the cosmic unredeemed state of Jewish existence, not the immediate problems of Jewish distress and assimilation. The conceptual matrix of their intentions was still primarily messianic. It seems likely that, initially, Alkalai's innovative messianic speculation was activated by the anticipation, prevalent in certain traditional Jewish circles, of 1840 as the year of redemption and the need to offer explanations for its dismal failure to appear. One line of rationale advanced by Alkalai was that the expectation of a one-time event of redemption was mistaken; hence, the mining of textual sources to prove that it is correctly to be understood as a process, in stages. Another admissible contention was that 1840 as the anticipated year of redemption was conditional upon the generation being worthy of it, leading to the conclusion that the faults of the generation must be sought out and eliminated with repentance and good deeds. Hence Alkalai's adoption of the concept of collective as well as individual repentance.[55]

Similarly, it is instructive that the Damascus blood libel of 1840 stimulated the innovative thoughts of both Alkalai and Kalischer, not in the first instance on account of the appalling victimization of Jews (it was, after all, only one more manifestation of perennial Jewish suffering in the *galut*) but rather because of the successful intervention of Adolphe Crémieux and Moses Montefiore, two outstanding Jewish notables of Western Jewry, who personified the ideal of Jewish emancipation in the Diaspora. In his work *Minhat Yehuda*, written in the wake of the Damascus libel, Alkalai enthused at the observation that "so great an event had never occurred from the day Israel was exiled from its land . . . such a deliverance was undoubtedly a beginning of the redemption by the hand of God."[56]

One must note the significant contrast between the crucial role that the problematics of emancipation and Jewish distress was to occupy in the ideological formulations not only of Pinsker but also of the rabbis of Hibbat Zion and its tangential and ambiguous role in the thinking of Kalischer and Alkalai. They were not unaware of the emancipation process's dangers to traditionalist Judaism, manifested in lapses from religious observance and in the activities of the reformist rabbinical assemblies in Germany during the 1840s. Yet Kalischer glossed over the unfolding implications of emancipation, from which contemporary traditionalist rabbis were generally withdrawing defensively and with growing orthodoxy, and instead interpreted the gaining of civil rights by Western Jews as a sign of approaching redemption. For Kalischer *the* salient factors appear to have been the emergence of Jewish notables who commanded wealth and had influence with the gentile rulers and the appearance of Christian advocates of Jewish restoration to Zion. Hence, his recurrent contentions that "the beginning of redemption will come when the spirit of [Jewish] philanthropists will be aroused and when gentile rulers will wish to gather some of the dispersed of Israel into the Holy Land."[57] It is the same confinement to messianic categories of thought that led Kalischer and Alkalai uncritically to applaud the Alliance Israélite Universelle. They fixed their greatest hopes upon that society as if blind to the fact that its underlying assumptions were modernist and emancipationist.

The essentially messianic conceptual matrix of Kalischer's and Alkalai's thought becomes all the more evident when one examines their visions of the goals to be attained by the anticipated return to Zion. Theirs was an unmistakably eschatological vision. As we have noted, it was not as antithesis to emancipation that they advocated return to Zion. What Kalischer appears to have envisaged was an interim period of Jewish return to Zion and settlement there, concurrent with and complementary to the advancing emancipation of Jewry in the Diaspora. This period of human endeavor and natural means would mark the beginnings of the redemption (*athalta de-geula*). Ultimately, however, the day of divine redemption, universal in its compass, would dawn, having been quickened by fulfillment of the first stage of return to Zion through natural means. It was this very anticipation of redemption that facilitated Kalischer's and Alkalai's apparently sanguine view of emancipation's harmful consequences. For the quickened stages of redemption would, as it were, outflank and eclipse the process of emancipation.

Perhaps the most conclusive of all the indications of his essentially messianic motivations was Kalischer's preoccupation with the question of whether or not the sacrificial cult of the temple might be reestablished in Zion. Kalischer engaged intensely in halakhic discussion of this question, and as early as the 1830s he concluded not only that it was permissible but that it was a required stage on the path to messianic redemption. It was the acme of the "deeds from below through which would come the deeds from above." The process anticipated by Kalischer involved the ingathering to Zion of enough Jews to make it what he termed "a settled land" (*eretz noshevet*) and the reinstitution of sacrifices on the site of the ancient temple in Jerusalem. Thereafter would follow the war of Gog and Magog and finally the miraculous ingathering of all the exiles and the fulfillment of all the prophecies, not least of all the revival of the dead (*tehiyat ha-metim*).[58]

Moreover, Kalischer and Alkalai implicitly envisaged the resettlement of the land as an enterprise conducted and fulfilled wholly by observant Jews. The entire return and settlement process envisaged would forfeit its messianic value if there were to be breaches in religious observances. Kalischer was at pains to assure Rabbi Azriel Hildesheimer, one of the leading orthodox rabbis in Germany, that there was no cause for concern that the settlers would default on the observance of sabbath and the precepts dependent upon The Land. He denied any likelihood that such travesties would occur and considered coercion a legitimate means of ensuring this. He himself planned to ascend to The Land in his old age and to undertake supervision of religious observances at the Mikwe Israel agricultural school.[59]

In sum, the conceptual matrix that motivated Alkalai and Kalischer and shaped their intentions belongs to the realm of traditionalist messianic anticipation rather than to the modernist, nationalist ideology of Zionism. Innovators they certainly were, insofar as their interpretations rendered the traditional sacred sources compatible with realistic human endeavors to resettle Eretz Israel, but the motives and the rationale for their innovation remained firmly ensconced in the traditionalist frame of reference. In other words, theirs was not yet a nationalist "imagining." This is not to deny that the stimuli for these innovations in religious thought might well have come from their awareness of

European national movements around them and from exposure to the early effects of advances toward civic emancipation in western and central Europe. But the inference that they were aware of this nationalist effervescence is not sufficient to bear out the conclusion that their own conceptual matrix was nationalist. It seems more likely that this awareness served their essentially traditionalist messianic motivations rather than vice versa.

As far as is known, the same essentially messianic conceptual matrix that animated Alkalai and Kalischer appears to have applied, with some nuances, also to other rabbis who associated themselves with mid-nineteenth century ideas of resettlement in Eretz Israel, notably Rabbis Eliyahu Gutmacher (1796–1874) and Natan Friedland (c.1808–1883).[60] On the other hand, at least one rabbi who actively associated himself with the Colonisationsverein is known to have expressed ideas that clearly exhibited a nationalist imagining. He was Rabbi Josef Natonek (1813–1892), who was born and lived in Hungary.

Natonek, however, was a product of the special circumstances of midcentury Hungarian Jewry in which governmental interference had introduced compulsory secular education in advance of full civic emancipation. This resulted in early linguistic acculturation of Hungarian Jews. In conjunction with other factors unique to the Hungarian sociopolitical environment, the communities were atomized into conflicting religious modes and congregations.[61] These ranged from those of the ultraorthodox disciples of the famous Moses Sofer, (known as the Hatam Sofer) to the assertive religious reformers who were known in Hungary as "Neologues." In that context, Natonek was a rather obscure personality who evinced a moderate strain of reformed Judaism. Certainly he represented a rabbinical type very different from Rabbi Kalischer. He was probably far closer to the Breslau conservative-reform school of Rabbi Zecharias Frankel and the historian Graetz, which in the previous chapter we identified as a part of the ethnicist intelligentsia. By the same token there was some affinity between Natonek's ideas and those of Moses Hess. Indeed, after Natonek got wind of Hess's *Rome and Jerusalem* in 1862, he entered into correspondence with him. Hess reported: "I am not surprised that two people who agree with each other in their main conception concerning the messianic idea of Judaism also interpret many particulars of our doctrine and history in almost the same way."[62] Hess later wrote supportive articles in the French and German press on Natonek's activities in Paris in collaboration with Kalischer, particularly on his proposals to the Alliance Israélite Universelle.

In the 1850s, Natonek was first a teacher in a Jewish school and then rabbi in Jaszbereny, Hungary.[63] Apparently an able linguist, he wrote in German and Hungarian and authored theological and philological works. In contrast to Kalischer, who, as we noted, glossed over the problematics of emancipation, Natonek explicitly appealed in 1860 to his congregation to pray that the Jews not be granted emancipation in Hungary, on the grounds that their homeland was not there but in Jerusalem. His preachings in this vein aroused the disapproval of the Hungarian authorities, and it seems that it cost him his rabbinical position in Jaszbereny. He was, however, accepted as rabbi in another town. In an unpublished manuscript written in German in 1851 and titled *Die Göttliche Offenbarung durch Moses* (The divine revelation through Moses) he drew comparisons with the rising national consciousness of other small nations:

Whereas powerful nations have declined and unknown peoples have reached world power . . . as regards Israel's liberation—since it still awaits the help of God—there is not the smallest sign. . . . For God has never revived a dead person who has committed suicide. Is not Israel bringing upon itself a national suicide, when it rejects the influence of world events which awaken national consciousness [*nationalen Bewustsein*]?[64]

Natonek's views found their fullest expression in a book in Hungarian called *Mesias* (Messiah) and subtitled *An Essay on Jewish Emancipation, of Equal Advantage for Jews and Christians*, which appeared in 1861 under the pseudonym Abir Amieli but was promptly banned from publication by the authorities. In it he criticized the advocates of emancipation and raised the banner of Jewish national revival as the preferred alternative:

Since in our time the national idea [*nemzetisegek*] is the guiding principle of liberalism, therefore my dispersed Israelite nation cannot give up its national rebirth, all the more so because it has been divinely destined to fulfil a great mission. . . . The Jewish people, which has been divinely endowed with the finest spiritual qualities, ought not to go begging for the meagre crumbs of equal rights when it could richly enjoy its national independence. . . . I do not nurture bold illusions that God will establish the independence of the Israelites by miracles, since for thousands of years God has ceased performing his miracles and transferred them to the realm of reason. . . . Divine Providence has chosen our time for the fulfillment of miracles by practical means. We are therefore obliged, first and foremost, to believe in the possibility of our national independence and to recognize this idea as the essence of our beliefs. . . . we are obligated to achieve the independence of Israel so that the miracle of our existence may take place.[65]

In the light of the text of *Mesias*, Natonek might well be described as a *maskil* rabbi who consciously sought to harness the power of Jewish belief for Jewish national revival. In the introductory remarks to *Mesias* he explicitly presented his credo:

Since I introduced myself to the reader as an orthodox Jew I also ought to make clear my personal credo. As a human being I am a zealous believer in God, and as an Israelite I am very liberal; but it is not possible for my faith to overcome my liberalism [*szabadelvuseg*], and I shall also not allow my liberalism to overshadow my Jewish nationalism. Each has its definite measure; that is to say while my religion should bring happiness to humanity, my liberalism should bring religious influence to bear upon my nation. . . . I regard it as the most sacred precept of my faith to free my nation by means of the power of its religion.[66]

Notwithstanding the great difference in their underlying conceptions, the common practical program of the Colonisationsverein obviously made it possible for Rabbi Natonek to collaborate closely with Rabbi Kalischer and to accept his moral authority. Indeed, in 1867 he resigned from his rabbinical post and traveled widely throughout Europe and to Constantinople seeking support for their proposals concerning funds and diplomatic schemes to further Jewish settlement of Eretz Israel. These included the notion that the cooperation of the sultan of the Ottoman Empire be gained in return for payment. To be sure, from a reference to Natonek in Kalischer's extant correspondence it is evident that he disapproved of Natonek's extremism in "proposing that political control be taken from Ishmael."[67] Kalischer considered such a notion flagrantly contrary to the homiletical tradition that there was a divine adjuration not to "hasten the [messianic] end" by force. Resettlement in the peaceful manner envisaged by Kalischer, however, was not contrary to that adjuration. Moreover, Natonek did not share Kalischer's position on the need to renew the sacrificial cult; he adopted the view that when the time came sacrifices would not take the form of offering up animals on the altar but rather of work for the good of the homeland. Nor did he share Kalischer's conviction that religious observance should be enforced in Eretz Israel by use of religious sanctions such as the *herem* (excommunication). Natonek held that "the period of the *herem* has passed."[68]

In deference to Kalischer, Natonek appears to have repressed his extreme notions for the duration of his diplomatic endeavors undertaken on behalf of their common program between 1865 and 1867. But thereafter he freed himself from restraints, and his nationalist rhetoric became very explicit, abounding in expressions such as "Judaism of today is an edifice without foundations, lacking its natural bases—nationality and language. . . . A new edifice of the House of Israel must and will arise on the national foundations of nationality and language" and the statement "There can be no doubt that we are standing on the threshold of a nationalist crisis, which will open the way to a new era of national revival. The reconstruction of the House of Israel on the natural foundations of nationalism and language must and will come."[69] Having given up his rabbinical position, in the 1870s Natonek lived in Budapest, where in 1872 he founded and began to edit a weekly periodical in German called *Das Einige Israel* (Israel—one people), which described itself as "an organ dedicated to the unity of Israel and the preservation of its religious values." Through this medium he avidly propagated his nationalist ideas.

For our inquiry into the origins of the Zionist ideology it remains an instructive fact that Natonek's voice produced even less resonance within European Jewry than did those of Kalischer, the traditionalist rabbi, on the one hand, or Hess, "the socialist rabbi," on the other. As is evident from his repeated use of pseudonyms, Natonek functioned within an environment largely hostile to his ideas. Owing to its banning, *Mesias*, Natonek's major ideological exposition, never gained any exposure to the Jewish public. Indeed, a copy was discovered only as late as 1948 in the library of the National Museum in Budapest. His periodical, *Das Einige Israel*, expired after only seven issues, and thereafter, Natonek appears to have withdrawn from public life. Not entirely so, however; some articles by him appeared in *Ha-magid* (but under a pseudonym) during 1881, at the time when groups of Hovevei Zion began to be formed. His life and activity may thus be said to bridge the time hiatus between the circle associated with the feeble Colonisationsverein of the early 1860s and the emergence of a loose congeries of associations sharing an Eretz Israel–oriented nationalist ideology in the 1880s. Still, the evidence falls far short of suggesting a consequential chain of influence leading directly from his ideas and actions to the formation of Hibbat Zion.[70] It cannot be said of Natonek's ideas, any more than those of Moses Hess, that they constitute in a historic sense the origins of the Zionist ideology. True, they both produced ideas that qualify for the description "nationalist," and since these were clearly Eretz Israel–oriented, they also might be called proto-Zionist. But they stand in phenomenological rather than causal or consequential relationship to the ideology articulated by the nationalist Jewish intelligentsia in the period of Hibbat Zion and thereafter. They were in this sense precursors.

Yet the relationship of Alkalai's and Kalischer's ideas to those later evident in Hibbat Zion calls for a different historical assessment. On the one hand, it remains doubtful whether their thought qualifies at all for the description "nationalist." At any rate there is no scholarly consensus that it be so regarded. On the other hand, there are reasonable grounds for concluding that their ideas bear a consequential relationship, not merely a phenomenological similarity, to those that prevailed in the Hibbat Zion period and even beyond it. However one important caveat is necessary: this applies only to the orthodox rabbinical participants in Hibbat Zion. In sum, their significance for our understanding of Zionism's ideological genesis lies in their ground-breaking reinterpretations relating to settlement in Zion and messianic expectations *within* traditionalist thought. They were not the only active messianists in Jewish history. But their particular brand not only broke with the regnant passive messianism of Jewish life, it also responded to modernity by seeking to exploit modernity itself for the quickening of the divine messianic end. They created a school of interpretation within the traditionalist universe of discourse that in due course facilitated the participation of orthodox Jews in the Eretz Israel–oriented nationalist movement that came to be known as Zionism. In this sense they were more than precursors; they opened the conceptual corridor that led to that stream within Zionism that has come to be known as orthodox or national-religious Zionism.

The historical record of their ideas demonstrates the resilient diversity of response to changing times within the nineteenth-century traditionalist rabbinate of Europe; indeed, it shows that religious traditionalism had an inherent path of its own to Jewish nationalism. Theoretically, one might say, it could have done the job of Jewish restoration to Zion by itself. In practice, however, it proved incapable of launching such an enterprise on its own and merely converged with the secularized intelligentsia's initiative. After 1880, orthodox rabbis (including a few who had earlier identified with the Colonisationsverein's endeavors) explicitly drew upon the Alkalai and Kalischer school of interpretation to legitimize their participation in Hibbat Zion,[71] and as we have already noted in the previous chapter, they even made a bid for hegemony over its activities. However, when the intelligentsia firmly grasped the helm of the nationalist enterprise, this very fact repulsed the larger part of the traditionalist rabbinate. Cooperation with transgressors of religious precepts, they objected, could only distance, rather than advance, the redemption. Ironically, in order to justify continued cooperation with the secularized intelligentsia, those rabbis who persevered within the Zionist movement at the turn of the century found it necessary to subdue the messianic motifs inherited from Kalischer and his associates. As we shall see, the founders of the organized party of religious Zionists known as Mizrahi argued that the Zionist movement itself was devoid of messianic meaning and was concerned primarily with the alleviation of Jewish distress.

PART TWO

The Variegation of Zionist Ideology

CHAPTER THREE

General Zionism

―――――◆・◆・◆―――――

Common Denominators

A S W E H A V E S E E N, the emergent Hibbat Zion groups of the early 1880s were the first to articulate an ideology pertaining to the idea of a return to Zion and its restoration as a homeland for the Jews that not only transcended the messianic idea but also produced extensive social results and a continuous ideological development. It is possible to trace from Hibbat Zion onward the continuous development of a highly ramified nationalist ideology within the framework of an organized movement. As we shall now show, this came to be known as Zionism.

Underlying this ideology was the axiom that the Jews are a single, distinctive entity, possessing national, not just religious, attributes. This understanding of the nature of the Jewish entity distinguished the adherents of Zionism sharply from those who abjured the national attributes of the Jewish entity and advocated the panacea of diasporic emancipation and integration. The common denominator for all the ramifications of Zionist ideology reflected three dimensions: diagnosis of a given problematic situation, proposal of a solution and suggestion of means for attaining that solution. As we have already posited in a previous chapter, in historical retrospect this common denominator might be formulated thus: First, the situation of the Jewish entity under conditions of dispersion is critically defective, not just in a messianic sense but emphatically in a worldly sense; second, the solution lies in territorial ingathering of Jews in Eretz Israel (or failing that, transitionally in another territory) under conditions of autonomy at least and sovereignty at best; third, these purposes should be effected by political diplomacy, settlement activities, and the revival of Jewish national morale and culture.

Within the framework of these propositions, the contours of ideological diversity were very wide. Conventional historical memory has it that there were three schools of Zionism in the formative years of the movement—political, practical, and cultural. The "politicals" contended that diplomatic efforts to attain international sanction were the prerequisite for practical settlement of Eretz Israel and that cultural programs were not the business of the Zionist Organization. The "practicals" argued that, irrespective of diplomatic endeavors, settlement activity ought to have priority and that success on the political front would, in the end, issue mainly from the facts established on the ground. The "culturals" expected little to come of diplomatic endeavors and held that top priority should be given to cultural revival in the Hebrew medium and the raising of national consciousness both in the Diaspora and in the context of practical work in Eretz Israel. There is some justification for this threefold division but only at the operative level of ideology, since the differences merely revolved around allocation of priorities in regard to agreed means. However, at the fundamental level of ideology—of underlying premises concerning the very nature of the problem Zionism was meant to address and concerning the ultimate ends envisioned—the so-called practical school of thought hardly stands on its own. At this deeper level there really were only two rival integrative conceptions.

One conception emphasized the external dimension of the Jewish situation— the "problem of the Jews," their physical distress and psychological malaise brought on by their alien status everywhere. It was a nationalist conception essentially functional in character. It called for a contractual mobilization of members of the Jewish ethnic group in order to solve their common problem by negotiating with the outside world for the creation of a new sovereign civic entity for the Jews like that possessed by other nations. Hence, according to this conception, political-diplomatic measures took precedence over all others deemed necessary for functional resolution of the problem. This nationalist conception might be labeled functional.

The alternative conception stressed the internal dimension of the Jewish situation—the "problem of Judaism," that is, the saving and regeneration of Jewish national-cultural individuality. It was a nationalist conception of romantic character, one postulating or imagining an organically evolved Jewish nation, crippled by historical misfortune yet driven by an immanent impulse to restore its national integrity. Part and parcel of the nationalist mode of Hibbat Zion (although not coextensive with it), it advocated a corrective for the course that practical settlement activity was taking, one that placed emphasis on cultural renaissance, not, to be sure, instead of practical settlement endeavor but more precisely as its essential prerequisite and concomitant. This nationalist conception might be labeled organic.

As a rule (although not without exceptions), it might be said that the social bearers of these two different integrative conceptions, the functional and the organic, were, respectively, the two major types of Jewish intelligentsia that we identified in the first chapter of this work: one that rebounded from the course of integration into European culture and society and another that had always been ethnicist in its ideological orientation. The contrast between these two types found its sharpest expression in that between the ideological expositions of Theodor Herzl, on the one side, and Asher Ginzberg (who came to be best known by the penname of Ahad Ha'am) on the other side. The geographical locus of Herzl was, of course, central-western Europe, or to be more exact, Austria-Hungary, Germany, and France; that of Asher Ginzberg was czarist Russia. Accordingly, in many respects the ideological contrast between these two thinkers assumed the appearance of one between the Zionists of central-western Europe, where formal emancipation of the Jews had taken place in the course of the nineteenth century, and the Zionists of the Russian Empire, where such formal emancipation was not reached until the revolution of 1917.

However, this is too simple a division, for there were émigrés from Russia in university centers such as Berlin, Vienna, Berne, and Paris who shared Ahad Ha'am's nationalist mode yet enthusiastically embraced Herzl's new initiative as a program of action. Furthermore, within Hibbat Zion the outlines of what was to become the Herzlian approach are discernible in the ideological formulations of that part of the Russian Jewish intelligentsia that reached a Jewish nationalist position on the rebound from belief that integration was attainable even in Russia. Leo Pinsker was the outstanding example. His ideological outcry of 1881, *Autoemancipation*, which we discussed in an earlier chapter, prefigured the essentials of Herzl's analysis.[1] Moses Leib Lilienblum was another important example. His ideological development took him from a traditionalist upbringing to enlightenment and the belief in religious reforms as a vehicle for integration into the broader society and thence to a belief in Socialist reconstruction of that society, before he finally arrived at Jewish nationalist affirmation. Outliving Pinsker (who died in 1891, before the appearance of Herzl), Lilienblum continuously challenged Asher Ginzberg's ideological conception with an alternative that correlated in major respects with that of Herzl, and this on Asher Ginzberg's eastern European home ground.[2] Lilienblum insisted that the revival of the body of the Jewish people had priority over the revival of the spirit, and he refuted Asher Ginzberg's premise that a cultural center could sustain the Jewish Diaspora. Jews would inevitably lose all Jewish national identity and assimilate. He argued that Jewish nationalism, like that of other nations, was essentially a response to a common external enemy. In the Jewish case that enemy was antisemitism. Spiritual cultural aspirations alone were insufficient. Only appeals for real normalcy, such as those of Pinsker and Herzl, could stir a people toward national revival. Indeed, "there would be nothing wrong with gaining even a lowly State like that possessed by the Serbs," even if it meant being under Turkish sovereignty.[3] The correlation of these two seminal conceptions of Zionism, the functional and the organic, with west-central Europe and czarist Russia, respectively, is thus valid only in the most general sense and if one overlooks important exceptions.

The Functional Nationalist Conception

We come now to an examination of the functional nationalist conception, that which conventionally is rendered as "political." It was this that Theodor Herzl called Zionism, which is not to say that Herzl actually coined the term. But it can be said that when he founded the Zionist Organization at the congress he convened in 1897, the semantic evolution of the term "Zionism" reached its final form, retained to this day. It had first appeared some seven years earlier in the columns of *Selbst-Emancipation* (Self-emancipation), a journal produced in Vienna by Nathan Birnbaum (1864–1937).[4] Birnbaum was to undergo an extraordinary ideological odyssey traversing socialism, the advocacy of Diaspora autonomy for Jews, Zionism, and finally a full circle return to strict religious orthodoxy. In the early 1890s, however, he was perhaps the foremost Jewish nationalist intellectual outside Russia, and *Selbst-Emancipation* both reflected and influenced the intellectual concerns of mainly émigré students from Russia in the Viennese Kadima (Forward) Society and the Russian-Jewish Scientific Society in Berlin. As first used by Birnbaum the adjective *Zionistisch* (Zionist) began to replace *Jüdisch-national* (national-Jewish), in the first instance to emphasize the Eretz-Israel orientation in contrast to efforts directed toward the settlement of Jews in other countries. In this sense it was congruent with the term Hibbat Zion. However, it soon began to be differentiated from Hibbat Zion when Birnbaum used *Zionismus* (Zionism) to signify the intention of creating a political organization or party in contrast to the philanthropically supported settlement activities that characterized Hibbat Zion's record. With *Selbst-Emancipation*'s issue of May 18, 1893, it was no longer called "organ of the Jewish nationalists" but "organ of the Zionists."

Herzl was no more aware of the semantics of the term Zionism than he was of the ideological and programmatic formulations that had preceded him, not even those of Pinsker that had appeared in German some fifteen years before Herzl's work *Der Judenstaat* (The Jew's state). In that work, Herzl used the term "Zionist" loosely to describe the known efforts to settle in Palestine and the philanthropic backing of such efforts. When the student intelligentsia societies in Vienna and Berlin rallied to him, he was exposed to their usage of the term, and by December 1896 he was using Zionism as the term to describe his own program, which gave primacy to political-diplomatic efforts to attain international recognition and sanction for the establishment of a state for Jews.[5] This Zionism stood in contrast to his use of the terms "national-Jewish" and "Zion Societies" to describe the Hovevei Zion or Hibbat Zion phenomenon. What was later to be called "political Zionism" was *the* Zionism of Herzl, the ideological formulation that, in the words of the program adopted at the congress in Basel of 1897, aimed, first and foremost, "to create for the Jewish people a home (*Heimstätte*) in Palestine secured by public law."

There can be no doubt that Theodor Herzl's role in the history of Zionism was primarily in the creation and organizational propulsion of the movement and in dramatically publicizing it rather than in formulating its ideology. Yet the glare of this truth should not blind one to the significance of his ideological contribution. It was in important respects both seminal and far-reaching. This owed less to the profundity of his formulations—there was much in them that was simplistic and fantastic—than the fact that they so boldly and lucidly propounded the outer limits of the nationalist idea as applied to the Jews, namely, the complete congruence of the Jewish entity with a sovereign polity, a *Judenstaat*, a state of Jews. There were various strands of thought in Hibbat Zion that had envisioned the imminence of an autonomous Jewish homeland, but no one until that time had so straightforwardly articulated the will to full sovereignty.[6]

Born in Budapest in 1860 into a well-to-do family of already attenuated Jewish content; educated in the Magyar and German languages and attendant cultural ambiences, with a distinct preference for the German; qualifying in law at the University of Vienna and attaining considerable renown as a litterateur and journalist, Herzl certainly may be described as a convert to Jewish national identity. He did not grow into it organically through uninterrupted continuities of ethnic assertiveness as did the core of the intelligentsia who had formed Hibbat Zion in eastern Europe.

Yet the popular notion that Herzl was an assimilationist whose sudden conversion was caused by the Dreyfus case of 1894–1895 (the notorious trial and conviction of a Jewish officer in the French army on a charge of treason later proved false) is mistaken. A plethora of research into Herzl's life has revealed significant levels of Jewish identification going back to his childhood. "An acculturated but socially Jewish milieu" is Steven Beller's recent summing up of the environment in which Herzl was situated for the major part of his life.[7] Stirred by his exposures to antisemitism in Vienna of the 1880s and early 1890s, his private records show a growing concern with the Jewish problem. It erupted into a veritable obsession some time before he witnessed the Dreyfus case as Paris correspondent of his Viennese newspaper.

True, Herzl's transformation was marked by tortuous psychological complexity. His cogitations on the Jewish question reveal a soul rent by poignant ambivalence. At one moment he is smarting with indignation and hurt Jewish pride at the damning charges of racist antisemites. At the next moment, having internalized the ambiguous endorsement of civic equality for the Jews characteristic of most gentile liberals, he was plagued by Jewish self-contempt and desperately casting about for paths to collective Jewish self-improvement. In the end, he postulated that Zionism was the only way to accomplish this goal. But in the interim he privately speculated on—among other bizarre ideas—the notion of a demonstrative collective conversion to Christianity of the younger generation of Jews. It would be predicated on a new understanding with the pope to do away with antisemitism.[8] Herzl himself, together with like-minded organizers of this program, would remain a Jew, but the way would thus be prepared for the dignified self-dissolution of Jewish identity in the next generation.

Weighed in the balance of everything else known about Herzl's erratically vacillating notions as he grappled with his Jewishness, it is doubtful whether this fleeting fantasy or other momentary contemplations of personal baptism warrant labeling him as an ideological assimilationist.[9] Herzl never actually became identified with any publicly voiced, programmatic advocacy of assimilation in the sense of total effacement of Jewish identity. The conventional integrationist ideology of the Jewish intelligentsia, which envisaged a continuation of some modicum of at least confessional-religious identity under conditions of full civic emancipation, may have been stretched to its limits by Herzl, but he never actually breached it. On the other hand, he took no noteworthy interest in the institutional life, religious or secular, of the communities in his place of domicile, whether Vienna or Paris. For these reasons he may be regarded, in the final analysis, as personifying the intelligentsia type described in chapter 1 of this book as the noninstitutional integrationists.

Returning to Herzl's ideological contribution to Jewish nationalism, a certain dialectic should be noted. The social and political values that he had internalized from the gentile milieu into which he had aspired to be integrated—and his attendant Jewish self-reproach—were not effaced by his transformation. They were incorporated into his particular vision of a full-blown nationalist solution as well as into the details of his practical proposals. These idiosyncrasies of Herzl's personality and ideological transformation have been subjected to more biographical scrutiny than those of any other of the founding fathers of Zionism.[10] Not the extravagant idiosyncrasies of Herzl's personal vision, however, but the essentials emanating from his categorical rejection of the integrationist way form the really significant part of his contribution to Zionist ideology as a whole. Insofar as the originality of that contribution is in question, it should be noted that Herzl formulated his conception of a Jewish national solution to the Jewish problem while still in a state of ignorance concerning similar formulations dating back as far as Moses Hess's *Rome and Jerusalem* of 1862 and Leo Pinsker's *Autoemancipation* of 1882. Hence, it may be said that Herzl's *Der Judenstaat* was an original, although not unprecedented, ideological and programmatic work.

The Problem of the Jews

As set forth in *Der Judenstaat*, the first premise of Herzl's diagnosis of the Jewish problem (much like that of Pinsker's *Autoemancipation*) was that the contemporary situation of the Jews was one of grave distress because they remained immutably alien in all gentile societies. "No one will deny the plight of the Jews. In all countries where they live in appreciable numbers, Jews are persecuted to a greater or lesser degree."[11] Civic emancipation had not proved to be a solution; indeed, it had exacerbated the plight of the Jews. "Everywhere we have sincerely endeavored to merge with the national communities surrounding us and to preserve only the faith of our fathers. We are not permitted to do so. In vain are we loyal patriots, . . . we are decried as aliens. . . . The equal rights that the law may call for have almost always been nullified in practice." Full assimilation, by which Herzl meant "not only externals in attire, certain ways of life, customs, and speech, but also conformity in feeling and manner" was impossible. "Perhaps we could succeed in merging with the peoples surrounding us everywhere without leaving a trace if we were only left in peace for two generations," he speculated, "but they will not leave us in peace. After brief periods of toleration their hostility towards us erupts anew time and again." Moreover, Herzl's reading of the situation allowed for no qualitative distinction between different parts of the Diaspora. "The Jewish question persists wherever Jews live in appreciable numbers," he asserted, "wherever it does not exist it is brought in together with Jewish immigrants."

Herzl opined that the remote cause of antisemitism was the loss of the Jews' assimilability in the Middle Ages; the immediate cause was a product of the emancipation itself. Arguing that present-day antisemitism was not to be confused with the religious hatred of former times, although it still retained a religious tinge in certain countries, he held that it was largely "a consequence of the emancipation of the Jews" since the upward mobility of the Jews had made them into "fearful rivals of the [gentile] middle class." Yet the host societies hesitated to withdraw emancipation because that would drive Jews into the ranks of the revolutionary parties! But the very impossibility of getting at the Jews only aggravated the hatred.

"I believe I understand antisemitism," Herzl claimed. "I view it from the standpoint of a Jew, but without hatred or fear." What he meant by this was that he acknowledged objective, hence "understandable" factors in the causation of antisemitism, including the Gentiles' "supposed need for self-defense." Herzl's private diaries and letters abound in evidence that this "understanding" of antisemitism derived from the internalization of some of its disparaging images of the Jew. Such was his use of the pejorative term *Mauschel*, a corruption of Moses that was a common antisemitic description of the Jewish trader type.[12] To be sure, Herzl was careful to avoid such negative Jewish self-images in *Der Judenstaat.* By his lights, what emancipation of the Jews in Europe had failed to accomplish for Jewish self-improvement, Zionism would surely remedy.

By the same token, Herzl was able to adopt an unembittered, coldly rational, even optimistic and instrumental attitude to the factor of antisemitism. This contrasted sharply with Pinsker's pessimistic, despairing view of Judeophobia as an ineradicable gentile sickness. Herzl's insight was that out of enlightened, rational self-interest the antisemites themselves, or at any rate their governments, were bound to be amenable to negotiation over a solution for the Jewish problem. With characteristic imaginative flair he sought to manipulate the problem itself in order to dialectically generate a creative solution—the distress of the Jews would become the motor power of their national restoration; the antisemitism of the European powers would make them cooperate in an international project that promised to rid them of the Jews. "The Jews will leave as honoured friends, and if some of them return later, they will be given the same kind of reception and treatment at the hands of civilized nations as the citizens of other foreign states."[13]

It was this diagnosis that led Herzl to his nationalist conception encapsulated in the slogan: "We are a people, one people."[14] The contemporary distressful condition of Jews (the *Judennot*), rather than any romantic glorification of an ethnic past, was thus the wellspring of Herzl's nationalism. "We are a people—our enemies have made us one without our volition. . . . Affliction makes us stand by one another." And thence he arrived at the operative conclusion that "the Jewish Question is neither a social nor a religious one, even though it may assume these and other guises. It is a national question and to solve it we must first of all establish it as an international political problem which will have to be settled by the civilized nations of the world in council."

As expounded in *Der Judenstaat,* Herzl thus posited a nationalism of a functional and contractual nature, not an organic and romantic nationalism such as characterized most of the Jewish intelligentsia of eastern European domicile or origin who had given rise to Hibbat Zion. It was a nationalism of choice, a choice to which one was driven by elimination of other options, not a nationalism erupting deterministically out of deep-seated ethnic consciousness. Much that is known about Herzl's earlier thoughts and behavior accords with the sentiment, so obvious in *Der Judenstaat,* to the effect that if only Jews would be "left in peace" to assimilate, that would be the best course to take. Aware, however, of the impropriety of so negative an attitude to Jewish nationality, he did make an effort to counterbalance it: "I have already referred to our 'assimilation'. I am not saying for a moment that I desire it. Our national character is too famous in history and, despite all degradations, too noble to make its decline desirable."[15]

An important observation is called for here. It would appear that in his years as a university student in Vienna Herzl absorbed some pan-German, race-conscious nationalist sentiments.[16] Be that as it may, the absorption of such ideological strains in the course of his eclectic ideological odyssey is immaterial to our evaluation of his contribution to Jewish nationalist ideology. What counted was that which was publicly known and enduringly so, and these were his two major Zionist works—*Der Judenstaat* and *Altneuland*—as well as his public speeches, especially at Zionist congresses. The mode of nationalism there expounded was devoid of romantic race consciousness. It was highly humanistic and permeated with a strong sense of universal mission. Throughout both works the Zionist project is presented no less as a contribution to mankind as a whole, as a light unto the nations, than as a particular solution for the parochial problem of the Jews. The last sentence of *Der Judenstaat* declared: "The world will be freed by our freedom, enriched by our riches, and made greater by our greatness. And whatever we attempt there for our own welfare will spread and redound mightily and blessedly to the good of all mankind."[17]

In this respect, too, one discerns the indelible marks of his earlier liberal-integrationist outlook. That outlook's characteristic mission ideal is not jettisoned together with his rejection of integration as a social solution; it is merely transferred by Herzl from the diasporic arena to the national-state arena that he aspired to create. Thus, he countered Vienna rabbi Dr. Guedemann's upholding of the universal mission through dispersion with the assertion that "there is nothing to prevent us from being and remaining the exponents of one humanity on our own home soil as well. To achieve this purpose we need not actually continue to reside among the nations who hate and despise us."[18] To be sure, Herzl added something of his own to the mission formula, something that has been described as the "new Humanism," which replaced the providence of God with the doctrine of progress by scientific advance in a spirit of tolerance and human brotherhood.[19]

Herzl's Vision

If the distinctive mark of Herzl's diagnosis was its categorical rejection of emancipation and integration as a solution to the Jewish problem, what was distinctive about his vision of the state for Jews was that it would exemplify the very ideals that had informed the emancipation-integration ideology. The aspired-for end product was the same—not an anomalous dispersed people alien to European culture but an enlightened Europeanized Jew, not a uniquely *Jewish* state but a copy of an idealized European state for Jews.

The outlines of Herzl's vision were already traced in *Der Judenstaat*, but they acquired a fuller exposition in his novel, *Altneuland* (Old new land) of 1902,[20] which described, through the eyes of a distinguished European visitor, the development, institutions, and society of an imaginary Jewish state in Palestine some twenty-five years after its establishment. Herzl's aim was less to provide an accurate blueprint for the Jewish state than to infuse as wide a readership as possible with optimism and enthusiasm by showing what great prospects modern technology could provide for practical realization of a great moral and socially progressive vision. This might be done better through the genre of utopian novel than by a political treatise. At any rate, Herzl's literary impulse got the better of him, since he had in fact always been anxious to avoid the utopian label. In *Der Judenstaat* he had declared, "At the outset I must guard my plan from being treated as a utopia,"[21] and he contrasted it with Dr. Theodor Hertzka's *Freiland* (Freeland), published in 1890, which Herzl described as a fantasy with nothing to indicate that it could really be set in motion. The considerations that he had brought to bear in order to prove that his project was realistic were threefold. First, the reality of Jewish distress would act as the driving force. "The present plan," he wrote, "contains the utilization of the driving force that exists in reality . . . the distress of the Jews." It was, he claimed, "powerful enough to run a great machine and transport men and merchandise." Second, the self-interest of the world: "The Jewish State is something the world needs and consequently it will come into being." Third, and possibly the point most persuasively made by Herzl in *Altneuland*, the technological means now at man's disposal rendered the project possible.

By the time *Altneuland* was published, Palestine had been adopted as the locus for the Jewish state. Initially, however, Herzl—again much like Pinsker before him—had entertained the acceptability of a territory other than Palestine (Argentina was a salient alternative) and said as much in *Der Judenstaat*.[22] That an alternative territory had not been totally eliminated from Herzl's program again became evident in 1903, when the British government tentatively suggested the granting of a territory in East Africa for Jewish colonization. Having been frustrated at every turn of his extensive diplomatic activities aimed at gaining a charter for colonization from the Ottoman regime, Herzl favored taking up the East Africa offer. This precipitated a crisis for Zionism to which we shall return in another context.

As described in *Altneuland*, the Jewish state was a distillation of the best that the experience of the states of Europe could teach. It was an exemplary product of the most advanced technology and a model society reflecting the highest values of tolerance, social welfare, and enlightenment. Culturally, it was rather inchoate: secular, cosmopolitan, and pluralist rather than distinctively Jewish. Even the Hebrew language was limited to the role of prayer and other traditional functions; Yiddish was spoken in the rural areas, but German predominated as the language of commerce and culture. It was definitely a state *for the Jews* rather than a *Jewish* state. Religion was respected but kept in its place as the private affair of its adherents.

The society depicted in *Altneuland* was undoubtedly an authentic expression of Herzl's personal predilections based on his own experiences and values. This tallies with everything revealed by his plentiful private diary and correspondence records. Included, for example, is Herzl's clear preference for a political system that countervailed mass democracy with an element of aristocratic control, a preference reinforced by Herzl's experience of the deficiencies exhibited by the fin-de-siècle political system of France, which he witnessed as a correspondent of the *Neue Freie Presse* of Vienna.

But the idiosyncrasies of Herzl's political and social ideas, while of great historical interest for understanding the person, are hardly material for appreciating his ideological influence on Zionism. Indeed, *Altneuland* aroused about as much disagreement and controversy among Zionists as it did enthusiasm for the Zionist movement. We shall have to return to this issue when we consider the irate reaction to *Altneuland* of Asher Ginzberg (Ahad Ha'am) and his school of thought. What *was* of profound and enduring importance as a contribution to Zionist ideology was the broad sweep of Herzl's vision: normalization of the Jews in the sense of no longer being dispersed and devoid of a national home. It was a simple polarization: all Jews who needed or desired to would live in an independent state of their own, while all who preferred to remain outside of it could now successfully assimilate into the majority societies. Belief in science and technology, their limitless prospects and human benefit, is another salient feature of Herzl's vision as depicted in *Altneuland*. The country that has consummated the goals of Zionism is blessed with the most advanced applications of electric power that Herzl could imagine at the turn of the twentieth century. There are elevated electric trains and a great canal from the Mediterranean to the Dead Sea providing hydroelectric power.

The application of technological progress with superlative central planning is matched only by the social progress of the country. The influences of those nineteenth-century utopian ideas that answer to the description of "mutualism" are especially evident in the country's cooperative farming units. *Altneuland* combines the best of Utopian Socialist mutualism with the best in capitalist free enterprise. So that talent and effort may have their due reward, its socioeconomic system allows for individualism and wage differentials. Yet it manages to avoid extremes of poverty or wealth. In *Der Judenstaat*, Herzl had already envisaged the seven-hour working day and had advocated the system of *assistance par le travail* that he had learned in France, that is to say, the provision of state-sponsored work relief to ameliorate the condition of unskilled workers. This is now implemented together with other such progressive measures as free schooling.

All of these exemplary attributes apply equally to all citizens of the country,

Arab and Jew alike. To the implications for Herzl's view of Jewish and Arab claims to the country we shall return in a chapter of this book that focuses specifically on that important issue. For the present, it should be noted that, above all, the society described by Herzl is a place of tolerance, that which the Jews had always hoped for but not found in the societies of Europe. It answers faithfully to a diary entry of August 6, 1899, in which Herzl noted: "My testament for the Jewish people: Make your State in such a way that the stranger will feel comfortable among you."[23] At one point in the novel, it is related that an intolerant nativist party headed by a certain Rabbi Geyer advocates the exclusion of Gentiles, but his party is defeated.

The only aspect of the society described in *Altneuland* that was perhaps not so progressive was its political system. It reflected his somewhat conservative political predilections, his reservations about unrestrained power of the masses in a simple democracy. As we have already noted above, he preferred a system that allowed for aristocratic restraint upon the masses. The presidency is described as a purely honorary position for a seven-year term. The legislature, although an elected congress, sits only a few weeks each year. The country is devoid of ideological mass parties. It is run by enlightened, talented bureaucrats rather than politicians. Indeed, we are told that "politics here is neither a business nor a profession," and "our courts have repeatedly ruled in slander suits that the term 'professional politician' is an insult."[24]

In all, what Herzl described was a "New Society" rather than a conventional national-state. It is a postnational state, a polity that transcends and betters the contemporary European state. As David Littwak (a personality modeled on David Wolffsohn, who was to succeed Herzl as president of the Zionist Organization) tells the European visitor Kingscourt: "We have no state, like the Europeans of your time. We are merely a society of citizens seeking to enjoy life through work and culture. . . . We are not a state. . . . We are a commonwealth. . . . We are simply a large cooperative association which is called the New Society."[25]

Herzl's Means

In the final analysis it was less in theorizing than in the creation of the instruments for attainment of Zionism's objectives that Herzl made his most important contribution. At the ideological level, the measures adopted by Herzl rested on the premise that when an endangered people is nationally incapacitated for whatever reasons, a group of its members may step forward and save it. This was an application to the collective sphere of the Roman juridic principle relating to the *negotiorum gestio*.[26] As in the case of individuals, the *gestor*—that is, the manager or caretaker of the incapacitated other's affairs—has a moral warrant derived from a higher necessity. "At present the Jewish people is prevented by the diaspora from conducting its own political affairs. Yet it is in a condition of more or less severe distress in a number of places. It needs, above all things, a *gestor*."[27]

According to Herzl's plan as outlined in *Der Judenstaat*, that corporate *gestor* was to be called "the society of Jews," an organization that would devise the plans and take the necessary steps for the establishment of a state. It would educate the Jews to national consciousness, find a suitable territory for a state, and negotiate with the Great Powers for the granting of an internationally sanctioned political charter to settle it systematically and form a sovereign state for Jews. It would, in short, be a state-creating agency. Its foremost task, taking precedence over all others, would be political-diplomatic in nature. "The entire plan is in essence perfectly simple," stated Herzl, "let sovereignty be granted us over a portion of the earth's surface that is sufficient for our rightful national requirements; we shall take care of everything ourselves."[28] Alongside this agency there would be created "The Jewish Company," to finance the project, see to liquidation of the economic interests of the Jews in the countries from which they were to emigrate, and organize the economic substructure of the new society. He envisaged it as a joint stock company, incorporated in England and subscribed to in the first instance by wealthy Jewish financiers.

As it happened, however, no bodies with such names came into existence. What Herzl managed to create in 1897 was something known as the Zionist Organization, a worldwide transnational framework comprising federations of local Zionist societies in different countries. Herzl was the president, with executive powers vested in a general council (Greater Actions Committee) and a central executive (Smaller Actions Committee). Anyone who subscribed to the Basel Program formulated at the 1897 congress and paid the annual tax, the shekel (one shilling or its equivalent in other currencies), was regarded as a Zionist and had the right to vote. At the second Zionist congress, held in 1898, it was decided to establish a bank as the financial instrument of the organization. It was founded as a joint stock company in London under the name of the Jewish Colonial Trust. The fifth Zionist congress, held in 1901, established the Jewish National Fund for the acquisition of land in Palestine as the inalienable possession of the Jewish people.

If the essence of Herzl's diagnosis was his identification of postemancipation Jewish distress, and the essence of his vision was a sovereign society of Jews, the crux of the means he advocated was political diplomacy. As a totality, his ideas amounted to a Jewish national conception that came to be labeled "political Zionism." Its operative implication was the primacy of political-diplomatic endeavors to attain an internationally sanctioned charter leading to territorial sovereignty for the Jews. In the context of all that had preceded Herzl, this meant that the Hibbat Zion pattern of small-scale settlement resting upon philanthropic resources was to be held in abeyance until attainment of the charter providing international sanction. Once this was achieved, a rationally planned mass emigration of Jews to Palestine would be implemented, stage by stage, until all Jews but those who were well integrated in their diasporic environments and wished to assimilate totally had been concentrated in the sovereign Jewish society. It followed from these assumptions that the old style of philanthropically aided, gradualist settlement carried on by Hibbat Zion was not only futile but, insofar as it assumed the appearance of infiltration without full legal blessing, detrimental to the achievement of Zionist goals.

Ironically, implicit tactical considerations dictated a dilution of the publicly declared aim of Zionism. The Basel Program did not speak of a "state," as did unequivocally Herzl's booklet *Der Judenstaat*. Also ironically, on the one hand, the Zionist Organization exemplified the new political mode that had begun to develop in the period of Jewish emancipation. For it was a mass movement, democratically based and aiming to exert a measure of political power in the interests of Jewish nationalism. On the other hand, Herzl's style of "personal diplomacy," such as that which he conducted with the antisemitic Russian minister, von Plehve, had much in common with the old Jewish intercessionist mode known as *shtadlanut*.[29]

In the summer of 1903, Joseph Chamberlain, Britain's colonial secretary, indicated to Herzl Great Britain's readiness to consider a Jewish settlement in its East Africa protectorate. Herzl informed the sixth Zionist congress, which met in August 1903, of the offer, suggesting that although Palestine remained the ultimate objective of Zionism, the offer merited positive consideration. The immediate proposal put before the congress was that an expedition be sent to investigate the territory and report back on the suitability of the project. The proposal precipitated a major crisis at the congress. The Russian members of the Actions Committee categorically declared their opposition and demonstratively left the congress hall, followed by the entire body of the "Anti-Ugandist" camp, appropriately dubbed Zionei Zion (Zionists of Zion). The vote yielded a majority of 295 to 178 in favor of the proposal, with 98 abstentions, and it was only after Herzl passionately assured the Zionei Zion delegates that he had not abandoned Palestine as the ultimate goal that they consented to return to the congress hall. But the rift was not healed. It tarnished Herzl's image in the eyes of the Zionist movement in Russia, where Menahem Ussishkin led a vigorous campaign of opposition to the very notion of a territory other than Eretz Israel.

A combination of factors, not least of which was the vocal opposition of the English colonists in the protectorate, led to a perceptible cooling of the British colonial office's attitude, and the Zionist investigatory commission also came up with an unfavorable report. When Herzl died on July 3, 1904, this issue was still exciting divisive passions and acrimony throughout the Zionist movement. The opponents of the scheme scored a decisive victory at the seventh Zionist congress, held in Basel in July 1905, when a resolution rejecting out of hand all colonization schemes other than that in Palestine gained an overwhelming majority. However, led by Israel Zangwill, the Anglo-Jewish novelist, some forty diehard supporters of any suitable territorial solution seceded from the Zionist movement and formed the Jewish Territorial Organization (ITO).

In sum, Herzl's entire strategy focused almost exclusively on diplomatic efforts to attain an internationally recognized charter for the reestablishment of Palestine as a national home for the Jews. All other considerations and tactics were subordinated to this single-minded objective; hence, Herzl's admonition that Zionists not be deflected into involvement with the politics of the countries of their present residence, especially not in any way that might raise objections from the authorities in those countries. He urged Zionists to focus their "shared aspirations exclusively on the settlement of Palestine, and not on the organization of the Jews in their present countries of residence."[30] Especially dangerous for the free development of the Zionist Organization in its main center, czarist Russia, would be the involvement of Zionists with any activities that could be construed either as revolutionary sedition or as serving local nationalist aspirations. Herzl repeatedly appealed to Russian Zionists to avoid this danger. For example, on his visit to St. Petersburg in August 1903, directing himself to those in his audience whom he knew to have Socialist proclivities he said:

Those who say that a person can be a Zionist and also do other work in which they see the salvation of the Jewish people, do not serve any useful purpose. . . . The [Basel] program as it is, has gained wide sympathy throughout Europe. But, if it is covered up by other questions, they will stop believing us and will assume that the program of Basel is a front for other things. . . . All those who say I am distant from the idea of progressive social thought do me a great wrong. But now under existing circumstances, it is premature to concern oneself with the realization of these ideas. Zionism needs the whole man and not half ones. . . . When I consider your situation, my brethren, I tell you: you are not doing the right thing by mixing Zionist principles with principles of another kind.[31]

It also followed from Herzl's single-minded policy that the Zionist Organization should avoid internal controversies of a divisive nature. This meant particularly questions of "culture" that challenged the authority and convictions of the rabbinical stratum and their flock. As we shall see when we discuss this important question in another chapter of this book, Herzl tried to subdue and circumvent persistent attempts of the segment of Zionists associated with the ideas of Asher Ginzberg (Ahad Ha'am) to raise this issue at Zionist congresses. On the other hand, Herzl's own call, at the second Zionist congress in 1898, for "conquest of the communities" by Zionists, was in effect an appeal for greater involvement in the institutional life of Diaspora Jewish communities.[32] To be sure, Herzl obviously intended this to be limited to the ousting from communal Jewish leadership positions of the oligarchic stratum of Jews, mostly wealthy and personally well integrated in the majority society. They mostly adopted an anti-Zionist stance. However, this call could be—and was sometimes so interpreted by some Zionists—but a variation on Asher Ginzberg's ideas. As we shall see, Ginzberg spoke of "preparing the hearts" of Jews, in the sense of raising their national and Hebrew-language consciousness. There was, consequently, some blurring of the lines between Herzl's idea of "conquering" the communities and the broader range of involvements that came to be called in Zionist parlance, *Gegenwartsarbeit* (literally, "present-day work").

The Ideological Lieutenant: Max Nordau

Clear and cogent as was Herzl's exposition of Zionism, it was exceeded in eloquence by that of his close associate Max Nordau (1849–1923), a medical practitioner by profession but better known as a literary personality. Nordau's early upbringing, as well as his passage to Zionism, had much in common with those of Herzl. He too was born in Pest, Hungary; grew to maturity in a German-language European cultural ambience (although after 1880 he was domiciled in Paris); and attained a considerable reputation as a journalist and writer. Instructed in childhood by his father, Gabriel Suedfeld, who had been ordained as an orthodox rabbi, he had a more substantial grounding than Herzl in Hebrew and Jewish tradition.[33] However, he, like Herzl, moved away from the Jewish ambience—curiously indicative of this was his change of name from Suedfeld (Southern field) to Nordau (Northern meadow)—and in due course he too came to personify the type of integrationist European intelligentsia barely associated with any Jewish communal institutions, who underwent a return to Jewish particularism in its nationalist form.

Nordau endorsed and adopted the Zionist ideology as expounded to him by Herzl when they first got to know each other in the summer of 1895.[34] His own testimony was: "The growth of antisemitism first awakened in me the awareness of my duties to my people."[35] However, closer scrutiny of Nordau's biography has revealed that his conversion was not an entirely sudden revelation, nor was his ideological conceptualization of Zionism a total inversion of earlier ideals and ideas.[36] There is evidence that the influence of his traditional upbringing was never totally eclipsed. His orthodox religious mother lived in his home until his fifty-first year of life, and in works written during the period of his apparent estrangement from Judaism there are references to the Jewish problem. Moreover, it is doubtful whether he ever espoused a wholly cosmopolitan outlook, for he recognized the important role of mankind's national divisions. However, his conception of the nation had been essentially cultural. That is to say, he held that not prescriptive factors such as race or birth but rather culture—meaning, above all, language—was the proper criterion for national belonging. It was in this cultural sense that he had regarded himself as a German, even though he was not so by domicile.[37]

Nordau's literary fame, or notoriety, depending on the viewpoint of the contemporary observer, derived from his vehemently censorious critique of certain trends—modern in the contemporary context—in European art, literature and political behavior, which he condemned as the "degeneration" of society. Regression to irrationality, egotism, and nihilistic social disorder were the root evils that he excoriated in books such as *Die conventionellen Lügen der Kulturmenschheit* (The conventional lies of society), first published in 1883, and *Degeneration,* first published in 1892. Nordau was a secularist and a positivist who was convinced that civilization's progress depended on rationalism and the natural sciences. He was an advocate of human "solidarity." As he used the term, it meant a kind of utilitarian moral conviction that, in doing what was beneficial for mankind, one was doing what was good for oneself, and conversely, in doing what was harmful for mankind, one was harming oneself. "The flourishing of mankind is your Garden of Eden," he wrote, "its degeneration—that is your Hell."[38] This concept was largely coextensive with liberalism. His was a bourgeois liberalism in the late-nineteenth-century sense of espousing concern for progress based on an orderly balance between the dignity of the individual and the mutual responsibility of all the individuals constituting the common societies of mankind. The ultimate human "solidarity," which alone could raise brute life to the level of humanity, depended on the fusion of mind and love, in other words, rationality and consideration of one's fellow man. Nordau's rationalist liberalism was also reflected in the fact that he conceived of the state not in organic but in contractual and functional terms. It was a civic framework whose purpose was to order the relations between its citizens for the enhancement of their security, freedom, and happiness. He deplored the signs of a fin-de-siècle regression to irrationality and disorder, warning that it was paving the way to dictatorship, state worship, and human alienation, in short, to the destruction of the sense of human solidarity.

In the context of his perception of European society's retreat from rational liberalism into irrational degeneracy, of which rising antisemitism was one major symptom, Nordau, by the time of his meeting with Herzl, was coming around to recognition that the real determinants of national belongingness were not subjective-volitional factors such as language but rather the objective factor of ethnic origin. It was this realization that predisposed him to endorse the Zionist diagnosis of the Jewish situation as espoused by Herzl. In Zionism he found a psychological and ideological release from the depression and helplessness he felt in the face of the irrational and illiberal trends engulfing European society. Losing hope for the capacity of European society to heal itself from the virus that he considered had infected it, and recognizing, in that context, that Europe was rejecting even the most acculturated Jews (like himself), he turned to Jewish nationalism as advocated by Herzl.[39] He formed the conviction that Zionism's aspiration to provide natural conditions of existence for the Jews in their own land was part of the necessary reordering of the world on the path to true human solidarity, that "as long as the Jewish question exists, as long as justice is denied us, civilization is written down a lie, and every diplomatic conference for the codification of the laws of comity and humanity is a farce."[40]

Some writers have debated the question of whether Nordau's adoption of Zionism was consistent with the fundamentals of the outlook propounded in the writings that had made him famous.[41] Be that as it may, in the context of the present work it should be noted that Nordau's Zionism bore the marks of his earlier liberal "solidarianism" at least insofar as he, like Herzl, propounded a conception of Jewish nationalism that was functional (as opposed to organic and romantic) and imbued with a sense of mission to mankind. "My ideal," he wrote, "is to see a Jewish people in the land of the fathers, ennobled by a two thousand year-old firmness of character, . . . an instrument of wise progress, a champion of justice, an apostle and personifier of brotherly love."[42] However, in this, as in other respects, his contribution to the storehouse of Zionist thought consisted less in innovation than in providing a brilliant supportive gloss on the ideas expounded by Herzl. His speeches included "State of the Nation" keynote addresses at a sequence of ten Zionist congresses. "No, ladies and gentlemen," he told his audiences repeatedly, "assimilation is not the remedy for the Jewish problem [*die Judennot*]. The assimilation of some Jews is possible. Assimilation of the Jewish masses . . . is in the foreseeable future impossible, and it is also undesirable."[43]

Moreover, outliving Herzl, he remained until the end of his life (1923) the standard-bearer of "political" Zionism, consistently defending it against the inroads of the "practicals" and the counterconception propagated by Asher Ginzberg, which called for the primacy of cultural renaissance and the creation of a cultural center in Palestine. The clash with Asher Ginzberg came to a head over the latter's harsh criticism of Herzl's *Altneuland* and Nordau's even harsher literary counterattack. In an exposition of superlative clarity, titled "Der Zionismus" and published in 1902, Nordau incisively laid down the principle that "the premise of political Zionism is that there is a Jewish nation." He defined its distinguishing character thus: "The new Zionism, known as political Zionism, distinguishes itself from the old, religious, messianic form, in that it disavows all mysticism and no longer identifies itself with messianism. It does not expect the return to Palestine to be brought about by a miracle, but rather seeks to accomplish it by its own efforts."[44]

Although cognizant of what he termed the "inner impulse of Judaism" as a factor in the emergence of Zionism, like Herzl he placed greater emphasis on the "external influences." These were the nationalist ideas that had come to dominate European thought and ubiquitous antisemitism. But he contended that for most

Zionists the role of antisemitism was as a catalyst that redirected their thought. Having resolved on Zionism, it would remain for them an imperative "even if antisemitism were to disappear completely from the world."

Most illuminating of all Nordau's ideological formulations was the distinction he drew between the two faces of the Jewish problem: "Jewish misery has two forms, the material and the moral." In eastern Europe (and likewise, he added, in northern Africa and western Asia), where probably nine-tenths of all the Jews lived, Jewish distress meant "the daily distress of the body; anxiety for every following day; the painful struggle for the maintenance of bare life." The other face of the Jewish problem was in the European West. There the struggle of existence was somewhat easier: "The question of food and shelter and of security of life tortures them to a lesser degree. Here the distress is of a moral nature." It meant wounded honor and loss of self-respect. The Western Jew, aspiring to assimilation, alienated himself from his Jewish roots and natural brethren only to be callously spurned by the gentile society and nation. "He has lost the home of the ghetto, the land of his birth denies itself to him as a homeland . . . that is the moral Jewish distress which is more bitter than the material one, for it is the affliction of the more highly differentiated, prouder, more sensitive beings."[45]

Another distinctive, although not unique, contribution by Nordau to the storehouse of Zionist ideology was his emphasis on physical education as a means for rescuing the Jew from the "degeneration" wrought by centuries of ghetto existence. Here one must note the combined influence of his medical insights and his internalization of emancipated middle-class European values. Gymnastics rather than sport (since the latter was not specifically designed to perfect the human body) was his therapeutic prescription for restoring the nervous and bodily health of the Jew and hence his comportment and dignity. In his speech to the second Zionist congress, in 1898, he declared: "We must consider once again creating a muscle Jewry [*Muskeljudentum*]."[46] He was instrumental in the founding of "Bar Kochba" gymnastic societies, which spread to many Jewish communities in Europe. Nordau's impassioned call for "muscle Jews" was one of many tributaries to the ideological streams of Zionism that emphasized physical regeneration as a therapeutic value. Herzl had similarly been much taken up with the notion of dueling. In Russian Zionism and in Palestine Jewish self-defense was the other side of the coin. After the First World War, Jabotinsky and his Revisionist Zionism raised Nordau to the pinnacle of the pantheon of Zionism's founding fathers but, as we shall see, enveloped the notion of physical prowess in a veil of military values, of discipline and ceremony.

The Organic Nationalist Conception

At bedrock level the cleft between the functual conception spearheaded by Herzl and the organic conception that characterized most of Hibbat Zion and was most profoundly formulated by Asher Ginzberg is attributable to the two types of Jewish intelligentsia that had converged to form the Jewish national movement to be known in due course as Zionism. Having come to Jewish nationalism on the rebound from the frustrated aspiration for integration into gentile European society, Herzl's diagnosis of the problem rested squarely on the material and psychological distress of the Jews, the *Judennot*. In sharp contrast to this was the focus on internal regeneration of the Jewish entity to which Ahad Ha'am had arrived as a natural emanation of the ingrained ethnicism of his Russian-Jewish milieu.

Born in 1856 into a traditionalist Hasidic background in the small town of Skvire in the Kiev province, Asher Ginzberg was married off by his parents at the age of sixteen. His education was thoroughly traditionalist, although he evinced an early interest in medieval Jewish philosophy, particularly that of Maimonides, and he did have some random exposure to literature of the Hebrew *haskala*. It was only in his twenties that he haltingly began an autodidactic exploration of European secular thought. He contemplated qualifying himself to enter a university and in his mid-twenties even left his wife and children and went to Vienna with that purpose in mind. However, as he later explained, he lacked the confidence to carry out so bold a venture and soon gave it up.[47] After he moved to Odessa in 1886, his autodidactic immersion into secular learning intensified, encompassing contemporary works of history, moral philosophy, psychology, and sociology.

From a socioeconomic point of view, no less than from an intellectual viewpoint, Asher Ginzberg may be regarded as a prototype of eastern European intelligentsia, which as we noted in an earlier chapter was seldom independent of middle-class occupations. His father was a well-to-do merchant, and for the major part of his life Asher too earned his livelihood in a middle-class occupation. For a time he was an independent merchant. Later he was employed in the Wissotzky firm of tea merchants, and from 1907 until he emigrated to Palestine in late 1921 he served as its branch manager in London. Only for a short period between 1896 and 1902 did he earn—or rather eke out—his livelihood from a purely intelligentsia occupation, when he founded and edited the Hebrew monthly *Ha-shiloah*, to which he applied his exacting standards and meticulousness with the aspiration of making it an equal of the best journals of enlightened culture and thought in Europe.

The nationalist ideology of Asher Ginzberg began to take articulate form when he made his literary debut in 1889 with an article titled "Lo zeh haderekh"

(This is not the way), which appeared in the Hebrew periodical *Ha-melitz*. In this article he subjected the Hibbat Zion settlement program to criticism from the perspective of his broader conception of Jewish nationalist goals. He chose to sign this article and his many writings that followed with the pseudonym Ahad Ha'am (one of the people). Henceforth it was as Ahad Ha'am that he came to be famous. He later explained with a show of modesty: "The idea of this pen-name was to make it clear that I was not a writer, and had no intention of becoming one, but was just incidentally expressing my opinion on the subject about which I write as 'one of the people.'"[48]

The Problem of Judaism

Ahad Ha'am's diagnosis of the problem that had generated Jewish nationalism focused not on the material distress of the Jews but on their cultural malaise. Not antisemitism but disintegration of Jewish cultural distinctiveness under the combined impact of civic emancipation and secular enlightenment was identified by him as the critical defect of the Jewish condition. On the one hand, the influence of ossified orthodox Judaism was in irreversible decline, while on the other, assimilation and attendant attempts at reform of Judaism were simply a new form of self-abnegation, of "slavery in freedom." "The Jews cannot survive as a scattered people now that our spiritual isolation is ended," wrote Ahad Ha'am, "because we have no longer any defense against the ocean of foreign culture which threatens to obliterate our national characteristics and tradition."[49]

The roots of Ahad Ha'am's premise that the primary issue for Zionism was the "problem of Judaism" rather than the "problem of the Jews" are embedded in his modern Enlightenment-induced understanding of Jewish identity itself. This conceptual foundation of Ahad Ha'am's ideas is of such far-reaching importance for Zionist ideology as to merit separate and more detailed treatment, and to this I shall accordingly return in part 3 of this book. In the present context, discussion is confined to Ahad Ha'am's ideas on the purposes and tasks of Zionism in contrast to those of Herzl.

Ahad Ha'am's shifting of the emphasis away from the "problem of the Jews" does not mean that he failed to recognize the severity of antisemitism as a cause of Jewish distress. Indeed, as a down-to-earth realist, Ahad Ha'am was convinced that there was no way for Jews, by their own actions, to eliminate the phenomenon of antisemitism. But Jewish nationalism should not be predicated, in the first instance, upon that problem. To his understanding, the Jewish national movement was an organic outcome of the inherent character of the Jewish people: its instinctive will to life. It was valid and necessary irrespective of the distress precipitated by antisemitism. Nor was it realistic to expect a quick and complete solution to the Jewish problem. As late as 1914, Ahad Ha'am reiterated in a letter to one of his former followers in Palestine:

> Now I have explained dozens of times that I do not regard it as at all impossible that in course of time Palestine may support a population of millions; and my question is not how all the Jews will find a living in Palestine, but how they will get there. If, that is, they go gradually—and no other way is possible—then, even after millions of our people have been settled in Palestine, the majority will still be in the diaspora, because the natural increase in the diaspora countries will offset the exodus to Palestine.[50]

Total physical removal of Jews from their diasporic situation was thus beyond the realm of the possible; belief in such a possibility belonged purely to the realm of messianic religious faith, which he did not share. It did not behoove Zionism, as an enlightened secular national movement, to engage in such messianic illusion, and Herzl's political Zionism was, in Ahad Ha'am's view, doing just that. He described Herzl's circle as "The New Zionists whose Zionism is born of antisemitism" and contrasted them with the "old Hovevei Zion, who look to Palestine for other things besides physical ease and the solution of the 'Jewish Problem' in its economic and political aspects."[51]

Given this conception, it is not surprising that Ahad Ha'am was unimpressed by the first Zionist congress convened by Herzl. In his view, since it was grossly unrealistic to think that Zionism could solve the material problem attendant upon Jewish existence in the Diaspora, what the Zionist congress ought to have addressed was the "moral" (*musari*) problem. *Moral* was here used by Ahad Ha'am not in the ethical sense but in the sense of self-esteemed cultural identity. True, at the congress he had heard Nordau's brilliant exposition of the moral problem, a speech that, in Ahad Ha'am's eyes, was one of the congress's few redeeming features. Yet he regarded Nordau's analysis as something applicable only to the "western" Jew, who

> after leaving the ghetto and seeking to attach himself to the people of the country in which he lives, is unhappy because his hope of an open-armed welcome is disappointed. He returns reluctantly to his own people and tries to find within the Jewish community that life for which he yearns—but in vain. . . . Jewish culture has played no part in his education from childhood, and is a closed book to him. So in his trouble he turns to the land of his ancestors, and pictures to himself how good it would be if a Jewish State were re-established there—a State arranged and organized exactly after the pattern of other States. Then he could live a full, complete life among his own people, and find at home all that he now sees outside, dangled before his eyes, but out of reach. . . . The eastern form of the moral trouble is absolutely different from the western. In the west it is the problem of the Jews, in the east the problem of Judaism. The one weighs on the individual, the other on the nation. The one is felt by Jews who have had a European education, the other by Jews whose education has been Jewish. The one is a product of antisemitism, and is dependent on antisemitism for its existence; the other is a natural product of a real link with a culture of thousands of years which will retain its hold even if the troubles of the Jews all over the world come to an end together with antisemitism,

and all the Jews in every land have comfortable positions, are on the best possible terms with their neighbours, and are allowed by them to take part in every sphere of social and political life on terms of absolute equality.[52]

When the East Africa proposal surfaced in 1903, Ahad Ha'am regarded it as the logical outcome of the misguided, nationally superficial Herzlian conception. Unsparingly attacking those Russian Zionists who had fallen in with Herzl's project, he reiterated the practical-cultural conception of Hibbat Zion as he had always understood it:

. . . we had an ideal. We knew even then that the tiny *yishuv* in its present form could not succeed, and that Palestinian colonization could not solve the problem of Jewish misery; we knew also . . . that we could not achieve a national revival in Palestine *in the political sense*, for who knows how long. But our ideal was the *spiritual revival*. We saw that in the spiritual sense the Jewish people was undergoing a process of progressive disintegration and decay; and we hoped to stem this process by the gradual establishment of a national center in Palestine. This was to be achieved by means of colonization on a small scale, but with proper method and system. And this settlement in Palestine, thoroughly Jewish in spirit, would restore unity to our people and re-create our impaired sense of continuity with our great past. . . . Our remote ideal was that in course of time the number of Jews in Palestine would grow, political conditions would change, and there would be a new generation of Jews . . . who would know how to free themselves and their country at the appropriate time.[53]

"Then came Herzl," complained Ahad Ha'am, "who laid all the emphasis on the material Jewish problem and made Palestine an immediate political ideal." The result was that the moral ideal was incrementally abandoned and pressed by the deteriorating situation of the Jews, Eretz Israel was abandoned. All that was now left, asserted Ahad Ha'am, was "a political movement, which will henceforth concentrate its attention mainly on looking for a country in which to settle distressed Jews." But the adherents of the original Hibbat Zion conception, he averred, had "never looked to Palestine for a remedy for our material troubles, and therefore we have no reason to go elsewhere. What we are looking for in Palestine cannot be found anywhere else; nor can be it proved that it is not obtainable in Palestine."

After Herzl's death in 1904, Ahad Ha'am explained in one of his letters to a colleague: "From the preface of the third volume of my essays you will know that I do not believe that 'messianism' can survive the 'messiah' [Herzl]. Zionism is in process of freeing itself from the messianic illusion, and it is bound as a matter of course to eject all the foreign elements which joined it, only because it was given a messianic turn." Accordingly, he expressed his hope that before long Zionism "will become once more a movement of national revival on historical lines, and consequently a movement limited in numbers with no mass appeal, because it cannot solve the economic problem of the masses."[54]

The Vision of a "Spiritual Center"

As envisaged by Ahad Ha'am, the objectives of Zionism in the foreseeable future thus contrasted sharply with Herzl's sweeping maximal vision. They focused on the creation of a "spiritual center" in Eretz Israel. There the Jewish cultural heritage would find free expression, receptive to the best currents of enlightened modernity yet faithful to its own individuality.

For this purpose Judaism needs at present but little. It needs not an independent state, but only the creation in its native land of conditions favourable to its development: a good sized settlement of Jews working without hindrance in every branch of culture, from agriculture and handicrafts to science and literature. This Jewish settlement, which will be a gradual growth, will become in course of time the centre of the nation, wherein its spirit will find pure expression and develop in all its aspects up to the highest degree of perfection of which it is capable. Then from this centre the spirit of Judaism will go forth to the great circumference, to all the communities of the diaspora, and will breathe new life into them and preserve their unity; and when our national culture in Palestine has attained that level, we may be confident that it will produce men in the country who will be able, on a favourable opportunity, to establish a state which will be a *Jewish* State, and not merely a State of Jews.[55]

Spelling this out further, Ahad Ha'am explained that the important desideratum was that the center provide conditions for "a complete national life" and this involved two things: "First, full play for the creative facilities of the nation in a specific national culture of its own, and secondly, a system of education whereby the individual members of the nation will be thoroughly imbued with that culture, and so moulded by it that its imprint will be recognizable in all their ways of life and thought, individual and social."[56]

This fixing of Zionism's objectives on no more than a national-cultural center rather than a sovereign state raises the question of whether the attainment of cultural autonomy for Jews within the context of multinational Russia or Austria-Hungary would not have been a better alternative. The historian Simon Dubnow (1860–1941), a friend of Ahad Ha'am and in some respects a kindred spirit, was the leading exponent of a rival ideological orientation that advocated just this, arguing on grounds of realism that Palestine could never become anything more than a peripheral factor in Jewish life. The real locus of Jewish cultural survival had to be eastern Europe, where the overwhelming majority of the world's Jewish population was situated.

The premises of Ahad Ha'am and Dubnow concerning the national-cultural identity of the Jews were highly convergent. Indeed, in certain respects, these two thinkers were closer in outlook than Ahad Ha'am was to Herzl.[57] Ahad Ha'am too disapproved of those who adopted "a negative attitude toward the diaspora." But he made a distinction between the subjective and the objective dimensions of such an attitude. "In a subjective sense all Jews adopt a negative attitude toward the diaspora . . . they would gladly put an end to this state of things if it were possible." Under modern conditions, diasporic Jewry no longer had "any defense against the ocean of foreign culture, which threatens to obliterate our national characteristics and traditions, and thus gradually to put an end to our existence as a people."[58] However, he advocated an attitude toward the Diaspora that was subjectively negative but objectively positive. The objective dimension consisted "in refusing to believe in the possibility of transferring all the Jews in the world to Palestine, and consequently in refusing to accept the proposition that we cannot survive in the diaspora. On the contrary, it holds that dispersion must remain a permanent feature of our life, which it is beyond our power to eliminate, and therefore it insists that our national life in the diaspora must be strengthened."[59]

Thus far, Ahad Ha'am was at one with Simon Dubnow. However, he insisted that there be no illusion: "National autonomy in the diaspora cannot give us the possibility of full and complete national life" because "our position among the nations is unique, and . . . the rest of the world will never be induced to admit that we have national rights in the territories that belong to other nations." It was no use comparing the Jews to other small nations in Russia and Austria-Hungary that aspired to national autonomy, since each of them had lived in its national territory for generations and had once been independent. Only the Jews were a foreign people with a national culture that belonged elsewhere.[60] Yet this position did not mean that Ahad Ha'am refused to have any truck with efforts to attain cultural minority rights in the Diaspora. He agreed that autonomy "to the greatest possible extent" should be "worked for wherever possible." But as he phrased it in one of his letters to Dubnow: "In my view, national work in the diaspora can be of use only as a stepping stone to our national home in Palestine . . . *without the centre in Palestine* this diaspora work cannot satisfy our craving for a full national life."[61] Thus, Ahad Ha'am did not concur with Dubnow's view that national autonomy in the Diaspora could ever provide a satisfactory solution for the problem of national-cultural survival. A spiritual center in the Jewish homeland, he insisted, was an absolute prerequisite for maintaining a meaningful cultural life in the Diaspora.

What exactly would communicate itself to the Diaspora? Ahad Ha'am spoke of "spiritual influence," which today might be labeled psychological—the center would restore self-respect to Diaspora Jews, "strengthen their morale," and "increase their sense of unity." But he had in mind much more than that: profound cultural influence, revivified language, creative literature, exemplary mores and modern thought, which would "provide a suitable content for their life as Jews."[62] It is only in the reciprocal relationship between the center and that major part of the Diaspora in eastern Europe where some degree of cultural autonomy was possible that such transfer of cultural attributes could take place in any meaningful sense. It is quite evident that Ahad Ha'am had no such expectations from the Diaspora of western Europe and the New World.[63] This is the inference required if we are to grasp the meaning of Ahad Ha'am's concept of the spiritual center.

In an essay of 1892 on Pinsker's pamphlet *Autoemancipation*, Ahad Ha'am had depicted the future national center in terms comprehending not only spiritual life but also prosaic occupations and activities:

A national spiritual center *for Judaism*; a center which is held in esteem and affection by the whole people, and binds the whole people together in unity; a center of Torah and learning, of language and literature, of physical labor and spiritual purity; a true miniature of the Jewish people as it ought to be: so that a diaspora Jew thinks himself fortunate in being able for once to see with his own eyes the center of Judaism, and on returning home says to his friend: "Would you like to see the truly typical Jew, rabbi or scholar or writer, farmer or craftsman or businessman? Then go to Palestine, and you will find what you want."[64]

Yet his use of the term "spiritual center" was an abiding cause of misunderstanding, many critics interpreting it to mean an entity devoid of normal economic and occupational life, and consequently caviling at the absurdity of the notion.[65] The lack of clarity was compounded by some of Ahad Ha'am's rhetorical statements, such as when he told a major conference of Russian Zionists at Minsk in the summer of 1902: "The establishment of a single great school of learning or art in Palestine, or of a single academy of language and literature, would in my opinion be a national achievement of first-rate importance, and would contribute more to the attainment of our aims than a hundred agricultural settlements."[66]

In response to his critics, Ahad Ha'am was at pains to explain that his use of the adjective *spiritual* was meant to describe the nature of the *influence* the center would have on the Diaspora, not the nature of the center itself: "When we use the word 'centre' metaphorically in relation to human society," he wrote, "what we mean is that a particular spot or thing exerts influence on a certain social circumference, which is bound up with and dependent on it, and that in relation to this circumference it is a centre."[67] He went on to explain: "'Spiritual' means that this relation of centre and circumference between Palestine and the lands of the diaspora will of necessity be limited to the spiritual side of life. The influence of the centre will strengthen the Jewish national consciousness in the diaspora; it will restore our independence of mind and self-respect; it will give to our Judaism a national content which will be genuine and natural." "But it is obvious," he wrote, "that a national centre cannot come into existence, and cannot create a new type of life, if it is purely spiritual. It must obviously include all the elements necessary to a nation, from agricultural labourers and craftsmen to the purest intellectuals."[68]

A related moot point, one that was later to gain increasing significance for those who considered themselves to be his ideological heirs, was whether such a national spiritual center required that there be a Jewish majority in Palestine. It cannot be said that Ahad Ha'am himself was unequivocal on this question. It is on record, however, that he did at least once state: "Palestine will become our spiritual center only when the Jews are a majority of the population and own most of the land. Then they will automatically control the institutions that shape the culture of the country, will impress their own spirit and character on the whole of its life, and will thus create the new pattern of Jewishness which we need so desperately and cannot find in the Diaspora."[69]

As conceived by Ahad Ha'am, the process of upbuilding the center was itself part of the national renaissance, but programmatically what was required above all was that Zionism engage in extensive educational and cultural work in the Diaspora alongside what was being done in Eretz Israel. Gradualism and the primacy of quality over quantity were of the essence of the strategy proposed by Ahad Ha'am. "One solid excellent colony, whose quality attracted the people's love to the Land of Israel," he wrote in his introduction to *Al parashat drakhim* (At the crossroads) in 1895, "would be more important than ten precarious colonies that required the protection of lovers of Zion."[70]

Although vis-à-vis Herzl's political Zionism, Ahad Ha'am purported to represent the cumulative ideological stance of Hibbat Zion, he had long in fact been an internal critic of the primarily practical and philanthropic direction that Hibbat Zion was taking. His view was that the revival of Jewish national sentiment and the creation of a committed elite embodying the values and attributes of a modernized Jewish national culture was the precondition for the success of settlement activities. The mistake of Hibbat Zion was to neglect or even give up the deeper work of national revival—which meant mainly Hebrew publicistic activity and the development of modern "enlightened" schools both in the Diaspora and among those newly settled in Eretz Israel—and to attempt the settlement of Eretz Israel with hopelessly inadequate resources. Consequently, Hibbat Zion was faltering and failing to fulfill its early promise. He held up the vision of a broad national cultural renaissance leading to, and in turn modeled upon, an exemplary miniature Jewish society in Eretz Israel.

To advance this conception of the Hibbat Zion enterprise, Ahad Ha'am set about shaping a cultural elite for the Jewish national movement, a cadre of nationalist intellects and educators who would guide the work of national spiritual revival. Founded in 1889 and named Bnei Moshe, it took the form of a clandestine society on the lines of the Freemasons, with attendant lodges, initiation ceremonies, rules, and passwords. The society demanded that members be of impeccable moral fiber, know Hebrew (although in practice this was not consistently sustained), and be selflessly dedicated to the cause. Its membership never exceeded about 160, although the spread of its lodges went beyond Russia and Palestine and included also Germany, France, Britain, and even the United States. The leading lodges were in Odessa, Vilna, Warsaw, and

Jaffa. Bnei Moshe was a short-lived experiment whose significance lay mainly in its contribution to the shaping of a modernized Jewish cultural identity, and it is in that context that we shall have to return to it in a later chapter.

After Bnei Moshe dissolved in 1897, Ahad Ha'am abandoned whatever active leadership role he had previously undertaken and withdrew into the publicistic activity that was his true metier.[71] He was sorely disappointed with the blind rush of Hibbat Zion members to Herzl's banner, and, as we have mentioned, appalled by the "new" Zionism's emphasis on antisemitism as the crux of the Jewish problem, on its advocacy of political means to the exclusion of all else, and above all, on its apparent lack of interest in the Jewish cultural heritage and the revival of the Hebrew language.

His attack on Herzl's approach, sustained in numerous essays from the time of the first Zionist congress onward, came to a head over Herzl's publication of *Altneuland* in 1902 and the East Africa proposal that he brought before the fifth Zionist congress in 1903. In Ahad Ha'am's view, *Altneuland* illustrated all the faults of Herzl's implausible conception. *Altneuland* was not really an expression of anything inherently Jewish; it was nothing more than a universalized European clone state, an expression of self-abnegation and collective assimilation to gentile culture. Particularly irritating was its ill-concealed disregard for the revival of the Hebrew language—German was the language of elite education and business while the population at large spoke a plurality of languages brought from the Diaspora. "Everywhere one sees similar sights . . . European people, European customs and European inventions. We find not a single distinctively Jewish impression in any place."[72] Typically, *Altneuland* had a Jewish Academy modeled on that of France in all except one respect: "That it does not concern itself with the Hebrew language and culture, in the same way that the French Academy does with the French language and culture." That was apparently considered too "nationally chauvinistic" for the Jewish society.[73] Ahad Ha'am ridiculed Herzl's depiction of massive immigration in so short a period and his utopian description of all the technological wonders that would be attained within a mere twenty-five years. With biting sarcasm he caviled at some of the absurdities depicted in *Altneuland*, for example, the idyllic ingenuity of the New Society in finding enough land for all the millions of Jews who had left the Diaspora without having to take away anything at all from the Arab population!

The clash between the two conceptual matrixes of Jewish nationalism in its Zionist form—the functional and the organic—peaked in the controversy over the East Africa proposal of 1903. As we have seen, the proposal was, by Ahad Ha'am's lights, a wholly reprehensible but entirely logical outcome of all the faults and fallacies of Herzl's "new" Zionism. He regarded it as the final bankruptcy of the whole Herzlian program to which, regrettably, so many members of Hibbat Zion had succumbed.[74]

The Way to "Synthetic" Zionism

After Herzl's premature death in 1904, without having attained the political charter upon which his entire strategy had revolved, the antithetic conception of Jewish nationalism that had animated Hibbat Zion gradually gained ascendancy in the Zionist Organization, although not without a protracted internal struggle between the so-called practicals and politicals. Herzl's immediate successor as president of the Zionist Organization, David Wolffsohn, sustained the effort to steer the organization on the political-diplomatic course set by Herzl and consequently continued to stem demands for increased practical work. However, the entire constellation of political circumstances, both internationally and within the organization, militated against him. The political Zionist camp was weakened in numbers once the diehard protagonists of the East Africa scheme, led by Israel Zangwill, seceded in 1905 to form the Jewish Territorial Organization (ITO). As it turned out they were to spend themselves in a futile search for a territorial alternative to Palestine. Moreover, the Young Turk revolution of 1908 soon proved to be markedly inclement for Zionist political designs on Palestine.

After the eighth Zionist congress (1907) the "practicals" gained considerable ground. They were headed by Menahem Ussishkin (1863–1941), who had become president of the Odessa committee of the Zionist Organization in Russia in 1906 and who earlier had led the bitter resistance of the Russian "Zionists of Zion" to the East Africa scheme. An important gain for the practicals' program was the decision to establish a Palestine Office to initiate and coordinate practical settlement activities on the spot and also the decision to spend one quarter of the movement's budget on work in Palestine. The Palestine Office was set up in 1908 under the charge of Arthur Ruppin (1876–1943).

At the eleventh Zionist congress in 1911 the practicals virtually gained control of the Zionist executive with the election of Otto Warburg (1859–1938) as president in place of Wolffsohn. Ahad Ha'am, having attended that congress as an observer—it was only the second time that he had attended a congress, the first being in 1897—was able to express some satisfaction at the turn of developments he had witnessed. "There were some very gratifying features," he wrote to one correspondent, noting that many new delegates, mainly from western countries, displayed a healthier understanding of the Jewish cultural heritage and the national ideal.[75] To be sure, what these developments signified was progress rather more in the field of practical colonization investment than in that of education and culture, which Ahad Ha'am valued above all.

The newer political policy and the older practical policy were mutually exclusive only as long as Herzl was able to hold up the imminent prospect of obtaining the aspired-for charter. To the extent that this prospect receded or could not be demonstrated, the logic of the situation dictated that Zionist policy take a more long-term view and adopt a synthesis of means—that is, continued, if more discreet, political activity conducted concurrently with carefully regulated settlement work as well as progress in the cultural-educational sphere.

That it hardly made sense for even those who had the strongest reservations about Herzl's exclusively political emphasis to advocate practical work to the total exclusion of political-diplomatic endeavors is illustrated by the fact that Menahem Ussishkin, regarded as the exemplar of the practical approach, articulated a call for a synthesis of both in his major programmatic statement, *Unser Programm* (Our program), which first appeared in 1904 in a Russian Zionist periodical and in 1905 was published as a booklet in Vienna.[76] Ussishkin averred that there were three legs to the political renaissance of any nation: "The people, the land, and the external circumstances." Tracing past policies, he distinguished three main phases in the development of the national movement. The first was the Hibbat Zion phase, lasting for some ten years, until 1891. He found fault with Hibbat Zion for failing to understand "the necessity of becoming an open movement and revealing itself to the world's public eye." After 1891 came the second phase: reinforcement from spiritual Zionism. But again it was unbalanced. The spiritual Zionists in Hibbat Zion "diverted attention from the external factors and also from the need to organize the nation; everything focused on a single principle—internal spiritual regeneration."

Ussishkin, while appreciating the contribution of Ahad Ha'am, did not allow himself to be confined by his ideas. He refused to regard the goal as "some kind of spiritual center, nor as simply a philanthropic settlement project." Then came Herzl and the first Zionist congress. This inaugurated the third and most glorious phase since the Basel Program in principle reflected all three vital dimensions of the national movement. But the same mistake of one-sidedness was repeated: the organization's efforts were concentrated solely on one aspect of the program, "diplomacy and the external legal formalistic aspect." In the result, seven years of exclusively diplomatic endeavor had led to a blank "stone wall," until the most desperate, misguided step of all was taken, the East Africa proposal. Now Ussishkin's program declared: "spiritual Zionism and diplomatic Zionism are none other than two forms of a single political Zionist essence." Furthermore, the land had to be de facto settled and worked by the people even before it became de jure theirs, and this meant persistent practical work concurrent with spiritual and diplomatic work. "Endeavors in all three directions at one and the same time; this is the only wise program for the liberation movement."

The notion of such a synthesis of means was soon thereafter aired at a milestone conference of Russian Zionists held in 1906 at Helsingfors. But at that important gathering the synthesis was conceptualized within the even broader context of a program of *Gegenwartsarbeit* (work in the present), a term connoting political and cultural work then and there in the Diaspora. Moreover, "political" was understood to be inclusive of the demand for rights to cultural autonomy for the Jews in the Russian empire, reflecting a new post-Herzlian nationalist perspective, long-term and dualistic. Alongside work for and in Eretz Israel, the Zionist program of action was now meant to include not only promoting but also institutionalizing the Jewish national entity in the Diaspora. The conference adopted a resolution that called for "continuous, energetic and planned work in Eretz Israel, concomitant with political activity which is consonant with the political character of our movement."[77]

Chaim Weizmann credited himself retrospectively with invention of the term "synthetic Zionism," but he in fact adopted rather than invented it. Although he was certainly not the only one to call for a synthesis, he was on record speaking in that vein at gatherings of Zionists in England in 1906 and 1907 and then at the Zionist congress in the Hague in August 1907.[78] Be that as it may, the circumstances of Weizmann's rise to prominence thanks to his role in the attainment of the Balfour Declaration of November 1917 made him the Zionist leader associated in historical consciousness with the "synthetic Zionist" formula. The Balfour Declaration was, albeit in a considerably attenuated form, in the nature of a political charter for creation of a Jewish national home in Palestine. It stated:

His Majesty's Government view with favour the establishment in Palestine of a national home for the Jewish people, and will use their best endeavours to facilitate the achievement of this object, it being clearly understood that nothing shall be done which may prejudice the civil and religious rights of existing non-Jewish communities in Palestine, or the rights and political status enjoyed by Jews in any other country.[79]

Although the attainment of this important declaration by no means put an end to the need for Zionist political activity, it rendered obsolete the old notion of holding practical work in abeyance. By the same token, it opened the way for greater educational and cultural endeavor. In short, the logic of the situation dictated willy-nilly a policy that sought to advance on all fronts. As president of the Zionist Organization after 1919, Weizmann, more than anyone else, personified this policy of synthesis which in effect became synonymous with "general Zionism."

Genesis of General Zionism

As a political party within Zionism, General Zionism emerged more by default than by design. In the early years of the Zionist Organization's existence there were no political parties. There were only territorial federations (*Landesverbande*), that is to say, single, comprehensive membership organizations in each country. These sent representatives to the annual (after 1903 biennial) congresses. All of the organization's adherents were therefore "general" Zionists. Moreover, the same was true of the organization's elected leaders not only at the outset but even after Britain assumed the mandate over Palestine in 1922. Theodor Herzl and his successors in the presidency of the Zionist Organization, David Wolffsohn (1905–1911), Otto Warburg (1911–1920), Chaim Weizmann (1920–1931 and 1935–1946), and Nahum Sokolow (1931–1935) were all general Zionists in the sense that their electoral mandate to Zionist congresses derived from various territorial federations.

However, the Zionist Organization's constitutional structure changed with the emergence of distinctive ideological groups. The forerunner of these was a short-lived formation of mainly student intelligentsia that was known as the Democratic Faction. It emerged in 1901, and its character will be discussed in part 3 of this book in the context of secular-religious tensions within Zionism. Largely in reaction to it, the Mizrahi national-religious party was formed in 1902. There followed the Poalei Zion (Workers of Zion) Socialist party, which obtained recognition in 1907 as a "separate union" (*Sonderverband*), the name by which such ideological groups with branches in various countries came to be recognized in the Zionist Organization's constitution. The ramified ideological development of the national-religious and the labor Zionists will be described in later chapters. In the present context suffice is to note that by virtue of their greater cohesiveness the "separate unions" grew stronger from congress to congress. Whereas in 1921, 73 percent of all the delegates to the twelfth congress were representatives of territorial federations—that is, general Zionists or, as they were at that time commonly called, *stam Zionim* (plain Zionists)—ten years later, at the seventeenth congress (Basel, 1931), the general Zionists constituted only 53 percent of the delegates.[80]

In the 1920s two groups emanated from the hitherto undifferentiated ranks of general Zionists. One was the Al Ha-mishmar (On Guard) faction in Poland headed by a rising leader, Yitzhak Gruenbaum (1879–1969). At the thirteenth Zionist congress (1923) this faction (initially calling itself Democratic Zionists) mustered twenty-one delegates, having been joined by like-minded Zionists in some other countries, including personalities such as Nahum Goldmann (1894–1982), Max Soloveitchik (1883–1957), Robert Stricker (1879–1944), and Moshe Glickson (1878–1939). Forming an international union in 1925, they became known as the Radical Zionists. What unified them was dissatisfaction with President Weizmann's policies. They considered him too conciliatory and passive in regard to the British mandatory power. They also opposed his plan for constituting an expanded Jewish Agency for Palestine in partnership with prominent Jewish philanthropists, notwithstanding the refusal of such persons to subscribe to nationalist Zionist ideology. The creation of such a broad Jewish Agency had been anticipated in a clause of the League of Nations' mandate to rule Palestine with which Great Britain was entrusted in 1922. In the interim the Zioinist Organization was to fulfill the same functions vis-à-vis the British government. Weizmann believed that the cooperation of wealthy and influential non-Zionists in countries like Britain, the United States, and Germany was vital for the satisfaction of the financial needs of the Zionist enterprise in Palestine. The Radical Zionists held that inviting these non-Zionist plutocrats into partnership was a gratuitous vitiation of Jewish nationalism.[81]

On the other hand, the Radical Zionists were at one with Weizmann in regard to the practical development of Jewish settlement in Palestine and were supportive of the practical settlement work and social program of the labor Zionists there. Although not Socialist themselves, they recognized the primacy of labor settlement and labor institutions such as the General Labor Confederation of Eretz Israel, known as the Histadrut. On this score, they were at variance with the second emanation out of the broad body of "plain" Zionists—the Zionist Revisionist Organization created by Vladimir Jabotinsky in 1925. For the Revisionists not only vehemently attacked Weizmann's policies but militantly challenged the hegemony of labor Zionists in Palestine, branding both as travesties of the pristine political Zionism of Theodor Herzl to which they purported to return. The nature of this revisionism will be considered in a later chapter.

It was only at the sixteenth Zionist congress (Zurich, 1929), that an attempt was initiated to organize all the members of the territorial federations into a comprehensive political group. The initiator was Dr. Isaac Ignacy Schwarzbart (1888–1961) of Galicia. In 1931, on the eve of the seventeenth congress he managed to convene a world conference of General Zionists, with the participation of delegates from some thirty-four countries. It formed a World Union of General Zionists. However, from the outset it was evident that its ideological unity was flimsy. The participants shared no more than a common belief that the Zionist Organization ought not to be encumbered by extraneous "special points of view" (the term used in the Zionist Organization's constitution of 1921 to define the character of "separate unions").[82] They held fast to the straightforward goals of Zionism as laid down in the Basel Program of 1897. But this proved to be a precarious bond as soon as it became necessary to take operative policy decisions facing the Zionist movement. By the time the fourth world conference of General Zionists convened at Cracow in 1935 it was evident that political unity could not be maintained. A distinct split ensued. One section—designated, for want of a more suitable name, General Zionists A—supported both Weizmann's policies in relation to the British mandatory power and the labor movement's enterprises in Palestine. In 1936 they formed a General Zionist faction within the Histadrut called Ha-oved Ha-tzioni (the Zionist Worker) to which was affiliated a number of settlements and also youth movements in the Diaspora. Another section—General Zionists B—was almost as critical of Weizmann's policies as were the Revisionist Zionists and also opposed the hegemony of labor institutions in the *yishuv*, where its affiliates sought to set up a separate workers' organization outside the Histadrut general trade union. This section reflected middle-class interests and demanded greater allocation of the Zionist Organization's funds for private economic initiative.

In contrast with the other political groupings in the Zionist Organization, the General Zionists failed to create and develop institutions of their own in Palestine in a manner that could coalesce and fortify their following there. Furthermore, all efforts to unify the General Zionists durably proved futile. Although a new World Confederation of General Zionists, headed by the American Zionist leader Israel Goldstein (1896–1986), was formed after the twenty-second Zionist congress (Basel, December 1946), it too failed to attain unity; and after the creation of the State of Israel in 1948 the General Zionists there founded two competing political parties: the adherents of Group B formed the General Zionist Party, later renamed the Liberal Party, whereas the adherents of Group A formed the Progressive Party, later renamed the Independent Liberal Party. In the world Zionist Organization framework, Group B assumed the name World Union of General Zionists (Brit Olamit), and Group A called itself the World Confederation of General Zionists (Hitahdut Olamit). However, the latter adopted the view that identification with particular political parties in Israel was no longer justifiable, thereby leaving its former counterpart, the Progressive or Independent Liberals, without direct representation in the world Zionist Organization.

In the period until the creation of Israel, Group A of the General Zionists drew their support mainly from a considerable section of the Zionists in Poland, the Zionist Federation of Great Britain, a part of the Zionist Organization of America (ZOA), the vast women's Zionist organization in America (Hadassah), and the General Zionists of Germany and South Africa. In Palestine it was supported by the Histadrut-affiliated group of General Zionists known as Ha-oved Ha-tzioni, and by Aliya Hadasha (the New Aliya), an organization founded in 1942 by Zionist leaders from Germany, recently settled in Palestine. Group B of the General Zionists also drew its main strength from Poland, particularly from Galicia, which was its special stronghold; from the majority of the Zionist Organization of America, especially after its leadership passed in the 1940s to Abba Hillel Silver (1893–1963); and from the Organization of General Zionists in Palestine.

Ideological Bases of General Zionism

As Isaac Schwarzbart himself, the person who most labored to unify all general Zionists, diagnosed it retrospectively, General Zionism "was a compound of many views but not an ideological entity . . . the heterogeneous composition of General Zionism inevitably resulted in a process of dissipation and refraction."[83] The amorphous nature of the political formation that Schwarzbart managed to pull together was reflected in the discomfort its adherents experienced in attempting to shake off the negative image of being a party by default. That is to say, the defining of a General Zionist as one devoid of real views, belonging neither to the Mizrahi, the labor parties, nor the Revisionists, or worse yet, one who is devoid of positive ideals, whether religious or social. The main thinkers of the General Zionist school of thought engaged endlessly in largely futile efforts to arrive at a more positive definition.[84] The writer and newspaper editor Moshe Glickson (1878–1939), a leading thinker of General Zionism, complained in 1929: "Whosoever today says 'General Zionism' means Zionism devoid of either positive religious ideals or specific social ideals. And this is one of the main reasons for the decline and weakening of Zionism today. No spiritual satisfaction can accrue from pure negation."[85]

Various attempts to offer a positive definition were made. Moshe Kleinman (1870–1948), a Hebrew and Yiddish writer and editor of note, composed a comprehensive exposition of the General Zionist outlook, in which he submitted that "it is Zionism itself, its first and basic frame, it is the Zionist Organization itself first and foremost."[86] Yitzhak Gruenbaum, the important leader of the Radical General Zionists in Poland preferred to describe the ideological position of General Zionism as "unqualified Zionism" (*tzionut le-lo levai*).[87] Selig Brodetsky, the foremost spokesman of General Zionism in Britain, called it "unhyphenated Zionism." He refuted the charge that General Zionists were merely those Zionists not personally involved in the upbuilding of the "national home," that is, merely philanthropists. Arguing, moreover, that "in the Zionist Organization party divisions are very imperfect and misleading," he pointed out that it was "quite false to suggest that General Zionists are necessarily neither socialists nor religious." (Indeed, Brodetsky himself was a long-standing supporter of the Labor Party of Britain). So far from being a Zionism of merely negative definition, General Zionism was in fact "a complete Zionism, a pan-Zionism, which embraces all shades of opinion and interest, which is identified with all phases of Palestine work, and which works for the complete unity of all Zionist endeavor." On the contrary, argued Brodetsky, it was labor Zionism that implied a negation, "namely that Zionism without socialism is undesirable or impossible." Likewise, revisionism implied a negation, "namely, that a Zionism which does not define final aims, and that takes account of realities in regard to practical policy, is not Zionism."[88]

Notwithstanding this amorphous nature of General Zionism, it is possible to extrapolate the core ideas that it entailed. In essence, General Zionism was coterminous with "synthetic Zionism." Thus, in an exposition that appeared in 1919, one finds Moshe Glickson critically evaluating and then simultaneously endorsing the seminal nationalist ideas of the Zionist movement's founding fathers, Herzl and Ahad Ha'am.[89] He goes on to emphasize three basic principles of Zionism. The first he calls "the idea of the collectivity." It postulates in quintessentially nationalist terms that "there can be no solution for the individual in Israel outside of the collective solution for the Jews." The other two principles were the idea of practical self-help and the idea of the nation's "moral mission." From this synthesis the major exponents of General Zionism adduced an overriding ideological proposition, namely, "the primacy of the national interest" (*ha-primat ha-leumi*). In Schwarzbart's words: "The guiding idea of General Zionism of every shade is preference of the national interest to any party interest."[90]

Of course, General Zionism's contention that it alone was the true guardian of the national interest was highly disputable. Schwarzbart had to admit that each of the parties in the Zionist Organization believed that its program was supremely in the national interest. What the General Zionist principle therefore boiled down to was the subordination of class interests to the nationalist goals of the Zionist movement—that is to say, nationalist primacy over any and every ancillary ideological "ism" or social class interest, whether of labor or of employers, and mobilization of every available resource, private enterprise no less than national capital (i.e., funds raised from the Jewish people).

In a booklet that appeared in 1936, another editor and writer of note, Felix Weltsch (1884–1964), offered a more philosophically grounded exposition of this principle.[91] Weltsch traced the development of a positive ideological conscious-ness among General Zionists. Initially, they were simply Zionists devoid of any intra-Zionist partisan awareness. Then the splitting off of the separate unions of Zionists, Mizrahi, and Poalei Zion made them aware of being General Zionists but only in the negative sense. The next stage was the formulation of a conscious ideology, in which a General Zionist was not simply one who did not adhere to any particular political party point of view but one who upheld a positive General Zionist program and saw it as a value in itself. He defined this value thus: "The positive General Zionist is 'General' not because he votes neither for the right nor the left, but rather because he consciously chooses the middle way [*die Mitte*]." "The middle way and unity as conscious ideals," he asserted, were the hallmarks of the true General Zionist. The task of their party was to resist and overcome the tendency of Zionism to tear itself apart self-destructively between the conflicting tendencies of social and political policy in a world acrimoniously divided between the Fascist Right and the Marxist Left.

Weltsch went on to draw distinctions between various manifestations of "the middle way." The true middle way of General Zionism was not a lazy middle way born of weakness, indecisiveness, and compromise or resting on illusions as to the conflicting policies at issue in the Zionist movement. To the contrary, it was a middle way arrived at out of strength, calling for daring, and based on a realistic understanding of the issues, "through the discovery of which something new emerges, something that was not there before, that raises man out of his state of doubt and dilemma." This was not a weak compromise nor even only an artificial synthesis but a "creative middle way" (*schöpferische Mitte*). "The General Zionist always strives for the creative middle way and only settles for duality [*Zweigeleisigkeit*] and synthesis when a creative solution is not possible and in so far as it is not possible." Hence, General Zionist ideology, as propounded by Weltsch, was a force for "unity and wholeness of the movement . . . a centripetal, not a centrifugal force." Its task was "to reconcile opposites, to hold together the wings, and to drive the whole movement forwards."

The question arises: Was General Zionism the "Liberal Party" of Jewish nationalism? Of course, the relationship between nationalism and liberalism is inherently problematic. Liberalism, after all, begins with the fundamental value of individual liberty. Its ideal society is one in which individual liberties are maximized. It champions the autonomy of the individual and is wary of the powers of the state. In the context of a nationalist movement, which is by definition highly collectivist, liberalism is necessarily constrained and very much a relative quantity. At the least it needs must express itself in the urging of significant restraints upon the collective for the sake of individual liberty.

It is noteworthy that neither Weltsch nor any other of the leading exponents of General Zionism made any effort to stake a claim to liberalism as a political ideology and to depict theirs as *the* Liberal Party of Zionism. Indeed, the development of General Zionism until the creation of the State of Israel does not exhibit any marked concern with liberal values in the sense delineated above. Its major concern was not individual liberties but protection of the collective whole against adulteration with extraneous value systems, particularly socialism of the type that advocated class warfare and hostility toward private enterprise. The concept of "primacy of the nation" was, after all, a quintessentially nationalist principle. It connoted the ideas that the first principle of allegiance was to the nation as a function of organic ethnic kinship and that the individual's life could be considered meaningful only through the prism of the nation. In the final analysis, this nationalist principle was a common denominator of all schools of Zionism and therefore fails to mark off clearly the General Zionist ideology.

It cannot be said that the major personalities in General Zionism came to Zionism out of a particularly liberal ambience any more than did other Zionists of eastern European background and central European higher education. It is instructive to note how, in an essay that he wrote in 1919, before he had settled in Palestine, Moshe Glickson grappled with a core problem relevant to the liberal world outlook—"the individual and the collective" (*prat u-klal*).[92] The historical context in which this essay was written was the trauma of the First World War, which, according to Glickson, was preceded by the great individualistic upsurge that accompanied economic liberalism. Then the war itself produced the opposite psychosis of total submission to the collective in the form of the nation. Now that the war was over, an opposite reaction of extreme individualism was again becoming prevalent. The thrust of Glickson's argument was a passionate appeal for balance and harmony between these two extreme tendencies. "How great is the error of that outlook, which sees in these two [the individual and the collective] different and disparate things, a and non-a . . . for is not the whole personality, in all of its life and actions, values and strivings, only a part of the nation? And is not the nation but a simple sum of its individuals?" He argued that, from a psychological point of view the individual and the nation were inseparable. They were simply "two layers of the soul, two dynamic spheres of life."

The nation is not a metaphysical entity, not a mystical ethereal thing that exists outside of the tangible existence of Reuben and Simon and Levy etc.; nor is it merely a logical abstraction . . . the nation is inside Reuben and Simon etc., it is Reuben and Simon themselves insofar as they are more than only a personality. . . . As Spinoza would put it: these two are not different substances, but rather two "descriptions of substance," that may be likened to two measures in geometry, length and width.

Glickson was here adumbrating the same quintessentially nationalist conception to which we have referred, according to which the individual was inseparable from the nation and bore the indelible stamp of the nation. His appeal was for a creative synthesis, for "the secret key to harmonization of the individual and the collective." Such harmony did not mean, he explained, merely peace between opposing elements, in which each side consents not to provoke the other but rather reciprocal understanding between them, the adjustment and correction of both in order to produce and move forward with a new creative harmony. This formulation, it will be noted, was very much in consonance with that of Felix Weltsch.

Arguably, Glickson and most of his fellow General Zionists were liberals in the general sense of favoring individuality, both social and economic, within the limiting parameters of the national cause. Yet clearly, the main thrust of all their ideological emphases was not the upholding of abstract principles of political liberalism but rather the aforementioned appeal for *a middle way*. It may therefore be said that General Zionist ideology was overwhelmingly concerned with the operative level of ideology, with means rather than with the dimensions of diagnosis and vision. Hence, it called for the rejection of all "class egoism" as patently injurious to the collective national purpose. Hence too, it was at pains to uphold the precedence of Zionism's elected national institutions in Palestine. It advocated a unified stream of national education and it opposed political-party domination of employment bureaus.

Of particular importance was the call of all General Zionists, Groups A and

B alike, for "national regulation" of labor relations in Palestine. In their first platform, formulated in 1927 prior to the fifteenth Zionist congress, there appeared a demand for "a general national labor-constitution, that would be obligatory for both sides [employers and workers] and would stipulate specific norms for all matters and conditions of labor."[93] However, there was never unanimity as to precisely what mechanisms were required to effect this. Some General Zionists were inclined to concur with labor leaders like David Ben-Gurion that no more was feasible or desirable than separately negotiated collective contracts between specific employers and workers, binding them not to resort to strikes or other sanctions prior to submission of labor disputes to arbitration. But official resolutions of the General Zionists implied a more compelling mechanism of labor dispute arbitration. Arguing that the call for national regulation of labor relations was of the essence of General Zionism's striving for the middle way to national unity, Moshe Glickson advocated establishment of an institution of compulsory arbitration. "A supreme national authority in labor matters, embodied in a general labor constitution of the *yishuv* that would be fully obligatory on both sides and that would set clear and specific norms in labor affairs."[94] He countered Ben-Gurion's assertion that this was not workable unless under the authority of the state (an authority not possessed by the Zionists in Palestine) with the argument that "this was after all the unique character of our [Zionist] movement, that it undertakes national tasks without possessing state power; in place of coercive means we can apply only the national will, public pressure, the national consensus."

Although in the economic sphere liberalism is historically associated with principles of laissez-faire and free enterprise, it cannot be said that General Zionism's championship of free enterprise was derived from abstract liberal principles. It stemmed, rather, from purely nationalist purposes in some combination with the narrower middle-class economic interests of part of its following. Furthermore, General Zionists were not particularly notable as advocates of freedom of religion and separation of state from religion. Nor did questions of civic rights, or of Jewish–Arab relations particularly, engage the General Zionists. To be sure, some persons who may be categorized as General Zionists became associated with groups that advocated compromise for the sake of peace with the Arabs of Palestine. The first of these was the Brit Shalom (Covenant of Peace) association founded in 1925. But as will be shown in a later chapter, these groups also included persons of labor Zionist affiliation. They cannot be considered concomitants of General Zionism as such.

It is a telling fact that in General Zionist thought prior to the creation of Israel use of the term "liberal" was rare. Apart from anything else, for General Zionists from Germany in particular, the term "liberal" was semantically too closely associated with anti-Zionist Reform Judaism.[95] Group B of General Zionists did sometimes use the term "liberal" in regard to the economic sphere, but its defense of private enterprise and objection to Socialist economic measures are probably better attributed to middle-class employer interests than to abstract liberal principles. As for Group A, it consistently favored a planned economy and the imposition of restraints no less upon free enterprise than upon labor. It is therefore not insignificant that its major spokesmen, the most prominent of whom was Moshe Glickson, editor of the newspaper *Ha-aretz* (The Land), refrained from using the term "liberalism" as a political self-description.

Equally instructive in this regard is the example of Fritz (Peretz) Bernstein (1890–1971), the General Zionist leader from Holland, who after settling in Palestine in early 1936 became editor of the newspaper *Ha-boker* (The Morning) and rose to the leadership of Group B of the General Zionists, which ultimately came to call itself the Liberal Party of Israel. One searches in vain in his writings for any fundamental or systematic articulation of a liberal political philosophy. Even in the post–State of Israel period he invoked the term liberalism only vaguely, almost as an afterthought, rather than as an ideological premise. Thus, in a typical speech, delivered at a conference in 1960, Bernstein placed primary emphasis on attaining the purely nationalist objectives of Zionism by whatever economic and social means were most effective. "But it is correct to say," he added as if as an afterthought, "that this approach which weighs up the utility of means in the light of the set aim, seeks to rely on methods and on principles that reflect in many respects the direction of liberalism."[96] It was only tardily that the two sections of General Zionism in the State of Israel began to lay claim to the title "liberal." Group A, which formed the Progressive Party (later the Independent Liberals) and was part of the Confederation of General Zionists in the world Zionist Organization, began to pay more attention to questions of civic rights; whereas Group B, which at first was called the General Zionist Party of Israel and thereafter adopted the name Liberal Party (and was part of the World Union of General Zionists in the world Zionist Organization), continued to place its major emphasis on economic aspects—private enterprise and the defense of middle-class interests against labor hegemony.

In the prestate period the ideological orientation of the progressive wing of General Zionism may be illustrated at its most articulate from the pen of Yehezkel Kaufmann (1899–1963). Kaufmann was an intellectual of note, a historian and biblical scholar, whose mammoth work analyzing Jewish national thought, *Gola ve-nekhar* (Exile and alienness), will engage our attention in a later chapter. Although he was neither a spokesman nor even an active political participant in General Zionism, in the 1930s he wrote a number of publicistic essays that profoundly expressed the progressive General Zionist critique of both Socialist Zionism and its archrival, Revisionist Zionism.

The thrust of Kaufmann's critique of Socialist Zionism was that its Marxist class-warfare rhetoric was a fallacious and self-delusive exercise that succeeded only in provoking an equally excessive suspicion and hatred of the labor movement on the part of the Revisionist Zionists. The truth was that Zionism and the movement of national redemption neither should nor could be realized through class warfare. Class warfare ran counter to the very logic of the Jewish socioeconomic and political condition. How could one have class warfare when there was no full-grown economy to overturn in the first place? Nor was there an established working class such as existed in other countries. The Jews were an overwhelmingly middle-class population, only a tiny part of which was attempting to transform itself into a working class in Palestine. He deplored the fact that the labor movement had tied itself "to a theory of social revolution which it was not able in practice to realize and indeed did not really strive to realize. Furthermore, it became tied to a theory of social revolution that was to come about in an economy that had not yet been created, and through a class that had not yet come into existence. All that readily existed was the revolutionary theory itself."[97]

Kaufmann debunked the seminal Socialist-Zionist theory of Ber Borochov, who, as we shall see anon, had contended that the "extraterritorialist" situation of the Jewish Diaspora made it impossible for a Jewish proletariat to be integrated into basic industries. Kaufmann argued that the problem had never been one of socioeconomic class but rather the fact that all Jews were ethnically alien in relation to the majority society. Moreover, there was no solid evidence to show that Jews in the Diaspora could not enter into the basic industries if they were so motivated. The truth was that "Jewry in western Europe has shown no tendency to become proletarianized. It rooted itself increasingly in the middle class."

In sum, Kaufmann denied the very proposition that there was any necessary connection between the fulfillment of Zionism, which he characterized as "national redemption," and the fulfillment of socialism. He postulated that while the attitude of Zionism toward socialism, as toward liberalism, ought not to be one of negation, it had realistically to recognize the limitations of both for the needs of a national movement. He deprecated all rhetoric hostile to private enterprise and labeled as "utter utopia" the notion of a wholly "workers' society." In reality, national fulfillment in Eretz Israel would become possible only on the basis of a pooling of all resources, not the least of which derived from private enterprise. Not to recognize that the success of the private economy in which he worked was a prerequisite for the worker's own welfare was myopic.

Yet notwithstanding this criticism, Kaufmann fully acknowledged the indispensable value, even primacy, of the labor movement as the backbone and pioneering thrust of Zionist fulfillment. His plea was for the labor movement to free itself from misguided and unnecessary Marxist rhetoric. Then it would be able to carry out its historic role, enjoying the overwhelming support of all Zionists. Therein lay the difference between the progressive General Zionist approach and that of the Revisionist Zionists. Kaufmann disapproved of revisionism's dogmatic and vehement assault upon labor's primacy in the settlement and development of the land. He also charged it with an "exaggerated valuation of the political foundation of Zionism." He argued that for genuine political Zionism the final goal was not the state structure itself but the creation of an ethnically settled land of Jews. This could not be obtained without the social transformation that was being wrought by the Zionist labor movement, which the Revisionists so scornfully dismissed. Nor could this be done without organized labor and the placing of restraints upon the selfishness to which capitalist private enterprise was prone. Kaufmann therefore defended the labor movement's principle of "the conquest of labor" as long as "its ultimate purpose was national redemption and not the social revolution."

Finally, Kaufmann rejected the very notion of nationalist "monism," which, as we shall later see, was the core of Revisionist Zionist ideology. He contended that self-realizing Zionism could not realistically be "monistic." The Zionism of Herzl had in fact been permeated by ideas of social reform, such as a seven-hour workday and cooperative settlements. Moreover, he deplored revisionism's adoption of some of the elements of European fascism—admiration of military glory, the idea of the dictator-leader, the blind hatred of Marxism, the use of brute force. In mitigation, however, Kaufmann noted that there was an important difference: because in Palestine the state was in British hands, revisionism's clash with the labor movement, even if it bore Fascist marks, was not over control of the state; it was only for hegemony over the national movement. This averted the chance of the Revisionists gaining control of the state itself, implementing a Fascist policy, breaking the workers' organizations and suppressing freedom.

CHAPTER FOUR

National-Religious Zionism

Emergence of a National-Religious Organization

A S WE HAVE SEEN in an earlier chapter, religious traditionalism had a path of its own to Jewish nationalism, one rooted in the messianic essence of Jewish religious faith. If we are unable to describe so-called precursors such as Rabbi Zvi Hirsch Kalischer as "nationalists," in regard to the rabbis within Hibbat Zion, such as Shmuel Mohilewer, there can be little doubt that the term "nationalism" becomes applicable. Their thought transcended the messianic conceptual matrix, making it possible for them to comprehend the Jews as an entity more comprehensive than the aggregate of those who were observant of Jewish religious law and traditions. Although never ceasing to believe in an ultimate messianic outcome from Jewish return to Zion, they concurred in essentials with the mundane and material analysis of the Jewish condition propounded by the nationalist Jewish intelligentsia. Hence, they were able to bring themselves to cooperate with it within Hibbat Zion.

Those rabbis who, together with other Hibbat Zion members, rallied to Theodor Herzl's call for a world Zionist Organization were confronted in 1901 by the emergence of an organized faction at the Zionist congress. Called the Democratic Faction, it comprised young émigré intelligentsia centered in German and Swiss universities. One of them was Chaim Weizmann. In addition to demands for more democratic practices in the Zionist Organization, the Faction advocated a concerted program of cultural and educational work predicated on the secularist premises of Ahad Ha'am. As such, we shall have cause to return to this subject in a separate chapter. In the present context, suffice it to say that this provoked a strong reaction on the part of eastern European orthodox rabbis for whom any notion of secularized education for Jews was like holding up a red rag to a bull. The very concept of secular culture (*kultura*, as it was called in turn-of-the-century Hebrew) was anathema to orthodox Jews, for whom it signified secularism's destructive onslaught on the Jewish religion. This precipitated the creation in 1902 of their own political faction, under the leadership of Rabbi Yitzhak Yaakov Reines (1839–1915) and in cooperation with some "political" Zionists who were at one with the orthodox in disqualifying cultural-educational matters from the Zionist program. They called this faction Mizrahi, an acronym for *merkaz ruhani*, meaning "spiritual center" but at the same time connoting "east," the traditional direction of prayer to Jerusalem.[1] As it happened, Mizrahi long outlived the ephemeral Democratic Faction, remaining a permanent party structure within the world Zionist Organization until the establishment of Israel, after which it was succeeded by the National Religious Party. Mizrahi's more secular members, however, had very soon quit, leaving it with a purely orthodox-observant membership.

Mizrahi in turn gave birth to a daughter movement called Ha-poel Ha-mizrahi (the Mizrahi worker). It emanated from a younger generation that had begun to be organized within the Mizrahi framework as Tzeirei Mizrahi (the Young Mizrahi), at first within Polish Jewry after the First World War and later in the Jewry of other countries, including Germany of the late 1920s and the 1930s. It took shape as a political framework in Palestine during the period 1919–1923, which is conventionally known in Zionist historiography as the Third *Aliya*. Its social composition differed from that of the mother organization, Mizrahi, for, with few exceptions its founders were not practicing orthodox rabbis, but rather orthodox youth, a major part of whom came from Hasidic backgrounds. This was, in a sense, ironical since all the great Hasidic rabbinical luminaries were firmly aligned with the orthodox religious opposition to Zionism. One scholar has suggested that the Hasidic roots of these young settlers "provided them with inveterate mystical channels and symbols for fomenting religious fervour capable of transcending the here and now and undermining institutionalized patterns."[2] Be that as it may, exposed to the accelerated modernizing influences of life in Poland and the adjacent new national states that emerged after the First World War, as well as to the influence that radiated from the upsurge of the Zionist labor movement in Palestine, these youths were motivated to seek a synthesis of orthodox observance and labor pioneering values of patently secular derivation, thereby freeing themselves much more thoroughly than had the Mizrahi rabbis from the constraining links still retained with the great centers of orthodox religious learning in Europe.

The immediate circumstances that led, in 1922, to the creation of Ha-poel Ha-mizrahi, which became an organization within the World Mizrahi Federation, were related to the need of such young Mizrahi settlers to create a social framework that would enable them to be employed as workers in Eretz Israel, while at the same time maintaining a suitable ambience for full orthodox religious observance. "We seek a life of labor and creativity based upon traditional Judaism," the founding manifesto of Ha-poel Ha-mizrahi stated. "We cannot engage solely in spiritual matters and confine ourselves to the four cubits of *halakha* [Judaism's legal code]. Nor can we rest content with the external nationalist trappings of language and country and forsake our Torah which is the basis of our national culture."[3]

In Palestine Ha-poel Ha-mizrahi went far further than Mizrahi had done in creating its own social and labor institutions. It established labor employment bureaus and a sick fund and sponsored agricultural and artisan cooperatives. These institutions paralleled on a small scale those of the increasingly dominant secular labor Zionist movement. Consequently, Ha-poel Ha-mizrahi in effect came to subsume its progenitor, Mizrahi. By 1927, in the election to the fifteenth Zionist congress, it polled some 55 percent of the total number of votes gained by the national-religious camp of Mizrahi and Ha-poel Ha-mizrahi together. By 1946, when the elections to the twenty-second Zionist congress took place, Ha-poel Ha-mizrahi had 78 percent of those votes.[4] Consequently, after the creation of the State of Israel it was the Ha-poel Ha-mizrahi element that dominated the National-Religious Party in Israel's Knesset (parliament).

Much as the break with a Hasidic background may well have had a dialectical effect on the young Mizrahi generation in Poland, so the influence of orthodoxy as it had developed in Germany seems to have left its mark on a secondary wave of Ha-poel Ha-mizrahi settlers originating from there. They had severed themselves from the ambience of neoorthodoxy—a phenomenon to which we shall shortly return—which favored exposure to secular learning and civic integration. Consequently, when the young national-religious generation in Germany was further exposed to labor movement values, it tended to adopt an ideological synthesis that was able even to endorse socialism. From the 1930s onward this ideological synthesis facilitated the creation of a number of kibbutz communes modeled entirely on the economic and social values of the secular prototypes created by the Zionist labor movement but in which the life of their members was ordered with fidelity to the *halakha*. This marked the pinnacle of ideological and practical confluence between national-religious Zionism and secularized labor Zionism.[5]

Religious Accommodation of Nationalism

Yet even those orthodox rabbis of Mizrahi who committed themselves unreservedly to the Zionist movement continued to experience great difficulty in accommodating the concept of nationalism to their universe of discourse. It was absolutely fundamental to orthodox Jewish belief that the unit of mankind contemporarily known as "Jews" was created by God through the revelation of his covenant (*brit*) with their ancestors, the Children of Israel. In the eyes of the Mizrahi rabbis it had become conceivable that the terms of that covenant, comprehensively laying down the mores, values, and rituals binding on all generations of Jews, were commensurate with those attributes that modernity ascribed to the term "nation." But in the final analysis their transcendental understanding of Jewish identity still rendered it conceptually inconceivable to regard that covenantal system as in any sense *a function of* the nation; to the contrary, it was the very *source of* the nation!

Equivocations and contradictions concerning Jewish self-definition as nation and religion abound in the ideological expositions of the leading figures in Mizrahi. Yitzhak Yaakov Reines, the founding father of Mizrahi is a case in point. In some writings he seems to recognize the ethnic-national entity as one broader than religion—that is to say, religion as a component of Jewish ethnicity. For he uses the term *amamut*, defined as "the race, the language, the religion, and the special land—in which is included political governance." "Ethnicity" would seem to be an apt translation of his usage of the word *amamut*, since he goes on to relate it to the formation of the nation: "For the *amamut* is the thing that fuses and unites all the members of the *uma* [nation]," he writes. (The territory, he adds, is ultimately necessary to protect this ethnicity and allow it to develop freely.) However, in the same breath, he gives primacy to religion, contending that it is religion that endows this ethnicity with distinctiveness, "for it [religion] alone made Israel a unique people from the very beginning, and only through it does Israel's ethnicity exist. Should, God forbid, the observance of Torah and commandments fall away, undoubtedly the ethnicity would disintegrate and disappear."[6]

Another example of the interminable and indeterminate semantic grappling with the concepts "nation" and "religion" that characterized the leading exponents of national-religious thought may be taken from the writings of Rabbi Yitzhak Nissenbaum. He was born in Bobruisk, Russia, in 1868 and served for a time in the 1890s as Rabbi Mohilewer's aide and secretary of the Hibbat Zion religious center, known as Mizrahi (but not to be confused with the Mizrahi organization created in 1902), that Rabbi Mohilewer headed in Bialystok. He was an early supporter of Herzl's new initiative but during the debate on the East Africa scheme he identified with the Zionists of Zion opposition. In 1901 he settled in Warsaw, and in 1902 he participated in the founding conference of the Mizrahi faction in Vilna. However, holding to the conviction that there should be a unitary Zionist organization, he held back from becoming a formal member until 1919. Thereafter he rose to the leadership of Mizrahi in interwar Poland, becoming its president in 1937 and contributing weightily to religious Zionist ideology. He perished at the hands of the Nazis in the Warsaw ghetto during the Second World War. Nissenbaum affirmed that "the religion of Israel is national from beginning to end." But in diametrical opposition to the Ahad Ha'amist school of thought, he argued that "the concept 'Hebrew national elements' without religion is absurd."[7] The Jews were unique among the nations because in their case the elements of religion and nation were absolutely indistinguishable from each other. This was attested to by the fact that "the Hebrew nation cannot incorporate the members of other religions. The Hebrew religion is the sole soul of the Hebrew nation, and just as no person can incorporate the soul of another—'a *dybbuk*'—so the Hebrew nation cannot suffer any other soul, strange and alien to it."[8]

In an attempt to cope with the semantic difficulties raised by this conceptual inseparability of religion from nation, Nissenbaum preferred to dispense with the term "nation" in the case of the Jews and instead use the term *yahadut*, in the sense of Jewry or Jewishness, for he explained: "The word *yahadut* is derived from the word Jews, and it has a double meaning; the totality of Jews—the nation, and the essence of the Jews—their Torah and the culture of their forefathers, or in one word tradition in its broadest sense."[9] He reasoned that "the concept *yahadut* is not at all a synonym for the concept religion (*dat*), it is rather something wider. It contains within it as well as religion, also Torah and also—nation." It meant the totality of Jews, that is to say, "the nation of Israel living according to the tradition of its fathers."[10]

Yet in the very same discussion, Nissenbaum cannot avoid recognizing a distinction between the two spheres, religion and nationalism, when he writes: "Religion is the sum total of the beliefs and practical commandments by which we are differentiated from the adherents of any other religion; and nationalism is the sum of the feelings and possessions by which we differentiate ourselves in relation to other peoples."[11] Moreover, by 1934, when the confrontation with the organized orthodox opponents of Zionism, Agudat Israel (the Association of Israel), necessitated clearer semantic distinctions, one finds Rabbi Nissenbaum upholding "the principle of the unity of the nation" in cooperation with secularists and condemning Agudat Israel's separatism and its view of the term "nation" as nothing but a conceptual surrender to secularism.[12]

Similarly, Rabbi Yehuda Leib Ha-Cohen Fishman, also known as Maimon (1875–1962), another major spokesman of Mizrahi and one of its most prolific writers and editors, drops semantic equivocations when he polemicizes against Agudat Israel, which he accuses of following the western European neoorthodox tendency to seek integration into the national tissues of the gentile host society: "Whereas according to the view of Agudat Israel religious Jewry condescends to make us over [purely] into the adherents of a single religion and unique faith, according to the outlook of Mizrahi the religion of Israel helped to make us become both a single people [*am*] and a unique nation [*leom*]. That is the fundamental difference between Mizrahi and Agudat Israel."[13]

A particularly pungent illustration of the inherent difficulty that the orthodox rabbis of Mizrahi had in coming to terms with the modern conception of nationalism may be found in the early 1930s in the writings and speeches of Rabbi Moshe Avigdor Amiel (1882–1946), who after serving as rabbi in Antwerp was elected as chief rabbi of Tel Aviv in 1936. Submitting a line of reasoning reminiscent of Yehiel Michel Pines, whose objections to secular nationalism we cited in an earlier chapter, Amiel argued that, notwithstanding the many divisions that had arisen in the Jewish people, none—not even Reform Judaism—had refuted "that most fundamental of principles":

I mean the fundamental principle that Rabbi Sa'adia Gaon encapsulated in the concise saying: "Our nation is not a nation except by its Torah," which means . . . that Israel is not a people like other peoples. . . . Then Zionism came . . . and refuted—if not explicitly then at least implicitly—this most fundamental of principles. According to its conception we are a nation like all the nations and indeed that is the end goal that has to be accomplished; to be but one of the many nations of the world.[14]

Debunking the notion, long a staple of Mizrahi ideology, that the return of freethinkers to Zionism augured their further return to Jewish religious observance, Amiel deplored the failure of his colleagues to recognize that there was a fundamental contradiction between the secular ideology of nationalism and the authentic self-understanding of Judaism. He all but concurred with the virulent orthodox opponents of Zionism in Agudat Israel that the secular conception of Zionism as nationalism was a mortal threat to Jewish religion, for it posed as a complete alternative aimed at replacing authentic Jewish belief and observance. It sought to legitimize emulation of the gentile nations, instead of upholding the uniqueness of the Jews as a nation purely by virtue of their covenant with God. "[Secular] nationalism is not merely a partial recognition of the truth, it is worse than secularism in general," he asserted. Secular nationalism was tantamount to "taking a foreign idol, to which one bows down and says: 'These are your Gods, O Israel.'"[15]

It should be borne in mind that Amiel's harking back to earlier orthodox negations of the Zionism of freethinkers was voiced in the 1930s. Witnessing the inexorable ascendancy of secular Zionist ideologies and perhaps influenced by what was happening in Europe at that time, he went so far as to contend that secular nationalism was morally reprehensible. According to Amiel, only as a function of religion—as Zionism should rightly have been comprehended— was nationalism morally tenable. In a speech to the world conference of Mizrahi in Cracow in 1933 he declared: "Nationalism in its conventional meaning amongst all the nations has its true source in the crude egoism to be found in all animals, by which each is concerned only for its own survival and struggles for its existence . . . except that in place of the private 'I' of animals there is the 'collective I.' But the foundation and source is the same."[16]

In the throes of his bitter assault on the secular ideologies of Zionism, Rabbi Amiel did not shrink from the charge that "the nationalism of secular Zionism draws its sustenance from hatred, the hatred of the gentiles for Israel." By contrast, he claimed, "our nationalism draws from love—the love of Israel for God and for all who are created in the image of God."[17]

In summation, perhaps Mizrahi's ambiguous ideological conception of Jewish nationalism might best be rendered comprehensible by employing the distinction between fundamental and operative ideology. At the fundamental level an unbridgeable abyss divided it from all secularized understandings of the nation as a more comprehensive unit than religion and hence of religion merely as a component of the nation. However, at the operative level, national-religious ideology recognized that there was a social circumference wider than the core of orthodox observant Jews and that it marked off a social unit answering to the description "nation" in the usage of the modern gentile world. This de facto rather than de jure cognizance of the concept of nation was the operative ideological license for cooperating with those who had a secular modern understanding of the nation. By the 1940s, after more than half a century of national-religious development, which included the emergence and ascendancy of Ha-poel Ha-mizrahi, one finds rather less of this tortuous equivocation over recognition of the nation in modern terms. Thus, for example, a comprehensive exposition of the ideology of Mizrahi, published in 1946, stated quite unequivocally that Mizrahi upholds the view "that it behooves us to affirm the nation as a single unit."[18]

The National-Religious Subculture

The part of orthodox religious Jewry that clung to Hibbat Zion and thereafter to Zionism, notwithstanding the major rabbinical defections during the 1890s and in the early years of the Zionist Organization, developed an increasingly distinctive subculture. It was a subculture in the sense of having its own norms of interpretation, identification and sources of charismatic authority.[19] Of course, its constituents did not perceive themselves as anything other than authentic interpreters of traditionalist Jewish law and lore. But in objective point of fact they were internalizing new elements of nationalist-mediated modernity while subjectively interpreting them as authentic emanations of Judaism's sacred textual sources.

Contemporary descriptive labels of this subculture included terms such as "religious Zionism" and "orthodox Zionism." However, because the word "orthodox" acquired connotations of a confessionalist approach, according to which the Torah was meant to be the code of a religious rather than a national entity, by the end of the First World War the term "national-religious" had become prevalent in ideological representations. It is indeed a particularly apt label in the context of our account here.[20] The national-religious subculture may be considered but one of three sociologically identifiable subcultures of religious orthodoxy. The other two were the neoorthodox subculture that had developed earlier in Germany around the teachings of Rabbi Samson Raphael Hirsch (1808–1888) in Frankfurt am Main and the congeries of ultraorthodox subcultures that had first developed in Hungary among the pupils of Rabbi Moses Sofer known as the Hatam Sofer (1762–1839).

Whereas the reform movement of Judaism, which had made great inroads into German Jewry by the mid-nineteenth century, viewed much of the *halakha* as an impediment to Jewish integration into its mainly bourgeoisie reference group in the majority society, Samson Raphael Hirsch reaffirmed the early Enlightenment position of Moses Mendelssohn (1729–1786) that *halakha* was the essential obligatory component of Judaism. He undergirded it with a coherent philosophical formulation and a theodicy that depicted the Jew as a partner in the task of perfecting a world intentionally created imperfect by God. He viewed emancipation as an act of progress toward the ultimate perfection of the world. The Jew had a unique role to perform in this universal process precisely by living in dispersion according to the strict letter of the *halakha* while at the same time participating in the civic life around him.

The aphorism *Torah im derekh eretz*, which is best translated as "living according to Jewish law together with civic life," encapsulated the principle underlying neoorthodoxy. Torah connoted the unimpaired validity of the *halakha* at the particularist level of the Jew's life. As such, Hirsch's approach, while tending, like Reform Judaism, to a confessionalist representation of Judaism, could not efface its national attributes as Reform attempted to do. It did, however, subordinate the national to the confessional: "Unlike other nations, where the law is created for the nation, in Israel the nation was created for the law," wrote Hirsch.[21] *Derekh eretz* connoted, inter alia, gaining academic and vocational education, engaging in a regular economic occupation, and generally deporting oneself in conformity with the manners of the majority civic society. As may readily be understood, this neoorthodox outlook was inimical to the notion of reviving Jewish national aspirations. It was an adjunct of the overall emancipation and integration ideology that captured the minds of most leaders of Jewish communities in Germany, western Europe, and the New World in the course of the nineteenth century. In this respect, ironically, neoorthodoxy found itself in the same camp as Reform Judaism, to which it was in every other respect sharply opposed.

Within the transformation process from traditionalism to orthodoxy, the antinomy of *Torah im derekh eretz* was the aphorism *hadash asur min ha-torah* (the new is forbidden by the Torah), attributed to Rabbi Moses Sofer, one of the most influential rabbinical figures of the first half of the nineteenth century. By the mid-nineteenth century, his successors in Pressburg, Hungary, had formed a self-secluded, rigidly observant prototype of the contraacculturative phenomenon that may be called ultraorthodoxy. This early ultraorthodoxy was reinforced and amalgamated in the late nineteenth century by the products of a new type of enlarged yeshiva (academy of talmudic study) in eastern Europe, such as those of Volozhin, Telz, and Mir, supported by solicitation of outside funds.

Conformity to the standardized norms set by the charismatic rabbinical heads of these yeshivas displaced the local and family norms that had characterized traditional religious life. Out of the rigidly cohesive and insular "societies of scholars" constituted by these yeshivas there emanated the sectarian ultraorthodox phenomenon known today as the *haredim* (literally, the God-trembling or God-fearing).[22]

Against this background, the upholders of the national-religious outlook faced a dual ideological challenge involving two different universes of discourse. In addition to their ongoing confrontation with secular schools of Zionist ideology, they had to face up to the sustained assault of those orthodox Jews who vigorously opposed Zionism within their shared homiletical universe of discourse. All three subcultures were responses to the challenge of modernity, to the identity crisis precipitated by the defection of increasing numbers from traditionalist observance as a result of secularism and reformed religion. Ultraorthodoxy's response was one of self-isolation. It barricaded itself within the four cubits of the *halakha*. The national-religious subculture had common ground with the ultraorthodox only inasmuch as they both opposed abandonment of the *halakha* and attempts to integrate into the national tissues of the environing gentile majority. With the neoorthodox, the national-religious had in common their response to modernity not by self-isolation from its influences but rather by regarding modernity as an opportunity for improving the condition of the Jews in the world. At a fundamental level, however, the national-religious approach clashed with the neoorthodox inasmuch as it endowed Jewish nationhood in itself with primary religious value. This, neoorthodoxy refused to do.

Since Mizrahi's social resources were embedded mainly in eastern Europe, its rabbinical leadership stratum did not relinquish its bonds with the traditionalist yeshiva institutions and charismatic rabbinical authorities there. It was not uncommon for notable rabbis to pass from one sphere to the other. Consequently, by and large, the Mizrahi rabbis were far too self-constrained to undertake innovative halakhic initiatives.[23] They experienced difficulty in arriving at unanimity over the resolution of practical incompatibilities between halakhic prescriptions such as the sabbatical year, which required that the fields be left fallow every seventh year, and the basic needs of a modern economy and society.[24] Politically, the lines of demarcation began to be more clearly drawn with the founding of Agudat Israel in 1912 as an organization comprising both neoorthodox and ultraorthodox elements, explicitly aimed at opposing the pretensions of the Zionists to represent all of Jewry in the international forum. But even this political division did not yet cut all the ties that bound the national-religious subculture to the rabbinical authorities and institutions centered in eastern Europe. As we shall see later, it was not until the 1920s, with the emergence of the subideology of *Torah ve-avoda* (Torah and labor) that bolder initiatives at halakhic innovation began to be taken.

The Orthodox Assault

The common denominator of Zionist diagnosis of the Jewish condition was, as we have seen, the proposition that the condition of the Jews in the dispersion is gravely defective, not only in a messianic but also a mundane sense. It might be said that all three subcultures of orthodoxy concurred in this proposition up to a point. Certainly in a theological sense, *galut* (exile) was a defective condition of existence; *geula* (redemption) was the vision of the ultimate, perfect condition for which all longed. Even in regard to some mundane aspects of Jewish distress and the complete performance of the precepts of Judaism, there could be agreement that life in the *galut* was defective. As Rabbi Nissenbaum stated in one of his ideological essays, "All Jews ['that are not infected with the plague of assimilation,' added the editor of Nissenbaum's writings in a footnote] admit that the *galut* is a punishment for Israel and not a mission. But some regard it as a kind of hell aimed at purifying us from our sins and therefore they end up singing its praises and calling it 'the crown of the Torah,' that is to say, the crown of thorns of the Torah."[25]

It was only Reform Judaism, an appalling distortion in the eyes of all three orthodox subcultures alike, that balked at this proposition, turning the dispersed condition of the Jews from a temporary fault into a permanent virtue. Where the national-religious school parted most substantially from the other two schools of orthodoxy was in regard to the remedy it proposed for the defective essence of *galut*: return of Jews to Zion and the restoration of Zion to the Jews in a modern national sense, involving not only self-help but also cooperation with members of the Jewish nation who had abandoned observance of the halakhic precepts of the Jewish religion.

The ideological clash between the national-religious approach, on the one side, and the neo- and ultraorthodox, on the other, was conducted on two interrelated but analytically separable levels: one was theological, involving, as it were, the covenantal relationship between Israel and God; the other was mundane, involving the perceived vital interests of rabbinical halakhic authority in its struggle against freethinking secularists who appeared to be advocating a substitute national-secular identity.

The orthodox religious critique of Zionism had already taken shape in the Hibbat Zion period, reinforced by waves of disaffection in reaction to the ascendancy of the secularized intelligentsia in the 1890s. In 1900, only a few years after the founding of the Zionist Organization, there appeared a compendium of major rabbinical opinions, including some of the foremost luminaries, such as Rabbis Eliyahu Haim Maisel of Lodz, Haim Soloveitchik of Brisk, David Friedman of Karlin, and Shalom Dov Ber Shneersohn, the Lubavitcher rebbe.[26] As was characteristic of the rabbinical universe of discourse, this polemic launched against Zionism spared no possible line of argument and drew upon any source in the vast sea of homiletical literature that could be shown to have the slightest bearing on the issues in dispute. At the mundane level it refused to see in Zionism anything but a campaign to supplant the supremacy of rabbinical authority and lead Jews away from observance of the precepts of Judaism. Moreover, it accused the Zionists of attempting to substitute the true identity of the Jew as the chosen creation of God by virtue of his eternal covenant, with a new heretical form of so-called national identity.

Over and over again, the rabbinical opinions presented in this compendium made such accusations as that the Zionists "have already made it publicly explicit that their purpose is to eradicate the foundations of religion—and to this purpose they also seek to capture all the centers of Jewish life,"[27] and that "it is open and known that their entire intention and thought is to destroy the foundations of the religion of our holy Torah."[28] The Lubavitcher rebbe was one of the most forceful and uncompromising opponents of Zionism quoted in this compendium of diatribes. He said, inter alia:

And their entire desire and intention is to remove the burden of the Torah and the commandments and to uphold only their nationalism. This is to be their Judaism. One of their movement's leaders recently set this forth before the eyes of all Israel in a published statement of calumny against all of Judaism, daring to say that a Jew does not have to observe the Torah. . . . They utter with their lips that there are commandments of the Torah that are a disgrace to Israel. And this they seek to instill in the hearts of the youths whom they want to capture in their schools, in order to implant in them the poison of heresy . . . and make nationalism their flag.[29]

In the same vein, another collection of rabbinical opinions, published in 1902, this time the product of major Hasidic luminaries in Poland, declared that "the very essence of the Zionist idea is nothing other than the complete uprooting of the religion of Moses and Israel" and that "Zionism itself is based on the denial of divine providence, the doctrine of reward and punishment and of the hoped-for redeemer. The nationalism of which they speak fulfills itself in nothing other than the destruction of sacred religion."[30]

To this basic line of attack were added various practical objections. One was the impossibility of transforming Jewish townsmen into farmers since it was "contrary to the laws of man's nature." Another was that "the notion of hundreds of thousands of Jewish settlers in Eretz Israel in the midst of the other peoples who populate it, and even more so the creation in it of a Jewish state and safe refuge internationally guaranteed, is contrary to all reason."[31] Particularly pungent was the castigation of those orthodox Jews who misguidedly lent their support to the heresy of Zionism. They were depicted as aiders and abetters of these terrible destroyers of the traditional Jewish order. Their claim that cooperation with nonbelievers and transgressors was justified since return to Zion would serve to return them to the religious fold was contemptuously denied. To the contrary, asserted the Lubavitcher rebbe, the inevitable consequence of this new heresy, Zionism, was all too obvious:

The Zionists are far more cunning [than plain secularists] in their evil. They have made nationalism a substitute for Torah and commandments. . . . After this assumption is accepted, anyone who enters the movement regards himself as no longer obliged to keep the commandments of the Torah, nor is there any hope consequently that at some time or other he will return, because, according to his own reckoning, he is a proper Jew in that he is a loyal nationalist. . . . It is clear on logical grounds that not only does the Zionist idea fail to bring near those who have distanced themselves from Israel, but it has even driven them further away. Moreover, it has even led right-thinking Jews to tear from their hearts every concern with the holiness of the Torah, faith in God and the fulfillment of the active commandments. For it has deprived them of the basis of the obligation of Torah and commandments altogether, and has instead planted in their hearts the belief that through nationalism they are complete Jews.[32]

But there was another dimension of the orthodox polemic, shared quite as much by many of the proemancipation neoorthodox as by the isolationist ultraorthodox, that went beyond mundane reasoning, touching the theological core of traditional Jewish faith. This was the charge that Zionism signified not only a loss of faith in God's providence but even a rebellion against God himself. In this regard there was frequent invocation of a venerable homiletical source concerning certain oaths by which God was supposed to have adjured his chosen people and the nations of the world: "One, that Israel shall not go up [all together as if surrounded] by a wall . . . the second that Israel shall not rebel against the nations of the world, and the third that God adjured the idolaters, that they shall not oppress Israel too much."[33]

It followed that the ordained task of the Jew was obdurately to persist in observance and study of the precepts of the Torah, patiently and quiescently awaiting the miraculous coming of the Messiah in God's own chosen time. "It never occurred to our brethren the children of Israel, upholders of the Torah and commandments," stated *Sefer da'at ha-rabbanim* (The book of rabbinical opinions) "that there could be redemption other than by the will of the holy one, blessed be He, to redeem us. And we are full of hope that, . . . at the time of His choosing to redeem us he shall send us Elijah the Prophet with the righteous messiah the son of David. Only this we are obliged to do: preserve and observe all the commandments of God which are more pleasant than gold and sweeter than honey."[34] Although this principle of faith did not in itself preclude going up to live or be buried in Eretz Israel, such an act was legitimate—indeed meritorious—only if it was to the purpose of purifying and perfecting that study, piety, and strict observance of the Torah. It could never be justified if it were associated with Jewish transgressors involved in any attempt to "force the end." As the Lubavitcher rebbe contended: "Our Godfearing brethren know . . . that it is their duty to bear the yoke of exile because it is the Divine Will that in this way their sins shall be atoned up to the time when the Lord will have mercy on us and speedily redeem us."[35] As we had occasion to note in an earlier chapter, in the Hibbat Zion period some eminent rabbinical authorities at least entertained the notion of a program to resettle Jews in Zion on condition that the entire project be directed and carried out exclusively by orthodox-observant Jews. On the other hand, the uncompromising Lubavitcher rebbe explicitly declared: "Behold even if these people were in consonance with God and his Torah, and even if there were reasons to think that they will attain their goal," we must not listen to them in this matter of trying to reach redemption by our own power."[36]

For yet other *haredi* opponents of Zionism, the principle so characteristically epitomized by the homily of the three oaths assumed dogmatic proportions so great as to lead to the absolute proscribing of Zionism as a satanic force, an abominable obstacle on the path of messianic redemption. Indeed, in later years, invoking the punishment alluded to in the three oaths homily, Rabbi Joel Teitelbaum, the luminary of the Satmar Hasidic sect, went so far as to suggest that were it not for the sins of the Zionists against God, the Holocaust in the Second World War might not have been inflicted on the Jews![37]

Marginalization of the Messianic Dimension

On the theological level, the response of the national-religious school of orthodoxy to the critique of its orthodox opponents drew upon the tradition of messianic interpretation that had been set by the "precursors" associated with the Colonisationsverein für Palästina (Hevrat Yishuv Eretz Israel) of the 1860s, which we discussed in part 1 of this book. Rabbi Mohilewer adopted Rabbi Kalischer's conception of the messianic process as one requiring a natural stage of settlement in the Holy Land.[38] In addition, he and other national-religious rabbis associated with Hibbat Zion vigorously refuted the severe charge that cooperation with the *maskil* intelligentsia was forbidden under any circumstances.[39] Yet in rebutting the harsh criticism of Hibbat Zion being voiced by many important rabbinical authorities, the national-religious rabbis tended to marginalize the messianic dimension of their outlook. This was reflected in a collection of rabbinic opinions published in 1891 by Rabbi Abraham Yaakov Slutzki, one of the foremost religious proponents of Hibbat Zion.[40] In his introductory essay, Slutzki admitted, rather apologetically, that some rabbis within Hibbat Zion did associate its program for settlement of Eretz Israel with the "beginnings of the future redemption." However, his own view was that "the idea of settling in Eretz Israel was sufficiently lofty on its own, without adding any other object." In the same vein, Rabbi Shmuel Yaakov Rabinowitz, a foremost spokesman of the rabbis who associated themselves with Hibbat Zion, explained that "in the Zionist movement in our time there is no hastening of the end [of days] and no messianic movement, no 'ascending of the walls', no rebellion—Heaven forbid—against the gentile nations, but only a striving in a natural way to realize a possibility suited to the circumstances of life in our time and to our situation amongst the nations."[41]

This marked the beginning of a tendency that was to crystallize into a policy with the founding of Mizrahi at the turn of the century. If cooperation with misguided transgressors was reasonably defensible in a program aimed at rescuing Jews from persecution and distress, it was less justifiable as any putative stage of messianic redemption. Hence, it was prudent to marginalize, if not suppress, the messianic motif. One example of this approach may be found in a booklet published in 1899 by the Hebrew writer Eliezer Eliyahu Friedmann, a religious Jew but not a rabbi.[42] It was a point-by-point rebuttal of the Lubavitcher rebbe's objections to Zionism. Friedmann tried to show that what mattered was less how a Jew anticipated the manner of the messianic coming than his sure belief in its coming. "For this belief and this name, 'messiah,'" he explained, "assumed different forms and images . . . consequent upon the changes in the situation of Israel amongst the various nations." At times, when there were signs of an improvement in the attitude toward Jews on the part of the rulers of the nations in whose midst they were domiciled, they formed an expectation of the messianic age drawing near by natural means. But when the situation deteriorated and looked hopeless, they resorted to the hope of a purely miraculous messianic redemption. Then "they imagined the messiah as an angel of the God of Hosts descending from the heavens to the earth in the form of a poor man riding a donkey, who would perform multiple miracles and change the order of nature." With the progress of civilization many countries granted civic rights to the Jews. Yet their situation was far from alleviated—here Friedmann showed his transcendence of the messianic conceptual matrix—"because Israel is a people, a nation, unique and salient amongst peoples, and it does not assimilate among the other nations." He went on to argue that even where there was civic equality there were eruptions of hatred against the Jews. "For they still considered the Jews aliens. And Israel, for its part, never abandoned its hope and faith in its own future to again be a people living in its own inherited land." In the light of these developments, argued Friedmann, a third conception of the coming of the messiah should be obvious, one that falls decisively between the two earlier conceptions, namely:

In the end of days God will perfect the process with great miracles . . . for eternity. But all these miracles will take place only after the children of Israel will arouse themselves to make preparations for them; after a great settlement of Israel will have been accomplished in the land of its fathers and it will have been adequately prepared and become fully capable of being an independent people; after these preparations have been made by the children of Israel with the "agreement of the powers" [the allusion is to Zionism's Basel Program].

The result was, claimed Friedmann, that freethinkers who had drifted away from their nation, considering themselves to be Germans or Poles of the Mosaic persuasion, were now returning. It was this that had led to the creation of the Zionist Organization. In this context, declared Friedmann: "Behold, the belief in the coming of the messiah, Hibbat Zion and Zionism are one and the same thing, for they depend one upon another like links in a chain." Zionism was really nothing new. It was the two-thousand-year-old "hope and faith in the coming of the messiah, but according to a political conception." It was therefore not important which of the three particular conceptions of the messiah a contemporary Jew held, "as long as he believes in the return of the children of Israel to the land of their fathers to be there a special people living on its land."

Thus, Zionism was in no sense a breach of the divine adjuration—the homily of the three oaths—not to "hasten the messiah." It constituted, purely and simply, "preparation for the redemption." Accordingly, it behooved every orthodox Jew to identify with Zionism and, noted Friedmann, it was instructive that in failing to do so the orthodox opponents of Zionism, like the Lubavitcher rebbe, were in fact allying themselves with the reprehensible reformers, that "degenerate limb in the body of Israel which scoffs at all the holy things of Israel and denies its own people."

When Rabbi Yitzhak Yaakov Reines (1839–1915) founded Mizrahi in 1902, he went further than Friedmann's undogmatic but still messianic-related justification for orthodox association with Zionism. He tried to make a clear-cut separation between the Zionist Organization and messianic faith. Reines was born in Karlin, Lithuania, and studied in the famous Volozhin yeshiva. Although he served as a rabbi in a number of different towns in Russia, his name is associated primarily with the Jewish community in the town of Lida, where he founded a yeshiva that pioneered the incorporation of some secular studies following part of the government curriculum as well as the traditional talmudic curriculum. In the 1860s the young Rabbi Reines had sympathized with the Colonisationsverein für Palästina led by Luria and Rabbi Kalischer, and in the latter years of the Hibbat Zion period he had become active.

Reines was among those rabbis who welcomed the advent of Herzl, although it was not until the third Zionist congress (1899) that he was a delegate. He committed himself enthusiastically to Herzl's leadership and conception of a Zionist Organization embracing all Jews, secularized and orthodox alike. Of course, in common with all the rabbis who had followed Mohilewer into the Zionist Organization, he demanded that it do nothing incompatible with Jewish religious observance. What was envisaged was a division of spheres such as Rabbi Shmuel Yaakov Rabinowitz had proposed in his treatise "Religion and Nationalism": "We shall divide . . . our work on the ship of Israel into two. Let the 'enlightened' amongst us, the knowledgeable equipped with the weapons of science, those who are familiar with the ways of the gentiles and with politics . . . do the work of the engine of our ship. . . . But let them also allow . . . the rabbis of Israel . . . to supervise the direction taken by our ship."[43]

Accordingly, Rabbi Reines's clear preference was for a cohesive Zionist movement, which, even if led in all material matters by erstwhile near-assimilated freethinkers like Herzl, would honor the spiritual authority and guidance of the rabbis. He could not agree to the adoption by the Zionist Organization of the cultural and educational program insistently advocated by those who shared Ahad Ha'am's approach. A man of deep national-religious conviction but of moderate disposition, he initially pleaded—at times with great passion—that the movement had no business engaging in anything but its diplomatic and practical activities. Failure to observe this principle would only be schismatic and farther alienate the vast mass of orthodox Jews, who otherwise would gravitate naturally toward Zionism.

But as we have explained earlier, when some of the "enlightened" secularized intelligentsia formed their Democratic Faction in 1901, energetically insisting that the Zionist Organization undertake cultural-educational work in a modern secularized mold, Rabbi Reines reluctantly came to terms with reality. Calling together the national-religious rabbis and other "moderates" (as he preferred to call the political Zionists who concurred with his opposition to the secular cultural militants), he founded the Mizrahi faction in 1902. Even then he consistently preferred that all educational and cultural activity remain *outside* the official orbit, not only of the Zionist Organization but also of Mizrahi. There were, however, others in the founding circle of Mizrahi, including the writer and historian Ze'ev Jawitz, who pressed for active engagement in independent educational work on the part of Mizrahi itself. As we shall later see, when we focus specifically on the culture clash with the Democratic Faction, Reines was again driven to a pragmatic compromise. At the Minsk conference of Russian Zionists in 1902, he agreed to the proposal that there be a division of localized (that is to say, still not centralized by the official Zionist Organization) educational-cultural work into two streams, one conducted by the modernists and the other by the orthodox. In 1911 this finally became the modus operandi of officially sponsored Zionist cultural and educational initiatives in Palestine—an arrangement whose legacy until today is two official governmental streams of schooling in the state of Israel, one national-secular and the other national-religious.

At its founding, however, the basic postulate of Mizrahi was that the Zionist

Organization ought to concern itself purely with those political, diplomatic, and material matters that were the vital common interests of Jews, religiously observant or not. As Mizrahi's founding manifesto of 1902 stated: "[Mizrahi] sees fit to divide the experience of Zionism as a generality into two spheres: [one;] the sphere of the body . . . which requires only financing and energetic diplomatic activity aimed at obtaining for our people a safe refuge in the land of our fathers recognized by international public law. And [two;] the spiritual sphere which is the real animator of Zionism."[44] "Spiritual" meant both the theological realm of messianic speculation, and the mundane sphere of cultural-educational work. Neither was the Zionist Organization's legitimate concern. Paradoxically, this implied the conscious repression or at least marginalization of what Mizrahi itself called "the real animator of Zionism!" From the outset this paradox rankled within the camp of national-religious orthodoxy. Not only was Mizrahi's inherent messianic propensity never entirely eclipsed within the ranks, but an alternative conception was postulated by an independent spiritual force of great charisma, Rabbi Avraham Yitzhak Ha-Cohen Kook.

Be that as it may, the fact is that Mizrahi's founding father, Rabbi Reines, was at pains to deny that the Zionist Organization had any messianic pretensions or significance. Mizrahi's manifesto, issued under his imprimatur, skirted the messianic issue almost entirely. The case it presented for participation of orthodox Jews in the Zionist movement through the medium of their own Zionist party rested on earthly, realistic grounds. It assured such Jews that now they "no longer need have any fear of being swamped by false ideas" of the freethinkers in the larger Zionist Organization.[45] It spoke of Jewish distress, of the ravages of assimilation, of the need to return to the integrity of life according to the Torah, and of the settlement of Eretz Israel as "a commandment of the Torah." But conspicuously absent was the seminal national-religious interpretation of the anticipated stages of redemption, commencing with resettlement of the promised land, that had been propounded by Rabbis Alkalai and Kalischer. This motif was marginalized notwithstanding the fact that it can be found in abundance in the writings of Reines himself.[46]

Instead, Rabbi Reines emphasized support for the program of Herzl's functional, political Zionism. He claimed that Zionism did not "convey any sign or note of the idea of redemption" and insisted that, so far from pretending to messianic redemption, Zionism "only endeavors to improve the material condition of the nation and to uplift its honor." Reines differentiated between the mundane program of Zionism and the ultimate redemption: "For the redemption in itself is above any and every natural phenomenon or human endeavor, and belongs entirely to the lofty realms of miracles and wonders."[47] For all the genuine regard in which he held Herzl as the prodigal son returned to lead his people, Reines did not depict him as any harbinger of the messiah. "Truly one ought to see the matter in simple terms," wrote Reines. "Here comes to us this man to announce a simple [i.e., not miraculous] solution, not pretending to the general redemption. He only shows the way to improve the situation of Israel and to raise its status and pride by trying to find a place for a safe refuge."[48]

It remains a moot point whether the position adopted by Reines was purely tactical, that is, in order to blunt the barbs of criticism being leveled against those orthodox Jews who participated in the Zionist movement. It does, however, seem that his overall conception differed substantively from that originally propagated by Rabbis Alkalai and Kalischer, which had identified the age of emancipation as a sign that the messianic process was about to begin. He seems to have formed a more mundane cyclical-interactionist view of events since the age of emancipation began.[49] Civic emancipation had opened the way to assimilation, which in turn triggered a reaction on the part of the Gentiles—antisemitism. This then served to return the wayward freethinking Jews to renewed Jewish identification—Zionism. "Providence turns events around so that the Gentiles renew persecution [of the Jews] and thereby [Jewish] religion and belief is strengthened," wrote Reines.[50] In his writings, unlike those of Kalischer, persecution of the Jews is a salient motif: "For not a day has passed in all the days of the *galut* on which there has not been spilled Jewish blood, and there is not one inch of the globe wherever the Jews have trodden that was not marked by the blood of Israel."[51] His grave concern with Jewish distress in the *galut*, compounded by his perception of the antisemitic reaction to emancipation brought him to the conclusion that it was of the greatest urgency to find a radical solution to the Jewish problem.

Accordingly, it seems that Reines concurred substantively in Herzl's diagnosis of the Jewish problem. At the same time, noting the phenomenon epitomized by Herzl, of "return to the nation," Reines formed the impression—or perhaps the wish-fulfilling delusion—that such return signified the beginning of "return to the religion."[52] Therefore, according to the conception with which Reines informed the initial ideological outlook of Mizrahi, the role of Zionism was strictly mundane: to find a safe refuge from distress and, by returning the wayward, consolidate the Jewish nation. It behooved all Orthodox Jews to support it. By joining Mizrahi they would collectively influence the secularized Jews in the Zionist Organization to return to Jewish observance.[53] It was Reines's ideological stance that made it possible for the majority of Mizrahi's delegates to the sixth Zionist congress in 1903 to support Theodor Herzl's painfully controversial proposal that the Zionist Organization consider acceptance of the British government's offer of a stretch of territory in East Africa for Jewish colonization. To this paradoxical development we shall return in a later chapter.

Elevation of the Messianic Dimension

In contrast with Mizrahi's normative tendency to repress the messianic cadences of the modern Jewish return to Zion, there was a lone contemporary voice that outspokenly vested that return with overriding messianic-redemptive significance. It was that of Rabbi Avraham Yitzhak Ha-Cohen Kook, regarded widely as the foremost mystic luminary of Jewish orthodoxy. After distinguishing himself as a brilliant young scholar in the famous Volozhin yeshiva of Lithuania and gaining considerable spiritual stature while serving as rabbi in the Lithuanian town of Boisk, Kook chose to ascend to Eretz Israel to become rabbi of Jaffa from 1904 to 1914. He proceeded to serve as the first chief Ashkenazi rabbi of Palestine from 1921 until his death in 1935.

From the outset, Rabbi Kook held highly idiosyncratic opinions that conformed neither with those of the orthodox religious supporters of Zionism nor with its orthodox opponents. Already at the turn of the twentieth century he evinced not only a mystical rapture for the idea of return to Eretz Israel but also a warm embracing of the flowering of nationalism in Jewish life. In 1901 he published an essay, "The Mission of Israel and its Nationhood," in which he inverted the thesis of Ahad Ha'am concerning the relationship between the religion and nationalism of the Jews. Whereas Ahad Ha'am portrayed the Jewish religion as an instrumentality of the "national will to life," Kook portrayed the factor of nationalism as a God-given instrumentality for preservation of religion. According to Kook the very purpose of national feeling and national attributes such as language and territory was to fortify and enhance the Jews' capacity to observe the code of life revealed in Sinai. This was the divine intent in vesting his revealed Torah in a whole nation rather than in individuals selected out of humanity in general. Hence, it behooved orthodoxy to regard Jewish nationalism positively, not to recoil from it in fear of secularization. "It is for us to concern ourselves with the task of fostering and deepening the national motive and to make room within the sacred precincts of tradition for the consequences of Jewish nationalism. Then it will take root and grow in our midst, doing its good and faithful work."[54] To the secular nationalists of Ahad Ha'am's ilk he appealed for recognition that the observances of religion were the most invaluable of nationalist assets, for nothing could bind the nation together more than its religion. Surely they should realize that the precepts ought to be observed even if only from nationalist motives. At the same time he warned that if they insisted on making nationalism a substitute instead of a coordinate of religion, the orthodox masses might be turned away from the path of Jewish nationalism.

Notwithstanding this embrace of modern nationalism, Rabbi Kook criticized the founding of Mizrahi. But he did so on theological grounds quite the opposite of those voiced by all orthodox opponents of Zionism. Whereas, as we have seen, they inveighed not only against association with secular nationalism but also against the supposed breach of God's adjuration not to attempt to force the messianic redemption, Kook considered as wholly objectionable Mizrahi's denial of Zionism's messianic significance, signified by its concurrence in the principle that "Zionism has nothing to do with religion." To the contrary, Mizrahi should see it as its holy task "to declare openly that, notwithstanding its trust in Zionism in general and identification with the nationalist conception, it opposes this single clause that has been inscribed in Zionism ever since the first congress." In his view it made "a mockery of all Mizrahi's ideology" and "had to be deleted from the platform of Zionism."[55]

Rabbi Kook's paradoxical approach relegated him to a unique position neither entirely in nor entirely out of Zionism in general and Mizrahi in particular. In fact he was never a member of Mizrahi. Indeed, at one point he ventured into an independent initiative that aspired to attract the masses of orthodox Jews who could not reconcile their beliefs with membership of a secular Zionist movement even if this were done through the medium of Mizrahi. To this end, he founded in 1918 a separate organization called Degel Jerusalem (Flag of Jerusalem), initially with headquarters in London, where he then resided, and branches in a number of countries. He intended it to stand "in a fraternal relation to general Zionism, but not as a branch of its organization." It would seek to "to revive the nation's soul in all its natural purity" on the "fullness of God's sacred foundation," in the way Kook had always believed the Zionist movement itself should act.[56] However, Degel Jerusalem proved to be an ephemeral enterprise, and by 1921 it had petered out.

Only in terms of his unique application of mystic traditions of Jewish thought to the challenges of modernity does the paradox in his approach find its integral resolution. His perception of the Zionist movement and the process of Jewish return to Zion derived neither from positive evidence nor from rational deduction but rather from the umplumbable depths of his mystical faith. The philosophical dimensions of Rabbi Kook's thought lie beyond our scope here. Suffice it to say that in addition to the Kabbala's mysticism, he drew on medieval Jewish thought and also on exposure, via Hebrew Enlightenment literature, to some nineteenth-century streams of philosophy, including the Hegelianism of Nahman Krochmal.[57]

Kook's outlook was not devoid of a universalistic human dimension, for in his eyes both Israel's exile and its redemption mirrored the cosmic alienation and ultimate redemption of all mankind. "Israel as a unique nation, blessed by a profound sanctity and aspiration for the divine, has an influence on all the nations of the world; it refines the national soul of each nation and elevates them to greater spiritual heights."[58] Yet, above all, an overriding ethnocentrism, sanctioned by religious belief, characterized all of his thought. He enveloped the fundamental belief in the chosenness of Israel with rapturous mystic faith. He was utterly convinced that "the collectivity of Israel [*knesset Israel*] is the very essence of all human experience . . . and Israel's history is the essence of all human history . . . it represents humanity's pinnacle of spirituality."[59] Typical of his statements, repeated in manifold ways, was the following: "Among all nations, according to the changing circumstances of humanity, there are individuals who can attain to the superlative heights of righteousness, but there is no other nation in the world, the soul-stamp of which is justice and the most inward inspiration of which is to attain divine righteousness, other than God's people."[60] "The spiritual quality of the collectivity of Israel differs qualitatively from the spiritual attributes of every other nation," he wrote. "In every other nation the focal point of its collective life style is based upon the economic factor in its various forms. . . . But in Israel the focal point is the Divine attribute that inheres in the soul of the nation."[61] Indeed, the imprint of divinity on the Jewish nation was indelible and eternal: "Though buried under heaps of stagnant delusion, foul practice and intellectual depravity, the impact of the Divine on the Jewish character can at no time be erased."[62]

Hence, all historical events affecting Israel, no matter how apparently atomized, contrary, or degenerate, were set on a predestined course toward restored wholeness. On this premise Rabbi Kook applied the explanatory device of dialectics to resolve all the apparent contradictions in perceived historical manifestations. Thereby, every antithesis, no matter how apparently wrong-headed and awry, was bound to issue in the synthesis that advanced Israel toward the divine thesis. Accordingly, he was utterly convinced that the secular nationalists were serving the revival of ultimately pristine Torah Judaism, despite their own conscious selves as rebellious heretics against the tradition. "The fact that there are men who express their love of Israel, while their hearts are removed from Torah, its study and observance, is because their love is still unripe, as it is said 'and our vines have tender grapes.'"[63] "What these nationalists really want, they themselves do not know," he averred. So powerfully united was "the spirit of Israel" to "the Spirit of God," that "the Divine Spirit enters into the inwardness" even of a Jew "who says that he has nothing to do with the Spirit of God, the moment he admits that he desires to share in the spirit of Israel."[64]

Kook was convinced heart and soul, as only a mystic could be, that by some divinely ordained dialectical logic the manifestations of nonobservance and even heresy among the pioneer settlers of Eretz Israel were a necessary phase in the working out of the messianic process. Typical of his writing is the following:

As it is impossible for wine to be without yeast, so it is impossible for the world to be without the wicked. And even as the yeast ferments the wine and keeps it in its proper strength so the vulgar desires of the wicked bring sustenance and strength to the vital current of all men—the average and the saintly. . . . The yeast are the bearers of wickedness and atheistic defiance that must be expected in the age immediately preceding the messianic era.[65]

Kook was convinced that the heretical and rebellious Zionist pioneers would in due course return to religious observances and beliefs "as already happened in the days of Ezra." For Ezra had enlisted "the very dregs of society who desecrated the sabbath even in Eretz Israel. Yet this resulted in the rise of the Second Temple and the spread of the oral law." "So, in our own time," he held, "the rebellious sinners will surely repent, influenced by the Holy Land's radiant spirit, and guided by the worshippers of God and lovers of Israel who patiently and lovingly work together with them."[66]

Kook taught that "repentance inheres in Israel. The arousal of desire in the whole nation to return to its Land, to the essence of its spirit and character, reflects the glow of repentance. It is an inner return, despite the many veils that obscure it."[67] Put in another way—and Kook's writings are a veritable kaleidoscope of variegated conceptual images repeating the same core ideas in different ways—there was (in the language of kabbalistic mysticism) a cosmic divine spark in all natural and human manifestations. Accordingly, nothing in the cosmos and, a fortiore, in God's people Israel, however apparently alienated from the divine source, was entirely devoid of a divine spark. The ultimate messianic redemption would consist in the liberation of all the divine sparks to reunite the cosmos with its divine source. Moreover, all the apparently negative manifestations that were evident in secular nationalism and the weakening of religious life were the necessary messianic phase known as *ikveta de-meshiha* (the footsteps of the messiah). Kook explained that this stage, "mirrored in Eretz Israel's manifestly providential revival, is designed to fortify Israel's material foundations . . . whose enhancement will release the Jewish people's divine spirituality, so that the entire Torah will be restored to its former strength, to become a light unto the world."[68]

In essence Rabbi Kook's approach harked back to that of Rabbi Kalischer but with one weighty difference: whereas the latter, in the context of his time, conceived of return to Zion and its upbuilding wholly as acts of religious Jews, Rabbi Kook's theological conception came to embrace the activities of secularized Jews as well. Although it never meant actual approval of any breach of orthodox religious observance, this embrace was made possible not only by Rabbi Kook's elaborate mystical dialectics concerning the unfolding messianic process but also perhaps by a certain empathy with the inner search of the idealistic Zionist pioneers for a reintegrated Jewish identity.[69] This was a search, on the one hand, for liberation from the constricted Judaism of the *galut*—a desire that Kook also experienced, although purely from within orthodoxy— yet, on the other hand, for continued anchorage in the Jewish cultural heritage.

In later chapters of this book we shall take a closer look at this ambivalence of the secular pioneers.

The paradoxical implications of Rabbi Kook's conception of Zionism are manifold. From a liberal outsider's perspective it might well be considered nothing but an extreme expression of ethnocentrism, albeit justified in sublimely religious terms. From a secular Jewish national viewpoint it might be, and indeed historically was, welcomed as an operatively tolerant (if patronizing and self-delusive) version of religious orthodoxy. Conversely, in the context of orthodox-religious Jewry, Kook's conception, although undeniably rooted in authentic Jewish belief, might be—and indeed is to this day—regarded by some as *the* consummate interpretation of Zionism's religious significance and yet by others (not least of all the contemporary *haredim*) as an entirely errant interpretation.

It should be emphasized, however, that although Rabbi Kook was highly respected and loved in Mizrahi circles and both the institution of the chief rabbinate of Palestine and his co-occupancy of the office were very much a Mizrahi initiative, not his approach but rather that of Rabbi Reines was the formative factor in the development of Mizrahi up to the time of Israel's establishment in 1948, if not longer. Neither the full significance of Rabbi Kook's ideas nor indeed the full scope of his writings was known to his contemporaries. Although his subsuming of the Zionist return to Zion within a holistic, dialectical conception of the unfolding redemption was reflected in isolated essays that appeared as early as 1901 and in sparsely collected form in the 1920s (notably *Orot ha-tehiya* [The lights of revival]), they did not have a major impact on national-religious Zionists. It was only after his death and, indeed, after the establishment of the State of Israel that more comprehensive editions of his essays were published. It is indicative of Rabbi Kook's limited influence on Mizrahi that even on certain important matters of *halakha* Mizrahi's rabbinical leaders did not follow Rabbi Kook's opinions; notably in their acceptance in 1919 of the eligibility of women to elect and be elected to public office, contrary to Kook's view.[70]

This is not to say that national-religious ideology ever entirely dispensed with the messianic perspective. Although tactically suppressed or marginalized, it was never abandoned out of conviction. This is abundantly evident in copious writings of most of the national-religious rabbis, not least of all those of Rabbi Reines himself, as we have noted. Even the most down-to-earth and politically hardened of Mizrahi's political leaders, Rabbi Meir Bar-Ilan (1880–1949) is a case in point. Son of the famous Rabbi Naftali Zvi Yehuda Berlin of Volozhin, Meir Bar-Ilan also studied with the great talmudic luminaries Rabbis Eliezer Gordon and Haim Soloveitchik. He became active in Mizrahi after the schismatic debate over the East Africa project; moved to Germany, where he edited an important, although unofficial organ of national-religious Zionism, *Ha-ivri* (The Hebrew);

and spent the First World War years in the United States, becoming head of the Mizrahi organization there. After the war he settled in Palestine and rose to the presidency of the world Mizrahi organization, adopting a staunchly maximalist and activist political line in the affairs of Zionism as a whole.[71]

Typical of Rabbi Bar-Ilan's mundane and realistic political orientation was his criticism of the messianic-evocative excitement exhibited by some religious personalities (including, of course, Rabbi Kook) after the Balfour Declaration and the conquest of Eretz Israel by the British. Opposing the labeling of these events as "the steps of the Messiah," he cautioned his Mizrahi colleagues that "there is nothing better for our national body than silence on the matter of the end of our exile and the beginning of our redemption." It was unrealistic and could only result in disillusionment.[72] Yet by the late 1930s and the 1940s, one finds Rabbi Bar-Ilan himself invoking messianic rhetoric in relation to events of the time. "We are approaching the period of the messiah, we already see his feet [drawing near]," he said, "if we complete what is still lacking, doing that which is required of us, we shall experience his coming, we shall be worthy of it.[73] On one occasion in 1940 he exposed the tactical considerations involved in the earlier suppression of messianic allusions when he explained: "There were days when Zionism constituted a danger, a danger of defiling the messiah's sanctity [*akhilat ha-mashiah*] . . . hence Mizrahi arose and declared to all those who distanced themselves from the work of reviving The Land and reviving the nation out of fear that Zionist work might defile the sanctity of the messiah: 'Zionism is sacred, The Land is needed, but the messiah prevails [as a separate matter] and do not touch my anointed.'"[74]

In a comprehensive survey of Mizrahi's ideology that appeared in 1946, its author, Dr. Yeshayahu Wolfsberg (Aviad), certainly endorsed the secular analysis, as might be expected of a leading Ha-poel Ha-mizrahi intellectual, but did not omit the messianic aspect. "Zionism according to the conception of Mizrahi," wrote Wolfsberg, was also "a critical way station on the path to the complete redemption." It meant not only "entry into the historical arena" but was also "the beginning of the heartbeats of the redemption."[75] Adopting allusions that bore the imprint of Rabbi Kook's thought, which otherwise was not at all salient in his exposition, Wolfsberg stated: "The very daring of [secular] Zionism hints at a messianic spark in its conception; for whence comes this optimism and daring to act and to build as if such hopes are justified? In Zionism there is, it seems, an assumption, a supposition of some messianism, however amorphous." Indicative of even Wolfsberg's ambivalence was his rather self-contradictory attempt to qualify this affirmation of the messianic significance of Zionism. In one breath he stated: "Mizrahi's view does not blur the lines and mix spheres. The path and essence of Zionism are not of messianic identity." In the next breath, harking back to Kalischer and Alkalai, he declared: "Thus will be the redemption of Israel—at first little by little. Zionism, according to the view of Mizrahi is this 'little by little' and perhaps only the beginning of little by little."[76]

In summation, the national-religious ideology transcended the messianic conceptual framework without denying it. The messianic aspect was inherent in the ideology, but it was not absolutely fundamental to it. When it was not serviceable, as in the beginnings of Mizrahi, it was marginalized. When it was serviceable, it was invoked. In this respect, one important scholar, Yosef Salmon, has suggested a useful analytical distinction between "suppressed messianism" and "eruptive messianism."[77] Only much later, after the creation of the State of Israel and the Six-Day and Yom Kippur wars of 1967 and 1973 did it erupt to become the most salient motif of national-religious ideology. It then took the form of an extraparliamentary popular movement calling itself Gush Emunim (The Block of the Faithful), which had emerged largely under the spiritual mentorship of Rabbi Zvi Yehuda Kook, son of the great Avraham Yitzhak Ha-Cohen Kook. Balking at the ancillary role that religious Zionists had historically been satisfied to play in the power structure of Zionism, this movement claimed inheritance of the pioneering ethos of Zionism. It set itself the task of settling the territories that had come under Israel's military rule as a result of the 1967 war. Moreover, Gush Emunim vigorously expounded an ideology based on a fundamentalist interpretation of divinely endowed right to the whole of Eretz Israel, according to which it was halakhically impermissible to give up an inch of the land now providentially restored to Israel.[78]

The Mundane Dimension

As we have seen, closely interlaced with the theological objections to Zionism were the objections to cooperation with secularized Jews. Indeed, if anything, the theological was ancillary to the mundane. Indicative of this is the fact that even within the Agudat Israel organization founded in 1912, with the purpose of challenging the claim of the Zionists to represent the interests of Jews in the world, there developed a subsidiary school of thought that sought to implement its own form of exclusively orthodox return to, and Jewish restoration of, Zion. Its leader was Rabbi Yitzhak Breuer (1883–1946).[79]

Much of national-religious ideology revolved around the refutation of orthodox objections to participation in a movement together with—moreover, led by—secularized Jews.[80] One of the most compelling justifications for cooperation with secularists was that Jewish distress was so critical as to answer to the supreme halakhic principle of "saving of life" (*pikuah nefesh*), which overrides all other religious precepts. Rabbi Mohilewer, prevented by his infirmity from attending the first Zionist congress, sent a message containing a classic articulation of this plea:

Although there are differences in the realm of matters between man and God, and although some of us hold others to be transgressors, yet it behooves us to liken the situation to the outbreak of a terrible fire in one's home, endangering all its contents, material and human. In such a situation, if there should come another person, even be he considered a religious transgressor, to save one's home and all one's possessions, would one not accept him with love and joy? Behold my brethren are we not, all of us, in this situation today! A terrible fire has broken out in our midst, awesome flames, and we are all endangered. Those who hate us have burst forth and multiplied, their numbers reaching many millions, and were it not for the restraints exercised by state authorities they would already have devoured us alive. And now, when we have found brothers in this dire hour of need with arms outstretched to help us, to do all within their power in order to save our people and to rescue it from these straits, will any of us dare to reject them? Let all ponder the matter well and let no one break the covenant of brethren![81]

A less dramatic warrant for cooperation with secularists was given by Rabbi Reines. He argued that just as in charitable affairs and economic life orthodox Jews were obliged to work together even with nonbelievers and transgressors, so too in the Zionist enterprise, "all the more so when what is involved here is cooperation in public matters whose purpose is the benefit of the whole public."[82]

Another example of such justifications may be cited from the writing of Rabbi Yitzhak Nissenbaum, the great Mizrahi leader in interwar Poland. He refuted the charge that cooperation with secular Zionists constituted a "carrying out of a commandment by means of transgression" (*mitzva ha-ba'a be-avera*) by asserting: "In a place where it is vital for a multitude to carry out a command-ment . . . it is permissible even if it involves a transgression." He reasoned that "the mishnaic statement . . . 'do not join up with evildoers' [*al tithaber la-rasha*] applies only to an individual . . . and only in a private matter . . . but not to a great congregation of people and to matters that affect the entirety of the nation of Israel."[83]

Apart from such pretexts, the rabbis who persisted in associating themselves with the Zionist Organization were sustained by the belief that the process of return to Zion would ultimately influence free-thinking and wayward Jews to return to the true path of Jewish life and observance. In his point-by-point rebuttal of the Lubavitcher rebbe's diatribe against Zionism, to which we have already referred, Eliezer Friedmann argued that "it was not Zionism that turned these people into 'opponents of God and his Torah.'" On the contrary, they were "free thinkers by dint of their education and their situation from childhood onward," and Zionism now was bringing them back to Judaism.[84] In the same vein, Rabbi Shmuel Yaakov Rabinowitz argued in 1900 that thanks to the efforts of the Zionists many youngsters who had "grown up devoid of Torah, spending their time in lighthearted amusements . . . now have come to hear the word of God." "Distant ones have been brought close," he claimed, "and it behooves us to reach out to them."[85] It is difficult to know whether such assertions are to be accounted for as naïveté and wishful thinking or whether the national-religious rabbis were constrained to argue thus, notwithstanding their own inner doubts. Certainly they were hard put to fend off the incensed reaction of the rabbinical opponents of Zionism to the all too evident nonreligious and antirabbinical views of the larger part of the contemporary Zionist intelligentsia.

Other than this apologetic motif, Mizrahi's ideological diagnosis of the Jewish problem was fully in consonance with that of secular Zionism, particularly as articulated by the functional nationalist approach of Theodor Herzl and Max Nordau. In a sense, this was paradoxical since the mode of nationalism to which national-religious Jews accommodated themselves was inherently organic and hence closer to the ingrained ethnicism of Ahad Ha'am than to the functional conception of Herzl. Furthermore, early Mizrahi, like Ahad Ha'am, spoke more of a spiritual *center* than of a sovereign state, and, at core, its concern was more with the "problem of Judaism" than "the problem of the Jews." But these apparent commonalities were more than counterbalanced in national-religious eyes by the manifest threat of Ahad Ha'am's essentially secular conception, which posited an alternative mode of identity to that determined by the *halakha*. Hence, it was more palatable and serviceable for Mizrahi to appear as allied to the functional conception of Herzl, which represented Zionism as essentially a project for relief of Jewish distress.

In Yeshayahu Wolfsberg's ideological summation, to which we have already referred, he speaks in terms indistinguishable from those of the secular Zionists, of "the collapse of the nation as a result of emancipation." He dwells on the abnormal condition of *galut*, and even the "shame of *galut*."[86] Rabbi Nissenbaum likewise identified "the *galut*" as the fundamental defect of the Jewish condition. "This is the source of all the poison that runs through all of our organs," he wrote, "and for as much as the *galut* is perpetuated, so the danger is heightened that its poison will spread into all the recesses of our soul." "Judaism must return to Eretz Israel," he declared, "there to fortify a place as speedily as possible, before the *galut* manages to destroy us body and soul."[87]

However, over and above its commonality with the diagnosis made by secular Zionists, national-religious thought perceived the defects of the dispersion in relation to the particularities of Jewish religious life. In so doing it identified the major defect of the *galut* condition less in terms of antisemitism than in terms of the disruption of Judaism's integrity (*shlemut*) as a complete way of life dictated by the fullness of the *halakha* and Jewish tradition. Yeshayahu Wolfsberg lucidly articulated this theme as follows:

As a religious movement Mizrahi sensed the tragedy of a dismembered life. Religious life in all the days of the *galut* was but a torso. . . . There was no possibility of observing the commandments applicable only in the Land of Israel. The communities and their leaders did not have the authority to conduct the affairs of the Jews purely on the basis of the *halakha* and the legal authorities [*poskim*]. We were dependent on others, their mercy, their arbitrariness, and the evil of diverse regimes. "*Dina de-malkhuta dina*" [the law of the kingdom is the law] became a governing principle, introducing an alien tendency. . . . The *galut* in its course stifled the creativity within us in every respect. . . . The observance of the sabbath became a sacrifice and an ordeal, *kashrut* [the laws of ritual slaughter and the dietary laws]—a matter of caution and circumspection. . . . Faith and the *halakha* do indeed demand sacrifices, but these were inordinate. The sanctity of the sabbath and the observance of the commandments ought to be, first and foremost, the natural forms of life of a nation whose constitution is religious.[88]

Accordingly, claimed Wolfsberg: "Mizrahi represents the integrity of Judaism, its comprehensive inclusion of all the traits of our people, its culture and its aspirations."

Ideological Innovation of Ha-poel Ha-Mizrahi

As we have seen, the original messianic impulse in national-religious ideology traversed an uneven course. Repressed in the early years of Mizrahi, it at last erupted forcefully after the emergence of the State of Israel in the form of the Gush Emunim movement—and even then, almost as if in delayed reaction, only after the 1967 and 1973 wars. When it did so erupt, it was out of the ranks of the mainly Israel-born and -bred young generation associated with Bnei Akiva, the youth movement created by Ha-poel Ha-mizrahi. The apparent paradox is compounded, for in Ha-poel Ha-mizrahi even more than in its parent organization, Mizrahi, the messianic motif had been relegated to the ideological periphery.

To be sure, the ideological fundamentals of Ha-poel Ha-mizrahi were the same as those that underpinned Mizrahi's ideology from the outset. It was not free of the same inherent tensions, including those relating to the messianic dimension. However, with far less ambivalence than Mizrahi, it broadened the focus of Jewish solidarity to emphasize preservation of the nation and not only observance of Torah. Some of its ideologues—Shlomo Zalman Shragai is a notable example—also tried to stretch the innovative potential of the *halakha* farther to cope with modern national needs. Its diagnosis of the Jewish condition shifted the emphasis overwhelmingly to the mundane plane, to the extent even of absorbing values derived from the labor Zionist movement, at least of the non-Marxist variety. What is more, the adjunct national-religious movement of young religious pioneers that emerged in Germany, called Bahad (an acronym for Brit Halutzim Dati'im, meaning Union of Religious Pioneers), explicitly endorsed socialism and created a grouping of orthodox-observant kibbutz communes in the 1930s.

Shmuel Haim Landau (1892–1928) was perhaps the foremost exponent of the ideology that incubated in Ha-poel Ha-mizrahi and came to be epitomized by the slogan *Torah ve-avoda* (Torah and labor). Emerging out of a Hasidic background in Poland, he became a leader of its junior section, Tzeirei Mizrahi (Young Mizrahi), and settled in Palestine in early 1926. There he was acknowledged as the foremost leader of Ha-poel Ha-mizrahi, but his career was cut short by his untimely death at the age of thirty-six. In the expositions of leading thinkers of Ha-poel Ha-mizrahi such as Landau there is far less equivocation than in Mizrahi over recognition of the nation as an entity that subsumes the religion. In terms hardly distinguishable from the usage of secular nationalists, Landau speaks of people (*am*) and nation (*uma*) as a "living body in itself, a collective 'I', and not only an aggregate of individuals." Through this organic unit "the individual connects with, and relates to, the world; to all of creation and human experience, and through it he becomes a partner in mankind and the cosmos as a whole."[90]

According to Landau's exposition, the purpose of the religious commandment of settling Eretz Israel (*mitzvat yishuv Eretz Israel*) was not to express piety or messianic anticipation. Its purpose was the revival of the nation. He accorded the nation a religious value at least as high as that of Torah itself: "For surely we were already taught by the sages of Israel that 'Torah was created for Israel?'" he averred.[91] Here the contrast with the neoorthodox position as had been expounded by Samson Raphael Hirsch in Germany is at its most pungent. As we have noted, according to Hirsch, Israel was created solely for the Torah.[92] In the light of later developments in national-religious Zionism it is of interest that, by the same token, Landau also accorded primacy to the nation over The Land: "For [the principle is that] The Land is for Israel; not Israel for The Land."[93] It is particularly noteworthy that Landau also questioned the conventional religious formula "our nation is a nation only by its Torah" on the grounds that "it contradicts the very essence of the nationalist idea."[94] Torah, he reasoned, is to be understood in two senses. One is the code of laws and precepts that the Jew is commanded to obey and observe; the other sense is "as the spirit of the nation, the source of its culture and the soul of its life; the public-national foundation emanating from the Torah." Likewise, the purpose of *avoda* (labor) was not just "for the sake of morality and social justice" but above all for the revival of the nation.[95] In sum, Landau's exposition amounted to conceptual acknowledgment of the nation as an entity more comprehensive than the religion and of the primacy of nationalist purposes within the religious code itself. Here was a religious imagining of the "nation" wholly consonant with that of secular imaginings.

In the ideology of *Torah ve-avoda* the diagnosis of the Jewish condition was predominantly mundane and nonmessianic. It followed much the same lines as characterized secular Zionism, combining Herzl's functional nationalist emphasis on "the problem of the Jews" with Ahad Ha'am's on "the problem of Judaism." Of course, the latter motif was infused with a meaning quite opposite to that expounded by Ahad Ha'am. There could be agreement with Ahad Ha'am that part of the problem was the disintegration resulting from the attempts (ultimately futile) of Jews to assimilate into other nations and the misguided fabrication of a "reformed" Judaism. But whereas Ahad Ha'am all but discounted orthodoxy and focused on the lack of a viable secular Jewishness, the primary defect identified as "the problem of Judaism" by *Torah ve-avoda* was the deterioration of conditions for maintaining an *integral religious life* in the *galut* and the attendant self-constriction and narrow-mindedness of the orthodox rabbinical authorities. This distorted the Jew's attitude toward simple productive labor. It incapacitated him and even distorted his soul; hence, the dire need for *havra'at ha-nefesh* (healing of the soul) of orthodox Jewry. In Landau's words:

All who look into the spirit of the Torah, the spirit of original Judaism, know that the Torah of Israel is a Torah of life; a Torah that influences, embraces and merges with life; it does not fight and oppose life. . . . [But in the *galut*] when difficulties multiplied and the conditions of living underwent change the [orthodox] Jew was distanced from worldly life . . . little by little he began to form in his mind a negative outlook . . . and worldliness became for him the symbol of evil incarnate. . . . Instead of the Hebrew Torah of life there emerged only abstract religion which has nothing in common with life as it is. Religion and life began to be antagonists.[96]

Lamenting the loss of the original expansive wholeness of Jewish religious life as a result of the ravages of modernity was a motif already long prevalent in Mizrahi ideology. But Ha-poel Ha-mizrahi now intensified and sharpened it. In a sense, it was the equivalent but antinomical version of Ahad Ha'am's "problem of Judaism." As Yeshayahu Bernstein (1902–1986), who emerged out of a Hasidic background in the Ukraine to become, after settling in Palestine in 1922, a leader of the left wing of Ha-poel Ha-mizrahi there, once wrote: "In our aspiration to build up The Land we wish first and foremost to provide a solution for what is called 'the problem of Judaism.' Or in the language of the Kabbala, 'the exile of the Divine spirit.'" Attributing to the influence of alien culture in the *galut* that which he described as "our great spiritual decline, the terrible emptiness in our lives increasingly deprived of content and taste," he drew the conclusion that the Jew "had to return to the cradle of his culture, Eretz Israel, for 'the revival of integral Judaism.'"[97]

This sense of impairment in Judaism's integrity in general and perception of degeneration in the orthodox religious establishment in particular was Ha-poel Ha-mizrahi's ideological trademark. But it also evinced subsidiary themes common to—and obviously influenced by—secular labor Zionism. Thus, Landau could state:

A people that has no earth and whose natural living vitality has dried up . . . ceases to be a "people" as such. Parasitism, whether conscious or not, becomes its second nature, parasitism of the individual and of the collective. It sees itself always carried on the shoulders of others, dependent on, and permanently in need of them; perceives itself as an adjunct of others and not as an entity in its own right. Hence, the negative attitude to productive labor, the lack of respect for the worker as a partner in [divine] creation and the feeling of pity mixed with contempt for he who "must," alas, be a working man.[98]

A characteristic of national-religious ideology, whether of the Mizrahi variety or of Ha-poel Ha-mizrahi, was the conceptual denial of actual innovation. This was a function of the universe of discourse of orthodox religious believers, according to which all truth and all instruction for moral social living inheres self-sufficiently in the Torah. "We must find an answer to all the questions of the world and of life, Israel and humanity. . . . We ought not to search and find worldly solutions outside of the Torah," stated Shlomo Zalman Shragai, another personality of Polish Hasidic background, who, after settling in Palestine in 1924, became a leader of Ha-poel Ha-mizrahi. He reasoned that the very thought of searching outside of the Torah detracts from its integrity as a consummate *torat hayim* (way of life).[99]

Hence, the exponents of *Torah ve-avoda*, no less than those of Mizrahi ideology in general, were constrained to demonstrate that all the principles they upheld, so far from being new, were inherent attributes of authentic Jewish religion. Thus, they strained to show, on the strength of chapter and verse from the biblical and talmudic sources, that insistence on the value of labor, for example, was not anything new. As one typical Ha-poel Ha-mizrahi ideologue stated: "We do not come to innovate. The basis for all our existence and essence is the Torah of Judaism, but in its full scope and integrity. . . . Labor is commanded to us in the Torah, and just as we immerse ourselves into all other commandments, so we must penetrate also to the soul and spirit of this commandment."[100] By the same token, the exponents of this ideology felt compelled to deny that the juxtaposition of concepts in the slogan *Torah ve-avoda* represented an artificial synthesis of two disparate value systems. "It should be clear to us that our slogan '*Torah ve-avoda*' is not a combination of two different slogans," stated one typical writer, "but the direct consequence of our Ha-poel Ha-mizrahi world-outlook, a world-outlook in which is reflected original, authentic and integral Judaism."[101]

The rationale for the integral relationship between Torah and *avoda* may be illustrated from one well-known essay by Rabbi Yeshayahu Shapira, the son of a great Hasidic rebbe in Poland and himself one of the few ordained rabbis in the leadership of Ha-poel Ha-mizrahi (although he too did not practice as a rabbi). He became a leading figure in its left wing after settling in Palestine in 1920. The essay addressed itself to the objection, quite cogently raised by some within Mizrahi, that the Torah recognized no difference between the worker and the trader or those engaged in any other occupation. They adduced that since the *shulhan arukh* (the authoritative codification of the main laws of Judaism) contained no section dealing expressly with labor as such, this showed that it was not among the primary values or duties of Judaism. Indeed, if anything, the *halakha* contained many more sections concerning commercial occupations. Nor was there anything in it that cast doubt on the moral value of private property. The only requirement was that economic relations must be ordered fairly and justly. Therefore, said these critics, Ha-poel Ha-mizrahi's elevation and extolling of the laborer above all other occupations, not to speak of the affinity it showed for socialism, was alien to the Torah.

In response to this, Yeshayahu Shapira pointed out that the upholders of *Torah ve-avoda* had never maintained that labor was obligatory as a dictate of the *halakha*:

> But none of us has said anything of the kind. If there were such an express statement in the *shulhan arukh* there would be no room for argument. All we say is that labor is intrinsic to the Jewish ideal since, apart from its value for the reform and welfare of society, it is also regarded as a possible way of living a perfectly just life. . . . One should learn not only from *halakha* but also from *agada* [the homiletical literature]. . . . [The value of labor] finds expression not only in Jewish law but also, and mainly, in what is beyond the strict letter of the law [*lifnim mi-shurat ha-din*].[102]

Shapira contended that the values of labor and social and economic equality derived precisely from this principle of going beyond the strict letter of the law. He pointed to the biblical commandments of the jubilee year, the cancellation of debts in the seventh year and the prohibitions on interest, all of which indicated disapproval of capitalist acquisitiveness.

Vision and Means

Compared to the clear diagnostic dimension of religious-national ideology, its vision of the future was obscure. Its manifest inclination to romanticism contributed to this obscurity. This romanticism, to be sure, differed from that of secular Zionism, for it was predicated entirely on the orthodox universe of discourse, according to which perfection already inhered in the sacred sources of Judaism. Only man's faulty or limited understanding veiled its consummate answers to all of life's questions. Accordingly, a putatively perfect, original Jewish society embodied in the ancient sacred sources was vaguely evoked as the model for the vision of the ideal future; the "restoration of the glory of the past," or, in alternate wording, "the renewal of our life as of yore." As one Ha-poel Ha-mizrahi writer put it: "Torah and *avoda* are said in the same breath. . . . Torah and *avoda* are but one life form, modeled on the good society of the past. And if we speak of the society of the future, we mean nothing but that which already existed, that which in our view is the symbolic example which we must all acknowledge." The same writer affirmed the value of labor but rejected the Socialist label inasmuch as it was copied from new sources extraneous to Judaism itself. "Not so with us. We must turn the direction of history backward—to the past we direct our eyes. We must engage ourselves with that which came before us, to renew our lives as of yore."[103] This genre of romanticism, by its very nature, left only a vague afterimage as to the future form of the restored past.

The main factor that obscured the visionary dimension of national-religious ideology was, however, the tension between its messianic impulse, subterranean but potentially eruptive, and the mundane reality of the Zionist project. On the one hand, for national-religious Jews return to Zion, its resettlement by Jews, and its restoration to Jews as a national home was the envisioned *athalta de-geula* (beginning of redemption). As such, the ultimate redemptive form it would take was the concern of God, not at all of man. On the other hand, however, the Zionist project represented an interim period of unknown duration in which the nature of the society being created by the human "awakening from below" was most decidedly the concern of national-religious Jews. It might thus be said that, by their lights, while at the fundamental level the visionary or utopian dimension of ideology was *ultra vires*, at the operative level it signified very definite requirements.

In a sense, the interim premessianic vision of national-religious Zionism was the converse of that conjured up by Ahad Ha'am. It was a vision of a national home where the public and personal lives of Jews would provide an exemplary model of the wholeness of religious observance and the spiritual elevation and expansiveness of the Torah as an all-embracing way of life. This model was epitomized by the slogan *Eretz Israel le-am Israel al pi Torat Israel* (The Land of Israel for the People of Israel according to the Code of Living of Israel). Rabbi Yitzhak Nissenbaum once expressed this along lines remarkably analogous to Ahad Ha'am's vision:

When Mizrahi says a "religious Eretz Israel" it is maximalist. . . . It aspires to making our religion or Torah comprehend all of life in Eretz Israel, that of the individual and family, public and national life and also social-political life. . . . Mizrahi demands that the sabbath and festivals be strictly observed in public life, that public kitchens and other public institutions act in accord with the demands of the Torah. It demands that the prevailing language of the Jewish people in The Land be its ancient national language. All of this together must imprint the Hebrew stamp on this land, so that [here he closely parallels Ahad Ha'am] whosoever comes to The Land and observes its life will feel that this is a Hebrew land; Hebrew by virtue of its form and content. He will see in the Hebrew settlements, not Gentiles speaking Hebrew and not—as someone once expressed it with reference to the Emek [the valley of Jezreel known for its many secular pioneering settlements]—speaking and thinking as Gentiles; not forms of life borrowed from alien lands and peoples. Rather, he will see before his eyes the original Hebrew life as we know it from the demands of our ancient Torah.[104]

Nissenbaum held the view that the Torah was not intended in the first instance for a subjugated and dispersed people. "Judaism was meant from the beginning to be for a polity and a nation," he argued, "and if this question of

'Judaism for a polity' in its full scope possibly still belongs to 'the laws relating to the messianic period' then nevertheless important parts of it can demand from us solutions in the not too distant future."[105] National-religious ideology sometimes spoke of a "Torah-state" but was never conclusive as to its meaning. It could mean a state wholly under the authority of the *halakha*, that is to say, some sort of theocratic polity. Alternatively, it could mean a secular polity whose consensual reference point for ultimate moral authority is Judaism as interpreted by the halakhic authorities; a state whose public life (the Sabbath, *kashrut* [dietary rules], marriage, and divorce,) conforms with the stipulations of the *halakha*. Yeshayahu Bernstein, in an extensive essay on this subject written not long after the establishment of Israel, had to admit that those who talked of a Torah-state were unable "to suggest a detailed practical program for the conduct of the state and the maintenance of its services according to the Torah."[106] However, he argued realistically that national-religious Jews need not have such a complete program. They could advance gradually towards it with "religious demands on the path to a Torah-State." One vital step in that direction would be to satisfy the need for a unified authoritative rabbinical voice capable of making halakhic decisions on matters arising from the new conditions of statehood.

This meant the revival of a Sanhedrin, an idea whose most important and fervent advocate had long been the foremost Mizrahi leader in Palestine, Rabbi Maimon. He made energetic efforts to research the entire halakhic question of renewal of the Sanhedrin. Resting on the authority of Maimonides, he contended that the rabbis of Eretz Israel were entitled to renew it on their own, and he urged Mizrahi to initiate the venture as a major priority. However, all his efforts were to no avail. Both at conferences of Mizrahi and in the council of the chief rabbinate (whose institution Maimon had regarded from the outset as a step in the direction of a renewed Sanhedrin) his proposals were repeatedly evaded or shelved. It proved impossible to attain the requisite measure of consensus for so bold a venture. The atomization of rabbinical authority and its inherent conservatism were insurmountable obstacles. Maimon, himself a lifelong opponent of Reform Judaism, complained bitterly that some rabbis even thought it would serve as a sanction for halakhic permissiveness tantamount to reform of religion.[107]

Thus, national-religious Zionism was never able to form a unified rabbinical authority, nor to formulate a coherent plan for its amorphous vision of a Torah state. To be sure, there was one remarkably original and profound intellectual endeavor to reconcile the contradictions between a modern democratic national state and the requirements of the Torah. It was the exposition of Rabbi Haim Hirschensohn (1857–1935), who was born in Safed, the scion of a family that had come from Pinsk, Russia, as early as 1847. Although Hirschensohn associated himself with Mizrahi from its foundation, he never became a leader or exerted any noteworthy influence on the movement. It is probable that his obscurity resulted largely from the circumstance that as early as 1903 he accepted a rabbinic pulpit in an orthodox congregation in New Jersey (USA). In the light of his views, it is paradoxical that he remained there for the rest of his life while concurrently immersed in his profound religious composition on the halakhic implications of the Jewish national renaissance and the vision of renewed Jewish sovereignty.[108]

Relying in important respects on the halakhic authority of Maimonides but influenced perhaps by familiarity with the American model of nonethnic, covenantal nationhood, Hirschensohn expounded a conception of the Torah as the expression of a dual covenant (*brit*) entered into by the free will of the Children of Israel. In its one aspect this covenant embodied the obligation to abide faithfully by the code of living revealed by God and interpreted in accord with changes in human society and knowledge by the succeeding generations of halakhic authorities. This was, in other words, the religion of Israel. However, in its other aspect the covenant was an intrahuman commitment to constitute a nation, and in this respect the Jewish nation was no different from others in the world. Here, it should be noted, Hirschenshon contradicted the conventional credo of all orthodoxy that Jewish uniqueness, by virtue of God's covenant, rendered it entirely incomparable to the nations of the world. "I am also a Mizrahi-ite," stated Hirschensohn, "but not because I consider the nationality of Israel to be its religion—as many religious Jews and Mizrahi Zionists mistakenly say. The truth is that the religion of Israel is a national religion, but the nationality of Israel is not purely national-religion. Religion is just one of the conditions of life of the nation . . . which it morally advances and spiritually enriches, but it is not the nationality itself, just as enrichment is not life itself although it sustains life."[109] An attendant implication of Hirschensohn's analysis was that a secular Jew, in the sense of one who renounced the terms of the covenant between God and the Children of Israel in its religious aspect, nevertheless remained a Jew in the full sense inasmuch as he continued to abide by the aspect of the covenant expressed in Jewish nationhood.

Over and above these implications of Hirschensohn's conception—so remarkably novel in the context of conventional orthodox thought—his analytical distinction between the national and the religious dimensions of the covenant with God made it possible to envisage a democratic Jewish national polity, that is, one in which an elected government was held accountable to the body of citizens constituting the nation, not to the rabbinate. Indeed, Hirschensohn's intellectual enterprise consisted largely in the elaboration of this compatibility, thereby constituting the kind of program for a Jewish state that was otherwise lacking in the ideology of national-religious Zionism. However, it remains a fact that Hirschensohn's cogitations remained shrouded in obscurity, eliciting no more than isolated publicistic discussion in national-religious circles.

In practice, whatever visions of a Torah state existed in the national religious camp were thwarted by the realities of building a modern society out of predominantly secularized people. It found itself preoccupied with a constant holding action against the overwhelming impact of secular modernity on the development of the Zionist project. As we shall show in a later chapter, having failed to prevent the Zionist Organization from adopting a secularized cultural-educational program, Mizrahi yielded by agreeing to a dual-stream policy. The religious cultural-educational stream was to be solely the responsibility of Mizrahi.

The Ha-poel Ha-mizrahi offspring of the national-religious camp, of course, differed from its Mizrahi mother movement in that it adopted a labor movement social policy. Its attempt to fuse this with Torah became a component of Ha-poel Ha-mizrahi's otherwise vague vision of a Torah state. Furthermore, since by the 1930s it all but subsumed its begetter organization in Palestine, this facilitated a political alliance between the secular labor movement and national-religious Zionism, an alliance that was to endure from 1935 until well into the period of Jewish statehood.

Before considering the operative implications of Ha-poel Ha-mizrahi's social policy, it should be noted that this departure from the mother movement's conservative social stance involved it in advocacy of certain distinctive means for its program of Zionist activity. These were epitomized by the slogans "the holy rebellion" (*ha-mered ha-kadosh*) and "renewal of the Torah" (*tehiyat ha-Torah*). The former expressed a spirit of rebellion against conventional orthodox authority in the Diaspora. Partly a generational factor and partly influenced by the example of the secular Zionist labor movement, it was reflected in rhetoric whose gravamen was that in the *galut* the established rabbinical authorities and institutions had become constricted and distorted. Only a truncated observance of the Torah's true spiritual content was possible in the Diaspora. The full realization of the Torah's prescriptions for the Jew's life and for drawing out the uplifting spiritual expansiveness of the Torah required a return to Jewish national existence in Eretz Israel.[110] Typical of this rebellious rhetoric was the declaration of Yeshayahu Bernstein:

A revolution must take place in our life! The *galut* has moved us so far from the path of Torah that today, in the name of Torah and religion Mizrahi battles against those who seek to follow its path wholly. . . . Against this we shall rebel with all our strength, in the name of all that is dear and holy to us. . . . We have proclaimed the great revolution in the life of Judaism and we wish to bring that rebellion into the ranks of Mizrahi. . . . We believe that with combined forces and a mighty will . . . we can remove all that is rotten in the life of the *galut*, all the fraud that was introduced into religious Jewry contrary to its true nature, and in its place we shall fulfill our work of recreating our original life in the spirit of our written and oral Torah—an Eretz Israel of religious-labor.[111]

The concept "renewal of the Torah" connoted the impulse of Ha-poel Ha-mizrahi to tackle actual problems of modernity in a Jewish religious society.

As we have noted, the Mizrahi rabbis had been too much a part of the institutionalized orthodox elite in general to venture into innovations that involved adaptation of the *halakha* to the needs of modernity in society and state. The pioneering element within Ha-poel Ha-mizrahi was more innovative, and this found expression particularly in the development of the religious kibbutz, which, having adopted the principle of Jewish self-labor, sought solutions for such sabbath-observance problems as the bearing of arms and milking of cows.[122]

Attitudes toward socialism varied within Ha-poel Ha-mizrahi from one pole—those who rejected it and insisted on only those values that are inherent in Judaism—to another—those who favored open cognition of the value of socialism as understood by secularists. Indeed, in 1924 it split into a left-wing faction that joined the Histadrut (the General Federation of Trade Unions established in 1920 by the secular labor Zionists, whose nature we shall discuss in the next chapter), and a right wing that maintained an independent existence in close relationship with Mizrahi. However, in 1927 the left-wing faction parted from the Histadrut, and Ha-poel Ha-mizrahi was reunified. In the meanwhile the world *Torah ve-avoda* movement (consisting of Ha-poel Ha-mizrahi in Palestine and Tzeirei Mizrahi and He-halutz Ha-mizrahi in the Diaspora) federated with Mizrahi in 1925 to form the World Mizrahi Organization. In 1929, Ha-poel Ha-mizrahi created its own youth movement, Bnei Akiva (Sons of [Rabbi] Akiva).

On balance it may be said that Ha-poel Ha-mizrahi's social orientation tended toward that wing of the secular labor movement that not only was non-Marxist but even had strong reservations concerning the adoption of the very term "socialism." (These distinctions within the secular labor movement will be discussed later.) Generally recoiling from the Socialist label because of its association with Marxist materialism, atheism, and the doctrine of class warfare, Ha-poel Ha-mizrahi eschewed conflict and favored harmonious relations between employer and worker. It held that the attainment of better working conditions depended more on interpersonal moral values than on class interests. As a typical contributor to its social thought wrote:

True, Judaism is not based on a Socialist regime. As is well known, the social regime that characterizes it is primarily based on recognition of the right to property. Judaism is social [*sotzialit*] on the basis of its laws and moral demands, but not Socialist. Nevertheless, we are able to say not only that Judaism does not oppose a regime of social reforms . . . but also that it even regards it positively.[113]

He argued that this social policy emanated from such general principles as "Love thy neighbor as thyself" and "Do that which is just and right." He pointed to the kind of socialism advocated by Gustav Landauer as the one most closely approximating to the spirit of Judaism since it "bases its whole system of socialism on the moral social progress of mankind." From this he adduced that Ha-poel Ha-mizrahi could not possibly agree to the tactic of class warfare. "The socialism of Judaism had to be based on love and not hatred," he averred, "on moral social progress on the one hand, and the exemplary models of cooperation as advocated by Landauer, on the other hand." Accordingly, the accepted attitude of Ha-poel Ha-mizrahi toward strikes followed the ruling of Chief Rabbi Kook that in labor disputes the workers should take the employers to court and only if the employer refused did the workers have the right to resort to the strike weapon.[114]

In the 1930s the labor orientation of Ha-poel Ha-mizrahi toward socialism was strengthened by the accretion of settlers belonging to the Brit Halutzim Dati'im (Bahad, the Union of Religious Pioneers). Its "Rodges group," so named after its training farm in Germany, arrived at the end of 1929 and laid the foundation for the creation of a religious form of kibbutz commune. These settlers recognized the legitimacy of class struggle and were explicitly Socialist in their rhetoric. Still, in 1933, at the third world conference of the *Torah ve-avoda* movement, Yeshayahu Bernstein although relatively a left-winger, avoided explicit use of the term "socialism." He proposed that the movement define itself as a "Zionist religious national labor movement."[155]

Notwithstanding the division between Mizrahi and Ha-poel Ha-Mizrahi on social policy, they advocated much the same approach in regard to the place of religion in the Zionist project. At the least they insisted on the rule of the *halakha* in the public activities of Zionism and the Jewish population of Palestine. Moreover, precisely because they shunned the sect-like separatism of Zionism's orthodox opponents, they experienced an abiding imperative to impose halakhic norms on the life of all Jews. Rabbi Yitzhak Nissenbaum gave explicit vent to this ideological imperative when he wrote:

Judaism is a private matter, that is to say, individuals are obliged to observe it, but also a public and national matter, that is to say, the public and the nation should observe it as a collective and should also see to it that the individuals—members of the public and sons of the nation—will observe it. . . . So you wish to interfere in the private lives of each and every individual—it will be objected on all sides. Yes! we shall answer candidly. Not only do we wish but indeed we are obliged to interfere in the private lives of each and every one inasmuch as "Judaism"—that is to say the demands of the Torah and the demands of the nation—interfere with them.[116]

In like vein even Shlomo Zalman Shragai of Ha-poel Ha-mizrahi wrote, "And even if we shall succeed in consolidating public forms in the spirit of the Torah, this is not our main aim, but rather our aim is religious revival and that the life of every individual (and *ipso facto* of the whole public) will be a religious life and then *ipso facto* the building of the land and its public form will be an edifice of Torah."[117]

In a sense this was an ideological compulsion comparable to that which drove

Socialist Zionists to shape the society of the national home in accordance with Socialist principles. The consequent tension with secularists could be, and generally was, ameliorated by compromise arrangements allowing for observance of halakhic norms at least in the public sphere. But the national-religious compulsion to influence the lives of all Jews by imposing halakhic norms wherever possible provoked far less tractable tensions. Secular Jews saw it as encroachment on the private sphere of life contrary to the accepted canons of modern nationhood. This facet of the means advocated by national-religious ideology was, and remains to this day, a constant, potentially volatile source of tension.

CHAPTER FIVE

Labor Zionism

The Challenge of Marxist Rejection

GREAT AS ARE the problematics of grafting liberal values onto the stem of nationalism, they are probably exceeded by those attendant upon attempts to graft socialism onto the same stem. In the case of Zionism, the contrast between these two grafts is striking. Whereas, as we have noted, liberal ideology attained only weak political and institutional expression in the development of the Jewish community in Palestine, Socialist Zionism attained virtual hegemony by about 1935 and, moreover, sustained it well into the post–State of Israel period. The cumulative influence of Socialist ideology upon Zionists, especially in eastern Europe and in Eretz Israel, was so enormous that it is hardly possible to exaggerate its importance.

From the outset those who sought a synthesis of Jewish nationalism with socialism had to contend with the basic fact that in Marxist terms the Jews hopelessly failed to qualify as a nation. Their destiny was to be assimilated. Consequently, at the turn of the century, the very premises of Zionism met with almost universal hostility from most schools of Socialists. Karl Marx had treated national differences as no more than a passing phase in history that would weaken with the expansion of trade and world markets in the advanced stages of capitalism. Nationalism belonged, by his lights, to the ephemeral superstructure of human society's dialectical evolution rather than to its substructure. It would lose its significance in the ultimate classless society. The *Communist Manifesto* stated:

The working men have no country. We cannot take from them what they have not got. Since the proletariat must first of all acquire political supremacy, must rise to be the leading class of the nation, must constitute itself *the* nation, it is, so far, itself national, though not in the bourgeois sense of the word. National differences and antagonism between peoples are daily more and more vanishing owing to the development of the bourgeoisie, to freedom of commerce, to the world market . . . the supremacy of the proletariat will cause them to vanish still faster.[1]

Theodor Herzl addressing the second Zionist congress, Basel, August 1898

Chaim Weizmann addressing the twenty-first Zionist congress, Geneva, August 1939

Yehuda Leib (Leo) Pinsker

Ahad Ha'am (Asher Ginzberg)

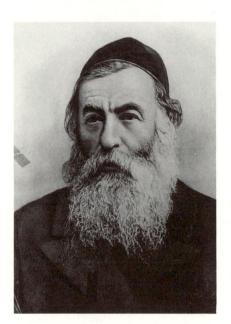

Rabbi Yitzhak Yaakov Reines

Rabbi Avraham Yitzhak Ha-Cohen Kook

Ber Borochov

Nahman Syrkin

Aharon David Gordon

Chaim Arlosoroff

Chaim Weizmann and David Ben-Gurion

Menahem Ussishkin   Rabbi Meir Berlin (Bar-Ilan)

Ze'ev (Vladimir) Jabotinsky

Berl Katznelson

Yosef Haim Brenner

Yitzhak Gruenbaum   Rabbi Yitzhak Nissenbaum

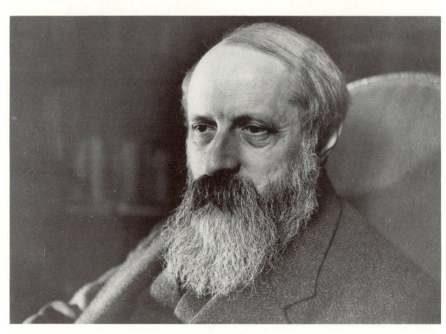

Martin Buber

At most, Marx came selectively to acknowledge the positive role of *some* nationalisms. His criterion was whether or not the national movement in question accelerated the disintegration of the feudal-absolutist monarchies in central and eastern Europe, thereby turning the wheels of history faster in the deterministic direction of the revolution. By this yardstick he justified the attainment of national independence for the older, historically established nations, such as the German, Hungarian, and Italian states, but denied such justification to the "history-less" peoples of southern and eastern Europe. Polish nationalism, for example, passed the test because the attainment of Polish national independence would weaken czarist absolutism.

As for the Jews, since Marx regarded their distinctive identity to be entirely dependent on their function in the dialectically sequential economic systems of feudalism and capitalism, there could be no Marxist justification of a Jewish nationalism. The entity identifiable as Jews was destined for dissolution, and the best that any progressive Jew could do was to cast his lot with the forces that were advancing toward the inevitable triumph of the proletariat and the creation of the classless society.

In broad outline this view became the accepted orthodoxy in all Socialist parties that claimed a Marxist patrimony. Jewish nationalism was also negated by most non-Marxist revolutionaries, non-Jewish and Jewish alike. One of the earliest Jewish examples was Ilya Rubanovitch of Odessa, a member of the Russian Narodnaya Volia (People's Will) revolutionary movement, who was arrested in 1881 and subsequently deported from Russia.[2] Even the founders of the first major Socialist organization of Jewish workers, the Allgemeine Yiddishe Arbeter Bund in Russland un Lita (the General Jewish Workers' Organization of Russia and Lithuania, commonly known as the Bund), founded in Vilna in 1897, subscribed in principle to this ideological conception. Its declared theory differed only in terms of strategy from that espoused by those Jews who individually cast their lot with whatever Socialist revolutionary forces emanated from the society in which they were domiciled. The Jewish Bund's founders considered that, if Jews were to be educated toward socialism and mobilized for the ultimate proletarian revolution and classless society, it was a strategic necessity that Jewish workers be organized in a separate Socialist framework functioning in the home language (Yiddish) of the overwhelming majority of Jews in the Russian Empire and taking account of whatever peculiarities applied to the specific situation of Jewish workers. To be sure, the Bund gradually came to adopt the demand for a degree of cultural-national autonomy, not only as a provisional strategy but also as a permanent feature of the Socialist revolution's envisaged goal.[3]

However, in relation to Zionism, the Bund continued to draw upon the same Marxist-rooted critique: Zionism was excoriated as a utopian diversion of energy from the real immediate needs of the Jewish workers and from their strategic confluence with the universal proletarian revolution. It was branded as a bourgeois-inspired and -led movement in alliance with Jewish religious clerical-ism. It was a misguided reaction to antisemitism and a dangerous opiate that blunted and stilted the class consciousness of Jewish workers and diverted them from the class struggle. As was resolved at the Bund's fourth conference, held in May 1901:

> The conference regards Zionism as a reaction of the bourgeois classes to the phenomenon of antisemitism and to the abnormal civic status of the Jewish people [in Russia]. The conference views the ultimate goal of political Zionism, i.e. the acquisition of a territory for the Jews—as an objective of little value, because such a territory would be able to contain but a fraction of the whole nation, and thus would be incapable of solving the Jewish question. Hence, to the extent that the Zionists seek to concentrate the whole of the Jewish people, or even only a major part of the Jewish people, in a single land, they pursue a utopian goal. Furthermore, the conference holds that Zionist propaganda inflames nationalist feelings and hinders the development of class consciousness among the Jewish proletariat.[4]

Although the earliest Socialist critics of Zionism were mostly of Jewish birth and it was primarily the Bund that targeted the Zionist movement for concerted attack, gentile Marxist Socialists also sustained the ongoing criticism of Zionism in much the same terms. Perhaps the most informed and profound of these critics was the preeminent ideologue of German Social-Democracy, Karl Kautsky. Similarly to Marx, he accounted for the contemporary survival of the Jews as a distinctive entity in terms of their role in commercial capitalism. But unlike Marx, Kautsky had a sympathetic attitude toward the Jews as an entity and empathized with their historical experience of suffering. Moreover, he recognized the existence of a Jewish proletariat and assigned to it a positive role in the revolutionary class struggle. Yet he too did not regard the Jews as qualifying for recognition as a legitimate nation since they had neither the requisite territoriality nor the necessary attributes for nonterritorial national autonomy. He too regarded Zionism as an artificial and retrogressive phenom-enon, a regrettable self-segregation that constituted an obstacle to the desirable assimilation of Jews and a hindrance to their participation in the revolutionary class struggle. Although not devoid of sympathy for the attainments of Jewish workers in Palestine, he dismissed Zionism's attempt to create a national home in Palestine on practical grounds. He was convinced that the combined effect of Arab opposition, economic nonviability, and the inevitable collapse of Anglo-French imperialist domination of the area would eventually bring this venture to naught.[5]

In the period preceding the First World War, it was only among Marxists in Austria that a reorientation toward the national question came to the fore, providing potential justification for some form of Jewish nationalism. The signal ideological innovation of Otto Bauer and Karl Renner (alias Springer) was the proposition that within a multinational political framework such as the Austro-Hungarian Empire the basis of nationality should be the choice of each individual as to which national unit he belonged and the right of each such national unit to cultural autonomy irrespective of whether it was territorially concentrated or not. Cultural autonomy included the right of each nationality to its own language and schools. The overall framework of the polity would be preserved by a federal parliament with overriding authority in the political and economic spheres.

Yet even within this conceptual framework, Otto Bauer (himself a Jew by birth), categorically disqualified the Jews from recognition as a legitimate national unit.[6] Although Bauer defined the nation as "an aggregate of people bound into a community of character by a community of fate," he followed in the steps of Marx in treating the Jewish nationality as a mere illusion.[7] Not only did the Jews have no territory of their own, they even lacked the linguistic and other uniform cultural prerequisites for being reckoned a separate nation. The Jewish entity was wholly the product of the Jews' economic function in preindustrial capitalist society. The advance of capitalist production would inevitably lead to their assimilation.

On the other hand, Karl Renner's version of this Austro-Marxist reorientation toward the national question did not quite so categorically exclude the Jews. Furthermore, there were some other Socialists in Austria who took a more positive view of Jewish nationality, notably Engelbert Pernerstorfer, who recognized the right of the Jews to self-definition as a nation and even went so far as to speculate that the Jews of eastern Europe might require an independent state to ensure the survival of their nationality.[8] These Austro-Marxist notions of national-cultural autonomy were an ideological pathbreaker for Jewish nationalism. Their influence can be discerned not only in the constrained form of Jewish nationalism that came to be adopted by the Socialist Bund but also in the liberal theory of diasporic nationalism propounded by the eminent historian Simon Dubnow.[9] Also, the Zionist movement within the Russian Empire, at its Helsingfors conference of 1906, gave the stamp of approval to Jewish demands for a degree of national-cultural autonomy in the Diaspora, alongside its aspiration for a restored Jewish homeland in Eretz Israel.[10]

During and after the First World War the branching out of increasingly diverse Socialist schools of thought in the world improved the disposition toward ideological syntheses of socialism and Jewish nationalism, including Zionism. In the ranks of the reconstituted Second International (after 1923 the Labor and Socialist International), which encompassed most of the world's Socialist parties that believed in evolutionary parliamentary methods, there was a marked modification of hostility to Zionism. Several resolutions were passed recognizing the right of the Jews to a national home in Palestine, and the International's chairman, the Belgian Emile Vandervelde, visited Palestine in the

1920s. Eduard Bernstein (himself a Jew), the "revisionist" Socialist antagonist of Karl Kautsky in German social democracy, evinced sympathy for Socialist Zionist attainments in Palestine in the 1920s.[11]

In the Third International (The Communist International, or Comintern, 1919–1943), however, hostility toward Jewish nationalism, particularly in its Zionist form, was rampant. To be sure, for Lenin, Zionism was a marginal issue; it was the Bund that the Bolsheviks regarded as a serious threat to the organizational and ideological centralization of the Russian Social Democratic Workers' Party. Stalin, who was to become the Soviet Union's first Commissar of Nationalities, elaborated on Lenin's views with acerbic dogmatism. In his "Marxism and the National Question" of 1913, he defined the nation as "a historically evolved, stable community of language, territory, economic life, and psychological make-up manifested in a community of culture." But his disqualification of the Jews was incisive:

What sort of nation, for instance, is a Jewish nation that consists of Georgian, Daghestanian, Russian, American and other Jews, the members of which do not understand each other (since they speak different languages), inhabit different parts of the globe, will never see each other, will never act together, whether in time of peace or in time of war? No, it is not for such paper "nations" that the Social Democratic Party draws up its national program. It can reckon only with real nations, which act and move, and therefore insist on being reckoned with.[12]

In sum, for decades following the Russian Revolution, it may be said that across a wide spectrum of claimants of the Marxist ideological heritage any Jewish claim to being a legitimate nation was disqualified. From Russia's Stalin through Germany's Otto Heller, who combined Stalin's arguments with those of Kautsky (by then a "renegade"),[13] and on to Trotskyites like Abraham Leon (a Jew),[14] Jewish nationalism in general was condemned as an ideologically illegitimate diversion from assimilation. Zionism in particular was excoriated as a utopian delusion and reactionary tool in the hands of the bourgeoisie and capitalist imperialism.

Foundations of Socialist-Zionist Synthesis: Nahman Syrkin

Notwithstanding the Marxist legacy of hostility toward any notion of Jewish nationalism, sporadic and inconsequential attempts to forge an amalgam of Socialist ideas and Jewish nationalism may be traced back as far as Moses Hess's writings in the 1860s. As we have seen in an earlier chapter, Hess held up a quasi-messianic vision of a regenerated Jewish nation in its own homeland exemplifying the Socialist ethics that inhered in the Jewish prophetic tradition. In the mid-1870s, Aaron Liberman, who was born in Vilna but had fled to London to join other expatriate Russian revolutionaries, was perhaps the first not only to postulate a synthesis of socialism and Jewish national affirmation but also to argue that the Jews should form an independent unit within the international Socialist movement. In the mid-1880s, Chaim Zhitlovsky (1865–1943) was already intellectually engaged in a search for a Socialist form of collective Jewish self-emancipation.[15] However, it was not until the late 1890s that the first seminal exposition of what became Socialist Zionism was penned. Its author was Nahman Syrkin (1868–1924).

Born in Mohilev, in czarist Russia, into a middle-class family, Syrkin's traditionalist Jewish education was supplemented with study at a Russian Gymnasium. In his teens he was already attracted both to Hibbat Zion and to Russian revolutionary circles. In 1888 he left Russia, and it was at a Berlin university that he gained a doctorate in 1903. That Syrkin's brand of socialism, although conforming to the class-structure analysis of society, diverged from contemporary orthodox Marxism was already evident in his first published book, which appeared in German in 1896, titled *Geschichtsphilosophische Betrachtungen* (Observations on the philosophy of history). It refuted doctrinaire historical determinism and affirmed the important role of human volition in history.[16]

He was among the most active in the early student Zionist circles in Berlin, which consisted almost entirely of young émigré intelligentsia from Russia. But as Syrkin later phrased it in a memoir, it was he who "undertook the thankless task of being a socialist among Zionists and a Zionist among socialists,"[17] and as such he already stood out at the early Zionist congresses. In Berlin he made attempts to form a Socialist-Zionist circle, which issued in no more than one short-lived periodical in Yiddish and another in Hebrew.[18]

Following the logic of nonromantic Socialist realism, in the 1903–1905 crisis over the proposal that the British offer of a territory in East Africa be considered by the Zionist Organization, Syrkin took a proterritorialist position. Indeed, from 1905 to 1907 he was one of the leaders of a group calling itself the Zionist Socialist Workers' Party (SSRP), which adopted a territorialist platform. But after moving to the United States in 1907, he abandoned territorialism and joined Poalei Zion (Workers of Zion) there. Poalei Zion was the common name adopted by various worker Zionists groups that had mushroomed in Russia at the turn of the century and that were consolidated there by 1906 into an adamantly "Zionists of Zion" antiterritorialist wing of Socialist nationalism. To this development and its moving spirit, Ber Borochov, we shall return later in this chapter. From 1909 until his death in 1924, Nahman Syrkin, based in the American branch, was a leading figure in the World Confederation of Poalei Zion, which had been constituted as a party within the Zionist Organization in 1907.

The vacillations in Syrkin's ideological odyssey, particularly his excursion into territorialism and his failure to sustain an independent following for his particular ideas, had left him rather on the periphery during the formative first decade of labor Zionism. Yet of all the ideologues in the founding generation, it was Syrkin who came closest to formulating the ideological rationale that most fitted the praxis characteristic of mainstream labor Zionism. This evaluation of Syrkin's significance will become evident as our survey unfolds in this chapter.

The seminal formulation of Syrkin's nationalist-socialist synthesis was a booklet that he published in 1898, in German, titled *The Jewish Question and the Socialist Jewish State*. It was patently intended as a Socialist-Zionist alternative to what he interpreted as the bourgeois Zionist conception of Theodor Herzl's *Der Judenstaat*, published only a few years earlier, in 1896. The main lines of Syrkin's Zionism were, to be sure, very much in tune with Herzl's in that they were unequivocally maximalist and remained so consistently throughout his organizational meanderings. He too envisaged a mass exodus of European Jews and the planned settlement and construction of a Jewish state in Palestine or, failing that, in another suitable territory. However, the particularities of his *diagnosis* of the Jewish problem carried indelible marks of his Socialist outlook. This was, as already stated, decidedly not of the orthodox Marxist (i.e., determinist-materialist) ilk. For that very reason Syrkin's exposition in this seminal booklet may be said to attest to the all-pervasiveness of the terms of discourse that Marx had set for almost all varieties of contemporary socialism. For Syrkin's was essentially a socioeconomic analysis of the Jewish condition that looked at antisemitism through a class prism. Where he diverged from these terms of reference was in his prognosis and vision, rather than in his descriptive and diagnostic presentation.

Although Syrkin recognized the religious-psychological roots of hatred between Christian and Jew, his account of the emergence of the Jewish problem was drawn in the dialectical and class terms of Marx's *Communist Manifesto*, which predicted the inevitable worldwide triumph of the proletariat over the bourgeoisie. With typically dialectical argumentation, Syrkin spoke of "the contradictions of bourgeois society . . . which will lead to its breakdown. The very freedom and equality which bourgeois society once proclaimed, but which it now denies, marshal the forces that will spell its doom."[19] Typical of the class focus was the following:

Anti-semitism, which serves to unite the various classes in capitalist society, is not equally intense in each class. In dormant form, it pervades society, because it is a product of the class structure. However, it reaches its highest peak in declining classes: in the *middle class*, which is in the process of being destroyed by the big capitalists, and within the decaying *peasant* class, which is being strangled by the landowners.[20]

Syrkin's diagnosis started from the Marxist premises that "the history of all human society past and present had been the history of class struggle" and that European society had reached the stage of critical class conflict between the declining bourgeoisie and the rising proletariat. Hence, the members of the bourgeoisie, according to Syrkin, "stand between the capitalist class and the proletariat and live in constant fear of falling into the latter. The more wretched their positions become, the fiercer their internal conflicts, the more they are driven to become vampires who feed on the working class." It was this middle class that suffered most from Jewish competition in the competitive struggle: "The Jewish storekeeper was at dagger points with his Christian neighbor over a customer; the Jewish broker attempted to beat his Christian competitor. Competition from the Jew was all the harder to face because natural selection had made him an especially fierce adversary in business." Thus did antisemitism become "the mainstay of the social-political program" of the middle class. And since the lower middle class contained "the most vulgar elements of society, their antisemitism, too, was of the most vulgar type." In terms of the same class analysis, Syrkin added that a second repository for antisemitism was the scum of proletarian society—"those floundering in the decaying peasant class but not absorbed into the productive proletariat which at least have their labor power to sell."[21]

The prognosis that issued from this diagnosis was that the more intense the class struggle became and the more the capitalist order was thrown into disorder, the more antisemitism would grow. "The classes fighting each other will unite in their common attack on the Jew," especially since "the dominant elements of capitalist society, i.e., the plutocrats, the monarchy, the church, and the state, seek to exploit the religious and racial struggle as a substitute for the class struggle."[22] Furthermore, since antisemitism permeated all of society, "Jewish suffering affects every class of Jewry—the proletariat as well as the intelligentsia, the middle class as well as the upper bourgeoisie." Hence, the Jewish worker shared a common fate with the Jewish bourgeois, and this called for national solidarity despite class differences. Syrkin insisted that "Zionism can be accepted by each and every class of Jew." "There can be no more foolish argument than to maintain that the Jewish class struggle conflicts with Zionism," he averred. "Why should the Jewish proletariat, which will be the first to be helped by Zionism in the material sense," he asked, "reject it merely because the other classes of Jewry have also adopted Zionism for national and ideological reasons?"[23]

Of course, as we have said, the standard Marxist contention was not only that ultimately the triumph of the proletariat would resolve this problem of antisemitism but also that Jews should abandon any separatism in the interim; for, whereas there might be justification for some national divisions during the struggle of the proletarians for the ultimate cosmopolitan classless society, the Jews, having long ceased to qualify as a nation, ought to throw themselves from the outset into the cosmopolitan struggle. Here Syrkin took issue with Marxist dogma most energetically. Although there can be little doubt that he was driven, at core, by a deeply ingrained Jewish ethnicism, the ideological rationale he offered avoided romantic nationalist rhetoric. Not the organic evolution of a

Volksgeist (national spirit) but the solidarity stimulated by oppression was emphasized. Although implicitly agreeing that the Jews were indeed nationally deficient, he argued that "nonetheless the enemy has *always* considered the Jews a nation apart and they have always known themselves as such. Though despoiled of all external national characteristics—being dispersed, speaking all languages and jargons, possessing no national property . . . —they have been a distinctive nation the fact of whose existence was sufficient reason for being." The fact that hatred, discrimination, and other impediments afflicted Jews belonging to all classes of society was sufficient proof that they were an identifiable collective entity with a collective consciousness sufficient to qualify them for recognition by Socialists as a nation. The recognition of a common need to free themselves from oppression and suffering had created a sense of Jewish national solidarity. After all, Syrkin argued, "the socialist movement staunchly supports all attempts of suppressed peoples to free themselves."[24] He invoked proof that at various national and international Socialist congresses the right of nations to self-determination had consistently been proclaimed. It was through internationalism rather than cosmopolitanism that socialism would attain its objectives. Hence, all Socialists should support also the national emancipation of the Jews.

Syrkin contended that if contemporary Zionism appeared reactionary, this was simply because the Jewish masses had not taken a firm hold of the Zionist Organization. Jewish Socialists were to blame, for they had failed to join the movement and shape it in their way. "The present reactionary form of Zionism does not free Jewish socialists from their obligation toward the Jewish problem and toward the conception of a Jewish renaissance. On the contrary, it places upon them the duty of illuminating this profound national phenomenon and transforming it into a socialist movement."[25] Turning the tables on Zionism's Socialist opponents, the main thrust of whose argument was that Zionism was a purely bourgeois emanation, Syrkin accused them of, in fact, blindly copying the Jewish bourgeoisie's yen for personal assimilation. "The Jewish bourgeoisie adopted assimilation and dropped the ballast of its Jewishness so that it might swim more freely in the waters of the stock exchange." Whereas Socialists of all other national minorities shunned assimilation, only in the case of the Jews "have the socialists inherited assimilation from the bourgeoisie and made it their spiritual heritage"![26] That Socialist Jews should adopt the same aspiration toward assimilation as did the Jewish bourgeoisie was unconscionable.

The Socialist Way to Statehood

Syrkin did not deny that in the final analysis "the social revolution and cessation of class struggle will normalize the relationship of the Jew and his environment."

Ultimately, there would be "the blending of all the nations into a higher unity, the creation of one humanity with a common language, territory and fate." But he insisted that "socialism will solve the Jewish problem only in the remote future," since in the meanwhile "Jewish suffering has a specific characteristic with which socialism cannot deal."[27] The economic structure of the Jewish people, its lack of political rights, and its peculiar position in society combined to place it in a singular situation that could not be improved solely through the Socialist struggle. Moreover, citing examples from the record of the Social-Democratic Party of Germany and the French Socialists during the Dreyfus Affair, Syrkin argued that "it often happens that, for tactical and opportunistic reasons, Socialist parties adopt passive attitudes or even abet attacks on the Jews."[28] On these grounds he rejected the blind dogma that the class struggle exhausted all the expressions of social life. "Class struggle is the main driving force of history, but it is a misconception to explain all social life, in its manifold expressions, in terms of this alone." "When a people is endangered," he averred, "all parties unite to fight the outside enemy, though in normal times the classes fight each other."[29]

Having established that all classes of the Jews could agree on the need for a Jewish state, Syrkin assigned to the Jewish working class the task of determining what form it should take. He charged that whereas contemporary political Zionism was striving for a Jewish state based on the rights of private property, adequate means for the creation of the Jewish state could be provided only by the workers and in accordance with Socialist principles. Not only was the Socialist way to Jewish statehood a value in itself, since "it is inconceivable that people will agree to the creation of an autonomous state based on social inequality, for this would amount to entering into a social contract of servitude," but it also was a practical necessity, "for the wheels of the Jewish state cannot be turned without the strong arms of the Jewish workers." If the venture were conducted on capitalist lines, it would not be viable. "Since the entire effort at colonization would be taking place in an underdeveloped country, wages would be depressed far below any level of subsistence that a European Jew could find acceptable. Most of the workers would therefore be recruited from among the native populace because they would work for less." The entire enterprise would disintegrate in no time. Also, for technological reasons it would be impractical for "within the climate of petty capitalism, it is not possible to mechanize agriculture and create large industries."[30]

In sum, Syrkin declared that "the Jewish state can come about only if it is socialist; only by fusing with socialism can Zionism become the ideal of the whole Jewish people—of the proletariat, the middle class and the intelligentsia." He infused this plea with a pseudomessianic vision claiming that "the messianic hope, which was always the greatest dream of exiled Jewry, will be transformed into political action."

Because the Jews are forced to find a homeland and establish a state, they therefore have the opportunity to be the first to realize the socialist vision. This is the tragic element of their historic fate, but it is also a unique historic mission. What is generally the vision of a few will become a great national movement among the Jews; what is utopian in other contexts is a necessity for the Jews.[31]

In a curious mixture of Jewish and Christian messianic metaphors he waxed eloquent, revealing the subterranean depths of religious-ethnicist feeling beneath his Socialist terms of discourse: "Israel is like a sleeping giant, arising out of the darkness and straightening up to his unknown height. . . . His tragic history has resulted in a high mission. He will redeem the world which crucified him. Israel will once again become the chosen of peoples!"[32]

Much as Syrkin's diagnosis of the Jewish problem overlapped in essentials with that of the "bourgeois" Herzl, notwithstanding all Socialist rhetoric, so too most of the means Syrkin proposed were consonant with the program of political Zionism as propounded by Herzl. For, accepting interclass cooperation in the settlement enterprise, Syrkin affirmed the need not only for an overall Zionist organization but also for raising national capital and founding a national bank to finance the entire enterprise. As soon as the land was acquired and legally secured, colonization should proceed on advanced Socialist cooperative lines so that the means of production would belong to the settlers themselves and the length of the workday, together with other labor conditions, would be regulated according to Socialist principles. Again like Herzl, he considered Eretz Israel, the ancient Jewish homeland, to be the country of first preference, but he made allowances for the possibility that, should efforts to obtain Palestine fail, "then the Jews would have to acquire some other land." However, he diverged from Herzl's diplomatic policy when he suggested that "the best and most honorable way" was to secure Palestine in alliance with other oppressed nationalities in the Turkish empire through a common stand against the Turks." These included such nations as the Macedonians, Armenians, and Greeks.[33]

Another divergence of Syrkin from Herzl's prescriptions related to diasporic activities. Since Syrkin accepted that "the majority of Jews will for years to come remain in the countries where they now live," he advocated a two-pronged program: involvement of Jewish workers in local social struggles as well as participation in the Zionist Organization. On the one hand, as a matter of "human dignity," Socialist Zionists ought to react to their conditions by fighting for economic improvement and political rights. This meant participating collectively as Jews in the struggle of the local progressive Socialist forces in each Diaspora country. He could not accept Herzl's earnest admonition that Zionists refrain from such involvements. "To urge the masses to withdraw from this struggle in the name of Jewish autonomy in Palestine would be suicidal, spiritually and economically. . . . To answer the driven thousands seeking employment and shelter with the slogan of a future socialist society is to give stones instead of bread."[34] On the other hand, Syrkin also advocated that Socialist Zionists concurrently activate a party of their own within the framework of the worldwide and interclass Zionist Organization.

Counterattack on the Bund

As we have noted, Socialist Zionists had to confront the pungent attacks not only of cosmopolitan Marxist Socialists but also those of the formidable Jewish Socialist labor movement known as the Bund. The Bund's pivotal charges against Zionism were that it was a project for the aggrandizement of the Jewish bourgeoisie, that it was utopian, and that it deflected Jewish workers from their true historic role as participants in the class struggle wherever they were domiciled. In this critique of Zionism, the Bund differed from the views of cosmopolitan Marxists, whether Jewish or not, only insofar as it advocated *collective* Jewish participation in the class struggle, incrementally adopted the demand for cultural autonomy, resting on the Yiddish language, and assumed an attitude of "neutrality" in regard to the question of whether Jews had a national future of their own.

Syrkin did not care to deny that at that time the Zionist Organization was dominated by members of the Jewish bourgeoisie. However, balking at simplistic Marxist dogma, he vigorously refuted the charge that their motivations were bourgeois economic interests. "Zionism is bourgeois not because it reflects the class interests of the burgeoisie, but because the class and psychological awareness of the masses has not yet begun to express itself within Zionism." The bourgeoisie "did not come to dominate Zionism on the strength of its class interests, but by virtue of its national feeling and its spiritual interests."[35] That it had assumed the leadership of Zionism was the fault of the very Jewish Socialists who criticized Zionism. Had they thrown in their lot with Zionism, they could have usurped the bourgeoisie and taken over the reins of the national movement.

Counterattacking the ideology of the Bund, Syrkin charged it with a blind, myopic mimicking of the Austrian Social Democratic Party "without understanding that the Austrian program fitted the Jews about as much as a 'streimel' fitted a 'Greek.'"[36] The Bund was futilely trying to copy a solution that could apply only to those national minorities that were territorially based.

The form of national autonomy that a suppressed people, whether dispersed amongst another nation or concentrated in one territory, can demand for itself is dependent upon the elements of its national life that remain from the days of its national independence. Nations that are concentrated in a circumscribed territory of their own, can demand also political independence, as in the case of Poland for example, and this subsumes freedom for their national culture and for national development in every respect.[37]

This could never apply to the Jewish case because the Jews lacked the necessary national bases. They did not have their own territory, law, and self-governance. They were even deficient in respect of national language. "If a people demanded for itself national autonomy, this meant that it wanted its own national language . . . to be the language of schools and universities; that it should be possible to use it in political meetings, in the courts of law and in governmental institutions, and that the other nation should not forcefully impose its language upon it."[38] For law to be a nation's own it had to be an authentic outgrowth of its own unique history and life-style, not those of another people. "National self-governance means—governance in accordance with the laws of the nation itself, as they still exist in the life of the nation." What remained of the Jewish community institutions—the kahal—was not an adequate basis. As for Yiddish, Syrkin cast doubt on its qualifying for the fulfillment of a genuine national cultural role. "The jargon lives as a language amongst the Jews only out of cultural poverty, not as an outgrowth of national feeling. . . . The jargon is the fruit of the cultural and political galut of the Jewish nation."[39] The Jews would not fight for Yiddish; they would inevitably seek integration into the dominant language.

Syrkin's contention was, in short, that the demand for national autonomy was not feasible for a nation like the Jews, uprooted from its natural territorial environment, attenuated in regard to its original national language, and randomly interspersed among other national groups that were, by contrast, indeed so rooted. He argued that precisely the Austrian example proved how groundless was the Bund's program: "He who wishes to uphold the example of Austria as a model for the Jews of Russia must take as his example not the Poles, the Czechs or the Ruthenians in Austria, but the Jews of Austria. For if he does not do so—the comparison is entirely invalid." The fact was, argued Syrkin, that even in Galicia, where the Jews were relatively more highly concentrated than elsewhere in the Austro-Hungarian Empire, they would never have national autonomy. Hence, he scoffed, the Bund's program amounted to no more than "vanities, childish notions, reactionary stupidity—in which no person could seriously believe."[40]

In sum, Nahman Syrkin laid the ideological foundation for a Socialist Zionism informed by the universe of discourse that Karl Marx had created. But he did so very selectively, emphasizing the role of volition as well as deterministic factors and taking issue with all the major contentions of Marxist Socialists who negated Jewish nationalism in general and its Zionist form in particular. He offered a rationale for interclass cooperation rather than class struggle in the framework of the Jewish national movement and set forth a vision, as well as a program of action, for the construction of a Socialist Jewish society from the ground level upward, largely on cooperative principles. As we shall see, in broad terms this was the direction taken by mainstream labor Zionism from about 1910 onward.

However, Syrkin's formulations were not initially adopted as the ideological program of the scattered workers groups that mushroomed in Russian Jewry at the turn of the twentieth century. These groups generally went by the name Poalei Zion (Workers of Zion), which at the beginning denoted little more than an occupational differentiation from other Zionists associations. In some cases, notably the Minsk Poalei Zion (one of the first to be formed), their aims were limited to promoting Zionism among working-class Jews and identifying with efforts to advance their working conditions. Unlike Syrkin, who functioned in Berlin's circle of Jewish émigré intelligentsia, the tone-setters of these diverse Russian Poalei Zion groups functioned in interaction with a Jewish proletariat of significant mass, part of which had already been captured by the powerful Socialist Jewish workers' organization, the Bund. Stimulated by local Russian influences and political events, especially those attendant on the abortive revolution of 1905, their ideological development branched out in a number of diverse directions, representing what were perceived to be the major options beckoning Russian Jewry. Those who placed primary emphasis on the struggle for Jewish national autonomy within a more democratic Russia, formed the Jewish Socialist Workers' Party, known by the initials SERP. They were also called Seimists, because they advocated Jewish autonomy and the creation of a Jewish Seim, that is, a representative parliamentary institution. Their ideologues included Chaim Zhitlovsky, who was associated with the Russian social-revolutionary movement (but whose mercurial career underwent numerous ideological vicissitudes). Those who adopted a territorialist program, under-girded by a Marxist rationale, went under the name of the Zionist Socialist Workers' Party (SSRP), one of whose ideologues was Jacob Lestschinsky (1876–1966). Yet another grouping of Poalei Zion in Poltava, Ekaterinoslav, and other southern Russian centers gradually was consolidated into the Jewish Social Democratic Workers Party–Poalei Zion, which inventively combined a Marxist ("social-democratic" in contemporary usage) ideological rationale with an adamant preference for Palestine as the only territorial objective. The pivotal personality responsible for the latter's consolidation, as well as for the crystallization of its ideological program and its development into the most historically consequential of all of the emanations of the Poalei Zion phenomenon, was a brilliant ideologue, Ber Borochov.

Materialist Jewish Nationalism: Ber Borochov

Ber Borochov (1881–1917), whose prolific theoretical cogitations made him the ideologist par excellence of Socialist Zionism was a young intellectual (he died at age thirty-five), whose father was a *maskil* adherent of Hibbat Zion and had provided Ber with a secular education. During 1900–1901, Ber was concurrently in the Social Democratic organization in Ekaterinoslav and in the local Zionist circle, but he left the former after encountering some antisemitism there.[41] No one made a more systematic attempt than he to rationalize in Socialist terms the fundamental propositions common to the Zionist ideology as a whole. Although his distinctive contribution to the storehouse of Zionist ideology was the rigidly Marxist formulation, articulated most comprehensively in Poalei Zion's "Our Platform" of 1906, Borochov's biography in fact reveals a fluctuation of ideological formulations. They commenced with a general Zionist exposition, only tinged with Socialist nuances, close to the synthesis propounded by the Russian Zionist leader Menahem Ussishkin in his "Our Program," to which we referred earlier. Beginning in the winter of 1905–1906 and continuing until 1915, Borochov made an apparent ideological volte-face. He became the proponent of a rigidly dogmatic materialist and determinist rationale but one that, instructively, did not change the ultimate Palestine-oriented objectives of the first phase. (Palestine rather than Eretz Israel was the preferred term, signifying a purposive repudiation of any romanticism or religiosity). From about 1915 until his premature death in 1917, a period that included a formative exposure to the working-class ambience of the United States, he turned nearly full circle back to the less dogmatic positions from which he had started, a development quite disconcerting, one should add, to many of his ardent followers in Russia. They found themselves, as it were, straining to save "Borochovism" from Borochov.

In the first phase of Borochov's Zionist career, 1904–1905, he was a traveling propagandist for Menahem Ussishkin's Zionei Zion (Zionists of Zion). His primary ideological enterprise was to translate Ussishkin's "Our Program," which, as we noted earlier, was essentially a Zionist synthesis of political and practical motifs, into the current Marxist-Socialist universe of discourse. This was reflected in two seminal essays: "On Questions of Zionist Theory" and "On the Question of Zion and Territory." Although elements of determinism and materialism are salient in these essays, they are more than balanced by conventional general Zionist motifs emphasizing volitional and idealistic factors.

The diagnosis of the Jewish problem offered by Borochov in this phase rested on an understanding of antisemitism that did not differ substantially from Pinsker's or Herzl's. It was, he argued, rooted not in religious differences or particular objective conditions of class or economic competition but in the ineradicable sociopsychological phobia of the alien, hopelessly exacerbated by the Jews' lack of a homeland. "The Jews in the Diaspora have always been considered outsiders. Not merely foreigners or people from another country, but a mass of aliens marked by distinct social, psychological, and, especially, physical traits."[42] It followed that all classes of society, not excluding the proletariat, were infected with antisemitism. "They have always treated us like strangers. We have never been seen as members of another people but as strangers, so small in number that our very weakness and vulnerability served as a stimulus to various kinds of persecution and acts of violence, and so numerous that we became a thorn in the flesh of the people of the land, always the object of its animus and awaiting its next blow."[43] National homelessness was thus the basic defect in the Jewish condition.

It was only as a secondary graft onto this primary diagnosis that the early Borochov introduced a line of analysis that drew upon Marxist terms of discourse. The irresistible deterministic sweep of advancing capitalism was displacing the Jew's economic role, the factor that had ensured his survival in feudal societies. He reasoned, indeed, that because Russia was moving more directly from feudalism to the higher stages of capitalism than had the countries of western Europe, the Jews there were "being rendered more thoroughly superfluous than in the west, and no reform will save them from isolation."[44] The idea that Jews should be proletarianized could provide no solution. At most, Jews were reduced to being a "luft-proletariat," eking out a living as artisans and in petty home industries. They were unable to enter employment in industrial manufacturing "because of antisemitism from both employers and workers and other factors such as the sabbath laws and their inability to compete physically with robust peasants streaming to the cities."[45]

Nor was emigration a solution. The same socioeconomic factors attendant upon advancing capitalism applied everywhere. Jews simply carried with them, as it were, the antisemitic reaction to themselves. "Restrictions are already being placed on our entry to those countries, and soon they will be barred to us completely," predicted Borochov presciently.[46] Furthermore, nowhere was the position of the Jews being bettered by national liberation of the nation in whose midst they lived, or by progress toward democracy or even proletarian revolution. "So long as Jew-hatred exists, hatred of us as strangers, progress will only make our position more sensitive." Among the examples Borochov gave was that of Morocco. Inevitably, progress there would bring about an uprising of the indigenous Moroccan population for whom everything European was alien and hateful. "And is not such a revolution bound to bring destruction on the Jews there?" he asked. "Will not their fury turn against the Jews who are defenseless rather than against the European predators who are well defended? . . . These Jews will pay for the first steps of militant progress with their lives." It was futile for the Jews to expect their collective salvation from any anticipated social revolution. Not only would "the socialist cataclysm on which our optimists rest their hopes not come so soon if it comes at all" but also, since Jews were in the final analysis regarded as aliens, they would everywhere find themselves rejected equally by the forces of revolution and reaction.

Up to a point Borochov's reasoning was thus very much in line with the thought of Nahman Syrkin, whom we discussed earlier. As such it pointed to a territorial solution, not necessarily in Palestine. But justifying the viewpoint of Ussishkin's Zionists of Zion was of the essence of Borochov's enterprise. It was in this respect that he presented his most ingenious—or perhaps disingenuous—ideological exposition. Employing the empiriocritical terms of discourse of the Russian Marxist Alexander Bogdanov,[47] he marshaled what purported to be empirical-realistic reasons to demonstrate that Palestine alone was suitable as the territorial framework for the Zionist solution to the Jewish problem.[48] Whereas Jewish migrants encountered resistance to their integration into countries of established capitalist industries, Ottoman Turkey did not yet have a developed capitalist economy, nor were there adjacent capitalist countries. Furthermore, it was too weak to withstand the wish of those Great Powers who would be interested in resolving the Jewish problem in Palestine. Whereas the established population of whichever other territory the Jewish migrant reached would sooner or later turn against him, in Palestine the native population itself could be assimilated, culturally and economically, into the incoming Jewish population, for the fellaheen had a natural racial affinity with the Jews. After all, they were "direct descendants of the Judean and the Canaanite population with a very small addition of Arab blood."[49]

If the early Borochov thus incorporated materialist-determinist elements in his diagnosis of the Jewish position, he certainly did not yet hold that the solution could be accomplished solely by deterministic processes. On the contrary, he underscored the need for volitional pioneering activity, arguing that whereas socialism's victory was inevitable—only its birth pangs could be shortened by human endeavor—the Jewish problem required a phase of "therapeutic" treatment to set the stage for the deterministic processes that would ultimately lead the Jews back to Palestine. "It is the very essence of the Zionist movement," he wrote, "that it can only begin through the mobilization of conscious and organized pioneers."[50] It was necessary first to have a wave of pioneers motivated by idealism, the desire to redeem the nation and revive the Hebrew language and culture. Returning to the soil of their traditional homeland, they would therapeutically lay the foundation for the processes that would follow with deterministic momentum.

With the founding, largely on Borochov's initiative, of the Jewish Social Democratic Workers' Party–Poalei Zion in Poltava in early 1906, his ideological orientation underwent a transformation. It took on a rigidly materialist and determinist cast aimed at providing ideological weaponry for the confrontation with the Marxist critique of Zionism in the Russian context.[51] This was crystallized, in the party's "Our Platform," first published in Poltava in 1906, an extensive document that summed up Borochov's Marxist theorizing on the question of nationalism and applied it in specific detail to the Jewish national problem.

The gravamen of his theory was that the development of nations and nationalism was explicable in legitimate materialist terms as a facet of the substructure of human society rather than merely as an artificial reflection of the superstructure. He demonstrated this by adding to Marx's concept of "relations of production," which constitute the economic substructure of society, the concept of "conditions of production." "In this conception of the 'conditions of production,'" he explained, "we have a sound basis for the development of a purely materialist theory of the national question. For in it is contained the theory and the basis of national struggles." These conditions vary considerably. They are "geographic, anthropological and historic." The historic conditions include "both those generated within a given social entity and those imposed by neighboring social groups."[52] Whereas the relations of production (i.e., the respective relations that persons have to the means of production) account for class differentiation and solidarities, the conditions of production account for national differentiation and the development of nations.

A nation is, according to Borochov, "a community developed in the same conditions of production whose members are united with one another by a feeling of kinship derived from a common historic past."[53] Much as class conflict is the outcome of the dialectical tension between the existing relations of production and the changing forces of production, nationalism is generated when a nation's conditions of production are inadequate or abnormal, that is, incommensurate with its forces of production. "Every disparity . . . between the *forces of production*, while they are in the process of development, and the *conditions of production* which hinder this development, results in a *national* problem which can be solved only by the emancipation of the oppressed nation."[54] Given normal conditions of production, the class struggle should ensue, and the proletariat has no cause to uphold nationalism. However, as long as the conditions of production are inadequate or abnormal—and this is what happens to oppressed nations—the workers legitimately have a provisional common interest with the bourgeoisie.

Such abnormal conditions tend to harmonize the interests of all members of a nation. . . . Class antagonisms are abnormally mollified while national solidarity exerts a more potent influence. . . . Under such circumstances, the mother tongue, for example, assumes greater significance than that of a mere means to preserve the local market. . . . The cultural aspects assume an independent significance, and all the members of the nation become interested in *national self-determination.*[55]

Thus, as long as the capitalist system prevails, workers are nationally differentiated, notwithstanding the transnational bonds created by their depressed economic condition and by their common interest in the future Socialist world order. They legitimately experience a sense of national solidarity with the bourgeois class of their nation in addition to their sense of international solidarity with workers of all nations. Borochov rejected "the widespread fallacy that the proletariat has no relation with the national wealth and therefore has no national feelings and interests."

> No class in a society is outside the conditions of production of that society. It therefore follows that the state of these conditions of production is of vital concern also to the proletariat. . . . If the general base and reservoir of the conditions of production, the territory, is valuable to the land-owning class . . . serves the bourgeoisie as a base for the capture of the world-market, and serves the middle-classes of society as the consumers' market . . . then *the territory also has its value for the proletariat, i.e., as a place in which to work.*[56]

This was also the reason, for example, that "the English worker must protect his place of employment not only against the profit considerations of the capitalist but also against the immigrant worker." However, studiedly avoiding any hint of romanticism, Borochov noted that all talk of "national spirit" and "cultural-historical essences" were nothing but "empty phraseology."[57] He was at pains to stress that "the national struggle is waged not for the preservation of cultural values but for the control of material possessions, even though it is very often conducted under the banner of spiritual slogans. Nationalism is always related to the material possessions of the nation, despite the various masks which it may assume outwardly." In the same vein, he tried to draw a distinction between "national" and "nationalistic." "Each class has a different interest in the national wealth and therefore possesses a different type of 'nationalism,'" he argued. The workers were "national," whereas the bourgeoisie was "nationalistic."

The thrust of the argument was that nationalism is progressive—hence, legitimate in Marxist terms—when it is evinced by the proletariat of an oppressed nation, one struggling to assure a "strategic base" for the pursuit of its class struggle. "Genuine nationalism in no way obscures class-consciousness. It manifests itself only among the progressive elements of oppressed nations." Its minimum program was "to assure the nation normal conditions of production, and to assure the proletariat of a normal base for its labor and class struggle." Once this goal had been achieved, "a sound class struggle" could ensue, aimed at the maximum of international socialism.[58] This was the case for the progressive nationalism of Socialist Zionism.

Borochov deepened his diagnosis of the Jewish problem by analyzing the economic condition of the Jews in Russia through the use of the 1897 Russian census statistics.[59] He drew the conclusion that the anomaly of the Jews was reflected in their abnormal economic structure. The percentage of Jews in any given level of production "varies directly with its remoteness from nature." Neither Jewish capital nor Jewish labor was to be found in the basic industrial means of production. The root cause of this anomaly was Jewish landlessness. Whereas the major part of a normal, territorially rooted nation draws its livelihood from natural resources—the soil—and from generating society's basic means of production in heavy industry, the Jews inordinately find employment in intellectual occupations. Jewish labor participates but little in the basic stages of production that are nearest to nature, such as agriculture, mining, and manufacturing, and is mostly concentrated in the last stages of production, such as the distribution of commodities for consumption, and in commerce and the liberal professions. Consequently, as capitalism advanced, machines increasingly doing the work of men in the lighter forms of production, Jewish labor would be displaced. Given the standard Marxist prediction that as capitalism advanced, so wealth was increasingly concentrated in fewer and fewer hands, large capital enterprises progressively swallowing up smaller ones, the end result for the mass of Jews would be compounded economic distress. Their petit bourgeoisie would be depressed into the upper working class, which, in turn, would be displaced. Consequently, relief would be sought increasingly in migration out of Europe.

As we have noted, in the early stage of his theorizing, Borochov had reasoned that Jewish emigration would inevitably gravitate toward Palestine. In his materialist-determinist phase, commencing in late 1905, he tightened and sharpened his depiction of this spontaneously deterministic process—his "prognostic Palestinism," as it came to be known. Almost entirely ignoring romantic and religious attachment to Eretz Israel, he argued that Palestine was uniquely suited as the territorial solution for the Jewish problem. This was so by virtue of its underdeveloped economy and its position in the Ottoman Empire. Only there would Jewish petty capital find it possible to invest into the development of basic industry and agriculture. Thereafter Jewish labor would inevitably follow Jewish capital. Hence, "the land of spontaneously concentrated Jewish immigration will be Palestine." The process was a matter of *stikhinost*, a Russian word derived from a Greek root, best translatable as "elemental spontaneity."[60] In arguing the case for such "prognostic Palestinism," Borochov described Palestine as a sort of "international hostel" owing to its own inchoate cultural-ethnic character and its exposure to a variety of foreign national and religious interests. The fact that its consumer population had such varied habits and tastes had reinforced its impenetrability by heavy capital and industry. The incoming Jews would thus be able to succeed in "developing Palestine's productive forces, and assimilating the local population economically and culturally."[61]

Much as the iron logic of dialectical materialism had led Marx to say that the task of the ideologically conscious proletariat was limited merely to lessening the birth pangs of the inevitable classless society, so the logic of Borochov's "prognostic Palestinism" limited the volitional task of the ideologically conscious Jewish proletariat. This meant allowing the Jewish bourgeoisie wide leeway and political support in order to expedite its predetermined task of building up the Palestinian economy. Stimulated by the profit motive, the bourgeoisie would draw on its capital reserves and use the Zionist Organization as its national instrument. This justified participation in the world Zionist Organization and in raising "national capital" from Jews everywhere, for it created the necessary preconditions that would ultimately generate a Jewish working class ready to conduct the class struggle alongside the workers of all nations. To be sure, in 1909 Borochov hardened his attitude toward the Zionist Organization. He revised his previous affirmation of full Poalei Zion participation in the Zionist congress and advocated withdrawal. For tactical reasons he considered it to be in the best interests of Poalei Zion to leave the Zionist congress in the hands of the bourgeoisie, while it devoted itself wholly to work within the ranks of the Jewish proletariat.[62]

During the last stage of Borochov's life, influenced by his experiences in American Poalei Zion and in the formation of the Jewish Congress movement there, he jettisoned the major part of his purported Marxist orthodoxy. Upon his return to Russia in August 1917 he openly declared to the third Poalei Zion congress convened in Kiev his cognizance of Zionism's emotional significance as the elemental "striving for a home." That was to say, it was far more than a strategic base for the class struggle! "Our terminology must be made richer and more elastic," he advised.[63] The veil was lifted from his former strictly materialist ideological rhetoric:

Twelve years ago . . . we did not attach any significance to form and to the aesthetic aspects of life. It had to be that way, for then our battle was fought on two fronts: the Bundist and the General Zionist. Lest we be confused with the latter we had to be cautious in our terminology . . . now we can and must employ an emotional terminology. Now we can and must proclaim Eretz Israel—a Jewish Homeland![64]

Moreover, admitting that what had motivated the previous "mechanical conception" was the need to countervail the General Zionists' assertion that the will of the nation was the sole determining factor in Zionism, he now openly advocated a program of proletarian initiative in the constructive development of the Jewish sector in Palestine. Borochov now made a profound admission: "Years ago we said: Zionism is a stychic process. Our only task is to remove all the obstacles which interfere with this process. And we left the creative work to the bourgeois Zionists. . . . We erred formerly when we contended that natural emigration waves were already under way. General Zionists were closer to the truth." "Our experiments in Palestine have taught us a new lesson," he now averred, "cooperative colonization in which the worker plays a very great role is also the way to a Socialist society in Palestine . . . we must originate inde-pendent activities in Palestine. We cannot merely content ourselves, as we have done until now, with the work of bourgeois Zionists and with our critical attitude towards it." Yet he remained against participation of Poalei Zion in the Zionist congress, which he still regarded as virtually a bourgeois General Zionist tribune. He preferred to be affiliated with a world Jewish Congress that could serve as "a national tribune having a semi-parliamentary status."[65]

The foremost scholar on Borochov's life and thought, Matityahu Mintz, has argued that this last phase of Borochov's ideological position is best seen as a synthesis of the previous two phases rather than as a total repudiation of his materialist-determinist phase of 1905–1915. He argues that it does not mean that Borochov totally abandoned his prognosis of a "stychic" migration to Palestine and of the capitalist development that was to take place there before a class war could begin to be waged. Rather, it represented his return to the view that an initial pioneering and avant-garde action on the part of the Zionist worker party itself was necessary. He still believed that the stychic process would eventually unfold itself.[66]

Borochov's Ideological Legacy

Whatever may be one's evaluation of the degree of inner consistency in Borochov's ideology, given the alternating phases in his actual expositions, it is hardly surprising that he left an ambiguous legacy for the labor Zionist movement. The strictly materialist-determinist "Borochovism" of his middle period became the canon of an avowedly Marxist wing of Poalei Zion, which sought, however unsuccessfully, affiliation with the Communist Third International (the Comintern). Irreconcilable differences regarding such international alignment, as well as strategy for attainment of Socialist objectives in Palestine (since 1918 under British administration), precipitated a schism in the World Confederation of Poalei Zion (Brit Olamit Poalei Zion). After a crucial conference held in Vienna in 1920 the left wing exited and came to be known as Left Poalei Zion (*Poalei Zion Smol*). Its independent development was in turn punctuated by turbulent ideological instability and splits of the kind typical of extreme left parties everywhere in the interwar and postwar years. In Soviet Russia the greater part of it—and in Palestine one segment—transmuted into Communist parties.[67]

We shall need to devote further attention to Left Poalei Zion later in this chapter. For the present suffice it to note that it clung dogmatically to Borochov's prognostic vision of a Palestinian wage-earning proletariat poised to launch class war against a capitalist economy that was expected to be introduced into Palestine by the Zionist bourgeoisie under the protective umbrella of British imperial power. Moreover, pursuant to the policy advocated by Borochov in 1909, it dissociated itself from the world Zionist Organization proper.

The ideologically more moderate and flexible wing of Socialist Zionism, was coextensive with the World Confederation of Poalei Zion after 1920. Its leaders in Palestine included personalities destined for historic roles, such as David

Ben-Gurion, Berl Katznelson, Yitzhak Ben-Zvi, and Yitzhak Tabenkin. They too were able to lay claim to Borochov's ideological legacy on account of its inherent ambiguities regarding the role of "therapeutic," voluntaristic pioneering. A selective approach to Borochov's ideological output was evidenced in the published collections of his works, edited by Zalman Shazar and Berl Locker,[68] both of whom belonged to the mainstream of Socialist Zionism (that is, the right wing of Poalei Zion). Its organizational development will now be traced briefly before we focus on its ideological content.

In Palestine during the crucially formative pre–World War I wave of Zionist settlers from Russia known as the Second *Aliya*, a Poalei Zion party had been founded at the end of 1905 by a group of about sixty workers. Yitzhak Ben-Zvi was one of the founders, and David Ben-Gurion joined this group after his arrival in September 1906. At the end of the First World War they reached an understanding with "nonparty" workers, mainly belonging to several agricultural unions. The non-party-aligned participants included some important future luminaries, notably, David Remez, Berl Katznelson, and Yitzhak Tabenkin. In the interests of greater unity and comprehensiveness, in 1919 they allowed their party to be subsumed by an entirely new framework, called Ahdut Ha-avoda (Unity of Labor). As its name suggests, Ahdut Ha-avoda aspired to unification of all Jewish workers in Palestine in a comprehensive trade-union-cum-political-party framework. We shall return later to the ideological significance of this innovation. In practice it failed to attain so comprehensive a form, since a major section of the workers declined to give up its independent political existence. It soon had to settle for playing the dominant political role in a broader, truly comprehensive framework of trade unions and workers' enterprises founded in 1920, the Histadrut Ha-klalit Shel Ha-ovdim Ha-ivrim Be-Eretz Israel (the General Federation of Hebrew Workers in Eretz Israel, commonly known as the Histadrut).

After the World Confederation of Poalei Zion split in 1920, Ahdut Ha-avoda became the Palestinian component of the right wing. It had relinquished its trade union and various social functions in favor of the Histadrut and reverted to being a conventional party. Its core role in the continuing World Confederation of Poalei Zion, which participated actively in Zionist congresses throughout the 1920s, was further enhanced when it united in 1930 with its former rival, Ha-poel Ha-tzair (the Young Worker). The latter, founded in October 1905, was also a unique emanation of the formative Second *Aliya* wave of settlers. Its leading figures included such prominent personalities as Yosef Aharonowitz, Yosef Sprinzak, and Eliezer Shohat. Abjuring socialism in any formal political sense and, a fortiori, rejecting Marxist doctrine, they had long resisted unification with Ahdut Ha-avoda's avowed Socialists. Their resistance had been a major factor in the failure of Ahdut Ha-avoda's 1919 initiative to subsume all political and trade union activity in one comprehensive framework.

Ha-poel Ha-tzair was unwilling to do more than cooperate in the forming of the Histadrut. On the world Zionist Organization plane, in 1920 Ha-poel Ha-tzair had joined forces with a congeries of like-minded Tzeirei Zion (Youth of Zion) groups in the Diaspora to form a worldwide political party called Hitahdut Ha-poel Ha-tzair-Tzeirei Zion (the Union of Ha-poel Ha-tzair-Tzeirei Zion, or the Hitahdut for short).

When these two wings of labor Zionism at last united in 1930 to form Mifleget Poalei Eretz Israel (the Workers' [or Labor] Party of Eretz Israel, best known by the acronym Mapai) and not long after formed a World Union, they were well set to grasp the political leadership of the Zionist Organization as a whole. This leadership role they indeed assumed from the Zionist congress of 1933 onward.[69] In 1935 their foremost leader, David Ben-Gurion, having been a front ranker in Ahdut Ha-avoda and the dominant member of the powerful Histadrut's secretariat since its founding, was elected chairman of the executive of the Zionist Organization and Jewish Agency for Palestine. Thenceforward, Mapai enjoyed virtual hegemony over the world organization, although always requiring coalition arrangements with other Zionist parties, primarily that segment of the General Zionists (Group A) that consistently supported Chaim Weizmann's candidacy for presidency of the Zionist Organization—Jewish Agency. Weizmann in turn depended on the support of Labor.

Mainstream Poalei Zion Ideology

Overall, the mainstream trend of Poalei Zion ideology tended increasingly to acknowledge idealistic, voluntaristic factors in its program of action for the fulfillment of Zionism's objectives on Socialist lines. Consequently, it moved closer to Nahman Syrkin's views. This was the case particularly in Austria-Hungary, whose imperial framework included the major concentration of Jews in the largely Polish-inhabited province of Galicia, but also in post–World War I independent Poland as a whole and in the United States of America, whose Jewish immigrant generation sustained a small but significant Poalei Zion presence. Moreover, as we shall see, in Eretz Israel too the trend was distinctly away from doctrinaire Borochovism.

The preeminent ideologist in the Austrian arena of Poalei Zion was Shlomo Kaplansky (1884–1950). Born in Bialystok, Russian Poland, Kaplansky studied mechanical engineering in Vienna and became a leader of Poalei Zion in Austria, serving for a time also as secretary of the World Confederation of Poalei Zion. After settling in Palestine in 1912, various tasks in the Zionist Organization took him back to Europe (from 1913 to 1919 at the Hague, from 1921 to 1924 and again from 1929 to 1931 in London). After returning to Palestine in 1931, he became head of the Technion Institute in Haifa, a position he held until his death after the creation of the State of Israel. Kaplansky did not feel called upon to prove the legitimacy of Jewish nationalism in quite so rigidly doctrinaire terms as had Borochov. The ambience of Austro-Marxism, whose distinctiveness lay precisely in the recognition of national frameworks as legitimate vehicles for the advance toward socialism, enabled Kaplansky to set out from the premise that the Jews were self-evidently a national minority. In a seminal essay of 1911 on the subject of class war in relation to the Jewish question,[70] he applauded the recognition given by Austrian Social Democrats like Viktor Adler, Engelbert Pernerstorfer, and Karl Renner to the view that "internationalism does not mean the mixing together of nations, nor even a-nationalism, that is to say, absence of nations." He traced this recognition as far back as Ferdinand Lassalle's endorsement (so claimed Kaplansky) of Fichte's conception of the nation as a matter of consciousness, the consciousness of ethnic-cultural distinctiveness expressed as a unique national spirit. National differentiation was a manifest social reality from which flowed the right of each national unit autonomously to solve its social problems and realize common Socialist objectives in its own way.

Yet Kaplansky's ideological frame of reference was still Marxist. Thus, echoing Borochov's "conditions of production," he stated: "History creates in each nation specific socio-economic conditions; it shapes a pattern of interacting social forces at various stages of development. In accordance with the specific conditions of life and pace of development of each nation—the proletariat being a part thereof—there are differences in the circumstances of its social struggle and in the basis for its class conflict." Accordingly, Kaplansky averred that the existence of a self-conscious Jewish nation incorporating its own proletarian class was empirically self-evident. "National consciousness developed as a natural result of the national experience. The Jewish people lives in practice its own distinctive national life and has its own special problems and social tasks." Hence, he also granted that the existence of the Bund as a specifically Jewish workers' movement, seeking its own place in a national federative framework of socialism, was an outcome of the reality of national differentiation. But he took issue with the Bund's belief that the Jewish national unit could viably realize its social objectives while it had a merely diasporic status in the midst of other territorially based national units. Kaplansky asserted that the Jewish situation was uniquely anomalous. Its Socialist objectives were realizable only through radical transformation of its condition by reconstructing its social foundations in its own national territory, Palestine.

Kaplansky's diagnosis of the Jewish problem, in contrast with that of Herzl, did not place primary emphasis on the failures of civic emancipation and the attendant rise of antisemitism.

For us the Jewish question is a phenomenon rooted in the Jewish nation's internal conditions of life. Even were there to be a country whose inhabitants love the Jews, this would not obviate the possibility of there being a Jewish question. . . . In Vienna I did not see hatred of Czechs; the Viennese deny the existence of a Czech question. Yet in the consciousness of the Czech workers in Vienna, who experience the danger of being assimilated, there has long been a Czech question in Vienna. And just as the anti-Czech riots in Vienna (1909) were only an incidental-external phenomenon and not the crux of the Czech Minority Question, so antisemitism, even if it leads to pogroms, is not the essence of the Jewish question.[71]

What assuredly *was* the essence of the Jewish question, according to Kaplansky, was the increasing socioeconomic distress of the Jews. Along lines compatible with Nahman Syrkin's diagnosis no less than Borochov's, Kaplansky argued that this socioeconomic distress was the result of being an extraterritorial national entity in the age of advancing concentration of capital. The Jewish bourgeoisie was being depressed downward into the Jewish working class which, in turn, was being occupationally blocked and displaced by the rapidly growing proletariat belonging to the territorially based national majorities. The first memorandum of the World Confederation of Poalei Zion addressed to the office of the Second Socialist International was largely formulated by Kaplansky. It stated:

The Jewish nation is situated in many countries, under the rule of different govern-ments . . . yet nevertheless is united nationally by the common conditions of development of its productive life, as well as by its history, traditions and culture. . . . There exists a Jewish question for the Jewish proletariat and it is the result of the material dependence and economic weakness of the Jewish people. . . . At a time when petty industry is doomed to displacement in its hopeless struggle against advancing heavy industry, and when masses of peasants uprooted from the land and destined for proletarization are being absorbed into the capitalist system . . . Jewish artisans, devoid of property and work, are being denied access to the new heavy industries. . . . Because of national competition from the masses of non-Jews on the verge of proletarization who still hold to reactionary superstitions and because of the retarded development of the Jewish industrial proletariat, together with the class displacement of wide strata of the Jewish people, peculiar obstacles arise on the path of the Jewish proletariat to class struggle and cripple its strategic position.[72]

Kaplansky contended, much as had Nahman Syrkin before him, that the Jewish bourgeoisie characteristically sought its way out of Jewish distress through the path of assimilation. He too accused Jewish Socialists who opposed Zionism of uncritically adopting "the spiritual legacy of the liberal bourgeoisie." But that was not the chosen path of the masses of Jewish workers, "for they struggle for the means to survive, to develop and determine their fate as Jews; Jewishness for them is not something from which to escape."[73] Emigration was another attempted outlet on the part of Jews, but, argued Kaplansky, "one could not compare Jewish migration with the flight of the masses of peasants and agricultural workers displaced by the owners of large landed estates (from Italy, Hungary, Poland, Ireland etc.)." That emigration was the product of the relics of feudalism in the economic system of the modern period. It took place because

advancing capitalist industry could not keep pace with the peasants' abandonment of the old feudal estates. They "leave their lands of birth, despite the
advancing victory of industry, whereas the Jews wander out *because of* the
development of great industry." But emigration was no real solution in the long
term. The Jewish emigrants "transfer their poverty from Eastern Europe across
the ocean, filling the sweatshops. . . . This migration is in no way the last
station on the Jewish proletariat's path of suffering." Kaplansky pointed further
to the reaction in Britain to such waves of Jewish migration—the 1905 Aliens
Act—and to the fact that in the United States the trade unions were demanding
the closure of the ports to would-be immigrants.

Another leading spokesman of the World Confederation of Poalei Zion in the
international forum was Leon Chasanowitsch (1882–1925). He was one of the
founders of Poalei Zion in Russian Poland. After suffering arrest by the czarist
authorities, he went to Galicia, where he edited Poalei Zion's Yiddish paper, *Der
Yiddisher Arbeter* (The Jewish Worker). During the First World War he served in
Poalei Zion's headquarters in the Hague, and after the war he was editor of the
party's Yiddish daily, *Die Tsayt* (The Times), in New York.

Chasanowitsch, like Kaplansky, echoed the materialist-determinist universe
of discourse. He presented the Zionist project for colonization of Palestine not
as a matter of religious belief, but as the necessary working out of "an historically
dictated process." He quoted the official statement of the World Confederation
of Poalei Zion to the effect that it stood "on the foundations of Socialist
doctrine" and strove for "the destruction of the capitalist order and of bourgeois
class domination through the economic and political class war of the proletariat
and the nationalization of the means of production."[74] However, all this rested
on the premise of Socialist internationalism—"that the internationalism of the
working class does not exclude, but rather includes, progressive, defensive
nationalism; that socialism does not require self-abnegation and self-renun-
ciation of nations but, on the contrary, first creates the possibility for the free
continuance of national individualities."[75]

Chasanowitsch objected to an exception being made to this principle solely
in the case of the Jews, who alone were told to renounce their nationality. This
demand, he declared, was "indefensible precisely from a Socialist standpoint
because the assimilation of the Jews . . . is not only an anti-national but also
an anti-social phenomenon of the highest degree." The possibility of assimilation, he argued, was restricted to the thin upper layer of the bourgeoisie. The
broad masses of the Jews would remain unaffected. Those who advocated it
were attempting "to loosen all social bonds," and to push "a wedge between the
intelligentsia and the national masses."

In much the same vein a 1918 publication of the American branch (which
spelled its name Poale Zion) succinctly summed up the common planks of the
World Confederation of Poalei Zion.[76] It set forth the basic premise: "Poale

Zion considers the Jewish people as one nation dispersed in various countries and leading everywhere an abnormal economical [*sic*] life." It asserted that the Jewish masses were more exploited than most non-Jewish workers because they lacked an agrarian class, and urban social ostracism and discrimination subjected them "to greater inequality of economic opportunity and to more horrible forms of poverty than most non-Jews are compelled to endure." The ultimate root of the problem was the fact that Jews "do not enjoy the right and power to determine their own fate as a nation. . . . The dominating national group considers itself *the* nation, looks with suspicion and jealousy upon the national activities of the minority groups and tries to bring about their enforced assimilation." Moreover, the Jewish minority suffered the most since "the prejudice of centuries" aggravated the situation. The result was "ostracism, antisemitism, economic boycotts, and even massacres."

The publication went on to state that Poalei Zion recognized that "the fundamental cause of Jewish poverty, like that of all poverty, was the capitalist system," and it accepted that there was "only one radical solution for this unendurable state of affairs—socialism." But this could best be attained on national lines. There was no conflict between socialism and "progressive nationalism," since "socialism is *international* and not *cosmopolitan*." Cosmopolitanism meant assimilation. It was undesirable because it involved surrender of individuality and loss of self-reliance and self-respect. "A people that is humiliated and is made to feel that its own speech and culture are of negligible importance is one that can also be more easily exploited."

Moreover, the attempt on the part of the Poale Zion to create a Jewish state in Palestine through the aid of methods of modern labor is in perfect conformity with that phase of socialism that undertakes to organize the economically undeveloped world, not for the sake of exploitation for a mother country, but for the purpose of increasing human productivity and bringing that productivity in normal relationship with the rest of laboring humanity.

The American Poalei Zion statement then went onto the offensive against its opponents in the Socialist camp. It countercharged that "the cosmopolitan ideal that involves the assimilation of smaller groups within an ever-growing unit is a capitalist attitude that is an outgrowth of imperialistic tendencies in modern society." In Jewry it was the wealthy bourgeoisie who were assimilationists, deliberately fostering the illusion that the Jews were merely a religious sect and trying to destroy Jewish national consciousness. Jewish Socialists who advocated assimilation were knowingly or unknowingly "a pawn in the hands of the ambitious bourgeoisie." Against the Socialist Jewish Bund's claim that the solution for Jewish distress lay in improvement of the workers' economic conditions in the Diaspora, it posited that "Jewish economic conditions are determined by Jewish national abnormality . . . to ignore the national woes of the Jewish people while trying to solve their economic difficulties is a ghastly mockery."

In sum, given their broadly Marxist terms of reference, the common diagnostic emphasis of all Poalei Zion everywhere was that the root of Jewish distress lay in the abnormal economic condition of the Jews in an age of advancing concentration of capitalism. The Jewish national unit was hopelessly disabled; it could not form a proper proletariat to participate in the class struggle that must inevitably give birth to new classless societies. The alternative, assimilation, was both impossible and undesirable. It served only the upper segment of the Jewish bourgeoisie. The more rigidly Marxist the argument, as in the mid-years of Borochov, the more the *impossibility* of proletarian assimilation was stressed; the less rigidly Marxist the argument, as with Kaplansky and the American Poalei Zion, the more the *undesirability* of assimilation was stressed. The solution offered by Poalei Zion ideology was regeneration of the Jewish nation on working-class Socialist lines in its own homeland, Palestine or Eretz Israel. The ultimate vision was of a normalized Jewish nation taking its place as an equal member in an international order of Socialist national societies.

The Ideology of "Constructivism"

In Palestine, under Ottoman rule, the small Poalei Zion party that had been formed in late 1905 by Second *Aliya* members from Russia initially held to the theoretical guidelines posited by Borochov at about the same time. The first ideological platform of Poalei Zion, formulated at a conference in the town of Ramle in October 1906, opened with the words "The history of mankind is the history of national and of class struggle" and virtually recapitulated the essence of Borochov's thesis concerning the conditions of production:

The means by which man creates the material necessities for his life and the natural and historical conditions of production differentiate mankind into societies and classes. A given set of conditions of production, once it begins to constrict the development of forces of production in that society, drives it to take possession of a foreign economic base—a territory—and this arouses opposition from the other affected society. Thus arises a national struggle.[77]

The platform went on to describe the socioeconomic situation of Palestine as still being largely feudal although with incipient middle-scale capitalist development, mainly in the agricultural sphere, brought in by Jewish immigrants. It predicted, in Borochov's prognostic terms, the gradual penetration of such capital and an attendant growing need for educated and energetic workers, one that could not be filled by the local less educated Arab workers. It further predicted that Jewish migration would inevitably follow the entry of capital into Palestine because "the Jewish masses were being displaced from all spheres of production and are forced to emigrate" and because "in countries of high capitalist development this is blocked by more and more obstacles."

The founders of Poalei Zion thus conceived of their Zionist Socialist role as that of providing the therapeutically required pioneer avant-garde, which would commence the task of creating a Jewish working class in Palestine. Since most of the Second *Aliya* pioneers were young, in their early twenties on the average, and in Russia had rarely been proletarians, agricultural or urban, this also meant that they were consciously seeking *downward* social mobility—a most unusual sociological phenomenon, explicable only in terms of their intensely ideological motivation. Given the economic conditions prevailing at the time, their basic aspiration was to gain employment as agricultural wage laborers in the existing farming settlements established by their predecessor settlers who had emanated from the Hibbat Zion phase of Jewish nationalism. In the period 1882 to 1900 some twenty such settlements had been founded, containing about 5,200 persons.[78] The problem was that those earlier settlers had long become accustomed to employing cheaper Arab wage laborers and were disinclined to replace them with less experienced, more expensive, and more demanding new immigrants. The minimal standard of living requirements of the aspiring Jewish wage laborers were higher than those of the Arab laborers who, besides, often could rely additionally for their subsistence on family plots in the Arab rural economy.

An attendant implication of the Poalei Zion ideology related to interclass cooperation. Again following Borochov's thesis, a division of national tasks was envisaged: while the bourgeoisie would administer the Zionist Organization and bring in the capital for economic development of the country, the Socialist Zionists of Poalei Zion would fulfill the crucial role of creating a healthy, fighting Jewish working class in Palestine, poised to wage class war in due course.

However, by 1909 the harsh realities of the situation were becoming manifest. There was no significant inflow of capital, nor were the aspiring wage workers finding employment in anything like sufficient numbers. The "conquest of labor" (i.e., wage labor), as the current slogan had it, was being frustrated at every turn, and indeed, many who had come with this Second *Aliya* wave were leaving the country.[79] Greater realism began to displace abstract theorizing, and the Poalei Zion of Eretz Israel began to diverge from the doctrinaire ideologizing of its progenitors in Europe. They tended incrementally toward a new strategy and attendant ideological rationale. Withdrawing from the aspiration to be employed purely as wage laborers, they began to experiment with a variety of forms of self-employing settlements. One of these was a small commune called Degania, near the Sea of Galilee. This was the progenitor of the unique commune form known as the *kvutza* and later the kibbutz. Another was a cooperative settlement project that had long been advocated by an economist of note and a prominent personality in German Zionist circles, Franz Oppenheimer. Opposed by the rigidly doctrinaire Borochovists of Russian Poalei Zion but supported by Austrian and American Poalei Zion, Oppenheimer's proposals gained endorsement by an international conference of the World Confederation of Poalei Zion held at Cracow in December 1909. Kaplansky, of the Austrian delegation, and Syrkin, who came as one of the American representatives, were among its advocates. Most significantly, the Poalei Zion delegation from Eretz Israel now came out in support of the plan. Oppenheimer's project was duly adopted as an official Zionist Organization project, and an initial attempt to implement it was the creation of the first cooperative settlement, Merhavia, in the Jezreel Valley.

The ideologically sanctioned ideal increasingly became not wage labor employed by Jewish farmers and orchard owners but joining a cooperative group or commune and participating thereby in the upbuilding of an embryonic societal system with its own political units and network of cooperative collective settlements, labor unions, social and health services, and self-defense force that would ultimately subsume the entire national project in Palestine. The implication for interclass cooperation within the Zionist Organization framework was one of practical dependence but ideological reservation. The bourgeois component of the Zionist Organization was expected to raise the national capital that would fuel the development of this workers' societal infrastructure, which in due course would encompass and subsume the Zionist enterprise in its entirety. This betokened a shift in the imagining of the nation-in-the-making. Rather than as a reproduction of existing European nations divided horizontally into a dominant middle class challenged by a rising working class, it was now to be imagined as an almost monolithic single-class nation in genesis. Ultimately, "nation" and "working class" were to be wholly coextensive.

One manifestation of the search for a new course was an extraordinary venture lasting from 1921 to 1929 known as the Gedud Ha-avoda (Labor Battalion). Its members were idealistic young pioneers from postrevolutionary Russia who arrived between 1919 and 1923—the Third *Aliya*.[80] At its peak the Gedud Ha-avoda numbered about 650 members, although many more passed through its ranks. The members were divided into units (*plugot*), each of which was a commune that offered itself as hired labor to whatever state or other work projects were available. A few of these commune units constituted agricultural *kvutza* settlements, but most were nonsedentary. They worked all over the country in a variety of occupations, mainly, as it happened, in government-sponsored road building. All earnings went into a common treasury that provided, within its financial limits, according to the supremely egalitarian principle of "from each according to his ability to each according to his needs." The principle of equality applied not only to the individuals constituting each commune unit of workers assigned to any particular enterprise but also to the division of income arising from each separate commune unit. The utopian-like vision that inspired this venture was that of an ever-expanding, centrally directed network of wage-earning laborers or self-employed communes that, together, formed a general countrywide commune. In this way a national Jewish society would evolve on fundamentally Socialist lines.

This innovative social experiment was soon disrupted, however, when a section of the Gedud's members that had formed an agricultural commune, Ein Harod in the Jezreel valley, became dissatisfied with both the administration and principle of the common treasury. In 1923, Ein Harod split off and served as the agriculturally based center of an independent grouping of workers employed also in various urban occupations as well as in several other agricultural settlements. Ein Harod became the prototype of the kibbutz, differing from the earlier intimate and relatively self-centered *kvutza*, whose prototype was Degania, in that it sought to attract and absorb new pioneering settlers from the Diaspora and to be a large commune engaged in as wide a range as possible of industrial as well as agricultural pursuits. But by 1927 the tendency was for the Ein Harod settlers to shed their central coordinating function in what was originally envisaged as a composite commune network, and instead the Ha-kibbutz Ha-meuhad (United Kibbutz), as it was called, became a federal association of several effectively autonomous kibbutz communes. By 1939 this federation encompassed thirty-three kibbutzim with a population exceeding twelve thousand and constituted the backbone of the avowedly Socialist-Zionist segment of the labor movement in Palestine.

As for the Gedud Ha-avoda itself, its always precarious economic basis was greatly damaged by the severe economic crises, with attendant unemployment, that afflicted Palestine in 1925–1926. This exacerbated disagreements over the administration of the common treasury. Moreover, the Gedud was plagued by chronic dissension over such issues as subordination to the authority of the Histadrut, of which it was a component; its potentially rival relationship to the Ahdut Ha-avoda party, to which many of its members belonged; and fundamental ideological questions of Socialist orientation toward Soviet communism. In late 1926 the Gedud split into a left wing and a right wing. Disintegration ensued after an important segment of the left wing, headed by one of the Gedud's original founders, Menahem Elkind, became totally disillusioned with the prospect of ever creating the envisaged comprehensive commune in the realities of Palestine. In 1927, Elkind went so far as to lead a return of some eighty members to Russia, where, after a period of work in an agricultural commune modeled on those in Palestine, they ended up, in a twist of ironic tragedy, bitterly persecuted by the Soviet regime.

The incipient reorientation of praxis that we have been discussing found ideological expression in the term Socialist "constructivism," a neologism that was in vogue by the 1920s. It harked back to the original program of action proposed by Nahman Syrkin in his "The Jewish Question and the Socialist

Jewish State." Indeed, after the First World War, Syrkin's direct influence was brought to bear on the deliberations of the World Confederation of Poalei Zion.[81] The personality whose thought both reflected and influenced the constructivist labor ideology most profoundly was Berl Katznelson (1877–1944), generally known simply as Berl.

Born in Bobruisk, White Russia, Berl's early education was that of the traditional *heder* (religious schoolroom) and of a home in which he was exposed somewhat to *haskala* (Hebrew Enlightenment) literature and also was taught the Russian language. As early as adolescence he was dually attracted to Zionism and the revolutionary ambience that led up to the abortive Russian Revolution of 1905. Initially, he vacillated indecisively between various alternative trends, including that of the Zionist Socialist Workers' Party, which favored a territorial solution other than Palestine, and the Seimists (members of the Jewish Socialist Labor Party), who directed most of their efforts to the attainment of Jewish autonomy in Russia. But in 1909, aged twenty-two, he decided to settle in Eretz Israel. Like David Ben-Gurion and other contemporaries of the Second *Aliya*, he started out as an agricultural laborer in various Jewish settlements. But unlike Ben-Gurion, he chose not to associate himself with either of the political parties that had come into existence. Instead, he turned his efforts to the creation of an Agricultural Workers Union and became a leading figure among those known as "the nonparty" workers. After serving together in one of the battalions of Palestinian Jews that had been formed under British command toward the end of the First World War, he and Ben-Gurion joined forces to become the prime movers of the attempt to form Ahdut Ha-avoda. As we have said earlier, this was emphatically meant to be not a political party in the conventional sense but an all-inclusive association of the Jewish workers in Palestine incorporating political, social, and educational activities as well as trade union functions. As such it implied the abandonment of the Borochovist theories of Poalei Zion's founders in Eretz Israel and the triumph of Katznelson's nonparty principle. Indeed, it meant Poalei Zion's self-dissolution and the incorporation of a majority of nonparty members in the new framework.

In the comparative context of modern Socialist experiments, this conception calls to mind French syndicalism, but the difference between the two goes to the very essence of constructivism's ideological uniqueness. Syndicalism was intent on radically changing an existing capitalist society. It did not concern itself particularly with the national character of the society. Spurning all cooperation with the regnant bourgeois class even in the parliamentary sphere, it aimed to deploy as its ultimate weapon the great strike that would finally overturn the old system. By contrast, the constructive socialism of the Zionist labor movement set out to take pioneering responsibility for the creation of a new society—an essentially *national* society—from the foundation upward and to this end was willing to cooperate with the Zionist bourgeoisie. In essence, the ideology of constructivism was predicated on ultimately nationalist purposes; it reflected the ascendancy of the particularist, nationalist strain over the universalist Socialist strain within mainstream labor Zionist ideology.

As envisaged by Berl Katznelson, the constructivist conception underlying Ahdut Ha-avoda aimed "to shape the life of the Hebrew nation in Eretz Israel as a community of workers (*kehilat ovdim*), living freely and equally on its own labor, in possession of its own resources and controlling its own labor, economy and culture."[82] Whereas for members of the Poalei Zion party this constructivist formula marked a distinctive if incremental ideological divorce from earlier conceptions, Berl Katznelson came to it with natural ease. He had never been enamored of Borochov's Marxism; Syrkin's approach was much closer to his heart. Although he certainly regarded himself as a Socialist, he perceived the working class as a vehicle for social progress and cultural creativity rather than as an instrument for gaining political power. Unlike Yitzhak Tabenkin (also a nonparty man of the Second *Aliya*, although in Russia he had belonged to Poalei Zion) or David Ben-Gurion, with whom he worked closely in a spirit of mutual respect, Berl Katznelson never fell under the spell of Lenin's image as the prototype of the totally dedicated, iron-willed revolutionary leader, the tactical genius who never lost sight of the strategic end goal. His deep-seated humanism led him to deplore the Soviet authoritarian model of socialism. A system that suppressed all individuality could not qualify as true socialism. Indeed, he was acutely sensitive to the danger that, exposed to misguided adulation of the Russian Revolution, idealistic Jewish youth, whether in the Diaspora or in Israel, might be drawn into Socialist universalism. He worked as indefatigably to counter this danger as he did for the unity of all Jewish labor.

Berl Katznelson's unique status and influence as ideological mentor of mainstream labor Zionism rested at least as much on intangibles such as his engaging personality, his communicativeness to youth, and his eloquent articulation of profound humanistic reflections as they did on the official positions he occupied. The latter included his founding editorship of the Histadrut's daily newspaper, *Davar*, and Am Oved, its publishing house. His articulations of constructivism were always informed by a profound humanism and sensitivity to tradition. They embraced the social program of labor Zionism but also went beyond it into the sphere of culture and secular identity, as we shall have cause to note in a later chapter devoted to that aspect. Typical of his expressions was the following:

Primitive revolutionism that believes in total destruction as the panacea for all society's evils reminds one in some ways of a child who attempts to discover how his toys work by breaking them. Against this primitive revolutionism our movement, by its very nature, offers constructive revolutionism. It too does not acquiesce at all in the defects of the existing world; it perceives the need for profound revolution. But, knowing how limited is the creative potential of destruction, it directs its efforts towards construction which alone ensures the value of revolution.[83]

As we have noted, the founders of Ahdut Ha-avoda failed to achieve its original objectives. Within a year, Berl Katznelson too had to settle for a compromise: the creation of the Histadrut (General Federation of Hebrew Workers in Eretz Israel).[84] This federation of workers' trade unions and parties, while even more broadly based than Ahdut Ha-avoda and taking over all its intended trade union functions and "workers community" tasks, did not eliminate party differences. Berl even came round to agreeing that Ahdut Ha-avoda should perform to all intents and purposes as a political party within the new framework. Henceforward, he, like Ben-Gurion, poured all his efforts into promotion of the Histadrut as the embodiment of the constructive Socialist approach.

As founded in December 1920, the Histadrut was composed of trade union associations as well as cooperative associations. But its structure was that of a general trade union based on direct individual membership rather than a federation of trade unions with block memberships. Each individual member, upon joining the Histadrut, was assigned to a particular occupational union. Membership was open to all Jewish workers who did not "exploit" the labor of others. This provided a broad definition of the term "worker," which included for example, professionals, a large teachers' union, and a clerical workers' union. But it developed into something much more than a federation of trade unions. It created labor exchanges and undertook activities in land settlement, work contracts, vocational training, and cooperative marketing. It also created medical services and was involved in defense and in the reception of immigrants as well as in the promotion of *halutz* (pioneer) immigration by the dispatch of emissaries to the Diaspora. In due course, it also created a workers' bank and a vast network of economic enterprises. Politically, it functioned as a democratic parliamentary system, the various political parties that participated in it competing for governance within the Histadrut. In its formative first decade, the Ahdut Ha-avoda party succeeded in dominating the Histadrut, with David Ben-Gurion, officially one of three joint general secretaries, effectively its dominant executive officer.

Under Ben-Gurion's stewardship the Histadrut constituted itself also as a *hevrat ovdim* (alternatively translatable as a workers' commonwealth or company) whose shareholders were coextensive with the Histadrut's membership. In principle, the *hevrat ovdim* controlled all economic activities of the Histadrut, whether conducted by small independent groups of cooperatives or by direct contracting agencies. The Histadrut was thus simultaneously a general trade union, a central wholesaler, and a vast holding company. But the secret of its phenomenal growth (within two decades it had become the largest employer and creator of employment in the Jewish sector of Palestine) lay in the fact that in the final analysis its ideological inspiration remained not socialism as an end in itself but an attempted synthesis of Socialist values with the essentially nationalist aims of Zionism. In praxis this translated into the principle that all profits of the Histadrut (as a "workers' company") were automatically committed for reinvestment. Hence, the fact that every individual member of the Histadrut was a shareholder in its manifold enterprises was theoretical because the members could not consume its dividends. On the other hand, phenomenal economic growth was facilitated. Another secret of the Histadrut's growth lay in membership of its Kupat Holim (sick fund or health system) being obligatory for all Histadrut members; conversely, access to the invaluable services of the sick fund was conditional upon membership of the Histadrut.

In sum, the Histadrut was a unique workers' institution enjoying comprehensiveness and influence unequaled by that of comparable institutions in any other contemporary industrial society of the non-Communist world. By 1932 it encompassed a membership of over thirty thousand, constituting some 75 percent of the organized workers in the country, a level sustained consistently thereafter well into the period of Jewish statehood. This gave it a preponderant influence over the labor market. David Ben-Gurion, who, as we have noted, was undoubtedly the key personality in directing the affairs and development of the Histadrut as an essentially national constructive institution, once rhetorically idealized its unique character as follows:

The Histadrut is not a trade union, not a political party, not a cooperative society, nor is it a mutual aid association, although it does engage in trade union activity, in politics, cooperative organization and mutual aid. But it is much more than that. The Histadrut is a covenant of builders of a homeland, founders of a state, renewers of a nation, builders of an economy, creators of culture, reformers of a society. And this covenant is based not on a membership card, not on legislation, but on a common fate and destiny—a commonality for life until death.[85]

From Class to Nation: David Ben-Gurion

It may be said without fear of any scholarly contradiction that in the final analysis Ben-Gurion's socialism was subordinate to his nationalism. But this is not to say that his socialism was insincere or no more than a thin veneer.[86] At least one important aspect of the Socialist world outlook that was deeply ingrained in him was the unshakable conviction that the destiny of human society lay with the working class. Indeed, there was a period of his life—in the early 1920s—when he evinced considerable admiration for Lenin's model of revolutionary working-class leadership and the radical transformation of Russian society that it had effected. To be sure, it was not the practice of dictatorship (so-called of the proletariat) that captivated his imagination but only Lenin's exemplification of what utterly single-minded, yet tactically flexible pursuit of an ideal could attain. But only the thinnest of lines separates such admiration of means from approbation of its related ends. Ben-Gurion's attribution of moral primacy to a class category of humanity rather than to the individual meant that he was far from being a thoroughly liberal democrat. Because of his teleological view of history, according to which the working class carried the social process forward toward an ideal messianic-like end, he did not recoil in principle from the notion that an avant-garde political elite, which "knew" what was best for all, might have to coerce the majority of individuals composing society.[87]

Yet even while the new Soviet society still exerted a magnetic attractiveness, Ben-Gurion explicitly upheld the primacy of national objectives. In the same breath as he is on record as having told the 1924 conference of his Ahdut Ha-avoda party: "We may regard as important the moral strength inhering in communism, in the dictatorship of the idea that subjects all life to it," he also unequivocally declared: "We must ask ourselves: What are we doing in Eretz Israel—is our main aim to realize here communism or socialism? I would answer: No. We came to this land to realize one particular thing . . . Zionism, the upbuilding of The Land [of Israel] for the purpose of building a new nation."[88] Equally indicative of his ideological conception, in the same speech he then proceeded to reiterate his fundamental conviction that the crucial question regarding the work of building was not what forms of workers' settlements were preferable—whether the kibbutz commune was preferable to the *moshav* cooperative form was the immediate question that had occasioned Ben-Gurion's statement—but to whose authority would all workers' enterprises of whatever kind be subject. The crucial principle was "working-class rule over all workers' economic enterprises."

Of course, for Ben-Gurion, as for all Socialist Zionists, whether following the seminal guidelines of Syrkin or of Borochov, the precondition for the Jew taking his rightful place in the Socialist future of mankind was the reacquisition of his territorial homeland. Only there could Jews create a working class that would fulfill its role, alongside the destined role of the working class everywhere, in determining the ideal future of mankind. Although he was a member of Poalei Zion in Palestine, he never quite adhered to the Borochovist theory embodied in its initial program. He was among the first to veer toward the kind of from-the-ground-upward Socialist program that Syrkin had originally proposed. "The question was not whether Eretz Israel after it was built up, would adopt a Socialist regime," submitted Ben-Gurion in a typical statement, "but rather— what are the social foundations upon which the country would be built? The difference of opinion [in Zionism] was not only over the final goal, but also over the way to the goal."[89] Its construction from the base upward had to be on the basis of Jewish labor, not the labor of Arabs, and the society in genesis had to bear the indelible social imprint of the Jewish working class.

In this, as in most respects, Ben-Gurion echoed and elaborated ideological positions common to all mainstream Socialist Zionists. After all, his greatness in the pantheon of Zionist history lay more in the sphere of innovative political praxis than in that of seminal thought. His emphatic articulation of the proposition that there was a complete identity between the development of the working class and the genesis of the nation reflected the official ideological goals of the Ahdut Ha-avoda party as formulated at its founding in 1919: "To shape the life of the Hebrew nation in Eretz Israel as a community of workers, free and equal, that lives by its own toil, controls its possessions and organizes its labor, its economy and its culture as it sees fit."[90] No one was more responsible for translating this proposition into practice in the political and institutional life of the Jewish sector in Palestine than was Ben-Gurion. In the process he mediated in great part the transition to constructive socialism.

In innumerable speeches, articles, and other statements, Ben-Gurion enunciated the identity of worker interests and national interests and expounded the conception of the re-created Hebrew nation in Eretz Israel as a virtually exclusive "working-class nation." "The worker has never experienced any contradiction between his class needs and desires and his national interests and aspirations," he averred in a typical statement. "The worker who recognizes his class-mission and is faithful to his historical destiny fulfills at one and the same time two missions that are in effect one: the mission of class and the mission of the nation as a whole." By contrast, he argued, "it is the objective fate of all the other classes that their class interests must, sooner or later, clash explicitly or implicitly, with the needs of the nation and of *aliya*." This was not a matter of bad intention, he explained. It was simply "a function of the inner logic and nature of private capital that it should seek profits and exploitation," and thereby default on the national cause.[91]

This ideological conflation of class (i.e., working class) and nation was the premise underlying the slogan *mi-ma'amad le-am* (from class to nation) that Ben-Gurion was avidly expounding by the early 1930s. It provided the rationale for the hegemony of the working class over the nation and for deployment of the national capital raised by the Zionist Organization to fuel the burgeoning settlements, cooperatives, and industrial enterprises encompassed by the *hevrat ovdim* of the Histadrut.

As long as these constructive economic initiatives enjoyed the recognition and support of the Zionist Organization, Labor Zionists felt no compelling need to oust its mainly middle-class general Zionist leadership. But the great influx of predominantly lower-middle-class immigrants from Poland in the mid-1920s, known as the Fourth *Aliya*, precipitated a grave challenge to labor's claims on national capital. Jabotinsky's Revisionist Zionists and elements of the civic sector in Palestine and of the General Zionists (B group) vociferously decried the preferential treatment accorded the labor economy and called for a shift of priorities toward private enterprise. This acutely exacerbated political conflict in the Jewish sector of Palestine, and Ben-Gurion sharpened the thrust of his claim that only the working class exhibited complete identity with national needs and goals. Ben-Gurion's slogan "from class to nation" acquired another dimension—the drive toward assumption of the directorship of the Zionist Organization.

The economic collapse that came in the wake of the Fourth *Aliya*, reaching its peak in 1925–1926, was grist for the mill of the arguments wielded by Ben-Gurion and his Labor Zionist associates. "The crisis in The Land and in Zionism," he contended, "has revealed with tragic clarity that there can be no separating labor in The Land from the national movement; the fate of the project and the fate of the movement go hand in hand." He drew the conclusion that "it was the obligation of the Hebrew worker to renew and to heal the Zionist movement just as it had renewed and healed the settlement project in The Land; it was his duty to conquer for himself a guiding and leading position in Zionism just as he had done in the *yishuv*." He exhorted the council of the Histadrut in January 1929 not to follow "the path of isolation from the nation, but to take up a position at its head." He called for a transition "from working class to working nation." "That is the national destiny of the working class," he declared.[92]

One could not, however, make a bid for governance of the Zionist Organization without recognizing its plural class and political composition. The former near total ideological conflation of nation and working class had to give way to a more realistic, less monolithic ideological formulation. The outcome might be described as a dialectical synthesis between the Borochovist separation of roles—middle-class capital infusion into Palestine on the one side, working-class preparation for class war on the other side—and the constructivist imagining of the evolution of an exclusively working-class nation. Now there was a certain recooptation of the middle class into the constructive process as a whole. The vision of creating a unique, exclusively working-class nation from start to finish was broadened to include the contribution of an active middle class. By 1932, Ben-Gurion was declaring:

Truth to tell, the workers do not deny that private enterprise can be a factor in Zionism. . . . The workers have always welcomed that private capital which created work opportunities for *olim* and expanded the absorptive capacity of The Land, and they will always welcome any capital that will build settlements and factories with Hebrew labor. Eretz Israel must serve as a refuge for all sectors and classes of the nation, capitalists as much as those without means. Zionism has to save not only the body and soul, but also Jewish property from the dwindling of resources and destruction that await it in the *gola*.[93]

This implied far greater interclass cooperation in working toward a common nationalist goal of Jewish statehood. But it also made it urgent for the working class to take over the reins of leadership in the Zionist Organization worldwide. By 1935 such labor hegemony had virtually been accomplished. In the elections to the Zionist congress of that year, the labor faction, since 1932 united as never before in the World Union of Poalei Zion–Hitahdut, got 48.8 percent of the vote. In that year too, Ben-Gurion, since 1933 a member of the Zionist Organization–Jewish Agency executive, was elected chairman of that body. Although Chaim Weizmann was reelected as president, his position depended on the labor bloc, and thenceforward Ben-Gurion was to become the most powerful political figure.

Non-Socialist Labor Zionism

The veering of Socialist Zionism in Palestine toward constructivism was greatly reinforced when Ahdut Ha-avoda amalgamated in 1930 with the far less class-conscious segment of labor Zionism known as Ha-poel Ha-tzair. Together they now formed Mapai, which became the dominant mainstream of labor Zionism, first in Palestine and, after 1935, also in the Zionist Organization as a whole. Here it is necessary to backtrack somewhat in our narrative. Ha-poel Ha-tzair had been formed in late 1905 by a founding group of some ninety mostly agricultural workers and some intelligentsia-type educators and writers. Some had belonged to the youth groups known as Tzeirei Zion (Youth of Zion) that mushroomed in eastern Europe. These groups were an outgrowth of general Zionism, but their distinctiveness in that context derived from their members being youths (mostly the sons of lower-middle-class families) who were more activist than their seniors in the Zionist Organization and expressed this particularly in the emphasis they placed on personally transforming their own lives by choosing to live in Palestine as workers. Within the milieu of the radical movements to which such youths were exposed in eastern Europe, their distinctiveness lay in rejection of the ideology of the Socialist Bund, as well as of all territorialist tendencies within Socialist Zionism, and also in their reservations concerning the highly class-oriented ideology of Poalei Zion.

The various Tzeirei Zion groups were, in the main, an amorphous entity from the ideological point of view. However, in the wake of the First World War years and the Russian Revolution certain political-ideological trends developed. One was influenced by Russian populist, social-revolutionary ideas. Another was a liberal-democratic trend that rejected the Socialist label, whether populist or Marxist. The adherents of this trend in Russia were known as the *Trudoviki* (toilers). During the 1920s, splits developed between various factions. In March 1920, at a conference in Prague, the mainstream of Tzeirei Zion joined with Ha-poel Ha-tzair of Palestine to form a "world union," that is, a worldwide political party within the Zionist Organization. Known as the Hitahdut, the short form of Hitadut Ha-poel Ha-tzair-Tzeirei Zion (Union of Ha-poel Ha-tzair and Tzeirei Zion), it accorded Jewish national goals primacy over any considerations of international working-class solidarity.[94]

The diasporic Tzeirei Zion component of the Hitahdut world movement, although never unequivocally identifying itself as a Socialist entity, tended ideologically more toward Socialist alignment than did its Palestinian component, Ha-poel Ha-tzair. The founders of Ha-poel Ha-tzair decidedly did not wish to be identified as Socialists. They regarded themselves as a vanguard of workers dedicated purely to the national upbuilding of Eretz Israel in a spirit of social justice and equality. To be sure, initially (until about 1910), like Poalei Zion members, their immediate goal was to become wage laborers in the twenty or so Jewish settlements that had already been established in Palestine. But, unlike Poalei Zion members, they had little enthusiasm for Socialist slogans calling for class consciousness, class war, and international proletarian solidarity. The early draft programs of Ha-poel Ha-tzair's founders characteristically avoided any mention of socialism. Its task was defined as "action for the fulfillment of Zionism in general, and concern for the conquest of labor by Jews." It spoke merely of "protecting the interests of Jewish workers, expanding their numbers and improving their economic and spiritual condition."[95]

To the Zionist congress of 1907 Ha-poel Ha-tzair presented a manifesto that included criticism of the well-to-do armchair Zionists who failed to make substantial financial contributions for practical work in Palestine. "Only persons utterly dedicated to our idea with all their hearts and strength should stand at the head of our movement," it demanded. It called on the congress to "recognize that labor in Eretz Israel has no value if it is not performed by Hebrew workers."[96] In another platform, drafted in spring 1908, the attitude toward socialism is left to the individual member on the grounds that "socialism will not have any material bearing on Zionism until the Jewish people will have created a national economic basis in Eretz Israel."[97] Joseph Aharonowitz, one of Ha-poel Ha-tzair's foremost leaders, reflected these ideological emphases when he stated that Ha-poel Ha-tzair aimed "to create in Eretz Israel a Hebrew population healthy in body and spirit, capable of serving as a center for national and human creativity for the entire Hebrew nation dispersed throughout the Diaspora." He stipulated its basic principles as "a Jewish majority, a foundation of healthy economical labor, moral education on national foundations—upright workers who do not live by the exploitation of others' labor and who bear high the flag of the prophets of justice and equality."[98]

However, as it became evident that this goal, designated the "conquest of labor," was being frustrated by the veteran Jewish settlers' practice of employing Arab labor, Ha-poel Ha-tzair began to adopt the idea of forming groups that would be given access by the Zionist Organization to publicly owned land on which to establish independent rural settlements. In these the principles of self-labor would be maintained. In practice, therefore, the direction taken by Ha-poel Ha-tzair was converging with that taken by the members of its rival, Poalei Zion. However, Ha-poel Ha-tzair refused to merge with the avowedly Socialist Ahdut Ha-avoda party formed by Poalei Zion and nonparty workers in 1919. It was repulsed by the militant Socialist phraseology to which it considered the members of Ahdut Ha-avoda to be addicted. Not class retrenchment but pioneering self-labor was its purpose, creating Jewish settlements that would serve organically as embryonic cells of the future Jewish society.

Ha-poel Ha-tzair persisted well into the 1920s with this adamant rejection of all class-centered proletarian slogans. It regarded class struggle as an unwarranted disruption of the national effort to regenerate a healthy working population of Jews in Palestine and deprecated Poalei Zion's adoption of Socialist phraseology as a form of assimilation unworthy of the Jewish national renaissance. Ha-poel Ha-tzair also insisted on the Hebrew language as the sole national medium, whereas some diasporic constituents of the World Confederation of Poalei Zion advocated the use of the Yiddish language. As Eliezer Shohat, one of its preeminent leaders, explained, Ha-poel Ha-tzair certainly did not identify with those who opposed socialism in the sense of social justice and equality. But it simply had no need for the Socialist label and certainly opposed those Jews whose socialism did not stem from the actual conditions of Jewish life, for that was no more than imitation and self-negation. A programmatic statement proposed by him stated that "the subject of Ha-poel Ha-tzair's idea was the entire nation and not one class of the nation" and "the national idea is an end in itself and not a means to another aim." It insisted that only by self-example would this end be attained. Ha-poel Ha-tzair's concern was primarily labor, not "the worker and the workers of the world," and it did not believe that class war could do any good for the regeneration of society. At most it was merely an instrument to be used with reluctance, not something fomented and used with joy, "as some other parties were wont to do."[99] In the same vein, the decisions of the annual conference of Ha-poel Ha-tzair in 1919–1920 defined its aims as follows:

1. The upbuilding of Eretz Israel on the foundations of self-labor and national ownership of land;
2. The establishment of Jewish society in Eretz Israel on foundations of social justice (*tzedek*) and equality in the economic, cultural and political senses;
3. The Hebrew language as the absolute foundation of our lives and our national culture, both in Eretz Israel and in the Diaspora;
4. The preparation of the nation in the Diaspora and its Hebrew-language education towards labor and ascent to Eretz Israel.[100]

The worker-intellectual who articulated and epitomized the ideology of Ha-poel Ha-tzair at its most refined was Aharon David Gordon (1856–1922). He summed up its essence in a letter to Ahad Ha'am in late 1911 that he drafted in the name of a group of workers to which he himself belonged at Ein Ganim near the farming village of Petah Tikva: "Our aspiration is to prepare a path in the movement for our people's regeneration, so that in place of its being by force of circumstance a parasitic people, it may again become a working people, living on its own labor. . . . Or, in one word, our striving is toward labor."[101]

The Legacy of A. D. Gordon

The especially captivating feature of Aharon David Gordon's life as a Zionist was the fact that at age forty-eight he settled in Eretz Israel to become a worker alongside the young settlers of the Second *Aliya*. Born in Podolia, in the Ukraine, into a traditionalist family, he grew up in a rural village environment on an estate that was managed by his father. He in turn took up the same rural but essentially white-collar vocation and continued in it for twenty-three years, during which time he identified, but in obscurity, with the Hibbat Zion movement. In 1904 he settled in Eretz Israel, initially working as a plain day laborer at the settlement of Petah Tikva, thereafter in the Galilee and finally in the first *kvutza* commune, Degania, where he died in 1922.

Although not formally a leader, nor even consistently a member, of Ha-poel Ha-tzair, Gordon carried great moral authority with that party's followers. Moreover, by virtue of his personal life as well as his writings he exemplified the Ha-poel Ha-tzair school of thought in labor Zionism. Intellectually, Gordon came close to cogitating a complete philosophy of life, but its profounder levels probably escaped the attention of most of his contemporaries.[102] Our concern here is more with the popularly perceived import of his ideas as they both reflected and affected Ha-poel Ha-tzair and in due course infused much of the ideology of the various Zionist youth movements that emerged in Europe, especially the youth movement aligned with Ha-poel Ha-tzair and named after him, Gordonia.

The Archimedes point of Gordon's thought was the individual as a social being. His premises were largely intuitive or postrational in the sense that, although recognizing the role of "intellectual consciousness" (*hakara*) he considered it insufficient for man's creative self-fulfillment. The experiential dimension (*havaya*) of man's life was vital. "Intellectual knowledge," he wrote, "is only part of immediate experience or the visible manifestation of the hidden light of immediate experience—the real basis of all human perception. . . . Take away immediate experience and nothing is left."[103] As both an emanation of cosmic nature and a social being, man could fulfill himself optimally only through the potential for "expansion of self" which countermanded the tendency to "contraction of self." "In the actual life of man one can observe these two fundamental aspects of life, expansion and contraction, as acting and activating forces. . . . On the one hand, a tendency to a life of pleasure, the satisfaction of desires . . . to inane selfishness that knows only oneself. On the other side, an unseen opposing tendency, a hidden longing for the spiritual life above pleasures."[104] The tension between these two tendencies within man was to be found in all dimensions of life, in esthetics no less than ethics. In terms of moral principle, Gordon contrasted his concept of "expansiveness" with the egoism accounted for by rational utilitarian philosophy as well as with the converse Christian emphasis on altruism.

Although Gordon's thought was diametrically opposite to Marxism in any form, there was one commonality of importance—he too condemned capitalist society's turning of man's labor into a commodity to be exploited and sold. This was, in his eyes, the deepest wound that could be inflicted on the dignity and self-worth of man. But his conception was not in any sense materialist. It substituted Marxist identification of the economic processes of production as the basis of all social relations with the proposition that labor in the sense of man's "cooperation in creativity" was the basis. For Gordon, labor was not only a rational value for the individual's expansion of self and his social relations; it was the key to a cosmic religious experience that bonds man to nature. Whereas all socialist prescriptions for man led, in Gordon's view, to *mechanistic* social organization—impersonal, manipulative, exploitative, and detached from nature—*his* prescriptions were for *organic* social units rooted in nature. The family was the basic organic social unit, and the nation was but an elaborate extension of the family. National individuality was the product of what he termed a "cosmic" relationship between the nation and its original territorial environment. "In nationalism," he wrote, "there is a cosmic moment, a moment when you may say that the spirit of the physical nature of a people's homeland becomes fused with the spirit of the people." Moreover, he added, the same cosmic element imprinted the national individuality on the "personal 'I' in each one of us," that is to say, on each and every individual member of the nation.[105] In this sense Gordon was a thoroughgoing nationalist. For all his emphasis on the individual being, he also held that man virtually had no meaningful existence except through participation in the life of the nation. "Where there is no 'nation man' relation, there is no 'man,' no individual man," he wrote: "The nation may be likened to a funnel; at its wide receiving end infinite existence is poured in, while through its concentrated restricted end the funnel empties its contents into the soul of man. The nation, therefore, is the force which creates the spirit of man. It is the link which unites the life of the individual to the life of mankind and to the world at large."[106]

There could hardly be a description of the relationship between the individual and the nation that better illustrates what Hans Kohn has called nationalism as a "state of mind." In Gordon's outlook humanistic nationalism was as organic a manifestation of the natural order of man as was the family. It stood in contrast with unnatural, mechanistic frameworks such as state institutions and political parties, not excluding those that advocated socialism. Hence, the society advocated by Marxist Socialists was no less mechanistic in the final analysis than was capitalist society.

Gordon was in favor of all things organic. What was organic was in nature. Individually and nationally "man should return to his source, to nature, on condition that he be neither a slave nor a master of nature but a trustworthy companion to nature in life and a trustworthy partner in creation."[107] No doubt there was in this much Rousseau-like romanticization of nature and a strong strain of reaction to urbanized industrial society. For example, Gordon bemoaned the "gross sensuality" that was replacing love: "There is no longer altruistic love, no longer faith, or idealism, or justice or truth."[108] But it would not quite be accurate to describe him as an antimodernist, since he explicitly averred that a return to nature did not imply a turning back of the clock: "It seems to me that no such demand has been or will be made. This is absurd. Man cannot turn back or yield up what he has conquered or acquired. . . . Man seeks to grow, to progress, to strike out on new paths; these paths however, must not stretch backward but forward."[109] What he sought was a highly qualified pattern of progress such as would temper human alienation and preserve man's communion with nature. In sum, the prescriptive message of Gordon's world outlook was that without withdrawing into the past, man must re-create the conditions for a creative life of individual self-expansion. He could accomplish this only through the experimental dimension that derives from labor close to nature in organic social units.

It should be stressed that notwithstanding the confluence in practice between most of Gordon's operative prescriptions and the constructivist program adopted by mainstream Socialist-Zionists, he himself explicitly and adamantly repudiated the idea of being a Socialist. "I am as far from Socialist ideas in the form they have assumed in our time as Judaism is far from materialism, and I am as far from party warfare in its proletarian sense, as the spirit of Israel is from envy and hatred,"[110] he once wrote. When Socialist ideas were wrongly attributed to him, he was at pains to deny this. He insisted that he was speaking "in the name of nationalism, free from socialism in any form." "What we have before us is not nationalism and socialism—it is nationalism that comprehends everything," he wrote, explaining: "Social justice [tzedek] in all its shapes and forms, as between man and his fellow-man and between nation and nation, we demand not in the name of socialism but in the name of nationalism."[111]

Within the context of this world outlook, the basics of Gordon's diagnosis of the Jewish problem—that which Zionism was to resolve—had more in common with Ahad Ha'am's school of thought than Herzl's. By the same token they diverged significantly from the emphases not only of Borochovism but even of Syrkin and the constructive Socialist school of thought. His nationalism was patently of the organic integral kind, not the covenantal civic kind, and his diagnosis of the Jewish problem rested less on the material distress of the Jews than on the deterioration of Jewish cultural individuality under diasporic conditions. Unlike Herzl, A. D. Gordon was not of the opinion that Jewish assimilation was structurally impossible. Nor had he ever entertained the notion that, were it possible to assimilate, this might be the answer for the Jewish problem. "To say that we cannot assimilate is sheer sophistry," he wrote, and he rejected the idea that "idle negation, an inability to die is the foundation for the existence of the nation." After all, religion was no barrier since in modern times one may live without religion, he argued. His answer to the question, why not assimilate, was not dissimilar to that of Ahad Ha'am's idea of a "will to life." He too postulated that there was something within the Jew "which fights for his individual existence." "What then is this peculiar stubborn something which one cannot put a finger on, that does not want to die and does not let us die?" he asked, and answered: "It is our national individuality—that cosmic moment together with the historic moment . . . which is one of the fundamental principles of the personal 'I' in each one of us."[112]

But Gordon differed from Ahad Ha'am in that his diagnosis of the Jewish problem focused, in the first instance, not macrocosmically on the problem of the collective attributes of Jewish culture such as language, literature, and the absorption of modern intellectual enlightenment but microcosmically on the individual personality of the Jew. He never tired of reiterating that "the revival of our collectivity will certainly not be possible except through the revival of the individual."[113] The crux of the collective problem of the Jews, as understood by Gordon, was that the loss of the Jewish homeland had deprived them of what he called "the cosmic moment" in their national life.

The cosmic moment in national independence is not ours in the diaspora; that we must seek in Eretz Israel. In the diaspora the historic moment operates within us; it upholds us and prevents our dying, but it is unable to give us life. There in the diaspora we have, of necessity, no national or creative life. From a creative standpoint we are parasites physically, and perhaps, to a greater degree, spiritually. There our national individuality naturally is restricted, has shrunk, is all but destroyed.[114]

The long years of Diaspora had deprived the Jew of the quality of labor linked to nature. "We lack the fundamental elements; we lack labor, labor by which a people becomes rooted in its soil and in its culture," he wrote, adding:

To be sure, not every individual among other peoples exists by labor. Many among such peoples despise labor and search for a way of life that can maintain itself on the labor of others. But the majority of a living people works in normal fashion; work is ingrained in their lives, and so it is carried on as an organic function. A living people always possesses a great majority to whom labor is its second nature. Not so among us. We despise labor. Even among our workers there are those who work because of necessity and with the continual hope of someday escaping from it. . . . We must realize how abnormal we are in this respect, how alien labor has become to our spirit and not alone to the individual life, but also to the life of the nation.[115]

The vision that A. D. Gordon conjured up for Zionism was not maximalist in the sense of implying the return of all Jews in the world to Eretz Israel. He made allowance for the continuation of Jewish life in the Diaspora and even for the possibility of productivizing it somewhat with more Jewish labor in emulation of the transformation wrought by those who returned to Zion.[116] Moreover, his firm reservations concerning mechanistic social structures led him to repress the goal of sovereign statehood in Zionism. Neither planning for sovereign statehood nor such related projects as the setting up of a Jewish military unit in the British army during the First World War appealed to him. His vision was of a society emerging out of a variety of organically evolving forms of community, such as the *kvutza* commune. In such a society the human alienation resulting from urban industrialization would be averted. "We hope to create a life not only strong enough to overcome city influences but to draw the city under the influence of the village," he wrote. Although he favored certain egalitarian principles upheld also by Socialist parties—notably, public ownership of land—and valued the constructive program of the Histadrut, he urged its directors not merely to create working class institutions and enterprises but to foster a new spirit of labor as a value in itself.

The spirit of the new life, of new creativeness, must penetrate labor and industry. The builder, the carpenter, the tailor, the factory worker . . . must feel that he and the others for whom he is working are bound not alone by an economic tie, but by a spiritual, human bond. Like us, the farmers, he must strive toward the goal wherein the important thing for him must be not the wage he receives for his work, but the work itself—the product of his labor.[117]

The foundation stones being laid in Palestine were, as he saw it, "not merely for an improved system of economic life." "No less important than social justice," he opined, "is a pure, national, human brotherhood, a brotherhood toward all men."[118]

As for the relationship he envisaged between Zion and the Diaspora, here again it was much like Ahad Ha'am's. By virtue of its exemplary social order as well as its embodiment of the Jewish nation's national-cultural heritage, the Jewish society in Zion would serve as the national center of those who lived in the Diaspora. "Our attitude as sons of Eretz Israel toward that part of the nation which remains in the Diaspora is . . . the attitude of those who live in the center to those in the periphery."[119]

Given Gordon's diagnosis of the Jewish problem and his vision for Zion, it followed that no means were more important than Jewish self-labor in the upbuilding of the envisioned society. On this point he was in strong disagreement with Ahad Ha'am, who considered the employment of local Arab labor by

Jewish settlements to be an unavoidable reality. For Gordon there was nothing more repugnant than the idea of a "parasitical" restoration to Zion. "If an individual lives on the labor of others, this is but an ordinary social problem," he explained, "but if a whole nation should come seeking its revival, a nation that pretends to carry the flag of absolute justice . . . and establishes its revival on the basis of parasitism, does one have in the world so terrible a degeneration as this?"[120] Moreover, as we shall show in another chapter of this book, in Gordon's view the very right of the Jews to Eretz Israel was predicated on Jewish self-labor.

Above all, it followed from Gordon's premises and from the personal example he set that the whole process of Zionist regeneration had to begin with the individual Zionist: it demanded of each and every one that he "transform himself so that the *galut* Jew within him becomes a liberated Jew; so that the impaired, shattered, unnatural person within him may become a natural, healthy person true to himself."[121] These expositions calling for individual self-transformation and the primacy of self-labor both reflected and inspired the ideology of Ha-poel Ha-tzair as a whole. They made Gordon the profoundest exponent of this school of thought in labor Zionism, even if he was neither completely understood nor followed in every detail.

At this point a digression is called for in order to point out the affinity between Gordon's ideas and those of another important, if less direct, intellectual influence on labor Zionist ideology—that of the philosopher Martin Buber (1878–1965). Buber was born in Vienna but spent his adolescence in Galicia and studied at universities in Switzerland and Germany. He was one of the student intelligentsia who rallied to Herzl's call for a Zionist congress in 1897. However, from the outset he was much closer to Ahad Ha'am's organic Jewish nationalism and cultural school of thought than to the functional and political mode of Herzl. Together with other members of the student intelligentsia, including the young Chaim Weizmann, he founded the Democratic Faction in 1901 as an opposition group to certain aspects of Herzl's administration of Zionism, a subject to which we shall return in chapter 7 of this work. Buber's contributions to Zionist thought found expression throughout his many lectures and writings and in his editorship of *Der Jude* (1916–1924), the leading intellectual forum of German-speaking Jews. From 1924 to 1933 he taught at the University of Frankfurt and from 1933 to 1938 he directed the Jüdisches Lehrhaus (Jewish Academy) of the community in Frankfurt. In 1938 he settled in Palestine, where he became a professor at the Hebrew University.

Buber's thought had a ubiquitous influence on the Zionism of German-speaking Jews, especially in various student circles and youth movements. Its diagnosis of their postacculturated Jewish condition was encapsulated in his *Drei Reden über das Judentum* (Three talks on Judaism) published in 1911.[122] It offered an intellectual orientation to contend with the schismatic duality experienced by the type of young Jew who, on the one hand, felt alienated from orthodox religion and bourgeois Jewry and, on the other hand, sensed that he was alien to the essentially gentile religious-cultural ambience of the social environment to which he was supposed to be acculturating himself. In a sense Buber provided the young Jew who found himself in a social-psychological situation of suspension, between the Jewish group and the environing gentile society, with a self-affirming alternative to the not uncommon tendency toward Jewish self-hatred. He called on these young Jews to take a leap into positive affirmation (*Bejahung*) of their Jewish cultural heritage, to reintegrate their personal human identity in an avowedly Jewish fashion. Not, to be sure, by returning to the external observances of orthodox religion but to positive Jewish identity informed by the inner sense that he termed "religiosity." (Although Buber's attitude toward Jewish religious observance was highly nonorthodox, his thought was essentially religious). This is where Zionism entered. Self-fulfillment through Zionism was the medium for consummating this new integrity. From these premises there emanated the conviction that one should go up to Eretz Israel, there to participate in the process of Jewish national regeneration, which alone in the conditions of modernity was destined to demonstrate the universal significance of Judaism.

Although Buber's message was so particularly pertinent to the central European intelligentsia and youth movements, its influence also extended to several other Zionist youth movements that mushroomed throughout Europe in the interwar years. His philosophical interpretation of Judaism found its social ethos in the values of the dialogic "I-Thou" relationship between human beings and in community, through which the immediacy of God is experienced by man. However, the impact of his thought on labor Zionism lay not in his philosophical profundity but rather in its operative implications for the kind of regenerated Jewish society that Zionist youth set out to create. In this respect his vision was closely akin to that of A. D. Gordon, from whose example he doubtless drew. Gordon's "Letters from Eretz Israel" were published in Buber's *Der Jude* in 1916, and he made a deep impression at a conference he addressed in Prague in 1920. Of course, Buber's social vision also drew on other intellectual sources, notably the humanistic socialism of his friend Gustav Landauer and the distinctions drawn by Ferdinand Toennies between *Gemeinschaft* (organic community) and *Gesellschaft* (mechanical association). Like A. D. Gordon, Buber found grave fault in all forms of socialism that involved the imposition by state powers of its principles of equality and social justice, however meritorious in themselves. He too envisaged the ultimate product as a composite of community cells, held together by organic bonds of *Gemeinschaft*, as in the *kvutza* commune, rather than as a centralizing society of organizations serving the self-seeking ends of individuals and interest groups and held together, at worst, only by coercive authority or, at best, by negotiated resolutions of conflicting interests.[123] Thus, the social message that Buber's thought conveyed for Zionist youth aspiring to a life of labor in Eretz Israel was complementary to that of A. D. Gordon. To be sure, it was never quite as compelling, since it issued more from speculative thought than from the insider's personal example, as did Gordon's message. Buber's focus on interhuman dialogic relations, after all, lacked the operative clarity of Gordon's focus on "realizing oneself" through a life of labor, close to nature, and in a family-like community.

Gordon's ideas, mythically enhanced by the personal example he set, resonated throughout the various youth movements that came to constitute the most potent ongoing social wellspring of the Zionist movement. One youth movement, above all, modeled itself on his ideological legacy, even naming itself accordingly, Gordonia. Founded in 1922 in Galicia, Poland, it was associated with the Hitahdut World Union. Although never a blind copy of A. D. Gordon's ideas, Gordonia's ideology certainly acknowledged them as its primary inspiration.

The secret of Gordon's (as of Buber's) appeal for the youth movement generation lay in his posing of existential human questions about man in relation to his fellow man, society, and nature,[124] and his answering them optimistically with a life-affirming belief in the ability of man to perfect his society through the refinement of his positive feelings and attributes. Precisely his emphasis on the experiential, rather than the purely cognitive, found an echo in the youth movements. Socially, his appeal lay in his advocacy of the intimate rural worker's commune as the cell of the good society and the panacea for the ills of urban industrial society. As Pinhas Lubianker (later Lavon, 1904–1976), the foremost ideologue of the Gordonia youth movement expressed it in an article written in 1930, Gordonia found inspiration in Gordon's conception of the nation not just as the sum total of impersonal territorial and economic factors but as "a spiritual-cultural-cosmic entity rooted in the primary sources of life and linking man with nature, with the world, with society."[125]

After 1930, the members of Gordonia regarded themselves as the heirs and spiritual guardians of the extinct Ha-poel Ha-tzair party within Mapai. Substantively, the distinctive attribute of Gordonia's ideology was its firm rejection of Marxist historical materialism. Pinhas Lubianker spoke instead of what he termed a "realistic-synthetic" world outlook, which "perceives life . . . as a holistic unity of diverse forces and forms of expression" and "recognizes not only the economic forces of production but, equally, also moral imperatives and human volition."[126] Gordonia's main ideological emphasis was on the idea of personal "self-fulfillment" through becoming a *halutz* (pioneer) worker and participating in the upbuilding of Eretz Israel as a socially just and egalitarian society. It took its cue from Gordon's conceptions of *am-adam*, that is, man's self-fulfillment through the medium of his nation, of labor as the mediator of man's cosmic relation to nature, and of the intimate classless *kvutza* commune as the exemplary unit of society. This meant a distinct preference for the small *kvutza* rather than the large kibbutz that had emanated from the class-conscious ideological tradition of Gedud Ha-avoda.

Gordonia did not, however, adhere completely to A. D. Gordon's rejection of the Socialist label. Thus, for example, a resolution of the second countrywide conference of Gordonia in Poland, September 1929, explained: "The trend of modern socialism to develop in a manifestly national direction, . . . and the liberation of large segments [of the Socialist movement] from the influence of the primitive materialist conception, makes it possible for Gordonia to tie in the aspirations of Gordon . . . with the struggle of the general Socialist move-ment."[127] Nonetheless, Gordonia's identification with international socialism remained more restrained and reserved than that of its earlier established archrival in the youth movement arena, Ha-shomer Ha-tzair, which, as we shall note later in this chapter, underwent a radically leftist transformation in the 1920s. Gordonia rejected out of hand the latter's *étapist* theory, which postulated a two-stage theory of revolutionary socialism—in the first stage, interclass cooperation; in the second, the revolutionary objective of a dictatorship of the proletariat. Gordonia regarded this as "the reduction of Zionism to the level of a merely ancillary matter" and charged that it was reflective of "a Zionist-Communist orientation"; at any rate, one that would not be capable of withstanding the Communist influence, which leads to denial of the value of the nation altogether. Lubianker argued that the Zionist Labor movement did not develop its unique settlement forms in the first instance out of a desire to reform the world. "Even though none of us wishes to deny that this aspiration has a place in our hearts," he said, "first and foremost, ours was an aspiration for conquest of labor and conquest of soil."[128]

Chaim Arlosoroff's "People's Socialism"

Another ideological formulation that buttressed the turn toward Socialist constructivism was contributed by Chaim Arlosoroff (1899–1933). Owing to the tragic circumstance of his murder at the young age of thirty-four, his life might be likened to that of a brilliant comet in the labor Zionist firmament.[129] Born in the Ukraine but growing to maturity in Germany, at the young age of nineteen he produced a profoundly analytical exposition of what he labeled *Der jüdische Volkssozialismus* (translatable as Jewish People's Socialism). Associated politically with a branch of the Ha-poel Ha-tzair party in Germany, Arlosoroff went to Palestine in 1924, where he rapidly became prominent in the labor movement, rising in 1931 to the position of head of the Jewish Agency's political department. In 1933 he was murdered while innocently strolling one evening with his wife on Tel Aviv's sea front. Since some members of the Revisionist right wing of Zionism (whose ideology remains to be discussed in later chapters) were accused of the murder and put on trial—but later acquitted for lack of evidence—this tragic act not only suddenly cut off a brilliant political career but also set off an explosion in the already volatile relationship between the labor movement and the Revisionist Zionists.

Arlosoroff had a sound academic background. Under Werner Sombart's supervision he wrote a doctoral dissertation on Marx's theory of class and class war, in which he formulated a critique of the materialist reductionism that had become the standard Social Democratic Party interpretation of Marxist theory. He argued on the basis of analysis of Marx's earlier and later writing that it oversimplified the master's own more complex understanding and that the resultant doctrinaire oversimplification misled most Social Democrats into grossly underestimating the inherent significance of national-cultural differentiation within the working classes of all societies. Hence, the utter collapse of putative proletarian solidarity and its slogan that "the workers had no homeland" with the outbreak of the First World War. The working classes of the belligerents fell in line with the most aggressive nationalist jingoism.

Applied specifically to the Jewish situation, Arlosoroff's analysis bore the strong imprint of this First World War experience and had much in common with the Revisionist-Socialist critique of canonized Marxist class theory by thinkers such as Eduard Bernstein in Germany. Arlosoroff's Socialist vision and operative prescriptions also show the influence of Peter Kropotkin's social anarchist ideas—his writings include a sympathetic treatment of this Russian thinker—as well as traces of the romantic nationalism prevalent in the early German youth movements. Although embracing the moral social message of A. D. Gordon, Arlosoroff diverged from this mentor's repudiation of socialism and indeed did not entirely conform to Ha-poel Ha-tzair's characteristic reluctance to endorse the label.

Arlosoroff's term *Volkssozialismus* expressed the essence of his particular ideological formulation, which in most respects followed that of Nahman Syrkin and the less rigidly Marxist thinkers associated with Poalei Zion—Kaplansky, for example. The prefix *Volk* here indicated that the path to socialism as well as its ultimately consummated form were properly inseparable from the unique attributes and circumstances of each and every *Volk*, that is, each self-aware ethnic-cultural unit of mankind. Not cosmopolitanism but nationally differentiated socialism was the way and the ideal both ethically and realistically.

Arlosoroff asserted that *Schicksalsgemeinschaft*, meaning the sense of community of fate, counted for workers no less than for the bourgeois class. The worker too "loves his mother tongue . . . he too loves his native land, his native people . . . the sky of his native land, its fields and cities. He too bears within himself his people's culture. His essence and his spiritual life are those of his people."¹³⁰ "We have to go our own distinctive way," he argued, just as did the Russian populists, Narodniks, and social revolutionaries, who held that the Russian case rested on the world of the Russian peasant. In the Jewish case, class divisions were fluid and blurred; hence, the notion of "worker" had to be inclusive. It had to include anyone "who had no property other than his work power." It had to take in not only factory workers but also the far more numerous workers who were to be found in a variety of artisan skills and home industries as well as that preponderance of Jews engaged in commerce and the free professions, as long as they were self-employed.¹³¹

The thrust of Arlosoroff's argument was that socialism had to differentiate itself into a variety of Socialist peoples' movements, distinct from each other in respect of culture, language, orientation, scope, and method. He insisted, moreover, that the Jews, so far from being an exception in respect of whatever Social Democrats chose to recognize as a national entity, were an undeniable case in point. It was an entity, however, characterized by particular anomalies resulting from the national homelessness of the Jews and their consequent lack of an economic substructure of their own.

The unique reality of our diasporic situation creates a decidedly anomalous position and special anomalous conditions for our struggle. An independent economic organism, living and capable of life, does not exist. What exists in respect of a Jewish economy is inextricably dependent upon the economic conditions of the peoples in whose midst we are domiciled. We exist as it were in the interstices of alien rocks, strands woven by default into an alien cloth. Our economic body breathes with artificial lungs.¹³²

Arlosoroff's polemic with cosmopolitan socialism, while not incompatible with that of more Marxist-affirming Labor Zionists like Kaplansky or even Ber Borochov, did not rely purely on a materialist economic analysis of the Jewish problem. It was quite as much an avowedly idealistic recognition that the cultural traditions and social context of the working man's own national unit of mankind provided vital succor for his soul. This alone could counter the alienation experienced by the worker in an increasingly industrialized society. Arlosoroff accordingly conceived of the return to labor and to economic normalization of the Jews as a process that needed to draw upon, and in turn revitalize, cultural attributes such as the common historical memory, the Hebrew language, Jewish symbols, traditions, and festivals. These were recognized as factors of solidarity that cut across class differences, a national solidarity that was both morally defensible and practically necessary because the subservient, oppressed condition experienced by all Jews, irrespective of class, constituted them as what he called metaphorically a wholly "proletarian nation." Their nationalism was consequently a nationalism of hunger and deprivation, one that sought no more than the basic conditions for its material and cultural dignity and well-being.

Our nationalism is the nationalism of starvation . . . the entire nation is proletarian from the national point of view. We have no desire whatsoever for conquests, like that of the European nations who live proudly by their swords. . . . All that we desire is but to assure for ourselves that which would be the natural and sacred duty of any man to defend: our essential selfhood and culture, our existential experience and its future.[133]

Hence, "Jewish socialism had to be distinctly and unambiguously national," averred Arlosoroff, "not only national in the sense of the unity of the Jewish nation consequential upon its history and culture, but also national in the economic sphere."

Vis-à-vis General Zionism, Arlosoroff's thesis paralleled Nahman Syrkin's argument that, both ethically and practically speaking, it would be absurd to try to construct a new Jewish national society on purely bourgeois capitalist lines. Arlosoroff too held up the vision of a Jewish cooperative Socialist common-wealth as a model of possibly worldwide significance. Likewise, Arlosoroff's approach endorsed A. D. Gordon's spiritually uplifting exhortation that Jews return to a life of labor attached to the soil of their natural homeland. "Redemption, depends above all not on numbers and sums, but on the living link between people and land, a link that is created only through conquest of labor," he affirmed. "And as long as we have not acquired this link, as long as we have not seen to it that everything we create in Eretz Israel is the work of our very own hands—the cultural and social regeneration of the nation is no more than a vague gesture and a chimera. . . . As long as labor in Eretz Israel is not Jewish, Eretz Israel too is *galut*."[134]

When, after his settling in Palestine and entry into the leadership ranks of Labor Zionism there, Arlosoroff applied his basic concept of *Volkssozialismus* more specifically to the situation on the spot, his views contributed substantial ideological support for the tendency toward Socialist constructivism; for, more than anyone else, Arlosoroff laid bare the realities of the situation, showing that the class struggle idea was no more than empty rhetoric. As he posited in a speech to Ha-poel Ha-tzair's 1926 conference,[135] the basic aspects of class struggle were manifestly inapplicable in the case of the Jewish settlers in Palestine. In the first place, the political struggle that Socialist parties normally conducted with the objective of snatching power away from the capitalist class was meaningless in a society under British colonial rule and consisting, to boot, of two rival nationalities. Foreign rule subjected the Jewish capitalist to its dictates no less than it did the Jewish worker, thereby linking their fate in a national sense. Furthermore, the vertical confrontation between Arabs and Jews rendered horizontal class solidarity unfeasible. "There are two nations, one of which is a majority and opposes the aspirations of the minority—and this fact certainly blurs any political class war in the country."

A second basic aspect of the class struggle, calling for redistribution of wealth, also was meaningless since the economy was still too rudimentary to produce capitalist wealth in the first instance. While the worker employed in an existing economy might well conduct class war aimed at gaining his participation in the dispensation of produce, the Jewish worker had to concentrate on the task of creating the prerequisite economic infrastructure itself. Arlosoroff made an analytic distinction between class consciousness and the actuality of class. In Marx's terms the problem was how to inject subjective class consciousness into an objective economic reality of class, whereas the opposite situation prevailed in the Jewish labor movement of Palestine: the Jewish workers of Eretz Israel "perceived themselves as a class before they had actually become a class." There was thus "an impossible gap between consciousness and reality."

According to Arlosoroff, yet a third facet of the workers' class struggle was for his dignity, the raising of his status in society and share in its culture. In this respect only was the objective situation of the Jewish worker very advanced, for in Eretz Israel the renewal of national culture was manifestly being accomplished by the workers and their labor institutions more than by any other class. The intelligentsia—thinkers, academics, teachers, writers, musicians, artists—was nearly entirely identified with the labor movement. "The public influence of the worker here reaches heights unequalled in any other country," he wrote. "The organized worker leads the *yishuv* as a whole in respect of its political organization." In sum, the class struggle slogan was void of content; it was not in congruence with reality.

Hence, what was called for was not class war but "constructive socialism." Only the workers themselves were capable of constructing the necessary economic substructure for the society in the making. Arlosoroff argued that even the most advanced capitalist societies recognized that major aspects of the state, such as education, security, public health, and land reclamation, needed state intervention and regulation. A fortiori, this was true in the context of Palestine's rudimentary economy under the British mandatory government. Only the Zionist Organization was capable of undertaking these public sector tasks in spheres such as education and health. Private investment, inherently governed by the profit motive, would never create a national economy.[136]

Yet at the same time, Arlosoroff urged his fellow Ha-poel Ha-tzair members not to recoil from use of the term "socialism." In his above-quoted 1926 speech, he told his listeners that for some time it had been recognized by Socialists that socialism could not be subsumed "by one monolithic model." If anything, socialism in Eretz Israel, he predicted, would probably have to take on a form closer to the Danish model, primarily agricultural in context, rather than to those of Britain and Germany. He said that what really counted was socialism's actual content, and this had always been inherent in Ha-poel Ha-tzair's demand for "a just society, just from the point of view of the working man, a society devoid of exploiters and exploited." He averred that he knew of no other way to attain this except the way of socialism.

As we noted earlier, in 1920 Ha-poel Ha-tzair had refused to conclude a merger with Ahdut Ha-avoda on account of the latter's emphatically class-conscious Socialist doctrine. It settled only for joining the Histadrut, in which it became an inner opposition party attempting to counterbalance the dominating influence of the Ahdut Ha-avoda party. But Chaim Arlosoroff's explicitly Socialist ideological formulations served to draw out elements of Socialist consciousness that had not been entirely absent in Ha-poel Ha-tzair even before his advent. A more diversified and, overall, a more sympathetic outlook on socialism had gained ground within its ranks by the late 1920s. This smoothed the way to the ultimate merger with Ahdut Ha-avoda in 1930 to form Mapai.[137]

The Socialist-Zionist Left

With hindsight the constructivist orientation appears clearly as the dominant mainstream of the labor movement in Zionism. Yet the potency of the more radical Left should not be underestimated if one is to comprehend the ideological dynamics of Socialist Zionism within historical context. The split in the World Confederation of Poalei Zion at its 1920 conference in Vienna did not yet signify a decisive, clear-cut separation of those who held that socialism in Palestine ought to develop on its own constructive national lines from those who clung to the conviction that their task as a Socialist party was to create a working class poised for class war in close international alignment with Soviet Russia. Indeed, the right wing of Poalei Zion was not much less under the spell of the Russian revolutionary experiment than was the left wing. At the Vienna conference it did not oppose the Left's urge to seek acceptance into the Third International (the Comintern, or Communist International) in the first instance out of repugnance for proletarian revolution.[138] The crucial bones of contention lay not there but in the right wing's insistence that allowance be made for unique national differences such as would not preclude association with the Zionist Organization. This desire inclined it toward alignment with those Socialist parties that ultimately formed the Labor and Socialist International. These were parties that sought evolutionary and parliamentary, rather than revolutionary, paths to socialism.

As for the left-wingers of Poalei Zion, in applying for acceptance into the Third International, they averred with avid revolutionary rhetoric that their aim was "nationalization of the means of production and the establishment of the international soviet socialist republic." They endorsed as "the path to its realization . . . the dictatorship of the proletariat in the form of the soviet regime and the struggle of the working class in all countries for the direct conquest of rule over the state." On the other hand, they retained their Zionist affinity inasmuch as they concurrently called not only for "the transfer of the semi-proletarian strata of the Jewish people to productive labor" but also for "the direction of Jewish migration towards Palestine." Yet, notwithstanding all its efforts, the left wing of Poalei Zion failed to gain acceptance to the Comintern, which insisted on "the complete repudiation of the ideology" that posited the concentration of the masses of the Jewish proletariat in Palestine. In the Comintern's view this idea was "counter-revolutionary" and in the final analysis, only "served to strengthen the position of English imperialism in Palestine."[139]

Still recoiling from collaboration with the bourgeoisie, Left Poalei Zion remained outside the Zionist Organization till 1939, when recognition of the need to have a stake in that organization's enhanced control of resources for the development of Palestine, as well as the looming danger of war in Europe, caused it to rejoin. Meanwhile in a manner characteristic of parties of the radical Left in the shadow of Soviet communism, it had undergone periodic doctrinal turbulence and organizational splits. Some splinter groups, notably one in the Soviet Union, abandoned Zionism and joined Communist ranks.

In Palestine a small Left Poalei Zion party crystallized in 1923, but its adherents underwent two splits and reunifications between 1923 and 1946. The sources of dissension were at least as much social as ideological, one wing drawing mainly on immigrants from Poland and the other on those from Russia and also on the local youth of Palestine. The former wing (headed by Nahum Nir, Moshe Aram, and Yaakov Zerubavel) was oriented more to activity among the Jewish proletariat in the Diaspora and favored Yiddish as the language of the Jewish working masses. The latter (headed by Yitzhak Yitzhaki and Ze'ev Abramowitz) favored Hebrew and focused more on activity in Palestine. Still faithful to the Borochovist prognosis, Left Poalei Zion looked forward to largely "stychic" migration of Jews to Palestine and the growth of a capitalist economy there. Both wings held that the goal of a Socialist society in Palestine could not be attained purely by the constructivist approach. They insisted on the need for active class struggle. Moreover, they balked at the mainstream labor Zionist principle that the Jewish sector of the economy employ only Jewish labor, and they espoused the idea of a joint Arab-Jewish worker's union (an idea mooted earlier in the 1920s also within the mainstream but abandoned to all intents and purposes in the 1930s). At the same time Left Poalei Zion upheld the aim of attaining a Jewish majority in Palestine in the belief that the Arab proletariat would ultimately acquiesce to minority status if it were within the framework of a soviet workers' republic. Ascribing Arab opposition to Zionism primarily to the machinations of British imperialism, it opposed mainstream labor's reliance on Britain as the guarantor for Zionist objectives. It anticipated the ending of the mandate through a joint Arab-Jewish workers' anti-imperialist struggle.[140]

In 1946 the small Left Poalei Zion party of Palestine merged with a radical leftist faction that had been germinating within the mainstream emanation of Right Poalei Zion ever since the 1920 schism. To the development of this faction we shall return later in this chapter. It was a convergence that, in turn, led in 1948 to the forming of a new party that styled itself the United Worker's Party (in acronym, Mapam). This party entered the era of Jewish statehood with a markedly pro-Soviet political orientation.

Radicalized Youth: Ha-shomer Ha-tzair

The convergence of radical left Zionist Socialists to form Mapam in 1946 included a highly cohesive kibbutz-centered group known as Ha-kibbutz Ha-artzi shel Ha-shomer Ha-tzair (The Countrywide Kibbutz of the Young Guard). In origin a youth movement, it remained in essence an attempt to perpetuate certain characteristic youth movement values in social and political forms that transcended the youth generation itself. Ha-shomer Ha-tzair was not the first Jewish youth movement to emerge in Europe; it was preceded and paralleled by a similar development in German Jewry, notably the Blau-Weiss (Blue and White) youth movement consolidated in 1912.[141] But in more specifically Zionist context, Ha-shomer Ha-tzair became the classic prototype of the youth movement phenomenon, a phenomenon whose scale and historical importance cannot be overestimated in comprehending the remarkable diffusion and potency of Zionism as a national movement. Ha-shomer Ha-tzair was founded in 1913, on the eve of the First World War, in the Polish province of Galicia, which was then part of the Habsburg Austro-Hungarian Empire. During the war it spread into "Congress" Poland (central Poland), and thereafter it expanded into many other countries of the Diaspora as far afield as the United States and Argentina. The first members of the movement in Galicia started going to Palestine in 1920; they were mostly in the age group eighteen to the early twenties.

The social profile characteristic of Ha-shomer Ha-tzair in Galicia was that of youth from reasonably well-to-do middle-class families who attended secondary schools (mainly Polish-language but some German-language).[142] Although many came from families still rooted in the traditionalist Yiddish-speaking population centers of Jewish Galicia, the parents of others were already of the type that regarded themselves as "Poles of the Mosaic persuasion." By and large, it may therefore be said that the youths who joined Ha-shomer Ha-tzair were young intelligentsia in the making, caught between traditionalist Jewish society on the one side and assimilationist modernity on the other. In their confrontation with the mainly Polish population of Galicia and central Poland they recognized the reality that neither assimilation nor any symbiosis was possible. Experiencing rejection by the majority Polish society in spite of all attempts at linguistic and national identification with it, they were cast back upon their Jewish background and identity. Their belonging to Ha-shomer Ha-tzair reflected their search for an alternative identification, a social and spiritual fellowship that could dispel their sense of uprootedness and alienation.

Initially called Ha-shomer (after the self-defense association of that name formed in 1909 during the Second *Aliya* to guard Jewish settlements), the new name, Ha-shomer Ha-tzair, appears to have been adopted only in 1919, at which time it was estimated that there were in excess of seven thousand members in over a hundred branches throughout Poland and Austria. It had emerged out of a fusion of two earlier youth formations: the first, some scouting and athletic societies following the somewhat paramilitary pattern of the Polish Scouts organization and emphasizing scouting and communion with nature. The second component was some Tzeirei Zion societies comprising mainly secondary school and university students, which had come into existence in Galicia as in other eastern European Jewish communities after about 1903. These societies were already imbued with Jewish nationalist sentiment, and their programs focused on self-education in areas of "enlightened" Jewish knowledge. But the formative period of the new Ha-shomer youth movement was during the war, from 1915 to 1918, when many members were refugees in Vienna; a branch of some one thousand members there became the heart of the movement. In Vienna these youths, while still functioning within a Galician-Polish cultural frame of reference, were exposed to influences emanating from the earlier established German youth movements, gentile as well as Jewish. These included the ideas of Gustav Wyneken, a seminal personality in the German free youth movement. He stressed the exemplary moral values of a specific youth culture perceived as an end in itself rather than merely as a stage toward adulthood, a youth culture and community with a free and independent self-identity rejecting the philistinism of bourgeois culture and society. Another, related influence was that of the Jewish Blau-Weiss youth movement. A particularly potent intellectual influence of German-Jewish provenance was that of Martin Buber, to whose thought members of Ha-shomer Ha-tzair were exposed along with some of the kindred ideas of A. D. Gordon emanating directly from Palestine.

The milieu that prevailed within early Ha-shomer Ha-tzair and was carried across to the first *kvutza* communes established by its graduates in Palestine after 1920 was permeated both with romanticism and with a kind of introspective search for truth and authenticity. They perceived themselves not as a political party but as an *edah* (community), that is, an intimate fellowship of companions. Inspired also by the sense of being an elite, a spiritual and moral vanguard, this combination of attributes made for a remarkably enduring social and ideological cohesiveness.

Yet after exposure to the intensely party-political divisions in Palestine, the Ha-shomer Ha-tzair settlers underwent ideological politicization. The crystallization of their ideological platform by about 1927 is perhaps the example par excellence of the kaleidoscopic ideological configurations exhibited by the Zionist movement in the course of its development. Given the similarity of Ha-shomer Ha-tzair's particular ideological preferences to the postulates already to be found now in one, now in another, of the existing labor Zionist parties, the dogged constancy with which Ha-shomer Ha-tzair preserved its independent existence is remarkable. Indeed, it defies explanation in purely ideological terms. Rather, the cohesiveness of Ha-shomer Ha-tzair is attributable to the powerful bonds of a sectlike group rooted in the indelible common experiences of adolescence in the youth movement.

Thus, Ha-shomer Ha-tzair's members refused to merge into Ha-poel Ha-tzair despite the fact that in the youth movement they had imbibed social values precisely of the type that found expression in the intimate *kvutza* commune and were accommodated ideologically in the non-Socialist Ha-poel Ha-tzair party. Indeed, as we have noted, the ideas of A. D. Gordon and the kindred philosophy of Martin Buber were profoundly formative factors in the early Ha-shomer Ha-tzair youth movement. But Ha-poel Ha-tzair was a product of the pre–Bolshevik revolution intellectual climate and drew particularly on the Narodnik, or social-revolutionary, tradition in Russia, whereas the members of Ha-shomer Ha-tzair grew to maturity in the revolutionary Bolshevik climate. Moreover, the years 1926 and 1927, during which they were deliberating over political orientation, coincided with the labor movement's ideological reaction to a new right-wing assertiveness in the Zionist Organization. This arose in the wake of the mainly middle-class Fourth *Aliya* and the ensuing economic collapse and widespread unemployment in Palestine.[143] We shall explore the nature of this Zionist Right in the next chapter of this book. In the consequently polarized ideological atmosphere of the time, the intellectual leaders of Ha-shomer Ha-tzair, notably, Meir Yaari (who stemmed from Galicia) and Yaakov Hazan (from central Poland), began to formulate an independent political orientation. It metamorphosed the radical but naïvely nonpolitical social utopianism of their youth movement experience into a political radicalism that not only distanced them from Ha-poel Ha-tzair but even placed them to the left of Ahdut Ha-avoda.[144]

All the more unacceptable was the option, after 1930, of joining Mapai, which, by Ha-shomer Ha-tzair's standards, compounded the ideological faults of both of its components. According to Meir Yaari, Mapai lacked "educative power"; it was incapable of "directing the working class by the lights of a world-outlook."[145] On the other hand, Ha-shomer Ha-tzair's commitments, rooted deeply in the youth movement experience, to the *kvutza* commune as the seminal cell of the good society, to Hebrew rather than Yiddish as the national language, and to participation in the Zionist Organization, preempted the option of joining Left Poalei Zion.

The outcome of Ha-shomer Ha-tzair's radical politicization was a unique ideological alchemy of constructive socialism, nationalism, and Marxist rhetoric.

The inherent contradiction was resolved by the device of an *étape* (step) theory positing a two-stage strategy. This was already spelled out in April 1927 at the founding assembly of Ha-shomer Ha-tzair's collective framework, Ha-kibbutz Ha-artzi (The Countrywide Kibbutz): Given the fundamental problem that the dispersed Jewish people was "devoid of a productive and territorial economic basis," it followed that the "national and human experience of the Jewish nation in the Diaspora . . . will find its complete corrective only through the creation of a socialist society in Eretz Israel, which will be realized in two stages: (1) the establishment of a Hebrew national home in Eretz Israel on a productive self-dependent economic basis, (2) the social revolution."[146]

In the first stage, valid until the national home had been consolidated in Palestine, a constructive Socialist program was to be followed. But it had to be vigilantly monitored by the organized labor movement using the kibbutz and the Histadrut as its major instruments. At the same time, it was ideologically imperative to retain a "revolutionary perspective" based on an essentially Marxist understanding of the dialectical-material historical process, modified only by Borochov's correctives in regard to the legitimacy of proletarian nationalism and the special Jewish national need for normalization of the Jewish proletariat in Palestine. This perspective included the legitimacy of revolutionary class struggle leading to a dictatorship of the proletariat, a process that was envisaged as stage 2 in the *étapist* theory. Although affirming its participation in the Zionist Organization, Ha-shomer Ha-tzair, by dint of its "revolutionary perspective," relegated such participation only to the first stage. In its view, "the Zionist Organization will end its task as soon as there has been created an economic, cultural and political basis, self-dependent and no longer in need of national funds deriving from voluntary national efforts." The Zionist Organization was therefore in this sense but a temporary need, not a permanent fixture.

In the course of formulating this ideological amalgam throughout the 1930s and 1940s, its very complexity necessitated that it be imposed on the members of Ha-shomer Ha-tzair with a doctrinaire rigidity that contrasts ironically with the youth movement's original emphasis on the value of individuality. Instead, "ideological collectivism" in its kibbutz units became the treasured value ensuring Ha-shomer Ha-tzair's integrity as an independent political factor. In the application of this ideology to political praxis, advocacy of an ultimately binational, Arab-Jewish society became a major plank in its platform, a subject to which we shall have to return in another chapter of this book.

The Mainstream's Left Wing

It would be oversimplified, if not wholly mistaken, to ascribe the appeal of radically class-conscious, Soviet-oriented ideology solely to the self-defined Left of Socialist Zionism. The fact is that the Soviet Union exerted tremendous magnetism even within the mainstream of the Zionist labor movement. It must be borne in mind that many of its leaders and rank and file had been cradled nearly as much in the Russian revolutionary ambience as in Jewish religion and ethnicism. This remained the predominant reference point for their political culture. At one time or another, leaders like David Ben-Gurion and Yitzhak Tabenkin (1887–1971), for whom nationalist goals ever remained the compelling bottom line, evinced feelings of empathy for the spirit of the Russian Revolution. Their rhetoric, especially that of Tabenkin, was often more attuned to the world of red revolutionary socialism than to that of pink social reformism. Unrequited love for the Soviet Union, albeit less painfully than that experienced by the Left Poalei Zion, was their story too. They too nurtured the hope that the day would dawn when this "tragic misunderstanding" (so they often phrased it) on the part of Soviet communism would be cleared up and their Socialist Zionism would at last be recognized as a legitimate part of the international revolutionary Socialist movement. Yet at the same time, the leaders of mainstream labor Zionism, especially Berl Katznelson, lived in perpetual anxiety lest the flower of Socialist-Zionist youth, frustrated by the obstacles experienced in Palestine, should be enticed—by dint of this very affinity with the Soviet Union—into defection from the Jewish national project, as indeed happened to part of the Gedud Ha-avoda in the late 1920s. Hence, the intensely ambivalent ideological syndrome in relation to Soviet Russia that characterized mainstream labor Zionism.[147]

Phraseology emphasizing the revolutionary role of the working class and implying justification, if not idealization, of Soviet society, effervesced particularly in the segment of Mapai associated with the large kibbutz framework, Ha-kibbutz Ha-meuhad (the United Kibbutz), to which we have referred in an earlier context. Consequently, this leftist tendency also permeated the youth movements fostered by that faction inside and outside Palestine. Ideologically, it centered largely on the personality of Yitzhak Tabenkin of Kibbutz Ein Harod.

Tabenkin was a Second *Aliya* contemporary of David Ben-Gurion. Although born in the Belorussian town of Bobruisk, he grew up in Warsaw, where he first became active in Poalei Zion. He took sides with Ber Borochov against those who turned territorialist but had reservations in regard to Borochov's adoption of rigidly determinist theory. In this respect the more volitional emphases of Naham Syrkin appealed to him from the start. In 1912 he went to Palestine. Once there he preferred, like his relative, Berl Katznelson, not to join either of the two workers' parties but was involved in the earliest agricultural union activities in the Galilee and in the Ha-shomer self-defense organization. However, holding the conviction that all political and trade union functions should be integrated in one united framework, he was one of the founders of the Ahdut Ha-avoda party in 1919 and the Histadrut in 1920. He also associated himself for a time with the radically avant-gardist attempt to create a countrywide, all-purpose commune—the Gedud Ha-avoda. But he was one of those who opted to root themselves in the Gedud's settlement, kibbutz Ein Harod in the Jezreel valley, which became the nucleus of the union of kibbutz communes constituted in 1927 and known as Ha-kibbutz Ha-meuhad.

In ideological terms, Tabenkin belonged to the mainstream of Labor Zionism, alongside Berl Katznelson and David Ben-Gurion, inasmuch as he was first and foremost a nationalist, notwithstanding all of his vaunted Socialist rhetoric. Indeed, that his nationalism was less yielding and more militant than theirs is evident in the fact that he even more adamantly refused to recognize the national dimension of Arab claims on Palestine. He also opposed proposals for a partition solution of the conflict over Palestine, not only in 1937 but even in 1947. Yet he shared the basic assumption that underlay the Socialist-Zionist synthesis once it had entered into its constructive phase, namely, that there was complete congruence between the interests of Jewish nationalism and those of the Jewish working class. Hence, their shared conviction that the fulfillment of Zionism was critically if not entirely dependent on those Jews who would become workers in Palestine and construct a worker-owned economic infrastructure there. However, Tabenkin did not have Ben-Gurion's tactical flexibility in pursuit of their common objective.

A striking example of Tabenkin's divergent phraseological idiosyncrasies was his preference for the term "communism" rather than "socialism." Speaking at the milestone conference of Ahdut Ha-avoda held in May 1924 at Ein Harod, he declared:

The correct name for our movement should be the one applied to the labor movement since the days of Marx and Bakunin: the Communist movement. Accordingly, we might perhaps be called the Zionist-Communist movement, if not for the fact that the great schism in the international labor movement caused communism to acquire a political connotation that is now associated with the Third International.[148]

On closer analysis, it is evident, one might say, that Tabenkin meant communism with a small *c* and that the substantive content of the term "communism" as he used it, related not to the Bolshevik Communist regime and praxis but purely to underlying theoretical principles and to the ultimate social goal. These were, respectively, the abolition of private property and the capitalist form of the state, and the attainment of the ultimate principle (as he put it in the same 1924 speech): "To each according to his ability and talents, for society as a whole; to each according to his needs, from society as a whole." As he explained on another occasion: "I endorse only the scientific-revolutionary Socialist side of Marxism. In regard to the rest, I am as free as Marx himself."[149] This statement reflected his firm opinion that initially Marx's approach was not totally determinist, that in fact he had left considerable room for the volitional factor and that only later interpretations of Marx overrode the voluntaristic element.

The essence of Tabenkin's Socialist conception might perhaps more appropriately be called "communalism" or "communitarianism," for the kibbutz commune model of society was the heart and core of his entire approach. He was the most tenacious guardian of the vision, cultivated in the erstwhile Ahdut Ha-avoda and Gedud Ha-avoda, of a Socialist Jewish society constructed from the base upward, with a centrally directed network of egalitarian communes, urban as well as rural. These would ultimately constitute a purely workers' society—hence, a classless society—embodying the consummation of the Jewish national movement's most elevated aspirations. The founding of the Kibbutz Ha-meuhad in 1927 was intended to provide the vanguard and core of the process, inspiring and guiding the whole constructive program.

Most of Tabenkin's policy differences with Berl Katznelson and David Ben-Gurion stemmed from this "communalist" perspective. Whereas they regarded the Histadrut as a constructive instrument for Jewish national fulfillment, Tabenkin tended to regard it as an instrument for preserving working-class independence of action within the Zionist movement, resisting private enterprise and ultimately also abolishing private property. Tabenkin's interpretation of the slogan "from a class to a people," popularized by Ben-Gurion, was not, as Ben-Gurion understood it, that the representatives of the working class should take over the leadership of the Zionist Organization as a whole. It was rather that the working class should dominate the national enterprise in practice, excluding any bourgeois and capitalist role so that in effect the society being built in Eretz Israel would be an exclusively working-class society—hence, classless in the end result. As he put it on one speech in 1944:

From a class to a people, but not by abolishing class independence, and not even by achieving the supremacy of the working class, but by abolishing classes altogether. . . . From a class to a people, but not a working class which precedes the people but one which is the people. The Histadrut and the party are the people. In Marxist terms the abolition of the classes; in A. D. Gordon's terms: a "working people."[150]

Hence, again in contradiction of Ben-Gurion, Tabenkin objected to anything that smacked of *étatism* and consequently even to any premature jump into statehood as accepting the idea of partition, proposed in 1937 by the British Royal Commission, would have meant. Even as late as 1947 those who had seceded with Tabenkin from Mapai in 1944 to form yet another labor party still rejected partition and instead advocated an international mandate over Palestine to replace the British mandate. Tabenkin consistently argued that Jewish statehood should be regarded only as a final stage after generations of solid construction. In this, his political strategy clashed head-on with that advocated by Ben-Gurion in 1937, namely, accepting even a partitioned ministate in order to proceed from there to the building up of the society. According to Tabenkin, statehood was not a prerequisite of the construction process but vice versa.

Apart from such specific differences of policy, the sympathetic orientation of Tabenkin's following toward the Soviet Union was a chronically volatile issue within Mapai, since, as we have mentioned, the danger of defection from Zionism hung like a pall over it. To be sure, Tabenkin was far from being uncritical of the Soviet regime. His ideological cogitations were never systematic, and contradictions abounded. For all his revolutionary rhetoric, he disapproved of the use of political power to attain socialism and to impose it coercively from above in a centralized political system. This method ran counter to the most fundamental aspect of his own conception, namely, that the Socialist ideal proper could be fulfilled only by construction of the system from below, in a manner that would virtually render state power redundant. This was what he believed Ahdut Ha-avoda had set out to do in Palestine. Yet he was inclined to make some indulgent allowance for the different circumstances that had existed in Russia and led to the Bolshevik way. At times he even found it possible to positively compare the similarities in the soviet model to that of Ahdut Ha-avoda. One common factor to which he pointed was the combination of trade union and political functions that characterized both the soviet system and the original intention of Ahdut Ha-avoda, this in contrast to purely trade union syndicalism such as had found a following in France.[151]

It is illuminating of his conception that he was critical of the reformist or "revisionist" genre of European social democracy advocated by, among others, Eduard Bernstein. To Tabenkin's way of thinking, this too meant enforcing socialism from above, even if by parliamentary means. He deprecated the record of the Social Democratic type of party; it was marred by incremental compromise with the capitalist system. This meant loss of working-class "independence of action"—the value that he most vehemently upheld in the context of the Zionist movement. By contrast, the Bolsheviks, for all their faults, had at least achieved an uncompromising working-class revolution. This was the sense in which Tabenkin insisted on identifying his brand of socialism as "revolutionary." It connoted tenacious preservation of working-class independence of action rather than the taking up of arms or the staging of a coup d'état. It meant constructing, from the foundation upward, a "revolutionary"—in the sense of radically innovative—structure of communes and cooperative units that would evolve organically into a complete Socialist society. To his mind, therein lay the great virtue of Ahdut Ha-avoda's way to socialism. In a retrospective ideological summation made in 1948, Tabenkin contrasted both Social Democratic and Communist regimes in other countries with his version of the Socialist-Zionist way. "Within Zionism, we have achieved our success not through political reforms," he proudly averred, "but through immediate and continuous revolutionary changes."[152]

Tabenkin's adherence to the term "revolutionary" might therefore be regarded as no more than an atavistic clinging to phraseology harking back to the Russian revolutionary milieu from which he had come to Palestine. Notwithstanding his criticism of Soviet communism, he retained a sense of affinity with and admiration for the working class of the Soviet Union and the revolutionary fervor and daring of Lenin's Bolshevism. Much as happened in the Socialist Left throughout the world, during the Second World War and well into the 1950s, this sense was inflated by identification with the Soviets' heroic struggle against Hitler's Nazism.

Formally, Ha-kibbutz Ha-meuhad did not insist on "ideological collectivism" as did the kibbutz movement of Ha-shomer Ha-tzair. But in practice the educational direction given by its emissaries to the youth movements and pioneer trainees aligned with it in the Diaspora was prone to the doctrinaire in respect of Socialist class consciousness. In Palestine, this tendency was likewise prevalent in the youth movements associated with Ha-kibbutz Ha-meuhad—Ha-noar Ha-oved (the Worker Youth) and Ha-mahanot Ha-olim (the Ascending Camps). Although their attitude to the praxis of dictatorship in the Soviet Union was not uncritical and there was resentment at its intolerance of Jewish nationalism even in proletarian form, the Soviet system nevertheless was upheld as the preferred alternative to the capitalist-imperialist West. This antithesis was poignantly commanding in the 1930s atmosphere of severe polarization between Soviet communism on the one side and the ascendant Fascist parties and regimes in Europe on the other side. Tabenkin's following in Ha-kibbutz Ha-meuhad was augmented in the late 1930s and in the 1940s by the growth within Mapai of an urban-based faction centered in Tel Aviv. It too evinced an explicitly pro-Soviet orientation in addition to its militant social program within Palestine. In contemporary parlance, this faction was referred to rather vaguely as Sia Bet (Faction B).

In summation, while Tabenkin and his following in Ha-kibbutz Ha-meuhad had became part and parcel of the broad-based Mapai labor party when it was at last formed in 1930, they continued to perceive themselves as the true ideological heirs of the type of commune-based and avowedly class-conscious socialism that had animated the Gedud Ha-avoda in the early 1920s. Consequently, their very connection with Mapai was mediated by their primary allegiance to the kibbutz communes of the Ha-kibbutz Ha-meuhad as an elite vanguard. If, for Berl Katznelson or David Ben-Gurion, it was the executive of the Histadrut and, behind it, the executive of Mapai that should give ideological and political direction to the working class, for Tabenkin, that task rightly belonged to Ha-kibbutz Ha-meuhad—as a political-ideological collectivity and not merely an egalitarian socioeconomic unit. Moreover, Tabenkin curiously combined his militant Socialist rhetoric with a tenaciously uncompromising nationalism in matters of political policy and military preparedness. His affinity for revolutionary rhetoric went hand in hand with justification of violent means should all else seem to fail. Ultimately, the cumulative effect of Tabenkin's divergences proved schismatic for the mainstream Mapai party.

Tabenkin's following in Ha-kibbutz Ha-meuhad and Sia Bet constituted an inherent germinating opposition to the political and moral-ideological leadership, respectively, of Ben-Gurion and Berl Katznelson over mainstream Mapai.[153] The upshot was a split within Mapai that took place in 1944, issuing in a new party whose name harked back to the Ahdut Ha-avoda concept of the 1920s—Ha-tnua Le-ahdut Ha-avoda (the Movement toward Unity of Labor). In turn, it led in 1948 to a composite merger with Left Poalei Zion and Ha-shomer Ha-tzair to form Mifleget Ha-poalim Ha-meuhedet (the United Workers' party, whose acronym was Mapam). This marked, for the first time since 1919, the reappearance of an avowedly Marxist-Socialist but at the same time firmly Zionist party at center stage of Zionist politics. Its distinguishing mark was its pro-Soviet political orientation. Not only the Soviet Union's heroic war against the Nazis but also the diplomatic and indirect military support it rendered the new State of Israel (merely tactical and transient as was soon to become evident) were delusively invoked as expressions of revolutionary socialism's long-awaited recognition of Zionism.

The Halutz Ideal as Common Denominator

These potentially schismatic tensions had repercussions far beyond the Mapai party in Palestine. They were felt in the Diaspora particularly within the general organization of pioneer youth known as He-halutz (the Pioneer). This organization was founded at the end of the First World War in eastern Europe largely on the initiative of Joseph Trumpeldor. Trumpeldor was a heroic figure who had served as an officer in the Russian army and was wounded in the Russo-Japanese war. After settling in Palestine during the Second *Aliya*, he returned temporarily to Russia to organize He-halutz. Back in Palestine, he met with a tragic death while defending the Galilee settlement of Tel Hai against an Arab attack in March 1920.

In the interwar period, He-halutz developed into a massive worldwide network of training centers preparing youth for settlement in Palestine. In August 1921 a worldwide conference took place in Czechoslovakia, and it was decided to anchor the organization within the structure of the world Zionist Organization itself. In Soviet Russia, all overt He-halutz activities were banned by the Communist regime in August 1928. By then, Poland had become the main center of the organization's strength. Numbers fluctuated considerably according to changing conditions in each country as well as in Palestine, but He-halutz worldwide claimed 89,500 members in some twenty-five countries in

1935. It is estimated that between 1919 and 1939 about forty-five thousand of its pioneer trainees settled in Palestine, constituting one-third of all immigrants in the "worker" category for those years.[154]

He-halutz had begun as a nonpolitical movement open to all youths above the age of eighteen who regarded Hebrew as their national language and were preparing for work in Palestine. Its major activity was the creation of training centers, agricultural wherever possible, where prospective *halutzim* (pioneers) were prepared not only for work occupations but also for the kibbutz form of life. However, politicization proved unavoidable, and He-halutz became yet another arena for rivalry and consequent splits between the various political-ideological trends in the Zionist labor movement.

Apart from the inter-Zionist party rivalry within He-halutz fanned by kibbutz emissaries who disseminated the ideology of the party political groupings, it was beset by internal controversy over the relationship between those of its components that were funneled into it by the various youth movements and those who joined as independent individuals. The latter were known as *stam halutzim* (plain *halutzim*) and did not come into its training centers with a crystallized ideological orientation. In Poland particularly, they constituted the larger part of the organization. The youth movements, particularly the two most important, Ha-shomer Ha-tzair and Gordonia, constantly sought greater independence in establishing their own homogeneous training centers. Countervailing attempts to unite the youth movements were repeatedly frustrated, and disunity was compounded by the very attempt of He-halutz itself to sponsor a single youth movement in the early 1920s. It was called He-halutz Ha-tzair (Young He-halutz). In the prevailing circumstances of inter–youth movement rivalry, it in effect became but another politically aligned youth movement, one associated in practice with the Ha-kibbutz Ha-meuhad framework in Palestine. Ha-shomer Ha-tzair, for its part, channeled its members exclusively into its own Ha-kibbutz Ha-artzi framework, whereas Gordonia was associated directly with the Hever Ha-kvutzot (Association of *Kvutzot*) framework that comprised the originally smaller *kvutza* communes and was informed by the Ha-poel Ha-tzair ideological tradition.

Halutziut (pioneering), as an ideal value-concept, wielded ideological influence far beyond the framework of the He-halutz organization, although its empirical content varied with nuances in the ideological formulations of those who used the term. The Hebrew world *halutz*, in its modern usage, is translatable as "pioneer" or "avant-garde" insofar as these words connote persons who consciously go ahead of a broader mass of followers in carrying out a commonly conceived social project. A semantic history of the word reveals that, although used sporadically in relation to the Bilu settlers and during the Second *Aliya*, it was only during the Third *Aliya* (approximately 1919–1923), paralleling the burgeoning of the He-halutz organization, that it gained ubiquitous currency as the quintessential expression of the

Zionist labor movement's ethos.[155] Henceforward, it also became the commanding ideal of a variety of youth movements, influencing the lives of successive generations of Jewish youngsters aged from the early teens to the early twenties in almost every Jewish community in the world.

Since *halutziut* relates primarily to the realm of action, it belongs, in the first instance, to that dimension of Zionist ideology that in our analysis till now has been termed the "means." However, the composite qualities of this particular means may be said to have subsumed the common essence of all varieties of labor Zionism in regard also to the ideological dimensions we have labeled "diagnosis" and "vision." For the ideal of the *halutz* represented the antithesis of the repressed, unproductive *galut* condition of the Jew, as well as depicting the vision of the new liberated Jew in his national home, Eretz Israel.

The connotations of *halutziut*, in addition to that of a vanguard, included, above all, a twin concept—*hagshama*. Translatable as "realization" (in the sense not of perception but of materialization), *hagshama* was usually coupled with self, as "self-realization." Contrary to what present-day understanding of this term might indicate, it did not mean individualistic self-fulfillment. Rather, *hagshama* implied the conscious choice to fuse one's own search for personal fulfillment with the national need. It therefore meant the process of acting out one's convictions by personally ascending to Eretz Israel and undergoing the transformation to a life of labor. As the philosopher Martin Buber, who sang the praises of the *halutz*, described it: "These people [the *halutzim*] bound their own welfare to the welfare of the nation and The Land through labor. This bond was the essence of the change they brought about. By virtue of this they created a new type—of self-realization, of *halutziut*."[156]

The *halutz* ideal and the *halutz* type, respectively, were thus of inestimable importance in Zionist ideology and the Zionist movement. *Halutziut* was, in a profound sense, the critical point of conjunction between the ideology of Zionism and the praxis of bringing to the homeland the committed core who would build up the Jewish presence there. In the context of a national movement, most of whose adherents in fact remained where they were in the Diaspora or migrated to other Diaspora lands like America, the He-halutz organization prided itself on being the "realizers" par excellence of the Zionist ideology. Typically, an important memorandum submitted to the Zionist congress of 1935 appealed for allocation of more financial resources on the merits of "the vision that animates He-halutz and its enterprise: its fidelity to the highest of all principles of Zionism—to be a *magshim* (a 'realizer')."[157]

This individual imperative was compounded by a collective allegiance, namely, voluntary submission to the discipline and mutual responsibility of the collective Zionist labor movement. Indicative of this linkage was the He-halutz organization's stipulation that its members must join the Histadrut on their arrival in Palestine. Moreover, the collective framework that came to command almost automatic allegiance from the *halutz* was the kibbutz commune. *Halutziut* also implied a profound sense of mission. In this respect diverse interpretations were imposed on the concept in accordance with each particular school of thought. As early as 1915, Ben-Gurion had defined the tasks of the *halutz* very broadly as "preparation of the land and the creation of conditions for absorption in it . . . construction and science." The *halutz*, he said, was a person "armed with a mighty will and a sense of historical mission," one who "committed his own personal destiny" to the fulfillment of the Zionist cause.[158] Ben-Gurion's interpretation evolved, as we have seen, from "working class to working nation." This gave ever wider compass to the mission of the *halutz*. By contrast, Tabenkin's school of thought gave a more constricted interpretation to the mission of the *halutz*, one that implied the individual's convergence with the almost deterministic three-tier roles of the kibbutz as generator of the working class, the working class as generator of the nation, and ultimately the classless society of the Jewish nation as exemplary participant in a Socialist world order.

In sum, after making allowance for such nuances of interpretation, it may be said that the ethos of *halutziut* became the most salient and enduring common denominator of all schools of labor Zionism. Only the case of Left Poalei Zion calls for a caveat in this respect. Inasmuch as its adherents clung to the determinism of doctrinaire "Borochovism," they attached quite as little importance to voluntarist *halutziut* as they did to the constructivist approach in general. Yet they too founded a kibbutz, and their adherents included various individual members of other kibbutzim. Indeed, the resonance of the *halutz* ethos was so all-pervasive that segments of General Zionism—notably the Ha-noar Ha-tzioni (the Zionist Youth) youth movement associated with Group A of General Zionism—nurtured their own version of the *halutz* ethos. So too did national-religious Zionism. Even labor Zionism's greatest rival, Ze'ev Jabotinsky, sought to appropriate the *halutz* concept by invoking the words of Joseph Trumpeldor, who, in addition to being a founder of the He-halutz organization, uniquely doubled as a hero in the pantheon of Revisionist Zionism as well as in that of labor Zionism. According to Jabotinsky, Trumpeldor had defined *halutziut* in broader terms than those that had been sanctified in the He-halutz organization. He related a conversation with Trumpeldor held in the summer of 1916, in which the latter had said that it meant much more than simply becoming workers. It meant "people willing to do 'everything,' all that is needed by Eretz Israel . . . a plain steel rod. Flexible—but steel. Metal that can be shaped into whatever is needed for the national machine. A wheel is lacking? I am a wheel. . . . The earth must be dug up? I dig. There is a necessity to shoot, to be a soldier? I am a soldier. . . . I am the pure idea of service, ready for all."[159] However, Revisionist Zionism did not succeed in appropriating the concept of *halutziut*. Its historical role remained the almost exclusive possession of the labor Zionist movement.

CHAPTER SIX

Revisionist Zionism

Ze'ev Jabotinsky's Activism

THE EMANATION of plain or general Zionism that was to have the most far-reaching and at the same time most disruptive consequences was Revisionist Zionism. Its founder and enduringly dominant personality was Vladimir (Ze'ev) Jabotinsky (1880–1940), a brilliant and charismatic multilingual journalist, writer, and orator born and educated in the enlightened Russian-Jewish milieu of Odessa and exposed at a formative period of his early adulthood to the intellectual stimulus of the University of Rome. The formative influence of Jabotinsky's ideological maturation was not the world of religious traditionalism and yeshiva study, nor even the Ahad Ha'amian attempt to secularize the tradition, but rather extraneous European influences such as the liberal strains in Russian literature, the nationalist drama of Garibaldi and the Italian Risorgimento, and the Polish national revival.[1] Prior to the First World War Jabotinsky's Zionist career was that of a talented, up-and-coming general Zionist whose liberal-tinctured nationalist outlook was qualified only by a proclivity for militant gestures. In accord with the changed circumstances of the movement after Herzl's death, he was involved in the new course of Zionist policy adopted at the Helsingfors conference of Russian Zionists in November 1906. As we noted earlier, it favored Zionist involvement in the struggle for equal rights and autonomy for Jews alongside other nationalities in the Russian empire and marked a stage in the synthesis of the Zionist movement's political and practical work.[2]

It was during the First World War that the effervescent militancy of Jabotinsky first came to the fore in the dramatic fashion that was to become his trademark as a charismatic leader in Zionism. This was when he became the foremost advocate of decisive Zionist alignment with Great Britain and her allies through the formation of a volunteer Jewish military unit in the British forces that were to be arraigned against Turkey. This daring proposal went against the neutralist consensus in a movement that, after all, had roots and branches in countries on both sides of the battle fronts and had to look to the safety of the still weak and vulnerable Jewish settler presence in Ottoman-ruled Palestine. A Jewish unit in the British forces came into existence only after innumerable hurdles had been crossed by dint of the indefatigable efforts of Jabotinsky and a small number of like-minded Zionist personalities, one of whom was the journalist Meir Grossman (another was Chaim Weizmann, who, in this respect, concurred with Jabotinsky). In August 1917 the British government at last announced its intention to establish a Jewish regiment. Popularly known as the Jewish Legion, it became operational in Palestine only in the last phase of the First World War.

Henceforward it remained an enduring plank in Jabotinsky's political platform to advocate the continued maintenance of this Jewish Legion and, after failing to ensure this—the residual Jewish battalion was disbanded in 1921—the restoration of some such Jewish military formation as a recognized part of the British garrison in Palestine. This advocacy was predicated on his unshakable belief that it was the British Mandatory's solemn obligation not only to foster the development of the Jewish national home but also to facilitate Jewish participation in its protection until it attained sovereignty. His call for a Jewish Legion, rather than any underground secret Jewish military formations, was consistently his preferred policy. Even while heading a Jewish self-defense group in Jerusalem in 1919 and 1920, Jabotinsky sought British recognition of its legitimate role as the core of a restored official Jewish military unit. However, this goal was never attained. Instead, Jabotinsky's self-defense activities led to his being arrested and sentenced to fifteen years in prison. After much worldwide protestation he was pardoned, and subsequently his sentence was revoked.

Prior to Jabotinsky's creation in 1925 of the Zionist Revisionist Organization (Ha-histadrut Ha-tzionit Ha-revisionistit, known by the acronym Ha-tzohar) as a faction within the world Zionist Organization,[3] it was simply the strident militancy of his approach to Zionist policy vis-à-vis the British regime that distinguished him from Zionists in general and from Chaim Weizmann, the president of the Zionist Organization, in particular. For his conviction that the attainment of Zionism's goals was dependent on the link with Britain and his view that it could be shown to be in Britain's strategic interest to support Zionism were shared by Weizmann. But Jabotinsky charged the Mandatory authorities in Palestine with willful failure to carry out the letter and spirit of British obligations, and he voiced increasingly acerbic criticism of what he considered to be the meekness of Weizmann's policy and comportment in relation to the British government.

It was this dissatisfaction with Weizmann's Zionist executive that led, in January 1923, to Jabotinsky's resignation from that body on which he had served since 1921. After an interlude in which he limited his activities to journalistic activity outside the Zionist Organization proper, two conjunctions with like-minded "activist" elements catapulted him back into the Zionist political arena in 1924.[4] Activism in the contemporary context meant taking venturesome and imaginative initiatives to advance Zionist aims rather than waiting upon events. The first conjunction was with a young student group in the Latvian capital, Riga, which called itself Histadrut Trumpeldor (the Trumpeldor Organization), Joseph Trumpeldor being the much-admired hero, formerly an officer in the Russian army, who was killed while defending the isolated Galilee settlement, Tel-Hai, against Arab attack in 1921. Out of this nucleus Jabotinsky created what was to become a massive paramilitary youth movement that adopted in 1926 the name Betar, an acronym for Brit Trumpeldor (the covenant of Trumpeldor) as well as a place-name marking one of the last outposts that had held out against the Roman legions in ancient Judea.[5] The second conjunction was that between Jabotinsky and a group of like-minded activists associated with the Russian-language Zionist weekly *Razsvet* (the Dawn) that had moved from St. Petersburg to Berlin. An important earlier accretion to Jabotinsky's following was the young Russian-born journalist Meir Grossman, who had moved after the outbreak of the war from Berlin to Copenhagen in neutral Denmark, where the Zionist Organization relocated its wartime headquarters, and joined Jabotinsky's crusade for the creation of the Jewish Legion. Defying the views of the executive in Copenhagen, Grossman set up the Yiddish language *Di Tribune*, the first organ of Jabotinsky's activism, and in 1917 moved its place of publication to London when he joined Jabotinsky there.[6]

At the outset, then, the Zionist Revisionist Organization formed by Jabotinsky in 1925 was an activist wing of general Zionism purporting to offer a militant alternative policy or mode of operations to that practiced by the Zionist Executive headed by Chaim Weizmann. In ideological terms, Jabotinsky purported merely to be *revising* the existing Zionist program by applying the original, but now lapsed, vision and methods of Herzl to the changed circumstances of the post–Balfour Declaration era. He had the appearance of an opposition leader, an alternative to Weizmann's leadership, rather than the exponent of a new genre of Zionist ideology. As events unfolded, however, the acrimonious interaction between Jabotinsky's assertive nationalist "activism" on the one hand and the already well ensconced position of labor Zionist organizations in Palestine on the other hand, rapidly transformed the ideology of Jabotinsky's following into a nationalist mode that exhibited a distinctive *Weltanschauung*, a collective mentality and political style conforming in many respects to parties of the Right and in some even to the Fascist Right in various countries during the interwar years.

Jabotinsky's Integral Nationalism

Jabotinsky was a prodigiously prolific essayist, not only on matters of the day but also on fundamental issues of ideology. For all that, however, he was far from being a systematic theoretician. His ideological profile is very much like a jigsaw puzzle that must be pieced together from innumerable, often contradictory passages, varying with time and place, so that the end product remains largely indeterminate and confounds attempts at categorization in conventional terms such as liberalism on the one extreme or fascism on the other.[7] The difficulty experienced in attempting to define Jabotinsky's ideology and contextualize it historically and comparatively is further compounded by the unabating political controversy surrounding the man and his devotees.

One of the ideological subjects that Jabotinsky essayed to examine profoundly was conceptualization of the nation. It was on the subject of "national minorities" that he completed an academic dissertation at the (Russian) University of Yaroslav in 1912, and in a number of essays he theorized about concepts such as "race" and "the nation." Although not uninfluenced by Socialist ideas, particularly of the type to which he had been exposed by the philosophical and social thought of Antonio Labriola in Rome, Jabotinsky rejected Marxist materialist determinism in this as in other respects. Even if it be granted, he argued, that man's history was largely determined by the "means of production," it had to be recognized that these means, in turn, were an outcome of antecedent factors. These included the influence of natural climatic conditions, and the nature of the terrain in which a society developed. But the paramount factor was something inhering in the human being himself—this he called the "psyche." That Jabotinsky's usage of this term connoted not only what might today be called mentality but a compound of intelligence and creativity as well is deducible from the context of his discussion and from the kind of example he chose to illustrate his point: "For what is the psyche if not the ultimate tool of production?" he asked. Was it not that which enabled man to "identify his needs, look for solutions to satisfy them, learn from experience, make cooperative efforts and invent new technologies?" This "psyche," he contended, was the decisive factor in the formation of national character, as indeed it was in history generally.[8]

The next step in his theory was the induction that differences in this psychic factor correlated by and large with physical and, in turn, ultimately chemical (nowadays one would probably say biochemical or genetic) differences between peoples. He argued that just as at the individual level, "given the same conditions, climatic, geographical, historical, social etc., and given an equal level of personal biographical development, we will see that two individuals who differ physiologically will show different psychological reactions to absolutely the same stimuli," so at the collective national level "physical differences at all times accompany (how and why, this for the time is one of the secrets of nature) psychic differences." This physiological-psychic factor he equated with the term "race." In a nutshell, Jabotinsky's answer to the question "in what does the nation consist?" was that, above all, it consists in its distinctive psychic-racial composition.

Natural terrain, language, religion, shared history—all of these do not constitute the essence of the nation, they are merely descriptions of it; certainly these descriptions are enormously valuable, and they have great importance for stable national existence. But the essence of the nation, the alpha and omega of its distinctive character, is its special physical attribute, the formula of its racial composition. . . . In the eyes of the researcher who is interested . . . in objective first causes, in the final analysis when all shells arising from history, climate, natural surroundings, and outside influences, have been removed the "nation" is reduced to its racial kernel.

Conversely, by the same token, Jabotinsky inferred that this psychic-racial determinant of differences between nations also characterized the average individuals of each nation: "Each nation—being in the above mentioned sense a separate 'race'—has its own 'racial' psychology which permeates to a greater or lesser degree the personality of any average member of the group beneath and above the diversity of their individual physiognomies."[9]

Comprehended, as it ought to be, within its proper historical context there was nothing out of the ordinary in the earnestness with which Jabotinsky, writing in 1913, regarded race as a primary factor in the formation of nations. Like most contemporary nationalists (including Ahad Ha'am, who came to be considered as occupying a pole of moderate nationalism opposite to that of Jabotinsky) he was drawing on the prevalent intellectual climate of the turn of the century with its pervasive positivist influences. The positivist assumption that putatively observable and testable hereditary attributes accounted for differences between human groupings was in vogue. It is, however, evident that this conception of the nation remained a permanent feature of his ideology throughout his life. For, in an English version of his 1913 essay "Race" (drafted as late as 1939, when rabid Nazi-type racism, victimizing mainly the Jews, raged rampant in Europe) he reiterated its central thesis. To be sure, he added a disclaimer of any association with odious racism and "the accursed and sinister significance it conveys to the present generation." "I wish to remind the reader" he wrote, "that the phraseology of the marketplace is no scientific criterion; and that consequently one may be a firm adherent of all men's and all tribes' equality, yet as firmly believe that 'race' is a fundamental factor of all civilization and all history; precisely in the same way as one need not be ashamed to admit the importance of sexual motives in poetry because there is lechery too."[10]

Certainly, Jabotinsky had consistently and explicitly refuted racism in the sense of the theory that there were "pure" races, and its concomitants that some were innately superior to others and that this accordingly justified a hierarchy of domination and subservience. In one feuilleton depicting an imaginary debate with a racist antisemite, Jabotinsky, insofar as he agrees to use his opponent's terms of discourse, tries to turn the tables on him by contending that the Jewish race scores best on the true criterion of "superiority"—retention against all odds of its own sense of selfhood, its own individuality and values. In the final analysis, however, Jabotinsky rejects any racist terms of discourse and draws a clear distinction between loving one's own nation and claiming that it is inherently superior in any sense. "There is no such thing as superior and inferior races," he wrote. "Every race has its own characteristics, its own persona, admixture of talents . . . the races are all approximately equal in value."[11] Nor did Jabotinsky's psychic-racial determinism mean that one could neither leave nor join a nation. In his dissertation on national minorities, written in 1912, he treats individual self-definition as an adequate criterion for national membership, qualifying it only with the point that voluntary entry into another nation, somewhat like acceptance into a religion, required a procedure in which an official authority of that nation accepts the person and facilitates his merging into it.[12]

Given these significant qualifications of Jabotinsky's psychic-racial determinism, its application to Jewish nationalist ideology amounted to little more than another variation of the standard "myth" or ideological commonality of almost all schools of Zionist thought, namely, that there was a Jewish nation that originated in ancient times in the territory, climate, flora, and so on of Eretz Israel. In Jabotinsky's version, a particular psychic-racial factor constituted the formative essence of that nation. Substitute for this Ahad Ha'am's "will to life" and "moral genius" (which we shall examine in due course), or Aharon David Gordon's "cosmic" fusion of labor and land, or even the Socialist Ber Borochov's "conditions of production" (which we discussed earlier), and one arrives at much the same conclusion: that quite apart from the nation's dire need for a place of refuge from persecution, its therapeutic resuscitation and its renewed contribution to mankind were crucially dependent on its restoration to independence in that same territorial homeland.

Yet the fact that Jabotinsky chose to qualify his above-quoted affirmation that all races are equal in value with the word "approximately" may be indicative of the precariously thin line that divided his usage of the concept "race" from its usage in antisemitism and other manifestations of rabid racism. Indeed, it might be said that walking dangerously on a tightrope between conceptual alternatives was characteristic of most of Jabotinsky's ideological formulations. This is what makes it so difficult to resolve the question of whether his own claim to be at heart a liberal in the nineteenth-century mold is tenable.[13] Jabotinsky's penchant for rhetorical flourishes and hyperbole does not make the matter easier. Typical is this declaration, which he approvingly puts in the mouth of Garibaldi: "Yes I was a knight for all mankind, but I taught my people that there is no value in the world higher than the nation and the fatherland, there is no deity in the universe to which one shall sacrifice these two most valuable jewels."[14] Yet it is clear enough that, like another nationalist whom he admired, Giuseppe Mazzini, his ideal was a polycentric world order, a concert of nations. In his formulation of "the idea of Betar" (1934) he stressed the belief that "each and every nation makes its own contribution to human culture, with the stamp of its own unique spirit."[15]

Clearly, Jabotinsky upheld the fundamental nationalist premise that the nation, not mankind as an undifferentiated whole, was the necessary and desirable medium for human self-fulfillment. Typical was his statement: "I unreservedly believe that in the competition between these two [the nation and mankind] the nation has precedence."[16] Thus, on the plane of universal mankind and the nation, the nation had primacy. This much was unequivocal in Jabotinsky's thought. Not so were his diverse statements on the plane of the individual in relation to the nation. Here he walked a tightrope. On the one hand, in the same breath as he gave the nation precedence over mankind at large, he averred that "the individual has precedence over the nation."

In the beginning God created the individual. Every individual is a king equal to his peers—and an evil person is also a "king." Better that the individual should sin against the public than that society sin against the individual: for the good of individuals society was created, not vice versa; and the final end of time as in the vision of the days of the Messiah is the garden of Eden of the individual. . . . And "society" has no task other than helping the stumbler, consoling him and raising him up.[17]

Yet, on the other hand, as we shall see in the course of this tracing of his ideas, the very essence of his ideological preaching came to be that the individual waive his individuality, obey his chosen leaders with unreserved discipline, shun allegiance to anything that in any way qualifies or weakens the single consensual goal of self-determination for the Jewish nation in a state of its own. In this important respect, which goes against the core of liberal values, an abiding and unresolved tension attaches to the teachings of Jabotinsky. His averred liberalism remained ambiguous. What he gave with one hand, he took back with another.

Thus far, the ideological character of Jabotinsky's revisionism was not substantially different from that of general Zionism. As we noted earlier, General Zionists did not set out in the first instance to embody liberal values as a restraint on their nationalism. Where Jabotinsky's way differed from theirs—even the most activist of them, such as Yitzhak Gruenbaum's Radical Zionists in Poland—was precisely in the solution he offered for the General Zionists' dilemma of appearing to uphold an unvaryingly negative ideological posture; that is to say being *non*-Socialist, *non*orthodox and so on. As we saw, the most that General Zionist ideological inventiveness could offer was some idealization of the "middle way" as a value in itself. Jabotinsky, in contrast, came up with an ideological formula far more appealing to the Jewish public at large and compelling for his devotees, the idea of "monism":

The movement whose world outlook I here wish to explain adopts a standpoint in regard to social problems generally and class war in particular that we call "monism." This means: during the process of building up the Jewish state, and as long as that process continues, we firmly negate the view that from the point of view of Zionism any value and importance attaches to any class outlook whether it be proletarian or bourgeois. . . . We do not forbid any person from nurturing in the depth of his soul alongside of the Zionist ideal also a world outlook, opinions or even subsidiary ideals of another kind. These are the private affair of each individual. . . . But in accord with our Herzlian world outlook we do not recognize the permissibility of any ideal whatsoever apart from the single ideal: a Jewish majority on both sides of the Jordan as a first step towards the establishment of the State. That is what we call "monism."[18]

It is in this sense that one may label Jabotinsky's nationalism as an "integral" nationalism. But in historical reality "monism" came to mean more than merely the principle, shared by most General Zionists, that in the course of building the aspired-for Jewish state, Zionists should not be deflected by any other abstract ideals or social programs. As expounded by Jabotinsky, and even more as interpreted by his followers, especially in Palestine, it came to mean the active excoriation of one particular "ism" deemed to be the absolute antinomy of true Zionism, namely, socialism.

As we have seen, General Zionists too lacked consensus on the attitude to be adopted toward the labor Zionist movement. Some General Zionists (i.e., Group B) were potential allies of Jabotinsky in this regard. However, a major segment (Group A) had a high, if not uncritical, regard for the role of labor. In this important respect they were at one with Chaim Weizmann, the leader they most preferred to have at the helm of the Zionist Organization as a whole. By the same token, they found Revisionism's increasingly unrestrained offensive against the labor movement, its assertive attempt to dislodge it from commanding positions in the Jewish sector of Palestine, so unacceptable that this consideration overrode any other commonalities they shared. One of these commonalities, particularly with Yitzhak Gruenbaum's radical Zionist faction of General Zionists, was opposition throughout the 1920s to Weizmann's determined strategy of entering into a partnership with wealthy and influential non-Zionists—philanthropic plutocrats in the eyes of Weizmann's opponents. Much to the chagrin of both Gruenbaum and Jabotinsky, in 1929 Weizmann finally succeeded in forming this expanded Jewish Agency for Palestine on the basis of a fifty-fifty representation of the Zionist Organization and non-Zionists in various countries.

Jabotinsky's claim that his "monism" was true to the original Herzlian conception of Zionism was not without foundation. Herzl had indeed been averse to Zionists becoming involved with socialism or any other activities that might be deleterious to, or deflect them from, the goal of gaining a political charter for national self-determination. However, all of this related to activities in the Diaspora. In the changed historical context of the interwar years, when something like the aspired-for charter had been gained—the Balfour Declaration of 1917 enshrined also in the terms of the League of Nations' mandate over Palestine confirmed in 1922—and, more important, when labor Zionism had become the major generator of settlement and economic development in Palestine, Jabotinsky's idealization of "monism" wrought a metamorphosis in the character of his nationalist ideology.

The transformation was more than purely quantitative. What issued was no longer the functional nationalism of Herzl nourished by turn of the century liberal roots and utopian social ideals. It was rather what might be called an integral nationalism whose original liberal roots were being nibbled away, and in part even entirely eradicated. For "monism" translated into reality inevitably clashed with liberal values insofar as it meant regimentation of the Zionist enterprise and restriction of dissent or any deviation from the pristine national goal of statehood. Moreover, it could easily come to mean that in the final analysis the end goal sanctified all means; conversely, whatever obstructed that end, was morally reprehensible. "Zionism is beautiful, pure and clean and 'moral,'" declared Jabotinsky in a typical rhetorical flourish, "and if Zionism is 'moral,' then everything that delays it is immoral."[19] In the fray of the ideological battle against their opponents, the emotion-laden charge of treason to the national cause came easily to the lips of those who upheld such a tenet.

To be sure, the evidence is abundant that, notwithstanding his rhetoric, Jabotinsky himself never took the implications of his monistic or integral nationalism to its logical extremes; never jettisoned *all* liberal restraints. Again one must describe him as walking an ideological tightrope. What sustained his delicate balancing act was an ideological rationale that had two complementary facets. One was the distinction he made between stages of the Zionist program: the first—"during the process of upbuilding the Jewish state, and for as long as this process continued"—was the phase in which "monism" applied; the second, after the state had been attained, would be open to the marketplace of social ideals and programs. Jabotinsky averred that he himself nurtured, in abeyance, certain social ideals. "Many of us believe that at a future time Eretz Israel will indeed be a laboratory in which the remedy for redemption of human society as a whole will be revealed and realized in our own special way. But before we set about discovering that remedy, we are obliged, first and foremost, to build the laboratory."[20]

The complementary side of Jabotinsky's rationale was what one might today call a plea for "affirmative action." Because the Jewish people was underprivileged and persecuted, weak and incapacitated, its adoption of compensatory attributes was necessary and justifiable, even if these might by liberal standards and in other contexts be deemed vices. On this premise, Jabotinsky was able to declare his revulsion from such phenomena as militarism and disciplinary regimentation,[21] yet in the same breath call for militarization and discipline as the highest desiderata of the Jewish national movement. Indeed, he extolled military virtues, making the distinction that "only war is ugly," whereas "the military life itself has many worthy aspects, for which we yearn in our ordinary lives . . . these are, first of all, camaraderie, spartan simplicity, equality between rich and poor; secondly, the hygienic factor, the open air and physical culture; and thirdly, the very discipline of the military."[22] The appeal for militarization of the Zionist youth and for the incorporation of a military unit, legal and open, in the Zionist program in general were, without doubt, preeminent innovations in Jabotinsky's program. He argued that whereas other privileged nations might well allow themselves "to stop learning the skills of war, we are forced to begin learning these bitter skills,"[23] for physical weakness was in itself a provocation. The capacity of the weak to defend themselves would in the end prevent violence in the world rather than increase it.

The youth movement that Jabotinsky created and headed, Betar, was intended from the outset to be both a "school" and "a military camp"; the former as a training ground for the new dignified type of national Jew, the latter as preparation for the Jewish Legion, which Jabotinsky hoped to resuscitate with British sanction.[24] The ideal of the new type of national Jew, the antithesis of the stereotyped *galut* (exile) Jew, was epitomized by the concept of *hadar*, incorporated in the oath of the Betar member: "I shall surely strive for *hadar* in all my thoughts, in all that passes my lips, in all my deeds, for I am the son of kings." Jabotinsky explained *hadar* as follows: "A Hebrew word that is almost untranslatable into other languages. It comprehends some dozen different concepts: external beauty, pride, manners, loyalty." It was meant to encompass everything in the Betar member's daily life, from his table manners to his diction. He was to show dignity, pride, and generosity of heart, and his every word was to be honorable. *Hadar* signified "the comportment of the son of a king," a Jewish equivalent of the English aristocratic or gentlemanly attributes. Jabotinsky anticipated the day when the equivalent of the comment "Here is a true gentleman" would be "Here is a true *Betari*."[25]

The paramilitary aspect of Betar was explicitly expressed in the first clause of its constitution, which stated that "the Trumpeldor Organization is a part of the future Jewish Legion that is to be formed in Eretz Israel." The members and officers of Betar wore brown military uniforms, and great emphasis was placed on marching exercises and other aspects of military ceremony. At the time of Betar's founding in Riga in 1923 one of its first functions was a program of paramilitary training, conducted by a gentile officer. However, its members also underwent training for trades and agricultural labor in workshops and on farms. Until 1931 world Betar was directed from the center in Riga and only loosely connected with the world headquarters of the Zionist Revisionist Organization, situated variously in Paris and London. At the 1928 and 1929 world Betar conferences there was some controversy over its structure. The Latvian founding group, some of whose members had already settled in Palestine, favored a democratic structure and continued emphasis on training for trades and farming and was generally not alienated from the labor movement's pioneering activities. The contrary view, advocating a hierarchic military structure for Betar, emanated particularly from the small but increasingly assertive Betar group in Palestine. The hierarchical principle won out. One outcome of this more rigid structure was that the pioneering tendency of the original Latvian group was incrementally stifled.[26] Although *Rosh Betar* (the Head of Betar), Jabotinsky, was elected at the movement's world conferences, in the interim the entire structure functioned hierarchically with orders from above. *Rosh Betar* appointed a "commissioner" in each country and these in turn appointed "branch commanders" in each town.

Discipline was a key value with which Jabotinsky adjured Betar. In his exposition of "The Idea of Betar" he stated: "The structure of Betar is based upon the principle of discipline. Our aim is . . . to forge Betar into a world organism of a kind that will be capable, at a sign from headquarters, to carry out in the same instant with all its tens of thousands of hands the same act in every city and country. . . . For the highest achievement of a mass of free people is the ability to act together all as one with the complete exactitude of a 'machine.' Only free people of high culture are capable of this." Jabotinsky denied that discipline was incompatible with man's sovereign will or that it reduced man to a mere machine. He was at pains to explain that Betar's was a voluntary discipline not enforced against its member's will. One consciously chose to subject oneself to its discipline out of conviction and dedication to the cause. Likening this to a choir or orchestra he argued that "it is not the conductor who has forced one but rather the person himself, insofar as he himself strives for unity . . . his free will has brought him to the conviction that the most edifying attribute of a human mass is precisely this capacity to bring about a harmony between his personality and the personalities of others for a common purpose."[27]

He also drew a distinction between the implications of discipline in a voluntary organization and in a state, asserting that "there are limits to the most complete loyalty in organizations whose basis is, after all, free will and not state compulsion."[28] In a voluntary framework it was indeed not only unrealistic but even "a moral absurdity" to coerce, contrary to conscience, an individual or a minority of individuals so that they comply with the majority. "If the state forces its citizens to act against their consciences, then it is the state and not they that carries the blame," he reasoned. "But, in a voluntary movement it is wrong for any one to act against his conscience, and if he does so act, then he has only himself to blame, and he has no excuse."[29]

This was a particularly germane aspect of Jabotinsky's teaching since his career was punctuated not only by verbal dissent but also by independent actions that deviated from policies determined by the Zionist Organization's elected leadership. After helping to displace Weizmann in 1931 but failing to replace him in the leadership, the Revisionist Zionists attempted their own diplomatic and political initiatives while still being a constituent part of the Zionist Organization. The most notable of these initiatives was the launching in 1933–1934 of a massive petition campaign addressed both to the governments of various countries and to the British Crown. This was deplored as a breach of discipline by the majority leadership, and when the latter introduced a stricter disciplinary clause in the constitution forbidding independent initiatives, this provided the pretext for the demonstrative act of secession from the Zionist Organization, for which Jabotinsky had been itching since early 1932 if not earlier.[30] In 1935, Jabotinsky's Revisionist Zionists left the Zionist Organization and created what they called the New Zionist Organization (Ha-histadrut Ha-tzionit Ha-hadasha, known by the acronym Ha-tzah).

Related to the question of discipline is the democratic principle of majority rule. Here, more than in any other area of Jabotinsky's thought irreconcilable contradictions abound. Largely as a function of his abiding interest in the rights of national minorities, he had reservations concerning the dangers of majoritarian tyranny. Jabotinsky's advocacy of minority rights in Eastern Europe was predicated on the imposition of restraints upon ethnic or national majorities. Applying this to the South African situation, with which he became acquainted on visits in the 1930s, he recognized the unjust anomaly of white minority rule. But he evinced sympathy also for the claim of the whites, who had brought civilization to South Africa, not to be subjected to the rule of the Black majority.[31] Positing moral limits on the rights of a demographic majority was, of course, also germane to the Zionist claim for precedence over the Arab population in gaining national self-determination (a subject to which we shall return in a later chapter).

Applying this rationale to intranational and intraorganizational spheres in the early 1930s, Jabotinsky felt justified in claiming the right of the Revisionist Zionists to independence of action in matters of essence concerning which he dissented from the elected executive of the Zionist Organization. Likewise, in the sphere of labor relations, he argued that under certain conditions a minority of workers was morally entitled to refrain from striking with the majority: "If the workers refuse to submit the conflict to arbitration, the minority has the sacred right to decide for itself if the strike that is about to break out is justified or not."[32] Grappling with the theoretical problematica of these claims, he rested his position in the final analysis on his utopian, nigh anarchistic, ideal of absolute human equality—"each man a king." In 1938 he wrote:

Democracy was created under the banner of a war against various forms of minority rule; it was the opposite swing of the pendulum. However, blind identification of majority rule with democracy is not really correct. The value of democracy does not depend upon the subjection of forty-nine equal kings to a hundred or even of ten or one to a hundred. The essence of democracy is to be sought in the doctrine of consensus or compromise.[33]

Consensus was thus Jabotinsky's proffered solution for the dilemma. In the case of South Africa this might imply what today would be called some kind of consociational solution guaranteeing the white minority's interests in certain spheres. However, in Palestine, Jabotinsky categorically rejected compromise and consensus solutions, such as binational parity irrespective of the population size of the Jews and the Arabs. At most he promised certain minority rights for the Arab population in a Jewish national state. In the Zionist Organization and in the trade unions he demanded freedom of action for a minority. Yet in his own Betar organization he espoused absolute discipline and held this up as the model for the entire national movement. Moreover, in the Zionist Revisionist Organization, at one critical point in 1933, when the policy that he believed to represent the majority view of the rank and file membership was at odds with that insisted upon by the duly elected executive, Jabotinsky allowed himself the prerogative, as president, of cavalierly dismissing the executive and calling a plebiscite. This was condemned by his opponents as grossly undemocratic. It precipitated their splitting of Revisionist Zionism and creating the Jewish State Party. To a confidante he apologetically justified his actions in these words:

Do not believe the fiction, that I waived the principle of democracy. . . . I rebelled against the hegemony of the minority—against the situation whereby the representatives of ten percent wished to stifle the representative of ninety percent; and indeed the elections to our congress proved that my estimate was correct. One may argue whether the system of putsch is good; but one cannot deny that I struggled on behalf of the right of the majority, that is, for the fundamental principle of democracy.[34]

More than almost any other political leader in the Zionist pantheon—certainly more than Chaim Weizmann—Jabotinsky was an ideologue par excellence, in the sense that he perpetually engaged in the cogitation and formulation of ideological rationales for his actions. Of course, all ideological rationales may be reducible to political interests or tactics and to personal motivations. While it is not our primary concern to speculate with such reductionism, the correlation between the painstaking ideological rationale we have been discussing and Jabotinsky's record of dissent and indiscipline in relation to the Zionist Organization is transparently evident. Clearly, the bottom line is that, by temperament, Jabotinsky was acutely uncomfortable in the role of subordinate and exceedingly impatient with perpetually being in the opposition. He argued that "in our Jewish circumstances [i.e. in the Zionist Organization] the very concept 'opposition' is nothing but an absurdity and an impossibility," since its parliament assembled only once every two years, and in the interim the administration took no notice whatsoever of the voices of opposition dispersed ineffectually throughout the world. "No living person can bear this kind of passivity, and it is wrong for him to bear it. . . . It is a crime against the people to bury in this way forces, indeed, even—perhaps—

talents."[35] It is instructive that in one of his last utterances, a statement that was published posthumously, he reiterated: "In a voluntary association majority rule is possible only to the extent that the conscience of the minority does not see itself wounded by it. . . . When the matter touches fundamental principles, it is worse than foolish to remain within a voluntary association that seeks with all its might to execute a policy that the minority considers damaging to its highest ideals."[36]

The Radical Right Wing

If Jabotinsky never shed his liberal constraints, notwithstanding the contradictions in his ideological canons, the same cannot be said of all his followers. In the late 1920s and early 1930s a small but not insignificant circle in Palestine, who were known as "maximalist" Revisionists, formulated a distinctly antiliberal ideological trend, saturated with quasi-messianic rhetoric quite foreign to Jabotinsky's way of thinking.[37] This mutant Revisionist ideology took root in the wake of the 1929 Arab riots and murders of Jews, a traumatic experience that also caused some labor Zionist leaders to revise their political strategy.

The leading "maximalists" were a number of poets, writers, and political publicists, notably Uri Zvi Greenberg (1894–1981), Abba Ahimeir (1897–1962), and Yehoshua Heschel Yevin (1891–1970). Zionism was portrayed by them in glorious metaphorical terms as a movement for "redemption of the people" and its goal as *Malkhut Israel* (the kingdom of Israel). They espoused an avant-gardist, revolutionary ethos of might. It was an ethos that found a home in Jabotinsky's Revisionist camp, although in fact it derived as much from certain revolutionary trends of thought within the ideology of the Left (influenced by the Russian social revolutionaries' model and by that of the Bolsheviks) as from the ideology of the European Right. Indeed, both Uri Zvi Greenberg and Abba Ahimeir first vented their versions of that ethos in the 1920s in organs of labor Zionism.[38] Born in Bobruisk, White Russia, Ahimeir settled in Palestine in 1924, after completing a doctorate at the University of Vienna on Oswald Spengler, author of the famous *Der Untergang des Abendlandes* (The Decline of the West). From Spengler's ideas he derived a certain contempt for liberal democracy. As early as 1926 he wrote, but refrained from publishing, a panegyric to the historic importance of the idealistic assassin. Called *Megillat ha-sikarikin* (The Scroll of the Sicarii) it argued, inter alia, that "morally it is permissible to kill for public reasons, whereas not so for private reasons even if motivated by revenge."[39]

In the early 1930s, Abba Ahimeir became the leading figure of the maximalist circle. Impressed by the successes of various European Fascist movements, he vigorously urged the transformation of the Zionist Revisionist Organization into a duce-led revolutionary movement. It should assume power by force in order to reappropriate Eretz Israel in its entirety as a sovereign Jewish state.[40] Ahimeir also headed a minuscule and short-lived (1930–1932) group called Brit Ha-biryonim (Covenant of Brigands, the allusion being to the ancient Jewish zealots who rebelled against the Romans and assailed the Jewish moderates in the last days of the Second Temple period). In practice, this group did not go beyond demonstrative acts and virulent anti-labor propaganda voiced particularly in its mouthpiece *Hazit ha-am* (The People's Front). But Ahimeir flaunted his admiration for Fascist ideology and called upon Jabotinsky to become the duce of Zionism. "I nurtured my sympathy for fascism within me even before I came to The Land," he explicitly stated in September 1928, explaining that if he did not publicly display this sympathy earlier it was only because the time had not yet been ripe.[41] What exactly Jabotinsky's attitude to Ahimeir's views was remains a moot point. Certainly, in March 1932 he publicly expressed praise of Ahimeir in the columns of *Hazit ha-am*. "In Eretz Israel there lives a wonderful type of young Jew. His name is Abba Ahimeir," he wrote. "Greetings to you from afar Abba Ahimeir, our teacher and master."[42] Moreover, he accorded Ahimeir unreserved moral backing when in 1933 he was put on trial as an alleged accessory to the assassination of Chaim Arlosoroff, a charge from which Ahimeir and his associates were acquitted by the court (although they were sentenced to imprisonment on other counts) but which left a smoldering residue of hatred between the Labor and Revisionist camps of Zionism.

Ahimeir's Fascist sympathies led him even to evince some esteem for Hitler's movement until as late as April 1933. He and his associates considered Nazi antisemitism to be merely another manifestation of a widespread phenomenon, no worse than was prevalent in the decadent democracies.[43] Jabotinsky, however, had absolutely no delusions about the unprecedentedly serious nature of Nazi antisemitism. In February 1933 he dismissed sanguine opinions that were still issuing from some Jewish sources in Germany to the effect that the Nazis would not give priority to actions against the Jews. "Understand me," he wrote in an article that he sent to *Hazit ha-am*, "the Jewish question is no addendum to the other clauses in his [Hitler's] program, it is the very essence of his plan."[44] In May 1933 the banner headline of *Hazit ha-am* was: "Jabotinsky, the leader of political Zionism, declares war on Hitlerian Germany!" and he called for a worldwide boycott of Nazi Germany. At about the same time he at last began to express strong disapproval of Ahimeir's pro-Nazi innuendos. "The articles and columns of *Hazit ha-am* on Hitler and the Hitlerite movement are a knife in my back and that of us all," he wrote to Dr. A. Weinshal, chairman of the Zionist Revisionist Organization in Palestine. He warned that if one more line would appear claiming to recognize in Nazism any signs of a movement of so-called national liberation, he would "demand the expulsion of the editors from the party and cut off all personal relations with the people who thwart me with this cheap and brazen behavior."[45] Yet Ahimeir and his like-minded associates were never expelled from the ranks of Revisionist Zionism, and as we shall see, their basic conceptions ultimately prevailed in the underground military organizations that claimed to be the authentic progeny of Jabotinsky.

In the course of the 1930s, the poetry of Uri Zvi Greenberg contributed immensely to the heroic cult of power. He extolled and glorified the virtue of self-sacrifice in the national cause, and his verse was replete with such vitriolic declarations as "And I say a land is conquered with blood / Only that which is conquered with blood is sanctified for its people / . . . Blood will decide who rules here."[46] He depicted Jewish destiny eschatologically as hanging between the poles of catastrophe and redemption. For some members of the maximalist, radical Right, such as Yehoshua Heschel Yevin and, later on, Israel Scheib, Greenberg was nothing short of a "prophet" and "lawgiver" of biblical dimensions. Yevin translated the spirit of his prophetic message into an ideological formulation called "The Twelve Principles of the Constitution of Liberation."[47] It spoke not simply of a modern state but of "the Kingdom of Israel" that would be established "in the natural borders of the soil on which the Jewish nation was born" and declared that "Ishmael and Edom [the Arabs and the British] are only alien occupants—just as the Russians were in Poland or the Turks in Serbia." This heroic vision was advanced in emphatic contrast to the effete, ghetto-bespectacled outlook of Weizmann and the rot of Socialist Zionism, which, together, had reduced Zionism to the squalid objectives of a mere "national home" in Palestine. Their vision was to be realized not merely through resettlement but primarily through armed liberation from foreign occupation.

There is a direct continuity of ideology as well as of personnel between the ethos of might formulated by Uri Zvi Greenberg, Ahimeir, and their associates in Brit Ha-biryonim and the Lohamei Herut Israel (Lehi, Freedom Fighters of Israel) underground movement founded in 1940 by Avraham Stern. Also, Lehi's "Eighteen Principles of the Revival"[48] emphasized in quasi-messianic terms that "the Jews are a Chosen People," "that the homeland is Eretz Israel in the boundaries stipulated in the Bible" (i.e., from the Nile to the Euphrates as in Genesis 15:18), and that "the sword and the Book were given together from heaven." It too spoke of "the revival of the kingdom." It even called for the building of "the Third Temple as a symbol of the complete redemption."

In all, the inner and ongoing tension between Jabotinsky's brand of nationalism—integral but not unrestrained by liberal compunctions—and these decidedly nonliberal and quasi-messianic strains rendered Revisionist Zionism far less monolithic than its theory of "monism" purported to make it. In this regard, Jabotinsky, ever the ideologue par excellence, had an ideological rationalization: he preached tolerance for internal differences in the movement. "How important it is to work together with persons who truly belong to your own 'race'" (here he used this term in the sense of mentality and world outlook), he wrote, "not to coerce the conscience of a comrade, but rather to allow time for him or you to reconsider and recognize his or your errors."[49] Be that as it may, the vociferous presence of the quasi-messianic maximalist group in revisionism certainly exacerbated its rivalry with the Zionist labor movement. This is not, however, to say that it alone was responsible for the acrimonious confrontation that ensued. Also Jabotinsky himself contributed heavily to the offensive against the labor movement.

The Offensive against Labor

As we have seen, Jabotinsky's Zionist Revisionist party came into existence in 1925 on a relatively limited plank of activist opposition to that which it deemed the disastrously meek policy of Chaim Weizmann vis-à-vis Britain's mandatory responsibilities. The critical factor that broadened the base of the Revisionist offensive and consequently transformed its nature was the historical reality in Poland and in Palestine in the second half of the 1920s. In Poland the drastic deterioration of the Jews' economic and political situation was generating an unprecedented mass emigration to Palestine, the generally preferred outlet to the United States having been effectively blocked by that country's new restrictive immigration laws. In the Zionist lexicon this wave came to be known as the Fourth *Aliya*.

The Fourth *Aliya*'s reception in Palestine was a mixed and ambivalent one because it willy-nilly posed a challenge to the until then gradualist pattern of highly ideologically motivated pioneering *aliya* and the virtual hegemony already attained by the Socialist party Ahdut Ha-avoda and the Histadrut labor federation. In this context, the critical determinative factor in the internal politics of Zionism was Jabotinsky's broadening of his offensive to target the Socialist labor movement. He charged that, motivated by venal self-interest and a perverted class-war doctrine, it had allied itself with Weizmann's defeatist policies. At the same time, casting about for a mass constituency in the struggle to oust the Weizmann administration of the Zionist Organization, Jabotinsky focused heavily on the Jewish middle class in Poland and in Palestine.[50]

The upshot was that Revisionist Zionism was rapidly transformed into an aggressively anti-Socialist, pro-bourgeoisie party, perceived by the Zionist labor movement as an unprecedented threat to everything for which it stood and all it had attained in Palestine. Given the interwar context of bitter political polarization between Socialist parties of the Left and the mushrooming Fascist parties of the Right all over Europe and indeed the world, the ensuing conflict within Zionism escalated fiercely. Jabotinsky himself, reverting metaphorically to his favorite theory of psychic-racial determinism, in 1926 described the difference between the antagonists as one so vast as to constitute two hopelessly incompatible psyches or "spiritual races." "The main difference between us and them," he wrote to Dr. von Weisel, "is not programmatic, it is psychic; at times I almost have the impression (of course this is only a jest) that we stand before a mysterious race difference."[51]

The core of Jabotinsky's ideological onslaught against Socialist Zionism, as that of socialism generally, was his rejection of the very idea of class rule. The red flag, signifying class rule and the concept of dictatorship of the proletariat, was as much anathema for him, he claimed, as was the swastika of Nazism. He regarded it as the antithesis of the principle of human equality, of "each man a king," which, he claimed, was the essence of his own liberal outlook. Class rule was the source of every kind of reactionary oppression; the greatest enemy of individual freedom of expression. It meant rule by one segment of society, a minority segment, over all others for "class always constitutes a minority and never will be a majority."[52]

To be sure, Jabotinsky did not deny the reality of class divisions in society nor that all classes displayed selfishness. However, he contended that whereas "the proletarian movement has sanctified class egoism," at least the bourgeois class was capable of showing shame for its selfishness.[53] Balking at all idealization of the worker at the expense of the middle classes, he refused to pay obeisance to that sacred cow of most of the labor movement—manual labor. Indeed, he rejected the contention that the future of human societies rested with the proletariat. "Technology is displacing labor," he predicted. The task of the proletariat, as a factor in production, was declining with such great rapidity that the chances were that it would no longer fulfill any vital function in the economy of future societies. The muscle and manual power of workers would inevitably be replaced by the machines produced by brain power.[54] Consequently, it was the bourgeoisie rather than the proletariat that was destined to play the major role in society. Certainly, the Zionist project needed middle-class entrepreneurs. It was to them that most national capital should now be funneled, no longer to the workers' economy as had inordinately been the case until that time. He caviled particularly at the absurdity of the situation: the lion's share of the national capital contributed mostly by middle-class Jews was being handed over to the Jewish working class in Palestine, which then cynically was declaring class war against the very middle class that was thus financially sustaining it! With increasingly passionate rhetoric he affirmed the value and pride of being bourgeois. He noted that he himself, being a writer and journalist, belonged to the intelligentsia. But if the proletariat regarded the intelligentsia as bourgeoisie, so be it, declared Jabotinsky: "We have nothing to be ashamed of, bourgeois comrades!" For the bourgeoisie embodied the highest spirit of enterprise, and private incentive was a basic and necessary factor in the development of human creativity. "Hence, if there is a class that carries on its shoulders the mission of the future (a supposition which we, the bourgeoisie, do not believe in because we scorn class ideology and our belief is in the nation above all classes and in humanity above all classes); if there is such a class, then it is we the bourgeoisie, the enemies of the police state, the harbingers of individualism."[55]

It might be said that revisionism sought out and adopted the role of ideological champion of the Jewish bourgeoisie, rather than emanating from that bourgeoisie. The fact is that most of the General Zionist camp worldwide was unwilling to go along with Jabotinsky's ideas. Indeed, a considerable segment of the Jewish bourgeoisie, including some private entrepreneurs, manufacturers, and citrus growers in Palestine, recognized the preeminent role of labor in the Zionist renaissance and favored accommodations with it on both political and economic planes.[56]

Jabotinsky balked at the virtual monopoly wielded by the Histadrut labor union over the development of the Jewish sector in Palestine. Allowing that "workers ought to be organized," he tried to explain that "no-one wishes to break the Histadrut—God forbid. More precisely we wish to break (and we shall surely break) its demand for a monopoly and for power. That is an accurate statement. Yes, to break!"[57] This cry and accompanying instances of strikebreaking, as well as the creation of a rival "national" workers' union, were the most abrasive aspects of all in the confrontation between Jabotinsky and labor Zionism.

On the theoretical plane, Jabotinsky began to formulate a program of labor relations that bore the unmistakable imprint of contemporary Fascist corporative models. His proposal, aired in general outline at the third Zionist Revisionist Organization's congress (Vienna, 1928), involved the creation of an institute of national arbitration, or supreme economic council, that would determine the fair equilibrium between workers' wages in all sectors, on the one hand, and employers' profits on the other. The elected president of such a council would be a neutral person acting "above party," and each sector of the economy would be corporatively represented, that is, employers and employees together. It would encompass the supervision of neutral labor exchanges as well as arbitration. To all intents and purposes national arbitration would override all trade union activities. Further enhancing this corporative conception, Jabotinsky also mooted the idea of a "Trades Parliament" for the Jewish sector in Palestine. Representing trades corporations across the spectrum of economic life, it would function alongside the existing elected assembly and National Executive (Va'ad leumi) as a sort of senate for the corporative regulation of all economic relations.[58]

It is indicative of Jabotinsky's ambivalent oscillation between systems of liberal democracy on the one hand and Fascist models on the other, that, having made proposals derived from the latter, he nevertheless went to great pains to deny any advocacy of fascism and to reiterate his belief in democracy. Clearly, he was troubled by the failings he perceived in contemporary European examples of democracy. Plagued by too many doubts about laissez-faire liberalism ever to consider it as an adequate alternative to the kind of labor hegemony that he frustratingly confronted in Palestine, he saw distinct advantages in aspects of contemporary Fascist experiments. Yet he was anxious never to be tarnished by the brush of fascism. No doubt he recognized that it would jeopardize all his aspirations to win the support of the British public, always the axis of his diplomatic policies. But apart from that consideration, the evidence indicates overwhelmingly that, notwithstanding his doubts, in the final analysis he genuinely fell back on democracy as the preferable political system. His articles on the subject of democracy are revealing of his ambivalence. As if he were arguing with himself—or perhaps with the notions of some of his followers— they consist in recitation of the failings of democratic governments, concluded by reaffirmations that for all democracy's faults "so it is . . . there is no better system."[59] In this regard there is a particularly illuminating letter of Jabotinsky written in 1933 to one of his lieutenants. With mingled indignation and apologia, he admits that revisionism did have commonalities with Italian fascism. "Revisionism is not 'Fascist,'" he averred, "the only view it holds in common with Italian Fascismo is the negation of class war, the demand for arbitration as the only way to solve labour conflicts and the subordination of class interest to the interest of the nation." Yet this, he goes on to insist, did not derogate from revisionism's belief in "democracy, a parliamentary regime, freedom of thought, press and association."[60]

Jabotinsky also made great exertions to show that there was a substantive difference between his proposals and the Fascist corporative system. Not without some cogency—but carrying no weight with his labor Zionist antagonists—he argued that, whereas Mussolini's fascism was predicated on coercion by the state, his own proposals, by virtue of the prestate circumstances of the Zionist project, rested on voluntary submission to an arbitration system that had no ultimate coercive power. In an article written in 1935, for example, he explained that, as used by the ancient Roman lictors, the fasces (the bunch of rods with an ax in the middle) was a symbol of coercive discipline imposed by the state. The essence of Italian fascism was indeed the principle of state coercion, irrespective of the will of those subjected to it. But this could have no application whatsoever to the Jewish population of Palestine. "When we Jews speak of 'compulsory' arbitration in Palestine, what we mean is a free pledge by all concerned to renounce voluntarily any other method of settling industrial disputes and to accept (voluntarily) the arbitrator's judgement, however unpalatable. . . . The point is that this program is the reverse of Fascism."[61]

In the decade between the founding of the Zionist Revisionist Organization in 1925 and the creation of the New Zionist Organization that subsumed it in 1935, an escalating series of clashes over policies exacerbated the relationship between the Revisionists and the labor movement to the point of utter schism.

One of these was Weizmann's broadening of the Jewish Agency in 1929 to include non-Zionists, a measure that had the support of much of the labor movement but was vigorously opposed by the Revisionists. Even more bitter was the clash over the allocation of immigration certificates to Palestine for persons without independent means. The criteria set by the Mandatory authorities enabled the majority in the Zionist Organization to discriminate against Betar members in favor of *halutz* workers associated with the labor movement. Advantage was taken of this as a means of disciplining the Revisionists when they persisted with independent political initiatives. The issue of certificates was a source of unceasing acrimony, as was the control exercised by the Histadrut over the labor exchange. This led to the Revisionists' founding, in 1934, of their own Histadrut Ovdim Leumit (National Workers' Organization). Another source of rancor was the "transfer" agreement of April 1933 negotiated with Nazi Germany to facilitate the transfer to Palestine of German Jews' capital in the form of goods. Endorsed by the Jewish Agency and the Zionist Executive, this became a painfully controversial issue for Zionists across the political board because it undermined attempts to organize a worldwide Jewish boycott of German goods. The Revisionists were among the most fervent advocates of this boycott plan.

But it was the assassination of Chaim Arlosoroff on the Tel Aviv beach front in June 1933 that brought the clash with labor to its boiling point. Even after Abba Ahimeir and the other Revisionists accused of this crime were ultimately acquitted for lack of evidence, it was widely and persistently believed in the labor movement's ranks that they were indeed guilty. The Revisionists, for their part, believed this to be a planned blood libel on the part of the labor leaders.

The cumulative outcome of all these clashes (not without some violence, the labor camp generally having the upper hand) was a mutual demonization of labor Zionists and Revisionist Zionists. By 1933 the former's image of the Revisionists worldwide was as nothing less than a Fascist distortion of Zionism. Ben-Gurion had no apparent hesitation in declaring that Jabotinsky was treading in the footsteps of Hitler.[62] With equal venom, the Revisionists portrayed the Zionist labor movement as incorrigible Bolshevists, traitors to the Zionist cause who, motivated by philistine self-centeredness, had sold out to Weizmann's policies and were bent on totally dominating the Zionist enterprise.[63] In 1934, David Ben-Gurion at last got together with Ze'ev Jabotinsky in a series of private meetings in London. They not only found sufficient common ground actually to draft a proposed agreement for peaceful coexistence, but they parted on terms of mutual respect and even some affection. Yet their efforts came to naught when, having been submitted to a referendum of the Histadrut's members, the proposed agreement was rejected.[64]

Diagnosis, Vision, and Means

We have traced the evolution of Jabotinsky's Zionist ideology out of its general Zionist matrix, which in itself comprised a synthesis of Herzl's strain of functional nationalism and the practical-cum-cultural strains of Hibbat Zion, into a comprehensive ideological canon within an independent organizational framework. In sum, it became more ideologically self-contained than almost any other variety of the Zionist ideology. Perhaps the only other comparably holistic ideological subsystem was that of the Ha-shomer Ha-tzair segment of labor Zionism, which we discussed earlier. Yet, as we have noted, even Revisionist Zionism underwent a bifurcation. The mainstream adhered to Jabotinsky's integral but liberal-restrained ideological formulations in all major respects. To be sure, a segment of that ideological mainstream parted company with Jabotinsky in 1933 and formed the Jewish State Party under the leadership of Meir Grossman. However, that was precipitated by an essentially tactical difference relating to the question of whether or not revisionism should break away from the unified framework of the Zionist Organization. The Jewish State Party remained within it.[65] The really profound bifurcation of Revisionist ideology was between the liberal-restrained mainstream and a small but (with historical hindsight it may be said) significant section, that which we have labeled here the radical Right. The latter jettisoned liberal restraints and replaced the nonromantic functional strain in Jabotinsky's national ideology with a romantic quasi-messianism. Notwithstanding these qualifications, the relative wholeness of Jabotinsky's subideology of Zionism facilitates one's summing it up under the heads of diagnosis, vision, and means.

Jabotinsky's diagnosis of the Jewish problem was but a gloss on the seminal thought of Pinsker, Herzl, and Nordau. Like Herzl, Jabotinsky treated antisemitism with great gravity but located the root cause in the condition of national homelessness rather than in antisemitic prejudice in and of itself. At the same time, there was something of Pinsker's diagnosis in Jabotinsky's view of the antisemitic odium as an ineradicable pathology inherent in mankind. This combination of notions was facilitated by a distinction Jabotinsky drew between "the antisemitism of people and the antisemitism of things." The former was an immutable and ever-present subjective prejudice, rooted in the human illness of xenophobia, hatred of the other. The damage its bearers caused could perhaps be blunted, but mankind could not be completely healed of it. In this Jabotinsky was quite as pessimistic as Pinsker had been. However, more pertinent to the Zionist diagnosis was the objective dimension of antisemitism, "the antisemitism of things." This was caused by the condition of exile—that is, national homelessness—and the resultant alien status of Jews everywhere. "For the cause of our suffering is the very fact of *galut*, the seminal fact that we are a minority everywhere. It is not the antisemitism of people. It is in the first place, the antisemitism of things, the internalized hatred of the alien, inhering in every social economic body, that is the cause of our suffering."[66] But, again, like Herzl, Jabotinsky considered this to be a datum of reality that could be, as it were, deployed against itself. That is, by effectively posing the Jewish problem as one of objective international concern, the antisemites themselves could be persuaded, if only out of self-interest, to facilitate the "evacuation" of the Jews and the national solution proposed by Zionism.[67]

In the interwar historical context, when antisemitic political parties were on the ascendant throughout Europe and the Jewish situation—economic as well as in terms of civic rights—was fast deteriorating, Jabotinsky's emphasis on the objective antisemitism of things took on the form of a radical call for "liquidation of the *galut* before the *galut* liquidates the Jews." Perhaps more than that of any other brand of Zionism, Revisionist rhetoric was animated by a sense of looming catastrophe for European Jewry, although even this foreboding, it must be stressed, was very far from imagining the unimaginable Holocaust of planned annihilation that was to be perpetrated by the Nazis during the Second World War. Jabotinsky, in fact, was well off the mark in some of his specific predictions. As late as 1939 he was of the opinion that full-scale war would be averted. He also nurtured an entirely unrealistic estimation of the capability of Poland to withstand a German assault. This has not obviated the prevalence of a myth that Jabotinsky, more than any other Zionist leader, anticipated the catastrophe of the Holocaust.[68]

Since the supreme principle of "monism" dictated that ultimate social questions be held in abeyance until the attainment of statehood, the visionary dimension of ideology was not supposed to occupy much attention in Revisionist Zionism. This did not, to be sure, prevent Jabotinsky from speculating as to the kind of social system that was most desirable. But such speculations were in the nature of rhetorical weapons to provide his devotees, especially in Betar, with the ideological wherewithal to counter the labor Zionist movement's compelling social vision. That the ultimate Jewish state envisaged by Jabotinsky was to be an essentially liberal democracy is clear enough, notwithstanding the considerable relinquishment of liberal values and the leaning toward a corporative system of economic and labor relations that he so insistently advocated for the period while the state was still in the making. It should also be noted that, after the creation of the State of Israel, even the Herut (Freedom) party, which was formed in large part out of the radical Right of Revisionist Zionism and claimed the ideological heritage of Jabotinsky, adhered unreservedly to the principles and rules of parliamentary democracy. Enduring many years in opposition, it attained governmental power for the first time only in Israel's election of 1977.

The purely speculative part of Jabotinsky's ideological formulations was largely reactive to Socialist ideas. He purported to derive from the Bible a social ethos that could serve as an alternative to that of working-class-conscious socialism. In contradistinction to the fixed Socialist order that would once and for all do away with economic inequalities but that inevitably exacted a heavy price—stunting individuality and creativity, destroying private enterprise, and so on—Jabotinsky proposed that the biblical concept of the jubilee (*ha-yovel*) be adopted. He explained that "the idea of the jubilee is of an entirely different character" from that of socialism.

Its essence is the idea that from time to time society itself would undergo a major and thorough social revolution, changing everything, taking away from the rich whatever was superfluous and giving it to the poor. But after each such revolution—every individual would remain free to start afresh on his social struggle, again to strive for the bettering of his situation, again exercising his energies and talents.[69]

By dint of this formula of periodic social readjustment, Jabotinsky suggested that the virtues of social equalization would be attained without the disastrous defects of a fixed Socialist order. Private property, free competition, and the natural inequalities in earning power that resulted from differences in ability, enterprise, and endeavor would be preserved. Of course, simplistic as this notion was, Jabotinsky did not claim that under modern conditions the biblical jubilee could be adopted literally. Qualified experts would find the ways and means of applying the fundamental principle of the jubilee to modern conditions. For the interim, between each stage of radical readjustment and socioeconomic equalization, Jabotinsky advocated something taken from the ideas of Josef Popper-Lynkeus.[70] Accordingly, he toyed with a Hebrew acronym for the five "elementary needs" of man that ought to be ensured to all by the state: "In Hebrew, they could be expressed briefly and euphoniously in five words, each beginning with the letter "m": *mazon* (food), *maon* (shelter), *malbush* (clothing), *mora* (education) and *marpe* (medical assistance)." The provision of this minimum subsistence, of course, required very substantial state intervention and controls. It also called for legislation fixing working hours and working conditions, progressive taxation and a national insurance system.[71]

So much for Jabotinsky's speculation about the ideal social system, all of which was, in principle, deemed inapplicable while the Jewish state was still in the making. This brings us to the dimension that occupied by far the major part of Jabotinsky's ideological profusion—the dimension of means. One aspect of this related to the internal development of the Zionist enterprise in Palestine and the mobilization of the Jewish people worldwide. As we have seen, Jabotinsky energetically challenged the dominant strategic program shared by labor Zionists and the Weizmannite General Zionists alike, namely, gradual and qualitatively selective *aliya* and development of an exemplary society. He fervently advocated his "monistic" alternative program of subordinating all qualitative considerations to the quantitative goal of attaining a majority in Palestine and thence to the pristine nationalist goal of sovereign statehood. Much of what was involved in this alternative strategy was the internal affair of Zionism: avoidance of all rhetoric and practice of class struggle, institution of a binding system of labor arbitration, politically neutral labor exchanges, and allocation of the national capital raised by Zionist funds for private enterprise as well as collective settlements and labor enterprises, all of which we have noted earlier.

However, the seminal and enduringly major part of Jabotinsky's program of means related to matters external, hence to what was called politics. A typical Jabotinsky aphorism was "Zionism consists in—and so it will have to stay also in the future—ninety percent economics and only ten percent 'politics.' But this ten percent of politics is the conditio sine qua non of our success."[72] Large-scale immigration and attainment of a demographic majority in the shortest possible time depended above all on the British mandatory regime. Hence the major question was what exactly Jabotinsky advocated that the Zionist Organization should do in order to achieve these premier objectives.

Chronologically speaking, given that Revisionist Zionism emerged as an expression of activist opposition to Weizmann's leadership, Jabotinsky's first and foremost prescription was that the Zionist Organization should assertively demand that the British administer Palestine to the optimal advantage of the Zionist enterprise. Therein lay the thrust of his criticism of Chaim Weizmann's leadership: the charge that Weizmann was too meek, compromising, and ineffectual. Spelling out what the optimal advantage of the Zionist enterprise meant, Jabotinsky's formulation amounted to, in his words, "a colonization regime." This included ensuring what Zionists would consider a favorably inclined civil service in Palestine—from the outset of the British military administration, a major criticism of Jabotinsky having been that the local mandatory authorities were unsympathetic to Zionism. "The question of a pro-Zionist administration, that regards our Zionist aspirations sympathetically, is perhaps the pivot of our entire political problem," stated Jabotinsky.[73] Moreover, it meant a comprehensive range of administrative and legislative measures, including land reforms facilitating Jewish purchase of government-owned lands, state protection for local industries, and a fiscal system favoring settlement. Above all, it required vesting controls of the rate of Jewish immigration largely in the hands of the Zionist Organization itself so that the Jewish population might advance rapidly toward becoming a majority in Palestine. Of course, it also meant permitting the formation under British aegis of a Jewish component of the British military garrison in Palestine.

Since the reality was that neither the British government's view of its own interests nor even its interpretation of its obligations under the Mandate were congruent with these optimal advantages of the Zionist enterprise, the operative question became how one ought to go about obtaining satisfaction of Zionist demands. Jabotinsky's grappling with this difficult question took the lion's share of his prolific publicistic output and rhetoric. A typical declamation was the following: "By what means are we to attain these rights? . . . With the same means adopted by Dr. Herzl, that is to say, by dissemination of information and organization of public opinion, Jewish, English and of the whole civilized world. That is the singular meaning of the concept 'political offensive.'"[74]

Jabotinsky was convinced that the British government could be persuaded that its interests ultimately coincided with those of Zionism, that what some British personalities like Josiah Wedgwood[75] believed, could and would become accepted governmental policy. He attached enormous importance to acts of public demonstration—mass protest meetings, worldwide petitions,[76] and the like—as instruments of pressure upon a society that was as democratic and susceptible to public conscience as he believed Britain to be. This was his approach, notwithstanding other far less optimistic ruminations to which he gave vent in his writings to the effect that "man is to man a wolf" and ultimately only power counts.[77]

Jabotinsky's particular suggestions of the kinds of public pressure that should and could be brought to bear upon the British government were myriad and often contradictory. At times he vested all his faith in the capacity of the moral conscience of the civilized world and particularly the British public to win over the British government. At other times he spoke as if he believed that public pressure could coerce the British authorities against their will: "To gather together, to concentrate and to bring before the powers that be such factors of pressure that will force them to give in—entirely independently of the fact whether their attitudes had changed for the better or remained hostile as before."[78] At yet other times he cast about for alternative powers—Italy or Poland, for example—ostensibly to replace the alliance with Britain. But this was really a bluff. It was only another supposed form of pressure against Britain because he well knew that no viable alternative was available.[79]

In a symbolic sense the touchstone of Jabotinsky's differences with the Zionist Executive headed by Weizmann came to be the question of proclaiming the *Endziel*, the final aim, of Zionism. Theodor Herzl had, of course, openly advocated the creation of a *Judenstaat* (Jews' state). However, from the outset, the Zionist Organization itself, governed by realistic tactical considerations, had phrased the official aims of Zionism in equivocal terms: the Basel Program of 1897, which remained officially valid until at least the postwar congress of late 1946, had spoken of the creation of a *Heimstätte* (national home) as the aim of Zionism. True to his demonstrative élan, Jabotinsky adopted the position that Zionism should unequivocally declare its aim to be "the creation of a Jewish majority in Eretz Israel on both sides of the Jordan" and thence a Jewish state capable of resolving the worldwide Jewish problem.[80] Jabotinsky argued not only that failing to state this clearly fooled neither the Arabs nor the British but also that it was necessary to stem the lapse of Zionism into a defeatist minimalism that could only encourage the British to further appease the Arabs.

At the seventeenth Zionist congress, in mid-1931, the Revisionists made a symbolic but crucial issue of their demand that the congress state publicly that Zionism's intent was for Palestine, meaning both sides of the Jordan, to be a "*Judenstaat* i.e. a *Staatswesen* (Commonwealth) with a Jewish majority."[81] The issue of stating the final aim was exacerbated by a statement that Weizmann was reported to have made during the congress to the Jewish Telegraphic Agency, which included the words: "I have no sympathy or understanding for the demand for a Jewish majority. A majority does not necessarily guarantee security. . . . A majority is not required for the development of Jewish civilization and culture. The world will construe this demand only in one sense, that we want to acquire a majority in order to drive out the Arabs."[82]

The upshot was that the Revisionists were able to create an enormous anti-Weizmann rumpus. Although the congress expressed disapproval of Weizmann's words in the interview, it shared his underlying view that leaving the original Basel Program's statement of aims intact was still the better part of political wisdom. When the labor camp managed to stymie the Revisionist resolution by using a procedural ploy of "moving to pass to the order of the day" without putting it to the vote, there was an uproar of protest, and Jabotinsky demonstratively tore up his delegate's card. This symbolic issue became the most salient pretext for the final secession in 1935 of the Revisionists from the world Zionist Organization.

All of this was regarded by Chaim Weizmann and the labor Zionist leadership as facile and futile demonstrativeness. So far from seriously influencing British policy, they thought it could more likely harm the progress of the Zionist enterprise by provoking ever greater Arab resistance and reinforcing those political forces in Britain that were already inimical to Zionist aspirations. Believing that they had a firm grip on political realities, they held fast to a gradualist, pioneering strategy of practical settlement and socioeconomic development. Only in the late 1930s and, finally, after the British White Paper of 1939, which virtually promised the creation after ten years of an Arab Palestine with no more than a Jewish minority, did David Ben-Gurion, chairman of the Zionist Executive, determine that the international situation warranted a change in strategy, a new phase of "fighting Zionism" and an international reorientation aimed at bringing American pressure to bear upon Britain.

In the final analysis, the end goal of Jewish statehood was no less ensconced in Ben-Gurion's Zionist ideology and even in that of Chaim Weizmann than it was in Jabotinsky's revisionism. The real differences—and they were crucial in the history of Zionism—were on the strategic level—that is, by what means was the goal to be achieved? Another enduring commonality that must be noted was the premise that only through the medium of Britain could that goal ultimately be reached. This "orientation towards Britain," as it was termed in Zionist phraseology, was shared by Jabotinsky throughout his life. Again, the real difference between him and Weizmann revolved around the question of by what means that medium was to be influenced so as ultimately to facilitate the fulfillment of Zionist aspirations.

Whatever may have been the extenuating circumstances in the international situation of the late 1930s, it is a matter of historical record that Jabotinsky's New Zionist Organization, created as a vehicle for untrammeled pursuit of his alternative Zionist strategy, failed to produce any significant impact on British policy. In the end, those who laid claim to Jabotinsky's ideological legacy resorted to a new strategy, tantamount to a radical revision of revisionism itself as it had for so long been espoused by their erstwhile mentor. Their strategy was violent resistance aimed at totally dislodging Britain from control over Palestine. This brings one to the question of Jabotinsky's relationship to the underground military organizations that, on the face of it, ran so contrary to his orientation on Britain, namely, the Irgun Tzvai Leumi (IZL, National Military Organization) and the Lohamei Herut Israel (Lehi, Fighters for the Freedom of Israel).

The IZL arose in 1937, having evolved out of a splinter group of the self-defense organization, the Hagana, which was secretly directed by the Zionist Executive. This splinter group, known as Hagana B, had been formed in 1931 by an alliance of Revisionist Zionists with some General Zionists and Mizrahi religious Zionists, all of whom chose to secede from what they considered to be the Labor-dominated Hagana. Lehi, in turn, was formed out of a secession from the IZL in 1940. The conventional wisdom cultivated by in-house memoirs and historical accounts has been that the IZL underground and, in its wake, the Herut political party, which issued from it after the establishment of Israel in 1948, were in direct line of continuity with the ideology of Jabotinsky. More recent historiography, executed with greater thoroughness and objectivity,[83] has revealed very significant differences and even outright clashes between Jabotinsky and such key younger personalities in the development of these underground groups as Avraham Stern and Menahem Begin. Stern was an important figure in the IZL before seceding from it in 1940 to form Lehi. Begin became the head of Betar in Poland in March 1939, and, having come to Palestine in 1942 as a soldier of the Polish army in exile, he became the commander of the IZL in 1944, when it launched its uprising against the British regime in Palestine.

It is evident that Jabotinsky, although nominally the supreme commander of the IZL, was hesitant and ambivalent about its break with the Hagana's policy of self-restraint in the face of Arab acts of violence against Jews in 1936.[84] The fact that Jabotinsky's endorsements and blessings of the IZL's actions followed events rather than initiating them is partly accountable in terms of his difficulties in having to be a remote-control clandestine commander. Effectively barred from entry into Palestine after 1929, he operated mostly from Paris until 1936 and thereafter from London. Obviously, he also needed to avoid any association of the underground with the New Zionist Organization or even Betar, both of which he headed officially. But there also were incompatibilities between the strategy he had consistently advocated and an alternative strategy espoused by Stern, Begin, and like-minded associates in the right wing of the Revisionist camp.

As we have already noted, Jabotinsky's strategy, sustained from the start to the finish of his career and served throughout by his brilliant ideological rhetoric, rested on the premise that the Jewish state could and would be attained through the medium of Great Britain's mandatory responsibilities over Palestine. In overall perspective, whatever alternative speculations he entertained are accountable as passing doubts, changes of mood, and tactical adjustments, all only human in the circumstances of a political career punctuated by many frustrations and difficulties.[85] Given Jabotinsky's abiding assumption that Britain's own interests could be shown to be compatible with Zionist aspirations, moral pressure in the form of public appeals, mass petitions, and unequivocal demands on the part of the Zionist Executive were the means that he espoused. In the light of this pivotal strategy, even the role of the IZL was conceived by Jabotinsky essentially as a *demonstration* of Jewish determination and capacity for resistance should Zionism's legitimate claims on Britain be frustrated. That is, in the final analysis, it was to serve merely as a radical means of pressure, *not* as an ultimate instrument of outright rebellion aimed at overcoming British power and "liberating" Eretz Israel in the manner of Garibaldi's liberation of Italy.

Precisely therein lay the fundamental division that rapidly developed after 1937 between Jabotinsky and those younger leaders, notably Stern and Begin, who were, albeit in divergent ways, to give the Lehi and the IZL undergrounds their determinate form as would-be instruments of rebellion to the finish against Britain. Stern, who was in direct line of inheritance from the quasi-messianic call for a revolutionary Zionism voiced by Abba Ahimeir and Uri Zvi Greenberg, had long nurtured this approach. Indeed, he showed disrespect for Jabotinsky and, while carrying out secret assignments, including arms procurement for the IZL in Poland in the late 1930s, busied himself with the formation of secret IZL cells within Betar unbeknownst to Jabotinsky and contrary to his wishes.[86] At about the same time, Menahem Begin, the up-and-coming young leader of Betar in Poland, was reaching operative conclusions similar to those of Stern via a more conventional Revisionist Zionist route.

The gravity of the cumulative departure from Jabotinsky's basic strategy became publicly evident in the debates of the third Betar world conference held in September 1938 in Warsaw. At that conference, Menahem Begin vented a barely disguised call for the new course of armed rebellion. "Cavour would never have achieved the liberation of Italy without Garibaldi," he declared. His call represented a radical reorientation predicated on the opinion that the long-time

Revisionist strategy of pressurizing Britain to recognize its putative interest in the Zionist project was a bitter delusion. This meant out-and-out rebellion in whatever form was available and with whatever alternative powers—Poland, for example—could be persuaded to cooperate. Later, after Stern had created Lehi, his search for alternative allies led him even to the extreme of making an approach to a diplomatic representative of Nazi Germany in the Middle East. The ends so sanctified the means that even an alliance with Satan was justified. However, the Germans spurned this approach.[87]

At the 1938 Betar conference, both Jabotinsky's interjections during Begin's impassioned speech and his reasoned response made it clear that he regarded Begin's words as misguided bravado. Jabotinsky's acquiescence in Begin's call for a change in the wording of a clause of the Betar oath was no more than of symbolic and rhetorical significance. The conference agreed to the change from "I shall not raise my arm but for the defense of my people" to "I shall raise my arm for the defense of my people and the conquest of my homeland." Far more important was the fact that Jabotinsky firmly rejected Begin's comparison with the liberation struggle of other nations. Pointing out that those nations had the crucial strategic advantage of being soundly barricaded as a majority in their own countries, he said: "Not a single strategist in the world would claim that, under the present circumstances, we could do what Garibaldi and de Valera did. This is just talk. Our situation bears no resemblance to that of the Italians and the Irish, and if you think that what Mr. Begin has suggested is the only way and you have the necessary arms—go ahead and commit suicide."[88] Jabotinsky proceeded to reaffirm his faith in moral power. "What finally counted in the world was conscience," he averred. "I respect it. It was wrong to ridicule it." He warned the gathering that if one despaired of there being a conscience, the alternatives left were drowning "in the Visla river" or communism. The arousing of conscience in the world was precisely what he believed could be achieved by "an outbreak of Hebrew heroism in Eretz Israel." In sum, the role that Jabotinsky envisaged for the IZL was no more than to demonstrate Jewish determination and heroism, not actually to wage a war of liberation to the finish.

Having stressed the differences between Jabotinsky and the more radical right wing of Revisionist Zionism, a caveat is necessary: these differences were matters of strategy; they related to the ideological dimension of means. That is, they might be considered differences at the level of operative ideology. In the case of Lehi it is arguable that this operative level coincided with a deeper difference in fundamental ideology: Jabotinsky's integral but functional and liberal-restrained mode of nationalism, on the one hand, and the radical Right's mode of quasi-messianic nationalism and its unrestrained ethos of naked power on the other. In the case of the IZL, the divergence from Jabotinsky's time-honored strategy was not necessarily coordinate with such a fundamental ideological mutation or deviation. After all, utter disillusionment with Britain or with the possibilities of peaceful progress toward the attainment of Jewish statehood could lead to the notion of a coup-like usurpation of power over Palestine without involving a change in fundamental Zionist ideology.[89] It therefore remains tenable to regard the IZL as it developed both during and after Jabotinsky's life as the natural progeny of fundamental ideological elements in Jabotinsky's mode of Jewish nationalism.

PART THREE

Fundamental Issues

CHAPTER SEVEN

Zionism as Secular Jewish Identity

Z IONIST IDEOLOGY involved far more than an innovatory political
program for the material welfare of Jews. It also redefined the nature of
Jewish identity in nationalist terms. It was the legacy of emancipation
and enlightenment, discussed in an earlier chapter, that made this nationalist
redefinition possible. Exposure to modernism in respect of the application of
scientific criteria in order to expand the frontiers of knowledge about man, his
society, and its history inevitably challenged the traditionalist understanding of
Jewish identity. Belief in the *transcendental* origin of Jewish identity, that is to
say, its creation by a divine force outside nature, was placed in question. An
alternative understanding presented itself—Jewish identity as the *immanent*,
evolving product of natural, scientifically explicable developments within an
ethnic group that came to be known as the Jews.

The schism between the traditionalist, transcendental self-understanding on
the one side and the modernist, immanent self-understanding on the other side
is the great divide in modern Jewish identity. It both preceded the emergence of
Zionist ideology and affected a wider range of Jews than was encompassed by the
Zionist movement. Within Zionism itself these two contradictory self-
understandings coexisted, however uncomfortably. The national-religious Zionists, although accommodating the modern concept of the nation, clung to the
traditionalist belief that this unique nation had been brought into existence by
the terms of an essentially religious covenant emanating from God, whereas the
secularized Jewish intelligentsia posited the natural evolution of a Jewish nation
generating a culture of which religious faith and precepts formed a part—for the
major period of the nation's history a dominant part, but only one part
nonetheless. The aspiration toward a renaissance of Jewish culture that was to be
accomplished by Zionism was predicated on the secularized understanding of
Jewish identity as an outcome of immanent processes in the history of the
nation. Religion was neither wholly coextensive with Jewish culture nor its
original source; it was merely one of the ingredients of Jewish national culture.

It was the condition of *galut* that had endowed religion with so inordinate an influence on Jewish existence, enabling it to consume, as it were, the nation.

The Secular National Jew: Ahad Ha'am

For the ethnicist intelligentsia, which, as we have argued, provided the core of Zionist ideology, the task of Zionism was to redress this distortion by reviving the secular dimensions of Jewish culture while incorporating only those elements of the religious heritage that were malleable and consonant with modernity. In the formative early decades of Hibbat Zion and the Zionist Organization, the foremost articulator of that intellectual enterprise was Ahad Ha'am. In this respect, although there is no reason to doubt his own denial of direct intellectual indebtedness to Peretz Smolenskin, it may be said that, phenomenologically, Ahad Ha'am was Peretz Smolenskin's successor, making his literary debut in 1889 some four years after Smolenskin's death.[1]

If the biographical passage of Ahad Ha'am from a traditionalist upbringing to secularized enlightenment and the search for a workable synthesis of the two was typical of the reforming ethnicist Jewish intelligentsia in eastern Europe, the particular Enlightenment ideas that he adopted were rather idiosyncratic. Teaching himself Russian and German and later on also English, French, and some Latin, he was particularly attracted to the thinking of Auguste Comte, as mediated by Russian thinkers like Pisarev, and to that of the British empirical philosophers and moralists John Locke, David Hume, John Stuart Mill, and Herbert Spencer. At first he read them mainly in German translation, later increasingly in the original. In sum, he was intellectually captivated by late-nineteenth-century positivist thought on religion and society.[2]

The thrust of this positivist thought was its attempt to derive knowledge exclusively from the empirical or "positive" sciences, rather than from abstract reasoning (i.e., metaphysics). In particular, the popular ideas of Herbert Spencer, for whom Darwin's doctrine of evolution served as the central unifying and organizing principle of all true knowledge, occupied an important place in the intellectual milieu into which Ahad Ha'am entered. Such conceptions came to inform his understanding of Jewish survival in the past and of its prospects in the future. In particular, they led him to posit the workings of a collective "will to life" (*hefetz ha-kiyum*), of an instinctive nature, and to consider the beliefs and precepts of the Jewish religion as a function of that will to life, rather than as its cause. Moreover, these conceptions informed his understanding of the nation as a biological-cum-cultural unit broader than religion. It enabled him to relegate religion to the status of a subsidiary aspect of culture and to shift his Jewish self-understanding from the traditionalist transcendental basis to a secular immanent basis.

Yet it cannot be said that Ahad Ha'am's expositions constituted a consistent philosophical system. His thinking was quite eclectic and not confined to purely positivist categories. At times his use of the concept "national spirit" (*ha-ruah ha-leumi*) was hardly distinguishable from the metaphysical abstractions of Hegel, and purely idealistic rationales abounded in his writing. Thus, the nationalist message he conveyed, while positing a will to life, did not rely on its power deterministically to ensure Jewish survival. Instead, he idealistically exhorted the nation to accomplish its unique moral purposes, without which survival itself would be meaningless. In his preface to the second edition of his famous book of essays, *Al parashat drakhim* (At the crossroads), Ahad Ha'am admitted that "although the national feeling [viz., the will to life] is the cause of our existence . . . knowledge of the cause does not suffice. We seek also to endow our survival with a purpose." Given the suffering and tribulations that the Jew had always undergone, it was necessary for him to know that he lives and suffers "not only because he cannot die, but because he ought to live."[3] It was the purpose embedded in the national spirit that gave meaning to the life of the Jew.

Reduced to simple terms, it may be said that Ahad Ha'am conveyed a double message to the individual secularized Jew: in positivist terms it assured him that Jewish survival was a deterministic function of an instinctive will to life that could find alternatives even for the former indomitable role of religious faith and practice; in idealistic terms, Jews must actively will their survival as a nation, for, by the prototypically nationalist lights of Ahad Ha'am, there was no higher form of human association than the nation. Its attributes—such as its language, the territory with which it was associated, its literary heritage—stood at the peak of the scale of values binding upon and endowing meaning and purpose to the lives of human beings. Much like the Italian nationalism of Giuseppe Mazzini, however, Ahad Ha'am's averted the hypernationalist or chauvinist potential of such organic nationalism by positing a quasi-religious moral purpose or mission for his own nation within a common mankind harmoniously comprising a plurality of nations.

Indeed, of all the national attributes that it behooved the Jew to value, none was held up higher by Ahad Ha'am than the moral values of the biblical prophets that had been distilled within the Jewish religious-cultural heritage. He countered the fascination of some Jewish nationalist thinkers (notably Berdyczewski, whose ideas we shall discuss later) with the ideas of Friedrich Nietzsche by arguing that Nietzsche's attribution of supreme value to the ideal of the *Übermensch* (superman) was nothing new to Judaism. The difference, however, was that, whereas Nietzsche exalted the superphysical, Judaism exalted the supermoral. But here he further contended that because of their exiled condition the Jews had so far failed to reach their ideal. "We have been unable to fulfil our mission in exile, because we could not make our lives a true expression of our own character, independent of the opinion or will of others."[4] Zionism's true purpose was to rectify this and to reset the Jews on the path to autonomous realization of their collective moral ideal.

Not religion but ethnic belonging was the basis for Jewish identity as proffered by Ahad Ha'am. For him the question "Why be a Jew?" was quite as senseless and unnecessary as it was for the most orthodox of Jews, although his reasoning was on secular lines. One was a Jew as naturally, immutably, and unquestionably, as one was a child of one's natural parents. Any attempt of a born Jew to pass as a member of any other nation was as self-abasing as it was self-defeating. Assimilation was no more than a form of inner slavery and spiritual degradation. The nation was an evolving organic entity, not a contractual association that one could join or leave at one's will or whim. In his polemic against Reform Judaism, which tried to reduce the bonds of Jewish identity merely to adherence to a covenantal belief system, he eloquently enunciated his plain, self-validating ethnicism: "I know why I remain a Jew; or rather, I can find no meaning in such a question, any more than if I were asked why I remain my father's son."[5] He commended the following statement to his readers:

For what reasons are we Jews? How strange is the very question! . . . We are incapable of being anything other than we are . . . as the love of a mother for her children . . . because the will to be a Jew is a natural force within us, a source of life for us; because Judaism resides within our hearts like the other feelings planted in man at the time of his creation—like parental love and love of the homeland. . . . Neither the Jewish outlook, nor the Jewish faith, are the original cause, the prime mover; but rather the Jewish feeling [*ha-regesh ha-yehudi*], an instinctive feeling, which it is impossible to define in words. Call it by whatever name you choose, call it blood kinship, call it racial feeling or the national spirit, but most appropriately of all call it: the Hebrew heart![6]

This ethnicist rationale for affirming Jewish identity did not dismiss the historic role performed by religion. However, positivist assumptions governed Ahad Ha'am's understanding of religion. He followed David Hume in explaining the origins of religion in immanent rather than transcendental terms, as the product of primitive man's fear in the face of the evil forces of nature.[7] He also adopted the view that morality was a function of subjective feeling. Furthermore, in the final analysis, it was not religion that created that moral feeling but vice versa—religion was its outcome:

The real relationship between religion and morals is, therefore, quite the opposite of what is usually held: although religion does support and validate the moral will of the people, the content of moral values is the result of other factors and it has its own lines of development. Religion gives vitality to abstract moral ideals . . . but the moral feeling [*ha-regesh ha-musari*] is what shapes the divine qualities in accord with each historical period.[8]

Hence, the displacement of rabbinical religious authority over the lives of Jews by advancing scientific knowledge—a process that he considered inevitable—did not ipso facto signify the eclipse of moral values. Rooted as Judaism's moral values were in the historically evolved experience of the Jewish nation—that is to say, in their "moral feeling"—they could not be sustained within a revitalized Jewish national culture in which rabbinical authority and influence was rapidly declining. The rabbinate and Jewish law no longer were the criterion. According to Ahad Ha'am's conception, "religion was only one of the forms constituting culture."[9] National culture was a phenomenon more comprehensive than religion. As he wrote to the American Reform rabbi and Zionist Judah Magnes in September 1910, "In my view our religion is national—that is to say, it is a product of our national spirit—but the reverse is not true. If it is impossible to be a Jew in the religious sense without acknowledging our nationality, it is possible to be a Jew in the national sense without accepting many things in which religion requires belief."[10]

Ahad Ha'am also made a distinction between Jewish religious belief and observance on the one hand and Jewish "religious feeling" on the other. Since Jewish religious morals, as well as beliefs and observances, were but a secondary outgrowth of the primary Jewish national culture, it was entirely possible that a Jew who, for intellectual reasons, no longer considered certain religious beliefs and practices to be binding upon him might nevertheless still be moved by the "religious feeling" that underlay those beliefs and observances. One could be "possessed of religious feeling, although without religious belief . . . beliefs can change completely, yet feeling may remain."[11]

It followed that, given the decline of Judaism in the sense of religion, in consequence of modernization and emancipation, the necessary evolutionary adaptation that the natural will to life could fuel was the modernization and revitalization of the national Jewish culture. It also followed that the modernized "national Jew," as Ahad Ha'am termed him, even if no longer bound *by* the authority and observance of traditionalist religious institutions, still could and ought to feel himself bound *to* the norms of "the national morals" and moved by the "religious feeling" that had animated the traditionalist religious forms in the first place.

No aspect of Ahad Ha'am's nationalist ideology was more significant—and, as we shall see, more controversial—than this insistence on his part that even the secular national identity of the new Jew was bound to a certain normative Jewish outlook; that is to say, beyond mere ethnic belonging and use of the Hebrew language, the "national Jew" was obliged to adhere to certain cultural norms. First and foremost of these was the distinctive moral essence distilled within the historic cultural heritage of the Jews. It was Ahad Ha'am's ambition to undertake a magnum opus that would explore and explicate definitively that moral essence.

This he never managed to do, but one may cull the gist of his thesis from a number of his essays.

One such essay, published in *Ha-shiloah* in 1899 and titled "The National Morality" in later collections of his writings, sought to clarify "the essence of Hebrew nationalism and the obligations which it places on its adherents."[12] Although not denying that there was a universal basis to all morality, he argued that every nation developed in the course of its history its own characteristic mode. There were certain principles and standards of morality that were applied or emphasized more in one national culture than in another. Indeed, what was considered ethical in one culture was sometimes considered unethical in another. Hence, the characteristic moral principles and standards of each nation constituted what was perhaps the most important of all its cultural attributes. The "national morals" were a faithful reflection of the "national spirit" no less than was the national language. On these lines Ahad Ha'am proceeded to argue that it behooved the national Jew to uphold the unique moral values of the Jewish people, rooted particularly in the biblical prophets, even if he had ceased to observe the laws and rituals of the Jewish religion. Not to do so would be to deprive the national Jewish culture of its essence.

Ahad Ha'am illustrated this point with reference to a contemporary drama written by Max Nordau, one of the newly established Zionist Organization's foremost leaders. The hero of this drama evidently was intended to reflect the spirit of Jewish nationalism as understood by Nordau. He was a Jew who, disappointed in his efforts to be fully accepted as a German, returned to his own people. Nordau's hero challenges a German Junker officer to a duel as an act in defense of Jewish honor. He says that as a Jew he is bound to do this. Here was an example, according to Ahad Ha'am, of cultural assimilation, for the true Jewish morality dictates nothing but contempt for the act of dueling and could never encourage such behavior. To further compound things, the hero is led into this situation in the first place by his love for and his desire to wed a gentile heroine. This prompted Ahad Ha'am to comment that, even if one assumed there to be nothing in the spirit of Jewish ethics itself that opposed such a marriage, there still remained further questions: whether, "given the dispersed and dismembered state in which we Jews are situated today, such marriages would not endanger Jewish existence? And if so, was preservation of his people's existence not a moral obligation binding the national Jew, to which end he ought to sacrifice also his personal happiness?" Ahad Ha'am was ready to accept that this hero might well be a "political Zionist," but "was he also a national Jew?" he asked. "Could a man be considered a national Jew when he was so remote from the spirit of his nation that in his very desire faithfully to carry out his moral obligation to it he is carried away by the emotions of an alien nation to the point of giving up his life, without even feeling that in doing so he is sinning against the spirit of the nation in whose name he speaks?"[13]

To be sure, Ahad Ha'am admitted in this essay that the example was a very simple one. The real gravamen of his argument was that there existed such a thing as "the national spirit" of the Jewish people from which there emanated moral norms "that applied to everyone, believers and non-believers alike." Hence, it was the Jewish national movement's task to foster study of the bases and implications of Jewish morality. It had to clarify, one way or another, "what are the obligations that the authentic national morality, without any alien admixtures, imposes on us in relation to ourselves and to others, and in what way it is possible for us, and it behooves us, to apply these obligations to our lives and outlook in the present?" By way of showing that such an enterprise was not unrealistic, he pointed to the efforts of men like Dr. Felix Adler in the United States, aimed at creating Societies for Ethical Culture independently of the authority of established religions.

In another essay, written some years later, in 1910, when he was living in London, Ahad Ha'am made a more profound contribution to his concept of "the national morality."[14] The essay was in response to a commentary on the Synoptic Gospels by Claude G. Montefiore, the leader in England of the trend of reformed Judaism that came to be known as Liberal Judaism. In that commentary Montefiore tried to show that Judaism and Christianity were in the final analysis not incompatible and that the teaching of the New Testament could be accepted as part of Judaism. Respectfully but sharply, Ahad Ha'am took issue with Montefiore's thesis. He illustrated the crux of his counterthesis with a famous talmudic discussion concerning a theoretical moral dilemma:

Imagine two men journeying through the desert, only one of whom has a bottle of water. If both of them drink, they must both die; if one of them only drinks, he will reach safety. Ben Petura held that it was better that both should drink and die, than that one should witness the death of his comrade. But Akiva refuted this view by citing the scriptural verse, "and thy brother shall live with thee." *With thee*—that is to say, thine own life comes before thy neighbor's (*Baba metzia*, 62a).[15]

Noting that Ben Petura was hardly known, whereas Rabbi Akiva was the acknowledged authority, Ahad Ha'am adduced that "we may be sure that through him the spirit of Judaism speaks." The implied premises of Akiva's judgment were as follows: Given that the saving of human life was an ultimate value, the standard of objective justice demanded that whatever life could be saved should be saved. Given further the equal value of all human life in the eyes of God, again by the standard of objective justice, he who, *ab initio*, possessed the means to save his own life should do so. Here was an example of a moral principle that had become normative to Jewish culture, and it differed from the norm of Christian culture. "If a man brought a question like this to a Christian priest," suggested Ahad Ha'am, "the priest would certainly begin to expatiate in glowing terms on the duty of a man to sacrifice his life for another, to 'bear his cross' in the footsteps of his 'Messiah' so that he might win the Kingdom of Heaven—and so forth." Judaism's morality, however, had always tended to the abstract religious and moral ideal and to the collective as mediator for the individual. Unlike Christianity, Judaism did not preach love as a value independent of social justice (*tzedek*). It demanded that one rise above sentiment and the personal factor and apply the standard of abstract impersonal justice, disqualifying equally egoism and altruism (which was merely inverted egoism.)

As with other examples chosen by Ahad Ha'am, the all too evident simplification need not concern us here. Suffice it to note the thrust of Ahad Ha'am's thesis, namely, that in the Jewish cultural heritage there inhered a distinctive morality, in this case one that differed from the equally distinctive morality of the Christian heritage. There was, in other words, an identifiable *essence* of Jewishness and the new "national Jew" remained bound to it no less than he was bound to the Hebrew language and literature, to Eretz Israel, and to identification with Jews as a collective social entity.

Notwithstanding Ahad Ha'am's conviction that this model of national Jewish identity on secular, yet still normative, foundations was bound to triumph, he did not discount the parallel continuation of Jewish identity on religious lines. He felt sure that in the long run Western Jewry "will not succeed, try as it may, in turning out only 'Jews by religion,' and gradually the national element will conquer the religious,"[16] but this was in regard to Western Jewry where Reform Judaism had taken hold. In regard to eastern European Jewry and the old community of traditionalist Jews in Palestine, Ahad Ha'am did not consider it likely that orthodox religion would be wholly displaced. Initially, it was his hope that the revitalization of Jewish life stimulated by the Hibbat Zion movement would affect also the traditionalists, that they too would make internal adjustments, bringing the life of traditionalist Jews more into tune with the general Jewish national revival. "Since Hibbat Zion would revive the national heart and fit it for modern development," he wrote, "it was bound to create, in the course of time, a similar change also in religious matters." He drew a distinction between reform and development:

Notwithstanding my opposition to religious reform I believe in religious development. Reform is an artificial thing . . . whereas development is a natural thing, which occurs imperceptibly, slowly, in the process of living, without intentionality, out of the necessities of living. The phenomenon of reform depends therefore on the will of the religious leaders, whereas the phenomenon of development does not depend on their will.[17]

Although orthodoxy's failure to undergo the requisite development disappointed him, Ahad Ha'am himself did not consider it practically expedient to adopt a dogmatic, uncompromisingly secular attitude.[18] This, for example, was evident in the position he adopted over the problem of religion's place in the

Hebrew gymnasium (high school) that had been created in Jaffa on the modernized lines advocated by Ahad Ha'am's school of thought. In 1908 the question had arisen as to whether the Bible should be studied by the pupils with or without covered heads. Writing from his residence in London, Ahad Ha'am advised the educator Menahem Sheinkin: "If the high school cannot continue to exist unless caps are worn in class and the Higher Criticism is excluded, I do not think that this should be made a question of principle." He argued that the important thing was that the pupils acquire a thorough knowledge of the Hebrew language, the Bible, and the Talmud—even if on orthodox lines—and an adequate knowledge of Jewish history, while concurrently getting a good general education. As long as this was achieved, "Eretz Israel will be very much better off from the cultural point of view" even if many of the pupils still adhered to their orthodoxy.

Do you expect all the Jews to become free-thinkers? I only wish we might have a real people in Eretz Israel, even if it were all orthodox—not in the uncouth fashion of the *haluka* [literally, "distribution"—the system under which money was collected in the Diaspora for the support of the Jews living in Eretz Israel] people, but decent civilized men like the Christian Englishmen whom I meet here. I should be very happy if I could hope to live to fight against orthodoxy of that type in Eretz Israel.[19]

Similarly reflective of his attitude is what he once told Joseph Klausner: "You seem to confuse intellectual compromise with practical compromise. . . . In every day life we do all sorts of silly things at the behest of fashion: why then must we insist on opposing religious observance, even at the risk of doing harm to our national movement?"[20]

In summation, it may be said that the nationalist ideology of Ahad Ha'am was an attempt to synthesize deeply ingrained traditional Jewish cultural elements with an enlightened modernism, heavily influenced by nineteenth-century positivist thought but never entirely free of idealism. On a positivist basis, Ahad Ha'am hypothesized three interrelated factors that both explained and justified the identity of modern free-thinking "national Jews." The first was the will to life, an instinct-like force fueling the national group's survival power in an unceasing evolutionary process of adaptation. Religious institutions and precepts had served as its major instrumentality in the absence of a territorially based polity. The second and third factors were the primordial "moral feeling" and "religious feeling" that inspired and shaped the evolving beliefs, institutions, and rituals of religion and that could also outlast these external religious forms when they were displaced by scientific knowledge. The idealistic motif in Ahad Ha'am's thought supplemented these positivist factors with the exhortation that the Jewish nation survive to provide cultural meaning for the life of Jews and to serve its moral purpose for mankind.

The seminal importance of Ahad Ha'am's thought for the inner development of Zionism lay less in the particular positivist concepts that he employed than in the implications of his approach for shaping the identity of the new "national Jew." It was to be a secularized identity but one bound by certain norms rooted in the religion-saturated cultural heritage of the Jewish nation. The fixing of these norms was predicated on the proposition that there was an identifiable essence of Judaism's heritage. It was, in sum, a secular identity of *normative* character that Ahad Ha'am epitomized and advocated, one bound to certain fixed philosophical outlooks and moral principles no less than to the Hebrew language, the Land of Israel, and the society of Jews.

The Hibbat Zion Phase

If Ahad Ha'am may be adjudged the most important thinker in the entire pantheon of Zionist ideology, it is not by virtue of philosophical profundity—which he displayed only in limited proportions—but rather because more than any other person he stimulated intellectual ferment over the ultimate meaning of the entire Zionist enterprise for the identity of Jews. As the seminal formulator of an ideological program for secular Jewish national identity, he provoked, willy-nilly, an ideological reaction from the orthodox religious segment of the Zionist movement, which has persisted to this very day.[21] Furthermore, even within that segment of the secularized Jewish intelligentsia that drew inspiration and guidance from Ahad Ha'am's writings, important aspects of his thought aroused spirited controversy. For his intellectual captivation by positivism cast his own synthesis of nationalist thought in a particular mold that did not necessarily fit others in the secularized nationalist camp. This accounted in part for the intellectual debate he aroused. But by far the most significant of the controversies that engaged the secular Zionist intelligentsia was precipitated by his avid advocacy of norms binding the secular Jew to a fixed world outlook and set moral principles as well as to respect for the religious sancta of the Jewish cultural heritage. Caught up in the ongoing debate were intellectuals and writers who had already settled in Palestine as well as others still situated in Europe.

In an earlier chapter of this book we referred to Ahad Ha'am's role in the founding of the Bnei Moshe society in 1889, whose purpose was to create a cultural elite for the work of national revival.[22] He formulated Bnei Moshe's main objective as "the renaissance of our people in the land of our fathers." It sought to "broaden the meaning of 'nationalism' and to make it a lofty concept, a moral ideal at whose center was the love of Israel . . . to strip the title 'national' of the materialist form which it has now assumed . . . and to elevate it to the level of a moral title, respected and loved in the eyes of the people." It aspired "in this way to educate on its lap, patiently, the generation that we seek."[23] As defined in Ahad Ha'am's formulation of Bnei Moshe's principles, the national values that were to be cultivated were "our fatherland and its [Jewish] settlers, the language of our forefathers and its literature, the memory of our ancestors and their history, the fundamental customs of our forefathers and their manner of national life through the generations."[24] In the type of schools that Bnei Moshe was to foster the pupils were to acquire these national values in addition to the attributes of modern European culture.

Ahad Ha'am's vision of Bnei Moshe was predicated on the assumption that the common nationalist denominator could bind together various elite intellectual elements, ranging from the highly secular who had personally broken with religious observances through to those who clung faithfully to orthodox religious observance. Bnei Moshe would "exalt above all, the general national flag"; its national work would foster the pure love of Jews for their nation, "a love which pushes aside all differences of opinion and private desires and draws together in unity all hearts, without factional differences."[25] Such unity presupposed, however, that the secularists retain a sense of respect for those religious traditions that had national value while the religious be open-minded about modern knowledge and education. In practice, it proved extremely difficult, if not impossible, to hold such an alliance together. The original Bnei Moshe oath, "in the name of the God of Israel and in the name of all that is dear and holy to me," was a source of dissension. In the Bialystok, Vilna, and Warsaw lodges, as well as in Jaffa, the tension between the two poles of secularism and orthodox religion resulted in various attempts to amend the society's rules and even to purge these lodges of dissenters.[26]

A particularly disruptive manifestation of the secular-religious tension in Bnei Moshe was the falling-out between Ahad Ha'am and Yehiel Michel Pines who occupied an important position in the settlement activities of Hibbat Zion in Palestine. Pines had settled there in 1878 as the representative of the Moses Montefiore Testimonial Fund, established by the British Board of Deputies with the object of advancing the economic welfare of the Jewish population. In 1887 he was appointed the representative of Hibbat Zion responsible for the administration of its agricultural colonies in Palestine. However, he soon fell out with the eastern European rabbis of Hibbat Zion over the question of how to observe the biblical sabbatical requirement that the fields lie fallow every seventh year.[27] As we have already noted in an earlier chapter, Pines was an extraordinary personality who combined religious orthodoxy with an open-minded attitude toward Enlightenment learning and on that basis had formulated what was probably the earliest version of Jewish religious-nationalist ideology. As such, he was a natural candidate for membership in Bnei Moshe, whose branch in Palestine he duly joined. However, his unique bridging of traditionalism and modernity (as well as a scandal concerning some allegedly fraudulent land purchases) made him the vortex of swirling controversies between the old and the new segments of the Jewish population in Palestine and eventually also within Bnei Moshe.[28]

Pines and a circle of like-minded supporters then drew nearer to the traditionalist Jewish community of Palestine (the "old *yishuv*"). In a series of pamphlets titled *Emet mi-eretz* (Truth from The Land), he pungently attacked the Ahad Ha'amist secularists of Bnei Moshe as well as those rabbis, notably Shmuel Mohilewer, who persisted in support of the Hibbat Zion movement in the face of what he regarded as its distortion by Ahad Ha'am and his kind. Pines campaigned against the secularizing influence of Bnei Moshe's Jaffa school. Its curriculum did not, to be sure, exclude study of religious laws and prayers, but the secular bias was all too evident in the way the secular subjects, Jewish history, and the Bible were taught. What is more, some of the teachers tended to flaunt their nonobservance. Pines declared that his love of Zion and belief in the resettlement of Eretz Israel remained as firm as ever. He had once supported the Bilu settlers because he then believed "in the power of the commandment to settle the Land of Israel since it would eventually restore those who had been estranged to the pasture of Torah and the commandments." But now he held the Bnei Moshe guilty of imposing their secularism on the movement and complained that "at the breast of this doctrine they are supposed to nourish a future generation!"[29] In "An Open Letter to Ahad Ha'am" he declared that Hibbat Zion, "in the form that it has now taken or that you [Ahad Ha'am] and your followers have dressed it up," failed to provide common ground for the "two types" of Jews, religious and secular. He averred that he too favored science and modern education and was a *Hovev Zion* (Lover of Zion), but he could not support the present form of Hibbat Zion, "which you have extricated from the temple of the religion of Israel and turned into a separate entity standing on its own."[30]

Bnei Moshe proved to be a short-lived phenomenon. Disrupted by such tensions between its secular and religious members, lacking strong leadership and criticized within Hibbat Zion itself on account of its secretive nature and elitist pretensions, it showed signs of disintegration by 1895, only six years after its inauguration. The important Jaffa lodge closed down in 1896. What remained was finally eclipsed by Theodor Herzl's groundbreaking initiative in calling together the first worldwide Zionist congress in 1897. Ahad Ha'am himself retrospectively described the whole venture as an "experiment that did not succeed."[31] This was perhaps too harsh a self-judgment. It is not insignificant that personalities who later played major roles in the development of Zionism received their ideological training within Bnei Moshe, including Chaim Weizmann, Leo Motzkin, Menahem Ussishkin, Shmaryahu Levin, and Haim Nahman Bialik. Moreover, it did foster publications of considerable significance, notably the *Luah ahiasaf* yearbook and the journal *Ha-shiloah*, which remained the preeminent forum of Zionist thought for decades after Bnei Moshe had ceased to exist. It also created some prototype Hebrew schools between 1892 and 1895, particularly in Jaffa but also in Russia.[32] Yet as an attempt to create a unified secular and modern religious elite on the basis of a common program for cultural renaissance of the nation, Bnei Moshe failed.

The Zionist Organization Phase

The meteoric advent of Theodor Herzl with the appearance of his *Der Judenstaat* in 1896 and his creation in 1897 of the Zionist Organization at the first Zionist congress in Basel inaugurated a dramatic new phase in the history of the Jewish national movement. As we have outlined in an earlier chapter, the highly critical reaction of Ahad Ha'am and kindred circles of the Hebrew-literate Jewish intelligentsia, mostly associated with Hibbat Zion, issued in an ideological position that has come to be known as cultural Zionism. They objected to the exclusive emphasis that Herzl placed on diplomacy aimed at attaining an internationally sanctioned, legal "charter" for systematic Jewish settlement in Palestine (or failing that, conceivably in an adjacent or other territory). They demanded that the Zionist Organization launch a comprehensive program of cultural renaissance rooted in the Hebrew language and the development of modernized schooling.

It was almost entirely in publicistic form that Ahad Ha'am vented his sharp critique of Herzl's exclusively political Zionism, for after the short-lived Bnei Moshe experiment he never again undertook a leadership role in any organizational or political sense. However, his influence as ideological mentor was discernible in the formation of the first political faction within the Zionist Organization. This was the Democratic Faction, which burgeoned promisingly in 1901 but faded out of existence in the course of 1903.

The Democratic Faction was the creation of members of the student intelligentsia, mostly stemming from eastern Europe and studying in German and Swiss universities. After the *numerus clausus* imposed in 1887 by the czarist government of Russia, the numbers of such students grew, reaching an estimated two thousand by 1899, compared with only 1,757 Jewish students studying in Russian universities.[33] Most of the émigré students were rooted in a thoroughly ethnicist Jewish identity, in the same mold as that of Ahad Ha'am but a generation later. Since the early 1890s nationalist Jewish student circles in various European cities had been engaged in plans for the convening of a unifying congress. They were on the point of achieving their objective when Herzl made his dramatic appearance in 1896. Responding to his call, by and large with enthusiasm, they were a visible presence when the first Zionist congress assembled in Basel in 1897. However, disenchantment with certain aspects of his policies and style of leadership soon set in. They were disturbed by the concentration of information and power within Herzl's inner circle, his apparent disregard for practical settlement activities, and his neglect of cultural work in deference to the rabbis.

As we saw in an earlier chapter, the foremost spokesman of the rabbis was Yitzhak Yaakov Reines. He earnestly appealed to the Zionist congress to recognize that the "question of culture was a disastrous matter for us" and should be excluded from the Zionist program.[34] The very concept of *kultura* (the Hebrew neologism for "culture" at that time) was anathema to orthodox Jews, for whom it signified secularism's destructive onslaught on the Jewish religion. It was grist for the mill of those orthodox rabbis who from the outset had warned that cooperation with secularists in the Zionist Organization was both mistaken and forbidden. Herzl was responsive to Reines's appeal. Whenever the question of culture was raised at the Zionist congress, Herzl endeavored to evade the issue. He sensed that it was a dangerously divisive issue and could only result in the loss to Zionism of the rabbis and their flocks. He held that the program of the Zionist Organization had to concentrate exclusively on diplomatic endeavors. To assuage the apprehensions of the rabbis, he repeatedly assured them from the congress podium that "Zionism does not intend anything that might wound the religious convictions of any section within Judaism."[35]

Chaim Weizmann, at the time a young chemist at a Swiss university, became the moving spirit of efforts to call together a Zionist youth conference comprising like-minded critics of Herzl's administration of the Zionist Organization. In the course of these efforts, he sought the advice and support of Ahad Ha'am, who, although not belonging to quite the same milieu as the student intelligentsia of Weizmann's generation, was almost universally regarded as their intellectual mentor. Ahad Ha'am characteristically declined the offer to take a prominent role in the initiative to create an opposition faction at the Zionist congress. To Weizmann he offered the advice that the youth conference he was trying to set up be removed from the official ambit of the Zionist Organization and that it function independently although, of course, in alignment with it.[36]

However, this advice was not heeded. Instead, Weizmann and his associates formed a faction that made its presence felt for the first time at the fifth Zionist congress in December 1901. It commanded 37 delegates of a total of 287.[37] Its leading personalities included Leo Motzkin, a mathematician; Berthold Feiwel, a writer; Zvi Aberson, its champion in ideological debates with the Jewish Socialist Bund; Shmaryahu Levin, a writer and brilliant orator; and Martin Buber, who was to become famous as a philosopher. Herzl, anxious as ever to avoid friction over the cultural question, tried by procedural means to defer debate on the Faction's resolutions until a new executive had been elected, which meant relegating it to the tail end of the congress. The Faction's members responded by demonstratively staging a temporary walkout in protest. In the end, however, the spirit of their demands was reflected in the resolution that was passed: "The Congress proclaims that an improvement in the level of culture, that is the education of the Jewish people in the national spirit, is one of the essential elements of the Zionist program, and it is incumbent on all its adherents to work towards its implementation."[38] The Faction's members were well represented on the Cultural Commission, which was supposed to pursue the subject further. They included Chaim Weizmann, Martin Buber, and Jacob Bernstein-Cohen, who was the key Zionist organizer in Russia. Moreover, Ahad Ha'am was also elected a member. But because the congress did not vote any funds toward such activity, the resolutions on culture remained frustratingly nominal.

The Democratic Faction's program was thrashed out in the first half of 1902 by a committee in which Leo Motzkin played the formative role.[39] Its ideological affinity with Ahad Ha'am's conceptions was manifest. The essence of Zionism was defined in terms of the striving for national cultural individuality, "an original Hebrew national culture in Eretz Israel."[40] Zionism's aim was "the revival of the Jewish people and its restoration as an organic unit." According to the program, "Zionism designates as Jewish cultural possessions, the past and present creations of the Hebrew spirit to the extent that they can be associated with general human culture." Moreover, it declared that "the injection of religious matters into the fundamentals of Zionism and its program is contrary to the national essence of Judaism" and called on Zionist leaders to desist from what it called "opportunism" in pandering to the rabbis' demands.

Although the program acknowledged the political goals of the Zionist Organization under Herzl's direction, affirming that "the complete liberation of the Jewish people will be made possible only through the establishment of a publicly, legally sanctioned refuge in Eretz Israel," it rejected the proposition that Zionism was in essence a reaction to antisemitism. Also, the emphasis it placed on the need to apply "scientific methods" to Zionist planning was fully consonant with the highly rational critique that Ahad Ha'am always applied to the national question. By this was meant such things as statistical inquiry into the actual conditions of Jewish existence in the Diaspora and the grounding of plans for practical work in Palestine on thorough research. Equally in conformity with Ahad Ha'am's ideas was the initiative taken by the Faction in furthering the project for creation of a Jewish university in Palestine, a matter in which Chaim Weizmann took a particularly energetic interest.

Although the Democratic Faction's program was thus the closest application of Ahad Ha'am's ideas since the demise of the Bnei Moshe society, it was far from being his own party. We have already noted that notwithstanding their regard for Ahad Ha'am as ideological mentor, the Faction's leaders did not accept his opinion that they should separate themselves from the Zionist Organization. Also, the Faction's program addressed some issues that did not particularly engage Ahad Ha'am's thought. One was its demand for the restructuring of the

Zionist Organization on the basis of ideological-political factions. Another was the stress placed on the "progressive" nature of Zionism. Although the Faction's program as a whole was far from being Socialist in character—the Socialist theorist Nahman Syrkin failed to find his place in the Faction[41]—it advocated that Zionism ought to act "according to principles that will limit, as far as possible, a class regime in the future Jewish state, despite the dominant materialist regime prevalent in the rest of the world."

The clash between the secular intelligentsia and the rabbinical stratum within the ranks of Zionism was, of course, at its most intense within czarist Russia. At the first conference of Russian Zionists, held in Warsaw shortly before the second Zionist congress (August 1898), several rabbis had proposed, without success, that a rabbinical committee be established alongside the Actions Committee of the Zionist Organization, with the purpose of overseeing educational, propaganda, and cultural activity.[42] Dissension over the cultural question came to a head at the second conference of Russian Zionists, which took place in Minsk in September 1902. By this time the Mizrahi organization, founded largely in reaction to the Democratic Faction, already commanded a substantial number of the delegates. However, the spiritual mentor of the Faction's brand of secular Zionism, Ahad Ha'am, was invited to be a keynote speaker.[43] In his speech he attacked the exclusively political version of Zionism that, so he complained, had become dominant under Herzl's leadership. Political goals were well and good but not if they meant the exclusion of cultural work.

Every true lover of Zionism [Ahad Ha'am warned] must realize the danger which it incurs through the diffusion of the idea that it had no concern with anything except diplomacy and financial transactions, and that all internal national work is a thing apart. If this idea gains general acceptance, it will end by bringing Zionism very low indeed. It will make Zionism an empty meaningless phrase.

By the same token he also maintained that "work for the national revival cannot be confined to material settlement alone." Zionism, in his view, had to take hold of both ends of the stick; it had to work for the creation of "an extensive and well-ordered settlement in our ancestral land," but at the same time it should not neglect the effort to create there "a fixed and independent center for our national culture, for learning, art, and literature." "The foundation of a single great school of learning or art in Palestine, the establishment of a single university for the study of language and literature," he declared, "would do more to bring us near to our goal than a hundred agricultural colonies."

Finally, in the prescriptive part of his address, Ahad Ha'am argued that the existing Zionist Organization was not capable of handling "the task of reviving the national culture." What was required was, therefore, to establish "a special organization for cultural work" that would function in cooperation with the existing Zionist Organization. He further proposed that within the cultural organization the secular national Jews and the orthodox national Jews, each independently and by its own lights, ought to foster Jewish cultural revival. There was a major task to be performed by each section. The orthodox had to reform their traditionalist education so as to imbue it with the national spirit, no less than the secular Zionists had to develop a new enlightened national education. The upshot was acceptance of Ahad Ha'am's compromise proposal by both the secularists and Rabbi Reines's Mizrahi—not, to be sure, that part of it that suggested separation from the Zionist Organization but only the idea of a two-stream solution. And this conciliatory outcome was clinched by an embrace between the major spokesmen on both extremes of the debate, Rabbi Reines and Chaim Weizmann, at the conclusion of the conference.

Notwithstanding Reines's implicit concurrence with Ahad Ha'am's proposal, there was reluctance within Mizrahi to relinquish the principle that neither the Zionist Organization nor Mizrahi itself should initiate educational projects. At the Mizrahi conference held in 1903 at Lida, the view prevailed that only at the local level should Mizrahi societies involve themselves in supervision and control of education "according to our religion and holy Torah."[44] Not until 1908 was a step taken in the direction of direct educational initiative, when Mizrahi in Frankfurt am Main took over responsibility for a school in Jaffa, known as the Tahkemoni school, which had fallen into financial difficulties.[45] No official Zionist support was sought for this, and at the ninth Zionist congress, which took place in Hamburg in 1909, Mizrahi held this up as an example of the principle that it still advocated.[46]

With the growth of the Zionist workers' parties in Palestine during the period of the Second *Aliya*, the secularists became more assertive. The "question of culture" erupted with renewed force at the tenth congress, held at Basel in 1911, when they sought to enforce cultural and educational projects in Palestine. At the end of the congress, a compromise proposal was suggested by the cultural committee, which included Rabbi Reines. It sought to delegate the direction of cultural activities in Palestine to the executive of the Zionist Organization while at the same time reassuring the orthodox that nothing prejudicial to religion would be done and that educational activities in the Diaspora would be left to local associations. A schism within Mizrahi's ranks became evident when one of its spokesmen, Hermann Struck (whose views represented mainly the German segment of Mizrahi), totally rejected the proposals. When the resolution was accepted by the congress, a split in Mizrahi indeed ensued. A group of members, mostly central European, abandoned the Mizrahi movement and shortly thereafter, in 1912, joined forces with other long-standing orthodox opponents of Zionism to form a new political organization of orthodox Jews sharing an anti-Zionist ideology—Agudat Israel (the Association of Israel).

In November 1913 a dramatic conflict erupted in the Jewish sector of Palestine over the primacy of the Hebrew language as the medium of education. It was precipitated by the attempt of the Hilfsverein, the leading philanthropic organization of German Jewry, to make German the language of instruction at a projected Technical College in Haifa (later known as the Technion). In the wake of this "language conflict," as it came to be called, the world Zionist Organization accepted financial responsibility for the Hebrew schools in Palestine established by the Hebrew Teachers' Association, champions of the Hebrew language in the conflict with the Hilfsverein. After a latent period owing to the First World War, this new direction was finally determined at a conference of the Zionist Organization held in London in July 1920. Modern Hebrew education in Palestine thenceforward became the responsibility of the Zionist Organization, but at the same time an autonomous authority effectively under Mizrahi control was established for a separate network of religious schools. Both systems were to be imbued with a common Zionist spirit, each according to its own lights. The dual solution to the cultural question thus became the rule. It continued when the State of Israel came into existence and persists until this very day.

Laissez-faire Secular Identity: Berdyczewski

The struggle over the "cultural question" was the most tangible expression of secular national identity in the program of Zionism. It emanated from Ahad Ha'am's view that Zionism called for a program of Jewish cultural renaissance in general and modernized Jewish education in particular. This view was shared by almost all of the ethnicist-rooted intelligentsia domiciled in, or stemming from, eastern Europe. This did not mean, however, that there was unanimous concurrence with the particular mode of secular national identity that Ahad Ha'am advocated. That mode, as we have seen, postulated the existence of an essential core of authentic Jewish cultural norms and insisted that these be accepted as binding by the secular national Jew. It was what might be termed a mode that commanded "normative" Jewishness. It might well be said that the Zionist ideology's profoundest and most persistent inner intellectual debate revolved on this critical point. The most influential antipode of Ahad Ha'am's position in this debate was articulated by a brilliant essayist and novelist named Micha Yosef Berdyczewski (1865–1921), also known as Micha Yosef Bin-Gorion.

The life and literary work of Berdyczewski was the very epitome of the ambivalence toward the Jewish religious heritage and the attraction to secular Western culture that characterized the nationalist Jewish intelligentsia of eastern Europe. The sheer poignancy and anguish that attended his onslaught on rabbinic traditionalism bespoke his ultimate rootedness in the old values. He was born in 1865, son of a rabbi in Medzhibozh, in the Russian-ruled province of Podolia, which was a stronghold of Hasidism. In his teens he groped toward

Enlightenment, the heroic books of the Bible, such as Joshua and Judges, serving as a passageway. There followed clandestine reading of advanced Enlightenment literature, ranging from Nahman Krochmal's *More nevukhei ha-zman* (Guide to the Perplexed of the Time) to Yitzhak Ber Levinsohn's *Beit Yehuda* (House of Judah).[47] Indeed, the discovery of this secret interest in Enlightenment heresy led to rejection by his father-in-law and the breakup of a marriage that had been arranged for him when he was only seventeen. After studying for a while at the somewhat more modern Volozhin yeshiva, in 1890 he broke with the world of the yeshiva and moved westward. He resided most of his life in Berlin, gaining his doctorate with a thesis on the relationship between ethics and esthetics. All the while he was gaining renown as a writer of novels and essays, mainly in Hebrew but also in Yiddish and German.

The dilemma of the uprooted, alienated *maskil* Jew, fettered by the chains of tradition and craving for the freedom of modern European culture, found supreme expression in his novels and short stories set against the background of the eastern European Jewish shtetl (small town). He also edited collections of Jewish legends and Hasidic lore. In his forays into historical writing, he tended to espouse the causes of personalities who rebelled against the authority of rabbinical Judaism. Although essentially an individualistic loner, Berdyczewski became the salient figure in the group of Hebrew writers known at the turn of the century as the Tzeirim (the young ones), who rebelled against what they regarded as the stifling weight of traditional rabbinic Judaism and who championed individual spontaneity and freedom.[48] Moreover, he had a deep influence on generations of Zionist intelligentsia who settled in Palestine, traceable in the thought of many a labor Zionist as well as in manifestations of the radical right and the Canaanite heresy (to which we shall return later in this survey).

Berdyczewski may be regarded as a direct successor of the nineteenth-century *haskala* revolt against religious traditionalism. But then, so too was Ahad Ha'am. There was, however, a major difference between the lines of *haskala* revolt followed by these two pivotal personalities. Ahad Ha'am took up the cudgels from those *maskilim* (for example, Moses Leib Lilienblum) who had attacked the established authorities of Jewish religion but at the same time nurtured some hope for internal reform of the religion. They had also evinced growing concern about the void that was being created by what they assumed to be the irreversible decline of religion in Jewish life. Since Ahad Ha'am shared this concern, he labored to formulate an alternative national Jewish identity bound by norms that would constitute a surrogate of sorts for the eclipsed religious authority and precepts. By contrast, in Berdyczewski's eyes religious authority was still a ubiquitous power, an unrestrained threat to free self-expression of the individual Jew in the present, no less than in the past. His concern was neither to reform the religion—a futile exercise, in his view—nor to fabricate a surrogate "national Judaism" lest the entire edifice of Jewish identity collapse but rather to break away completely from all religious authority and from all established norms. This escape was not, to be sure, into assimilation—Berdyczewski strongly affirmed Jewish identity itself—but in his view the normal, natural bonds of ethnicity would suffice for the preservation of Jewish identity. (He did not use the term "ethnicity," but his views were tantamount to affirmation of what today we would term ethnicity.) What was needed was not the imposition of newly formulated norms purporting to be distillations of the true essence of Judaism—as Ahad Ha'am proffered—but the "broadening of the cultural boundaries" of natural Jewish ethnicity. Hence, whereas most of those *maskilim* who came to adopt a nationalist program tended to seek compromise with traditionalism in the interests of national integrity, Berdyczewski thrust onward uncompromisingly with the *haskala* revolt.

At first Berdyczewski had a close relationship with Ahad Ha'am. He wrote articles that appeared in *Ha-shiloah* and for a time acted as Ahad Ha'am's assistant in its publication. Differences soon arose, however, over literary questions. Ahad Ha'am had reservations concerning Berdyczewski's tendency to inventive but ungrammatical style. He himself was a master of the essay form marked by grammatical care and terse rational argumentation. More important, Ahad Ha'am insisted that modern Hebrew literature set itself a nationalist purpose. He felt that the nascent Jewish literary energy of the contemporary generation could not afford to dissipate itself on universal themes. It should consciously restrict itself to issues that were intrinsically Jewish. Thus, poetry of the kind written by Saul Tschernichowsky (1875–1943), which abounded in Hellenistic, pagan, and universal motifs, was considered unsuitable for *Ha-shiloah*. Berdyczewski balked at this literary constriction.[49]

As soon became evident, the intellectual clash between Berdyczewski and Adah Ha'am ran much deeper than such differences over their respective literary outlooks. They espoused conflicting conceptions of the desired identity form of the secular national Jew. Berdyczewski sought to remove all cultural constraints, not only by encouraging literary creativity expressive of the whole range of human passions and concerns but also by rejecting any binding cultural norms such as those of "the national morality" as postulated by Ahad Ha'am. In the eyes of Berdyczewski and the Tzeirim circle of writers it was deeply regrettable that Ahad Ha'am had, so they argued, regressed from his original advocacy of the new national Jew's unlimited free thought. The crucial passage in Ahad Ha'am's writings that served as the basis for this charge had appeared in his essay of 1891, "Slavery within Freedom." There he had contrasted the natural self-affirmation of national Jews with the need of the assimilating Western Jews to justify their residual Jewish identity artificially by trumpeting their notion of a Jewish mission to the nations. In this connection he had written:

I at least have no need to exalt my people to heaven, to trumpet its superiority above all other nations in order to find a justification for its existence. I at least know "why I remain a Jew"—or, rather, I can find no meaning in such a question any more than if I were asked why I remain my father's son. I can at least speak my mind concerning the teachings and beliefs which I have inherited from my ancestors without fearing to snap the bond that unites me to my people. I can even adopt that "scientific heresy which bears the name of Darwin" without any danger to my Judaism.[50]

According to Berdyczewski, Ahad Ha'am had proceeded to propagate ideas that contradicted this original and commendable position. "If I may judge according to my heart about the beliefs and opinions bequeathed to me by my ancestors," he objected, "I am also permitted to pass judgment on those very values or even to reject them outright, without that rejection resulting in any severance from my people." "The people of Israel is an existential fact, not a world-outlook," he averred. "We are a people who happened to think in certain ways, but our being a people is not dependent on thinking in those ways. We shall not be compelled by an abstract Judaism of one kind or another. We are Hebrews and we shall follow our own hearts."[51] Unlike Ahad Ha'am, Berdyczewski did not seek some kind of synthesis with traditionalist Judaism that would be a modernized but still normative Judaism—a "national Judaism." Berdyczewski demanded not just a synthesis but "a revolution; a transvaluation of all the precepts of our lives till now."

Our heart, desiring life, feels that the revival of Israel is in the scales—Jews have precedence over Judaism; the living person has priority over the legacy of his forefathers. We must cease being Jews on the basis of abstract Judaism, and become independent, as a living, thriving nation. . . . Let us not restrict our ideas to fixed forms that command us what to think and how to feel. . . . What we need in our lives are not reforms but transformations, basic changes affecting all of our lives, thoughts and souls. Jewish learning and religion are merely aspects of life which, according to one's will and inclinations, may or may not oblige one. But the people of Israel has precedence over them: Israel comes before the Torah. . . . We shall no longer be able to solve the riddles of life or live and act according to the ways of our forefathers. We may be the sons and sons of sons of the generations that preceded us, but we are not their coffins. . . . A great responsibility rests upon our shoulders. All is in our hands! We shall either be the last of the Jews or the first of a new nation.[52]

In this passage, as in many others by Berdyczewski, the cry for a "transvaluation of values" reveals unmistakably the influence of Friedrich Nietzsche's ideas. There can be no doubt that they inspired, if not the content, then at least the form, of much that Berdyczewski espoused. The notion of the "new Hebrew" is clearly influenced by the example of Nietzsche's *Übermensch*. Berdyczewski followed Nietzsche in disdaining attributes of meekness, altruism, and passivity and in lauding boldness, heroism, and genius. He attributed the fault of "excessive spirituality" to the literature of the biblical prophets, the Talmud, and the medieval commentaries that had produced the Judaism of rabbinical traditionalism. Applying to Jewish history selective criteria in the use of the past, much as Nietzsche had advocated, he extolled the heroic, semipagan phase of Jewish history that had preceded the prophets and the whole corpus of oppressive rabbinical legalism.

Bemoaning the Jews' loss of appreciation for esthetic beauty and for intimacy with nature, he blamed this on the teachings of the diasporic rabbis. "Is it any wonder that generations [of Jews] came to despise nature," he wrote, "is it any wonder that we became a non-people, a non-nation, non-men? . . . Give us back our fine trees and fields! Give us back the world."[53] Yet the Nietzschean influence on Berdyczewski should not be overestimated. At core, Berdyczewski's views were essentially an expression, taken to extremes, of the secular revolt against rabbinical authority in eastern European Jewry.

A characteristic of Berdyczewski's essays was the repeated juxtaposition of contrasting symbols drawn from the history of the Jewish people. He repeatedly contrasted "the Book" (*ha-safer*) with "the Sword" (*ha-saif*). "The Book" signified the sum total of prescribed beliefs, precepts, and observances and the endless talmudic legalistic quibbling surrounding it. It was the source of the "excessive spirituality" of Judaism. In the same vein he contrasted the ethos "of daring and life" of Shammai with Hillel's "tenderness and humility, [his] submission to the yoke of life and excessive spirituality that suppresses life itself."[54] Another contrast was that between Yavne and Jerusalem. It was to Yavne that Rabbi Yohanan ben Zakkai escaped from Jerusalem when it was besieged by the Romans. There he reestablished the Sanhedrin, representing the numbing, legalistic, rabbinical Judaism that Berdyczewski deplored. Jerusalem, which held out against the Roman invaders, symbolized the authentic, heroic, and spontaneous values that he extolled. Nowhere is the contrast with Ahad Ha'am's valuation more stark than in Berdyczewski's charge that Moses and the biblical prophets were the source of the degenerative process that led to Yavne and the culture of the Book, for Ahad Ha'am taught that Moses and the prophetic tradition were the very epitome and essence of authentic Judaism.

For Zionist ideology the most far-reaching implication of Berdyczewski's outlook was the contention that there could be no liberation from the condition of *galut* without prior liberation from the past weight and present burden of normative rabbinical Judaism. By dint of his "transvaluation of values" he inverted the conventional wisdom concerning the causal relation between the exile and Judaism. By his lights, the exile was not the cause of Judaism's degeneration; rather the degenerate nature of Judaism (i.e., normative rabbinical Judaism crystallized out of the prophets, Yavne, etc.) was the original and ongoing cause of the exile!

Yet notwithstanding the radical thrust of his views, Berdyczewski was plagued by ambivalence and doubts. His writing is consequently shot through with contradictions. Whereas at one moment Berdyczewski speaks as if the heritage of the past is wholly dispensable, at another he recognizes, with Ahad Ha'am that there can be no cultural creativity without building upon the heritage of the past:

Culture is a possession of spiritual-heritage that comprises all human spiritual life and molds it into an historical-national form, fixed and distinctive of the given collectivity. In abstract terms one might say: culture is the eternal residue of everyday life and needs, a residue that is passed on from father to son and from generation to generation. Every son begins at the point where his father ended, and so each generation inherits [its culture] from its predecessor and undertakes the labor of advancing and perfecting it.[55]

At yet other times, Berdyczewski is reduced to deep frustration: "When we defeat the past, we ourselves are the defeated—and on the other hand, if the past is victorious, then again we and the sons of our sons are vanquished," he wrote. "Elixir of life and poison in one. Who will clear the path for us? Who will show us the way?"[56] Berdyczewski was thus a person in anguish, tortured and rent by the implications of his own radical revolt against rabbinical Judaism, pained by the stones he found himself throwing into the wells of his own Jewish identity: "Sometimes all my thoughts, all my meditations and the values I have destroyed, turn upside down before me. . . . Sometimes I feel I am killing myself."[57] Moreover, he was riddled by doubts as to whether the "new Hebrew" could ever really be realized. By contrast, Ahad Ha'am, although approaching Judaism from much the same secularist premises, had a calm and rational approach to the Jewish cultural heritage in its totality. He was not so plagued by ambivalence and doubt.

At the deepest level the difference between Berdyczewski and Ahad Ha'am lay in the clash between two conceptions of the Jewish heritage—the relativist conception of Berdyczewski on the one side and the essentialist conception of Ahad Ha'am on the other. Contrary to Ahad Ha'am, Berdyczewski rejected the notion that there was a permanent essence of Judaism, that it had a definable world outlook. There was no such thing as a constant single Judaism. Each generation formulated and lived by another variation of Judaism: "One generation goes and another comes, values go and values come."[58] The so-called essence of Judaism embodied moral values that were good before the giving of the Torah and became bad thereafter. What was considered good by Shammai was considered bad by Hillel. The God of Israel was seen at one time as "merciful and forgiving" and at another time as "jealous and vengeful." The God of Isaiah was not the God of Ecclesiastes; the God of Maimonides was not the same as the God of the Baal Shem Tov (founder of Hasidism). Berdyczewski contended that there really was no single "Judaism"; there were only Jews who thought and did.[59] "We wish to be what each one of us is according to his spirit and education and attitude to the world and all that it encompasses, just as is the case with every other nation," he declared.[60]

Adjunct to this relativism of Berdyczewski was his individualistic perspective, which clashed with Ahad Ha'am's collectivist emphasis. In this sense it might be said that Ahad Ha'am was the more pristine nationalist since, by definition, nationalist ideology posits above all that the individual's human self-fulfillment is impossible without his immersion in the national collectivity. For Ahad Ha'am the collective attachment of man was the primary natural phenomenon, whereas man's individualism was unnatural. For Berdyczewski quite the opposite was true: individualism was the natural healthy instinct of man, whereas his submersion into the collective was unnatural. Paradoxically, Berdyczewski's individualism therefore tempered his nationalism in the sense that it rejected uniformity of the nation. Yet it was at the same time a more radical nationalism than Ahad Ha'am's in the sense that it demanded a greater transformation. Berdyczewski's attack on Jewish religion was an attack on those dominant strains in Judaism that suppressed the natural individuality of the Jew. However, he did not deny that there had been other strains that had had the opposite effect—they had enhanced and liberated the individual. He held that whereas the nationalisms of other peoples provided a healthy balanced reciprocity between the creativity of the nation and the creativity of the individual, the domination of rabbinic Judaism had robbed the Jewish nation and the individuals it comprised of such reciprocity:

In every nation, nationalism is the only treasury in which human virtues are stored, in which the individual finds assurance for his actions and activities, and protection for his possessions. But with us the individual finds in nationalism an element in opposition to that which is in his heart. This contradiction is felt by each one of us. As soon as one begins to improve oneself and to aspire to higher culture, one feels it to a lesser or greater degree, knowingly or unknowingly. Moreover, amongst the nations of the world the sacrifice that one makes for one's nation is only in times of war when it is threatened by enemies, but in times of peace . . . the individual hardly knows such sacrifice. That is to say, he is not aware of living or having to live solely for the sake of his people. . . . But with us it is demanded of every individual that he constantly live for the sake of his people, that he sacrifice himself for it day by day and hour by hour.[61]

In sum, if Ahad Ha'am's ideal of the revivified national Jew might be called the collectivist "normative" model, then one might by contrast label Berdyczewski's as the individualist, existential, or laissez-faire model. On the continuum of secular Jewish identity produced by Zionist ideology these two models represented the most significant opposite polarities. Since both shared the same immanentist premises, together they were ranged against the transcendentalist religious models of Jewish identity whether ultraorthodox, neoorthodox, reformed, or even national-religious. Yet beyond that commonality they generated an inner tension for the secular identity of Zionists, a tension that prevails to this day.

Socialist-Zionist Secularism

Severe as was Berdyczewski's attack on religious traditionalism, it was sometimes exceeded by that of working-class Jews in eastern Europe and members of the Jewish intelligentsia there as well as at European universities, who came under the influence of radical Socialist ideas. The fusion of such ideas with the nationalist premises of Zionism provided a comprehensive belief system, a functional equivalent of religion. This served to relieve Socialist Zionists of some of the ambivalence toward their traditionalist roots that so tortured the souls of liberal literary intellectuals like Berdyczewski.[62] In the words of the preeminent theorist (at least for part of his short life) of Marxist Zionism, Ber Borochov, socialism was not only a political-social program: "No, socialism is a total world view that provides a solution for the deepest gropings and quests of man's spirit. And the foremost virtue of socialism is that it puts an end to all religious quests. For, through human, worldly means, it fulfills all those spiritual needs that religious faith in God sought to provide."[63] Indeed, Borochov was at pains to emphasize that precisely because socialism alone could provide Zionists with so complete a surrogate for one's existential needs, it could overcome rabbinical religious authority in a way that was not possible for bourgeois Zionism.

The attempt to destroy the authority and influence of religious institutions on the Jewish masses characterized not only the avowed devotees of Marxism who condemned religion totally as "the opiate of the masses" and relegated religious institutions to the dustbin of history. It also was characteristic of those Zionists who adhered to less materialist and doctrinaire varieties of Socialist radicalism. The foremost example was Nahman Syrkin, the seminal ideologue of what was to become mainstream, constructive labor Zionism. As we have shown in an earlier chapter, Syrkin was not a materialist Marxist; his socialism rested on idealist and ethical premises. Aspects of his socialism harked back to Moses Hess insofar as he evoked the biblical prophetic tradition and conflated Jewish messianism with the universal history of mankind. Yet if Syrkin's nonmaterialist philosophical standpoint restrained him from *tout court* condemnation of all religion, his attack on Jewish religion in its contemporary manifestations—the expression he used was "Jewish religion as practiced"—was no less vigorous than that of dogmatic materialist Marxists. In his 1901 proclamation to Jewish youth he declared:

The Jewish masses are steeped in ignorance, religious obscurantism, and talmudic anthropomorphism. The community rabbis, the "bought" state-appointed rabbis, the Jewish bourgeoisie and the government—all these are responsible for keeping the Jewish masses in this benighted state. Zionist socialism declares war on these forces of darkness in the name of the light, the truth and the idea of national renascence. Socialist Zionism sees in Jewish religion as practiced—which Heine described brilliantly as not a religion but a misfortune—the chief obstacle to culture, scientific knowledge and freedom. This religious praxis cripples the Jewish mind and spirit, prevents independent action, and keeps the people enchained. Socialist Zionism seeks to dispel this darkness and to bring into the nation the illumination of the Socialist national ideal.[64]

In like vein the short-lived newspaper *Ha-shahar*, which he attempted to launch in Berlin in 1903, set forth its editorial policy in blatantly antireligious terms: "*Ha-shahar* will freely cast light on Jewish history, on the Bible and on the evolution of religious faith, and will indeed 'desecrate the sancta of Israel' with true scientific knowledge."[65] He criticized the Zionist establishment for appeasing obscurantist rabbis in order to win their cooperation. Moreover, cynically rejecting any possibility of a balanced synthesis between modernism and traditionalism, he treated Ahad Ha'am's views as the futile rationalizations of the Jewish bourgeoisie: "The Zionism of the masses will not march arm in arm with sanctimonious religion, crowned by the traditions of the past. . . . Quite the contrary, the masses will draw from Zionism the strength to free themselves from the chains of the spiritual *galut*, and to be rid of the useless impositions of religious Judaism."[66]

Syrkin thus shared with Berdyczewski a radical rejection of the Jewish culture of the exile. His selective view of Jewish history also coincided at some points with that of Berdyczewski insofar as he too drew a contrast between biblical Judaism, the fruit of political independence, and talmudic practice of Judaism, the fruit of the exile, with its "collection of superstitions . . . customs, laws, prohibitions, constraints, casuistry." Indeed, some passages of Syrkin's early writings seem to echo Berdyczewski's; for example, "Yavne was built on the ruins of Jerusalem and is the exact opposite of national political freedom. The period of spiritual decline started with Rabbi Yohanan ben Zakkai."[67] On the other hand, whereas Berdyczewski regarded the prophetic tradition as a factor in the decline of glorious Israelite culture, Syrkin extolled that tradition.

In sum, give or take some differences of emphasis, on the continuum of secular Jewish identity the Socialist-Zionist model epitomized by Nahman Syrkin was located at the laissez-faire polarity rather than at the normative polarity associated with Ahad Ha'am. In tune with Syrkin's views, labor Zionists, even those of non-Marxist hue, appeared to uphold a less anguished version of Berdyczewski's outlook.

The existential, laissez-faire approach to the contents of Jewish culture and the identity of the national Jew was prevalent in the labor-oriented core of the Second *Aliya*. That wave of immigration, extending from 1904 to 1914, stemmed mainly from czarist Russia and encompassed some thirty-five thousand to forty thousand settlers, about half of whom later left Palestine. A part of this wave, estimated at about ten thousand to fifteen thousand, were laborers, although by 1914 only one thousand to fifteen hundred of them were actually engaged in agriculture, mostly as hired labor. This was the core that generated Zionism's ethos of pioneering labor in service of the nation. In respect of their Jewish identity profile, they were a remarkably homogeneous group. Most had emerged out of a traditionalist religious background but had abandoned it in their youth.[68] For them and thereafter for successive generations of the various pioneering youth movements and the He-halutz organization, the adoption of the pioneering ethos of Zionism meant transformation of one's life through the act of ascent to Eretz Israel and dedication to a life of pioneering labor. It also meant the creation of a new social order and a new type of Jew, usually designated by the term *ivri* (Hebrew).[69] In many respects this ethos served as a functional equivalent for traditional religion.

The ideological rhetoric of the Second *Aliya's* labor Zionist core was very much in tune with the views of Berdyczewski and Syrkin. It was antirabbinical, contemptuous of halakhic minutiae, and disdainful of the *galut*, past and contemporary. Although there were some countervailing Ahad Ha'amist influences, to consideration of which we shall return, the main ideological thrust was toward the divorce of the new Hebrew identity from all religious authority and influence and the "normalization" of Jewish national culture on a secular basis.[70] No one articulated this view more systematically than Yitzhak Avigdor Wilkansky, better known as Elazari-Volcani (1880–1955).

Volcani was an agronomist, having trained at agricultural colleges in Berlin and Koenigsberg. After settling in Palestine in 1908, he became one of the pioneers of its agricultural development. His role, however, extended into the intellectual sphere too: he was a notable figure in the Ha-poel Ha-tzair party, and he wrote studies not only on agricultural subjects but also on ideological issues. In 1913 he published an article in the journal, *Ha-poel ha-tzair*, titled "The National Theology."[71] Written in a florid Hebrew style that betrayed the indelible marks of his earlier yeshiva training as well as of later Hebrew Enlightenment influences, it constituted one of the most potent and unequivocal affirmations of secular Jewish identity in the entire corpus of Zionist literature. He was reacting to the European Zionist intelligentsia's current publicistic discussions, centered largely on Ahad Ha'am's ideas, particularly his essay *Al shtei ha-seifim* (Between two outlooks), published in 1910.

Volcani used the term "national theology" to describe what he perceived to be a trend of thought that subsumed Jewish nationalist ideas within theological categories of thought born of misguided metaphysics and nostalgia. The core of such national theology was the idea of Jewish mission, the notion that the existence and future of the Jewish nation was somehow dependent on a purpose beyond itself. He drew a parallel between the "cosmopolitan theology" of much European Jewish religious thought and the "national theology" of Ahad Ha'am and the attendant circle of cultural Zionist thinkers who were perennially locked in debate about the ultimate purpose of Jewish national life. The only difference was that the cosmopolitan theologists saw the purpose in Jewish dispersion, whereas the national theologists saw it in a miniature ingathering of exiles in a nuclear center that would create a superlative model of moral virtue. "Whoever, not seeing in the life of a people a purpose in itself, seeks in it some hidden mission," opined Volcani, "inevitably becomes entangled in vanities and leads himself and others astray."[72]

Launching a frontal attack on this phenomenon of national theology, Volcani championed the Jewish self-understanding of the thoroughly secular national Jew. He explicitly exposed its immanentist assumptions. The morals and values that Ahad Ha'am identified as distinctively Jewish, asserted Volcani,

did not descend to man from the heavens on high, but rather were lifted up by man from the earth to the heavens. . . . Man says that God created him in his image but in truth, as we know, every people creates its gods in its own image. Man created for himself a God to serve and offered himself up to that God to the very point of his own self-effacement; but in truth he enslaved his God to himself. His own perceptions, arbitrary desires, creations and doings he attributed to God. . . . And he called every war aimed at fulfillment of his desires a holy war, a war of the God of Hosts!

To this phenomenon he contrasted the way of the secularized Jew, "the self of the free Jew." "God has left him and belief has been cut out totally from his heart," wrote Volcani. "He cannot live with the illusion of a God because with uncovered eyes he witnesses the passing of historical events, and he stands on the shoulders of previous generations with full knowledge of how things happen."

According to Volcani, the secular Jew was in no need of illusions to numb his senses. He needed no myths to cope with the wonders of nature. Whatever was beyond his understanding or control today he would master tomorrow. "His creativity and his self-expression, these are his God!" Hence, the free Jew could relate to the sancta of his ancestors with complete equanimity. "The goals of the prophets of old may be regarded by him as broken tablets which have no place in our generation," he wrote. "All the possessions that we have inherited can be relegated by him to the storehouses of antiquity. . . . He may well see the pinnacle of all times in the wisdom of Greece rather than in the prophecies of Isaiah."

Volcani expounded the principle that "nationalism in general has nothing to do with religion." Since he refused to acknowledge any difference in *kind* between the religion and nationalism of the Jews and the religion and national-ism of other peoples, he saw absolutely no reason that Jewish religion could not be separated from Jewish nationality. He argued that a person born a Jew could never be detached from his Jewish identity no matter what his opinions were about the nature of Judaism. "Even the convert is a Jew despite himself; he is merely a traitor fleeing to the camp of the enemy; and the traitor may well be punished according to civil laws. But no one has yet invented a guillotine such as can cut him off from the body of his people." Although Volcani by no means favored the adoption of Christianity by Jews, he explained that this was not for "national philosophical reasons, but for tactical reasons," since acceptance of another religion results in the breakdown of the distinctions between the Jewish nation and other nations. However, he made it clear that this reservation about the freedom of a Jew to adopt another religion was only an "emergency measure and not a taboo for all generations." Once a secure and mature Jewish nation had emerged, speaking its own Hebrew language in its own territory, there would no longer be a need to oppose such things, any more than there was in other normal nations.

According to Volcani the "unique self" (*yihud ha-atzmiut*) of the Jewish nation was not obliged to develop on fixed normative lines. It would develop as an act of free creativity and an expression of the living self of the Jewish people in its own land, speaking its own language. What the Jews needed, he argued, was a corner, a refuge and shelter for its "unique self, and not for its holy spirit." It had to be a "a homeland for us and not a homeland for the nurturing of the prophets of God for the benefit of the whole universe. We wish to be a nation like all the nations; not a superior nation." He was confident that "living Jews will in the course of things create some kind of Judaism. It matters not whether it will or will not be in the spirit of the prophets." All that mattered was that it would be a working out of the national self. "In any event," he declared, "the non-prophetic Judaism of complete Jews will be more prophetic than the Judaism of *galut*-Jews."

In sum, Volcani made a forceful plea for Zionism's goal to be the development of a "nation like all other nations," whose life, like theirs, would be an end unto itself and not a means toward some sort of mission outside itself, no matter how virtuous. It would be a nation freed of obligatory ties not only to particular ideas and beliefs but also to the particularities of the Jewish religion itself; hence, the operative conclusion that Zionism's task was to dedicate itself exclusively to the material dimensions of *aliya*: settlement, the Hebrew language, and Jewish labor. The spiritual dimensions would follow naturally and spontaneously. Nostalgia for Jewish traditions and all the convoluted metaphysical debates about the nature and essence of Jewishness and its purpose were but an unnecessary and misguided diversion into national theology.

The Radical Secularism of Brenner

The intellectual of the Second *Aliya* who stirred up the most acute controversy over this open-ended secular understanding of the new Hebrew identity was the writer Yosef Haim Brenner (1881–1921). Like most of the Jewish intelligentsia of

Russia, he too had broken away from his traditionalist yeshiva upbringing. He was drawn into the Jewish labor movement and wandered to Bialystok and thence to Warsaw, where he eked out a living by teaching Hebrew and in 1901 produced a collection of short stories. After being drafted into the Russian army, he was smuggled out of the country in 1904 at the outbreak of the Russo-Japanese war. He then moved to London, where he published a Hebrew monthly called *Ha-meorer* (The Awakener) from 1906 to 1907. Returning to Russia, he worked as a typesetter on a Yiddish daily in Lvov. In 1909 he emigrated to Palestine. There he continued his publicistic activities, becoming the outstanding literary voice of the Second *Aliya* generation. In addition to many short stories and journal articles, Brenner wrote a play and several novels and translated several Russian and German works into Hebrew. In May 1921 he met with a tragic death at the hands of Arab attackers in Jaffa.

In the plethora of stories, essays, and letters that filled Brenner's short life, he gave vent to a rebelliousness against the authority of rabbinic halakhic Judaism that paralleled Berdyczewski's views and, indeed, was even more intemperate. Brenner vehemently condemned the *galut* as a moral disaster and attributed to it a variety of sins ranging from religious obscurantism to self-deprecating assimilation and economic parasitism. Indeed, Brenner's harangues against *galut* and the Jewish past were sometimes so harsh that he came close to justifying gentile hatred of the Jews.

For Zionist ideology the most far-reaching implication of Brenner's approach, as of Berdyczewski's, was this radical negation of the *galut*, not only in terms of its lack of viability for the life of Jews—a premise accepted by almost all Zionists—but also in terms of its moral unacceptability. Furthermore, the blame for both the objective condition of *galut* and its immorality was placed upon normative rabbinical Judaism itself. There could be no liberation from the *galut* condition without prior liberation from that Judaism. By his lights, that form of Judaism was not the result of the unfortunate condition of *galut*. Rather, the opposite was true: the unfortunate condition of *galut* was the result of that Judaism.

Brenner was also at one with Berdyczewski in rejecting Ahad Ha'am's attempt to formulate a binding, secularized "national Judaism" in lieu of the traditionalist religious Judaism. "This hybrid idea must be uprooted," he wrote, adding, "Ahad Ha'am once did so but afterwards regretted it. But we, his free Jewish friends, have naught to do with [religious] Judaism. Nevertheless, we are within the [Jewish] collectivity, by no means less than those who lay *tefillin* [phylacteries] and grow sidelocks." He countered Ahad Ha'am's view with bold affirmation of a laissez-faire receptivity to all beliefs and ideas.

The question of our Jewish life is not a question of religion, of the "survival of Judaism." . . . We say: it is a question of finding a productive place to work for ourselves as Jews. . . . Whether or not we fast on Yom Kippur, and whether or not we eat meat with milk, whether or not we keep to the ethics of the Old Testament, whether or not we are faithful pupils of Epicurus [i.e., heretics] in our world outlook, we do not cease to feel that we are Jews, live our Jewish lives, work and create Jewish modes of working, speak our Jewish language and obtain spiritual sustenance from our literature. We labor for a free national culture, defending our national honor and fighting a war for survival in every manner that such a war entails. . . . We reiterate to you: there is no Judaism outside of us and our lives. There are no permanent beliefs that are obligatory for us. . . . We are Jews in our very lives, in our hearts and feelings. We need no rational definitions, no absolute truths and no written obligations. Everything that is dear to us today, everything that has value for us, everything that springs from our own free nature—without any form of compulsion or coercion—this is our "Judaism," if one insists on using that word.[73]

Brenner's greater extremism was also evident in his contemptuous rejection of all rhetoric—whether orthodox, reform, or secular borrowings—relating to the notion that the Jews are "a chosen people." He excoriated this as shameful, self-deluding pretension: "I would with exquisite pleasure eliminate from today's Hebrew *sidur* [prayerbook] the notion "Thou hast chosen us" in any form. I would strike it out this very day. I would erase these false nationalist verses until not a trace of them remained. Such empty national pride and vain Jewish boasting will not help heal our wounds. Such fraudulent nationalist phrases are worthless."[74]

For Brenner, as for Berdyczewski, the basis of Jewish identity was thus ethnic kinship rather than the beliefs and observances of religion. Not prescriptive beliefs but the individual's innate feelings were the core of national identification. To the new national Hebrews he attributed "an instinctive national feeling, that endears to themselves their people, that is to say their own selves."[75] "We are, therefore, sons of the Hebrew nation who are faithful to ourselves," he declared, "who live within our own people and are unable to imagine a life for ourselves outside the bounds of our own people, for good or for bad."[76]

However, not only the rebellious negations that characterized Berdyczewski are to be found in Brenner but also the countervailing ambivalences. His writings too are punctuated with contradictions and doubts. The pathos of personal crisis pervades the whole, and Brenner vacillates. At one moment there is the almost nihilistic assertion of individuality and total freedom of thought; at another, cognizance of the Jew's deterministic bond with the national collectivity, the inescapability of Jewish national fate. Attendant upon this is the tension between Brenner's bold conviction that the Jewish character had to be changed and his nagging doubts as to whether this was possible in reality. Typical of his self-questioning is the following passage: "In order that our character should change as much as possible we must have our own environment. And yet, in order to create this environment by ourselves our character must first undergo a complete change. . . . The question is how can we, as ourselves, become other than ourselves?"[77]

Yet in the final analysis, Brenner's ambivalence is less anguished than Berdyczewski's, and his prescriptions are clearer. Whereas Berdyczewski, as we have noted, was subject to anxieties as to whether the break he so effusively advocated would not prove to be self-destructive of all Jewish identity, Brenner was unequivocal about the desired and necessary goal—the return of Jews to the Land of Israel and to labor. The doubts that plagued him related not to this crystal-clear prescription but only to the question of whether the Jews, crippled by their past, were capable of transforming themselves. The difference may at least partly be accounted for by the fact that the context in which Brenner spoke was one of action in the central arena of Zionist endeavor, Eretz Israel, whereas Berdyczewski's writing remained in the realm of pure reflection in the Diaspora context.

At a profounder level of analysis the contrast between Berdyczewski's views and those of Brenner boils down to the difference between the former's emphasis upon Judaism as a philosophical system and the latter's sociological emphasis.[78] Berdyczewski attributed the *galut*'s evils to Judaism as a confining system of beliefs and precepts, whereas Brenner attributed those evils to the socioeconomic characteristics conditioned by Judaism in the *galut*. Consequently, the operative solutions they offered diverged; Berdyczewski calling for a broadening of the boundaries of Jewish cultural norms, something that was as applicable in the Diaspora as in the revived Jewish homeland. In this way the tide of assimilation sweeping the Jewish intelligentsia could be stemmed: "Our young people were made to believe that spiritual attachment to the Jewish people necessarily meant faith in a fixed and parochial outlook, so they turned away and left us, for their souls sought another way."[79] Here Brenner differed. He held out no hope at all for the Jewish intelligentsia in the Diaspora since the pull of assimilation was a sociological phenomenon, and no ideological broadening of boundaries would help. Anything other than a social transformation accomplished by return to a life of self-labor in Eretz Israel was futile. The sole viable change was existential, not ideological. Only Jews living in their own land, with their own language and their own labor and common society, possessed the prerequisites for a meaningful Jewish future and culture. The Jew rooted in this way had complete freedom to adopt whatever beliefs and metaphysical ideas he chose. In this sense, Brenner's thought may be regarded as a radically Zionist extension of Berdyczewski's.

A controversy precipitated in November 1910 by one of Yosef Haim Brenner's essays might be cited as the most illuminating illustration of the conflict over the nature of Jewish national identity within the literary intelligentsia. Published in the periodical *Ha-poel ha-tzair*, the organ of the Zionist workers' organization of the same name in Palestine, Brenner's essay was one of his regular series titled

"In the Newspapers and Literature."[80] The context in which Brenner's comments were made was the widely reported wave of conversions to Christianity by young Jews in Europe. In characteristic fashion, however, he allowed himself various digressions, which included pungently provocative comments on certain Jewish religious beliefs.

The gist of Brenner's argument was that anxiety over the conversion phenomenon in the Diaspora was misplaced. Those European Jews who converted were already assimilated. Their conversion merely placed the final stamp on their prior desertion of the Jewish people. The preoccupation with this phenomenon in the Jewish press distracted it from concern with the real problems of the Jewish people: the need to relieve the material distress of the Jewish masses, to productivize them, to revitalize Jewish culture, and to build up Eretz Israel on sound national and social foundations. The real question was "the question of our Jewish lives, and not the question of the Jewish religion" or speculation on the comparative virtues of Judaism and Christianity.[81] Indeed, theological questions were of no consequence for the future of the Jewish people. They were peripheral to the true concerns of contemporary Jewish youth because religion, whether Christian or Jewish, had ceased to carry weight in their lives. Whatever spiritual ideals existed in religion could be accepted or rejected by contemporary Jews without their choices having significant bearing on matters of real concern, such as their personal freedom and their national identity.

Brenner went on to ask rhetorically: even assuming that a "free Hebrew," like himself were to be attracted to some aspect of Christianity, what of it? He raised the prospect of a Hebrew who "is thrilled by the image of the son of our people, the poor Jew Jesus of Nazareth," and averred that "a person can be a good Jew, wholeheartedly devoted to his people, without fearing the Christian legend as if it were some kind of ritually forbidden food." The universal spiritual ideas inhering in all religions were one matter, and the specific rituals and modes of life dictated by the various religions were quite another. The new Jew, creatively rooted in his own national land and language, was free to identify with any spiritual ideal of his choosing, not excluding those particularly associated with Christianity. If he did so, he did not thereby cease being a Jew.

As if these heretical views were not enough, Brenner spiced his essay with disrespectful references, such as the comment that he himself saw nothing worthy of admiration in the old religious "fawning before some kind of father in heaven and pleading that He provide a livelihood." He also gibed: "From the hypnosis of the twenty-four books of the Bible I have long liberated myself. . . . Also the 'New Testament' is our book, bone of our bone and flesh of our flesh." That Brenner was not merely trying to be provocative is attested to by some unpublished notes that he recorded about three years later. They show that he held obdurately to the same views. "No one can take from me the right to relate to Jesus and his apostles with deep feeling," he wrote, "just as I have the same right to scoff at them if I wish."[82]

The views expressed by Brenner in this essay raised a storm of controversy that dominated the intellectual milieu of the Jewish intelligentsia for well over a year. His statement had stretched the limits of the immanentist secular identity of the national Jew to the utmost, almost to the point of reductio ab absurdum. Indeed, in histrionic reaction, the Sephardic paper *Ha-herut*, edited by Haim Benatar in Jerusalem, not only accused Brenner and his compatriots in Ha-poel Ha-tzair of "heresy" and of "inciting towards conversion from Judaism to Christianity" but even insinuated that they were in the pay of Christian missionaries![83]

These wild accusations added fuel to the fire and produced a vehement reaction. Shocked by the appearance of such "brazen and crude" views in *Ha-poel ha-tzair*, a periodical partly sponsored by the Odessa Committee of the Zionist organization in Russia, Ahad Ha'am called for sanctions to be applied. He importuned the committee: "Surely you sense how insulting to the nation is this impertinence in regard to those very beliefs for which our people have given up their lives for thousands of years? And if you feel this, then surely you must also feel that you bear a responsibility not to provide such impudent persons with the means to print their views at the expense of the public."[84] The Odessa Committee did in fact decide to apply sanctions. It withdrew its financial support and made renewal conditional upon the exclusion of Brenner and a change in editorial policy. Joseph Klausner, a member of the committee and the successor of Ahad Ha'am as editor of *Ha-shiloah*, called Brenner's views "nonbelief [*apikorsut*; literally, Epicureanism] in its most deplorable form" and averred firmly that "only the blending of freedom of opinion together with respect for the past heritage can produce a renaissance."[85]

The Odessa Committee's sanctions provoked an indignant reaction among the Second *Aliya* settlers. A group of writers called together an emergency gathering to register their protest. The participants were preeminent writers of the new *yishuv*, including Eliezer Ben-Yehuda, Shai Agnon, Joseph Witkin, and Aharon David Gordon. It is noteworthy, moreover, that the prime movers of the gathering were Alexander Ziskind Rabinowitz and "Rabbi" Binyamin (pseudonym of Yehoshua Radler-Feldman), who were known to be observant of religious tradition. The meeting took place in Jaffa on February 11, 1911, and a resolution was passed condemning the Odessa Committee's action. Most of the opinions voiced at the gathering emphasized the principle of freedom of speech. They expressed their indignation at the Odessa Committee's particularly insulting setting of a condition that its financial support for *Ha-poel ha-tzair* would be renewed only if the periodical closed its columns to the offending Brenner and undertook to change its editorial policy. However, while all objected to this infringement of freedom of speech, some of the participants dissociated themselves from the substance of Brenner's view.[86]

In a broad array of Hebrew and Yiddish periodicals both in Europe and in Palestine, the leading lights of the contemporary Zionist intelligentsia participated in the controversy raised by the "Brenner incident." Of interest, in retrospect, are the views of the young David Ben-Gurion. He took a firm stand in defense of the principle of freedom of expression but without wholly identifying himself with Brenner's substantive views. Ben-Gurion regretted that Ahad Ha'am had apparently abandoned his former view that "the question of religion should not be mixed with the national question." Yet he considered that Ahad Ha'am was entitled to change his opinion and objected less to his consequent rejection of Brenner's article than to the action of the Odessa Committee at his behest. He charged Ahad Ha'am with "leading Hibbat Zion to Canossa" and criticized the Odessa Committee for kowtowing to the orthodox. Brenner was being charged with overstepping the bounds of legitimate opinion. "But what were these bounds?" asked Ben-Gurion. "Who is to judge until which point it is permissible and from which point it is forbidden? And in any event, who is entitled to place limits on matters of the heart? And what was freedom of opinion if not the removal of all divisions, reservations and fences that confine the thoughts of man?"[87]

The Hebrew organ of the world Zionist Organization, *Ha-olam*, published in Vilna, responded to the Brenner incident in an unsigned article that drew a distinction between freedom of thought, "which no man and no institution had the right to suppress," and the hurling of insults. Brenner may have had the right to reject the Jewish religion, but "he had no right to insult religious Jewry." *Ha-olam* took the position that the Odessa Committee was within its rights in withdrawing support, since "Zionism is not to be placed above Judaism, which has sustained the nation for thousands of years; and Herzl is not to be regarded as above 'Our Father in Heaven.'"[88]

The imposition of sanctions had diverted much of the debate to questions of freedom of speech and the relationship between financial support, censorship, and public responsibility. More to our purpose here, however, are the profound substantive issues manifest in this controversy, namely, the relationship between religion and nation and the proper nature of Jewish national identity. These questions continued to surface throughout the debate as article piled upon article and point and counterpoint vied. The editor of the periodical *Hed ha-zman* in Poland, Ben-Zion Katz, contributed one of the more profound examinations of these deeper questions in an article pertinently titled "Nationalism, Judaism and Religion."[89] In his view, Brenner's personal predilections concerning Christianity were less important than the fact that no small number of Jews was influenced by the essentially Christian ideas of Lev Tolstoy. He opined that although this did not mean that one should doubt their belonging to the Jewish nation, insofar as such Jews "in theory acknowledge the Christian ideal," they were nationally defective. Given the incitement to persecution and shedding of Jewish blood that the Christian legend had caused for centuries, he failed to see how a truly national Jew could regard the figure of Jesus with "religious enthusiasm" as Brenner had suggested.

Among the Zionist literati in Europe, support prevailed, by and large, for the substance of Ahad Ha'am's position in the affair. However, in a balanced and profound analysis that appeared in the Warsaw Hebrew newspaper *Ha-tzefira*, Simon Bernfeld adopted a lenient attitude to Brenner's rebelliousness, attributing it to the spirit of youth and noting that there was hardly any mature writer who had not done the same in his youth. (He mentioned, as an example, Yehuda Leib Lilienblum.) Moreover, he defended Brenner's right to express his opinions and disapproved of the Odessa Committee's action. He felt that the heresy of Brenner was less harmful to the Jewish people than the punishment meted out to him by the Odessa Committee. "What was uglier, the sin of Brenner or his punishment?" he asked rhetorically. But as to substance, Bernfeld categorically opposed Brenner, arguing forcefully that "as it is impossible to separate between the sun's power of light and power of heat, so it is impossible to separate between the nationalism and the religion of the Jews." Bernfeld contended that Judaism was not a religion in a conventional sense but rather a "cultural vision." He himself averred that he at one and the same time believed in the God of Israel and belonged to the Jewish culture. The elements of universal culture were filtered for him through Jewish culture. While religious belief was a matter of moral truth, belonging to Jewish culture was one of education and choice. If Brenner had only the sense of participation in Jewish culture but the religious belief eluded him, this did not mean he was deserving of punishment. Rather, he was to be pitied.[90]

Ahad Ha'am himself formulated a comprehensive response to the challenge of Brenner's ideas in his essay *Torah mi-tzion* (The law out of Zion), which he published in *Ha-shiloah*.[91] He pungently attacked those Jews who claimed they had a "free national consciousness" and "who were attempting to influence the young generation in Eretz Israel not only to become 'free of religious observances' but also free of anything that connects generation to generation in the national life." Although he did not grant any credibility to the accusation that Brenner and his likes were in the service of Christian missionaries, he nevertheless commented caustically that "were the English missionaries to know what views are now being spread amongst young Jews in Eretz Israel, they would be delighted and would regard it as 'the beginning of the redemption.'" "National consciousness 'free' of the national past was an absurdity unknown to any nation and tongue," he averred. The French Revolution, he noted, had failed to uproot elements of the national past and to wipe out all memory of even such things as the names of the months. He pointed also to the example of the United

States of America to illustrate the importance of a common cultural heritage in the formation of a nation:

Thousands upon thousands of people who come from the four corners of the earth to a certain country and find there "a place for productive work" [here he was quoting Brenner's words] do not yet constitute a nation and do not share a common national consciousness. All they share is common interests. Only now, after hundreds of years of productive labor in America are there beginning to appear signs of the formation of a new "American" nation.

Ahad Ha'am reiterated the core premise of his model of secular Jewish identity bound to norms rooted in the Jewish cultural heritage. Irrespective of one's religious belief or disbelief, one was bound to love and respect one's own cultural heritage. The question was not whether the attributes of one's own culture were better or worse than those of alien cultures; what counted was simply that they were one's own. "Have you ever heard," he asked rhetorically, "of a son who rejects his mother just because he has found another more beautiful than her?" By the same token, even a Jew who personally doubted the reality of a godhood could not deny the reality of the God concept as a real historical force in the cultural heritage of his people. No genuinely nationalist Jew could say that he had no part in belief in the God of Israel, "in that historical force that animated our people and influenced its spiritual quality and way of life for thousands of years." "He who truly has no part in the God of Israel; he who does not feel in his soul any affinity to that 'upper world' into which our forefathers poured their minds and hearts in every generation and from which they drew their moral strength, may qualify as a man, but a national Jew he is not, even if he 'lives in Eretz Israel and speaks the holy tongue' [quoting Brenner's words]." The same criterion applied to all the basic treasures of the Jewish cultural heritage, argued Ahad Ha'am, from the "Book of Books" to the land, Eretz Israel. Again invoking the example of other mature nations, he pointed to members of the English nation (he was at the time still living in England) who, irrespective of personal religious beliefs or disbeliefs, proudly celebrated the anniversary of the completion of the Authorized Version of the Bible in English as a precious national asset. How much more so should the national Jew appreciate the original version contributed to all of mankind by his own forefathers!

The Jewishness of A. D. Gordon

Two interrelated but analytically separable issues are discernible in the controversy evoked by the "Brenner incident." One was the principle of freedom of speech; the other was the parameters of the secular national Jew's identity. The range of responses evoked shows that even the labor sector of the Second *Aliya* was far from endorsing unanimously the laissez-faire extremism of Yosef Haim Brenner. Although there was a consensus in support of freedom of speech, many participants in the controversy leaned more toward the norm-bound secular Jewishness advocated by Ahad Ha'am. This was particularly true of Aharon David Gordon, who, as was shown in an earlier chapter, was an unusual personality and original thinker who became something of a legend in his own time and an emblematic figure for later generations in the pioneering youth movements.

Gordon addressed the Brenner incident in an open letter to his "worker comrades."[92] Since, as a matter of principle, he advocated full self-reliance of the Jewish workers in Palestine, he did not favor Ha-poel ha-tzair's acceptance of outside support from the Odessa Committee in the first place. Although therefore sympathizing with Brenner as a victim of such reliance and of the sanctions that resulted from it, he was in agreement with the substance of Ahad Ha'am's objections to Brenner's views. In a letter to Ahad Ha'am himself he assured him that Ha-poel ha-tzair's readers were far from negating Judaism or from "negation of the negation of Christianity." He explained that they could not imagine that these admittedly negative views of Brenner would arouse such alarm. But although most disagreed with Brenner's views, they saw no reason to censor them. For therein lay the difference between Eretz Israel and the *galut*: "In Eretz Israel the Jew does not need to feel his national pulse every hour, for in that sense he is completely healthy.[93]

Gordon's biography diverged from the typical pattern of the eastern European Jewish intelligentsia as well as from that of the Zionist settlers who formed the Second *Aliya*. When he decided to go to Palestine in 1904, he was already forty-eight years of age and was still observant of orthodox religious practices. After settling there, he gradually left off religious observances, but he never ceased being an essentially religious person. Thus, his passage out of a traditionalist religious upbringing was very atypical of that undergone by the young settlers of the Second *Aliya* in whose midst he now lived. His experience involved no abrupt traumatic break from traditionalism and was marked by no rebellious rejection and clash with rabbinical authority; it was a gradual personal transition that stretched, rather than snapped, the deeply traditionalist sources and symbols that remained his abiding inspiration.

Religion, as comprehended by Gordon, was an intuitive experience relating man to the infinite source of all being. "Religion, at bottom, is the pure, the human, relationship toward the essence of existence in all its phases; it is the expression of the living eternal question; it renews itself at all times; it is a vital force guiding life."[94] His sense of Jewish identity therefore allowed for belief in a transcendental source; less, however, one manifest in history as traditionalist Jewish religion perceived it than one manifest cosmically in nature and human fellowship. He paid scant attention, if any at all, to questions of divine revelation or to petitionary prayer, to the doctrinal aspects of Judaism or its ritual minutiae. Religion for him was, in short, a cosmic, not a historical, phenomenon, a personal rather than a collective matter. Yet an overriding nationalism was the context in which this mode of religiosity was conceived, for, according to Gordon's understanding, the intuitive experience identifiable as religion took place optimally through the mediation of one's nation. The creative nourishment of one's nation, in turn, depended upon its being in symbiosis with nature, thereby closing the circle of the individual man's relationship to the infinite.

It was on the basis of this chain of thought that Gordon elected to participate in the process that would restore the Jewish nation to its natural homeland environment, that is, to its cosmic source. This required of him that he undergo an individual occupational transformation—becoming a manual laborer—and take part in the practice of labor Zionism in Palestine. As an individual he thereby opened himself to the universal religious experience available only through the nationally mediated symbiosis with man's natural environment. The articulation of the necessity for this process of transformation, from the individual dimension to the national dimension and back to the individual, was the essence of his ideological contribution to Zionist thought. Phrased in another way, according to Gordon the potentiality for authentic religious experience inhered in Jewish nationalism insofar as that nationalism brought its adherents into a restored harmony or communion with the natural environment that had given rise to the national unit in the first place.

The links in this chain of thought were mystical and nonhistorical in nature. They amounted to a philosophical configuration very different from that of Ahad Ha'am's essentially rational understanding of Jewish culture as an immanent development of a historical nature. Yet he arrived at a model of Jewish identity whose praxis was consonant with that advocated by Ahad Ha'am. Both placed great emphasis on Jewish self-affirmation and Jewish cultural individuality. Both declared their revulsion from anything that smacked of assimilation. Gordon, although upholding the principles of equality and self-labor, condemning all forms of economic exploitation, and disapproving of private land ownership, considered the adoption of Socialist doctrines to be a form of assimilation and therefore undesirable. He preferred to draw social values from the wells of the Jewish religious-cultural heritage. He was against "entangling ourselves with foreign movements." "Personally I cannot reconcile myself to the idea," he wrote, "that when the Jewish people shall again become a living nation, this nation should not develop from within itself, but should be drawn along the roadway of others."[95]

This compound of deeply rooted personal religiosity together with firm ethnic self-affirmation placed A. D. Gordon much closer to Ahad Ha'am's upholding of Jewish cultural norms than to the laissez-faire identity expounded by Berdyczewski or Brenner and prevalent among Second *Aliya* settlers. This was so notwithstanding the fact that, sharing the Second *Aliya* ambience with Brenner, Gordon felt a strong fellowship with him. He could not concur with the tirades of Berdyczewski and Brenner against orthodox religious Judaism. "Whence stems all this pent-up hatred?" he asked. "All this unlimited disparagement for the religion of Israel, for the spirit of Israel, for all that inheres in us rather than emanates from the spirit of other peoples or fails to suit the tastes of others?" To the contrary, Gordon was moved to declare his fondness for the religion of Israel: "Until this day I love it to the depths of my soul, notwithstanding the fact that I do not observe its precepts and am not religious in the conventional sense. And I also remain fond of the rabbinical literature, even though, belonging to a different generation, there are matters in it which are not to my taste."[96] He wondered whether the difference between his feelings and those of his friend Brenner was a generational matter. Brenner, belonging to the generation of religion's sharp decline, had never experienced it when it was still vibrant, as had Gordon.

In an essay on the theme of Jewish "self-evaluation," Gordon explicitly favored Ahad Ha'am's self-evaluation, "based on our national individuality as it has expressed itself in our life from the beginning to this very day," over Berdyczewski's radical reevaluation, which he characterized as "the great doctrine of negating ourselves." Likewise, he saw Brenner's way as "an attack from within against that wretched self with the purpose of changing it radically, of transforming it into something different rather than of renewing it from within itself and helping it to become itself again."[97]

Although he appreciated the individualistic emphasis of Berdyczewski (which contrasted with the collective emphasis of Ahad Ha'am), he disapproved of its Nietzschean character. This he regarded as evidence of assimilation, of "the influence of an alien culture that has perverted even the most original amongst us."[98] To be sure, A. D. Gordon was not entirely consistent in this respect, for he himself adopted ideas and values from a patently non-Jewish cultural source, namely, the Russian-Christian thought of Lev Tolstoy that extolled physical labor and the peasant life in particular. For instance, he upheld individualism in Tolstoy's naturalist mode by contrast with Nietzsche's inconoclastic nihilism and his exalting of the individual "superman." Likewise, he followed Tolstoy in elevating the natural organic community over artificial, mechanistic social organization. These premises informed his definition of culture in a manner diverging from that of Ahad Ha'am. Whereas the latter spoke almost exclusively of high culture, especially in the sense of literary creativity, Gordon comprehended culture in the broad sense:

A living culture embraces the whole of life. Whatever man creates for the sake of life is culture: the tilling of the soil, the building of homes, the paving of roads. . . . Arrangement, method, shape, the way in which a thing is done—these are forms of culture. What a man does, what he feels, thinks, lives . . . these mold themselves into the spirit of culture. Higher culture draws its nourishment from science, art, beliefs, and opinions, from poetry, ethics, religion. Higher culture or culture in its restrictive sense, the culture to which we usually apply the term when we speak of culture, is the *butter* of culture. . . . But is it possible to make butter without milk or can man make butter from milk belonging to others, and will the butter then be his very own? What then are we seeking in Palestine if not that which we cannot find anywhere else in the world—the living milk of culture? Our object is not to create today an academic culture. . . . What we have come to create is a living culture . . . which will need only sufficient churning to produce butter, the higher culture.[99]

The Message of Berl Katznelson

If Aharon David Gordon was an unusual personality and his religious conception too abstruse and idiosyncratic to qualify as a representative voice of his generation, the same cannot be said of Berl Katznelson.[100] Berl—it was by his first name that he affectionately came to be known—was the preeminent ideological mentor of mainstream labor Zionism in Palestine. As we noted in chapter 5, he was also the foremost advocate of "revolutionary constructivism," a principle he sought to apply not only in regard to socialism but also in the cultural field. Accordingly, he advocated a mode of secular Jewish identity that, without ever being explicitly Ahad Ha'amist, veered very much toward the normative model envisaged by Ahad Ha'am.

To be sure Berl's broadly Socialist world outlook contrasted greatly with the essentially bourgeois orientation of Ahad Ha'am. Nor did he show any interest in the ongoing intellectual debate over Ahad Ha'am's conceptual framework, whether in regard to "the will to life" as the motor force of Jewish survival or in regard to the postulation of a moral and cultural essence of Judaism binding the national Jew. Berl's policy preferences in regard to the Jewish national move-ment, like those of the labor Zionist camp as a whole, were far closer to the maximal political goals of Herzl than to the minimalism of Ahad Ha'am, and he never explicitly endorsed Ahad Ha'am's ideological formulations. Yet his emotional ties to traditionalist customs were much like those of Ahad Ha'am. His literary style too drew heavily not only from biblical sources but also from the daily prayer book, the sages of the Second Temple period, and rabbinical *midrash* (homiletic literature).[101] Moreover, Berl's persistent urging that the major religious festivals be retained in the life of labor Zionists, albeit in innovative secularized forms, was tantamount to an endorsement of the practical implications of Ahad Ha'am's outlook.

As an intellect and an educational role model widely acknowledged in mainstream Zionist labor circles and especially in its youth movements, his eloquent disapproval of any manifestations disrespectful of Judaism's traditional sancta carried considerable weight. When in 1934 one of the youth movements associated with Mapai chose to open its annual summer camp on the eve of the Ninth of Ab (observed by religious Jews as a solemn fast day mourning the destruction of the Temple in Jerusalem by the Romans), Katznelson severely reprimanded them in the columns of *Davar*:

What is the value and what are the fruits of a liberation movement that has no sense of rootedness; that casts [the past] out of memory, that instead of imbuing its bearers with an appreciation of the nation's sources, blurs the memory of its origins. . . . Would we today be capable of a movement of revival if not for the fact that the Jewish people stubbornly preserved in its heart the memory of the [Jerusalem Temple's] destruction. . . . Such is the vitality of a symbol that crystalizes in the annals of a nation.[102]

He noted that the national memory had invested the Ninth of Ab with its bitterest experiences, dating from the destruction of the First and Second Temples through to the expulsion from Spain and until the outbreak of World War I in contemporary times. "By the simplest device, on a single day, the nation's memory was able to imbue every Jewish soul throughout the entire world with a sense of profound mourning."[103] Nor did he agree with those who averred that, for the pioneers who had returned to Zion, the Ninth of Ab should be converted from a day of mourning to a day of rejoicing. He regarded this as a distorted view that made light of the gravity of the contemporary Jewish situation. The Ninth of Ab had to remain a day of sadness as long as there were any Jews still in the Diaspora. The same awe and respect for major traditions applied to the festival of Passover, which embodied the loftiest fusion of universal and national values—"a people observing for thousands of years its exodus from the house of bondage." How could Zionist workers neglect such a festival!

In evaluating the nature of Katznelson's affirmation of certain Jewish festivals and customs, one cannot discount the residual emotional influences of his early upbringing in a traditionalist environment.[104] It is known that he refrained from eating pork even when, as a soldier in one of the Jewish Battalions of World War I, this meant subsisting, as he himself described it, solely on "tins of jam." However, the articulated rationale for this personal preference, no less than for his advocacy of collective Sabbath and festival observances, remained nationalist in essence. To his understanding, the cultural heritage of the past was an indispensable resource for national regeneration. Thus, he explained his refraining from eating pork primarily as an act of identification with the symbolic national significance of *kashrut*. By the same token he pleaded the case— unsuccessfully as it happened—of those orthodox soldiers who wished to retain their beards.[105]

In like vein was his insistence on the value of the Sabbath. If anything was worthy of selection out of the Jewish religious heritage for observance by secularized Jews, it was the Sabbath, for it epitomized the convergence of a basic national-cultural tradition with a great universal social value. "For me," he declared, "the Sabbath is one of the pillars of Hebrew culture and the first social achievement of the working man in human history."[106] It was a social and cultural treasure belonging no less to the Zionist worker than to orthodox Jews. He applauded the decision of the labor factions, convened in Lucerne at the time of the world Zionist congress in 1938, to keep the Sabbath as a day of rest from all labor. Not only political considerations that made it advisable to refrain from confrontation with religious elements in the Zionist movement motivated Katznelson. He declared that for him this was "a matter of the first order of importance, one on which depended the very existence of the race; a matter of social hygiene; a cultural-social-national matter."[107]

An innovating and creative generation does not cast the heritage of generations into the garbage bin. It examines and checks, rejects and selects. And sometimes it holds on to an existing tradition and adds to it. It may sometimes delve into the heap of scrap, reveal long-forgotten things, remove their rust and renew old traditions that may nourish the soul of the generation of renewal.[108]

By no means did this positive attitude to traditions derived from the Jewish religion mean that Berl Katznelson advocated a return to orthodox observance whether of the Sabbath or of the festivals and days of mourning. He assumed that they could be observed to full Jewish cultural satisfaction in a secularized spirit quite independently of their original transcendental quality. Indeed, he favored innovation: "I do not judge and stipulate rules on the question of the form that the festivals should take," he wrote. "A living feeling in the heart and the revival of the spirit will give rise to the appropriate forms."[109] Characteristically, while in the Jewish Battalions, Berl himself had proposed that the Passover seder (festive meal) be celebrated with an innovative collection of Hebrew poetry and prose rather than purely with the traditional *Hagada* (Liturgy for the Passover festive meal).[110]

One instructive way of appreciating the mode of Jewish identity that pervaded the labor wing of Zionism is to view it in the context of what some have labeled "civil religion."[111] This concept is used to characterize the development, under conditions of modernity, of a functional alternative to traditional religion—a symbol system that provides secularized people with a sense of ultimate meaning approximating that provided by religion. In this sociological perspective, the labor Zionist version of "civil religion" adopted numerous symbols and practices from traditionalist Jewish religion but transformed and complemented them with universalist, largely Socialist, values. Moreover, civil religion tended to stand in confrontation with traditionalist religion itself, often universal Socialist values and symbols offensively challenging those of the tradition.

In this light it may be said that the ideological formulations of Berl Katznelson that we have here discussed promoted the development of a civil religion for the Jewish sector of Palestine, particularly in the calendar of the labor segment and even more especially in that of the kibbutz communes. However, it is also evident that, toward the end of his life, Katznelson was worried by the apparent estrangement of the sons of the pioneering settlers from the Jewish cultural heritage and consequently also from the Jews of the Diaspora.[112] Perhaps he sensed that advocacy of this kind of highly selective observance of Jewish traditions was not sufficient to guarantee a viable Jewish identity, that reliance solely on spontaneous processes for the development of a modern national Jewish identity rooted in the past was misplaced.

Honor for Religion: Jabotinsky

If Berl Katznelson's ideological formulations in regard to Jewish religious tradition were an expression of nascent civil religion in the Zionist labor movement, for the Zionist Right a similar role might well be attributed to Vladimir (Ze'ev) Jabotinsky. However, the Zionist Right's variety of civil religion differed from that of labor Zionism in that, rather than universalizing the symbolic meaning system drawn from traditionalist Judaism, it tended to endorse and fortify that system's ethnocentrism.

Jabotinsky's secularized Jewish identity was evident in his personal nonobservance of religious precepts and in his wholly immanentist understanding of the origins of the Jews as an entity in history.[113] Early in his career he expressed the view that the Hebrew religion was a product of the national culture rather than vice versa. He commended Heinrich Heine's famous dictum that the religion had served the nation as its "portable fatherland." Nonetheless, "not religion, but national uniqueness . . . is the sacred treasure which our people has so stubbornly preserved and continues to preserve."[114]

Thus far, Jabotinsky shared common ground with the major part of the Zionist intelligentsia and not least of all with Ahad Ha'am. But as the quintessential political Zionist, Jabotinsky's disposition in regard to the Zionist program could not have been further from that of Ahad Ha'am. Also, their educational backgrounds were quite different—Ahad Ha'am came to Odessa after a wholly traditionalist upbringing, whereas Jabotinsky was born and bred in that modern center of Enlightenment. He was more culturally literate in Russian than in Hebrew sources, and unlike the purely autodidactic Ahad Ha'am, he had studied at a university (in Rome). Although he mastered Hebrew, in addition to a number of other languages, his voluminous writings drew nothing of note from rabbinical literary sources. In sum, his intellectual profile differed greatly from that of Ahad Ha'am.

Yet, the operative implications of Jabotinsky's Jewish self-understanding were entirely compatible with Ahad Ha'am's approach. As we have seen in an earlier chapter, in his search for a "monistic," nationalist social program as an alternative to the dualism of Socialist Zionism, he speculated vaguely about the possibility of adapting the biblical principle of the jubilee year to modern conditions. "If I were a king," he wrote, "I would renew the face of my kingdom according to the jubilee idea, and not according to Socialist theory."[115]

Amorphous and simplistic as was Jabotinsky's evocation of this biblical jubilee idea as a basis for a modern social program, it symbolized his proximity to Ahad Ha'am's norm-bound conception of Jewish secular culture. Moreover, although by a different route, Jabotinsky too came to regard the moral ethos of Judaism and its major sancta as indispensable assets of the national revival. That is to say, he recognized the instrumental value of religiously rooted cultural norms for the fostering of a wholesome Jewish nation and, by the same token, for the identity of the individual nationalist Jew. Indeed, political expediency aimed at gaining allies from the orthodox public, particularly in Poland, prompted Jabotinsky to incorporate what sounded like a proclerical clause in the constitution of the New Zionist Organization at its founding conference in September 1935. It stated: "The mission of Zionism is the redemption of Israel in its land, the revival of its polity and language and the rooting of the sancta of its Torah in the life of the nation." In ardently advocating the adoption of this clause, Jabotinsky explained that the nineteenth-century slogans declaring religion to be a private matter and calling for separation of church and state remained valid, but, he added, "history moves in dialectical fashion and today we are witness to a turning point that calls for considerable revision also in this sphere. The removal of clerical rule was a necessity, but it led to removal of God; and one may seriously doubt if this is a desirable outcome." He concluded that "it was a matter of the highest importance for the state—and in our case for the nation—that the eternal flame not be put out, that in the whirlpool of countless different influences that ensnare the youth of our time, and ofttimes mislead and poison it, this influence [of religion] remain alive, for it is without doubt the purest of all, the spirit of God."[116]

This demonstrative bow toward religion did not pass without disagreement within the New Zionist Organization's ranks, not least of all from Jabotinsky's son Eri, who was a self-declared atheist. Jabotinsky was at pains to explain to his son that the expression "the sancta of the Torah" referred to the sacred moral values "which even an atheist, qua atheist, would uphold." He said that although one could create a moral system independent of belief in any transcendental source, as he himself had done all his life, he now had become convinced that it was more correct "to treat of these moral principles as ones connected with the mystery beyond the reach of man." Moreover, he now averred that "religious pathos as such was sorely needed" and that he would be only too happy "were it possible to create a wholly believing generation."[117]

Another elaboration of what Jabotinsky had meant by "the rooting of the sancta of our Torah in the life of our nation" was addressed to a leader of the special organizational framework for orthodox Jews that he had formed to facilitate their association with the New Zionist Organization. He explained that solutions to social issues of the nation should be sought out "first of all in that treasure which is called 'our tradition.'" He declared that he envisioned an ideal state, an example to all the nations, "a state on whose pillars is pasted the trademark of the tradition. One pillar—will have its source in the Bible, the second—in the Mishna, the third—in Maimonides." This did not mean that modern science and learning would be ignored, he explained, but rather that the revived Jewish nation would demonstrate to the Gentiles that all the moral truths aimed at the perfection of the world were rooted in the Jewish tradition and that whatever was now being learned from them "was none other than an elaboration of things which they themselves had once learned from us."[118]

It is a moot point whether Jabotinsky genuinely underwent a transformation in the late 1930s from a thoroughly secular outlook to a certain religiosity or whether his expressions of views on religion were merely motivated by political expediency. There are some indications of uncertainty and wavering between an immanentist, rational outlook, on the one hand, and a postrationalist search for the transcendent on the other. For example, in an article that appeared in June 1939, he wrote:

The ambience of my education in old Russia and thereafter in old Italy, was permeated by a rationalist world-outlook. In the end this ambience brought me, subconsciously, to the view that rationalism alone is unable to reveal to me the sole truth worthy of knowing, namely: from whence came I and whither am I to go and what is the meaning of this hunger in my soul? . . . It is too late for me and my generation to return and fill it with meaning.[119]

In the final analysis, notwithstanding such sentiments and his many public statements stressing the importance of a religious dimension in national life, it is evident that for him religion remained subordinate to nationalism; the religious dimension was always more an instrument in the service of the nation than an independent, absolute value in itself. At the same time, whatever may have been the role of political expediency, there can be no doubt that Jabotinsky's policy produced a Revisionist Zionist stance vis-à-vis orthodox Jews that was far less confrontational than that evinced by labor Zionists.

Yet this observation does not hold for all of the ideological permutations spawned by the Zionist Right. Nor can one always neatly separate the intellectual strains of Zionist Left and Right. There were some surprising convergences issuing in manifestations that were ideologically significant although they remained politically peripheral. Such was the appearance of the tiny militant group bearing a Fascist orientation, called Brit Ha-biryonim and led by

Abba Ahimeir. The political implications of this emanation, extending to the formation of the Lehi underground military organization in the 1940s, have been traced in an earlier section of this book. In the present context we must note that their stretching of Revisionist Zionism to extremes also extended to the matter of religion. They favored religious traditions insofar as these could be pressed into the service of militant nationalism. They stridently extolled whatever strains of national assertiveness they could select out of the religion in Jewish history and contemptuously rejected whatever smacked of abstract spirituality and political passivity.[120] In their eyes, the Bible was the main repository of the positive elements, whereas theological spirituality and passivity were the unfortunate legacy of the Talmud and later rabbinical literature. In this respect they were manifestly the heirs of Berdyczewski's Nietzschean diatribes. Yet they certainly did not inherit his laissez-faire secularism, for they in effect endorsed Ahad Ha'am's advocacy of a norm-bound Jewish national identity. Indeed, Abba Ahimeir extolled the monistic uniformity and discipline imposed on a nation by religion. In his eyes it had the great virtue of making individual freedom congruous with conformity. Moreover, not a few of the leading personalities associated with this radical strain of Revisionist Zionism, including Avraham Stern, the founding head of Lehi, personally observed the Sabbath and the dietary laws. More important, however, than the largely instrumental affirmation of the Jewish religion as a nationalist asset was this ideological tradition's gross appropriation of Judaism's mythic messianic rhetoric. This extolled the unique eschatological destiny of the chosen people and its inherent right not only to attain absolute redemption in its homeland but also its prerogative to have dominion over other population groups domiciled there.[121]

Even more strikingly illustrative of the kaleidoscopic possibilities inhering in secularized Jewish identity and mediated by the Zionist enterprise was the radical abandonment of all such secular appropriation of religious observances, symbols, and messianic rhetoric by a tiny coterie of literary personalities who came to be known as Canaanites. Having first been immersed in the milieu of 1930s radical Revisionist Zionism, the founder of this "Canaanism" surfaced in the early 1940s with an ideological transmutation. Its leitmotifs were total dissociation from the Jewish religion and the modern rebirth of a postulated archaic Hebrew nation out of a Middle Eastern territorial matrix rather than out of the diasporic Jewish *ethnie*.

An Invented Identity: Canaanism

We have seen that all of the secular branches of Zionist ideology aspired toward a new type of Jew and of a modern, if not entirely new, culture of Jews as the outcome of Zionist settlement in Palestine. Moreover, those belonging to what has here been called the laissez-faire wing of secular Zionist ideology, as contrasted with the normative approach of Ahad Ha'am, anticipated with varying degrees of approval that this would lead to cultural incompatibility with Diaspora Jewry. In this outlook, taken to its logical extreme, there inhered the theoretical possibility of a complete break with Diaspora Jewry. This potentiality was signaled by the fact that the secularized pioneering settlers in Palestine gave semantic currency to the term *ivri* (Hebrew). It was a self-description that served to contrast their burgeoning homeland-based, Hebrew language identity with that of the *yehudi* (Jew) in the *galut*. Attendant upon this usage was the abstract noun *ivriyut* (Hebraism) as an affirmative ideological representation of the new, Hebrew-speaking, physically robust, close-to-nature, secularized culture of the Hebrew homeland.[122]

Yet none of the Zionist thinkers who applauded this new *ivriyut*, across the spectrum from the labor Left to the radical revisionist Right, regarded it as something discontinuous and incompatible with the Jewish past. They may have selected some phases of that past for censure and others for glorification, but their self-identification as Hebrews rather than Jews signified a transformation of long-existing Jewish identity, not an absolutely new identity. They never relinquished the premises that Jews, whether domiciled in Eretz Israel or in *galut* constituted a single ethnic unit and that their nationalism rested on this common ethnicity. The singular ideological innovation of an idiosyncratic but brilliant poet and writer named Uriel Halperin (1908–1981), who became better known by the pseudonym Yonatan Ratosh (he also used the names Uriel Shelah and A. L. Haran at various periods), was the rupturing of this ethnic basis for nationalism and its replacement with a postulated territorial-linguistic basis.[123]

Although, like several of the Zionist intelligentsia we have discussed, Ratosh was born in eastern Europe, a descendant of a long line of rabbis, his father had adopted a secular Zionist outlook and pioneered the institution of Hebrew language kindergartens in Warsaw. In 1920 the family emigrated to Palestine, where the father continued his work in that field. Uriel gained his Hebrew language education there and at the Hebrew University and was attracted to the radical wing of Revisionist Zionism. Its ethos of power and romantic invocation of the ancient Hebrew past were to find eloquent expression in his poems, the first of which was published in 1929, as well as in his publicistic writing. But his views had not yet broken out of the accepted boundaries of Zionist thought.[124]

In early 1938, Ratosh went to Paris, where he remained until the end of 1939. There he met Adia Gurevitch (1897–1975), whose pseudonym was A. G. Horon (Horon being the name of a Canaanite god). Horon was a kindred spirit whose historical depiction of the ancient Hebrews appears to have provided the catalyst for the transmutation of Ratosh's radical Revisionist Zionism into an alternative ideology of ultimately anti-Zionist character. Born in Kiev, Ukraine, Horon lived for a time in Turin, Italy, and then went to Paris in the late 1920s, where he studied Semitic languages and published historiographical articles on the ancient Hebrews and the Middle East. Having been active in the Betar paramilitary youth organization created by Ze'ev Jabotinsky, he participated in the founding conference of the latter's New Zionist Organization in the mid-1930s. There he is on record as having spoken out against Jabotinsky's adoption of a clause affirming the importance of religion in the national movement, declaring: "I am not a Jew from Yavne but a Hebrew from Samaria."[125]

Horon formulated a historical thesis according to which in the geographical region extending roughly between the Mediterranean and the Euphrates there had existed an ancient nation comparable in form and function to the ancient Hellenic nation.[126] Horon designated this region as Eretz Ha-kedem (the East Land; the Hebrew word *kedem* here encompassed two meanings: "ancient" and "eastern," or Ever Ha-nahar, meaning "the Land across the River," i.e, west of the River Euphrates). It was polytheistic and Hebrew-speaking, although in a variety of dialects, and included the Phoenicians on the Mediterranean coastline as well as other peoples, such as the Edomites, Moabites, and Ammonites. The covenant-bound tribes of Israel were only one of the political units within this broader ancient Hebrew nation and culture. The Land of Canaan was a geographical subsection of the region, and the peak of the nation's imperial greatness was under the House of David, when it encompassed the larger part of Eretz Ha-kedem.

It is noteworthy that this kind of speculative reconstruction of the past is a characteristic of many nationalist movements.[127] It is comparable to the evocation of classical Greece by modern Greek nationalism, of Cyrus's Persia by the Pahlavi dynasty in Iran, and of the heritage of the Pharaonic age by a strain of Egyptian nationalism, and to the manner in which, under Attaturk, the ideology of the new Turkish nationalism invoked reconstruction of the history of ancient Anatolia and the Hittites long before the rise of Islam.

In the mid-1940s, Ratosh, having been back in Palestine since late 1939, launched a Committee for the Consolidation of Hebrew Youth. He directed his appeal to that segment of the new Hebrew type that was closest to his heart—the young members of the dissident Jewish underground movements, the IZL and the Lehi. In a seminal document styled "An Epistle to Hebrew Youth,"[128] he called upon them to recognize "the deep abyss" that separated them from all of the Jewish *galut*: They were authentic Hebrews; the Hebrew language was for them a real mother tongue, and the homeland was "a real, actual, existing homeland," not "a solution to the Jewish Question . . . nor a solution for various emotional complexes of the Diaspora neurotics." The epistle appealed to them to liberate themselves from the choking bonds of the Jewish Diaspora. "If you will only remove the Jewish cobwebs from your eyes," it exhorted them, "you will see the vision of the great Hebrew future."

According to Ratosh's conception, not ethnicity but territoriality was the basis for nationalism and nationhood. Just as the nations of the New World, such as the United States of America, Mexico, or Australia, emerged on the basis of a shared territory, so would a broad Hebraic nation emerge in the natural territorial unit ranging from the Mediterranean to the Euphrates, a territory of which Eretz Israel formed an integral part. Moreover, just as the nucleus of settlers bearing a particular language and culture come to constitute the core of the New World nations (Englishmen in the United States, Spaniards in Mexico, and so on), so the new Hebrews—that is to say, those former Jews who had transformed themselves into Hebrews, "nativized" in Eretz Israel—were the potential core of the broader national-cultural unit that could ultimately emerge in the Middle East.

Of course, there remained the question of why the formative influence should emanate from those Hebrews rather than from the infinitely larger and more firmly rooted Arabic-speaking groups. In answer to this question, Ratosh proffered Horon's theory of the inherently Hebrew character underlying the culture of all the inhabitants of the territory under discussion. It was putatively a Hebrew character rooted in the ancient past and only artificially covered by imposed layers of extraneous languages, religions, and folkways. This monumentally fallacious interpretation enabled Ratosh to explain why the contemporary Arabic-speaking population groups, including those in Palestine, might be expected to assimilate into the revived Hebraic culture. He argued that there was no Arab nation to assimilate into, that from the standpoint of nationality there was a vacuum in Palestine. Had there existed a real Arab nation, the revived Hebrew nation could not have arisen there from the outset, just as it had not arisen among Jewish immigrants to Argentina or the United States.[129]

The following that Ratosh's new ideology came to command was minuscule—its active articulate core probably never numbered more than a dozen, all poets, novelists, or artists—but it certainly reflected a broader undercurrent of doubts and inclinations amongst those born or brought up in the Hebrew-speaking *yishuv*. Ratosh's circle reached its peak of activity only after the creation of the State of Israel, when it was able to produce its own organ, called *Alef* (the letter *alef*, symbolizing a new beginning, formed the logo of Ratosh's ideology), which appeared monthly or bimonthly from 1949 to 1953, reaching a distribution of about one thousand copies.[130]

The term that came to be associated with the ideological position propounded by Ratosh and his circle is *kena'aniyut* (Canaanism), its adherents being known as *kena'anim* (Canaanites, the singular form being *kena'ani*). Initially, however, they used the terms *ivri* and *ivriyut*, which, as we have noted, had gained currency in the terminology of the *yishuv*. Somewhat ironically, it seems that the label Canaanite was originally coined by the labor Zionist poet Abraham Shlonsky as a pejorative description of the heretical views aired by Ratosh's circle.

(Genesis 9:25 states: "Cursed be Canaan, a servant of servants shall he be to his brethren.") By the early 1950s, however, Ratosh's circle had itself adopted this designation in order to mark itself off positively from the Zionists' usage of the term *ivri*, which they considered to be fraudulent. In retrospect, it is therefore useful to distinguish between two usages of the term: Zionist Hebraism was the usage that remained within the confines of the Zionist consensus, and Canaanist Hebraism broke out of those confines and challenged Zionism. Although nurtured from the same source, the difference between the two usages was vast.

It is a moot point whether the eruption of an articulated Canaanist ideology in the 1940s rather than at any earlier time reflected the peak strength of widespread nativist Hebraic consciousness in the *yishuv* or, alternatively, was the defensive reaction of a declining circle to the resurgence of popular identification with diasporic Jewry in the wake of the Holocaust.[131] Certainly, Ratosh's "Epistle" demonstrated a pointed detachment from the terrible fate of European Jewry and indeed an implied concern lest misguided emotional identification with it would cause the young generation of Hebrews to backslide into conventional Zionism.

Yet there can be no doubt that Ratosh's Canaanist Hebraism was a dialectical offshoot of Zionist ideology in general and of the radical wing of Revisionist Zionism in particular. In that sense it ended up as a tiny but lethal "heresy" (as the historian Yaacov Shavit has aptly labeled it) in the very heart of the Zionist enterprise, Eretz Israel. It revoked the fundamental premises of all Zionist ideologies proper. Ratosh balked at the notion that the diasporic Jews in themselves were an actual or potential nation and wanted no part in any efforts to solve their supposed "Jewish problem." In a Canaanist document known as his "Opening Discourse,"[132] he declared emphatically:

There is no Hebrew except a Hebrew who is the son of the Land of Ever, Land of the Hebrew, to the exclusion of all else. And whosoever is not a native of this land, the land of the Hebrews, cannot be a Hebrew, is not a Hebrew and never was a Hebrew. And whosoever comes from the Jewish diaspora, from all its countries and for all its generations, from the beginning to the end of days, is a Jew and not a Hebrew. . . . And the Jew and the Hebrew can never be identical. Whoever is a Hebrew cannot be a Jew, and whoever is a Jew cannot be a Hebrew.

The vision of Canaanist ideology was of a revived Hebrew national culture within a restored Hebraic polity, encompassing not only the Arabic-speaking inhabitants of Palestine but all the inhabitants of the territory extending between the Mediterranean and the Euphrates. For attainment of this object, it was necessary to liberate the existing Hebraic nucleus from all diasporic and Judaistic influences and links. "As long as the land of the Hebrews is not cleansed of Zionism and the hearts of the Hebrews made pure of Judaism, all efforts will be in vain and every sacrifice a wasted one," declared Ratosh.[133] By the same token, the Arabic-speaking population had to rid itself of all Pan-Arabism because it obstructed the resuscitation of the ancient Hebraic essence that had been smothered by layers of imposed religions, languages, and political divisions over the centuries. To the question of why the Hebrew (formerly the Jew) should not be expected to integrate into a broader secular nationalism whose language was Arabic, Ratosh's Canaanism proffered an illusory if not disingenuous answer: such Pan-Arab nationalism was quintessentially Moslem sectarian, factionalizing the Middle Eastern population, immuring it within a medieval social structure and rendering it prey to European imperialism. Only the Hebraic nucleus had the necessary modern secular impetus that could re-create a glorious independent national culture in the Middle East.

Accordingly, the Canaanist program involved winning over to modern Hebraism all other inhabitants of the entire region, starting with minorities such as the Druse, the Maronites, and the Kurds and continuing with the larger population groups whose inherent Hebraistic potential had been suppressed by Pan-Arabism and Western imperialism. This process would, it was anticipated, require the use of force. Here was an aspect of Ratosh's ideology that emanated from his long-standing affinity with the radical, maximalist circle of Revisionist Zionists in Palestine and its ethos of power akin to that of European fascism. Ratosh insisted on describing the anticipated violence as "civil war." Indeed, this became his interpretation of the war of 1948. By his lights, it was in the nature of a civil war between the new Hebraic generation that at last had asserted itself and overridden the constraints of the Jewish-bound Zionist establishment, on the one side, and the forces of medieval Islamic-bound Pan-Arabism, propped up by British imperialism, on the other side.[134]

It should be noted, however, that various post–State of Israel transmutations of Canaanist ideology incrementally withdrew from this expansionist aspect, as also from the emphasis Ratosh placed on the supposedly historiographical basis of the ideology.[135] Advocating that the State of Israel must seek integration into the Semitic region through an alliance of various political units in a greater regional structure, they implicitly recognized the fallacy at the heart of Ratosh's original Canaanist ideology, namely, Ratosh's belief that Hebrew language and culture could be imposed upon the whole mid-eastern region[136]

Canaanism has engaged our attention because it was undeniably an emanation—one might say a reductio ad absurdum—of Zionist-mediated secular Jewish identity. It reflected contradictions, tensions, and tendencies that inhered in the secularization of Jewish identity within a nationalist framework. In the context of our analysis, it was a peculiar hybrid of intellectual strains. In some respects it is traceable back to the laissez-faire secularism of the Berdyczewski and Brenner school of thought. In other respects it is explicable as a dialectical outcome of radical Revisionist Zionism. Yet sight should not be lost of the fact that Canaanism was a *quantité négligible*, never encompassing more than a tiny coterie of adherents. Moreover, it was essentially a localized phenomenon. It had no resonance in the broader intellectual world of Zionism, and it is to the mainstream of Zionist ideology that we must cast back our attention.

Jacob Klatzkin's Radical Secularism

Within the mainstream Zionist intelligentsia, the seminal ideas of Ahad Ha'am, already set down before the First World War, continued to leaven the ongoing debate over the Zionist redefinition of secular Jewish culture long after he died in early 1927. Two outstanding thinkers who participated in that debate, critically engaging Ahad Ha'am's views during his lifetime and long thereafter, merit special consideration. They were Jacob Klatzkin (1882–1948) and Yehezkel Kaufmann (1899–1963). Neither was a founder of any political school of thought in the Zionist movement, but each, in his own way, contributed notably to the ideological storehouse of Zionism. In chapter 4 we noted Kaufmann's formulation of a progressive General Zionist ideology. Both took issue with Ahad Ha'am on substantive aspects of his analysis of the Jewish cultural heritage and its implications for the secular identity of Zionist Jews, and both were led to conclusions favoring a maximalist political program aimed at sovereign statehood, over Ahad Ha'am's minimalist concept of an autonomous cultural center in Zion.

Jacob Klatzkin was a Jewish intellectual, born in Russia but living in central Europe, who first became known as the editor of the Zionist Organization's organ, *Die Welt*, from 1909 until 1911. From 1912 to 1915 he was employed in the main office of the Jewish National Fund in Cologne. During the years of the First World War he edited the Swiss *Bulletin Juif,* which covered events of relevance to Jews in the countries at war. Thereafter he returned to Germany, where he founded the Eshkol Publishing House, noted for its publication of the German *Encyclopaedia Judaica,* of which he served as general editor. After ten volumes had appeared in German and a beginning had been made in Hebrew, the advent of the Nazi regime caused the suspension of this mammoth work, and Klatzkin sought refuge in Switzerland. Thence he moved to the United States, where he resided from 1941 to 1947. He returned to Switzerland in 1947. It seems that it was his intention to settle in Palestine, but he died in 1948 while still in Switzerland. His contribution to Zionist ideology was made in numerous articles in Hebrew and German that appeared in journals ranging from *Ha-shiloah* to *Die Welt* as well as in several volumes of essays.[137]

Klatzkin's ideological formulation of Zionism bridged the gap between those who had come to Zionism from an initially integrationist position (mostly central European Jews) and those, mainly living in, or stemming from, eastern Europe, whose Zionism had emerged directly out of a consistent Jewish ethnicism. His roots were intertwined with those of Ahad Ha'am, but his conclusions merged with those of Theodor Herzl insofar as he denied that the Diaspora had any long-term viability and envisaged an ultimately clear-cut alternative—the continuity of Jewish life in a Jewish state, on the one hand, and complete assimilation throughout the Diaspora on the other. Although respectful of Ahad Ha'am as a personality and writer, he rejected out of hand Ahad Ha'am's vision of a Jewish cultural center sustaining a continued Jewish Diaspora life.

Klatzkin was the son of a rabbi and had received a thorough traditionalist Jewish education, but, typical of the *maskil* intelligentsia of his generation, he broke away and left to study philosophy at the University of Marburg in Germany. In 1912 he gained a doctorate in philosophy from the University of Berne. Although he had studied under Hermann Cohen, who was a neo-Kantian, Klatzkin came to adopt a "vitalistic" approach in philosophy, which largely displaced pure reason and cognition in favor of emphasis upon the senses as the source of human vitality and purpose.[138] The underpinning that his vitalistic philosophical bent provided for his Zionist theory is evident in his pivotal thesis that abstract ideas did not constitute a factor in the definition of the nation.

Up to a point, Klatzkin's conception of the nation was quite in accord with that of Ahad Ha'am, for he too regarded ethnic kinship and feeling as the basis for organic development of the nation. However, as we have seen, Ahad Ha'am had gone on to posit that this organic development produced for each nation a unique national genius and that in the Jewish case this was reflected in a particular system of ideas, including ethics. On this point Klatzkin's vitalistic premises appear to have intervened. He balked at the notion that uniform ideational content of any sort was a precondition for the viability of the nation. Ideational *content*, such as particular beliefs and ethical values, was not the essential factor, he insisted, but only structural *form*, meaning common language and territory. "Would one make the creation and character of the German nation or the French nation depend upon philosophical systems, ideas, world-outlooks?" he asked rhetorically, "and do differences in such ideas enable us to distinguish between these two nations?"[139] Zionism's purpose was purely "to place the nation on an objective basis, namely, language and territory."[140] It was no part of its purpose to insist upon any uniformity in the realm of beliefs, philosophical ideas, and ethical principles.

On this score Klatzkin faulted Ahad Ha'am. He contended that the mistaken attempt to define Jewish national identity on the basis of putative fixed values and ideas—a so-called spirit of Judaism—had led Ahad Ha'am misguidedly to overemphasize the link with traditional sources as a national obligation. "Not value-contents but only objective forms are obligatory for members of the nation," Klatzkin asserted. Indeed, he depicted Ahad Ha'am's approach as no more than the other side of the coin of assimilationist Reform Judaism. The latter attempted to turn Judaism into a purely spiritual matter. It dispensed with objective attributes such as territory and language and retained only religious faith. According to Klatzkin, in proposing that Jewish national identity be based upon a putative "spirit of Judaism" commanding fixed ideas and moral principles, Ahad Ha'am was merely submitting the converse side of Reform's program, which he himself so sharply rejected. As opposed to both the Reform assimilationists and Ahad Ha'am, Klatzkin advanced a "third approach wholly nationalist in character, which places Judaism on an objective basis."

It posits anew that the Hebrew experience means neither religious precepts nor philosophical principles. It has transcended its former religious and abstract meaning and assumed a purely national meaning. We are neither a religious denomination nor the embodiment of a philosophical system; neither the bearers of a single belief nor of a single world-outlook, but rather we are the sons of one family, bearers of a common history. That which unites us and distinguishes us from others is not an objective covenant of ideas but a subjective covenant born of a common history and future. Hence, the holding of heretical beliefs does not disqualify anyone from belonging to the nation any more than holding supposedly correct beliefs includes one. A Gentile does not become a Jew by virtue of belief in the religion of Israel or a Jewish spiritual outlook, and a Jew does not cease being one if he balks at religious precepts or at that supposed spiritual outlook. In short, national consciousness neither demands nor negates any specific views and ideas.[141]

Klatzkin challenged the very assumption that one could identify an essence of Judaism, a "spirit of Judaism." Like Berdyczewski he contended that all one could find was a constant conflict and interaction of alternative ideas. For example, he argued, there had never been unequivocal clarity as to whether "our God is a God of peace, of mercy and compassion, or a God of war, a jealous and vengeful God."[142] Judaism had always been a religion of laws and observances, not of philosophical ideas. That was why the alien ideas incorporated in the mystical work, the Kabbala, and in Hasidism did not cause total schisms in Judaism, "for they affected only creed and not deed." The great sages of Judaism were full of contradictory ideas: "Our religion is not a church because it is not a system of beliefs but a system of deeds. It does not teach us philosophical essence and outlooks . . . it has no dogmatic principles. It is prescriptive in its law, free in its ideas."

Klatzkin questioned Ahad Ha'am's attempt to contrast a Judaistic essence in the moral realm—the concept of *tzedek*—with the Christian moral principle of love: "And what will you then have to say when one spiritual essence is compared with the other only to find that this meagre difference of idea does not suffice to make a significant distinction?" He reasoned that not subjective ideas but only national attributes of an objective nature, especially language and land, could define the Jewish entity. "There is no such thing as 'a national spirit'; there is only a national form," he averred. "Foreign ideas do not exclude anyone [from the nation], a foreign language and a foreign country do exclude one!" If Ahad Ha'am were justified in his contention that a national Jew's nonobservance of religious commandments was acceptable, then by the same token the national Jew should be free to abandon whatever specific ideas of a philosophical and ethical nature happened to be found in the tradition. Moreover, Ahad Ha'am's demand for uniformity of thought carried with it the danger of coercion and chauvinism. A liberal, nonchauvinistic nationalism was one that freed the individual as it freed the nation: "For there is no national freedom unless it is accompanied by human freedom. And there is no national revival worth fighting for unless it frees and repairs the human values in the national personality."

Although insisting on the purely objective factors of ethnic kinship, language, and territory as the bases of the nation, Klatzkin was at pains to explain that his view was not wholly deterministic:

On the contrary, the national view, too, requires an act of will. It defines its nationalism in terms of two factors: participation in the past and the will to continue participation in the future. Two bases are involved: an historically deterministic basis and a basis of historical will. A Jew who does not wish to continue his participation in the Hebrew nation, who breaks the covenant, balks at the suffering it entails and evades the common battle for the nation's redemption, thereby relinquishes his share in the past and secedes from the nation. By the same token, a person cannot become a convert to Judaism merely by accepting our religious observances or ideas; only the act of will to participate in the life of the Hebrew nation qualifies him for Judaism.[143]

It is the insistence upon the attainment of a Jewish territorial state that marks the confluence of Klatzkin's approach with that of Theodor Herzl's political Zionism. It should be noted, however, that this was by no means a total congruence of view: Herzl showed nothing like the understanding that Klatzkin had of language—that is to say, the Hebrew language—as the essential basis for Jewish nationalism. Furthermore, having come up against the frustrating obstacles to Jewish assimilation despite formal emancipation in west-central Europe, Herzl built much of his ideological exposition on the contention that assimilation was impossible as long as there was no Jewish state somewhere. Klatzkin, in contrast, argued that, with or without Jewish statehood, assimilation of Diaspora Jewry was not only possible but inevitable. "A people dispersed and divided amongst other peoples and lands must in the end be swallowed up by them when its religion no longer delays this."

Nor could assimilation be stemmed by the creation of a "spiritual center" in Eretz Israel as envisaged by Ahad Ha'am. The Jewish people had survived the long period of dispersion not on the strength of a unique system of ideas but because of specific *forms* of living that emanated from the observance of Jewish law and from the virtual autonomy it enjoyed up to the period of emancipation. But the power of these religious forms had lapsed, and there no longer were powerful divisions to isolate the ghetto and thereby preserve national distinctiveness in the Diaspora. Therefore "there was no valid analogy between the *galut* that preceded the *haskala* and the *galut* that followed it. They were two different *galut* conditions. . . . As long as our religion was intact, we were surrounded by a protective wall and we lived a national life, almost a political life, on alien soil."

Thus, although rooted in the same ethnicist premises as Ahad Ha'am, Klatzkin was led to much the same conclusion as the former believer in integration, Theodor Herzl. Klatzkin too envisaged polarization in the future: a full, normal national life in a Jewish state for the main body of Jewry and total assimilation of the remnant in the Diaspora. "Our people will then be divided into two," he conjectured, "a Hebrew collectivity in the land of Israel and a Jewish collectivity in the *galut* . . . two nations with different visages . . . the rift will widen." At the same time, he went far beyond Herzl in his castigation of *galut* life. In common with Berdyczewski, although with none of his ambivalence and doubts, Klatzkin not only denied the viability of the *galut* but also condemned it as an irredeemably undignified and even immoral existence:

Even if we were to assume that the *galut* is viable and that total assimilation will not inevitably ensue after the falling away of religion, we are obliged to state: the Judaism of the *galut* is not worthy of survival. The *galut* falsifies our national character . . . the *galut* corrupts the human in us . . . *galut* existence cannot be called life, not from a national perspective and not from a human perspective.[144]

These were the contentions out of which Klatzkin formulated the archetypal radical Zionist position that came to be known as "negation of the *galut*." It laid down as a central ideological tenet the proposition that the *galut* deserves to exist only as a corridor to redemption from itself through ascent to Eretz Israel. Yet *Gegenwartsarbeit*—that is to say, political and cultural activity in the Diaspora—was compatible with his viewpoint. "We must preserve Judaism in the *galut* as far as is in our capacity," he affirmed. But he also insisted that this must never be regarded as an end in itself. His cogent formulation of this important ideological position merits quotation at length:

The *galut* cannot survive, and all our endeavors to keep it alive can only have short-lived results. But far be it from us to scorn them. These temporary results can perform an important function if they serve the long-term purpose of constructing the nation in the Land of Israel. The *galut* cannot survive, and all our efforts to keep it alive are no more than unnatural and false. However, these efforts are not wasted, for we have no intention of building our future on the ruins of a *galut* that is about to collapse. Nor are we attempting to prop it up permanently. Rather, we are hoping to postpone its end and in the meanwhile to salvage some bricks for a new structure. The *galut* is not worthy of survival. What does this mean? It means when it has the pretension of being an end in itself. But it has merit when it serves as a means and a corridor towards another form of existence. The *galut* is worthy of existence for the sake of redemption from the *galut.* Thus the aspiration towards the Land of Israel imparts value to the *galut.* Without this goal, without the objective of The Land, the *galut* is nothing more than a life of deterioration and degeneration, an indictment of the nation and of man, a life of futile struggle and pointless suffering, of ambiguity, confusion and eternal impotence. It is not worth keeping alive.[145]

In this spirit Klatzkin offered guidelines for the behavior of Zionists while still situated in the Diaspora. They were not to get involved in the inner national life of the nations among whom they were domiciled; they were to preserve their consciousness of being aliens, of being in exile. "Let us not seek after authority and high office in alien states. We ought to maintain fences between us and their peoples and not become too involved." He objected particularly to the habit of taking pride in examples of Jews who had gained high office or other distinction as patriots or war heroes. He considered this undignified and self-disparaging, since such Jews epitomized assimilationism. Their deeds served other nations, whereas for their own people they did naught. "What Jews really ought clearly to state," he opined, was that "we do not take pride in Jews of that type." The greatest enemy of the Jewish nation was assimilation, and everything possible had to be done to fight it. Indeed, "national conversion" had to be equated with religious conversion. An assimilationist should not be regarded as a Jew any more than should a religious convert to Christianity. "The time has come," he proclaimed, "for national conversion to cancel membership of the Jewish people."

The Ultimate Critique: Yehezkel Kaufmann

Yehezkel Kaufmann was born in 1899 in eastern Europe and studied in the modernized yeshiva of Rabbi Haim Tschernowitz (Rav Tzair) in Odessa and later at the Academy of Oriental Studies in St. Petersburg. In 1918 he gained a doctorate from the University of Berne. He settled in Palestine in 1929, where he at first taught at the Reali High School, Haifa. After 1949 he lectured in Bible studies at the Hebrew University of Jerusalem and completed a multivolume history of the Jewish religion.[146] Kaufmann's signal contribution to the storehouse of Zionist ideology lay in his conscious attempt to examine critically the premises of Zionist thought and to offer an empirical historical analysis as a guide to the program of Zionism. The relationship between religion and nation and the nature of Jewish secular identity were major foci of this analysis.

Kaufmann's endeavor dated back as far as 1914, when he first subjected Ahad Ha'am's conception of Judaism to sharply critical scrutiny in the columns of *Ha-shiloah.*[147] In that essay he focused primarily on the debate between Ahad Ha'am and Berdyczewski as to whether, in the first instance, Judaism possessed a normative essence and whether, in the second instance, enlightened national Jews ought to consider themselves bound by it in their personal lives. Kaufmann dismissed Berdyczewski's charge that Ahad Ha'am had withdrawn from the position (expressed in his essay "Slavery in Freedom") that, happily, the enlightened national Jew could hold "any opinion in the world without it endangering his Jewishness." He argued that Ahad Ha'am had been consistent in positing the existence of a permanent, normative essence in Judaism. This view Kaufmann endorsed, but he contested Ahad Ha'am's interpretation of that essence. It was not a matter of particular moral principles such as *tzedek*, as claimed by Ahad Ha'am. Rather, it was rooted in a certain cognition: "cognition of the reality of God as revealed to the people of Israel in history" (in history, Kaufmann stressed, as opposed to metaphysical logic). This cognition of belief set the parameters of Judaism's normative essence. It provided a *masoret* (tradition) whose validity for Jews was independent of reason. Judaism's essence was, in other words, a unique form of religious faith, one rooted in historical revelation. Kaufmann argued that a godhead recognizable by metaphysical logic alone (such as some of the ancient Greek philosophers posited) did not endow a tradition in this sense because its principles remained dependent upon human reason.

Since Kaufmann thus affirmed that Judaism had an essence and was not simply the sum total of what Jews happened to think and do, he rejected Berdyczewski's call for a complete "transvaluation of values." "A Judaism whose values have changed is a contradiction in terms," he declared. "It is a mistake to think that Judaism in the past had periodically expunged its former content and refilled itself with new content." This did not mean that Judaism had been static or impervious to outside influences; "the barrel" (as he put it metaphorically) remained fixed by the tradition even though the wine changed and fermented and even though new wine from foreign vines was periodically poured into it. Hence, for instance, when Maimonides absorbed Aristotelian ideas, he synthesized them with the Jewish tradition. But the importance of Maimonides's contribution lay not in innovation of values; it lay in no more than innovative *interpretation*. It followed that Kaufmann concurred with Ahad Ha'am on the issue of Jesus as it had emerged in the debate over Brenner's comments. According to Kaufmann, the belief that Jesus was not whatever Christians believed him to be was part and parcel of the Jewish tradition; it inhered in the normative essence of Judaism as historically evolved. Since the Hebrew people did not accept Jesus in his time, it may never accept from him any influence as long as it remains true to itself.[148]

Up to this point, Kaufmann sided with Ahad Ha'am against Berdyczewski. However, he took issue with Ahad Ha'am's premise that the "barrel" of tradition could be maintained as the normative essence of Jewishness even after the core belief of the tradition had been removed. He argued that Ahad Ha'am failed to take cognizance of the enormous difference between Judaism possessed of the old faith and the new national Jewishness devoid of that faith. The functional difference between a relationship of "I believe" and one of "I feel" was not just quantitative; it was qualitative. "I believe" signified invincible faith, "I feel," merely romantic attachment. He noted that even Ahad Ha'am had sensed this—hence he had felt compelled to draw from the well of the tradition a binding ideological content that would endow the national Jew with a sense of purpose. This he thought he had found in "the national morals" epitomized by the principle of *tzedek*.[149]

Contrary to this view, Kaufmann argued that moral principles, even if they had a national coloration, never could provide the same life force for national distinctiveness as could religious belief. Furthermore, since moral ideas were inseparable from one's world outlook in general, "how can we demand of a person," Kaufmann asked, "that he subordinate his moral ideas to those of the 'national morals' when in other spheres we admit his right to think and to behave in whatever manner he pleases?" Nor was he convinced that significant difference existed between Jewish morals and Christian morals or those of other peoples. Even the vaunted principle of *tzedek* had tendentiously been selected out of the Jewish tradition by Ahad Ha'am, for it was mistaken to say (as in the example evoked by Ahad Ha'am concerning the talmudic difference of opinion between Rabbis Akiva and Ben Petura) that Ben Petura's opinion was not in accord with the spirit of Judaism. *Tzedek*, after all, represented only the minimum moral demand; above that no limit was set. While "*tzedek* was obligatory, love and compassion were optional." All were desirable in the Jewish tradition.

In another essay, one that appeared in 1920, Kaufmann stripped Ahad Ha'am's conception of a national *hefetz ha-kiyum* (will to life) of what he considered its empirically unacceptable positivist assumptions. He argued that only figuratively speaking might one perhaps call national feeling an instinct. In actuality, only the social nature of mankind was a matter of instinct, not the feeling for any particular social group. The latter was acquired, not instinctive. He likened the relationship between man's general social instinct and his particular national ties to that between sexual desire and love for a particular person:

Sexual desire is certainly a natural drive. But love of a particular woman is not implanted in a man by nature. Accordingly, national feeling, to the extent that it is a permanent factor, that is, to the extent that it involves a relationship with a specific historical society and is not conceived merely as a general anthropological disposition, is not a natural feeling but an acquired one. . . . Nature cannot implant in a person an attachment to a particular language, a particular land, a particular literature, customs and religion.[150]

His point was that, subjected to scientific scrutiny, the metaphor of an instinctive national will to life was reducible simply to the learned behavior of the individuals constituting any national social unit.

Kaufmann proceeded to argue that, since the general rule observable in history was for diasporic minorities to disappear through assimilation, Jewish survival was a historical exception that could only be explained with reference to some unique factor. That factor was the unique religious faith of the Jews:

> While the spiritual culture and life of the Jewish people in the Diaspora does contain secular-nationalist elements, there is no doubt that the element that has maintained and preserved all this culture and life, the element whose power to influence has been unique and which has been the cause of the Jewish people's unique national survival in exile, has been the religious element in our spiritual culture.[151]

Thus, religion was not, as Ahad Ha'am had claimed, merely a means used by the will to life within the nation; it was, in fact, the primary cause of Israel's self-isolation: "the very source of its national will." Kaufmann went on to explain that the factor of religion meant, in the first instance, its faith core, "the national monotheistic belief." Rituals and precepts and practices, were only the nuts and bolts of survival; the foundation itself was the Jew's unshakable faith in his covenantal relationship with the universal God. Given the unique survival-sustaining function of religion in the above sense, it followed that

> Anyone who thinks that some other "means" temporary or permanent can be found to replace religion in its demise (e.g. autonomy, Yiddish) is utterly mistaken. Certain elements in religious praxis did serve as a means against assimilation, and for religion in that sense there are substitutes. But religion in the sense of faith, the religious devotion that tied Israel with a living bond to its national culture, was not a means but, as we have said, the very source of the national will. With the extinction of the faith, the national will is also bound to perish.[152]

Kaufmann's conclusion was emphatic: there could be no surrogate for religion in ensuring Jewish survival, at any rate not in the modern Diaspora. Neither Ahad Ha'am's putative will to life nor his spiritual center would do.

This penetrating critique of Ahad Ha'am's ideas was extensively elaborated in the monumental four-volume study in Hebrew titled *Gola ve-nekhar* (Exile and alienness), which appeared between 1928 and 1932, marking the apex of Kaufmann's enterprise. To be sure, for all of this work's erudition and profundity, it proved to be so recondite and discursive as to make it inaccessible to all but the most intellectually qualified minds within Zionism. However, in some later writings, Kaufmann's main ideas were rendered more lucid and accessible, notably in a small but masterly critical study of Jewish nationalist thought titled *Bein netivot* (Between pathways) which he wrote in 1943.[153]

Methodologically, *Gola ve-nekhar* bore the stamp of European historical sociology associated variously with Fustel de Coulanges, Wilhelm Dilthey, Heinrich Rickert, and Wilhelm Windelbrand. Kaufmann sought to explain the

Jewish historical experience within the conceptual context of broader sociological generalizations. Since he emphatically rejected all notions of historical materialism and determinism, he did not endow these generalizations with the status of laws functioning independently of human will. They were, rather, empirically detectable regularities.[154] In *Gola ve-nekhar* the regularities on which he focused concerned the role of factors such as the ethnic community, language, and territory and the fate of diasporic ethnic minorities. One salient generalization arising from Kaufmann's inquiry was that common origin, kinship, and language (and less so a common territory) were the essentials of ethnic distinctiveness. Another was that not simple conquest of a territory but ethnic settlement and the successful implantation of the settlers' language and culture were what created an inalienable "natural homeland right." This in turn expressed itself in the ethnic group's unshakable, natural "sense of dominion" (*regesh adnut*) over a particular territory. It followed that because diasporic ethnic minorities could never share in that natural sense of dominion, they remained irremediably alien until they succumbed to assimilation, as they almost invariably did.

Within the context of these major historical-sociological generalizations, Kaufmann subjected the Jewish case to elaborately detailed scrutiny and emerged with far-reaching (and in part farfetched) operative conclusions for Zionism. The main thesis of *Gola ve-nekhar* was that the survival of the Jews was an exception to the general rule of assimilation, the explanation for which lay in the unique nature of Judaism as a religion at once universal in its validity for mankind and particular in its imperatives for the Jewish ethnic group. The Jewish religion was thus a unique force in history that ensured Jewish survival despite dispersion, one for which there could be no functional substitute.

In *Gola ve-nekhar*, Kaufmann also elaborated his long-standing criticism of Ahad Ha'am's notion of a will to life as a sort of biological drive or instinct. Concurrently, he contested Marxist determinism and found fault with Dubnow's historical theory, which, going far beyond Ahad Ha'am's notions, affirmed the possibility of a viable Jewish culture in the Diaspora. Furthermore, although himself convinced that the modern Diaspora was incapable of sustaining a viable Jewish culture, Kaufmann attacked the aggressive genre of negation of the *galut* preached by Berdyczewski and Brenner. It will be recalled that they excoriated the *galut* as an existence of shameful parasitism and degradation and placed the blame for it upon religious Judaism itself.

Kaufmann debunked not only these views but also Aharon David Gordon's kindred characterizations of the *galut* as a parasitic life detached from natural productive work. He argued that such views reflected crass ignorance and misinterpretation of history. The true historical record showed that even under conditions of dispersion Jews had never languished degenerately. Merchant and trading occupations were no less productive and worthy than any other occupation. The charge that Jews were economically parasitic was an insidious invention of antisemites, which Berdyczewski, Brenner, and their likes had shamelessly internalized. Their views were an exhibition of self-hatred. To be sure, Kaufmann fully recognized that the Zionist enterprise required idealistic Jewish productivity and pioneering, but he argued that this had nothing to do with characterization of the *galut*. The most economically productive of Jewish laborers or farmers situated outside a homeland—and therefore excluded from the enjoyment of "natural national dominion"—were as much in the *galut* as the least economically productive of yeshiva scholars.

According to Kaufmann, the *galut* was, in essence, not a state of nonproductivity but one of "alienness" (*nekhar*). This resulted from the lack of a national homeland, not from Judaism itself. The *galut* was a condition, unique to the Jews, of suspension between unattainable assimilation on the one side and hopelessly defective national existence on the other. "The fundamental mistake [of Berdyczewski] is that he sees the *galut* as 'sin,' whereas in truth it was not sin but disaster," wrote Kaufmann. "Not the 'spirituality' of the sacred moral teachings of Israel but the fruits of disaster were the cause of Israel's political destruction."[155] As for the accusation that the so-called servile morals of Judaism, its timidity and nonassertiveness, had supposedly caused the Jews to be in the *galut*, how was it, asked Kaufmann rhetorically, that those same values had not caused "exiled peoples" to emerge among Christians or among fatalistic Buddhists. Christianity, after all, had adopted the same basic values from Judaism and even emphasized love, compassion, and timid "turning of the other cheek" far beyond the normative teachings of Judaism.

Nor did Kaufmann endorse Berdyczewski's relativist denial that there was any ideational essence to Judaism. He pointed to an internal contradiction in Berdyczewski's position. If there were no such thing as a normative Judaism in the first place, how could he then claim that Judaism had forced itself upon the Jews and distorted their natural human instincts? Yet Kaufmann insisted on categorizing Berdyczewski and Brenner, and indeed also A. D. Gordon, as "spiritual Zionists" in common with Ahad Ha'am, despite the relativism that divided them from Ahad Ha'am. He justified this on the basis that they too "misguidedly thought that the central question was not the question of *geula* [redemption], that is to say the question of the *galut* as a social problem, but the question of cultural revival and survival."[156]

It should be noted that Kaufmann personally shared a secular Jewish identity with Ahad Ha'am and the other "spiritual Zionists" whom he so piercingly criticized. His was not the argument of those who insisted that all Jews must be religiously observant; it was an argument about historical-sociological verity. Kaufmann's uncompromising intellectual integrity dictated that the truth must be faced even if it did not suit ideological preferences. As early as 1920 he had noted: "Our situation is truly tragic: the situation of those who, having lost their religious faith without hope of recovering it, still cling to that entire national universe which depended upon that faith for its life."[157] He therefore left unanswered the question of whether and in what form secular Jewish identity was viable. On the one hand, he cast doubt on the value of cultivating a "normative" secular identity as advocated by Ahad Ha'am. On the other hand, he rejected Berdyczewski's relativism as to the nature of Jewish culture and his consequent laissez-faire or existential mode of identity. Since Kaufmann certainly did not advocate a return to religious belief as a viable option, his analysis implied that all *conscious* attempts to shape future Jewish identity through Zionism were futile. In the Diaspora it had no long-term future; in a territorial homeland it would develop spontaneously, as did the national-cultural identity of all territorial nations.

CHAPTER EIGHT

The Right to The Land

A T T H E H E A R T of the Zionist ideology was the claim to Eretz Israel, or Zion, as the national homeland of the Jews, hence, as the legitimate locus for the national self-determination of the Jews. The purpose of this chapter is to elucidate the articulated ideological formulations of this Zionist claim. The appropriate focus here is not the legalistic arguments over the relative obligations of the British mandatory power toward Jews and Arabs in Palestine, although these served the diplomatic efforts of the Zionists and consequently figure prominently in standard histories of the triangular relationship between Britain, Jews, and Arabs. Nor is it the record of negotiation attempts between Zionism and Arab personalities in and outside Palestine or the ideological dilemmas associated with the resort to force for defensive or offensive purposes.[1]

Rather, our focus is on the fundamental ideological formulations of Jewish right to Eretz Israel as they were conceived internally by the votaries of Zionism in its various schools of thought and projected externally in the forum of world public opinion. In this respect it is useful to apply the distinction that has been drawn between two dimensions of ideology, the fundamental and the operative. Our concern here is more with the fundamental dimension, which refers to the underlying fixed principles of ideology, than with the operative dimension, which reflects the tactical modifications made in the course of political action.[2]

From the outset, differences in Zionist perceptions of their claim were in large part a function of another and far deeper division in modern Jewish life—that between two self-understandings of Jewish identity. According to one self-understanding, Jewish identity had a transcendental source; it derived ultimately from the supernatural acts of God as revealed in the ancient history of the Children of Israel and recorded in the Bible. For the other self-understanding, as was shown in the previous chapter, Jewish identity emanated from the natural history of a particular unit of mankind. It considered the religious system of Judaism (including the very idea that God had endowed the Jews with their Jewish identity!) to have been self-engendered no less than had been their language or other facets of their culture. Since the Zionist movement from its inception comprised both orthodox religious Jews and secularized Jews, some ideological components of Zionism were subject to the same cleavage between transcendental and immanent interpretations. One such component was the claim that the Jews were entitled to seek their national salvation in the Land of Israel.

Divinely Endowed Right

The orthodox religious segment of Zionism has always perceived the Jews' right to Eretz Israel as part and parcel of the everlasting covenant between God and the Children of Israel.

And the Lord appeared unto Abram and said unto him, I am God Almighty. . . . I will establish My covenant between Me and thee and thy seed after thee throughout the generations for an everlasting covenant to be a God unto thee and thy seed after thee. And I will give unto thee and to thy seed after thee, the land of their sojournings, all the lands of Canaan for an everlasting holding: and I will be their God. (Gen. 17:1, 7, 8.)[3]

By these terms it matters not which peoples were the earliest inhabitants of The Land nor who presently occupy it. Nor, indeed, is the right to The Land an issue resolvable between nation and nation. God alone is Lord and possessor of all lands; He alone distributes lands to peoples. This article of faith is epitomized by the highly authoritative commentary of Rashi to Genesis 1:1, in which he states, "Should the nations of the world question the validity of Israel's title to the Holy Land by saying: 'You are robbers in that you have overrun the territories of the seven peoples' [that occupied The Land previously], Israel can retort: 'The whole world is the Lord's. He created it and gave it to whomsoever He saw fit. It was His will to give it to them [the Canaanite nations] and it was His will to take it away from them and give it to us.'"

Notwithstanding the Jews' exile from The Land and irrespective of the divine reasons for this condition (a subject upon which Judaism's sages pondered throughout the ages), the absolute perpetuity of the biblical covenant eliminated any notion that God had reallocated The Land permanently to any other people. No conquest could ever usurp Israel's right. Just as all the vicissitudes of fortune that afflicted the Jews (and of which the prophets warned) did not invalidate their chosenness for God's covenant, so too Eretz Israel remained irrevocably *theirs*, and their ultimate messianic return to it was guaranteed. By the same token, since God had given The Land to the Jews as a trust, it followed that the Jews themselves had no right to give it up: "And The Land shall never be given up [sold in perpetuity], for The Land is mine" (Lev. 25:23).[4]

The aforementioned articles of faith were common to all orthodox Jews, whether they joined the Zionist fold or not. Here one must note an important paradox: the very fact that the fundamental ideology of religious Zionism rested on belief in the divine promise, that is to say, on a thoroughly determinist basis, rendered it possible to make operative ideological modifications secure in the belief that the end goal of return to Zion was in any case predetermined by God. By contrast, secular Zionists, since they relied on no more than the interplay of human free will and other natural factors, had to assume that their end goal might never be reached unless they took the right choices. In this sense, as we shall see later in this survey, religious Zionists could sometimes be more flexible than their secular counterparts. Much as some rabbis could reject Zionism outright without impairing their absolute faith in the ultimate divine restoration to Zion, others, while affirming Zionism, could entertain operative options facing the Zionist movement that fell short of immediate access to Eretz Israel. Moreover, the less the orthodox Jews conflated the Zionist movement with the process of messianic redemption itself, the wider the range of acceptable options became. Such options could comprehend not only satisfaction (temporarily) with rights of Jewish settlement merely in parts of Eretz Israel but even adoption of settlement activity in another territory altogether (again temporarily). Conversely, it stood to reason that if the Zionist project in Eretz Israel was in fact a manifest stage within the divinely ordained process of redemption, any waiver of or deflection from resettlement activity—or worse still, any relinquishment of territorial control already attained—was unacceptable. Hence, the more the religious Zionists associated the messianic process of redemption with Zionism itself, the less flexible they became in regard to waiver of any part of the claim to Eretz Israel.

These characteristics of religious Zionist ideology first became evident when the Zionist movement faced a critical choice involving an alternative territory to Palestine. As we have noted in an earlier chapter, other territorial alternatives were contemplated at early stages of Zionism's development as a movement, not the least notably in two seminal expositions of the Zionist idea: Leo Pinsker's *Auto-Emancipation* (1882) and Theodor Herzl's *Der Judenstaat* (1896). Moreover, the prospect of being granted a strip of territory in Britain's East Africa Protectorate (the somewhat misnamed "Uganda Scheme") came to the fore, with convulsive consequences, at the sixth Zionist congress in 1903.[5]

The motivations of those Zionists who advocated positive consideration of this proposal—the immediate question at the congress was whether to constitute a committee to inquire into the proposal—were essentially pragmatic.[6] There was, however, a small number of congress delegates, notably the English writer Israel Zangwill (1864–1926) and the Hebrew writer Hillel Zeitlin (1871–1942), who held the conviction that Palestine, apart from being unattainable, was distinctly less advantageous than other conceivable territorial alternatives as a solution for the Jewish problem. These were the ones who seceded from the Zionist Organization after the seventh congress (1905) finally resolved to identify Zionism exclusively with Eretz Israel. Led by Israel Zangwill and augmented by some Socialist-Zionist circles who rejected the obsession with Zion as so much bourgeois romanticism, they formed the Jewish Territorial Organization (ITO). Its efforts were unsuccessful. After the Balfour Declaration of 1917 and Britain's assumption of the mandate over Palestine, it petered out, finally dissolving in 1925. Sporadic endeavors to similar ends, to be sure, were made by small successor organizations till 1948, all to no avail.[7]

As for Herzl himself, given his ambiguous record in regard to Eretz Israel, one cannot discount the possibility that, frustrated by the failures of his intense diplomatic efforts with the Ottoman regime, he was thrust back to the initial view evident in *Der Judenstaat*, namely, that in order to solve the Jewish problem the Jewish people needed a suitable territory, not necessarily Eretz Israel. Had the scheme for Jewish colonization in East Africa come to fruition, its political and practical implications might well have shifted the entire focus of Zionism away from Eretz Israel—a prospect scathingly deprecated by those Zionists who utterly refused to entertain the East Africa scheme and declared themselves Zionei Zion (Zionists of Zion).

Be that as it may, it is clear that Herzl's *ideological* formulations in respect of the East Africa proposal were never predicated on suspension of the claim that Eretz Israel was the inalienable homeland of the Jewish nation and the ultimate goal of Zionism. All his public statements in advocacy of a positive response to the East Africa offer were couched in assurances that this could never be a substitute for Eretz Israel. "If I forget thee O Jerusalem, may my right hand forget its cunning," he effused, in order to win back the trust of the mourning "Nay-sayers"—mostly the delegates from Russia—who staged a dramatic walkout from the congress hall. In urging the immediate need to ameliorate the desperate condition of Russian Jewry by finding an outlet for migration and directing it into an autonomous national framework, he emphasized that "the Jewish people can have no ultimate goal other than Palestine" and that "our views on the land of our fathers are and must remain unchangeable." A persuasive consideration that raised the credibility of Herzl's pleading was the manipulative notion that by acquiring official British sponsorship the cause of Zionism would at last attain an international status that would transcend the East Africa proposal, irrespective of its ultimate realization or lapse. "Whatever the fate of this proposal may be," he urged, "the Congress will recognize the extraordinary progress that our movement has made through the negotiations with the British government." Moreover, in the next breath, Herzl reported that on his recent journey to Russia he had received assurances that no obstacle would be put in the way of emigration directed by the Zionists and that the Russian government was willing to use its influence with the sultan of Turkey "in support of our efforts to obtain Palestine." "Now we can continue to strive for

Eretz Israel with renewed courage and with brighter prospects than ever before," he declared.[8]

Max Nordau, having set aside his initially negative reaction to the East Africa idea, rallied to Herzl's support and in like vein characterized it not as a desertion of Zion but as a *Nachtasyl* (night shelter or temporary refuge) that would consolidate national consciousness and ultimately serve as a stepping-stone to Zion. It would be a training ground into which "Jews would be brought as vagabonds, there to be groomed for citizenship—not for East Africa itself . . . but for Zion."[9] Whatever may have been the undeclared intentions or expectations involved in the East Africa interlude between 1903 and 1905, it therefore can be said that in the *ideological* sense, Zionism remained identified with and never waived its claim upon Eretz Israel.

This was the ideological context in which the national-religious Zionists of Mizrahi confronted for the first time a critical issue involving a waiver or suspension in some sense of the claim to Jewish national self-determination in Eretz Israel. Paradoxically, the historical record shows that so far from categorically refusing to countenance Herzl's proposal that the East Africa offer be favorably considered, the majority of Mizrahi's delegates to the Zionist Congress voted with the "ayes." The immediate motivation was undoubtedly the sense that one could not reject out of hand what promised to be a major outlet for mass Jewish migration from czarist Russia, where recently an unprecedentedly terrible pogrom had devastated the Jewish community in the town of Kishinev. Another consideration that counted was allegiance to the leadership of the by now legendary Theodor Herzl, whose attempts to keep the secular cultural Zionists at bay indebted them to him.[10] However, the apparent paradox of Mizrahi's position on this critical issue can be adequately explained only within the context of its inner ideological ambiguities over the relationship between Zionism and messianic redemption. These ambiguities have been explored in chapter 4 of the present work.

It was the repression of the messianic potential in Zionism that made it possible for the majority of Mizrahi's delegates to the sixth Zionist congress in 1903 to support Theodor Herzl's painfully controversial East Africa proposal.[11] Only by denying that the Zionist Organization was a manifestation of messianic redemption were those rabbis able to adopt this position, whereas, paradoxically, many of the secularized Zionists declared themselves to be faithful Zionei Zion and, on romantic as well as practical grounds, refused to countenance any proposed solution outside Eretz Israel.

To be sure, the East Africa proposal caused much heart searching within the ranks of Mizrahi. One dissenter was Rabbi Meir Berlin (later Bar-Ilan) who was to become president of the World Mizrahi Organization in 1916. Mizrahi's contemporary leader, Rabbi Reines, was ambiguous. He abstained in the crucial vote at the 1903 congress. Yet in his major speech to the congress he provided moral support for Herzl's proposal that the East Africa offer be favorably considered. Not only did most of the Mizrahi delegates cast their votes for it, but some rabbis in Russia were soon even justifying "Uganda" homiletically.[12] Moreover, even after the seventh congress (held in 1905) resolved to reject territorialist schemes, Mizrahi societies were not forbidden to support the deviant Jewish Territorialist Organization (ITO). Indeed, in correspondence with ITO's leader, Israel Zangwill, Reines continued to express sympathy for attempts, concurrent with those to settle Eretz Israel, to found autonomous Jewish settlements in other territories. In his view the latter would both relieve Jewish distress and, by fostering Jewish self-help, autonomy, and morale, serve the strategy of ultimate restoration to Zion.[13]

In sum, the Uganda proposal was neither depicted as an abandonment by Zionism of Eretz Israel nor perceived by contemporary orthodox Jews as in any way a waiver of the Jewish right to it. Hence, it did not, in fact, call into question the fundamental ideological proposition of religious Zionists that the Jewish people had a divinely endowed, exclusive right to Eretz Israel.

Of course, as we have seen in chapter 4, in contrast with the Mizrahi's normative tendency to repress the messianic cadences of the modern Jewish return to Zion, there was a lone contemporary voice that outspokenly vested that return with deep messianic-redemptive significance. It was that of Rabbi Abraham Isaac Ha-Cohen Kook, who served as Ashkenazi Chief Rabbi of Palestine from 1921 until his death in 1935. For a man of Rabbi Kook's deep religious faith the divine promise to the Children of Israel overrode everything else. As he once put it, to bring proofs and reasons for such things is like "holding up a candle to strengthen the light of the sun!"[14] The inherent logic of his consummate conflation of the Zionist enterprise as a whole with the beginning of the redemption runs counter to the notion that Zionism should in any sense compromise the Jewish nation's exclusive right to Eretz Israel. Consequently, as has become evident in present-day Israel, latter day devotees of Rabbi Kook's conception find it unconscionable to entertain any waiver whatsoever of actual or even potential Jewish gains in Eretz Israel.

Yet in his own lifetime, Abraham Isaac Ha-Cohen Kook never actually perceived the need to apply his messianic subsumption of Zionism to a critical decision affecting the Jewish right to Eretz Israel. Indeed, the only extant evidence of his attitude to the Uganda option indicates some understanding for those Mizrahi rabbis who supported Herzl's proposal. It is in the form of an open letter issued not long after he settled in Palestine as rabbi of Jaffa and the environing colonies. In this letter he took issue with Eliezer Ben-Yehuda, who, in the course of justifying the Uganda scheme, had contended that "all of us [Zionists] have turned our backs on the past and this is greatly to our credit." To this Rabbi Kook responded indignantly: "Without entering at all into the dispute between the 'Zionists of Zion' and the 'Ugandists,' there certainly are truly upright people in both parties who love their own nation and do not turn their backs on their past, just as there are such people also amongst those who oppose the Zionist Organization altogether."[15] It would thus appear that, notwithstanding the difference between their conceptions of the relationship between redemption and Zionism, Rabbi Kook did not differ substantially from the rabbis of Mizrahi in his perception of the Uganda project. In neither case was it perceived as a waiver of the Jewish right to Eretz Israel as irrevocably endowed by the divine promise.

Rabbi Kook died in 1935, some two years before the British Royal Commission of Inquiry, chaired by Lord Peel, raised the prospect of partition of Palestine. By then the Zionist project was well advanced, and the Jewish population of Palestine was 404,000, constituting some 29.5 percent of the total.[16] Because agreeing to partition meant actually giving up part of Eretz Israel, it put the fundamental ideological belief in the divinely endowed right to The Land to the test of practical policy as never before.

The memorandum submitted by Mizrahi to the Peel Commission was titled "Our Religious Right to Eretz Israel," and it averred that the source of the Jewish right is the divine promise. It argued somewhat speciously that this was not just "a mystic, subjective Jewish view but an objective historical reality which is openly expressed in the history of both the Jews and Eretz Israel."[17] If compared with the religious Zionist response to the East Africa offer of 1903, the response elicited by the partition proposal of 1937 certainly reveals a major shift away from Mizrahi's initial portrayal of the Zionist movement as a purely material remedy for Jewish distress. No religious Zionist expressed this more unequivocally than did Rabbi Meir Berlin (at the time honorary president of the World Mizrahi Organization) in his address to the twentieth Zionist congress in 1937. He explicitly placed the divine-right claim above any considerations of morality or existential need: "In our eyes Zionism is not just a response for hungry Jews, nor are we claiming our right for reasons of moral rectitude. Today's world does not function according to this principle. The basis of Zionism is that The Land is ours, and does not belong to the Arabs."[18] With similar recourse to fundamental belief, even *Netiva*, the weekly organ of Ha-poel Ha-mizrahi editorialized: "From a purely religious point of view there is no place for two opinions. Any conscious surrender constitutes a deliberate profanation of the sanctity of the country and of the sublime covenant between the Master of the Universe and the Patriarch Abraham, namely: 'To your seed I have given this land, from the River Egypt unto the great river, the River Euphrates.'"[19]

Nevertheless, the record of the great internal Zionist debate over the partition proposal of 1937 indicates that although the fundamental belief that the Jews had an absolute right to all of Eretz Israel by virtue of the divine promise was prevalent among religious Zionists, there was ambiguity on the operative question of whether acceptance of a partition proposal would indeed constitute a waiver of that right.[20] Rabbi Avigdor Amiel, at the time chief rabbi of Tel Aviv and an important Mizrahi leader, was one of those who had no doubt that it would. He averred that the Jewish belief concerning the sanctity of Eretz Israel applied not only to the messianic end of days but also to the present. Monetary sales of individual parcels of land were halakhically permissible but never any concession that implied a giving up of Judaism's sacred possession of the entire Promised Land. "Its sanctity cannot be the subject of bargaining and sale, and that is why the *halakha* states: 'Gentiles have no right of possession in Eretz Israel such as might impair its sanctity' [the reference is particularly to Maimonides's halakhic ruling in *Ha-yad ha-hazaka*, "*Hilkhot Akum*," 10,3]. And all the related laws are not 'laws for the messianic time' but practical laws applicable in every generation." The logic of Rabbi Amiel's argument was that since a partition agreement would involve surrender in perpetuity of parts of Eretz Israel, including some areas that had already come into Jewish possession, this would mean either a breach of the *halakha* or perpetrating a lie, or both. "Could we sign any agreement to the effect that we give up any part of Eretz Israel and assent to its being Ishmael's land, when even now this controverts the truth and the *halakha*?" he asked rhetorically.[21]

Yet there was also a substantial minority of national-religious Zionists who favored the partition proposal. They were mostly members of the Ha-poel Ha-mizrahi section, those from Germany setting the tone. Their line of reasoning was that partition was a political question, not a question of *halakha*. Opting for partition as the best alternative in the prevailing political circum- stances by no means meant that Jews relinquished their ultimate right to the whole of Eretz Israel as immutably promised by God. Thus, Dr. Erich Pinchas Rosenblueth argued that the partition proposal, while involving for the time political surrender of Jewish sovereignty over specific parts of the country, did not call into question the Jews' right to their country any more than, in the first place, the Balfour Declaration had served as the basis for that right. In political terms "the only solution was partition, a practical separation that facilitates for the time being partial fulfillment of the two conflicting aspirations [of Jews and Arabs]."[22]

Rabbi Yitzhak Unna, another prominent Ha-poel Ha-mizrahi figure, argued similarly against the mainstream Mizrahi opposition to partition. Although he could understand the economic, political, and strategic considerations weighing against partition, he failed to see the validity of the religious objections raised. That which was determined in the Torah was eternal and therefore could never be waived by any act. All that was involved in accepting partition was a political opportunity for untrammeled Jewish control over at least a part of Eretz Israel, thereby enabling the absorption of hundreds of thousands of their persecuted brethren from the Diaspora. "Who was so foolish as to believe that the establishment of a Jewish State would mean the messianic days had come?" he asked. After all, as the sages of Judaism had already noted, it was only in stages that the Children of Israel had conquered the Promised Land, and it was a fact that they had never ruled over the whole of the country. The key issue was not what percentage of The Land would be incorporated in the Jewish state but rather what would be its Jewish nature and whether it would be shaped in the spirit of the *halakha*.[23]

It is noteworthy that throughout this controversy no definitive *psak halakha* (halakhic ruling) was issued by the chief rabbinate of Palestine, an institution comprising two chiefs—one Ashkenazi (European) and one Sephardi (Moslem lands)—that was broadly representative of the *yishuv* in the spirit of Mizrahi's Zionism. This was not for lack of urging from religious Zionists that it do so but rather a true reflection of the highly ambiguous nature of the halakhic issues involved. In June 1937, Ashkenazi Chief Rabbi Hertzog was party to a public declaration rejecting partition on the grounds that the Jewish people had a divinely endowed right to all of Eretz Israel. Yet in May 1938, when the council of the chief rabbinate discussed its imminent evidence to the British government's committee appointed to examine the practical feasibility of partition (the Woodhead Commission), Rabbi Hertzog proposed that if asked categorically whether partition was permissible the rabbinate should answer that it was.[24]

The fact is that the question of partition did not produce an unequivocal halakhic response. The spectrum of positions adopted by the rabbis fell much more into the category of halakhic opinion (*da'at torah*) based largely on homiletical sources than of authoritative halakhic judgment (*din torah*) anchored firmly in prohibitions explicitly stated in the Torah. Differing conclusions were drawn from the same basic texts, such as the passage in Deuteronomy (7:2), which tells that when the Children of Israel took possession of Eretz Israel and dispossessed its inhabitants they were commanded not to make a covenant with them. The text contains the phrase *lo tehonem*, a prohibition that the talmudic sages and later rabbinical authorities interpreted to mean both "show no mercy to them" and "do not allow them to hold land."[25]

In the final analysis, the political predispositions of the major disputants determined their halakhic opinion. Rabbi Avigdor Amiel, whose firm rejection of partition on halakhic grounds was mentioned above, was an example; his earlier record on issues such as the response to Arab terror and the question of illegal immigration veered closely to the activism of Revisionist Zionists.[26] Another illustration of the aprioristic nature of the rabbis' halakhic preferences was the fact that anti-Zionist Agudat Israel rabbis were able to oppose partition not so much because of biblical prohibitions like *lo tehonem* but simply because partition would create a secular-dominated Jewish state. Indeed Agudat Israel's luminary, Rabbi Grodzinsky of Vilna, did not even regard *lo tehonem* as applicable in the given circumstances of British rather than Jewish rule over Palestine.

At all events, it is evident that even for religious Zionists the divine promise to The Land was certainly not the only consideration that entered the partition debate. Also the mundane considerations raised by secular Zionists (which we shall discuss later) exercised their minds, especially the need to provide a haven for Jews suffering persecution and distress and the economic and political viability of a partitioned territory. Indeed, it was by the hand of a Ha-poel Ha-mizrahi member named Reuben Gafni (Weinshenker) that the most thoroughgoing exposition of the Jewish "historical-legal" right to Eretz Israel was published only a few years before the partition issue came to the fore.[27] A lawyer by profession, Gafni presented the Jewish case with minimal reference to the divine promise. He emphasized the objective historical connection between the Jewish people and Eretz Israel, presented the case for Jewish self-determination from the point of view of international law, and explicated the objective "moral right" of the Jews to Eretz Israel. Since the arguments he presented in this work were of the same kind as those formulated by secular ideologists, we shall return to them later in this chapter.

For reasons of political interest, predicated on obdurate Arab opposition to partition, that need not detain us here, the 1937 partition proposal was soon shelved by the British government, and it was only after the Second World War and the Holocaust that partition again became the dominant proposal for a solution of the Palestine problem. At that point, Mizrahi acquiesced in it, however reluctantly, and marshaled arguments for the Jewish right to a state in Palestine that were much the same as those submitted by the secular Zionist groups. Indeed, a memorandum prepared by Mizrahi's Dr. Aaron Barth was prefaced by the statement: "The author is a religious Jew. But in order to convince every unbiased reader whatever his religious attitude may be, he made no mention in this survey of the promise contained in the Bible."[28] Chief Rabbi Isaac Hertzog opened his evidence to the Anglo-American Committee of Inquiry with the statement: "Gentlemen, the recognition of our right to establish our National Home in this tiny country is for us a matter of life and death. . . . To our Arab cousins with whom we have much in common and for whom we have both esteem and natural sympathy, Palestine, after all, represents but a fragment of a vast empire; for us it is the beginning and the end of all."[29]

In the formulations of Jewish claims presented by the Mizrahi to the Anglo-American Commission of Inquiry the divine promise remained the ultimate source of the Jewish right to The Land. "It is our strong conviction," it stated, "that no person, individual or representing any power, has the right to alter the status of Palestine to other than that which was established by Divine Right." At the same time, considerable attention was paid also to mundane arguments. Thus, the memorandum began by explaining that in regard to the problem of Jewish distress its views were "identical with those put forward by the Jewish Agency and its various bodies." Therefore, it wished to address itself more specifically to the spiritual aspects of the Jewish problem. In so doing, it argued that in addition to "unbearable suffering" the Jews faced the danger of spiritual-cultural extinction as a result of assimilation and inability to maintain Jewish precepts in the Diaspora. For this there was "but one cure, the very cure for the physical needs of the hopeless Jews remaining in Europe," namely, "to return the Jewish nation to its homeland to live a politically independent life." Furthermore, the memorandum stated, even "had the Jews been able to live normally and without this threat to their existence, they are still justified in this natural aspiration to return to their country and homeland just as every other nation demands and fights for the right to live on its own land."[30]

Not until after the creation of the State of Israel did Chief Rabbi Kook's infusion of messianic significance into Zionism issue in the fervent religious nationalism of Gush Emunim (the Bloc of the Faithful). The adherents of this movement dogmatically declared the divine promise to "the whole of Eretz Israel" to be the overriding, if not the sole, basis of the Jewish national claim, and its rabbinical authorities considered as contrary to *halakha* the relinquishing of any part of The Land that had fallen into Israel's possession.[31] The foremost of these authorities was Rabbi Zvi Yehuda Kook, son of Abraham Isaac Ha-Cohen Kook. He taught that the Torah prohibition *lo tehonem* now applied absolutely, proscribing any "irrevocable renunciation of territory in favor of a foreign nation."[32]

Having traced over the span of time the fluctuations of emphasis accorded to the divine promise as the alpha and omega of Jewish right, note must be taken of the problem that inhered in positing a putative divine promise as the conclusive basis for right to political sovereignty over a territory. By the accepted standards of objective judgment it was dubious whether an essentially subjective experience—which is what revelation of the divine promise is, no matter how resonant in some of the most influential cultures of the world—might qualify for recognition as a valid right. Doubtless, the dynamic progress of Zionism is inexplicable without reference to the phenomenal mythic force of this subjective experience. But this does not eliminate the moral defect inhering in any attempt to convert a subjective claim into an objective right. One might say that if such conversion were the universal rule it would create an infinite series of insoluble clashes between claims engendered by subjective beliefs. After all, the Jewish claim based on subjective experience of God's revelation, has come to be challenged with similar subjective "validity" by that of Christian and Moslem Arabs who believe that God has granted them a supersession of the Jews' former rights. That this difficulty was generally recognized by the spokesmen of religious Zionism is evident from the fact, already noted in our survey, that they invariably supplemented the subjective claim of divine promise with considerations of an objective nature. Notwithstanding the utterly compelling belief in the divine promise common to national-religious Zionists themselves, they did not treat it as an exhaustively sufficient basis for the Zionist case as presented to the outside world.

There was, however, a sense in which the religious claim to Eretz Israel was proffered on an objective rather than a subjective basis. Positing the "ground rule," as it were, that every religious system ought to be entitled to self-fulfillment according to its own lights, it was argued that of the three contending religions—Judaism, Christianity, and Islam—the one for whom Palestine (Eretz Israel for the Jews or Filastin for the Arabs) was the most vital prerequisite for self-fulfillment was Judaism. To the Royal Commission of Inquiry of 1936 the chief rabbinate of Palestine and the Mizrahi Organization submitted,[33] inter alia, that although both Christianity and Islam ascribe special importance to Palestine, they are not dependent on the country; their legitimate concern is only with the holy places. For Judaism alone the whole land is holy. It was no wonder that no nation aside from the Jews made its physical or spiritual creations in Palestine and the country lay desolate under foreign rule. Furthermore, even Christians and Moslems recognized the sanctity that Eretz Israel held for the Jews and referred to it as the Jews' "Promised Land."

In like vein, Mizrahi's memorandum to the Anglo-American Committee of 1946 contrasted the holiness of "Palestine as a whole and its every stone and every hillock" to what it claimed was the meager relationship of Islam to Palestine. It stated:

As to the Arab claim of a religious link with Palestine this is of a general Moslem character and has no special significance to the Arabs as a nation. . . . Palestine as such is not sacred to Islam, no specific Islamic precept is linked with Palestine. The Moslems have only certain Holy Places. . . . Jerusalem (or to be more exact two Jerusalem Mosques) only ranks third after Mecca and Medina. Its relegation in religious importance is evidenced by the fact that the prophet Mohammed, after only a short time, decreed that worshippers should no longer face Jerusalem when in prayer. He ordered instead that they turn to Mecca because the former practice was considered as a purely Jewish one.[34]

Chief Rabbi Isaac Hertzog, in his evidence before the committee in March 1946, made much the same submission:[35] "Other religions have holy places in Palestine. In the Jewish religious concept, every inch of Palestinian soil is sacred and this sanctity finds practical concrete expression in specific religious laws which apply with reference to the soil and produce of this country and of this country only." Formulated in this way, the Jewish religious claim to Eretz Israel was one that could be judged objectively after due consideration had been accorded to all the evidence presented by the advocates for each religion. James Parkes, the English scholar (an Anglican), compared in this way the rival claims of Islam, Christianity, and Judaism and concluded that Judaism's involvement with Palestine "indicates an intensity of relationship going beyond that of either of the other two religions."[36]

A particularly comprehensive exposition of this objective version of the religious claim was penned some years after the creation of Israel as a Jewish state by Solomon Zeitlin, at the time professor of rabbinic law and lore at Dropsie College in Philadelphia. On the strength of historical documentation, Zeitlin argued that there was a "vital difference in the historical ties, in the spiritual quality and the degree of the indispensability of Palestine for the wholeness of the religion in Judaism in contrast to the two daughter religions." Zeitlin pointed to evidence that for the early Christians Palestine as a whole was not holy. They spoke only of "Loca Sancta" (holy places), those associated with the life and death of Jesus. Christianity made Rome its center and emphasized the heavenly rather than the terrestrial Jerusalem. Pope Urban II was the first to call Palestine "Terra Sancta" (the Holy Land), when he appealed in 1095 for a crusade to wrest the land from Moslem rule. As for Islam, Mecca is its center, not Jerusalem, and the Koran mentions Filastin only peripherally in one Sura (the seventeenth), where there is an allusion to Mohammed's transportation from the sacred temple of Mecca to the temple of Jerusalem and his ascent to heaven from there. By contrast, terrestrial Eretz Israel was always inherently central to the precepts, rituals, and messianic self-fulfillment of Judaism. Zeitlin summed up his comparison as follows:[37] "In a word, to the Christians, only the places connected with Jesus' birth, his sojournings and the Holy Sepulchre are sacred. For the Moslems, only those places which tradition connects with Mohammed and Moses and other figures of their religion are sacred. For the Jews, Eretz Israel as a whole is a holy land."

The contentions thus articulated formed the objective dimension of the claims of Zionism insofar as they were couched in religious terms. Of course, their relevance to the dispute between Jew and Arab over Palestine was dependent on the problematic assumption that the authentic self-understandings of religious groups were objectively ascertainable. Moreover, they depended also on the questionable proposition that, in the first instance, the comparison between these self-understandings was a valid basis for determining rights to political self-determination in a disputed territory.

Judaism's Mission

Another variety of the Jewish religious claim to the Land of Israel found its most distinguished exponent in the philosopher Martin Buber (1878–1965). Although Buber was not himself an observant orthodox Jew, his exposition of the Jewish claim rested quite as much as did that of national-religious Zionists on transcendental revelation of a covenant that bound the Children of Israel and their descendants to fulfill a mission. According to Buber, that mission was the formation of a community that, by virtue of the particular values and precepts emanating from the covenantal terms originally set forth in the Bible, aspired to the optimal human relationship between man and man. Translated into the language of his own philosophical discourse, that was the dialogic I-Thou relationship. The spiritual experience underlying this was the essence of what Buber meant by Jewish "religiosity," which he distinguished from the regimented norms of "religion."

As we noted in chapter 6, Buber's genre of Zionism offered postassimilationist central European Jews a rationale for Jewish self-affirmation through involvement in the formation of a community in Eretz Israel that would endeavor to consummate the divinely inspired covenant. Whereas in the orthodox religious view Jewish right to Eretz Israel was absolute because it derived directly from God's promise, Buber's formulation consisted in an appeal to all of mankind to recognize the Jews' *need* for Eretz Israel as the indispensable prerequisite for fulfillment of the unique Jewish contribution to mankind. As Buber tried to explain to Mahatma Gandhi, who, in a statement made in 1938, had criticized the Zionists for seeking divine sanction in the Bible:

Decisive for us is not the promise of the land, but the command, the fulfillment of which is bound up with the land, with the existence of a free Jewish community in this country [Palestine]. For the Bible tells us and our inmost knowledge testifies to it, that once, more than 3,000 years ago, our entry into this land was in the consciousness of a mission from above, to set up a just way of life through the generations of our people, such a way of life as can be realized not by individuals in the sphere of their private existence but only by a nation in the establishment of its society.[38]

According to Buber, that mission of the Jews could only begin to be fulfilled under conditions of self-determination in their own ancestral land. The Bible was the record of incomplete attempts to fulfill their mission, and then came the dispersion:

We went into exile with our task unperformed. But the command remained with us and it has become more urgent than ever. We need our own soil to fulfil it; we need the freedom to order our own life. No attempt can be made on foreign soil and under foreign statute. It may not be that the soil and the freedom for fulfillment be denied us. We are not covetous, Mahatma: our one desire is that at last we may obey.

But Gandhi had expressed the opinion that "Palestine belongs to the Arabs" and that it was therefore "wrong and inhuman to impose the Jews on the Arabs." In arguing thus, he was implicitly crediting the Arabs with a historical right to possession of Palestine. As we shall see in a later section of our present discussion, much of the Zionist Organization's official formulations invoked countervailing claims of Jewish historical right. Buber, however, never recognized the validity of historical right in the first place. Already in 1929 he had argued that although Jewish "right rests on the ancient link between us and The

Land, . . . this right differs from what is customarily called our 'historic right.'" He had gone on to explain that:

A historic right in this overall sense does not exist at all: every chapter in world history which is used as an authority for justifying a given right was preceded by another chapter, which in turn can support a different right. Consequently, it is impossible to claim a right in terms of time. Would not the remnants of those ancient peoples which were dispossessed by the Israelites have the right to question our "historic right?"[39]

To Buber's way of thinking, the ancient link between the Jews and the Land of Israel was significant not as the basis for any so-called historical right of repossession but rather because it gave rise to the covenantal Jewish mission that served "a perpetual good for all of humankind; and anyone who recognizes this will also acknowledge our right."

In this vein Buber responded in 1938 to Gandhi's statement: "But by what means did the Arabs attain the right of ownership in Palestine?" he asked rhetorically.[40] Since the answer was, manifestly, by conquest with a view to settlement, Buber contended that Gandhi's statement was tantamount to holding that conquest constitutes an exclusive right of possession. In place of the dubious morality of such a proposition, Buber invoked a religious proposition: "It seems to me that God does not give any one portion of the earth away so that the owner thereof may say as God does in the Holy Word script: 'Mine is the land.' Even to the conqueror who has settled on it, the conquered land is, in my opinion, only lent—and God waits to see what He will make of it."

Buber appealed to a higher morality, one that allowed for some agreement "by the representatives of humanity" on a just reordering of relations between nations and countries, allowing for such measures as colonization of unpopulated territories and intensified cultivation of lands. In terms of this higher morality, Buber submitted—and therein lay the real thrust of the argument— that the Jews' claim to Eretz Israel, as well as deriving from genuine existential need, served also for the ultimate good of mankind. "You are concerned, Mahatma, with 'the right of possession' on the one side," he censured Gandhi, "you do not consider the right to a piece of free land on the other side—for those who are hungering for it." In Buber's view, it was "the dogma of 'possession,' of the inalienable right of ownership, of the sacred status quo" that had led Gandhi unjustly to tell the Jews, "Hands off! This land does not belong to you!" He should, instead, have helped to establish a genuine peace, giving the Jews what they needed without taking from the Arabs what they needed. Buber insisted that "such an adjustment of the required living room for all" was possible if it were accompanied by intensified cultivation of all of Palestine's soil.

Upon this religious stem Buber grafted an argument common to most schools of Zionism, namely, what he called "the right deriving from creation and fertilization."[41] In his response to Gandhi he argued further that the Arabs had forfeited their claim to sole possession of the land because they had grossly neglected it. "Ask the soil what the Arabs have done for her in 1300 years and what we have done for her in 50. Would her answer not be weighty testimony in a just discussion as to whom this land belongs?" Moreover, linking this point with his formulation of the Jews' primary claim—their need for the land in order to fulfill their covenantal mission—Buber added that the Jews wished to fructify Palestine, not for themselves alone but also for the benefit of their Arab neighbors:

The Jewish peasants have begun to teach their brothers, the Arab peasants, to cultivate the land more intensively; we desire to teach them further; together with them we want to cultivate the land—to "serve" it as the Hebrew has it. The more fertile the soil becomes, the more space there will be for us and for them. We have no desire to dispossess them: we want to live with them. We do not want to rule, we want to serve with them.

An analytical distinction may be made between the objective and the subjective bases of Buber's exposition. On the one hand, the objective basis of the claim was the burning existential need of the Jews and of Judaism for Eretz Israel as a "living heart and center." However, it should be noted that unlike the political Zionists, whose views will be considered below, Buber emphasized the *spiritual* need of the Jews more than their physical distress exacerbated by antisemitism. In this he followed Ahad Ha'am; he subordinated the Jewish nation's need for a physical refuge as a political unit to its need for a home or sanctuary as a community of culture. On the other hand, the purely subjective basis of Buber's exposition consisted in the assertion that the Jews were divinely endowed with a mission of the greatest importance for the good of mankind as a whole; a mission that could be fulfilled only if a national-cultural home was restored to them in Palestine. The defect of this claim, as of the orthodox religious claims considered earlier, lay in its subjectivity.

Since Christianity and Islam claimed revelatory experiences that, by their lights, subsumed or superseded those of Judaism, Buber's exposition of the Jewish mission as one totally dependent upon a center in Eretz Israel, entirely failed to oblige Moslems and carried weight only with certain Christian denominations whose own particularities of belief required the restoration of Zion to the Jews as prerequisite for the second coming of Jesus to redeem all of mankind. As for secular nonbelievers or adherents of the world's many other religions, Buber's claims could hardly be expected to command their support. Indeed, as Buber knew only too well, among the Jews themselves there existed, in Reform Judaism, a rival interpretation that perceived dispersion, and not national return to Zion, as the true prerequisite for fulfillment of Judaism's mission.[42]

In the light of the subjectivity of Buber's exposition and of its Eurocentric,

Judeo-Christian bias, Mahatma Gandhi was hardly likely to be dissuaded from his proclivity to support Arab claims in the conflict over the right to Palestine, for, as a Hindu, Gandhi was not bound by biblical evidence in the first place. Furthermore, as an Indian nationalist who strove for Hindu-Moslem brotherhood in a united India, Gandhi preferred to credit Moslem religious views, prevalent in the Khilafat movement in India of the early 1920s, according to which "as an article of Moslem faith," unequivocal Muslim control had to be maintained over the "Isle of Arabia," which included Palestine.[43]

If Buber's Zionist formulations carried objective moral weight, it was due less to their religious basis than to his cognizance of the rival Arab case, and his unswerving fidelity to the principle that moral ends did not justify immoral means. As he told a convention of Jewish youth in Antwerp in July 1932: "If the goal to be reached is like the goal which was set, then the nature of the way must be like the goal. A wrong way, i.e. a way in contradiction to the goal, must lead to a wrong goal."[44] At the same time Buber was a realist. His approach has aptly been characterized as "a believing realism."[45] He took account of the fact that in reality: "It is indeed true that there can be no life without injustice. The fact that there is no living creature which can live and thrive without destroying another existing organism has a symbolic significance as regards our human life. But the *human* aspect of life begins the moment we say to ourselves: we will do no more injustice to others than we are forced to do in order to exist."[46]

Consistent with his core conception of Zionism as an expression of "Hebrew humanism" and as the instrumentality for fulfillment of the Jewish mission as a whole, Buber considered the attainment of peace and understanding with the Arabs of Palestine as the touchstone of the whole enterprise. These conceptions and beliefs led him to support what might be termed "the compromise for the sake of peace camp" in Zionism. It took the form of the Brit Shalom (Covenant of Peace) association that functioned from 1925 to 1933 and was succeeded by a number of other organizations such as Kedma Mizraha (Toward the East), the Bond, and the Ihud (Union). Although not all of this camp's components followed Buber's conceptions (we shall return later in this chapter to further consideration of this form of Zionist ideology) they concurred in advocating, as an equitable solution to the Arab-Jewish conflict, national and political parity institutionalized in a binational state. To Gandhi, Buber mentioned that he belonged to a group of people (the group that called itself the Bond) that

considered it a fundamental point, that in this case two vital claims are opposed to each other, two claims of a different nature and a different origin, which cannot be pitted one against the other and between which no objective decision can be made as to which is just or unjust. We considered and still consider it our duty to understand and to honour the claim which is opposed to ours and to endeavour to reconcile both claims. We cannot renounce the Jewish claim: something even higher than the life of our people is bound up with the life of the Land, namely the work which is our divine mission. But we have been and still are convinced that it must be possible to find some form of agreement between this claim and the other. . . . Where there is faith and love, a solution may be found even to what appears to be a tragic contradiction.[47]

Another permutation of the claim to Palestine by virtue of a sense of mission, one that synthesized it with the values of secular labor Zionists, may be found in the teachings of Aharon David Gordon (1856–1922). Gordon's conception had much in common with that of Buber. To be sure, Gordon was the senior of the two, and his thought preceded the full articulation of Buber's ideas. Both considered return to Eretz Israel as a prerequisite for the fulfillment of the unique Jewish society prescribed in the bible. However, whereas Buber's exposition largely looked outward to the conscience of the gentile world, Gordon spoke exclusively to the inner Jewish conscience. If the essence of Buber's case lay in his appeal to the world to support the Jews' mission, A. D. Gordon's message was that only spiritual regeneration through a return to a life of labor in Palestine could actualize the Jewish right.

Both Gordon and Buber upheld an interpretation of the Jewish right to Eretz Israel that was inspired by a religious faith of sorts. In Gordon's thinking, religion meant the relationship of man to the infinite source of all being and of his own self, a relationship that was mediated by his natural and human environment.[48] But in contrast with the national-religious Zionists, Gordon, like Buber, invoked not the divine promise but the mission undertaken by the Jews. He wrote: "We have a deed to Eretz Israel, which has never ceased, and shall never cease, to be valid; this is the Bible; and not only the Bible, and not because our right to The Land was promised therein, but because it was in Eretz Israel that we created the Bible. . . . Works like these, the creation of the Bible alone, give us an eternal right to go on creating."[49]

The right to Eretz Israel derived from what the Jews had experienced and created in that land in ancient times, as recorded and demonstrated in the Bible. But that ancient right did not in itself suffice for its reassertion in modern times. Only a return to the working of the soil, and thereby a resumption of the creative process begun in the Bible, validated the modern Jewish right to Eretz Israel. Recognizing that the Arabs also exercised a historic claim to the same country, as well as a right by virtue of their working it, Gordon argued that, in the final analysis, Eretz Israel would belong to the people that prevailed in the contest over the quality of creative self-labor there. "Whoever works harder, creates more, gives more of his spirit, will acquire the greater moral right and deeper vital interest in The Land," he wrote. "Our strength lies in creative action; upon it we base our right to The Land now as ever; this is the justice of our claim." Furthermore, according to Gordon, that rivalry between Jew and Arab was to be "peaceful competition," constructive and beneficial to both peoples. This demanded of the Jewish settlers that they "take the utmost care" in their relations with the Arabs: "In buying land for example, there must be no infringement on the human rights of the Arabs, nor any dispossession of those who actually work on the land. Rather than wrong them in any way we must be ready to pay two, three, or indeed, many times the value of the land in order to compensate fully the real owners, those who live on, and work, the land."[50]

In the final analysis, so insisted Gordon, "there is no right, and no kind of ownership holds good, other than the right and the power of ownership through work." He therefore called unceasingly for the "genuine, political 'categorical imperative': to work." "In as much as we work," he exhorted, "the land will be ours, and if not—all the 'national homes' and 'blood and fire' will be of no avail."[51]

Historical Right, Existential Need, and Moral Precedence

One may usefully draw a distinction between the "mythic" and the "ideological" components of the Jewish claim to Eretz Israel. The former refers to the primordial, subjectively induced ideas that motivate the actions of groups— indeed, often masses—of people quite irrespective of their demonstrable objective validity. The latter refers to the rationalized formulations of putatively objective ideas that inspire and direct the actions of groups of people. In this sense, the religious claim fell into the mythic category, insofar as it rested entirely upon belief in the divine promise. Its ideological counterpart was at least partially reflected in what has here been described as the objective dimension of the religious claim, as well as in the appeal for the opportunity to fulfill the unique mission of Judaism. It found weightier expression, however, in what orthodox believers and secular Jews alike proffered as the "historical right" of the Jews.

One of the earliest invocations of historical right was made by Moshe Leib Lilienblum in 1882 when he wrote: "We have an historical right [to Eretz Israel] which has neither lapsed nor been forfeited with the loss of our sovereignty, just as the right of the Balkan nations to their lands has not lapsed with the loss of their sovereignty."[52] When posed in this way, historical "right" or "title" was inferred from the demonstrably objective historical connection of the Jews to Eretz Israel dating back to biblical times. This inference was implicit in the ideological formulations of almost all Zionist thinkers.[53] However, in the periods of Hibbat Zion and of Theodor Herzl's political Zionist regime, prior to any serious Arab ideological challenge to the Zionist project, historical right did not feature prominently in Zionist formulations. Theodor Herzl's statements were a case in point.

Herzl certainly regarded it as a self-evident truth that the Jews had a historical right. It is implicit in statements such as he made in his address to the second

Zionist congress (1898): "If there is such a thing as a legitimate claim to a portion of the earth's surface, all peoples who believe in the Bible must recognize the right of the Jews."[54] But the circumstances in which Herzl functioned, as the leader of a movement representing merely a segment of dispersed Jewries and lacking any real power to assert itself politically, nullified the value of appeals to historical rights as a basis for his diplomacy. Rather, his formulations reflected his fin-de-siècle, European-centered world outlook, one for which the right of the European powers to reorder and colonize the rest of the world was axiomatic. Within the boundaries of that ideological ambience, Herzl was both a liberal and a legalist. As a liberal he advocated paternalistic, benevolent colonialism, and as a legalist he considered it of the utmost importance that Zionists obtain recognized legal authority for the implementation of their plans. Hence, the aim of Zionism as formulated at the first Zionist congress held in 1897 (the Basel Program): "Zionism strives to create for the Jewish people a home in Palestine secured by public law." Hence, too, Herzl's indefatigable (yet abortive) endeavors to gain a legal charter from the Ottoman authorities. This combination of benevolent colonialism and legalism predisposed Herzl to ignore the local Arab population of Palestine and concentrate solely upon winning the approval of the Ottoman authorities in Constantinople, whether directly or through the mediation of the European powers.[55]

By the standards of Herzl's paternalist, Eurocentric liberalism, it was neither prudent nor necessary to deploy the notion of historical right. It sufficed to stress two rational, progressive benefits to morally justify the restoration of Zion to the Jews: first, its provision of a solution for the Jewish problem to the mutual benefit of the long-wronged Jews and of the various European states; second, the supposedly indubitable benefits it could bring to the Arabs. The former benefits were fully outlined in his *Der Judenstaat*; the latter occupied an important place in Herzl's utopian novel *Altneuland*. One of the novel's dramatis personae, the Arab Reshid Bey, blissfully recites to the European visitor Kingscourt the "blessings of Jewish immigration" for the country's Arab citizens: "employment, better food, welfare . . . these people are far better off than before; they are healthy, they have better food, their children go to school. Nothing has been done to interfere with their customs or their faith—they have only gained in welfare."[56]

It was only after the British government issued the Balfour Declaration in November 1917 and, consequently, Arab resistance to Zionism grew more intense that Zionist formulations increasingly tended to invoke the concept of Jewish historical right or title. The concept was deployed to counter the Arab claim to self-determination as the indigenous majority in Palestine. In the draft resolutions presented by the Zionists to the Paris Peace Conference in February 1919, there was no reference to the divine promise. They opened with the statement: "The High Contracting Parties recognize the historic title of the

Jewish people to Palestine and the right of the Jews to reconstitute in Palestine
their National Home" and went on to elaborate: "The land is the historic home
of the Jews; there they achieved their greatest development; from that center,
through their agency, there emanated spiritual and moral influences of supreme
value to mankind. By violence they were driven from Palestine, and through the
ages they have never ceased to cherish the longing and the hope of a return."[57]

It is instructive to note, however, that this assertion of historical right or title
by no means exhausted the claim as presented by the Zionist Organization.
Indeed, the document stated that the claims of the Jews with regard to Palestine
rested upon five main considerations. The first was the above-quoted historical
claim; the second invoked the existential need of the Jews: "The conditions of
life of millions of Jews are deplorable," it stated, and there was a dire need for
"fresh outlets" of emigration to relieve the situation. "Palestine would offer one
such outlet," it argued. To the need to relieve material distress the document
added the spiritual need of the Jews. Although Palestine was not large enough
to contain more than a proportion of the Jews of the world and the greater part
of the fourteen millions or more scattered through all countries would remain in
the Diaspora, a Jewish National Home in Palestine would provide them with a
vitally needed center whose influence would "permeate the Jewries of the world,"
inspire them "with a new hope," and indeed, "help to make them even more
useful citizens in the lands in which they dwell." The fourth and fifth
considerations invoked in this statement were vaguely similar to those emphasized by Martin Buber, to which we referred earlier: that "such a Palestine would
be of value also to the world at large" and that the land of Palestine itself was in
need of redemption after centuries of neglect and desolation.

Perhaps the most systematic statement of an official nature ever made of the
Zionist case was a memorandum titled "The Historical Connection of the
Jewish People with Palestine," which the Jewish Agency for Palestine submitted
to the Palestine Royal Commission in 1936.[58] This statement traced the Jewish
connection with Eretz Israel from the biblical period through the first exile to
Babylon, the return from Babylon, the Maccabean era, the period of Rome and
Byzantine rule (70–637 C.E.), Arab invasion and rule (637–1096), the era of the
Crusaders (1096–1187), the rule of the Ayubides and Mamelukes (1187–1517),
and the Turkish era (1516–1917). It also described the periodic movements of
return of Jews to Zion, traced the various mystical messianic manifestations of
the connection with Eretz Israel, and finally, explained the modern Jewish
national revival that gave rise to the Lovers of Zion movement (Hibbat Zion)
and the Zionist Organization founded by Theodor Herzl.

The pivotal points of the Jewish historical case as outlined in this memorandum were, first, that in ancient times the Jews were by force deprived of their
sovereignty:

Even after the [Roman] conquest of Jerusalem they did not give up the struggle for their independence. . . . Fifty years later they rose again in a great national insurrection and for many months defied the Roman forces until at last they were crushed. It was as a result of that devastating defeat that the Jewish political power in Palestine was finally destroyed. Yet for centuries after that destruction the Jews continued to cling stubbornly to the country, and it was only the policy of extermination and expropriation pursued by the Romans and Byzantines which in the end drove the bulk of the Jewish people out of Palestine.

Second, throughout the centuries of their exile, the Jews continued to regard Palestine as their homeland: "The Jewish liturgy and religious rites, their sacred and secular liturgy, the provisions of rabbinical law and the folklore of the Jewish diaspora—all these bear testimony to the intense attachment of the dispersed communities to the national home." Third, despite all manner of restrictions, subjection, and persecution, the Jews continued to maintain some presence in Palestine, and Jews as individuals and groups never ceased to return. "Century after century has seen movements of reimmigration. To go back and live in the Holy Land was regarded as the fulfillment of a sacred duty. . . . The present wave of immigration and settlement is only the latest phase of a movement that has never ceased since the destruction of the Jewish State." Fourth, the Zionist phase of return did not involve the displacement of "indigenous statehood" because this had not existed ever since the Jews were dispossessed of it in ancient times. "When the Jewish Commonwealth was destroyed by the might of Imperial Rome, . . . the land of Palestine disappeared from the political map of the world. It became a backward province of successive empires. It never again attained indigenous statehood. It was only in the Balfour Declaration that both the Jewish People and the land of Palestine reappeared as political entities."[59] Fifth, the sui generis case of the Jewish historical connection nullified comparison with other historical instances of former dominion:

It is asserted that it might similarly be pleaded that the Italians had a claim to a national home in Great Britain because that country had once formed part of the Roman Empire. The conclusive reply to that sophistic argument is that the Italians were never settled in England and that they have, and always have had, a home of their own in Italy, whilst the Jews are not merely the ancient rulers but also the former settlers of Palestine and never had and to this day do not possess any other national home. It is because of that homelessness and because "they have never forgotten" that the Jews have a claim to the restoration of their national life in Palestine.

In sum, the gravamen of this entire memorandum was that the demonstrable "unparalleled character of the Jewish historical connection with Palestine" proved that the Jews were legitimate claimants to Palestine and not "intruders in an Arab country."

One of the most comprehensive Zionist expositions of historical right was a book published in 1933 by a religious Zionist, active in Ha-poel Ha-mizrahi,

Reuben Gafni (Weinshenker, 1903–1971).[60] Gafni brought his legal training to bear on the subject in an attempt to explicate the Jewish case without recourse to the divine promise. After surveying the political history of Palestine from ancient times and comparing the historical record of the Jews' relationship to it with that of the Arabs, he offered an exposition of the "national-historical right" of the Jews to self-determination.

Gafni drew a distinction between claims in terms of "historical interests," "historical right," and "historical connection." Historical interests merely meant claims for right of access to a particular territory for the conduct of activities therein, commercial, religious, educational or the like—for example, the historical interests of France in Syria or the right of access of the Christian churches to holy places. Such rights could legitimately be claimed not only by states but also by nonstate bodies such as churches. The invocation of historical right, argued Gafni, had been applied mainly in disputes between one state and another concerning political rule over a given territory. The state claiming such a right did so on the strength of the fact that it had ruled it at some time in the past. Such was the case in the disputes over Alsace-Lorraine between Germany and France; over Posen, between Poland and Germany; and over Vilna, between Lithuania and Poland. The validity of this type of claim was very much a moot point in international law since an endless series of claims going back into the past would lead to serious disorder in the world. Hence, in such cases a plebiscite of the population inhabiting the territories in question was a feasible solution.

The Jewish claim to Eretz Israel, submitted Gafni, was different. Here was a matter not between rival claimant states but between rival nations, one of which claims the right to self-determination in the territory in question by dint of predominant habitation, whereas the other claims it by virtue of historical connection. In such a case a plebiscite of the local population was irrelevant because that population was itself one party to the dispute. Other criteria had to be applied to determine which claimant was entitled to the disputed territory. These criteria involved much more than simply the current population size belonging to the claimant nations or the aggregate of private property held by them. More important was the spiritual and cultural value of that territory for the claimant nation. This, in turn, was a function of the dimensions of creativity generated by that nation's past and present habitation of and relationship with that territory. It often happened that actual political control over a territory fell into the hands of one nation whereas, in a national-cultural sense it belonged much more to another nation, irrespective of the scale of that nation's current physical presence there.

According to Gafni, "historical connection" in this sense described the nature of the Jewish claim to Eretz Israel. It was valid not simply because the Jews were once its political rulers. More important were the facts that, despite displacement and dispersion, the Jewish nation had never relinquished its claim and had not in the meantime acquired another territorial homeland. In addition, Jewish spiritual and cultural creativity and the contribution of these to mankind as a whole were inextricably bound up with that territory. Moreover, having gained recognition explicitly in the preamble to the British mandate over Palestine, a valid document in international law signed by fifty-two countries of the League of Nations, historical connection became the basis for the Jewish claim in international law.

Furthermore, argued Gafni, this historical connection was also the basis for the moral case of the Zionist project. Pointing to the disparity that existed even in regular intranational law between the ideal of absolute moral justice or equity and the defective reality of formal justice, Gafni noted that this disparity applied, a fortiori, in international affairs. But the case of the Jews for national self-determination rested as much on the moral principles of ideal equity as on the formal realities of international law, in which brute power still played a predominant role. International equity, like intranational equity, required the application of universally accepted moral principles, such as "do not unto another that which you would not have him do unto you." Insofar as every nation in the world was entitled to self-determination, equity demanded that this apply also to the Jewish nation—the more so because of the Jews' grave material distress. Whatever concession was required on the part of the Arabs of Palestine—and this was not grave, contended Gafni, since they would enjoy full civic rights in Palestine while also being culturally attached to an Arab nation holding sovereignty in vast territories—was justified on the basis of the existential need of the dispersed Jews, persecuted and rejected everywhere: "The Jews are entitled to a homeland not only by virtue of their being a nation deprived of its national home but also because of their sufferings that have no solution except in Eretz Israel."

Gafni's exposition reflected mainstream Zionist ideology, particularly in respect to his differentiation between the two kinds of historical claim. It was echoed, for example, in a publication published in 1947 primarily for the internal educational needs of the Zionist Organization.[61] The author, Joseph Heller, had earlier been associated with Ahad Ha'am (who, it will be recalled, had lived in England from 1908 to 1922) and was one of the finer intellects of Anglo-Jewish Zionism. Heller drew the same distinction between two usages of the term "historical right". One was the assertion of a nation's right to reassume rule of a given territory merely because that territory was once, in the past, under that nation's rule. This usage was incompatible with the accepted standards of international justice. The second usage was the assertion that the abiding spiritual-cultural connection of a particular nation with a particular territory entitled it to restoration in that territory. Such was the case of the Jews, the stamp of whose national culture had been indelibly impressed on the Land of Israel, just as, conversely, The Land had continued to live in the national culture of the Jewish Diaspora. Moreover, the suffering and distress of the Jews could be relieved only by restoration of the nation to the territory to which it had such a historical right. Admittedly, the rights of other affected nations had to be taken into account, but the Jewish right could not be overruled by the present Arab majority any more than a village, situated on some great artery running through a defile in the mountains, had the right to block the communications of a whole nation simply because the majority in that village did not wish the traffic to pass that way. Therefore, argued Heller, "the Jewish claim to Palestine is justified both by history and by the present Jewish and international situation: it is a historic right in the true meaning of the term."

A more sophisticated intellectual contribution to the notion of Jewish historical right to Eretz Israel was made by Yehezkel Kaufmann in his monumental but highly discursive work *Gola ve-nekhar*, published in the 1930s, to which we have referred in another context. Kaufmann drew an analytical distinction between "the natural national right" to a territory and the "positive legal right" of political rule. The natural national right produced a sense of national property that, although different in character from private property, was as deeply rooted and powerful a social factor in history. Kaufmann, an intellectual antagonist of Marxist materialism, held that no less than economics, ethnicity, and ethnic attachment to "national land" were crucial factors in the development of human society. From time immemorial popular consciousness had associated territorial "country" and "inheritance" with specific ethnic groups in a manner not necessarily coincident with the boundaries of regnant political authority. Thus, the national territory of the Germans or Italians was one thing, and the actual states of Germany or Italy quite another. But the actualities of political rule did not efface the realities of lingering attachment to the concept of "the national land," a concept that, Kaufmann argued, was derived ultimately not from rule over a land but from "ethnic settlement." It was ethnic settlement that defined the area of national territory and created the concept of a national land:

When a tribe or people takes possession of a piece of territory and settles it to the extent that its ethnic culture holds natural sway over it, that tribe or people feels itself to be master of that territory; that territory thus becomes its national property, its area of private authority, its special preserve . . . hence settlement, culture and language roots and not political roots create the natural national right to a territory.[62]

Accordingly, Kaufmann argued that it was by virtue of its original ethnic settlement of Eretz Israel that the Jewish nation had an undeniable "natural national right," independently of political facts there. Moreover, it was a pivotal thesis of Kaufmann's *Gola ve-nekhar* that a nation could belong fully only in a territory to which it had such a natural national right—hence, the Jews' manifest failure to belong organically in any other territory in the world, their immutably alien status in exile. Emancipation and the rights of citizenship never sufficed; they were only of legal-political significance. What really counted was organic ethnic belonging.[63] According to Kaufmann, the purely rational conclusion of some of the early Zionists, like Leo Pinsker and Theodor Herzl, was territorialist in conception; that is to say, they thought that any suitable territory would be satisfactory to solve the Jewish problem. But Hibbat Zion and the masses of Jewry turned to Eretz Israel exclusively because of "the sense of natural historical ownership which the Jewish people has for the land of its past."[64]

However, it followed from Kaufmann's own logic that the Arabs had a natural historical right to ownership of the same land. This he had to admit, however reluctantly: "Eretz Israel is, it seems, the only land in the world to which two people have the right of possession. For no one can doubt that not Israel alone but also the Arabs have a historical right to the land."[65] Realistically appraising the resistance to Jewish aspirations in Palestine that the Arabs were bound to put up, he recognized that an Arab "movement of national revival had begun to effervesce."[66] Kaufmann's conclusion, although extremely divergent from the Zionist consensus, was consistent with his reasoning: he proposed a return to the general territorial idea. Since the Jews would ever remain aliens to the natural historical homelands of other peoples throughout the Diaspora and since Palestine could not serve as a complete solution owing to natural Arab resistance, a supplementary territory was needed to provide a secondary solution of "unhampered Jewish ethnic settlement" and national-cultural autonomy.[67] Of course, this proposal must be understood in the context of the 1930s, a time when the rise of Hitler and rabid antisemitic regimes throughout central and eastern Europe, on the one hand, and immigration restrictions by the Mandate regime in Palestine and by countries of the New World, on the other hand, revived Jewish territorialist schemes.

As for the conflict between Jews and Arabs in Palestine itself, Kaufmann took a position close to that of the mainstream of General Zionism. In debate during 1931 with the members of Brit Shalom, an association dedicated to the attainment of understanding with the Arabs through compromise (to whose views we shall return later), Kaufmann argued on the following lines:[68] He agreed with Brit Shalom insofar as universal moral standards required that "the fulfillment of our right must not lead to the displacement or impoverishment of the Arabs. We must not do anything to them which will cause them objective harm." He even suggested that "the authority to decide about this must rest with a neutral institution such as the League of Nations." However, he held that this did not by any means warrant Brit Shalom's premise that the Zionist enterprise required the assent of the Arabs in order to be morally and legally valid. The national historic right of the Jews to be the governing factor in Palestine was a valid "ethical-legal basis" for the Zionist enterprise, and it took on a positive legal form in the Balfour Declaration and in the Mandate. "If you think that Palestine is not the country of the Jews as long as the Arabs have not agreed to this," Kaufmann told the members of Brit Shalom, "then you abandon and annul our right altogether." Kaufmann's conclusion was much the same as that of Jabotinsky. He said that since Arab agreement, an "Arab Balfour Declaration," was an impossibility, one could only hope that "when they see that the clock cannot be put back, and when they realize that the creators of the 'national homeland' had no intention of harming the Arab nation," the Arabs would come to reconcile themselves to the existence of the Jewish national home. In the meanwhile the constructive work of Zionism had to go forward.

Our survey of the various ideological expositions of the historical claim to Eretz Israel makes it evident that the term "historical right" was both vague in meaning and of dubious import. In the final analysis all that could be established with objectivity was the irrefutable fact of the Jewish people's special historical *connection* with Eretz Israel, dating back to ancient times. This in itself, however, could not efface the equally objective fact that the Arabs of Palestine also had a historical connection, as well indeed as having the advantage of being the present majority of the country's population.[69]

Furthermore, even granted the fact of a unique and unbroken Jewish historical connection with Eretz Israel and (as was claimed by the Jews) its superiority in intensity and significance to that of the Arabs, whatever "right" emanated from these premises could not morally be treated as absolute and unlimited irrespective of its effect upon the Arabs. Conversely, by the same token, the "right" of the Arabs to self-determination qua majority population in Palestine could not morally be treated as absolute and unlimited, irrespective of *its* effect upon the Jews. What the claim of historical connection did establish, however, was relevance; the relevance of Jewish claims to the future national character and political status of the territory wrested from Ottoman imperial rule in the First World War and held since 1922 by Britain, under mandate from the League of Nations, under the name Palestine. It was precisely such relevance that the Jews lacked in relation to any other territory in the world—East Africa, for example.

In sum, by virtue of the Jewish nation's proven historical connection with that territory, its claim (represented by the Zionist Organization) to national self-determination therein was admissible both in the court of international law and, as it were, in the moral court of world public opinion. But admissibility of a claim did not yet mean attainment of a right. That required the marshaling of argumentation in terms of international law and at the same time called for the exposition of moral considerations.

The legal implications of the Jewish historical connection have been cogently expounded from the Zionist point of view by two notable scholars of international law, Nathan Feinberg and Julius Stone. Their argumentation started from the premise that the Jewish nation had become a recognized legal entity. Various states had made humanitarian interventions on behalf of Jews on occasions dating back as far as the Peace Congress of Westphalia in 1648 and becoming more frequent in the nineteenth century. But whereas these interventions had concerned themselves only with protection of the individual rights of Jews, the collective national attributes of the Jews at last gained international legal recognition during the First World War. This was the outcome of the principle of national determination as adopted by the principal Allied Powers in the formulation of their war aims and in the peace settlement after the war. According to Feinberg, "The Jewish question was raised to the level of a question involving a nation as a whole i.e., an entity entitled to separate national existence and to the organization of its life within the framework of the State."[70] Moreover, the Balfour Declaration of November 1917 followed by the official League of Nations mandate over Palestine of 1922 established international legal recognition of the Jewish nation's historical connection with Palestine. The preamble of the mandate specifically recognized "that the Mandatory should be responsible for putting into effect the declaration originally made on November 2nd, 1917 by the Government of His Britannic Majesty and adopted by the said Powers, in favour of the establishment in Palestine of a national home for the Jewish people" and added to this that "recognition has thereby been given to the historical connection of the Jewish people with Palestine and the grounds for reconstituting their national home in that country." This meant, Feinberg averred, "the de jure recognition of the Jewish people as a state-forming entity."[71]

The Zionist line of legal argumentation was that this international legal recognition outweighed whatever claims the Arabs in and outside Palestine put forward on the basis of the principle of self-determination. It invoked the accepted rule of intertemporal international law that "the legality of an action is determined in the light of the law in force when it was in effect and not of the law prevailing when its validity is challenged." Accordingly, Feinberg contended that there had never been agreement on whether self-determination of peoples was a binding rule of positive international law or merely a political principle or moral postulate. "But one point is clear beyond any doubt," he claimed, "it was not a binding rule of law at any of the many stages on the road towards the emergence of the State of Israel."[72]

Along similar lines but in writings penned after the establishment of the State of Israel, Julius Stone contended that the appropriate historical and legal context having been the First World War and the peace settlement that ensued, what was at issue was the reallocation of ex-Ottoman imperial lands. On their own evidences the Palestinians did not at the relevant time constitute a distinctive nation separate from the Arab nation as a whole. In that historical-legal context, Jews and Arabs appeared simultaneously as legitimate claimants for self-determination in Palestine. "The rival claimants were, only Jewish nationalism on the one hand and Arab nationalism (with, of course, further dynastic distributions within the Arab allotment) on the other." In other words, "Jewish and Arab claims in the vast area of the former Ottoman Empire came to the forum of liberation together, and not (as is usually implied) by way of Jewish encroachment on an already vested and exclusive Arab domain."[73]

In that context a vast territorial dispensation was made to the Arab nation as that nation then presented itself, providing in later decades for a plurality of independent Arab states. This massive attainment of the Arab nation was offset only by a minute territorial allocation, Palestine under British mandate, for the satisfaction of legitimate Jewish national needs. Whatever impairment was caused thereby to that section of the Arab nation that inhabited Palestine—and had to be satisfied with the enjoyment of minority and civic rights alone—was justified in the light of "the principle that where two rightful claims are in conflict, the amount of suffering that will be caused by failure to satisfy each one of them must be carefully weighed and the decision must fall in favor of that which will result in the least suffering."[74]

In the final analysis, therefore, the legal claim relied upon what might be described as a utilitarian moral principle: given the impossibility of an equitable solution equally satisfying to both claimants, the maximum of good and the minimum of harm should be done. Or as Chaim Weizmann phrased it in his evidence to the Anglo-American Committee of Inquiry of 1946; "move on the line of least injustice."[75]

Labor Zionist Formulations

This reasoning was equally evident in the ideological formulations of Socialist Zionists. For them the notion of historical right presented formidable ideological difficulties because major Socialist theoreticians condemned the concept. Karl Kautsky, for example, defined it as "the claim of a nation to the restoration of the boundaries of its state as they existed centuries ago, under entirely different circumstances."[76] Such a claim he branded as a reactionary blind for wars of conquest and territorial aggrandizement. It was the very antithesis of the progressive, democratic principle of "self-determination of nations," which called for plebiscites in disputed areas to determine the will of the people in regard to independent statehood.

Alsace-Lorraine was regarded by most Socialists as a case in point. It was in the name of historical right that Germany had annexed Alsace-Lorraine in 1870. Notwithstanding their belief that a blatant wrong had been perpetrated, many Socialists opposed French reannexation of Alsace-Lorraine during and after World War I. Governed by the principle of self-determination (versus historical right), they insisted on a preliminary plebiscite to determine the will of the population of Alsace-Lorraine. After the territory had reverted to France, there followed Hitler's notorious demand for its restoration to Germany, once again on the basis of historical right. This reactionary claim further discredited the notion of historical right in the eyes of international Socialists.

Following Marxist theoreticians like Karl Kautsky, Jewish Communists and also the Socialist Jewish workers' Bund caviled at the Zionists' invocation of historical right. Socialist Zionists who turned to territorialism followed suit. As well as despairing of the prospects of Eretz Israel on account of Arab resistance, they rejected religious and historical claims alike. They deprecated the "romanticism of the Cave of Machpelah, the Wailing Wall and Mother Rachel's Tomb"[77] and argued that "from a socialist standpoint, all means of production belong to the class which works them. The earth, from this standpoint, belongs to those who now work it; not to those whose forefathers at one time worked it."[78] Only in a place "where there was no native, hungering population; where large stretches of land have not yet been worked by anyone" was it feasible and legitimate, from a Socialist standpoint, to develop a Jewish territorial home.

Also, Chaim Zhitlowsky (1865–1943), who throughout his ideological permutations remained at heart sympathetic to labor Zionist settlement in Palestine, disqualified the invocation of historical right.[79] As late as 1936 he wrote:

There can be no talk of an absolute right to Eretz Israel; neither on the side of the Arab nation, nor of the Jewish. Also our so-called "historical right" to the land of our fathers is a pure fiction and its value is nil. Not long ago an Arab publicist rightly remarked that if the historical right to countries is to be recognised, Andalusia (in Spain) ought to belong to the Arabs. As we know from history, England once belonged to Rome and America to the Red Indians. Who now considers such historical facts? And why should we consider them? There is no such thing as "historical right."

Zhitlowsky opined that the notion of an absolute right of ownership by any nation over "its" land was unacceptable, no less on grounds of Socialist theory than on those of Jewish religion. He illustrated this by comparing Rashi's commentary on the passage of Genesis "for mine is the earth" (to which we referred at the beginning of this chapter) to the opinion shared by both Proudhon and Marx that no territory may be regarded as the exclusive property of any nation. Indeed, with the ultimate consummation of world socialism the borders of all lands would be eliminated.

According to Zhitlowsky, the Socialist world outlook prescribed that "the title to land belongs only to those persons—of whatever nation—who inhabit that land and work it with their own hands. That is, a worker's right by virtue of use." He argued that this "worker's right to possession of land" was exemplified no less in Zionist purchases of land in Palestine than in the Soviet Union's establishment of kolkhoz farms. On these Socialist grounds, Zhitlowsky rejected the demands of the Arabs that Jewish land purchases and Jewish immigration to Palestine be stopped.

No true Socialist may identify with the notion that the majority of any population, to be found within borders in any case determined by the diplomatic whims of the imperialist powers, has a right to do there whatever it wishes; at will to permit entry of others and forbid purchase of land. No Socialist is permitted to identify with such a demand, which is a slap in the face for the most important foundation of the social consciousness of right: the right of every human being to live in any place on our common mother-earth, be it in present Palestine or in Trans-Jordan or in the wilderness of Arizona, or wherever he chooses, and to draw from mother-earth his livelihood through his own labor; on condition, naturally, that in so doing he does not take away from any other human the piece of land from which he derives his livelihood by his own labor.

Given the severe ideological reservations held by Socialists on the notion of historical rights, special importance attaches to the materialist-determinist formulations of Ber Borochov, the seminal theorist of Poalei Zion. As we noted in chapter 5 of this book, in the first phase of Borochov's oscillating ideological odyssey he still attributed importance to volitional factors. In his early essay "On the Question of Zion and Territory," one finds the statement that the Jews have historical rights to Palestine, of which "it was not at all ridiculous to speak," since they happened to enjoy recognition not only in European public opinion but even by the fellahin (peasants) in Palestine.[80] At that time this invocation of historical right served his propagandist activity on behalf of the Zionists of Zion in Russia, who opposed any notion of a territorial solution other than Palestine. Indeed, Borochov went so far as to claim that one of the greatest advantages of Palestine was the racial compatibility between its autochtonous peasant population and the contemporary Jewish people. "It is a reasonable assumption," he wrote, "that the peasants in Palestine are the direct descendants of the residual rural population of the Jews and the Canaanites, with a light admixture of Arab blood."[81] Hence, he argued, the prospects of their being assimilated by the returned Jewish population were much better than would be the case in any other territory the territorialists could come up with.

However, this line of thought receded in the second, rigidly materialist, and determinist phase of Borochov's thought, first noticeable in late 1905 and early 1906 and already reflected in his formulation of "Our Platform." In that document, Borochov shifted the emphasis from the claim of racial kinship to the putative advantage of Palestine as an "international hostel" (not unlike Switzerland) of different languages, cultures, and religions, whose inhabitants consequently lacked a distinctive national character of their own.[82] But the main thrust of his theory was determinist. He invoked neither traditional hankering for Zion nor historical rights. Indeed, he explained that Poalei Zion's preference for Palestine "is not a matter of principle because it is not connected with traditions of the past." Rather, it was a matter of recognizing the structural socioeconomic reality (in the Marxist sense) that would inevitably turn the Jewish national migration toward Palestine. The rationale for this "prognostic Palestinism" formed the major part of Borochov's ideological inventiveness and, as such, has been discussed in chapter 5.

It should be remembered that these ideas belong only to the middle phase of Borochov's ideological development. In the years of World War I, which were the last of his short life, his thinking diverged from its earlier determinism, and he acknowledged the importance of historical and emotional factors in making Palestine the magnet for the spontaneous process of Jewish immigration, which he continued to predict. In the "Declaration to the Hollando-Scandinavian Socialist Committee" submitted by the Jewish Socialist Labor Confederation Poalei Zion in August 1917, which Borochov helped prepare, "the uninterrupted spiritual association of the Jewish people with its native soil" was not overlooked.[83]

Moreover, contemporaneously with Borochov's materialist phase, the Poalei Zion parties of Austria and of the United States refrained from such dogmatic determinism and sought a synthesis of materialist and idealist arguments for the assertion that Socialist-nationalist aspirations of Jews could reach fulfillment in Palestine alone. Thus, the draft program of the Austrian Poalei Zion, composed by Shlomo Kaplansky and discussed by its third conference in 1906, submitted—still in materialist terms—that "the Jewish stream of emigration must be directed to such a land whose geographical and economic situation can make possible large-scale industrial and commercial colonization." But it added—in idealist terms—that it had to be "a country which has a power of attraction capable of keeping the Jewish masses on the soil. . . . These prerequisites exist only in the historic fatherland of the Jews . . . which has . . . remained for thousands of years in the minds of the Jewish people as the only country of its future and its liberty."[84]

Berl Locker (1887–1972), who, throughout most of the period of the British mandate, served in the international forum as a spokesman for mainstream labor Zionism, composed, in 1936, a refined exposition titled "The Jews and Palestine: Historical Connection and Historic Right." Locker recognized that from a Socialist point of view, "historic right is a discredited conception" but argued that this was "because the conception has so often in history been misused in an attempt to justify injustice. And it is utterly wrong to suppose that every claim to historic right must per se be spurious."

The historic right of the Jewish people to Palestine is based on the one hand on such concrete historic formulations that there is no parallel to them among all the other "historic rights" while it is at the same time absolutely free from the negative and fictitious elements that are characteristic of those other "historic rights." . . . The aim of Zionism is not to establish an alien rule over the population and the resources of the country for the benefit of an outside Power, but to replant in its ancient home the people that was uprooted from it. Not to dominate and to exploit from without, but to come there to live and to work on the land, to build and develop it, to restore it and by its means to be itself restored—that is the aim of Zionism. Not to conquer a colony for a foreign "motherland", but to build up a home and a fatherland for a homeless people. Is it not obvious what a deep gulf lies between the two conceptions?[85]

The converse side of Locker's pleading of the exceptionalist validity of historical rights in the Jewish case was his qualification of the principle of national self-determination in the Arab case. He argued that it did not mean "the absolute right of every nation to have the sole say, no matter what the conditions, in deciding the future of the territory in which it lives." The right of self-determination was not unlimited and under certain conditions had to give way to the higher international interests of mankind as a whole. "And Zionism is one of those higher interests of humanity," averred Locker.

Although Locker thus pleaded the case for the validity of Jewish historical rights (at any rate as represented by Socialist Zionism), he did not rest Zionist claims solely, or even primarily, upon such historic right. He acknowledged that the exercise of Jewish historic rights was conditional upon their not annulling the rights of others and that, in fact, Jewish claims confronted historical counterclaims of the Arabs. But in accord with prevalent labor Zionist thinking, he denied that the Arabs were being seriously harmed. Moreover, he averred that even if it were argued that there was "a clash between two conflicting rights, each of them justified,"

even then it would still be an open question which of the two peoples should withdraw its rights in favour of the other—the Arab people who owns immense areas, to a large extent empty or only sparsely populated and little cultivated, and to whom Palestine is merely a small corner of their vast territory, so that even without this tiny land, they would not be a homeless people, or the Jews who have no home of their own anywhere in the world, who have for thousands of years been subjected to persecution, who are faced by the danger of physical and spiritual extermination, and to whom their return to this land is the sole opportunity they have of a renewed life of independence and creative effort. Any unbiased international tribunal capable of rising above petty sectional interests and political considerations would have to ask itself, before it reached any decision, which people's withdrawal from its rights would do least harm to the general interests of humanity as a whole. I do not think that in those circumstances we would lose our case.

It is thus noteworthy that in Locker's exposition, as in the others we have examined, historical right was not presented as a self-sufficient and unrestricted justification of the Zionist enterprise. It merely served to establish that Eretz Israel or Palestine was irrefragably *relevant* to the Jews, that the Jews were *legitimate claimants*. It showed, in Locker's words, that "from the beginning we have a stake in this land, because we have never abandoned our claim to it, because in every generation and throughout the whole period of our dispersion we have considered ourselves historically bound up with this land, not only with its past but also with its future."

Berl Locker was not a particularly original nor important thinker. His presentation of the Socialist-Zionist case merely reflected the prevalent view in the labor Zionist mainstream. Another articulate spokesman who may be cited by way of further illustration was Haim Greenberg (1889–1953), who, having left his birthplace in Bessarabia, Russia, first became one of the editors of *Ha-olam*, the Hebrew organ of the Zionist Organization, and then moved to America in 1924. There, as editor of the weekly *Yiddisher Kempfer* and the monthly *Jewish Frontier*, he became the leading theoretician of labor Zionism in the English-speaking Diaspora. Recognizing the limitations of any case based on historical right, Greenberg pleaded the Socialist principle of redistribution of property: "Group ownership of territories is also a form of private ownership which should be subjected to control and regulation by a broader human or international principle . . . the same criterion of justice—the assurance of the necessary minimum to every creature that is stamped with the 'image of God'—must also be applied to entire nations, races and tribes." Furthermore, he too stressed the Jewish existential need: "One may not say to the Jews: the world is already divided up; some received more and others less but there is nothing left for you and no-one is obliged to share with you, even though he possesses fields which he cannot or does not wish to cultivate."[86]

Thus, in summation, it must be noted that the Socialist-Zionist case, too, was reducible from so-called historical right to the plea of greater existential need and the application of utilitarian morality.

Jabotinsky's Formulation

Perhaps the most telling example of the ultimate reduction of the Jewish claim to Eretz Israel to the baseline of existential need may be found in the expositions of Ze'ev Jabotinsky, which must certainly be numbered among the most eloquent in the annals of Zionism. As the militant exponent of an integral brand of nationalism, Jabotinsky had no inhibitions about the proposition that the Jews had a historical right to Eretz Israel. Indeed, he claimed that "everything in The Land which was worthy of praise and glory belonged to us, to the Jewish people."[87] In contrast to the labor Zionists, Jabotinsky set little store by the actual achievements of pioneering settlement as the basis for the Jewish claim. Not those achievements but the historical facts that "Titus exiled the people of Israel from its land two thousand years ago" and that the exiles had never renounced their claim to their land thereafter was the real and sufficient basis for Jewish right.[88]

Yet Jabotinsky recognized, no less than did the labor Zionists, that neither historical right nor self-determination were principles of absolutely unlimited and universal validity. He too upheld existential need as the moral touchstone for the validity of historical rights—hence, the fallacy in the cavil frequently directed at the Zionists that if it be granted that the Jews have a right to Palestine, then the Arabs have the same historical right to Spain! "The first question is," Jabotinsky argued, "have you a need for land? If you have no need, if you have sufficient, then you may not rest your case on historical rights."[89] The same criterion of existential need was applied by Jabotinsky to the principle of self-determination, which "does not mean that he who has grabbed a piece of territory must always remain its owner, and he who was forcibly expelled from his land must remain the eternal wanderer."

Self-determination means a revision—a revision in the division of the globe between the nations, in such a manner that those who have too much should give up a part to those who have too little or nothing at all, in order that all of them should have a place in which to practice their self-determination. . . . Confiscation of a strip of territory from a nation possessed of great stretches of territory for the purpose of providing a home for a wandering people—that is an act of justice. And if that nation with so much territory does not agree (and that would only be natural) then it must be coerced.[90]

In like vein, Jabotinsky stated on another occasion: "We take our stand from the point of view of the 'jubilee': he who has nothing—one gives to him; he who has too much—one takes from him; he from whom has been taken, it is returned to him."[91]

A lucid exposition of existential need as the ultimate basis of the Jewish claim to Eretz Israel was made by Jabotinsky in his evidence before the Palestine Royal Commission of 1937. In that speech Jabotinsky professed to holding "the profoundest feeling for the Arab case insofar as that Arab case is not exaggerated." However, juxtaposing this prospect with the total homelessness of the Jewish nation, he denied that becoming a minority in one country was an unreasonable hardship:

It is not a hardship on any race, any nation, possessing so many National States now and so many more National States in the future. One fraction, one branch of that race, and not a big one, will have to live in someone else's State: well, that is the case with all the mightiest nations of the world. I could hardly mention one of the big nations, having their States, mighty and powerful, who had not one branch living in someone else's State. That is only normal and there is no "hardship" attached to that. So when we hear the Arab claim confronted with the Jewish claim; I fully understand that any minority would prefer to be a majority, it is quite understandable that the Arabs of Palestine would also prefer Palestine to be the Arab State No. 4, No. 5, or No. 6—that I quite understand; *but when the Arab claim is confronted with our Jewish demand to be saved, it is like the claims of appetite versus the claims of starvation* [emphasis added]. No tribunal has ever had the luck of trying a case where all the justice was on the side of one party and the other party had no case whatsoever. Usually in human affairs any tribunal, including this tribunal, in trying two cases, has to concede that both sides have a case on their side and, in order to do justice, they must take into consideration what should constitute the basic justification of all human demands, individual or mass demands—the decisive terrible balance of Need. I think it is clear.[92]

Thus, Jabotinsky did not differ substantially from labor Zionism in regard to the ultimate moral justification for the Jewish national claim to Eretz Israel. Where he differed was over the means to actualize that claim. For the very reason that he realistically anticipated implacable resistance on the part of the Arabs of Palestine, Jabotinsky was convinced that there was no possibility whatsoever of their "voluntarily agreeing" to the fulfillment of Zionist aspirations. Moreover, precisely because he respected their pride—so he averred—he knew that no social class of Arabs would be fobbed off by Socialist rhetoric or economic aggrandizement. Zionist negotiation with the Arabs was therefore futile.[93]

In Jabotinsky's view the moral justification of the Zionist enterprise derived from the relatively greater existential need of the Jewish nation, not from the acquiescence of the Arabs. Therefore, the alternative the Jewish people faced was clear-cut: either to succumb to national starvation or to save itself by self-assertion. He was convinced that only if and when the Arabs came to recognize the impossibility of overcoming the Jewish national entity in Palestine would there be any chance of their coming to terms with it. Hence, he advocated a policy aimed at erecting what he termed "an iron wall" unassailable by Arab resistance: "an iron wall, that is to say the existence of a force in Eretz Israel that in no way would be influenced by the pressure of the Arabs."[94] The supreme task of Zionist diplomacy was to wrest from the British Mandatory the means for erecting and maintaining this "iron wall."

As we have shown in a previous chapter, Jabotinsky believed that this object was attainable without breaking with Britain, by means of demonstrative political and moral pressure. But some of Jabotinsky's followers resorted to violent courses of action. These were the founders of the Irgun Tzvai Leumi (IZL) in the late 1930s and of the Lohamei Herut Israel (Lehi) in 1940. Abandoning the Hagana's policy of restraint, these underground groups not only countered Arab terror with their own terror but also rebelled against the British authorities in Palestine.

To complete this survey of the articulated ideological formulations of the Zionist claim to Jewish national self-determination in Eretz Israel, it is necessary to broaden our scope somewhat and encompass those schools of thought that mark the extreme poles of the Zionist ideology in regard to Jewish claims. One pole was the radical Revisionists, of which the Lehi was the most extreme offshoot. The other was what might, for convenience' sake, be called the Brit Shalom (Covenant of Peace) school of thought. In quantitative terms both were minuscule, accounting for no more than a few hundred adherents at their peaks. In both cases these adherents were concentrated in Palestine although enjoying some degree of support also in the Diaspora—the Brit Shalom school mainly in German Zionism, the radical Revisionists mainly in Polish Zionism.

Much as our examination of the religious Zionist formulations of divinely endowed right to Eretz Israel of necessity touched also upon the implications for praxis—tested mainly by the Uganda and partition proposals—so our scrutiny of these two ideological extremes cannot be separated from their actual policy implications. Finally, to balance our perspective, it will be instructive to refocus more specifically on center stage. This may best be accomplished by examining the ideological formulations and implications for praxis of the major personality who stood at the helm and steered the policy of the Zionist Organization in the thrust toward Jewish statehood—David Ben-Gurion.

Might Is Right: The Radical Revisionists

As we showed in chapter 6, in the course of the 1930s two significantly divergent Revisionist ideological trends became evident. One retained Jabotinsky's liberal restraints. The other was of authoritarian and nonliberal character, had Fascist sympathies, and was saturated with quasi-religious messianic rhetoric. It was spawned by a small circle of individuals in Palestine who were collectively referred to as "the maximalists" and particularly by Abba Ahimeir, who formed the short-lived Brit Ha-biryonim organization. If Jabotinsky's conception of Jewish right to Palestine rested on the rational and moral premises of the Jewish nation's historical connection and greater existential need, not so the fundamental ideological conceptions that animated the maximalist wing. As formulated by Yehoshua Heschel Yevin, "The Twelve Principles of the Constitution of Liberation," which expressed the radical Right's ethos, replaced the restricted concept of "a national home" with a heroic vision of *malkhut Israel* (the kingdom of Israel). This was a metaphorical allusion to a Jewish imperial realm extending to the borders of the biblical kingdom of Israel, one that could contain all the millions of Jews in the world. Proclaiming that "Ishmael and Edom [the Arabs and the British] are only alien occupants—just as the Russians were in Poland or the Turks in Serbia," it called for armed liberation from foreign occupation![95]

The romantic concept *malkhut Israel* was inseparably twinned with another concept, *regesh ha-adnut* (literally, "the sense of mastery" or "dominance"), a sense that the Jews had lost in the *galut* and for whose restoration the poet Uri Zvi Greenberg passionately called. It meant regaining the confidence and resolve to rule over a realm containing not only one's own national population but also others, just as most normal sovereign nations did (for example, as did the Poles over Ukrainians, Germans, and other minorities). The "Twelve Principles of the Constitution of Liberation" stated, in pointed contrast to the views of Weizmann and the labor Zionist leaders: "There is no place for talk of 'non-domination' and 'bi-nationalism.' The nation of Israel, like each and every nation within its territorial boundaries, can and must rule over other minorities that are situated on the historic territory of the Hebrew nation."

This ethos of power found its most thoroughgoing expression in the Lehi underground organization founded in 1940 by Avraham Stern. Lehi's "Eighteen Principles of the Revival"[96] paralleled in essence the quasi-messianic terms of "The Twelve Principles of the Constitution of Liberation." It too called for "the revival of the Kingdom" and declared that "the homeland is Eretz Israel in the boundaries stipulated in the Bible." Moreover, it categorically grounded the Jewish right to Eretz Israel upon might: "The Jewish people conquered Eretz Israel by the sword. There it became a nation, and there alone it shall restore itself. For this reason the people of Israel are the sole rightful owners of Eretz Israel. This right is absolute: it has not lapsed and cannot ever lapse." Accordingly, it spoke of "conquest—to liberate the homeland from foreign control," to which end all means were justified. It declared "war to the finish against all who stand in the way" and sought "alliances with all who are interested and are willing to assist." Furthermore, it called for "the revival of mastery [*adnut*] over the redeemed land" and "glorification of the Hebrew nation as the foremost military, political, cultural and economic factor in the East and the Mediterranean littoral." It also intimated that "the problem of foreigners [viz., the Arabs] will be solved through population exchange."

In sum, as enunciated by the radical wing of Revisionist Zionism, the assertion of Jewish right to rule over Palestine dispensed with ideological justifications, whether in terms of historical right or existential need and morality; indeed, it regarded them with contempt as a mark of weakness. It rested the Jewish case without moral scruple upon the fundamental proposition that might was right; it was by conquest that Eretz Israel had become the homeland of the Jewish nation in ancient times, and surely by conquest it would now be liberated from foreign rule.

To be sure, after the death of Stern at the hands of the British security police in 1942, Lehi underwent a series of convoluted ideological transformations, some of which appeared to contradict its original ideological stance.[97] Yet on closer analysis, it may be said that his successors, Natan Friedman-Yellin (Mor), Israel Scheib (Eldad), and Yitzhak Jazernicki (Shamir, who was later to become prime minister of Israel), remained true, at core, to the fundamental ideological positions of the "Eighteen Principles of the Revival" that had inspired Lehi as founded by Stern. These included the proposition that the right of Jews to Eretz Israel was self-validating, absolute, and exclusive—hence necessitating no justification beyond the fact of original conquest—and the corollary that the Arab inhabitants of Eretz Israel were, in the final analysis, aliens and therefore transferrable.

In regard to basic strategy, too, Stern's successors were faithful to their teacher.

They not only continued to treat Britain as Zionism's archenemy (the Arabs they considered merely as Britain's tool), not shrinking from personal terror against its representatives, but also sought to win over the support of another foreign power. In Stern's time there even had been a secret attempt to seek alliance with Nazi Germany![98] It was abortive. After 1944, Stern's successors veered toward seeking alliance with the Soviet Union. With ironic inversion of the key Revisionist principle of "monistic" nationalism, some of them came to adopt an ideological dualism that sought to synthesize Lehi's radical-right nationalist heritage with support for a workers' socialism cleansed of all liberal-tainted cosmopolitanism.[99] It was modeled on the halcyon nationalist-cum-socialist image of the Soviet Union during the Second World War years and on the eastern bloc "democratic republics." This shift necessitated an exposition of the Jewish right to Palestine and operative ideological positions on the Arab question that were more palatable for foreign (especially Soviet) consumption than were those of Stern's "Eighteen Principles of the Revival." Hence, Lehi began to appeal to the "progressive" elements of the Arab Middle East to cooperate in the struggle against the common enemy, British imperialism. It asserted that were it not for Britain's nefarious, intriguing instigation of Arab hostility toward the Jews, there would be no real conflict of interests between Arab and Jew.

A major political document that reflected this ostensible ideological trans-formation was Lehi's memorandum to the United Nations Special Committee on Palestine (UNSCOP) of June 1947.[100] So far from treating the Arabs as aliens having no rightful place at all in Eretz Israel, it assured them of equal citizenship as well as the preservation of their culture in a future Jewish state. To be sure, it spoke of population exchange but purely as a voluntary option for those Arabs who would prefer to live in Arab national states. (The exchange would be with Jews who lived in those states.) Although upholding the absolute Jewish right to Eretz Israel, the memorandum defined its historic boundaries as both sides of the Jordan, rather than as from the Nile to the Euphrates in maximal biblical terms. It then launched into a lengthy justification of Jewish historical rights, stressing, inter alia, the parallel with restoration of independent Poland's western lands "after seven hundred years under the yoke of the German conqueror." It also included an ancillary justification of a kind usually associated with a school of Zionism situated on the very opposite ideological pole—notably that espoused by Martin Buber—namely, the "need of the Jewish nation to regain the conditions for its unique national-cultural creativity" for the sake of all mankind.

It may thus be said that on the eve of the war of 1948 there was an ostensible return to the mainstream ideological tradition of Jabotinsky's more liberal mode of integral nationalism. It was, however, but the penultimate stage of Lehi's ideological gyrations, for during the war it reverted to positions on the Arab question essentially the same as those with which it had started out on its dissident course in 1940, notably the espousal of transfer of the Arab population.

This it justified on the fundamental ideological ground of exclusive Jewish right to Palestine as well as on the operative ideological reasoning that it was the only durable solution, given the refusal of the Arab population to accede to loyal citizenship in a Jewish state.

Jewish Rights in the Brit Shalom Tradition

The approach of Martin Buber, which was discussed earlier, was a major component of an ideological stream that cut across the divisions between various political groups within the labor and general Zionist camps and issued in a series of politically peripheral but ideologically significant Zionist associations, the first of which was Brit Shalom (literally, the Covenant of Peace but whose English designation was the Peace Association). Although founded in Jerusalem in 1925, Brit Shalom had roots within the Zionist movement in Germany and continued to enjoy support from that quarter.[101] It was an intellectual circle whose founders included Dr. Arthur Ruppin (1876–1843), who since 1908, as director of the Zionist Organization's Palestine office, had occupied a central position in the entire Zionist settlement enterprise; Samuel Hugo Bergmann (1883–1975), who became director of the Jewish National and University Library and professor of philosophy at the Hebrew University; the writer "Rabbi" Benjamin (pseudonym of Yehoshua Radler-Feldman, 1880–1957); Yitzhak Epstein (1862–1943), an educator and one of the founders of the Zionist school system in Palestine; Haim Kalvarisky (1868–1947), an agronomist; and Gershom Scholem (1897–1982) and Akiva Ernst Simon (1899–1988), who, respectively, became professors in the fields of Jewish mysticism and education at the Hebrew University. Their decision to form Brit Shalom arose from a shared conviction that the Zionist leadership was misguidedly overlooking the crucial importance of relations with the Arab population of Palestine.

Initially, the founders of Brit Shalom sought to investigate the prospects for Jewish-Arab understanding and to place their findings at the disposal of the Zionist executive. The association's statutes stated that the object was "to arrive at an understanding between Jews and Arabs as to the form of their mutual relations in Palestine on the basis of absolute political equality of two culturally autonomous peoples, and to determine the lines of their cooperation for the development of the country.[102] The approach soon adopted by Brit Shalom came to rest on the premise that an Arab-Jewish understanding was the vital prerequisite for the fulfillment of Zionism. Advocating a binational dispensation in Palestine, it wished to create

a state inhabited jointly by the two peoples living in this country under complete equality of rights, as the two elements which jointly and equally determine the destiny of this country, without regard for the fact which of the two is, at any particular time, numerically superior. Brit Shalom aspires to create here in Palestine a solid and wholesome Jewish community, to contain as many Jews as possible, without regard for the fact whether the Jews attain a majority as against the other inhabitants of this land or not, since the question of a majority in this country should in no way be linked with any advantages or privileges.[103]

The leading figures in Brit Shalom, although sharing this general orientation, were not wholly of one mind. Ruppin, who had taken the main initiative in its founding but sought to launch a debate rather than a political offensive, had withdrawn his participation by the end of 1931. He had found himself to be at odds with other members who, in search of compromise with Arab claims, were willing to acquiesce in the condition that the Jews agree to remain a minority in Palestine. This implied not only renunciation of intentions ultimately to form a Jewish state but also voluntary limitation of Jewish immigration to Palestine (a roof of 40 percent Jews was mooted in discussions with various Arab leaders). During 1933, Brit Shalom dissolved owing to the desertion of many of its members and its chronic lack of funds.

The underlying impulse that had animated Brit Shalom did not, however, die out. It found continuous expression in a series of successor groups constituted by varying combinations and alliances of like-minded Zionists. Kedma Mizraha (Forward to the East), which functioned actively from 1936 to 1938, included most former Brit Shalom members (Ruppin was one of the exceptions), with the addition of a number of veteran Sephardi Jews in Palestine. The association's declared aims were fostering "knowledge of the East, making cultural, social and economic ties with the nations of the East, and distributing correct information on the work of the Jewish people in Palestine."[104] But its membership covered a political spectrum too broad to permit full agreement on a solution for the Palestine problem. It was superseded by the League for Jewish-Arab Rapprochement and Cooperation founded in early 1939 by persons formerly active in Brit Shalom and Kedma Mizraha in cooperation with others associated with the Socialist parties Ha-shomer Ha-tzair, Left Poalei Zion, and Mapai. It also had the participation of some members of the Aliya Hadasha (New *Aliya*) group (comprising progressive-minded General Zionists who had come from Germany) and even some General Zionists (Group B). In reaction to the wartime Biltmore Conference of Zionists in 1942, (so called after the hotel venue in New York), which for the first time openly called for the transformation of Palestine into a "Jewish commonwealth," Ha-shomer Ha-tzair and Left Poalei Zion formally joined the League. It propagated the alternative policy of a binational Palestine. An overlapping but smaller group, known as the Ihud (Union Association), was formed in 1942 on the initiative of Judah Magnes.[105] It included Martin Buber, Ernst Simon, and other persons most of whom were concurrently associated with the League. The Ihud advocated an Arab-Jewish binational state in a self-governing and undivided Palestine, based on equal political rights for the two peoples of Palestine. Its activities ceased after the outbreak of the war of 1948 and Magnes's death in the same year but were revived in the 1950s by "Rabbi" Benjamin. Its journal, *Ner* (Candle), continued publication until 1964, thereby carrying the small flame of Brit Shalom's moral-political tradition into the era of Jewish statehood.

Throughout the Mandate period, Judah Magnes was a key figure within this tradition of thought, although he had not been a formal member of Brit Shalom.[106] Magnes was American-born and ordained as a rabbi in 1900 by Reform Judaism's Hebrew Union College, whose atmosphere was inhospitable to Zionism. Yet Magnes formed a firm commitment to Zionism while studying toward a doctorate from 1900 to 1902 in Berlin and Heidelberg. Back in New York he served as secretary of the Federation of American Zionists from 1905 to 1908 and settled in Palestine in 1922, an extraordinary act for an American-born Zionist. Magnes was closely associated with the founding of the Hebrew University in Jerusalem, becoming its chancellor in 1925. When the administration was restructured in 1935, he became its president, a position he occupied until his death in 1948.

Magnes was the quintessential dissenter. He was a Reform rabbi but tended to a conservative outlook. Although regarding himself as a disciple of the Ahad Ha'am school of Zionism, he in fact diverged from Ahad Ha'am's views in three important respects. First, the deeply religious underpinning of his Zionism stood in contrast with Ahad Ha'am's essential secularism. Second, his confidence in the viability of Jewish life in the Diaspora independently of the existence of a cultural center in Zion, exceeded that of Ahad Ha'am. Indeed, although Magnes never actually subscribed to Dubnow's advocacy of Jewish cultural autonomy in the Diaspora as an alternative to Zionism, his refusal to "negate the Diaspora" placed him closer to Dubnow than to Ahad Ha'am in that respect. "The despair theory of Zionism does not appeal to me," he wrote to Chaim Weizmann in 1914, "I have not despaired of the Jewish people and I believe in its eternity even without Palestine." He did, of course, believe that "with Palestine the people will live better and develop its culture more hopefully and with more achievements," but his operative conclusion was: "We must help one another to be Jews and live as Jews, be it here or there."[107] Third, his rejection of violence and self-declaration as a pacifist during the First World War had no parallel in Ahad Ha'am's outlook, nor did his consequent disparagement of the Balfour Declaration as an imperialist action unworthy of serving as the basis for the Zionist enterprise.[108]

The most acute expression of Magnes's maverick quality, however, was the internal resistance he offered to the mainstream of Jewish nationalist ideology and praxis. For Magnes was a cultural rather than a political nationalist, that is to say, one who affirmed the ethnicist aspects of nationalism but recoiled from their political translation into the demand for a state exclusively congruent with a single nation. "Very often a nation is confused or made synonymous with a political State and with a continuous territory," he complained, "but it is just this idea of nationality which we wish to combat from the beginning."[109] In the final analysis, Magnes placed a higher value on maintaining the moral purity of Zionism and the congruence of its ends and means than on attainment of sovereign statehood. It was his consistent opinion that "if we cannot find ways of peace and understanding . . . our whole enterprise is not worthwhile."[110] Hence, Arab-Zionist agreement was a necessary precondition for a worthwhile Zionism. In practice this translated into willingness to compromise with Arab claims over Palestine by suggesting a binational constitutional dispensation and agreeing to some limitation of Jewish immigration.

All of this did not signify that Magnes denied the validity of Jewish right to Eretz Israel, but it did mean that realization of this right by unworthy means was tantamount to its moral disqualification. His underlying assumptions determined his version of the Jewish case. Thus, consistent with his pacifist premises, Magnes did not focus on historical rights; they were, after all, ultimately derived from conquest, a morally unacceptable source. By the same token, he belittled the significance of the Balfour Declaration, agreeing in this respect with Gandhi's view that "the mandate has no sanction but that of the last war."[111] Recognizing that the Jewish historical connection to Eretz Israel was counterbalanced by the "natural rights" of the Palestinian Arabs, he shifted the focus to the principle of self-determination applied universally. "If self-determination be a true principle for other peoples, it is just as true for the Jewish people," he wrote in his letter to Gandhi. But then this principle applied as much to the Palestinian Arabs as to the Jews. Hence, the solution required mutual compromise—a binational dispensation that would provide a meaningful, though less than maximal measure of self-determination for Palestinian Jews and Arabs alike.

Magnes's affirmation of Jewish life in the Diaspora was another underlying assumption that colored his particular interpretation of Jewish rights. Like Buber, he portrayed Jewish existential need less in terms of physical distress than in respect of the Jews' need for "a spiritual and intellectual center." In his exposition to Gandhi he allowed that the Jews could possibly exist without a spiritual center, as their history until that time showed,

but they have never ceased experiencing the deep need for such a Center and of trying to establish it in Palestine on innumerable occasions. Such a spiritual and religious Center must, for the Jewish people, take on the qualities of a National Home. The Jewish people are not like the Catholic Church . . . Judaism is peculiar in this, that it derives its final authority out of the life . . . of ordinary everyday, hard-working human beings.[112]

In the final analysis, Magnes's exposition, like Buber's, was predicated on the assumed universal validity of the biblical heritage. This allowed him to "begin with the thesis that Palestine is sui generis." It was the land of which God said, "Mine is the Land" (Exod. 19:5; Lev. 25:23). Therefore, reasoned Magnes, "Palestine belongs in a very real sense to all the nations that have come under the influence of Judaism, Christianity and Islam." Spiritually and historically, it was of too great importance to say that it belonged to any of its inhabitants. "These inhabitants are privileged trustees (and must so act)."[113] One of Magnes's most trenchant formulations of this view was made in a letter he wrote to American Jewish leader, Felix Warburg, in 1929:

Palestine does not belong to the Jews and it does not belong to the Arabs, nor to Judaism or Christianity or Islam. It belongs to all of them together; it is the Holy Land. If the Arabs want an Arab national state in Palestine, it is as much or as little to be defended as if the Jews want a Jewish national state there. We must once and for all give up the idea of a "Jewish Palestine" in the sense that a Jewish Palestine is to exclude and do away with an Arab Palestine. . . . It must be our endeavor first to convince ourselves and then to convince others that Jews and Arabs, Moslems, Christians, and Jews have each as much right there, no more and no less, than the other: equal rights and equal privileges and equal duties. That is practically quite sufficient for all purposes of the Jewish religion, and it is the sole ethical basis of our claims there. Judaism did not begin with Zionism, and if Zionism is ethically not in accord with Judaism so much the worse for Zionism.[114]

With varying nuances of emphasis, other members of Brit Shalom shared the major premises of Magnes and Buber. Thus, Ernst Simon, while not arguing as an outright pacifist, commended the virtues of a postnationalist Zionism: "The world has not yet overcome its era of force and of the state as necessity, but we [the Jews] overcame it at the latest in the year 70 of the Christian era. We turned the national disaster into the fruitful seed of a new life. Zionism is not entitled to turn the wheel of history backwards." Indeed, he went so far as to argue further that the Jews, although themselves having outgrown the need for national statehood, should recognize with understanding that the Arabs had not yet done so and did not have the same postnational state resources as did the Jews. Perhaps by serving as "a living example of a non-state people out of choice," the Jews might be able to lead the Arabs in the same direction.[115]

In dialogue with Yehezkel Kaufmann, who (as we showed in the last chapter) had tried to debunk the idea of a mere spiritual center, Simon stoutly defended what he described as the Ahad Ha'amist position. Kaufmann had asked what point there was of making such great sacrifices in order to create in Palestine a mere autonomous community, rather than a state, when there already were just such communities in various countries of the Diaspora. Why Zionism rather than Dubnowian autonomism? Simon answered that Eretz Israel was the only country in which such an autonomous Jewish community could rest upon a normal structure of settlement and self-labor and upon the Hebrew language in life and culture. Moreover, it was the only country in which the Jews "could become together with the Arabs an authentic people enjoying real equality of rights and thus not just a 'national-minority.' "[116]

Simon reasoned from first principles that both Arabs and Jews had historical right to Palestine. However, he rejected the premise that such historical right provided the moral basis for either Arab or Jew to rule over it or to claim exclusive ownership of it. "Historical right is a metaphysical category, not a political one," he asserted. "It does not oblige the Arabs but only ourselves. It is a wholly internal category of Judaism." In other words, Jewish historical right was merely a subjective factor that motivated the Jews themselves; it could not be endowed with objective validity to sanction the conversion of Palestine into a Jewish state. Furthermore, Simon added, even if it were to have validity as the moral basis for Zionist aspirations in Eretz Israel, it would forfeit its validity if "wrong ways of realizing it" were adopted.[117]

The operative program of binationalism was the common denominator of the disparate political groups constituting that tradition within Zionism that sought compromise with Arab claims. They were not, however, of one mind on the level of fundamental ideology. Neither Ha-shomer Ha-tzair nor Left Poalei Zion, nor even all members of Brit Shalom shared the religious-moral underpinning of Magnes and Buber. Their Ahad Ha'amist preference for an autonomous cultural center falling short of statehood was also a source of disagreement.

Ha-shomer Ha-tzair was the most potent of the constituent elements in the alliance that favored binationalism in the 1940s. The graduates of this idealistic youth movement, who produced a network of vibrant kibbutz communes, had taken a sharp turn toward politicization on Marxist-materialist lines in the late 1920s.[118] Less formidable politically but equally intense ideologically was the Left Poalei Zion. As we have seen, it sought acceptance into the third Socialist International (the Comintern) and tended to dissociate itself from the "bourgeois" Zionist Organization (remaining outside it until the Zionist congress of 1939).[119] True to its Marxist materialist principles, Left Poalei Zion not only shunned religious claims of any description but also avoided the notion of historical rights. By contrast, Ha-shomer Ha-tzair's view of historical rights was much the same as that of the mainstream Labor Zionist movement. For example a statement made as late as 1947, while advocating a binational solution to the Arab-Jewish problem, included an exposition that echoed that of Berl Locker, which we discussed earlier. It quoted the Arab charge that "if the historical rights of the Jews to Palestine are upheld, a dangerous precedent is created whereby it might prove necessary to rechart the ethnographic map of the world in accordance with historical rights dating back to antiquity." In answer to this it stated:

In all the world there has been no other instance of a people demanding its historic rights to a country which, throughout its long and troubled history, was the only land in which, as a nation, it had ever been concentrated, and in which it had attained political independence. Furthermore, it creates no precedents, since the modern Assyrians, for example, are not known to be formulating any demands for the territory in Mesopotamia occupied by ancient Assyria. And, finally, there has never been a complete break in the continuity of Jewish settlement in Palestine, however limited the number of Jews in it, at any one time since their dispersal.[120]

As this shows, Ha-shomer Ha-tzair did not ignore the factor of Jewish historical connection to Eretz Israel. Yet its main emphases lay elsewhere. By its lights, whatever served working-class interests and advanced toward the ultimate classless society was ipso facto morally justified. Hence, its ideological articulation of the Jewish right to Eretz Israel rested heavily on the putative role of working-class Zionism in educating and socially liberating the Arab workers from the oppressive Arab effendi class and from Western imperialism.

To be sure, the mainstream of Socialist labor Zionism (namely, Ahdut Ha-avoda in the 1920s and Mapai thereafter) also indulged copiously in the claim that its form of Zionism was beneficial to the Arabs. However, its translation of this plea into trade union practice in the reality of Palestine was different from that advocated by Ha-shomer Ha-tzair or by Left Poalei Zion. In the 1920s, within Ahdut Ha-avoda the notion of a joint Jewish-Arab trade union had been entertained with much ambivalence. But its successor party, Mapai, abandoned the notion to all intents and purposes. At most it favored cooperation between separate Jewish and Arab unions. Ha-shomer Ha-tzair and Left Poalei Zion, each in its own way, continued to search for a relationship of workers' fraternity between Arabs and Jews that would be consonant with their Socialist principles, and on that score they found fault with the policy of mainstream labor Zionism. In the early 1930s, Ha-shomer Ha-tzair unsuccessfully called for the Histadrut to adopt a program gradually integrating Arab workers, starting with the permanent workers in the colonies and the towns, as two national divisions in a joint labor framework.[121] Left Poalei Zion followed a more extreme line, persistently calling for a completely unified labor framework devoid of national distinctions and engaging in independent labor activity in that vein outside the Histadrut.[122]

Ideology and Praxis of Ben-Gurion

The relationship between the fundamental ideological convictions that underpinned the Zionist claim to Eretz Israel, on the one hand, and the variety of operative justifications that were conjured up and juggled to serve Zionist praxis on the other is traceable in the record of many a Zionist leader. No better example may be chosen than David Ben-Gurion, undoubtedly the most important of all the labor Zionist leaders in Palestine of the 1920s and in the

Zionist Organization–Jewish Agency after his election to its executive in 1933 and to the position of chairman in 1935. It was Ben-Gurion, more than any other single Zionist leader, who led the thrust toward Jewish statehood in the 1940s. Moreover, the plenitude of personal documentary evidence that he bequeathed, thanks largely to his acute awareness of posterity, has rendered his thoughts and actions eminently accessible to historical research.[123]

Ben-Gurion was admirably representative of labor Zionism's highly moralistic self-image as an inherently just, progressive, and constructive movement: a nationalism with a human face that fused exemplary social values with national aspirations and that sought to serve the needs of its own people without being inconsiderate of those of other affected peoples. From the time of his *aliya* to Eretz Israel in 1906 until his declaration of Jewish statehood—indeed, until the end of his life in 1973—he projected this image of Zionism in a multitude of writings, speeches, and statements. Typical of his references to the rights of the Arab inhabitants of Palestine was the following, penned by him in 1918:

By no means and under no circumstances are the rights of these inhabitants to be infringed upon—it is neither desirable nor conceivable that the present inhabitants be ousted from the land. That is not the mission of Zionism. . . . The demand of the Jewish people is really nothing more than the demand of an entire nation for the right to work. However, we must remember that such rights are also possessed by the inhabitants already living in the country—and these rights must not be infringed upon. Both the vision of social justice and equality of all peoples that the Jewish people has cherished for three thousand years, and the vital interests of the Jewish people in the diaspora and even more so in Palestine, require absolutely and unconditionally that the rights and interests of the non-Jewish inhabitants of the country be guarded and honored punctiliously.[124]

On one occasion in 1928, in the context of an exposition described as a discussion between a Jewish worker of Palestine and a Russian Jewish revolutionary, he indulged himself with the following hyperbole: "According to my moral outlook we do not have the right to harm a single Arab child, even if by dint of such harm we should achieve all we desire. Our work cannot be built upon the rights of someone else." He added, however, that by the same token, "the Arabs do not have the right to deprive us of our rights."[125] As late as 1946 in his testimony before the Anglo-American Committee of Inquiry, Ben-Gurion offered the following paradigm for the Jewish case:

Our case, and I think you have just seen many such cases in Europe, is like that of the Jews who were forcibly expelled from their homes, which were then given to somebody else. Those homes changed hands and then after the Nazi defeat some Jewish owners came back and found their houses occupied. In many cases they were not allowed to return to their houses. To make it more exact, I shall put it in this way. It is a large building, the building of our family, say fifty rooms. We were expelled from the house, our family was scattered, somebody else took it away and again it changed hands many times, and then we had to come back and we found some five rooms occupied by other people, the other rooms destroyed and uninhabitable from neglect. We said to these occupants, "We do not want to remove you, please stay where you are, we are going back into the uninhabitable rooms, we will repair them." And we did repair some of them and settle there.[126]

Yet it is supremely characteristic of Ben-Gurion that at the same time, and often in the same breath, that he expressed himself in this moralistic way he also stuck rigidly to the fundamental assertion that Jews had the right to return to Zion and ultimately to become a majority there since in the *national*, as distinct from the civic, sense Eretz Israel was the inalienable homeland of the Jews alone. Ben-Gurion was, moreover, above all a man of praxis, a consummate strategist and tactician who never lost sight of his essentially nationalist, ultimate goal—Jewish sovereignty. In the final analysis, his nationalist goals overrode his vaunted moral concern for the rights of the Arab inhabitants of Palestine, just as they took precedence over his declared Socialist principles. Thus, on the labor front he consistently opposed the creation of a unitary labor union incorporating Arabs and Jews alike, advocating instead that Jewish labor should render assistance to a separate Arab labor union. Indeed, overall he favored a program of separate development for Jews and Arabs: two autonomous socioeconomic and cultural units.

Ben-Gurion's overriding Jewish nationalist goals dictated his strategy for the development of an economically sound and self-dependent Jewish society that could ultimately constitute a state with a clear Jewish majority. On the basis of these objectives, he explicitly defined "the Arab question," as it was referred to in Zionist parlance, not as an altruistic moral concern for the Arabs but wholly in terms of Jewish national needs. Indeed, he regarded the expression "the Arab question" as a misnomer; its real meaning was, in his view, nothing other than the question of how to fulfill the objectives of Zionism notwithstanding the reality of an Arab presence. The opening lines of his preface to a collection of his writings and speeches published in 1931 stated: "This anthology is dedicated to clarification of a tragic fateful question, incorrectly dubbed in Zionist discourse by the name 'the Arab question,' whose real significance is nothing other than the question of how to fulfill Zionism from the aspect of the Arab reality."[127] In an address to Brit Shalom in late 1924, Ben-Gurion explained: "For me an Arab question exists only on the basis of a Zionist stance: I want to solve in Eretz Israel the question of the Jewish people, that is, to concentrate it in Eretz Israel and make it a free people in its land. . . . First and foremost I am a Zionist . . . and only from that point on an Arab question arises."[128]

It is precisely in this respect that Ben-Gurion differed most emphatically from the views of Judah Magnes and some of the members of Brit Shalom and its successor groups. What he had in common with them was the declarative view that Arab and Jewish needs were not hopelessly irreconcilable, and in this regard both he and they differed in turn from Jabotinsky, who argued that the utter incompatibility of Arab and Jewish aspirations rendered negotiations no more than a futile exercise. But Magnes's approach derived from religious moral principles of universal, reciprocal applicability. This meant that Arab consent to Jewish actions was a moral imperative; it was a precondition for the fulfillment of Zionism as a moral movement, and to be an authentic expression of Judaism, Zionism had to pass the test of morality. It also meant a vision of Eretz Israel as a Jewish spiritual center of qualitative excellence; a vision not dependent on maximal concentration of world Jewry in Palestine. Magnes's conception of Jewish and Arab rights thus led him to seek negotiated compromise, which inevitably boiled down to acceptance of the irreducible demand of the Arabs that their majority status be guaranteed in perpetuum. Ben-Gurion's approach, in contrast, rested on the equally irreducible baseline of Jewish right to find full national refuge and self-fulfillment in Eretz Israel. This meant that Arab agreement to Jewish aspirations, while desirable, was not, as Magnes posited, a moral precondition for Jewish actions.

It also followed that agreement to perpetual minority status in Palestine would be tantamount to self-destruction of Zionism. As Ben-Gurion incisively told Magnes in 1935: "The difference between me and you is that you are ready to sacrifice immigration for peace, while I am not, though peace is dear to me."[129] On the grounds that the Jewish right to national fulfillment in Eretz Israel exceeded, rather than merely equaled, that of the Arabs, he adamantly rejected not only the operative implications of Brit Shalom's binationalist proposals but the very premises upon which they rested:

If your formula posits that Eretz Israel is of equal value for both Jews and Arabs, then you are missing the point and distorting the truth. Eretz Israel is not the same thing for the Jewish and Arab peoples. The Arab nation possesses many extensive countries, the area of which in Asia alone amounts to a third of that of all Europe. The economic, cultural and national existence of the Arab nation, its independence and sovereign existence is not connected with or dependent upon Eretz Israel. . . . This is not the case with regard to the Jewish nation. For the entire Jewish nation throughout its generations and dispersions this has been the one and only country with which its historic fate and destiny as a nation has been bound up. In this country alone can it revive and maintain its independent life, its national existence and unique culture. Only here can it establish its independence and sovereign liberty. And anyone who blurs this truth risks the soul of the nation. It is our duty to guard the rights and equality of our Arab neighbors, but we are deceiving ourselves if we say that Eretz Israel has the same significance for the Arab nation as it has for the Jewish nation. If the idea of bi-nationality means this, then it is nothing but a distortion of the truth and emasculation of the objective. Instead of this erroneous slogan I say: *Palestine is destined for the Jewish nation and for the Arabs domiciled there.* [Emphasis added.][130]

Ben-Gurion was willing to negotiate with Arabs, both of Palestine and beyond it, on phased progress toward Jewish majority status, to provide guarantees for Arab civic rights and cultural autonomy, and to ameliorate their sense of national deprivation by means of a federative link with a wider regional Arab political framework. But he absolutely rejected any Arab claim that Palestine belonged exclusively, in a national sense, either to its Arab inhabitants or to the pan-Arab nation and that they therefore were entitled to limit the Jews to perpetual minority status. It was on these premises that he conducted negotiations in the course of the 1930s, especially from 1934 through 1936, with a variety of Arab political personalities.

Given these absolutely fundamental ideological positions, many questions arise in attempting to explain Ben-Gurion's operative ideological declarations. Were his statements during the 1920s—so characteristic of the mainstream labor movement—that the progress of socialism would pave the way to Jewish-Arab accord in Palestine a result of naïveté? Were the repeated attributions of Arab hostility not to their burgeoning nationalism but rather to the interests of the effendi landowner class or to religious incitement or to criminal gang rioting a case of ideological self-delusion? That is, were they an ideological mechanism to cope with guilty conscience or to avert the cognitive dissonance that might result from even tacit recognition of an Arab national right to sovereignty over Palestine? Were Ben-Gurion's repeatedly declared opinions that Jewish and Arab needs were compatible and his initiation of negotiations in the early 1930s rooted in sincere conviction? Or were these merely tactical devices aimed at gaining time for the advancement of Zionist goals and at creating a posture of reasonableness in British eyes?

It may be beyond the capacity of the historian to answer these questions definitively. Some light may be thrown on the subject, however, by comparing what Ben-Gurion said in negotiations with Arab leaders with his expositions to fellow Zionists, as well as by comparing his public expositions with his private reflections and utterances. It certainly is evident that when he conducted his negotiations with Arab personages he did so frankly on the explicit premises that Jews were returning to Eretz Israel as of right and not by dint of British or Arab favor and that they were entitled to become a majority and to form a national state in the fullness of time. When he met with Awni Abd el-Hadi, the Istiqlal party leader in July 1934, he made the point that for the Jews "this land was everything and there was nothing else. For the Arabs, Palestine was only a small portion of the large and numerous Arab countries." Not at all obscuring the intention of the Jews to become the majority in Palestine, he tried to assuage his interlocutor with the thought that the Arabs would always remain a majority in their Middle Eastern territory as a whole. He compared their situation to that of the English minority in Scotland, who "were not a minority, because they were part of the United Kingdom, where they constituted a majority." "For the Jewish people," submitted Ben-Gurion, "it was essential that they be the majority, as otherwise they would not be independent." But the Arabs could never turn into a minority in the broader regional context.[131]

The bedrock premise upon which Ben-Gurion sought to rest all of his negotiations with Arab leaders was that what was at stake was not a local conflict between the Jews and the Arabs currently situated in Palestine but one between the entire Jewish nation dispersed worldwide and the entire Arab nation, spread over the whole Middle East and beyond it. On this premise he labored, with dubious success, to get Mussa al-Alami's agreement to the proposition that "the complete realization of the aspirations of the Jewish people in Palestine did not conflict with those of the Arab people. On the contrary, the two complemented one another; cooperation between the two peoples would be of benefit both to Palestine and to the other Arab states.[132]

In this respect there was no disparity between what Ben-Gurion told the Arab leaders with whom he met and what he repeatedly declared to his Zionist comrades. For example, in January 1930 at the merger convention of Ahdut Ha-avoda and Ha-poel Ha-tzair, which formed Mapai, he reiterated his premise that the baseline for "wrestling with the Arab question" was "the historic necessity that the masses of Israel settle in this land and here become a nation that is its own master." On that firm ground the Arab people had to be approached

not with words of falsehood and deceit, not with any concealment of our Zionist aspirations, but with words of truth and peace. We will put it clearly: come what may, we will not budge from here. No attack or obstruction will weaken the efforts of the Jewish people to settle once again in its land. . . . But we recognize your needs, and we know of your nationalist aspirations. . . . We wish to find a way to further our common interests as sons of one homeland. Not only shall we not harm you and you not harm us, but we shall help each other and work together—Is there no hope that these words of ours will be heard, even if not immediately?[133]

In a similar vein, at Mapai's first conference in late 1930, he declared that the first step along the path to understanding was to tell the Arab nation the whole truth, namely, that the Jewish nation numbering seventeen million, "by virtue of its historic will to live and survive aspires—is forced to aspire—to assembling the maximum possible number of its members in Palestine, in order to become an independent nation there." He submitted that only on the basis of Arab acceptance of this fact would understanding be possible but added that it was equally necessary for the Jews to recognize another fact, no matter how discomforting: "that for hundreds of years large numbers of Arabs have been living in Palestine . . . and that Palestine is their country, where they want to continue living in the future." "As inhabitants of this country, the Arabs have every right to benefit from Palestine," he declared, "but they do not have the right, as do owners of private property, to deny us the benefits of the country."[134]

These are typical examples of Ben-Gurion's public expositions expressing the precedence of Jewish national right over Arab rights. The record of his private reflections and utterances indicates that his characterization of the rival Arab entity was determined by conscious tactical considerations rather than by naïveté or ideological self-delusion.[135] Already well before the end of Turkish rule over Palestine, he had become aware of the local Arab population's implacable hostility to Zionism. In mid-1922, after experiencing a commercial strike organized by the Muslim Executive Council, he recorded the impression that "we are dealing here with a national movement." When more potent Arab disturbances occurred in 1929, the proven ability of its fomentors to mobilize the masses confirmed his recognition that the *yishuv* was confronting an Arab national political movement.[136]

Yet he composed a memorandum to the Socialist International concerning those disturbances in which he portrayed the violence as the work of vandals incited by religious fanatics and the effendis who feared the liberating effects of the Jewish example on the exploited fellahin.[137] This statement adhered to the conventional labor Zionist line that refused to acknowledge the existence of a national movement of Palestinian Arabs. It did not regard the effendi class as potential partners for negotiation but rather awaited the day when Arab peasants and workers would recognize that the effendis, and not the Zionists, were the cause of their woes.

As we have noted earlier, however, when Ben-Gurion reached the helm of the Zionist Organization in the early 1930s, he diverged from this line. He made efforts to negotiate with Arab leaders of the effendi class. But he changed his tactics in the wake of the Arab revolt that erupted in 1936. The evidence indicates that from that time onward he formed the increasingly firmer conviction that only the creation of accomplished facts and the gaining of deterrent strength would drive the Arabs to some form of understanding and indeed that a confrontation of might between the Arab national movement and Zionism was unavoidable. To be sure, he did not cease making negotiation soundings with Arab leaders, but there can be little doubt that he did so essentially with an eye to British governmental and public opinion. He said as much to his party's Central Committee on April 7, 1936: "The willingness of Jews to meet with Arabs and the refusal of the Arabs . . . is a weapon in our hands—that is, if the English know that the Jews want to talk with the Arabs, and the Arabs refuse. This is a card in our hand. . . . I don't want to forfeit this strategically important position."[138]

There is abundant evidence that Ben-Gurion's acceptance of the partition of Palestine proposed by the Peel Commission in 1937, aborted by the British government in 1938, and finally adopted by the United Nations in 1947 (on the basis of which the State of Israel declared its independence in 1948), marked a change in strategy for attainment of his unflinchingly fixed national objectives, rather than an embrace of abstract principles of just compromise.[139] Whereas until that time the strategy of the Zionist leadership of all ideological stripes had been first to become a majority in Palestine under the British mandatory regime and then to advance toward some form of sovereignty, Ben-Gurion (and Weizmann, for that matter) now advocated a strategic reversal of the order. It was now to become acceptance of statehood, albeit in a truncated area, which would then permit unlimited immigration and the equalling or even outnumbering of the Arab population in Palestine as a whole. This would then create a new dynamic in which Jewish national strength and resources might permit changes to the further advantage of Zionism.

Yet throughout the evolution of Ben-Gurion's strategic thinking and notwithstanding all his resourceful tactical twists and turns, his fundamental ideological position on Jewish and Arab rights remained remarkably consistent. It runs like a golden thread throughout his innumerable statements and formulations uttered both publicly and privately. One of the most succinct expressions of this may be found in his composition of a series of "Postulates for the Formulation of a Constitutional Regime in Eretz Israel" in 1929, a document that served as the basis for his strategy, and for the attendant negotiations he initiated with Arab leaders, between 1929 and the partition proposal of 1937. It stated categorically that "the present residents of the land alone do not possess the right of ownership and rule over the land" but gave the assurance that "all the inhabitants of the land without exception [would] enjoy full civic rights both as individuals and collectively." It laid down his postulates that "Eretz Israel is destined for the Jewish people and for the Arabs domiciled in it" and that "the right of the Hebrew nation is not conditional upon external agreement and does not depend upon the will of others." He averred that Jewish right to Eretz Israel

emanates from the unbroken connection of the Hebrew nation with its historic homeland, from the right of the Jewish people to independence and national revival in equal measure to that enjoyed by all other peoples, from the situation of the Jewish people in the exile as a minority deprived of a territorial base and dependent on the will of others, from the emigration needs of millions of Jews, from the depopulated state of Eretz Israel, from the possibilities of settlement and fructification of its soil and unexploited natural resources, from the Jewish settlement project in the country in recent generations.[140]

All of the factors mentioned in this document entered into Ben-Gurion's representation of the Jewish claim, but given the existence of Arab counterclaims, his case, like that of Jabotinsky, appealed in the final resort to the utilitarian moral principle. In his evidence to the United Nations Committee on Palestine of 1947 he summed it up thus:

One cannot ignore the fact that both communities living in Palestine are merely fragments of larger communities living outside—that both of them belong to these larger units and that their fates are inextricably bound up with the larger units. By depriving the Jews in Palestine of a national home, by preventing them from becoming a majority and attaining statehood, you are depriving not only the 600,000 Jews who are here, but also the millions of Jews who are still left in the world, of independence and statehood. In no other place can they have the desire to attain, nor the prospect of attaining, nationhood. In depriving the million Arabs of the same prospect, you do not affect the status of the Arab race at all. An Arab minority in a Jewish State would mean that a certain number of individual Arabs would not enjoy the privilege of Arab statehood, but would in no way diminish the independence and position of the free Arab race. The Arab minority in Palestine, being surrounded by Arab States, would remain safe in national association with its race. But a Jewish minority in an Arab state, even with the most ideal paper guarantee, would mean the final extinction of Jewish hope, not in Palestine alone, but for the entire Jewish people, for national equality and independence, with all the disastrous consequences so familiar in Jewish history. *The conscience of humanity ought to weigh this: where is the balance of justice, where is the greater need, where is the greater peril, where is the lesser evil and where is the lesser injustice?* [Emphasis added.][141]

Jewish Right and Partition

Having focused attention first on the two extremes of the Zionist ideological spectrum and then on the key figure effectively at the helm of Zionist praxis in the drive toward statehood, one ought not to overlook the fact that it was Chaim Weizmann rather than any of those we have discussed who was the preeminent spokesman of the Zionist movement in the international forum. The relationship between Weizmann and Jabotinsky was, of course, one of chronically bitter confrontation throughout the 1920s and 1930s. As for the radical Right and its emanations in the form of the IZL and the Lehi, they were anathema to Weizmann. The Brit Shalom tradition, on the other extreme, was arguably less incompatible with Weizmann's ideological orientation. For a short period around 1931 he appeared to veer quite closely to the operative remedies suggested by Brit Shalom.[142] Nevertheless, he never shared its fundamental ideological orientation insofar as it made the Zionist project morally conditional upon Arab acquiescence. With Ben-Gurion, Weizmann was in delicate political alliance for most of the period, but they too clashed, at times acutely, in the 1940s.[143]

Notwithstanding the differences in temperament, style, and policies between Weizmann and Ben-Gurion and the deeper ideological fissure that divided both of them from Jabotinsky and his Revisionist Zionism, they were all at one in articulating existential need and the utilitarian moral principle as the ultimate basis for the Jewish right to national self-determination in Eretz Israel and for its precedence over the claims of the Arabs. Whenever Weizmann had occasion to present the Jewish case, he did so in terms almost identical to those we have cited from the statements of Jabotinsky and Ben-Gurion. For example, to the Anglo-American Committee of Inquiry of 1946 he submitted:

I recognize fully that what I ask for will meet with considerable opposition on the part of the Arabs, . . . but there is no counsel of perfection in this world, and there is no absolute justice in this world. What you are trying to perform, and what we are all trying to do in our small way, is just rough human justice. I think the decision which I should like this committee to take, if I dare say this, would be to move on the line of least injustice. . . . I say there may be some slight injustice politically if Palestine is made a Jewish State, but individually the Arabs will not suffer . . . economically, culturally, religiously, the Arabs will not be affected. . . . We know what it is to be a minority. . . . The Arabs have a perfect guarantee; whatever Palestine may be, it will only be an island in an Arab sea . . . the position of the Arabs as a people is secure. Their national sentiments can find full expression in Damascus and in Cairo and in Baghdad, and in all the great countries which will, I hope, some day build up an Arab civilization which will equal the ancient glories of their people. Palestine is to the Jews what Baghdad, Cairo and Damascus all rolled together are to the Arabs, and I think *the line of least injustice demands that we should be given our chance.* [Emphasis added.][144]

Agreement on this ideological postulate was, however, one thing; operative policies were another. With the advantage of historical hindsight it may be said that of all the points of divergence and convergence that marked the internal debates over Zionist policy options, the most fateful concerned the proposal that Palestine be partitioned between Jews and Arabs. This option won the support of Weizmann and Ben-Gurion when it was first officially tabled in 1937 by the Peel Commission and again in the second half of the 1940s. On the other side it was opposed not only by Jabotinsky—and even more vehemently by the radical Right—but also by adherents of the Brit Shalom tradition. Their reasons, of course, were quite opposite. The Revisionist Right was adamant that all of Eretz Israel (including even Trans-Jordan) become a uninational Jewish state with civic and cultural minority rights for its Arab inhabitants, whereas those who purveyed the Brit Shalom tradition favored a unitary framework with a binational polity catering equally to Arab and Jewish national needs.

Yet partition in itself did not signify a moral imperative for Weizmann anymore than it did for Ben-Gurion, whose strategic adoption of the idea in 1937 we discussed earlier. Both settled for partition, not as a compromise for the sake of equitable justice but rather out of enlightened national self-interest. They perceived it, realistically and pragmatically, as the least disadvantageous of all the options available in the prevailing political circumstances.[145] To the United Nations Committee on Palestine of 1947, Weizmann stated:

We realize that we cannot have the whole of Palestine. God made a promise: Palestine to the Jews. It is up to the Almighty to keep His promise in His own time. Our business is to do what we can in a very imperfect human way. . . . If I, personally, came to the conclusion that partition is the best, I did so by a process of elimination. I know that one speaks of a bi-national state; of a sort of federal solution; . . . I do not think that this has the advantages of partition, which is final, definite and crystallized. Anything that leaves an uncertainty will leave room for pulling by the two forces. The Jews will want to get something better. The Arabs will want to push us out of what we have. Therefore I believe, although partition means a sort of Solomon's judgment, it is in the circumstances perhaps the better.[146]

Moreover, their acceptance of partition was conditional on the partition plan's providing a viable state primarily for the satisfaction of the Jewish national need. "The part of Palestine which would remain after partition," Weizmann insisted, "must be something in which Jews could live and into which we could bring a million and a half people in a comparatively short time." The mitigation of whatever harm was being caused to the national aspirations of the Arabs of Palestine was implicitly a secondary consideration. The advantages Weizmann chose to emphasize in his evidence to the commission were only two: "It is final, and it helps to dispel some of the fears of our Arab friends."

In other words, even when accepting the partition proposal the fundamental ideological position, held in common by Weizmann and Ben-Gurion, no less than by Jabotinsky, remained firmly predicated on the premise that in the *national* sense (as distinct from the civic sense) Eretz Israel belonged exclusively to the Jewish people. Had Eretz Israel been indivisible, like the proverbial babe brought before King Solomon, it would have had to become a Jewish state in its entirety. Since a territory is in fact divisible and since political realism dictated a territorial compromise, the Zionist leadership in 1946–1947 opted for a Jewish state in part of Eretz Israel. Having so opted, the ideological posture of Zionism was considerably enhanced in the international forum. It could be, and was, projected for world public opinion as a just compromise that provided a territorial framework for the national self-determination not solely of the Jews but also of the Palestinian segment of the Arab nation, which already had a number of states extending over vast territories. If Jewish statehood in Eretz Israel as a whole was the line of least injustice, how much more so was Jewish statehood in only a part of Eretz Israel.

Afterword

———◆———

T
HIS STUDY HAS sought to examine the ideology of Zionism in a
dual context, as an emanation of the modernization of the Jews and as
a phenomenon belonging to the genre nationalism. As such, it has
accounted for the genesis of the nationalist ideology that came to be known as
Zionism by approximately the mid-1890s in terms of the remarkably enduring
ethnic roots of Jewish ethnicity in Europe, notwithstanding modernization—to
be sure, an ethnicity whose most obvious, although not sole, attribute was the
Jewish religion. It has identified Zionism as manifestly a case of ethnic
nationalism sparked by a convergence in the early 1880s of ideas generated
within distinguishable categories of social carriers.

The seminal and most significant of these social carriers was that part of the
Jewish intelligentsia that not only was rooted in the objective reality of ongoing
Jewish ethnicity but also subjectively displayed an ingrained ethnicism. In the
course of the nineteenth century, this ethnicist section of the Jewish intelligentsia
resisted the tendency of another section, labeled here "integrationists." Aspiring
to incorporation with the national majority, they either were indifferent to the
fact of birth into a group stamped by the marks of ethnicity or consciously
endeavored to reduce the salience of those marks and to give the group the
appearance of a purely religious denomination.

The ethnicist intelligentsia, although also seeking civic and cultural integration into the national majority in whichever country it was domiciled, treasured
the historically evolved attributes of the Jewish *ethnie*—its religiocultural
heritage, the Hebrew language, and its association (at least symbolic) with its
particular territory, Zion. It was the crisis resulting from the breakdown of the
premodern integral identity of the Jews as an alien but largely autonomous
entity in European societies that generated this modern ethnicism. The ethnicist
intelligentsia was avidly in search of a cultural synthesis that would preserve
Jewishness while at the same time facilitating integration into the majority
society; a modernized interpretation of the age-old Jewish cultural heritage that
would reintegrate and sustain the identity of the Jew in modern times.

This phenomenon does not qualify for description as a nationalist ideology because it did not imply that it was necessary to attain congruence between the Jewish *ethnie* and a sovereign polity of Jews. But the nationalist potentiality that inhered in it became evident in sporadic eruptions of ideas that were not only unmistakably nationalist in character but were even proto-Zionist, in the sense that return of Jews to Zion and its restoration to the Jews was advocated. With historical hindsight the most striking and fully articulated of these eruptions were the views advocated by Moses Hess. A parallel, more traditionalist-rooted eruption of proto-Zionist views was that of Josef Natonek, who lived in Hungary. But their contemporary impact was very slight even though both associated themselves in the 1860s with a short-lived society for the encouragement of practical settlement of Eretz Israel. One might say that they represent historical but not historic facts.

It was only in eastern Europe, mainly in multinational czarist Russia, where the objective reality of distinctive Jewish ethnicity remained the dominant characteristic of the Jewish population's status and condition, that the ethnicist intelligentsia carried the most weight. There it assumed the form of an enlightened cultural transformation (the *haskala*) that elevated the value of the Hebrew language as its appropriate medium. In that ambience, by the 1870s an articulation of ethnicist ideology was identifiable, most clearly in the thought of Peretz Smolenskin, which justifies the appellation "nationalism" qualified only by the epithet "cultural." This cultural nationalism rejected the west-central European program of integration and its ancillary, Reform Judaism, and already posited that the Jews (or at least that critical mass of them concentrated in eastern Europe) merited recognition as a nation. It fell short of being unqualifiedly nationalist only insofar as it did not postulate the necessity for attaining congruity between the nation and a territorial polity. It would be anachronistic to call it Zionist, not only for the formal semantic reason that the term was not yet in vogue but also for the substantive reason that it did not specifically advocate return by Jews to Zion and restoration of Zion to the Jews as an essential ingredient of its nationalist program. Nevertheless, its exponents were precisely that stratum of intelligentsia that came to constitute the heart and core of an Eretz Israel–oriented nationalist ideology. This developed in the Hibbat Zion movement after 1880 and finally matured as Zionism by the mid-1890s.

However, the spark that set off the national movement was the convergence between this ethnicist core and a part of the integrationist intelligentsia that changed its ideological orientation. There were a few such cases by the late 1870s—in Russia, Eliezer Ben-Yehuda was one example—but after 1881 the phenomenon became widespread throughout Europe. Theodor Herzl and Max Nordau were the prototypes of such a turning to the new national ideology. Therein lay the role of antisemitism in generating Zionism. Although this modern racist transmutation of age-old Jew hatred, which emerged largely in reaction to the very emancipation of the Jews, was already taken into account by the ethnicist intelligentsia, it had never been the crucial factor in their motivations. Not so the motivations of the former integrationists. Clearly, they were driven toward Jewish national identification by the impediments, frustrations, and injuries to their dignity experienced personally as individuals or as part of the collective Jewish entity.

The Eretz Israel–oriented national movement, known after 1880 as Hibbat Zion and after the mid-1890s as Zionism, was further augmented by a third convergence: that effected by a segment of orthodox rabbis and their following of religious Jews primarily concentrated in the countries of eastern Europe. These drew upon a tradition of messianic interpretation, as well as on programs for resettlement of Eretz Israel that had first been formulated around the middle of the nineteenth century by a small coterie of traditionalist rabbis, the most notable of whom where Alkalai and Kalischer. It has here been argued that the traditionalists had a conceptual corridor of their own to Jewish nationalism. But based as it was on a belief in the divinely ordained origins and destiny of the Jews, the rabbinical stratum that favored resettlement of Zion experienced great difficulty in accommodating the modern conception of the nation as an "imagined" entity more comprehensive than the body of religious Jews.

The resulting modus vivendi between the secularists and the religious Zionists harbored an enduring inner tension. It was precisely the orthodox religious Zionists' sense of national responsibility that impelled them to seek ways of ensuring, if not imposing, a religious character on Zionism as a movement and on the *yishuv* as its practical project. This tendency was both a reaction to and in turn a stimulator of the ever-growing secularized intelligentsia. The latter were the successor generations of Jewish ethnicists, and their seminal intellect was Ahad Ha'am. They were themselves perennially engaged in an inner intellectual ferment concerning the relationship between their Jewish traditionalist roots and their absorption of European cultural modes and intellectual trends. This study has focused on the inner tension between what has here been termed the normative mode of secularized identity espoused by Ahad Ha'am, on the one hand, and the existential or laissez-faire mode espoused by a variety of Zionist intelligentsia on the other hand. Illustrative of this tension in Palestine as early as 1910 was the controversy sparked by the views of Haim Yosef Brenner. The reductio ad absurdum spawned by extreme secularization, conflated with certain right-wing trends in Zionism, was the peripheral "Canaanite" heresy that surfaced briefly in the 1940s. Although the latter has proved to be a passing aberration, the fundamental tensions between the normative and the laissez-faire modes of secular Zionism endure until the present time.

The initial stage of diversification of Zionist ideology has been traced in this volume largely as an emanation of the threefold convergence that sparked the nationalist movement. The ethnicist intelligentsia, although ambivalent in relation to its traditional cultural sources, was unequivocally committed to an organic conception of Jewish nationalism. But that part of the integrationist intelligentsia, of which Theodor Herzl was the prototype, having rebounded from its integrationist intentions, formulated an essentially functional conception of Zionism. This distinction became blurred with the passage of time. The plain Zionists, who became General Zionists by the late 1930s, represented a synthesis of both approaches. As for the national-religious rabbinical stratum, while adjusting to the modern conception of the nation, it remained in tension with the secularized elements in the Zionist Organization. At the same time it was also engaged in an ongoing ideological conflict with the large segment of orthodoxy that remained opposed to Zionism but with whom it still shared the same orthodox religious universe of discourse.

Political diversification of the Zionist ideology through the incorporation of ancillary isms began to be evident at the turn of the century. However, it was mainly during the period of the British mandate over Palestine—the period of "the Jewish National Home"—that the political diversification of Zionist ideology was intensified, primarily on issues of policy vis-à-vis the mandate's administration and over ways and means of developing the *yishuv*. As a diasporic nationalism dispersed over many different countries, it is not surprising that its intelligentsia absorbed a rich variety of sociopolitical ideologies. In accord with the diversified ideological milieus to which Zionists were exposed in different places and at different times, they were impelled to formulate ideological syntheses. The most potent of these was that relating to socialism. By virtue of the formative role that labor Zionists of various ideological hues played in the development of the *yishuv*, its leaders attained virtual hegemony over the entire Zionist movement by the mid-1930s. This study has focused on the fundamental nationalist essence of Zionist ideology. In the final analysis national purposes overrode other ideological proclivities, whether Socialist, liberal, conservative (or even Fascist for a tiny group of Revisionist Zionists that evinced such a tendency). Yet, given the all too human reality of ideological inconsistencies and ambiguities, there is no sound reason to doubt the often passionate conviction of the adherents of a Socialist world outlook, in particular, that they were forging a genuine synthesis of their nationalist and Socialist values.

Rather more amorphous was the synthesis of nationalism with liberal political and social values that initially characterized the main body of Zionists. These liberal values were mainly transposed from the emancipationist milieu that had earlier nurtured many of the integrationist Jewish intelligentsia in Europe. By and large, it was a European type of liberalism that, especially in the interwar period, incorporated ideas of social reform and therefore was able to find common ground with at least some positions on the wide spectrum of labor Zionism. However, that broad body of plain Zionists who became General

Zionists never explicitly regarded itself as the Liberal party of Zionism. Its self-image was essentially that of the guardians of the primacy of nationalist objectives and exponents of the middle way, unadulterated by other isms.

The liberal inheritance of the Zionist intelligentsia was at its most problematic in the Revisionist Zionist movement created by Jabotinsky after 1925. Jabotinsky emerged out of a liberal ideological background (in the nineteenth-century Russian mold) that combined strains of both the organic and the functional conceptions of Jewish nationalism. Diverging initially from the Weizmann-led executive of the Zionist Organization on questions of operative policy, in the mid-1920s he proceeded to infuse the Betar youth organization and Revisionist Zionism that he founded with an integral nationalist ideology. It borrowed symbols and ideas from contemporary conservative, authoritarian, and in some respects also Fascist, parties of contemporary Europe. Jabotinsky himself never abandoned all liberal restraints, but by the late 1930s the distinctly nonliberal ideological strains had gained the upper hand in Revisionist Zionism.

As is all too evident to this very day, in the final analysis the most enduring and intractable of all the problems with which Zionism had to cope was the resistance issuing from the Arab population of Palestine, a problem at the same time inseparable from relations with the British government, which held the mandate to rule Palestine. Policy differences over strategy and tactics in regard to the Arab question compounded all the social-policy issues that divided the various Zionist parties. Skirting these operative issues, the present study has attempted to extrapolate the fundamental ideological question as to what, in the first instance, constituted the right of Jews to seek national self-determination in Palestine. It has revealed far greater unanimity than might appear to be the case in the light of the sharp policy differences that punctuate the history of the Zionist movement. The common denominator extending across the whole spectrum of Zionist ideologies was that which has here been described as the plea for recognition of the greater existential need of the Jews and the attendant appeal to a "utilitarian" moral principle of following "the line of least injustice" in the circumstances. Yet the actual resolution of the tragic clash between Jewish and Palestinian nationalist claims is still the most critical of all the questions facing the State of Israel as the embodiment of the Zionist enterprise.

This study has not pretended to encompass the totality of Zionism's phenomenal impact on the modern history and contemporary condition of the Jews. It has not been able to exhaust the ramifications of Zionism even in the ideological sphere on which it has focused its attention. In particular, the impact of varying societal environments in different countries has not been considered at all. Such variables undoubtedly affected the ideological character of Zionism in ways that, as it were, cut laterally across the horizontal ideological variegation that has been described in this volume. They caused Zionist ideology in general to take on a variety of different *modes*, normatively characteristic of Zionists in each political-cultural region of the world in which Jewish communities are to be found. They account for the sometimes highly significant differences between the normative self-understanding of Zionists in communities such as those of Germany, Britain, and the United States, not to speak of others located in predominantly Moslem North Africa and the Middle East. The study of these normative modal variations requires specialized inquiry into the development of Zionism within the specific societal and political context of each and every country. This was far beyond the scope of the present volume. However, cognition of regional modalities ought not to obscure the common transregional kernel and essence of the Zionist ideology. It has been the purpose of this study to explicate that kernel.

Certainly, when viewed in comparative regional perspective, one feature of Zionism that becomes salient is its functional role as a medium for the expression of Jewish ethnic identity, or, in ideological terms, ethnicism. This function was ubiquitous; it has been noted in regional studies of Zionism in Germany and England as well as in the multinational states of eastern Europe. The specific character of such ethnicism appears to be determined differentially according to the ethnic-national composition of the environing society. Thus, taking South Africa as one example from the societies of the New World, in the context of the castelike divisions of the multiethnic pluralism of South African society, compounded by the sociocultural dualism of the dominant whites, Zionism attained a normative status of unusual prevalence and potency in the life of the community. Yet there too the normative modality of Zionist ideology, being more ethnicist than nationalist, was quite compatible with continued life in the Diaspora.

Indeed, in terms of the definitions of ethnicity, ethnicism, and nationalism that formed the basis of the present study's perception of Zionism, one may usefully distinguish between two axes of its development. The first, which formed the subject of this study, is its linear progression on a time axis from ethnicism to a qualified nationalism (call it cultural nationalism) and thence to unqualified nationalism. Concurrently, on a latitudinal axis across diverse geographical regions, for the overwhelming majority of Zionism's adherents it amounted to an ethnicism that fell short of becoming nationalism in the full sense. This was all the more so in Britain and the countries of the New World, of which the most important was, of course, the United States of America. Consequently, Zionism assumed a vicarious character, almost as if it had undergone a mutation. The Jewish communities there remained the only loci of residual Zionist ideology in the Diaspora after the Holocaust, the insulation of the Jews of the Soviet Union, and the relatively massive migration to Israel of Jews from North Africa and the Middle Eastern Arab countries. In sum,

Zionism, as it manifested itself in the New World countries, is more accurately described as an expression of Jewish ethnicism rather than of nationalism.

In the contemporary Diaspora Zionism continues to be in essence a manifestation of such Jewish ethnicism. It consists in the positive valuation of those attributes that constitute and characterize the Jewish *ethnie*—its religion, its languages (today almost exclusively Hebrew), its historical memory and folklore, and its association with the territory traditionally identified as Eretz Israel—today the State of Israel. The residual Zionist ideology of diasporic Jews devolves on the centrality of Israel in the public consciousness of almost all diasporic communities. Most of these communities evince a desire and propensity to continue their diasporic life. To this end Israel serves as a source of identification and pride and a major cultural resource as well as a place of refuge in case of need. But simultaneously its safety and welfare also arouse dire concern. Present-day Zionism as positive valuation of Jewish ethnicity—in other words, as ethnicism—is reinforced to the extent that the countries of Jewish domicile experience a revival of ethnicity in general. This is true, although in different ways, not only in the eastern European countries currently undergoing powerful ethnic-national convulsions but also in Western countries, inasmuch as they are becoming increasingly amenable to programs of ethnic multiculturalism. The latter tendency, identified by some as a characteristic of postmodernity, implies that the state relinquishes the thrust of cultural homogenization, substituting for it an open-mindedness to the need and right of its citizens to foster diverse ethnic-cultural supplementation.

With the hindsight of nearly half a century since the creation of the State of Israel in 1948, it is apparent that the Zionist Organization has accomplished its major objective—a sovereign Jewish state in the traditional homeland of the Jews. It is equally clear that Zionism is far from fulfilling the ultimate ethnic-nationalist purpose of attaining congruence between the *ethnie* and its own territorial polity. To be sure, demographic projections do indicate that within the next half-century the State of Israel will probably contain a Jewish population larger than that of any community in the Diaspora. This is due primarily to the low birthrate in the Jewish communities of the Diaspora and to the attritions of assimilation. Yet a significant minority numbering millions will doubtless remain in diasporic communities. Moreover, given modern conditions of communications and travel and the natural movements of population to and from Israel, it is doubtful whether the idea of reaching complete congruity of the *ethnie* and the state carries weight any longer. It is evident, furthermore, that the residual World Zionist Organization is gradually being eclipsed in terms of authority, membership, resources, and functions. Structurally, it has long been overshadowed not only by the authority and functions of the State of Israel itself but also by the Jewish Agency framework that it renewed in the late 1960s as an equal partnership between its own representatives and those of the major fundraising organizations in the Diaspora. The latter, although initially non-Zionist, have since endorsed the aims of post–state Zionism as defined in the Jerusalem Program of 1968.

Yet the decline in significance and gradual eclipse of the Zionist Organization is only one side of the coin. The other is the well-nigh ubiquitous triumph of the Zionist ideology in all of contemporary Jewish life. Zionism as the primary expression of Jewish ethnicism has passed out of its "utopian" phase and become the consensual ideology to which most Jews throughout the world subscribe. Its ideological linchpin is the idea of "the centrality of Israel in Jewish life." This idea remains, however, open to two major trends of interpretation: One considers Israel's centrality as an inherent attribute of the Jewish situation under conditions of modernity. It upholds *aliya*, meaning the act of personal settlement in Israel, as an ideological imperative. It also warns that the Jewish Diaspora continues to be vulnerable to antisemitism. But above all, it contends that the attrition caused by the majority culture renders the Jewish communities of the Diaspora (not excluding even its major concentration in northern America) incapable of guaranteeing the creative future of a distinctive Jewish culture.

The alternative interpretation, while no less committed to identification with and support for Israel, regards Israel's centrality as a contingency rather than an inherent factor of the modern Jewish condition. It envisages the Diaspora, particularly in its North American location, as a viable entity coexisting and mutually interacting with the Jewish society and culture of Israel. It accordingly refutes the idea of personal *aliya* as an ideological imperative, although, to be sure, in pragmatic terms it appreciates the importance of immigration to Israel from all countries.

Possibly, in this antithesis of interpretation there inheres the seed of a new dialectic that may yet prove ideologically schismatic in Jewish life. On the other hand, the shared contemporary Zionist proposition that Israel is central for Jewish life mitigates the tension between these two interpretations. Nothing of the intensity and bitterness that characterized the pre–State of Israel clash between Zionists and their Jewish opponents is currently evident. Present engagement with this issue may prove to be but the last heartbeats of the age of Zionist ideology. It may eventually peter out, leaving way for as yet undiscernible ideological dynamics in the life of the Jews as an entity, a major part of which constitutes a nation but whose other parts will remain units of a postmodern, largely religious ethnic group.

Notes

Abbreviations of Libraries and Archives

CZA   Central Zionist Archives, Jerusalem
JIA   Jabotinsky Institute Archives, Tel Aviv
JNUL   Jewish National and University Library, Jerusalem

1. Social Origins of Jewish Nationalism

1. I have chosen not to venture into the vast labyrinthine literature on the term "ideology" and the infinite variety of definitions that have been and continue to be offered. As broad and flexible a working definition as possible has been adopted, bearing in mind that the context in which the term is here employed is that of nationalist aspirations rather than of intrastate politics. The phrase "comprehensive cognitive map" is borrowed from Edward Shils's treatment of ideology in the *International Encyclopedia of the Social Sciences*, ed. David L. Sills (New York, 1968), vol. 7, pp. 66–76, and reproduced in revised form in Edward Shils, *The Intellectuals and the Powers and Other Essays* (Chicago and London, 1972), pp. 23–41. The term "ideas" is meant to subsume also underlying values, while the qualifying words "coherent" and "set of" [ideas] emphasize that these ideas are not random; they can be analytically formulated as a series of logically related propositions. The emphasis on the "action-oriented" quality of these ideas and their "call for action" is of importance in distinguishing between ideology and the coherent set of ideas aspired to by social scientists when analyzing the same realities as those addressed by ideologists. My terminology draws upon Carl Friedrich's use of the phrase "action-related systems of ideas" in his working definition of ideology. See Carl Friedrich, *Man and His Government* (New York, 1953), pp. 89, 90.

2. Hugh Seton-Watson, *Nations and States: An Enquiry into the Origins of Nations and the Politics of Nationalism* (London, 1977), p. 5.

3. Hans Kohn emphasized that "nationalism is first and foremost, a state of mind, an act of consciousness. . . . it recognizes the nation-state as the ideal form of political organization and the nationality as the source of all creative cultural energy and of economic well-being. The supreme loyalty of man is therefore due to his nationality, as his own life is supposedly rooted in and made possible by its welfare." Hans Kohn, *The Idea of Nationalism* (New York, 1944), pp. 10, 11, 16. In the same vein, Jacob Katz predicates his analysis of Jewish nationalism upon the observation that "it is the transforming of ethnic facts into ultimate values." Jacob Katz, "The Jewish National

Movement: A Sociological Analysis," in *Jewish Emancipation and Self-Emancipation* (Philadelphia, 1986), p. 90.

4. Ernest Gellner, *Nations and Nationalism* (Oxford, 1983), p. 43.

5. Katz, "Jewish National Movement," p. 90.

6. Seton-Watson, *Nations and States*, pp. 383–415.

7. Anthony D. Smith, *Theories of Nationalism*, 2nd ed. (London, 1983), pp. 192–210. Smith's definition of *ethnie* appears with slight variations in a number of his works. This formulation is from Anthony D. Smith, "The Myth of the 'Modern Nation' and the Myths of Nations," *Ethnic and Racial Studies* 11, no. 1 (January, 1988), p. 9. For a more comprehensive discussion, see Anthony D. Smith, *The Ethnic Origins of Nations* (Oxford, 1986), esp. pp. 21–46. Cf. John Armstrong's elaborate typology of the emergence of national identity, which locates Zionism as an "archetypal diaspora." John A. Armstrong, *Nations before Nationalism* (Chapel Hill, N.C., 1982), esp. p. 288.

8. See Richard G. Hovannisian, *Armenia: On the Road to Independence* (Berkeley, Calif., 1967).

9. Hans Kohn and Carleton Hayes both date nationalism from this period. According to Hugh Seton-Watson, "the doctrine of nationalism dated from the age of the French Revolution but nations existed before the doctrine was formulated." He distinguishes two categories of nations, the old and the new. The old are those that had aquired national consciousness before the formulation of the doctrine of nationalism, notably the French and the British. Seton-Watson, *Nations and States*, pp. 6, 7. Elie Kedourie opens a seminal study on nationalism with the statement "Nationalism is a doctrine invented in Europe at the beginning of the nineteenth century." Elie Kedourie, *Nationalism,* 3rd ed. (London, 1966), p. 9.

10. Gellner, *Nations and Nationalism*, passim.

11. Kedourie, *Nationalism*, passim.

12. Benedict Anderson, *Imagined Communities: Reflections on the Origins and Spread of Nationalism* (London, 1986), pp. 13, 14.

13. Gellner, *Nations and Nationalism*, pp. 101–109.

14. See Haim Rabin, "The National Idea and the Revival of Hebrew," *Studies in Zionism* 7 (spring 1983), pp. 31–48. Also, Mitchell Cohen, *Zion and State: Nation, Class and the Shaping of Modern Israel* (Oxford, 1987), pp. 55–57.

15. Smith, *Theories of Nationalism*, p. 108.

16. The "primordialists" referred to are mainly Edward Shils and Cliffort Geertz. See, e.g., Edward Shils, "Primordial, Personal, Sacred and Civil Ties," *British Journal of Sociology* 7 (1957), pp. 113–145; Clifford Geertz, "The Integrative Revolution," in *Old Societies and New States*, ed. Clifford Geertz (Harmondsworth, U.K., 1963); and Clifford Geertz, "Ideology as a Cultural System," in *Ideology and Discontent*, ed. David Apter (New York, 1963).

17. Smith, *Ethnic Origins of Nations*, pp. 12, 13.

18. Smith, *Theories of Nationalism*, pp. 231, 236.

19. Ibid., pp. 133–136, 237; Anthony Smith, ed., *Nationalist Movements* (London, 1976), p. 21.

20. Smith, *Theories of Nationalism*, p. 249. Elsewhere, Smith prefers the term "neo-traditionalism" rather than "traditionalism"; see idem, *Nationalism in the Twentieth Century* (London, 1979), pp. 30ff.

21. Smith, *Theories of Nationalism*, p. 255.

22. John A. Armstrong (see n. 7 above) treats of the Jews as an "archetypal diaspora: a dispersed ethnic group that persistently maintains a sacral myth." He suggests that there

is no purely definitional way of distinguishing ethnicity from other types of identity. The ethnic group is defined by "boundary mechanisms" of exclusion; "ethnicity is a bundle of shifting interactions rather than a nuclear component of social organization." It has a "complex shifting quality over a long period of time transmuting into classes or religions." He further categorizes the Jews, together with the Armenians, as "middle-men minorities" and "mobilized diasporas" characterized by their "extraordinary accumulation over the centuries of skills and aptitudes required in modernizing polities." See Armstrong, *Nations before Nationalism,* esp. pp. 206–213. Cf. Smith, *Ethnic Origins,* esp. pp. 116–119. Smith concurs in essentials with Armstrong's analysis of the premodern Jewish *ethnie.*

23. The so-called Edict of Tolerance, issued by the Hapsburg emperor Joseph II in 1781 (and extended to Galicia in 1789), sought to reform the Jews' occupations, institutions, and customs to fit them for integration. For example, they were no longer permitted to operate inns or be tax collectors, and they were to adopt family names and conduct their business affairs in German, not Yiddish.

24. Particularly seminal contributions to the historical literature on this transformation are Jacob Katz, *Exclusiveness and Tolerance* (New York, 1961), *Out of the Ghetto* (New York, 1978), *From Prejudice to Destruction* (Cambridge, Mass., 1980). For an overview of the period, see also Shmuel Ettinger, "The Modern Period," in *History of the Jewish People,* ed. Hillel Ben-Sasson (London, 1976). Another volume examining the transformation in a number of separate countries is Jacob Katz, ed., *Towards Modernity: The European Jewish Model* (New Brunswick, N.J., 1987). In the same vein, see also Jonathan Frankel and Steven J. Zipperstein, eds., *Assimilation and Community: The Jews in Nineteenth-Century Europe* (Cambridge, 1992).

25. See Shmuel Ettinger, *Ha-antishemiyut ba-eit ha-hadasha* (Antisemitism in the modern period) (Tel Aviv, 1978), also Shmuel Ettinger, "The Origins of Modern Anti-Semitism," *Dispersion and Unity* 9 (1969), pp. 17–37. A succinct survey of different approaches is Todd M. Endelman, "Comparative Perspectives on Modern Anti-Semitism in the West," in *History and Hate: The Dimensions of Anti-Semitism,* ed. David Berger (Philadelphia, 1986), pp. 95–114.

26. An analysis providing a sweeping comparative overview of these processes throughout the nineteenth century and into the twentieth is Calivin Goldscheider and Alan S. Zuckerman, *The Transformation of the Jews* (Chicago, 1984). Deriving from social science perspectives, their approach emphasizes not Jewish intellectual factors but structural factors of the environing society that forged ethnic cohesion through economic, social, and political interactions. Their overall thesis, vigorously argued, is that modernization did not destroy Jewish ethnic cohesion; it merely transformed the bases of that cohesion.

27. Jacob Katz's works (see n. 24 above) analyze this phenomenon of transformation without loss of distinctiveness, emphasizing, as well as external deterministic factors, the inner volition of Jews to retain their distinctive collective character. See also David Sorkin, *The Transformation of German Jewry, 1780–1840* (New York, 1987). Sorkin's central thesis is that the outcome of the processes associated with emancipation in Germany, far from being disappearance through assimilation, was an internalization by Jews of German (bourgeois) culture. This crystallized into a distinctive German-Jewish subculture, "invisible" to its own members. To be sure, Sorkin states: "The subculture should not be confused with what contemporary parlance calls an 'ethnic' community." (See n. 7 of Sorkin's introduction, p. 181.) By the terms defined here, even if most German Jews were not "ethnicist" (insofar as they were unconscious of their distinctive-

ness or, if accused of purposely retaining it, would vigorously refute the charge), their subculture still constituted part of the ongoing Jewish *ethnie*. That is to say, if, as Sorkin demonstrates, their distinctiveness was more other-defined than self-defined, such German Jews may be said to have been characterized by "ethnicity" but not "ethnicism."

28. See Jacob Katz, "Orthodoxy in Historical Perspective," *Studies in Contemporary Jewry*, vol. 2 (Bloomington, Ind., 1986), pp. 3–17; Moshe Samet, "The Beginnings of Orthodoxy," *Modern Judaism* 8, no. 3 (October 1988), pp. 249–270. Cf. Samuel C. Heilman and Menahem Friedman, "Religious Fundamentalism and Religious Jews: The Case of the *Haredim*," in *Fundamentalisms Observed*, ed. Martin E. Marty and R. Scott Appleby (Chicago and London, 1991), pp. 197–264, esp. pp. 199, 211–213. Since the typology of religious groupings within Jewry from the late eighteenth century onward is a source of much semantic confusion, a definition of the terms I have adopted here is advisable. Orthodoxy, not unlike its antithesis, secularism, is best understood as a *process* of change affecting the norms of religious behavior and thought that were once common to Jews in premodern traditionalism (i.e., while society was still uncontestedly tradition-bound). This process involved heightened defensiveness against the challenge of secularization and religious reforms, strict reaffirmation of traditional norms, and in some cases, secession from the institutional structure of the Jewish community. Such "orthodoxization" affected the rabbinical stratum throughout Europe in varying degrees. Neoorthodoxy is a term best reserved for the particular form of orthodoxy associated with Rabbi Samson Raphael Hirsch in Germany. It conflated the defensive reaffirmation of traditional norms characteristic of all orthodoxy, with a less characteristic welcoming of emancipation, secular learning, and accommodation to external norms of civic behavior and dress. In contemporary Jewry this distinction has all but disappeared, leaving "orthodoxy" as the generic term for Jews committed to traditionally interpreted *halakha*, accommodative of modern secular civic life, and not associated with any alternative reformed (i.e., nonorthodox) institutional frameworks. The "ultraorthodox" or *haredi* (God-fearing, said to derive from the verse in Isaiah [66:5]: "Hear the word of the Lord, you who tremble [*ha-haredim*] at his word") are those groups, both *misnagdic* and hasidic, who have taken their reactive self-segregation to such extremes as, inter alia, rejection of most forms of secular learning and retention of distinctive dress. Their original strongholds were in Hungary, Galicia, and the Old *yishuv* of Eretz Israel.

29. See Todd M. Endelman, "Conversion as a Response to Antisemitism in Modern Jewish History," in *Living with Antisemitism: Modern Jewish Responses*, ed. Jehuda Reinharz (Hanover, N.H., and London, 1987), pp. 59–83.

30. For Mendelssohn's view concerning the irrelevance of the messianic restoration to Zion for the civic loyalty of Jews, see Moses Mendelssohn, *Gesammelte Schriften*, vol. 3 (Leipzig, 1843), p. 366.

31. An example of an important research contribution that employs the term "national" is Isaac E. Barzilay, "National and Anti-National Trends in the Berlin *Haskalah*," *Jewish Social Studies* 21 (1959), pp. 165–192; see also Yehezkel Kaufmann, *Gola ve-nekhar* (Exile and alienness) (Tel Aviv, 1929), vol. 2, b. 1, pp. 1–34; Benzion Dinur, *Be-mifne ha-dorot* (At the turn of the generations) (Jerusalem, 1955, pp. 229–354; Dov Weinryb, "Tzionut etzel yehudei germaniya be-tekufat ha-haskala" (Zionism among Jews of Germany in the period of the *haskala*), *Knesset le-zekher Bialik* (Anthology in memory of Bialik) (Tel Aviv, 1936); also idem, "Yesodot ha-tzionut ve-toldoteha" (The foundations of Zionism and its history), *Tarbiz* 8 (1937), pp. 69–113.

32. Zecharias Frankel, "Die Symptome der Zeit," in *Zeitschrift für jüdische religiöse*

Interessen 2 (1845), pp. 1–21, as cited and translated in Mordecai Waxman, ed., *Tradition and Change: The Development of Conservative Judaism* (New York, 1958), pp. 48–50.

33. Rivka Horwitz, *Zecharia Frankel ve-reishit ha-yahadut ha-positivit ha-historit* (Zecharias Frankel and the beginnings of positive-historical Judaism) (Jerusalem, 1984), esp. pp. 18, 19.

34. See Shmuel Ettinger's introduction to Zvi Graetz, *Darkei ha-historia ha-yehudit* (The paths of Jewish history) (Jerusalem, 1969), esp. pp. 20–33; Eliezer Schweid, *Toldot ha-hagut ha-yehudit* (A history of Jewish thought) (Jerusalem, 1977), pp. 321–328; also Ismar Schorsch, ed. and trans., *Heinrich Graetz: The Structure of Jewish History and Other Essays* (New York, 1975), pp. 1–62.

35. The quotation is from Heinrich Graetz, *Die Konstruktion der jüdischen Geschichte,* trans. in Schorsch, *Heinrich Graetz,* p. 71.

36. Heinrich Graetz, *Geschichte der Jüden,* vol. 5, Magdeburg, 1860, pp. 1–8, as translated in Michael A. Meyer, *Ideas of Jewish History* (New York, 1974).

37. On Salvador's life, see Hanoch Reinholt-Rinot, "Joseph Salvador: hayav ve-deotav" (Joseph Salvador, his life and opinions), *Zion* 9 (1944), pp. 109–141, See also Michael Graetz, "Mekomo shel Joseph Salvador be-gibush toda'at ha-yihud ha-yehudi" (Joseph Salvador's place in the crystallization of a consciousness of Jewish particularity), *Zion* 37 (1972), pp. 41–65. An incisive analysis, demolishing the notion that he was a proto-Zionist, is Paula E. Hyman, "Joseph Salvador: Proto-Zionist or Apologist for Assimilation?" *Jewish Social Studies* 34, no. 1 (January 1972), pp. 1–21. On the general phenomenon of return to affirmation of Judaism via messianic ideas, see Michael Graetz, "Ha-meshihiyut ha-hilonit ba-mea ha-tsha-esrei ke-derekh shiva la-yahadut" (Secular messianism in the nineteenth century as a way of return to Judaism), in *Meshihiyut ve-eskatologia: kovetz ma'amarim* (Messianism and eschatology: A collection of essays), ed. Zevi Baras (Jerusalem, 1983), pp. 401–418. Also Michael Graetz, *Ha-periferiya hayta la-merkaz* (From periphery to center) (Jerusalem, 1982).

38. The passage appeared in Joseph Salvador's *Loi de Moise* (Paris, 1882). It is given here as translated in Hyman, "Joseph Salvador," p. 6. Cf. Nahum Sokolow, *History of Zionism, 1600–1918* (New York, 1969), pp. 176, 177.

39. Quoted in Benzion Netanyahu, ed. *Road to Freedom: Writings and Addresses by Leo Pinsker* (New York, 1944), p. 49; also David Vital, *The Origins of Zionism* (Oxford, 1975), p. 6.

40. See Isaac Levitats, *The Jewish Community in Russia, 1772–1844* (New York, 1943); idem, *The Jewish Community in Russia, 1844–1917* (Jerusalem, 1981).

41. Yehuda Slutsky, "Tzmihata shel ha-intelligentzia ha-yehudit russit" (The Growth of the Russian Jewish intelligentsia), *Zion* 25 (1960), pp. 212–237, esp. p. 213; also in Yehuda Slutsky, *Ha-itonut ha-yehudit-russit ba-mea ha-tsha-esrei* (The Russian Jewish press in the nineteenth century) (Jerusalem, 1970).

42. See Ezra Mendelsohn, *Zionism in Poland: The Formative Years, 1915–1926* (New Haven, Conn., and London), 1981, pp. 5–11. Mendelsohn notes moreover that the concept "nationality" was a lesser gauge of their ethnic cohesion than language, since it is likely that many orthodox Jews found Jewish self-description as a nationality rather than as a religion unacceptable or uncomfortable.

43. See Michael A. Meyer, "The German Model of Religious Reform and Russian Jewry," in *Danzig between East and West,* ed. Isadore Twersky (Cambridge, Mass., 1985), pp. 69–91.

44. Cited in Jacob S. Raisin, *The Haskala Movement in Russia* (Philadelphia, 1913), p. 238.

45. See Steve J. Zipperstein, "*Haskalah*, Cultural Change, and Nineteenth-Century Russian Jewry: A Reassessment," *Journal of Jewish Studies* 35, no. 2 (1983), p. 197.

46. David Gordon, "Be-shuva va-nahat tivasheun" (In rest and ease shall you be saved), *Ha-magid*, no. 14 (1863), reproduced in Getzel Kressel, ed., *David Gordon: Mivhar ma'amarav* (David Gordon: Selected articles) (Tel Aviv, 1942), p. 35. In terms of the definitions employed here, Gordon's predicating the ultimate restoration of Jewish nationhood on both civic emancipation in the Diaspora and divine redemption makes his perspective ethnicist rather than nationalist proper.

47. Peretz Smolenskin, *Ma'amarim* (Articles), vol. 4 (Jerusalem, 1925), pp. 243, 244; also vol. 2, pp. 141–147, selections of which are translated in Arthur Hertzberg, *The Zionist Idea* (New York, 1973), pp. 145–147.

48. See Yehuda Slutsky, "Tzmihata shel ha-intelligentzia." The account of the rise of the Russian intelligentsia that follows in this section relies on this important article. See also Michael Stanislawski, *Czar Nicholas I and the Jews: The Transformation of Jewish Society in Russia, 1825–1855* (Philadelphia, 1983).

49. Slutsky, "Tzmihata shel ha-intelligentzia," pp. 236, 237.

50. See Michael Confino, "On Intellectuals and Intellectual Traditions in Eighteenth- and Nineteenth-Century Russia," *Daedalus* (spring 1972), pp. 117–150.

51. See Eli Lederhendler, *The Road to Modern Jewish Politics: Political Tradition and Political Reconstruction in the Jewish Community of Tsarist Russia* (New York, 1989); also Jonathan Frankel, *Prophecy and Politics: Socialism, Nationalism and the Russian Jews, 1862–1917* (Cambridge, 1981), pp. 49–132, esp. pp. 51, 81.

52. On these historical circumstances, see Vital, *Origins of Zionism*, pp. 65–134; also Frankel, *Prophecy and Politics*, pp. 49–132. A concise summary is Jonathan Frankel, "The Crisis of 1881–82 as a Turning Point in Modern Jewish History," in *The Legacy of Jewish Migration: 1881 and Its Impact*, ed. David Berger (New York, 1983), pp. 9–22.

53. Quoted in translation in Vital, *Origins of Zionism*, p. 119, and in Frankel, *Prophecy and Politics*, p. 87, from Lilienblum's seminal article in *Razsvet*, no. 41 (9 October 1881), p. 1641.

54. On Am Olam, see Frankel, *Prophecy and Politics*, pp. 55–57, and Abraham Menes, "The Am Oylam Movement," *YIVO Annual of Jewish Social Science* 4 (1949), pp. 9–33.

55. Quoted and translated in Frankel, *Prophecy and Politics*, p. 98. On the extent of czarist government responsibility for the pogroms, see Hans Rogger, *Jewish Policies and Right-Wing Politics in Imperial Russia* (Berkeley and Los Angeles, 1986), esp. pp. 113–175; also Michael I. Aronson, "The Attitudes of Russian Officials in the 1880s toward Jewish Assimilation and Emigration," *The Slavic Review* 34, no. 1 (1975), pp. 1–18; Shmuel Ettinger, "Ha-diyun ba-nitzul ha-yehudi be-da'at ha-kahal ha-russit shel reishit shnot hashmonim la-mea ha-tsha-esrei" (The debate on Jewish exploitation in Russian public opinion at the beginning of the 1880s), in *Prakim be-toldot ha-hevra ha-yehudit bi-yemei ha-beinayim u-va-et ha-hadasha, mudkashim le-Yaakov Katz* (Chapters in the history of Jewish society in the Middle Ages and the Modern period, dedicated to Jacob Katz), ed. Emanuel Etkes and Yosef Salmon (Jerusalem, 1980), pp. 287–307.

56. The quotations that follow are from the English translation by D. S. Blondheim published by the Federation of American Zionists in 1916, as reproduced in Netanyahu, ed., *Road to Freedom* (see n. 39 above).

57. See, for example, Leo Pinsker to Yehuda Lev Levanda, October 26, 1883, in Alter Druyanov, ed., *Ketavim le-toldot Hibbat Zion ve-yishuv Eretz Israel* (Writings in the history of Hibbat Zion and the settlement of Eretz Israel) (Odessa, 1919; Tel Aviv

1925–32), vol. 3, no. 1182, cols. 568–574 (translated in Netanyahu, *Road to Freedom*, p. 60).

58. See Shulamit Laskov, *Ha-biluim* (The Biluim) (Jerusalem, 1979), and for a concise summary in English, see idem, "The Biluim: Reality and Legend," *Zionism* 2, no. 1 (spring 1981), pp. 17–70.

59. "Megillat takanot shel Bilu" (Scroll of regulations of Bilu), in *Tekufat Hibbat Zion*, ed. Shmuel Yavnieli, vol. 2 (Jerusalem and Tel Aviv, 1961), pp. 93–98. It is apparent from the text that this document was a draft proposal of regulations, but when and where it was drafted is unknown.

60. Ze'ev Dubnow to Simon Dubnow, October 20/November 1, 1882, in Druyanov, ed., *Ketavim le-toldot Hibbat Zion*, vol. 3, no. 1163, cols. 405–406. The letter is there reproduced as originally written in Russian. A Hebrew translation is given in Alter Druyanov and Shulamit Laskov, eds., *Ketavim le-toldot Hibbat Zion*, rev. ed. (Tel Aviv, 1982), vol. 1, pp. 522, 523.

61. Laskov, "The Biluim: Reality and Legend," pp. 28, 29.

62. Vital, *Origins of Zionism*, pp. 155–158.

63. Joseph Goldstein, "Ha-tenua ha-tzionit be-russia, 1897–1904" (The Zionist movement in Russia, 1897–1904) (Ph.D. diss., The Hebrew University, Jerusalem, 1982), pp. 268–269; idem, *Bein tzionut medinit le-tzionut ma'asit: Ha-tnua ha-tzionit be-russia be-reishita* (Between political and practical Zionism: The beginnings of the Zionist movement in Russia) (Jerusalem, 1991), tables on p. 167. These estimates are based on the number of shekels purchased. The shekel was the official membership certificate instituted by the Zionist Organization and entitled the purchaser to a vote for the world Zionist congresses held annually until 1901 and thereafter biennially.

64. Druyanov, ed., *Katavim le-toldot Hibbat Zion*, vol. 3, no. 1180, cols. 563–564. The occupations of some of the listed invitees are not identifiable; hence, the discrepancy in numbers. Rabbi Schwabacher, the "modern" rabbi of Odessa also was listed but was not included in the calculation.

65. These estimates were based upon analysis of an extant copy of the list of participants deposited in the CZA, Jerusalem. See Haim Orlan, "The Participants in the First Zionist Congress," in *Herzl Yearbook*, vol. 6 (New York, 1964–65), pp. 133–152.

66. Joseph Goldstein, "Some Sociological Aspects of the Russian Zionist Movement at Its Inception," *Jewish Social Studies* 47, no. 2 (spring 1985), p. 174.

67. Mendelsohn, *Zionism in Poland*, pp. 338, 339. Mendelsohn draws upon a vast collection of contemporary autobiographies preserved in YIVO Archives, New York.

68. See Walter Gross, "The Zionist Students' Movement," in *Leo Baeck Institute Yearbook*, vol. 4 (London, 1959), pp. 143–164. On the social origins of Zionism in German Jewry and its ideological character, see Jehuda Reinharz, "Ideology and Structure in German Zionism 1881–1933," *Jewish Social Studies* 42 (1980), pp. 119–146. Moshe Zimmermann, "Jewish Nationalism and Zionism in German Jewish Students' Organizations," *Leo Baeck Institute Yearbook*, vol. 27 (London, 1982), pp. 129–153; idem, "Mivne hevrati ve-tzipiyot hevratiyot ba-tzionut ha-germanit lifnei milhemet ha-olam ha-rishona" (Social structure and social prognosis in German Zionism before World War I), in *Uma ve-toldoteha* (The nation and its history), part 2: *The Modern Period*, ed. Shmuel Ettinger (Jerusalem, 1984), pp. 177–199.

69. This generalization is documented in Hagit Lavsky, "The German Zionist Leadership," to be published in a volume edited by Jehuda Reinharz and Anita Shapira.

70. Henriette Hannah Bodenheimer, *Prelude to Israel: The Memoirs of M. I. Bodenheimer*, trans. Israel Cohen (New York and London, 1963), p. 60.

71. "Opening Address at the First Zionist Congress" (August 29, 1897) as translated in Theodor Herzl, *Zionist Writings: Essays and Addresses*, trans. Harry Zohn, vol. 1 (New York, 1973), p. 133.

72. See Josef Fraenkel, "Colonel Albert E. W. Goldsmid and Theodor Herzl," in *Herzl Year Book*, vol. 1 (New York, 1958), pp. 145–153; also Stuart A. Cohen, *English Zionists and British Jews: The Communal Politics of Anglo-Jewry, 1895–1920* (Princeton, N.J., 1982), pp. 8, 26–29, 35–36.

73. Joseph Goldstein, "The Attitude of the Jewish and the Russian Intelligentsia to Zionism in the Initial Period (1897–1904)," *The Slavonic and East European Review* 64, no. 4 (October 1986), pp. 546–556.

74. See Yosef Salmon, "Teguvot ha-tzibur ha-yehudi le-hevrat yishuv Eretz Israel" (Responses of the Jewish public to the Society for Settlement of Eretz Israel), in *Sefer Shragai*, ed. Mordecai Eliav and Yitzhak Raphael (Jerusalem, 1981), pp. 15–39.

75. Israel Klausner, ed., *Ha-ketavim ha-tzioni'im shel ha-rav Zvi Hirsch Kalischer* (The Zionist writings of Rabbi Zvi Hirsch Kalischer) (Jerusalem, 1947), p. 297. On these "remnant rabbis," see Jacob Katz, *Leumiyut yehudit: Masot u-mehkarim* (Jewish nationalism: Essays and studies) (Jerusalem, 1979), pp. 286–289.

76. See Yosef Salmon, "Yehiel Michael Pines: From the Vision of Zionism to the Reality," *Modern Judaism* 8, no. 1 (February 1988), pp. 65–82.

77. On this type of "*maskil*-rabbi," see Shmuel Almog, *Zionism and History: The Rise of a New Jewish Consciousness* (Jerusalem, 1987), p. 171.

78. *Admor* (plural *-im*) is the acronym for *adoneinu, moreinu* (our master and teacher). The relationship of the traditionalist rabbis in Eastern Europe toward Hibbat Zion and the phases of defection from it are profoundly researched in Yosef Salmon, *Dat ve-tzionut: imutim rishonim* (Religion and Zionism: First encounters) (Jerusalem, 1990), pp. 112–149, 204–251, 314–339.

79. See Israel Klausner, *Be-hitorer am* (The national awakening) (Jerusalem, 1962), p. 356; also the letter of Rabbi Eliezer Gordon, head of the Telz Yeshiva, dated 3 Tammuz, 1889, reproduced in Yehuda Leib Appel, *Betokh reishit ha-tehiya* (At the beginning of the revival) (Tel Aviv, 1936), pp. 545–549.

80. The quotation is from Mohilewer's exposition of the anticipated nature of *geula* (redemption), written in 1875–1876, in Judah Leib Fishman, ed., *Sefer Shmuel* (Jerusalem, 1923), pp. 154, 155.

81. On Mohilewer's life and views, see Yosef Salmon, "Ha-rav Shmuel Mohilewer: rabam shel Hovevei Zion" (Rabbi Shmuel Mohilewer: The rabbi of Hovevei Zion), *Zion* 56, no. 1 (1991), pp. 47–78.

82. On the role of Edmond de Rothschild, see Dan Giladi, "Ha-baron, ha-pekidut ve-hamoshavot ha-rishonot be-Eretz Israel: Ha'arakha me-hadash" (The baron, the officials and the first settlements in Eretz Israel: A reevaluation), *Cathedra*, 2 (1976), pp. 59–68; also Simon Schama, *The Rothschilds and the Land of Israel* (New York, 1978).

83. On this insight into the dialectical relationship of Zionism as a synthesis derived from the thesis of traditionalism and the antithesis of modernism, see Ben Halpern, *The Idea of the Jewish State* (Cambridge, Mass., 1969), esp. p. 66.

84. For another application of Smith's theory to a particular nationalism, see John Hutchinson, *The Dynamics of Cultural Nationalism: The Gaelic Revival and the Creation of the Irish Nation State* (London, 1987). Hutchinson focuses on Irish "cultural nationalism" as the formative factor in the emergence of the independent Irish state. However, unlike the cultural Zionism propounded by Ahad Ha'am, which perceived Jewish cultural regeneration as part of the process of return to a territorial homeland, the

cultural regeneration of the Irish was directed against the state in which they were already domiciled. Its primary concern was "the regeneration of the historical community against the levelling power of the State." See also the perceptive comparison by Hedva Ben-Israel, "The Role of Religion in Nationalism: Some Comparative Remarks on Irish Nationalism and on Zionism," in *Religion, Ideology and Nationalism in Europe and America*, ed. Hedva Ben-Israel et al. (Jerusalem, 1986), pp. 331–340.

85. On this point see more in chap. 3, below. Semantic clarity has long been confounded by the interchangeable use of the terms "assimilation" and "integration" in the historiographical literature and indeed by the fact that contemporary nineteenth- and early-twentieth-century sources often used the term "assimilation" to describe the ideological position that I have here labeled "integrationist." In the interests of greater analytical clarity I reserve the label "assimilationist" for those Jews who advocated total dissolution of the Jewish entity as a programmatic option. Some scholars might prefer to term this "radical assimilation."

86. Cf. the similar perception of Shlomo Avineri, *The Making of Modern Zionism: The Intellectual Origins of the Jewish State* (London, 1981), pp. 4, 5. On the relationship between Zionism and antisemitism see Shmuel Almog, *Leumiyut, tzionut, ve-antishemiyut: masot u-mehkarim* (Nationalism, Zionism, antisemitism: Essays and studies) (Jerusalem, 1992), esp. pp. 221–241. Also Katz, *Leumiyut yehudit*, pp. 36–53.

87. See Anthony D. Smith, "Nationalism and Religion: The Role of Religious Reform in the Genesis of Arab and Jewish Nationalism," *Archives de Sciences Sociales des Religions* 35 (1973), pp. 23–43. In this article, Smith applied his hypothesis to the Jewish case but placed too great an emphasis on religious reform of Judaism as the progenitor of Jewish nationalism, and none at all on the role of traditionalists. This gives a somewhat distorted impression, as if Jewish nationalism were largely a product of central European Reform Judaism. In fact, the main thrust of Reform Judaism was anything but conducive to the postulates of Jewish nationalism, and the overwhelming majority of its proponents conducted an ongoing ideological battle against Zionism. The distinction that I have suggested between integrationist and ethnicist reformists provides a corrective to this distortion. Whereas Reform Judaism was the seedbed for a large part of the integrationists, it was rejected (or restrained) by the ethnicists, who considered it a form of assimilation and upheld the ethnic attributes of Judaism that Reform Judaism tried to repress.

88. On Birnbaum, see Joshua A. Fishman, *Ideology, Society and Language: The Odyssey of Nathan Birnbaum* (Ann Arbor, Mich., 1987). Also Yehoyakim Doron, *Haguto ha-tzionit shel Natan Birnbaum* (The Zionist thought of Nathan Birnbaum) (Jerusalem, 1988).

2. Ideological Precursors of Zionism

1. Benedict Anderson, *Imagined Communities: Reflections on the Origin and Spread of Nationalism* (London, 1983), p. 15.

2. Yehiel Michel Pines, *Emet mi-eretz titzmah* (Truth shall spring forth out of The Land), ed. Pinhas M. Grajewski (Jerusalem, 1895). Letter to Reuven Brainin, 14 Tevet 1895, in vol. 3, p. 24; letter to Ahad Ha'am (undated), in vol. 2, p. 17. CZA, 26.889.

3. On Pines, see Yosef Salmon, "Yehiel Michael Pines: From the Vision of Zionism to the Reality," *Modern Judaism* 8, no. 1 (February 1988), pp. 65–82; also Ehud Luz, *Parallels Meet: Religion and Nationalism in the Early Zionist Movement 1882–1904* (Philadelphia, 1988), pp. 91–98.

4. A succinct survey of Jewish reflection on *galut* is Chaim Hillel Ben-Sasson's entry under *Galut* in the *Encylopaedia Judaica*, vol. 7, pp. 275–294.

5. For an illuminating application of the distinction between active and passive messianism, see Jody Elizabeth Myers, "Seeking Zion: The Messianic Ideology of Zevi Hirsch Kalischer 1795–1874" (Ph.D. diss., University of California, Los Angeles, 1985). Also Jody Elizabeth Myers, "The Messianic Idea and Zionist Ideologies," *Studies in Contemporary Jewry*, vol. 7 (New York, 1991), pp. 3–13.

6. See Arthur Hertzberg's introduction to *The Zionist Idea* (New York, 1959), esp. pp. 17, 18; also Max Nordau's definition of Zionism in *Zionistische Schriften* (Berlin, 1923), p. 22.

7. Theodor Zlocisti, *Moses Hess: Der Vorkämpfer des Sozialismus und Zionismus, 1812–1875* (Berlin, 1921); Theodor Zlocisti, ed., and Getzel Kressel, trans., *Moshe Hess u-venei doro* (Tel Aviv, 1947); Isaiah Berlin, *The Life and Opinions of Moses Hess* (Cambridge, 1959); Edmund Silberner, *Moses Hess: Geschichte seines Lebens* (Leiden, 1966); Shlomo Na'aman, *Emanzipation und Messianismus: Leben und Werk des Moses Hess* (Frankfurt, 1982). See also David McLellan, *The Young Hegelians and Karl Marx* (London, 1969), pp. 137–159; Jonathan Frankel, *Prophecy and Politics* (Cambridge, 1981), pp. 6–28; and the most recent study, Shlomo Avineri, *Moses Hess: Prophet of Communism and Zionism* (New York, 1985). Both Frankel and Avineri show the salience of Hess's Jewishness in his early writings. The original title of Moses Hess's "proto-Zionist" work was *Rom und Jerusalem—die letzte Nationalitätenfrage*. It is reproduced in Horst Lademacher, ed., *Moses Hess: Ausgewählter Schriften* (Cologne, 1962). The quotations that follow are from the English translation: Moses Hess, *Rome and Jerusalem: A Study in Jewish Nationalism*, trans. Meyer Waxman (New York, 1943).

8. Hess, *Rome and Jerusalem*, p. 74.

9. Ibid., p. 58. Waxman anachronistically translates *Judenhass* as "anti-Semitism."

10. Ibid., pp. 165, 166.

11. Ibid., p. 147.

12. The first mention of Hess in Herzl's diaries is dated May 1897, and he read the whole work only as late as May 1901. Raphael Patai, ed., and Harry Zohn, trans., *The Complete Diaries of Theodor Herzl* (New York, 1960) vol. 1, p. 548; vol. 3, p. 1090.

13. Theodor Zlocisti, ed., and Getzel Kressel, trans., *Moshe Hess u-venei doro*; see Kressel's introduction, pp. 83–87, 109.

14. It was less evident in Hess's first work, *Die heilige Geschichte der Menschheit* (The holy history of mankind), published in 1837, in which Hess pointed to the this-worldliness of Judaism as opposed to the other-worldliness of Christianity and thence to the contribution that Judaism could still make for the future of mankind. See Avineri, *Moses Hess*, p. 22.

15. See Silberner, *Moses Hess*, pp. 184–192; Avineri, *Moses Hess*, p. 157, n. 32.

16. Hess, *Rome and Jerusalem*, p. 43.

17. Ibid., pp. 166, 260, 147, in that sequence.

18. Michael Graetz, "Le-'shivato' shel Moshe Hess la-yahadut: ha-reka la-hibur 'Romi ve-Yerushalayim'" (On the return of Moses Hess to Judaism: the background to 'Rome and Jerusalem'), *Zion* 45 (1980), pp. 133–153, reproduced in Shmuel Almog, ed., *Lifnei heyot ha-tzionut* (Before there was Zionism) (Jerusalem, 1981) pp. 175–197.

19. The term "quasi-messianic" is used here and throughout this work (see chap. 6 below) to describe messianic rhetoric not predicated on traditionalist or orthodox understanding of the messianic belief. This is not, however, to deny its mythic potency also for nonorthodox or secular Jews.

20. Hess, *Rome and Jerusalem*, pp. 46, 173–175.

21. See Shulamit Volkov, "Moses Hess: Problems of Religion and Faith," *Zionism* 3 (spring 1981), pp. 1–16.

22. For surveys of these restorationist projects, see Franz Kobler, *The Vision Was There: A History of the British Movement for the Restoration of the Jews to Palestine* (London, 1956); also Barbara W. Tuchman, *Bible and Sword* (New York, 1956). A recent reevaluation is Isaiah Friedman's introduction to the new edition of his *The Question of Palestine: British–Jewish–Arab Relations 1914–1918* (New Brunswick, N. J., and London, 1992), pp. xi–lvi. Like other studies, Friedman's focuses on the contribution of restorationist ideas to the creation of "a favorable climate of opinion" for Zionism in England, which he considers to be substantial. No studies have yet focused on the question of whether these ideas contributed substantially to the genesis of Jewish nationalism itself.

23. Edwin Hodder, *The Life and Work of the Seventh Earl of Shaftesbury* (London, 1886), vol. 1, p. 310.

24. Ibid., pp. 330–331. See also Geoffrey B.A.M. Finlayson, *The Seventh Earl of Shaftesbury, 1801–1885* (London, 1981), pp. 112–116, 264–265.

25. Quoted in Kobler, *The Vision Was There*, p. 66. See also Franz Kobler, "Charles Henry Churchill," *Herzl Yearbook*, vol. 4 (New York, 1962), pp. 1–66.

26. Jonathan D. Sarna, *Jacksonian Jew: The Two Worlds of Mordecai Noah* (New York, 1981), p. 119. Sarna characterizes Noah as a personality who combined two different types of ethnic leadership: the defender of the faith and the integrationist. See also Robert Gordis, "Mordecai Manuel Noah: A Centenary Evaluation," *Publications of the American Jewish Historical Society* 41 (September 1951–June 1952), pp. 1–26. Also Bernard D. Weinryb, "Noah's Ararat Jewish State in its Historical Setting," *Publications of the American Jewish Historical Society* 43, nos. 1–4 (1953/4), pp. 170–190.

27. Manuel Noah, "Discourse on the Restoration of the Jews, Delivered at the Tabernacle, October 28, and December 2nd 1844" (New York, 1845); reprinted in *Call to America to Build Zion* (New York, 1977) in the Arno Press collection America and the Holy Land (advisory editor Moshe Davis), p. 25.

28. See, e.g., Laurence Oliphant, *The Land of Gilead* (New York, 1881), p. 26: "It is somewhat unfortunate that so important a political and strategic question as the future of Palestine should be inseparably connected in the public mind with a favorite religious theory. . . . As far as my own efforts are concerned, they are based upon considerations which have no connection whatever with any popular religious theory upon the subject." In the light of Oliphant's religious eccentricities, his sudden resignation from his seat as an M.P. in order to join a religious community (the Brocton Colony in New England), and the important role that Christian ideas played in his life as a whole, it is doubtful if this disavowal should be taken at face value. For a comprehensive study of Oliphant's life, see Anne Taylor, *Laurence Oliphant, 1829–1888* (Oxford, 1982).

29. See Hess, *Rome and Jerusalem*, pp. 150–155; David Gordon, "Be-shuva va-nahat tivasheun" (In rest and ease shall you be saved), *Ha-magid*, vol. 14, 1863, reproduced in Getzel Kressel, ed., *David Gordon: mivhar ma'amarav* (David Gordon: Selected articles) (Tel Aviv, 1942), p. 36.

30. Nahum Sokolow, *History of Zionism, 1600–1918* (1919; reprint, New York, 1969). Cf. Adolf Boehm, *Die Zionistische Bewegung* (1920; reprint Berlin, 1934); N. M. Gelber, *Zur Vorgeschichte des Zionismus: Judenstaatprojekte in den Jahren 1695–1845* (Vienna, 1927).

31. See Sokolow, *History of Zionism* (1969), pp. 16, 17. In his preface (p. xxvii),

Sokolow explains: "In renewing the gradual evolution of the Zionist idea over such a wide field . . . I had to go back to the beginning of this idea and extend the meaning of Zionism to all aspirations and efforts tending in the same direction."

32. Boehm, *Die Zionistische Bewegung*, p. 55.

33. Dov Weinryb, "Yesodot ha-tzionut ve-toldoteha" (The foundations of Zionism and its history), *Tarbiz* 8 (1937), p. 71.

34. Ben Zion Dinaburg, *Mevasrei ha-tzionut* (Tel Aviv, 1938); also Ben Zion Dinur, *Be-mifne ha-dorot* (At the turn of the generations) (Jerusalem, 1955), pp. 9–18.

35. Ben Zion Dinur, "Ha-yesodot ha-idiologi'im shel ha-aliyot be-shnot 1740–1840" (The ideological foundations of the *aliyot* in the years 1740–1840), in *Bemifne ha-dorot*, pp. 69–79.

36. See, e.g., Jacob Katz, *Leumiyut yehudit: masot u-mehkarim* (Jewish nationalism: Essays and studies) (Jerusalem, 1979), pp. 230–238; also Shmuel Ettinger's "Ben-Zion Dinur ha-ish u-poalo ha-histori" (Ben-Zion Dinur the man and his historical work), which is the introduction to the fourth volume of Dinur's historical writings: *Dorot u-reshumot* (Jerusalem, 1978). See also the criticism of Dinur's interpretation of eighteenth-century rabbinical homiletics in Yosef Salmon, *Dat ve-tzionut: imutim rishonim* (Religion and Zionism: First encounters) (Jerusalem, 1990), p. 31. The specifics of Dinur's thesis concerning the *aliya* of Yehuda he-hasid and his disciples were refuted in Meir Benayahu, "Ha-'hevra kedosha' shel rabbi Yehuda Hasid ve-aliyato le-eretz Israel" (The 'Holy Society' of Rabbi Yehuda Hasid and its settlement in Jerusalem), *Sefunot*, bks. 3 and 4 (Jerusalem, 1960), pp. 133–182. Benayahu showed that the *aliya* connected with Yehuda he-hasid, so far from being innovative and a turning point in the direction of Zionism, was of a piece with the *aliyot* characteristic of that period; its inspiration was Sabbatean messianic.

37. Arie Morgenstern, *Meshikhiyut ve-yishuv eretz Israel ba-mahatzit ha-rishona shel ha-mea ha-yod tet* (Messianism and settlement of Eretz Israel in the first half of the nineteenth century) (Jerusalem, 1985). See also a brief version in English: Arie Morgenstern, "Messianic Concepts and Settlement in the Land of Israel," *Vision and Conflict in the Holy Land*, ed. Richard I. Cohen (Jerusalem, 1985), pp. 141–162.

38. Ibid., p. 159. Morgenstern did not, to be sure, claim that this reaction to the disappointment of 1840 was the only cause of the reversion to quietism.

39. See the symposium in Cohen, ed., *Vision and Conflict*, pp. 141–189, and esp. Israel Bartal, "Messianic Expectations and Their Place in History," pp. 171–181; also Bartal's detailed review of Morgenstern's book in *Zion* 52, no. 1 (1987), pp. 117–130.

40. See Jacob Katz's three studies on *Mevasrei ha-tzionut* (Precursors of Zionism), in Katz, *Leumiyut yehudit*, pp. 263–356.

41. See the letter to Mordecai Manuel Noah of January 1, 1822, from Edward Gans and Leopold Zunz of the Verein für Kultur und Wissenschaft der Juden in Berlin, reproduced in *Publications of the American Jewish Historical Society*, no. 20 (1911), pp. 147–148.

42. See Getzel Kressel, "Ha-hevra ha-rishona le-yishuv Eretz Israel" (The first society for settlement in Eretz Israel), *Zion* 7 (1941/2), pp. 197–205, reproduced in Almog, ed., *Lifnei heyot ha-tzionut*, pp. 197–206.

43. Haim Luria's letters to Moses Hess, August 26 and September 14, 1862, reproduced in Zlocisti and Kressel, *Moshe Hess u-venei doro*, pp. 243–245.

44. *Kitvei ha-rav Yehuda Alkalai* (Writings of Rabbi Yehuda Alkalai), vol. 2, ed. Yitzhak Raphael (Jerusalem, 1974), p. 696. The quotation is from *Nehamat ha-aretz* (The consolation of The Land), 1866.

45. *Ha-ketavim ha-tzioni'im shel ha-rav Zvi Kalischer* (The Zionist writings of Rabbi Zvi Kalischer), ed. Israel Klausner (Jerusalem, 1947), pp. 29, 129. The quotations are from Kalischer's major work, *Derishat Zion* (Quest for Zion), first published in 1862.

46. Katz, *Leumiyut yehudit*, pp. 299, 300. Katz points out, inter alia, that the example of other nationalisms was invoked by Kalischer only in writings aimed at a wider public, not at all in private letters. It should be noted that the passage quoted in n. 45 above, in which mention is made of the concept "national," appeared in an appendix to the second edition of *Derishat Zion* addressed to "the enlightened reader" (*korei ha-maskil*).

47. *Kitvei ha-rav Yehuda Alkalai*, vol. 1, p. 237.

48. Ibid., pp. 199–200. Rabbi Yehuda Bibas was born in Gibraltar (date unknown), lived in London for a time, then in Livorno, Italy, until 1831, and thereafter served as rabbi in Corfu. Toward the end of his life he settled in Eretz Israel. He died in 1852. Although obscurity clouds much of his life, it is apparent that he espoused human action as the prerequisite for divine redemption (i.e., "active messianism"). See Israel Klausner, "Ha-rav Yehuda Bibas: Ehad mi-mevasrei ha-tzionut" (Rabbi Yehuda Bibas: One of the precursors of Zionism), *Ha-olam*, no. 7 (1944). Also, David Benvenisti and Hayim Mizrahi, "Rabbi Yehuda Bibas ve-kehilat Corfu be-zemano" (Rabbi Yehuda Bibas and the contemporary Corfu community), *Sefunot* 2 (1958), pp. 303–330.

49. Extracts reproduced from Zvi Hirsch Kalischer's *Derishat Zion* and translated by Arthur Hertzberg in his *The Zionist Idea* (New York, 1973), p. 111.

50. Ibid., p. 112.

51. One particular passage of Alkalai's writings in his *Raglei mevaser* (The bringer of tidings) has been cited in support of the view that he merely used the homiletical discussion in this way. See Eliezer Schweid, *Toldot ha-hagut ha-yehudit ba-eit ha-hadasha* (A history of Jewish thought in the Modern period) (Jerusalem, 1977), p. 376. However, Jacob Katz dispels this inference. See Katz, *Leumiyut yehudit*, p. 331. The passage under discussion appears in *Kitvei ha-rav Yehuda Alkalai*, vol. 2, p. 630. It reads:

> The words of those who wish to draw the time of redemption nearer by natural means and by the actions of the rulers of nations are based upon common sense [*sikhlam ha-yashar*, could alternatively be translated as "rational thought"]. For the Lord awakened their spirit and the times taught them! And all the homilies and proofs are mere supporting evidence [*asmakhta be-alma*]. Since there is no authoritative tradition in these matters—and no one can know God's intention. And they serve only to disprove the words of those who tell the simple people that it is forbidden to engage in matters of the redemption and resettlement of The Land.

Both Kressel and Weinryb assumed that Alkalai and Kalischer merely used religious discourse as a necessary rationale for an already secularized purpose. See Getzel Kressel, *Rabbi Yehuda Alkalai—Rabbi Zvi Hirsch Kalischer* (Tel Aviv, 1942–43); Weinryb, *Yesodot ha-tzionut ve-toldoteha*, p. 72. An extreme example of the reading of later nationalism into Kalischer's writings is Sam N. Lehman-Wilzig, "Proto-Zionism and Its Proto-Herzl: The Philosophy and Efforts of Rabbi Zvi Hirsch Kalischer," *Tradition* 16, no. 1 (summer 1976), pp. 56–76.

52. See Yosef Salmon, "The Rise of Jewish Nationalism on the Border of Eastern and Western Europe," in *Danzig: Between East and West*, ed. Isadore Twersky (Cambridge, 1985), pp. 123–137, esp. p. 128; also idem, "Aliyata shel ha-leumiyut ha-yehudit be-merkaz Europa u-be-ma'arava" (The rise of Jewish nationalism in central and western Europe), *Ha-tzionut* 12 (1987), pp. 7–16.

53. See Salmon, *Dat ve-tzionut*, p. 37.

54. See Salmon, "The Rise of Jewish Nationalism." On the terms "neoorthodoxy" and "ultraorthodoxy" see chap. 1, n. 28.

55. See Katz, *Leumiyut yehudit,* p. 312.

56. *Kitvei ha-rav Yehuda Alkalai,* vol. 1, pp. 221–223. The Damascus blood libel of 1840 concerned the disappearance of Father Thomas, superior of the Franciscan Convent in Damascus. It was alleged that the Jews had killed him to use his blood for Jewish ritual purposes. A number of Jews were arrested, and some confessions were extorted by torture. Adolphe Crémieux and Moses Montefiore visited Damascus and took a leading role in the protests raised by Jews and Christians in various countries. The outcome was the release of the prisoners.

57. *Ha-ketavim ha-tzioni'im shel ha-rav Zvi Kalischer,* p. 40.

58. Ibid., pp. 41–46. These stages are described in Kalischer's *Derishat Zion,* supported with various proofs from the sacred texts. Salmon argues that Kalischer's emphasis on ritual sacrifices was prompted more by the challenge of Reform Judaism than by messianic anticipation. See Salmon, "The Rise of Jewish Nationalism" (n. 52 above). A contrary view of Kalischer's motivation for emphasizing the reinstitution of sacrifices is advanced by Jody Elizabeth Myers. Her account tends to confirm Jacob Katz's earlier judgment that Kalischer genuinely believed renewal of the sacrificial cult to be a necessary stage toward messianic redemption; that is to say, he did not raise the issue merely as an anti-reform polemic. Indeed, whereas Katz held that by the 1860s Kalischer had bowed to criticism of his views on the renewal of sacrifices and shifted his emphasis to actual settlement, Myers contends that he persisted throughout his life in his nigh-obsessive belief that renewing the sacrifices was vital. See Myers, "Seeking Zion: The Messianic Ideology of Zevi Hirsch Kalischer," esp. p. 104, n. 62; pp. 113–114. Also idem, "Attitudes Towards a resumption of Sacrificial Worship in the Nineteenth Century," *Modern Judaism* 7, no. 1 (February 1987), pp. 29–49.

59. *Ha-ketavim ha-tzioni'im shel ha-rav Zvi Hirsch Kalischer,* p. 185, and see Katz, *Leumiyut yehudit,* pp. 301, 335.

60. See Israel Klausner, ed., *Kitvei harav Natan Friedland,* 2 vols. (Jerusalem, 1980). On Rabbi Gutmacher, see Yitzhak Raphael, "Mi-igrot Zion," *Sinai* 17 (Jerusalem, 1944), pp. 324–337.

61. See Michael Silber, "The Historical Experience of German Jewry and Its Impact on *Haskalah* and Reform in Hungary," in *Towards Modernity: The European Jewish Model,* ed. Jacob Katz (New Brunswick, N.J., and Oxford, 1987), pp. 107–157.

62. Moses Hess to Rabbi Josef Natonek, August 7, 1862, reproduced fully in translation in Dov Frankel, *Reishit ha-tzionut ha-medinit ha-modernit: Josef Natonek* (The beginning of modern political Zionism: Josef Natonek) (Haifa, 1956), p. 98. This book's title is somewhat hyperbolic.

63. See Dov Frankel, *Reishit ha-tzionut ha-medinit;* also Mordecai Frankel, "Ha-rav Josef Natonek, hoge ha-tzionut ha-medinit le-or ketavav" (Josef Natonek, political Zionist thinker, in the light of his writings), *Kivunim,* no. 24 (August 1984), pp. 123–143. The quotations that follow are taken from Mordecai Frankel's translations from the German and the Hungarian in this article.

64. Mordecai Frankel, "Ha-rav Josef Natonek," p. 127 the unpublished writings of Natonek are in CZA, Jerusalem.

65. Ibid., pp. 130–131.

66. Quoted in Dov Frankel, *Reishit ha-tzionut ha-medinit,* p. 76.

67. Rabbi Kalischer to Rabbi Eliyahu of Graiditz, reproduced fully in Dov Frankel, *Reishit ha-tzionut ha-medinit,* p. 101.

68. Quoted from Natonek's introduction to his *Göttliche Offenbarung durch Moses*, in Dov Frankel, *Reishit ha-tzionut ha-medinit*, pp. 34, 41.

69. Quoted in Mordecai Frankel, "Ha-rav Josef Natonek," p. 132, and in Dov Frankel, *Reishit ha-tzionut ha-medinit*, p. 73. These statements were made in 1871 in the context of his comments on an annotated translation into German of the Song of Songs.

70. Dov Frankel's contention that Natonek was in fact the first "political Zionist" is a gross overstatement. He also speculates, without any real evidence, that Natonek's influence impinged on the households in Budapest of both Jacob Herzl, father of Theodor, and Gabriel Suedfeld, father of Max Nordau. Natonek was, however, related to the Raab and Stampfer families, who were members of the first orthodox group of Jews that left Jerusalem in an attempt to establish an agricultural settlement, Petah Tikva. This was in 1878, before the beginning of Hibbat Zion settlement.

71. This was evident, for example, in the major compilation of rabbinical opinions approving participation in Hibbat Zion: *Shivat Zion* (Return to Zion), which was edited by Abraham Yaakov Slutzky and published in two volumes in Warsaw, 1892.

3. General Zionism

1. Asher Ginzberg himself would not have approved of this correlation between Pinsker and Herzl. See "Dr. Pinsker u-mahbarto" (Dr. Pinsker and his pamphlet [1892]) in *Kol kitvei Ahad Ha'am* (Collected writings of Ahad Ha'am) (Tel Aviv and Jerusalem, 1959), pp. 43–45.

2. Moshe Leib Lilienblum, "Zekhut ha-kiyum ve-hoser ha-matara" (The right to live and the lack of a goal), in *Kol kitvei Moshe Leib Lilienblum* (Collected writings of M. L. Lilienblum) (Odessa, 1913), vol. 3, pp. 300, 301, 305; idem, "Bein ha-dimyon ve-ha-efshar" (Between the imaginary and the possible), vol. 4, pp. 247–249.

3. Ibid., "Tehiya meduma" (The illusion of revival), vol. 3, pp. 253, 254. See Shlomo Breiman, "Ha-pulmus bein Lilienblum le-vein Ahad Ha'am ve-Dubnow" (The controversy between Lilienblum, Ahad Ha'am and Dubnow), *Shivat Zion* 1 (1950), pp. 138–168.

4. On Nathan Birnbaum, see chap. 1 above. The semantic origin of the word *Zionism* has been meticulously examined in Alex Bein, "the Origin of the Term and Concept 'Zionism,'" in *Herzl Yearbook*, vol. 2 (New York, 1959), pp. 1–27. Bein traced the first appearance of the noun *Zionismus* to May 16, 1890. He cites a letter from Birnbaum to Motzkin, November 6, 1891, in which Birnbaum urges "the establishment of an organization of the national-political Zionist party in juxtaposition to the practically-oriented party that existed until now." He also cites an editorial written by Birnbaum on November 2, 1891, in which he speaks of Zionism meaning a "new course . . . to realize the aim by creating a large Zionist party for the instruction and education of the people."

5. Bein, "Origin of the Term," p. 23. According to Bein, the noun *Zionismus* first appears in Herzl's diary on March 1, 1896. He cites Theodor Herzl, *Tagebücher*, vol. 1 (Berlin, 1922), p. 353.

6. See Ben Halpern, "Herzl's Historic Gift: The Sense of Sovereignty," in *Herzl Year Book*, vol. 3 (New York, 1960), pp. 27–36.

7. Steven Beller, *Herzl* (London, 1991), p. 3. See also Andrew Handler, *Dori: The Life and Times of Theodor Herzl in Budapest (1860–1878)* (University, Ala., 1983); Joseph Patai, "Herzl's School Years," in *Herzl Yearbook*, vol. 3 (New York, 1960), pp. 53–75.

8. See Theodor Herzl, *The Complete Diaries of Theodor Herzl*, ed. Raphael Patai and trans. Harry Zohn (New York, 1960), vol. 1, p. 7.

9. Ibid., p. 4: "There might have been a time when I would have liked to get away

from it—into the Christian fold, anywhere. But in any case these were only vague desires born of youthful weakness. For I can say to myself with the honesty inherent in this diary—which would be completely worthless if I played the hypocrite with myself—that I never seriously thought of becoming baptised or changing my name."

10. A recent work is the concise but penetrating volume: Beller, *Herzl*. Some others of note are the pioneering study by Alex Bein, *Theodor Herzl* (Philadelphia, 1941); Desmond Stewart, *Theodor Herzl: Artist and Politician: A Biography of the Father of Modern Israel* (New York, 1974); Amos Elon, *Herzl* (New York, 1986); Ernst Pawel, *The Labyrinth of Exile: A Life of Theodor Herzl* (New York, 1989). An instructive reconsideration of Herzl's role in Zionism is Jacques Kornberg, "Theodor Herzl: A Reevaluation," *Journal of Modern History* 52, no. 2 (June 1980), pp. 226–252. Since Kornberg's illuminating full-length study of Herzl's way to Zionism, *Theodor Herzl: From Assimilation to Zionism* (Bloomington, Ind., 1993), reached me as my manuscript was being delivered to the publisher, I was unable to benefit from it as fully as I would have wished.

11. Theodor Herzl, *The Jewish State (Der Judenstaat)*, trans. Harry Zohn (New York, 1970). This and all the quotations that follow are from this edition in the following sequence: pp. 43, 33, 34, 43, 35, 48, 49, 33, 47, 33.

12. See, e.g., Herzl's article "Mauschel" (*Die Welt*, October 15, 1897) in Theodor Herzl, *Zionist Writings: Essays and Addresses*, trans. Harry Zohn (New York, 1973) vol. 1, pp. 163–168, where it is used with reference to the Rothschilds who had sorely disappointed him.

13. Herzl, *Jewish State*, p. 39.

14. Ibid., p. 33. The quotations that follow are, in sequence, from pp. 49 and 33.

15. Ibid., p. 48.

16. See Jacques Kornberg, "Political Symbolism and Mass Mobilization in the Thought of Theodor Herzl," *Proceedings of the Eighth World Congress of Jewish Studies* (Jerusalem, 1982), vol. 2 (English section), p. 158. But Kornberg concedes that, in *Der Judenstaat*, Herzl "directed his main appeal to Jewish need, not to *Volkish* enthusiasm."

17. Herzl, *Jewish State*, p. 110.

18. Herzl, *Complete Diaries*, vol. 1, p. 232.

19. See Joseph Adler, "Herzl's Philosophy of New Humanism," in *Herzl Yearbook*, vol. 3 (New York, 1960), pp. 175–198.

20. The translation used here is Theodor Herzl, *Old New Land (Altneuland)*, trans. Lotta Levensohn, with a new introduction by Jacques Kornberg (New York, 1960).

21. Herzl, *Jewish State*, p. 27. The quotations that follow are from pp. 28 and 29.

22. "Palestine or Argentine?" in Herzl, *Jewish State*, p. 52.

23. Herzl, *Complete Diaries*, vol. 3, p. 856.

24. Herzl, *Old New Land*, p. 256.

25. Ibid., pp. 79, 284.

26. Herzl, *Jewish State*, p. 92.

27. Ibid., p. 94.

28. Ibid., p. 49.

29. On Herzl's diplomacy, see David Vital, *The Origins of Zionism*, (Oxford, 1975), pp. 267–370.

30. E.g., Herzl to Professor Zvi Belkowski (Sofia), June 30, 1897, in Theodor Herzl, *Kitvei Herzl: Igrot mi-reishit ha-peula ha-tzionit ad ha-kongres ha-rishon* (The writings of Herzl: Letters from the beginning of Zionist activity until the first congress), ed. Alex Bein and trans. Dov Sadan (Jerusalem, 1961), vol. 2, p. 324.

31. Quoted in Joseph Adler, *The Herzl Paradox: Political Social and Economic Theories of a Realist* (New York, 1962), pp. 35, 36. See also Moshe Shaerf, "Herzl's Social thinking," in *Herzl Yearbook*, vol. 3 (New York, 1960), pp. 201, 202.

32. See *Stenographische Protokoll des II Zionisten-Kongresses, Vienna, 1898* p. 5. On the question of *Gegenwartsarbeit* in Herzl's time, see Shmuel Almog, *Zionism and History: The Rise of a New Jewish Consciousness* (New York, 1987), pp. 177–193.

33. See Meir Ben-Horin, *Max Nordau: Philosopher of Human Solidarity* (London, 1956), p. 211. Also Meir Ben-Horin, "Reconsidering Max Nordau," in *Herzl Yearbook*, vol. 2 (New York, 1959), pp. 153–170.

34. Herzl, *Complete Diaries*, vol. 1, p. 196 (July 6, 1895): "Yesterday with Nordau, over a glass of beer. Also discussed the Jewish Question of course. Never before had I been in such perfect tune with Nordau. Each took the words right out of the other's mouth. . . . We agreed on every point."

35. Max Nordau, *Zionistische Schriften* (Berlin, 1923), p. 486.

36. See Ben-Horin, *Max Nordau*, pp. 173–211.

37. See Moshe Halevy, "Darko shel Max Nordau el ha-tzionut" (Max Nordau's path to Zionism), *Ha-tzionut* 16 (1991), pp. 63–92, esp. p. 75.

38. Max Nordau, *The Conventional Lies of Our Civilization* [trans. from the German] (Chicago, 1886), p. 363.

39. Halevy, "Darko shel Max Nordau," p. 87.

40. Max Nordau, "Address to the Eighth Zionist Congress" (August 14, 1907) in *Max Nordau to His People*, ed. Benzion Netanyahu (New York, 1941), p. 172.

41. For the view that his Zionism was a break inconsistent with his former cosmopolitan liberalism, see P. M. Baldwin, "Liberalism, Nationalism, and Degeneration: The Case of Max Nordau," *Central European History* 13, no. 2 (June 1980), pp. 99–120. For the opposite view, see Ben-Horin, *Max Nordau*. According to Ben-Horin, Nordau's Zionism was an outgrowth of his "solidarianism."

42. Benzion Netanyahu, ed., *Max Nordau to His People*, (New York, 1941), p. 188.

43. Nordau, "Talk in the Hague" (April 10, 1900), *Zionistische Schriften*, p. 271.

44. Nordau, "Der Zionismus" (1902) *Zionistische Schriften*, pp. 18–38. This and the quotations that follow are from pp. 22, 23, 28.

45. Nordau, "Address to the First Zionist Congress" (August 19, 1897), *Zionistische Schriften*, pp. 40, 51.

46. Ibid., p. 72. See Almog, *Zionism and History*, pp. 108–118.

47. "Pirkei zikhronot" (Reminiscences), *Kol kitvei Ahad Ha'am* p. 494.

48. "Pirkei zikhronot," p. 468. For an illuminating discussion of Ahad Ha'am's choice of this pen name as "a combination of modesty and ambition," see Steven J. Zipperstein, *Elusive Prophet: Ahad Ha'am and the Origins of Zionism* (Berkeley and Los Angeles, 1993). Since this work reached me as my manuscript was being delivered to the publisher, I was unable to benefit from it as fully as I would have wished.

49. "Shlilat ha-galut" (Negation of the exile), *Kol kitvei Ahad Ha'am*, p. 400, as translated in Leon Simon, *Ahad Ha-Am: Essays, Letters and Memoirs* (Oxford, 1946), p. 213. *Unless otherwise stated, the translations by Simon cited in the endnotes that follow are from this particular volume.* "Slavery in Freedom" (1891) is the title of another famous essay by Ahad Ha'am. See *Kol kitvei Ahad Ha'am*, pp. 64–69.

50. Letter to J. Eisenstadt (London), April 21, 1914. *Igrot Ahad Ha'am* (Letters of Ahad Ha'am) (Jerusalem, 1924), vol. 5, p. 171, as translated in Simon, *Ahad Ha-Am: Essays, Letters, Memoirs*, p. 292.

51. Letter to Dr. M. Ehrenpreis, Odessa, December 22, 1897. *Igrot Ahad Ha'am*, vol. 1, p. 158, as translated in Simon, p. 247.

52. "Medinat ha-yehudim ve-tzarat ha-yehudim" (The Jewish state and the Jewish problem) (1897), *Kol kitvei Ahad Ha'am* p. 137, as translated in Hans Kohn, ed., *Nationalism and the Jewish Ethic: Basic Writings of Ahad Ha'am* (New York, 1962), p. 74.

53. Letter to A. L. (Warsaw), August 31, 1903. *Igrot Ahad Ha'am*, vol. 3, pp. 136–139, as translated in Simon, pp. 283–286.

54. Letter to Dr. J. Klausner (Odessa), October 16, 1905, *Igrot Ahad Ha'am*, vol. 3, p. 210, as translated in Simon, p. 288.

55. "Medinat ha-yehudim ve-tzarat ha-yehudim," *Kol kitvei Ahad Ha'am* p. 135, as translated in Kohn, p. 79.

56. "Shlilat ha-galut," *Kol kitvei Ahad Ha'am*, p. 401, as translated in Simon, p. 217.

57. See the introduction in Koppel S. Pinson, ed., *Simon Dubnow: Nationalism and History* (Philadelphia, 1958), pp. 53–57.

58. "Shlilat ha-galut," *Kol kitvei Ahad Ha'am*, pp. 399, 400, as translated in Simon, p. 214.

59. "Shlilat ha-galut," p. 403, as translated in Simon, pp. 220, 221.

60. "Shlilat ha-galut," p. 402, as translated in Simon, pp. 219, 220.

61. Letter to S. Dubnow (Odessa), September 22, 1907, *Igrot Ahad Ha'am*, vol. 3, p. 288, as translated in Simon, p. 265.

62. Letter to Dr. M. Ehrenpreis (Odessa), January 7, 1904, *Igrot Ahad Ha'am*, vol. 3, pp. 159, 160, as translated in Simon, p. 287.

63. See letter to S. Dubnow, London, December 18, 1907, *Igrot Ahad Ha'am*, vol. 3, p. 291.

64. Ahad Ha'am, "Dr. Pinsker u-mahbarto," *Kol kitvei Ahad Ha'am*, p. 47.

65. See, e.g., letters to Ehrenpreis (Odessa), January 7, 1904, *Igrot Ahad Ha'am*, vol. 3, pp. 159, 160; and to Dizengoff (London), July 15, 1912, vol. 4, pp. 283.

66. Ahad Ha'am, "Tehiyat ha-ruah" (The revival of the spirit), *Kol kitvei Ahad Ha'am*, p. 181, as translated in Simon, p. 97.

67. Ahad Ha'am, "Milim u-musagim" (Words and concepts), *Kol kitvei Ahad Ha'am* p. 393, as translated in "A Spiritual Center" (1907), Simon, pp. 203, 204.

68. Letter to Ehrenpreis (Odessa), January 7, 1904, *Igrot Ahad Ha'am*, vol. 3, p. 160, as translated in Simon, p. 287.

69. Letter to D.S. (Odessa), July 27, 1903, *Igrot Ahad Ha'am*, vol. 3, p. 129. See also "Shalosh madregot," (Three steps) (1898), *Kol kitvei Ahad Ha'am*, p. 153. Yet in an article entitled "Sakh ha-kol" (The summation), 1912, he was again equivocal on the question of whether a Jewish majority was necessary. See *Kol kitvei Ahad Ha'am*, pp. 421–428.

70. Ahad Ha'am, "Hakdama le-mahadura rishona" (Introduction to the first edition), *Kol kitvei Ahad Ha'am*, p. 3.

71. For recent reevaluations of Ahad Ha'am's motives and attributes as a political leader, see the comprehensive biography, Joseph Goldstein, *Ahad Ha'am: Biografia* (Ahad Ha'am: A biography) (Jerusalem, 1992); also, more succinctly, Joseph Goldstein, "Ahad Ha'am: A Political Failure?" *Jewish History* 4, no. 2 (fall 1990), pp. 33–48. In contrast to Leon Simon's depiction of Ahad Ha'am as an intellectual who was uninterested in political machinations (see Leon Simon, *Ahad Ha-Am: A Biography* [London, 1960], esp. pp. 298–327), Goldstein depicts Ahad Ha'am as a person who had political aspirations but always withdrew from taking on the ultimate responsibilities of power. Cf. Steven J. Zipperstein, "Ahad Ha'am's Politics," *Jewish History* 4, no. 2 (fall 1990), pp. 89–96.

Zipperstein describes his leadership style as a secularized version of traditionalist rabbinical authority.

72. Ahad Ha'am, "Altneuland," *Kol kitvei Ahad Ha'am*, p. 319.

73. Ibid.

74. "Ha-bokhim" (The weepers), *Kol kitvei Ahad Ha'am*, pp. 337–341.

75. Letter to J. H. Ravnitzki (Odessa), London, August 29, 1911, *Igrot Ahad Ha'am*, vol. 4, p. 244.

76. Menahem Ussishkin, *Unser Programm*, reproduced in Hebrew translation in R. Benjamin (Radler-Feldman), ed., *Sefer Ussishkin* (The book of Ussishkin) (Jerusalem, 1934), pp. 97–125. The quotations are from pp. 97, 98, 99. An English translation appeared as *Our Program: An Essay by M. Ussischkin [sic]*, trans. D. S. Blondheim (New York, 1905).

77. Cited from A. Rafaeli, "Veidot artziot shel tzionei russia" (National conferences of Russian Zionists), in *Katzir: kovetz le-korot ha-tnua ha-tzionit be-russia* (Harvest: Anthology on the history of the Zionist movement in Russia) (Tel Aviv, 1964), p. 97.

78. See Jehuda Reinharz, *Chaim Weizmann: The Making of a Zionist Leader* (New York, 1985), pp. 297, 298, 310.

79. The literature on the genesis of the Balfour Declaration is extensive. See particularly Isaiah Friedman, *The Question of Palestine, 1914–1918*, 2nd ed., expanded (New Brunswick, N.J., and London, 1992).

80. See the table of party representatives at Zionist congresses, Appendix V in Israel Cohen, *A Short History of Zionism* (London, 1951), p. 262. In 1921 there were 376 General Zionists out of a total of 512 delegates to the congress; in 1931, only 84 out of 254; in 1935, 128 (81 were Group A; 47 were Group B) out of 463.

81. On the genesis of the Jewish Agency, see Yigal Elam, *Ha-sokhnut ha-yehudit: Shanim rishonot, 1919–1931* (The Jewish Agency: Formative years, 1919–1931) (Jerusalem, 1990).

82. Articles 3 and 11 of the Constitution of the Zionist Organization (1921), *Stenographisches Protokoll der Verhandlungen des XII Zionisten-Kongresses in Karlsbad, 1–14 September 1921*, pp. 796, 797.

83. Isaac Schwarzbart, "General Zionism," *Struggle for Tomorrow: Modern Political Ideologies of the Jewish People*, ed. Basil J. Vlavianos and Feliks Gross (New York, 1954), p. 28.

84. See for example, Ben-Zion Mossinsohn, "Le-hagdarat ha-musag 'tzionut klalit'" (Toward a definition of the concept "General Zionism"), *Ha-tzioni ha-klali*, vol. 1, February 23, 1932.

85. Moshe Glickson, "Al ha-yesodot" (Foundations) (1929), in Moshe Glickson, *Im hilufei mishmarot* (With the changing of the guard), vol. 1 (Tel Aviv, 1939), p. 187.

86. Moshe Kleinman, *Ha-tzionim ha-klali'im* (The General Zionists), (Jerusalem, 1945), p. 63.

87. Yitzhak Gruenbaum, "Le-shem tzionut le-lo levai" (For the sake of unqualified Zionism), *Ha-aretz*, November 29, 1935, quoted in David Shaari, *Mi-"stam tzionut" le-"tzionut klalit"* (From plain Zionism to General Zionism) (Jerusalem, 1990), p. 96.

88. Selig Brodetsky, "General Zionism: The Mainstay of the Organization, An Analysis," *The Jewish Chronicle*, September 30, 1932. Another example of a General Zionist who was at the same time a supporter of socialism was Nehemia de Lieme of Holland. See the sketch on his role in Joseph Nedava, ed., *Sefer Peretz Bernstein* (Tel Aviv, 1961), pp. 207–212.

89. Moshe Glickson, "Hilufei mishmarot" (Changing of the guard), 1919, in his *Im*

hilufei mishmarot, vol. 1, pp. 3–17. See also his synthesis of Herzlian and Ahad Ha'amian ideas in "Al ha-yesodot," pp. 176–179.

90. Schwartzbart, "General Zionism," p. 35.

91. Felix Weltsch. *Allgemeiner Zionismus: Eine Ideologische Skizze* (General Zionism: An ideological sketch) (Prague, n.d. [c. 1936]. The quotations are from pp. 5, 6, 15, 17. This drew on ideas he explored more fully elsewhere in a work entitled *Das Wagnis der Mitte: Ein Beitrag zur Ethik und Politik der Zeit* (The daring of the middle way: A contribution to the ethics and politics of the times) (Kohlhammer, 1936).

92. Glickson, "Prat u-klal" (The individual and the collective), in Glickson, *Im hilufei mishmarot*, pp. 33–62.

93. Glickson, "Al ha-yesodot," p. 200. See also Shaari, *Mi-"stam tzionut" le-"tzionut klalit*," pp. 116–118.

94. Glickson, "'Mishtar borerut' ve-hukat avoda," (An "arbitration regime" and a labor constitution) (1935), *Im hilufei mishmarot*, p. 394.

95. See Shaari, *Mi-"stam tzionut" le-"tzionut klalit*," p. 28. Also Yigal Drori, *Bein yemin le-smol: Ha-hugim ha-ezrahi'im bi-shnot ha-esrim* (Between Left and Right: The civic circles in the 1920s) (Tel Aviv, 1990). This monograph distinguishes between two approaches in what were called the "civic circles" in Palestine. One was "liberal" (Moshe Glickson being its main spokesman); the other was "conservative" (Yehoshua Supersky being its main spokesman). However, the "liberal" school of thought as described by Drori favored state-controlled social programs and paid little attention to individual human freedoms.

96. See Peretz Bernstein, "Liberalizatzia eina liberaliyut" (Liberalization is not liberalism), *Sefer Peretz Bernstein*, p. 175. Also "Darka shel ha-tzionut ha-klalit" (The General Zionist way), *Sefer Peretz Bernstein*, p. 149. This article was published on December 4, 1959, reproducing text that first appeared March 26, 1943.

97. Yehezkel Kaufmann, *Be-hevlei ha-zman* (The tribulations of our times) (Tel Aviv, 1936), p. 120. This is a volume of essays. The quotation is from p. 120 of the essay "Milhemet ha-ma'amadot" (Class war), 1934. Those that follow are from pp. 133, 130, 146, 138, 141, 149, 158.

4. National-Religious Zionism

1. A detailed history of Mizrahi from an insider's vantage point is Yehuda Leib Fishman (Maimon), "Ha-tzionut ha-datit ve-hitpathuta" (Religious Zionism and its development), in *Azkara le-ha-rav A.Y. Kook* (In Memoriam: Rabbi A. Y. Kook), ed. Yehuda Leib Fishman (Jerusalem, 1937), pp. 78–366. There is no up-to-date authoritative history of Mizrahi.

2. Aryei Fishman, "'Torah and Labor': The Radicalization of Religion within a National Framework," *Studies in Zionism*, no. 6 (autumn 1982), p. 258. Fishman argues that the new radical values and norms they adopted were incorporated within traditional culture as part of Torah.

3. *Ha-poel ha-mizrahi* 2, nos. 6/7 (July/August 1925), pp. 179–181, reproduced in Aryei Fishman ed., *Ha-poel ha-mizrahi 1921–1935: Teudot* (Ha-poel Ha-mizrahi, 1921–1935: Documents) (Tel Aviv, 1979), pp. 152, 153. The translation used here is as given in Aryei Fishman, "'Torah and labor,'" p. 261.

4. See Fishman, "'Torah and Labor,'" p. 255.

5. See Aryei Fishman, *Judaism and Modernization on the Religious Kibbutz* (Cambridge, 1922).

6. "Orot: Leket ketaim mi-tokh sifrei ha-rav Y. Y. Reines," (Lights: A selection of Rabbi Y. Y. Reines's works), selected and edited by Ze'ev Aryeh Rabiner, in *Sefer ha-mizrahi, kovetz le-zekher Rabbi Yitzhak Yaakov Reines* (The book of Mizrahi: An anthology in memory of Rabbi Y. Y. Reines), ed. Yehuda Leib Fishman (Jerusalem, 1946), pp. 24, 25, 26. The quotation is from Yitzhak Yaakov Reines's *Or hadash al Zion* (New light on Zion), part 10, chap. 1.

7. Yitzhak Nissenbaum, *Imrei drosh* (Homiletical essays) (Warsaw, 1926), pp. 7, 8. Much the same thesis is repeated in a 1922 article: "Mahi ha-mizrahut" (What is Mizrahism?), in *Yitzhak Nissenbaum, ketavim nivharim: Ma'amarei yesod be-tzionut u-be-yahadut* (Yitzhak Nissenbaum, selected writings: Basic articles on Zionism and Judaism), ed. Eliyahu Moshe Genihowski (Jerusalem, 1948), pp. 107–119.

8. Nissenbaum, *Imrei drosh*, p. 20.

9. Nissenbaum, "Mahi ha-mizrahut?" p. 109.

10. Ibid., p. 28.

11. Ibid., p. 36.

12. "'Ha-mizrahi' ve-ha-'aguda'" (Mizrahi and the Aguda), 1934, in *Yitzhak Nissenbaum, ketavim nivharim*, p. 161.

13. Yehuda Leib Maimon, "Ha-mizrahi ve-agudat Israel" (Mizrahi and Agudat Israel) (1924), in Yehuda Leib Maimon, *Le-sha'a u-le-dor: Masot u-mehkarim* (For now and for the generation: Essays and articles) (Jerusalem, 1965), p. 203.

14. Rabbi Moshe Avigdor Amiel, "Ma anu?" (What are we?) (part 3), *Ha-tor* (The turtle-dove) 11, no. 17 (September 28, 1932), p. 5. See Eliezer Don-Yehiya, "Tefisot shel ha-tzionut ba-hagut ha-yehudit ha-ortodoksit" (Conceptions of Zionism in orthodox Jewish thought), *Ha-tzionut* 9 (1984), p. 77.

15. Rabbi Moshe Avigdor Amiel, "Shuv al ha-yesodot ha-ideologi'im shel ha-mizrahi" (Once again on the ideological foundations of Mizrahi) (part 3), *Ha-tor* 14, no. 34 (August 24, 1934), p. 3. See Don-Yehiya, "Tefisot shel ha-tzionut," p. 78.

16. Rabbi Moshe Avigdor Amiel, "Ha-yesodot ha-ideologi'im shel ha-Mizrahi" (The ideological foundations of Mizrahi), reproduced in Yitzhak Raphael and Zalman Shragai, eds., *Sefer ha-tzionut ha-datit* (The book of religious Zionism), vol. 1 (Jerusalem, 1977), p. 4.

17. Ibid., p. 5.

18. Yeshayahu Wolfsberg [Aviad], *Ha-mizrahi, ha-poel ha-mizrahi*, (Jerusalem, 1946), p. 21.

19. For a sociological analysis showing that this may aptly be described as a subculture, see Aryei Fishman, *Judaism and Modernization*, esp. pp. 9–27, 46–66.

20. See Mordechai Breuer, "Al ha-musag 'dati-leumi' ba-historiografia u-ba-hagut ha-yehudit" (On the concept "national-religious" in Jewish historiography and thought), in *Be-shvilei ha-tehiya* (In the paths of renewal), vol. 3 (1988), pp. 7–10. Initially, Mizrahi described itself as a *Histadrut tzionit-ortodoksit (A Zionist Orthodox organization)*. See, e.g., Nissenbaum, "Mahi ha-mizrahut?" pp. 106, 107. But there was never complete satisfaction with the term "orthodox." See, e.g., Wolfsberg, *Ha-mizrahi, ha-poel ha-mizrahi*, p. 41. Wolfsberg writes: "This name 'orthodox' does not really apply to our movement because it is a term alien to the spirit of Judaism: it is Greek in origin and Greek-Christian in significance. By definition it excludes practice and overemphasizes the dogmatic aspect."

21. Samson Raphael Hirsch, *Horev: A Philosophy of Jewish Laws and Observances*, trans. Isador Gronfeld (London, 1962), sect. 714, p. 571. For a comprehensive study of

neoorthodoxy, see Mordechai Breuer, *Modernity within Tradition: The Social History of Orthodox Jewry in Imperial Germany* (New York, 1992).

22. See chap. 1, n. 28. In regard to the ultraorthodox, or *haredim*, one scholarly opinion emphasizes the formative role of the disciples of the Hatam Sofer in midcentury Hungary. See Moshe Samet, "The Beginnings of Orthodoxy," *Modern Judaism* 8, no. 3 (October 1988), pp. 249–270. Another opinion emphasizes the role of the late-19-century enlarged type of yeshiva in Russia. See Menahem Friedman, *Ha-hevra ha-haredit: Mekorot, megamot, ve-tahalikhim* (The *Haredi* Society: Sources, trends and processes) (Jerusalem, 1991).

23. See Aryei Fishman, "Masoret ve-hidush be-havayat ha-tzionut ha-datit" (Tradition and innovation in the experience of religious Zionism), *Be-shvilei ha-tehiya*, ed. Avraham Rubinstein, vol. 1 (1983), pp. 127–148.

24. See Ehud Luz, *Parallels Meet: Religion and Nationalism in the Early Zionist Movement, 1882–1902* (Philadelphia, 1988), pp. 73–77.

25. *Yitzhak Nissenbaum, ketavim nivharim* p. 197.

26. Shlomo Zalman Landa and Joseph Rabinowitz, eds., *Sefer or la-yesharim* (The book of light for the righteous) (Warsaw, 1900). The protracted struggle over Hibbat Zion and Zionism within the religious public of eastern Europe from the early 1880s until the death of Herzl in 1904 has been thoroughly researched in Yosef Salmon, *Dat ve-tzionut: Imutim rishonim* (Religion and Zionism: First encounters) (Jerusalem, 1990), pp. 112–339, and in Luz, *Parallels Meet.*

27. *Sefer or la-yesharim*, p. 55. The words are those of Rabbi Haim Halevi Soloveitchik of Brisk.

28. Ibid., p. 20. The words are those of Rabbi Pinhas Eliyahu Rothenberg of Piltz.

29. Ibid., p. 58.

30. *Sefer da'at ha-rabbanim* (The book of rabbinical opinions) (Warsaw, 1902), p. 106.

31. *Sefer or la-yesharim* p. 92; *Sefer da'at ha-rabbanim*, p. 105.

32. This statement, made in 1903, is reproduced in Shalom Dov Ber Shneersohn, *Kuntres u-ma'ayan mi-beit Adonai* (A tract on: And a fount from the house of the Lord) (Brooklyn, N.Y., 1943). The quotations are, in sequence, from pp. 48, 47. The translation here makes use of that in I. Domb, *The Transformation: The Case of the Naturei Karta* (London, 1958), pp. 225, 226.

33. See Seder Nashim, Ketuboth, 111a, *The Babylonian Talmud,* (London: Soncino Press, 1936), pp. 713, 714. This talmudic discussion was based on a biblical passage in the Song of Sol. (Cant. 2:7.) "I adjure you, O daughters of Jerusalem, by the gazelles, and by the hinds of the field, [that ye awaken not, nor stir up love, until it pleases]." There is a division of opinion among scholars as to the historical significance of this homiletical tradition of the oaths. One view is that it carried little weight until it was deployed in the struggle against Zionism in the late nineteenth century. See Mordechai Breuer, "Ha-diyun be-shalosh ha-shvuot ba-dorot ha-ahronim" (The debate on the three oaths in recent generations), in *Geula u-medina* (Redemption and State) (Jerusalem, 1979), pp. 49–57. Another view is that it was prevalent throughout the generations and made a deep impression in Jewish life and halakhic literature even before the advent of Zionism. See Aviezer Ravitzky, *Ha-ketz ha-megule u-medinat ha-yehudim: Meshihiyut, tzionut ve-radikalizm dati be-Yisrael* (Messianism, Zionism and Jewish religious radicalism in Israel) (Tel Aviv, 1993), pp. 277–305.

34. *Sefer da'at ha-rabbanim*, p. 10.

35. Domb, *Transformation*, p. 228.

36. *Sefer or la-yesharim*, p. 57.

37. Yoel Teitelbaum, *Sefer va-Yoel Moshe* (The book of Va-Yoel Moshe) (Brooklyn, N.Y., 1961), pp. 5, 6. The punishment alluded to in the relevant talmudic discussion (and related by Teitelbaum to the Holocaust) is "If you will keep the adjuration, well and good; but if not, I will permit your flesh [to be a prey] like [that of] the gazelles and the hinds of the field."

38. See, e.g., Yehuda Leib Fishman, ed., *Sefer Shmuel* (Jerusalem, 1923), p. 153.

39. See S. Zvi Schechter, "Nimukeihem shel rabbanim bead shituf peula im ha-'maskilim' be-tnuat 'Hibbat Zion'" (Rabbinical reasons for cooperation with "the Enlightened" in Hibbat Zion), in *Mehkarim be-toldot am Israel ve-Eretz Israel* (Studies in the history of the Jewish people and Eretz Israel), ed. Aryeh Rappaport (Haifa, 1978), pp. 239–251.

40. Abraham Yaakov Slutzki, ed., *Shivat Zion* (Return to Zion) (Warsaw, 1891–92). On the significance of this work, see Salmon, *Dat ve-tzionut*, pp. 150–172.

41. Shmuel Yaakov Rabinowitz, "Hashkafa le-tova" (A positive viewpoint), *Ha-melitz* no. 156 (July 14, 1899), p. 2.

42. Eliezer Eliyahu (ben ha-rav) Friedmann, *El karyana de-igreta* (To the readers of the epistle [of the Lubavitcher Rebbe]) (Warsaw, 1899/1900). The quotations that follow are, in sequence, from pp. 4, 5, 6, 8.

43. Rabbi Shmuel Yaakov Rabinowitz, *Ha-dat ve-ha-leumiyut* (Religion and nationalism) (Warsaw, 1900), p. 116. See also Rabbi Josef Yaffe's statement in Slutzki, *Shivat Zion*, pp. 72–73.

44. *Kol korei* (Manifesto [of *Mizrahi*]) Adar 2, 1902, p. 1. A copy is in the Jewish National Library, Jerusalem.

45. *Kol korei*, p. 2.

46. See, e.g., the selection *Orot*, in *Sefer Ha-mizrahi*, pp. 17–20, (n. 6 above) in which Reines distinguishes faithfully in the Kalischer tradition between *geula nisit ve-tivit* (miraculous and natural redemption) and affirms *athalta de-geula be-derekh ha-teva* (the beginning of the redemption by natural means).

47. See Yitzhak Yaakov Reines, *Sha'arei ora ve-simha* (The gates of light and joy) (Vilna, 1899), p. 13; Yitzhak Yaakov Reines, "Orhot Israel" (The ways of Israel), *Beit ha-midrash: Mikdash le-tora u-le-hokhmat Israel* (The house of study: Sanctuary of the Torah and the wisdom of Israel), ed. Micha Joseph Bardyczewskaya, part 1, (Cracow, 1888), p. 70. See also Geula bat-Yehuda, *Ish ha-meorot: Rabbi Yitzhak Yaakov Reines* (The man of lights: Rabbi Yitzhak Yaakov Reines) (Jerusalem, 1985), p. 80; Eliezer Don-Yehiya, "Ideologia u-mediniyut ba-tzionut ha-datit—haguto ha-tzionit shel ha-rav Reines u-mediniyut 'Ha-mizrahi' be-manhiguto" (Ideology and policy in religious Zionism: Rabbi Isaac Jacob Reines's conception of Zionism and the policy of Mizrahi under his leadership), *Ha-tzionut* 8 (1983), pp. 103–146.

48. Yitzhak Yaakov Reines, *Or hadash al Zion* (New light on Zion) (Vilna, 1901/2), p. 78.

49. See Michael Zvi Nahorai, "Le-mahuta shel ha-tzionut ha-datit: Iyun be-mishnoteihem shel ha-rav Reines ve-ha-rav Kook" (On the essence of religious Zionism: An examination of the thought of Rabbi Reines and Rabbi Kook), in *Be-shvilei ha-tehiya* ed. Mordechai Eliav, vol. 3 (1988), pp. 25–38.

50. Yitzhak Yaakov Reines, *Shnei ha-meorot* (The two lights) (Piatrakov, 1913), p. 38, cited in Nahorai, "Le-mahuta shel ha-tzionut ha-datit," p. 29.

51. Reines, *Or hadash al Zion*, p. 124.

52. Ibid., p. 255.

53. See Luz, *Parallels Meet*, p. 237. Luz adjudges Reines's thought to be beset by a

debilitating internal contradiction. He argues that Reines "delivered two antithetical messages. He coaxed anti-Zionist orthodoxy to join his party, so that together the two groups could constitute the majority and increase the influence of religion within the Zionist movement. On the other hand, he demanded that the secular Zionists preserve the purity of political and practical Zionism, so that he would win converts from the orthodox camp." Ambivalence indeed marked Reines's approach. He wanted to allay the fears of the *haredi* rabbis and counter their objections and at the same time to ensure that the Zionist Organization did nothing inconsonant with religion. However, this was not necessarily an incompatible combination of intentions so long as he could demonstrate that the Zionist Organization itself had no messianic pretensions and that Mizrahi could look after and advance the interests of Zionism's orthodox adherents.

54. Avraham Yitzhak Ha-Cohen Kook, "Teudat Israel u-leumiyuto" (The mission of Israel and its nationalism), *Ha-peles* 1 (1901), pp. 45–53. The translation is as rendered in Jacob B. Agus, *Banner of Jerusalem: The Life, Times and Thought of Abraham Isaac Kuk* (New York, 1946), p. 63.

55. Avraham Yitzhak Ha-Cohen Kook, *Igrot ha-ra'aya* (Letters of Rabbi A. Y. Kook) (Jerusalem, 1961), vol. 2, p. 134.

56. Ibid., vol 3, 1965, pp. 163, 164, 173. See Yossi Avneri, "Degel Jerusalem," *Be-shvilei ha-tehiya* 3 (1988), pp. 39–58.

57. Works on the thought of Rabbi Kook abound. See Benjamin Ish-Shalom, *Ha-rav Kook: Bein ratzionalism le-mistika* (Rabbi Kook: Between rationalism and mysticism) (Tel Aviv, 1990); Eliezer Schweid, *Ha-yahadut ve-ha-tarbut ha-hilonit* (Judaism and secular culture) (Tel Aviv, 1981), pp. 110–142; Zvi Yaron, *The Philosophy of Rabbi Kook*, trans. Avner Tomaschoff (Jerusalem, 1991); Nathan Rotenstreich, *Jewish Philosophy in Modern Times* (New York, 1968), pp. 219–238.

58. Avraham Yitzhak Ha-Cohen Kook, *Orot* (Lights) (Jerusalem, 1961), p. 151. See also the quotations in this vein in Yaron, *Philosophy of Rabbi Kook*, pp. 245–257.

59. Kook, *Orot*, vol. 1, p. 138, as translated in Yaron, *Philosophy of Rabbi Kook*, p. 201.

60. Avraham Yitzhak Ha-Cohen Kook, "Ikvei hatzon" (By the footsteps of the flock [a reference to Cant. 1:8] (1906), in *Eder ha-yakar ve-ikvei ha-tzon* (A goodly price [a reference to Zech. 11:3] and the footsteps of the flock) (Jerusalem, 1967), p. 124.

61. Kook, *Orot*, p. 44.

62. Avraham Yitzhak Ha-Cohen Kook, *Hazon ha-geula* (The vision of redemption) (Jerusalem, 1941), p. 100.

63. Ibid., p. 82.

64. Ibid., p. 71.

65. Ibid., p. 89, as translated in Agus, *Banner of Jerusalem*, p. 212.

66. Kook, *Igrot ha-ra'aya* vol. 1, p. 348.

67. Avraham Yitzhak Ha-Cohen Kook, *Orot ha-teshuva* (The lights of repentance) (Jerusalem, 1979), pp. 122, 123.

68. Kook, *Orot*, p. 83.

69. See Schweid, *Ha-yahadut ve-ha-tarbut ha-hilonit* p. 127.

70. See Nahorai, "Le-mahuta shel ha-tzionut ha-datit," pp. 11–24. The first two volumes of his *Orot ha-kodesh* (The lights of holiness) were published in 1938, three years after Rabbi Kook's death, and a third volume appeared in 1950. The still incomplete *Igrot ha-ra'aya* also began to appear long after his death—the first volume in 1943, the second in 1946, and the third in 1965. On the virtual canonization of Rabbi Kook's writings in post–Six Day War Israel, see Gideon Aran, "Mi-tzionut datit le-dat tzionit: Shorshei

gush emunim ve-tarbuto" (From religious Zionism to Zionist religion: The roots of Gush Emunim and its culture) (Ph.D. diss., Hebrew University, 1987), pp. 109–112.

71. See Meir Berlin, *Mi-Volozhin le-Yerushalayim* (From Volozhin to Jerusalem), 2 vols. (Jerusalem, 1971); also the article and documents in Netanel Katzburg, "Ha-rav Meir Bar-Ilan u-mediniyuto ha-tzionit be-shnot ha-shloshim" (Rabbi Meir Bar-Ilan and his Zionist policies in the 1930s), *Niv ha-midrashiya* (spring 1970), pp. 212–241.

72. Meir Berlin, "Mehashvei kitzim" (Calculators of the end), in his *Be-shvilei ha-tehiya* (In the paths of renewal) (Tel Aviv, 1940), p. 33.

73. Berlin, *Be-shvilei ha-tehiya*, pp. 206, 207. The quotation is from an address entitled "El ha-noar" (To the youth), 1940. See also *Kitvei rabbi Meir Bar-Ilan* (Writings of Rabbi Meir Bar-Ilan), vol. 1 (Jerusalem, 1950), p. 264: "The State of Israel is a matter from heaven. . . . Is it not '*ikveta de-meshiha*' [the footsteps of the Messiah] writ large? Is it not '*athalta de-geula*' [the beginning of the redemption] on a large scale?" (1949). Rabbi Yitzhak Nissenbaum is another case in point. See Avraham Rubinstein, "Pa'amei mashiah ve-hevlei mashiah be-mishnato shel ha-rav Yitzhak Nissenbaum" (The heartbeat of the Messiah and the travails of the messianic coming in the thought of Rabbi Yitzhak Nissenbaum), in *Sefer Shragai* (Jerusalem, 1981), pp. 118–126.

74. Meir Bar-Ilan, "Tafkidei ha-mizrahi ba-shetah ha-kalkali ve-ha-dati" (The tasks of Mizrahi in the economic and religious spheres) (Nissan, 1940), *Kitvei rabbi Meir Bar-Ilan*, vol. 1 (1950), p. 113.

75. Wolfsberg, *Ha-mizrahi, ha-poel ha-mizrahi*, p. 27.

76. Ibid., pp. 12, 13, 25, 26.

77. See Salmon, *Dat ve-tzionut*, p. 19.

78. It has been shown that the progenitors of Gush Emunim were a group of youths who formed a group called Gahelet (Embers) in the 1950s. They were not at the time particularly captivated by the thought of Chief Rabbi Abraham Kook. Some of their number later studied under Zvi Yehuda Kook at the Rav Kook Yeshiva in Jerusalem. It appears that rather than emanating directly from Zvi Yehuda Kook's teaching, the future founders of Gush Emunim came with a predisposition to the thought of Rabbi Abraham Kook as interpreted by his son and chose to accept the son's spiritual guidance. They were "believers in search of a dogma." See Gideon Aran, "From Religious Zionism to Zionist Religion: The Roots of Gush Emunim," *Studies in Contemporary Jewry*, vol. 2 (Bloomington, Ind., 1986), p. 138. Cf. the different interpretation of Gush Emunim's political character in Janet Aviad, "The Messianism of Gush Emunim," *Studies in Contemporary Jewry*, vol. 7 (New York, 1991), pp. 197–216. See also Eliezer Don-Yehiya, "Jewish Messianism, Religious Zionism and Israeli Politics: The Impact and Origins of Gush Emunim," *Middle Eastern Studies* 23, no. 2 (April 1987), pp. 215–234.

79. See Rivka Horwitz, ed., *Yitzhak Breuer: Iyunim be-mishnato* (Yitzhak Breuer: Studies on his Thought) (Ramat Gan, 1988).

80. See Schechter, "Nimukeihem shel rabbanim," pp. 239–251.

81. The text of Rabbi Mohilewer's letter to the congress is reproduced in Yehuda Leib Fishman, ed., *Sefer Shmuel*, pp. 66–70. The quotation is from p. 68. On the way rabbis Mohilewer, Eliasberg, and Reines coped with modernity see Salmon, *Dat ve-tzionut*, pp. 39–41.

82. Reines, *Or hadash al Zion*, p. 223.

83. Nissenbaum, *Imrei drosh*, p. 158.

84. Eliezer Eliyahu (ben ha-rav) Friedmann, p. 19. See n. 42 above.

85. Shmuel Yaakov Rabinowitz, "Ezrat sofrim: Da'at rabbanim" (Author's section: Rabbinic opinion), no. 5, *Ha-melitz*, no. 90 (April 23, 1900). This series began with

Rabinowitz's own statement in *Ha-melitz* of March 30, 1900, under the title, "Rabbinic Opinions in Favor of Zionism."

86. Wolfsberg, *Ha-mizrahi, ha-poel ha-mizrahi*, p. 9.

87. Nissenbaum, "Ma-hi ha-mizrahut?" p. 198.

88. Wolfsberg, *Ha-mizrahi, ha-poel ha-mizrahi*, pp. 21, 22, 41.

89. See Fishman, *Judaism and Modernization*, pp. 72–79.

90. Shmuel Haim Landau, "Le-veirur shitateinu" (In clarification of our outlook) (1926), in *Kitvei Shmuel Haim Landau* (Writings of Shmuel Haim Landau), vol. 1 (Warsaw, 1935), p. 41.

91. Ibid., p. 38.

92. Landau's view of Samson Raphael Hirsch's neoorthodoxy is outlined in his "Oreita ve-Israel" (Torah and Israel), in *Kitvei Shmuel Haim Landau*, p. 2.

93. Landau, "Le-veirur shitateinu," p. 37.

94. Shmuel Haim Landau, "Ha-tzionut ha-datit ha-leumit" (National-religious Zionism) (1928), in *Kitvei Shmuel Haim Landau*, p. 62.

95. Landau, "Le-veirur shitateinu," pp. 38, 39.

96. Landau, "Al tafkidei tzeirei mizrahi" (On the tasks of Tzeirei Mizrahi) (1923), in *Kitvei Shmuel Haim Landau*, pp. 29, 30.

97. Yeshayahu Bernstein, "Le-mahuta shel histadruteinu" (On the essence of our organization), *Ha-poel ha-mizrahi*, year 1, nos. 8/9 (August 1924), pp. 18–22, extracted and reproduced in Aryei Fishman, *Ha-poel ha-mizrahi, 1921–1935: Teudot* (Tel Aviv, 1979), p. 159 (hereafter, Fishman, *Teudot*).

98. Landau, "Le-veirur shitateinu," p. 41.

99. Zalman Shragai, "Ba-mahaneh" (In the camp), extracted and reproduced in Fishman, *Teudot*, pp. 195, 196, from a series of articles in *Netiva*, year 9, no. 8 (March 7, 1934), p. 2; no. 16 (May 23, 1934), p. 2; no. 19 (June 13, 1934), p. 2.

100. Nathan Gorodensky (Gordi), "Mahuteinu" (Our essence), *Ha-poel ha-mizrahi* 1, no. 2 (April 1923), pp. 28–30. The quote is on p. 30.

101. S. H. Borokhuni, "Mahu ha-poel ha-mizrahi" (What is *Ha-poel ha-mizrahi*), *Ha-poel ha-mizrahi* 1, no. 5 (May 1924), pp. 1–5; and nos. 5/6 (June/July 1924), pp. 6–9, extracted and reproduced in Fishman, *Teudot*, p. 158.

102. Yeshayahu Shapira, "Ve-asita ha-yashar be-einav" (Thou shalt do what is right and good) (1929), in *Yalkut: Ma'amarim al ra'ayon torah ve-avoda* (Compendium: Articles on the idea of *Torah ve-voda*), ed. Nehemia Aminoah and Yeshayahu Bernstein (Jerusalem, 1931), pp. 38–43. The translation here is adapted from Yosef Tirosh, ed., *Religious Zionism: An Anthology* (Jerusalem, 1975), pp. 120–127.

103. Yitzhak Gur-Aryeh, "Sheifat ha-dorot" (The aspiration of the generations) (1927) in *Yalkut*, p. 45; originally in *Netiva* 2, nos. 14–16 (June 1927), pp. 252–258. Cf. Salmon, *Dat ve-tzionut*, pp. 24, 25.

104. Nissenbaum, *Yitzhak Nissenbaum, ketavim nivharim*, p. 164. This contrast with Ahad Ha'am's vision is ubiquitous in national-religious Zionism. See, e.g., *Ha-poel ha-mizrahi's* Yeshayahu Bernstein, "Merkaz ruhani" (Spiritual center), in *Yeud va-derekh* (Destiny and path) (Tel Aviv, 1956), p. 152.

105. Nissenbaum, "Ha-yahadut ha-temima," in *Imrei drosh*, pp. 8, 13.

106. See, e.g., Yeshayahu Bernstein, "Le-ba'ayat medinat ha-torah" (On the problem of the Torah state) (1956), in *Yeud ve-derekh*, esp. pp. 215, 205, 225.

107. See Geula Bat-Yehuda, *Ha-rav Maimon be-dorotav* (Rabbi Maimon and his times) (Jerusalem, 1979), pp. 600, 609; Yehuda Leib Ha-Cohen Maimon, *Hidush*

ha-sanhedrin be-medinateinu ha-mehudeshet (The renewal of the Sanhedrin in our renewed state) (Jerusalem, 1951).

108. See Eliezer Schweid, *Demokratia ve-halakha; pirkei iyun be-mishnato shel ha-rav Haim Hirschensohn* (Democracy and *halakha*: The thought of Rabbi Haim Hirschensohn) (Jerusalem, 1978).

109. Haim Hirschensohn, *Sefer malki ba-kodesh* (My king in holiness [reference to Ps. 68:25]), 6 parts, 1919–1928; parts 1–4 published in Hoboken, N.J.; parts 5 and 6 published in Seimi, Rumania. The quotation is from part 4 (1922), p. 244, cited in Shweid, *Demokratia ve-halakha*, pp. 27, 28.

110. Zalman Shragai, "Torat ha-mered ha-kadosh" (The doctrine of the holy rebellion), *Netiva*, year 19, nos. 16/17 (1944), pp. 2, 3. See Aryei Fishman, *Judaism and Modernization*, p. 60.

111. Yeshayahu Bernstein, "Al ha-ihud" (On unification), *Ha-ohala*, nos. 2/3 (1925), pp. 40, 41.

112. See Aryei Fishman, *Judaism and Modernization*, pp. 54, 115–140.

113. Avraham Yitzhak Yekutieli, "Torah ve-avoda be-tor hashkafat olam" (Torah and *avoda* as a world outlook), *Netiva*, year 2, no. 11/12 (April 16, 1927), pp. 199–201. Extracted and reproduced in Fishman, *Teudot*, pp. 181, 182. Yekutieli came to Palestine in 1914 and was a teacher in Petah Tikva and in Jerusalem.

114. See the questions and answers put to Rabbi Kook in *Netiva*, year 8, no. 7/8/9 (March 28, 1933), p. 343. See also Zalman Shragai, "Ha-poel ha-mizrahi ve-yahasei ha-avoda ba-aretz" (Ha-poel Ha-mizrahi and labor relations in Eretz Israel), *Netiva*, year 8, no. 10 (May 26, 1933), pp. 377, 378.

115. Cited in Shlomo Zalman Shragai, "Mahshevet Torah Ve-avoda" (The thought of Torah Ve-avoda), *Netiva*, year 10, no. 26/28 (April 12, 1935), p. 15.

116. Nissenbaum, "Mahi ha-mizrahut?" pp. 110, 111.

117. Shlomo Zalman Shragai, "Tafkid ha-mizrahi ve-avodato" (The role and task of Mizrahi), *Ha-tor* 9, no. 27 (May 10, 1929), p. 8.

5. Labor Zionism

1. Karl Marx and Frederick [*sic*] Engels, *The Communist Manifesto* (1848), trans. Samuel Moore (1888) (London, 1948), p. 149. See also Solomon F. Bloom, "Karl Marx and the Jews," *Jewish Social Studies* 4, no. 1 (January 1942), pp. 3–16; Robert Wistrich, "Marxism and Jewish Nationalism: The Theoretical Roots of Confrontation" *The Jewish Journal of Sociology* 17, no. 1 (June 1975), pp. 34–54. Also J. Carlebach, *Karl Marx and the Radical Critique of Judaism* (London, 1978); Walter Laqueur, *A History of Zionism* (London, 1972), pp. 416–437.

2. See Jonathan Frankel, *Prophecy and Politics: Socialism, Nationalism and the Russian Jews, 1862–1917* (Cambridge, 1981), pp. 128ff.

3. See Koppel S. Pinson, "Arkady Kremer, Vladimir Medem, and the Ideology of the Jewish *Bund*," *Jewish Social Studies* 7, no. 3 (July 1945), pp. 233–264; Moshe Mishkinsky, "The Jewish Labor Movement and European Socialism," in *Jewish Society through the Ages*, ed. Haim Hillel Ben-Sasson and Shmuel Ettinger (New York, 1971), pp. 284–296.

4. Ber Borochov, *Ketavim* (Works), ed. L. Levita and D. Ben-Nahum, vol. 1 (Tel Aviv, 1951), appendices, p. 366. See also Henry J. Tobias, *The Jewish Bund in Russia: From Its Origins to 1905* (Stanford, Calif., 1972), pp. 115–118.

5. See Karl Kautsky, *Rasse und Judentum* (Stuttgart, 1914), trans. and rev. as *Are the Jews a Race?* (London, 1926). Cf. the penetrating reappraisal of Kautsky's views on the

Jewish question in Jack Jacobs, *On Socialists and "The Jewish Question" after Marx* (New York, 1991).

6. See Otto Bauer, *Die Nationalitätenfrage und die Sozialdemokratie*, 2nd ed. (Vienna, 1924), pp. 366–381.

7. Ibid., p. 135.

8. Engelbert Pernerstorfer, "Zur Judenfrage," *Der Jude: Eine Monatsschrift*, vol. 1 (Berlin and Vienna, 1916/1917), pp. 308, 309, 313. See Edmund Silberner, "Austrian Social Democracy and the Jewish Problem," *Historia Judaica* 13, no. 2 (October 1951), pp. 121–140; also Wistrich, "Marxism and Jewish Nationalism," pp. 43–54.

9. Koppel S. Pinson, ed., *Dubnow: Nationalism and History* (Philadelphia, 1958). See Pinson's introduction, pp. 3–72, and the translation of Simon Dubnow's "Letters on Old and New Judaism," pp. 73–241.

10. See Joseph Goldstein, *Bein tzionut medinit le-tzionut ma'asit: Ha-tnua ha-tzionit be-russia be-reishita* (Between political Zionism and practical Zionism: Russian Zionism, the formative years) (Jerusalem, 1991), pp. 82–85; also David Vital, *Zionism: The Formative Years* (Oxford, 1982), pp. 467–475. On the working out of the idea of national-cultural autonomy in practice, see Oscar Janowsky, *The Jews and Minority Rights, 1898–1919* (New York, 1933).

11. The World Confederation of Poalei Zion joined those parties that formed the so-called Two-and-a-Half International in Vienna (February 1921) after they had seceded from the disrupted Second International (1899–1914) but refused to join the Communist Third International (Comintern, 1919–1943). When attempts to unite the rump of the Second International and the Two-and-a-Half International culminated in a congress held in Hamburg in May 1923, seven Poalei Zion delegates attended. The World Confederation of Poalei Zion continued to be a member of the ensuing Labor and Socialist International. See the brief survey in Schneier Levenberg, *The Jews and Palestine: A Study in Labour Zionism* (London, 1945), pp. 113–121. Also Ezra Mendelsohn, "The Jewish Socialist Movement and the Second International, 1889–1914: The Struggle for Recognition," *Jewish Social Studies* 26, no. 3 (1964), pp. 131–141; Walter Laqueur, *A History of Zionism* (London, 1972), pp. 423–425; Robert Wistrich, "Eduard Bernstein and the Jewish Problem," *Jahrbuch des Instituts für deutsche Geschichte*, vol. 8 (Tel Aviv, 1979), p. 255.

12. Joseph Stalin, "Marxism and the National Question" (1913), translated from the Russian in Joseph Stalin, *Marxism and the National and Colonial Question* (London, n.d.; Moscow, 1950), pp. 11, 12. See Wistrich, "Marxism and Jewish Nationalism," p. 51; also Norman Levine, "Lenin on Jewish Nationalism," *Wiener Library Bulletin* 33, no. 51/52 (1980), pp. 42–55.

13. See Otto Heller, *Der Untergang des Judentums* (Vienna, 1931), pp. 173, 174.

14. See Abraham Leon, *The Jewish Question: A Marxist Interpretation* (New York, 1970); originally *Conception materialiste de la question juive* (Paris, 1946).

15. See Frankel, *Prophecy and Politics*, pp. 28–44, 127–128.

16. Although this book was also an outcome of his philosophy studies, the thesis for which he received the degree of doctor of philosophy was completed only in 1903. Also of an epistemological nature, it was titled *Empfindung und Vorstellung* (Sensation and idea). See Marie Syrkin, *Nahman Syrkin, Socialist Zionist: A Biographical Memoir and Selected Essays* (New York, 1961), pp. 58, 59.

17. Syrkin, *Nahman Syrkin*, p. 42.

18. Ibid., pp. 28–85. In 1901, Syrkin tried to form a group called Hessiana; in 1902, another called Herut (Freedom).

19. Nahman Syrkin, "The Jewish Problem and the Socialist Jewish State," as reproduced in English translation in Marie Syrkin, *Nahman Syrkin*, pp. 257, 259.

20. Ibid., p. 265.

21. Ibid., pp. 265–268.

22. Ibid., p. 267.

23. Ibid., pp. 274, 282, 281, in that sequence.

24. Ibid., pp. 271, 274.

25. Ibid., pp. 301, 302.

26. Ibid., pp. 271, 272.

27. Ibid., pp. 268, 270, 276.

28. Ibid., pp. 277, 278.

29. Ibid., p. 282.

30. Ibid., pp. 283, 282, 284, in that sequence.

31. Ibid., p. 284.

32. Ibid., p. 285.

33. Ibid., pp. 289, 288, in that sequence.

34. Ibid., p. 297.

35. Nahman Syrkin, "Ha-tzionut ve-ha-Bund" (Zionism and the Bund), in *Kitvei Nahman Syrkin* (Writings of Nahman Syrkin), ed. Berl Katznelson and Yehuda Kaufman, vol. 1 (Tel Aviv, 1939), p. 220.

36. Ibid., pp. 226–227. The "streimel" was the type of headgear worn by orthodox Jews in eastern Europe on festive occasions.

37. Ibid., pp. 221, 222.

38. Ibid., p. 222.

39. Ibid., pp. 226, 223, 224, in that sequence.

40. Ibid., pp. 227, 228.

41. The most authoritative study is Matityahu Mintz, *Ber Borochov: Ha-ma'agal ha-rishon, 1900–1906* (Ber Borochov: Circle One, 1900–1906) (Tel Aviv, 1976); idem, *Zemanim hadashim zemirot hadashot: Ber Borochov, 1914–1917* (New times, New tunes: Ber Borochov, 1914–1917) (Tel Aviv, 1988).

42. "Le-she'elat tzion ve-territoria" (On questions of Zion and territory), in Borochov, *Ketavim*, vol. 1, p. 36.

43. "Le-she'elat ha-teoria ha-tzionit" (On questions of Zionist theory), in Borochov, *Ketavim*, vol. 1, p. 40, as translated in David Hardan, ed., *Sources: Anthology of Jewish Thought*, vol. 2 (Jerusalem, 1971), p. 36.

44. "Le-she'elat tzion ve-territoria," p. 41. For a comprehensive discussion of these ideas of Borochov, see Frankel, *Prophecy and Politics*, pp. 338ff.

45. "Le-she'elat tzion ve-territoria," p. 41. In this respect Borochov concurred with the members of the earliest Poalei Zion group—the Minsk Poalei Zion—who propounded a theory of Jewish nonproletarianization.

46. This quotation and those that follow are from "Le-she'elat ha-teoria ha-tzionit," pp. 14, 15, as translated in Hardan, ed., *Sources*, pp. 25, 45.

47. See Matityahu Mintz, "Borochov ve-Bogdanov" (Borochov and Bogdanov), *Ba-derekh* (On the path) 1 (September 1967), pp. 96–122, who argues that Borochov's intellectual preference was for Alexander Bogdanov's version of Marxist materialism.

48. "Le she'elat tzion ve-territoria," p. 140.

49. Ibid., p. 148.

50. Ibid., p. 53.

51. See Frankel, *Prophecy and Politics*, pp. 359–363, which discusses alternative

explanations for Borochov's volte-face or transformed doctrine of 1905–1906. Frankel suggests that it may well have been less a political maneuver than "a sudden re-evaluation analogous to a religious conversion."

52. "The National Question and the Class Struggle," (1905), in Ber Borochov, *Nationalism and the Class Struggle: A Marxian Approach to the Jewish Problem*, ed. Abraham G. Duker (Westport, Conn., 1972) (first published in 1937 by Poale Zion-Ze'ire Zion of America and Young Poale Zion Alliance of America, New York), pp. 137, 138. The quotations that follow are from this English version.

53. Ibid., pp. 142, 144.

54. Ibid., p. 162.

55. Ibid., pp. 164, 165.

56. Ibid., p. 157.

57. Ibid.; the quotations are, in sequence, from pp. 159, 150, 141, 144, 150.

58. Ibid., p. 166.

59. See ibid., pp. 59–74, for Borochov's "The Economic Development of the Jewish People,"

60. "Our Platform," in Borochov, *Ketavim*, vol. 1, p. 280. I owe this apt translation to Mitchell Cohen; see Ber Borochov, *Class Struggle and the Jewish Nation: Selected Essays in Marxist Zionism*, ed. with an introduction by Mitchell Cohen, p. 21.

61. Borochov, *Ketavim*, vol. 1, pp. 282, 283.

62. See Matityahu Mintz, "Ber Borochov," *Studies in Zionism* 5 (spring 1982), p. 44.

63. "Eretz Israel in Our Program and Tactics," in Borochov, *Nationalism and the Class Struggle*, p. 125.

64. Ibid., p. 127.

65. Ibid., pp. 127, 128, 130, 131.

66. See Mintz, "Ber Borochov," pp. 45, 46.

67. See Elkana Margalit, *Anatomia shel smol: Poalei Zion smol be-Eretz Israel, 1919–1946* (Anatomy of the Left: Left Poalei Zion in Eretz Israel, 1919–1946) (Tel Aviv, 1976).

68. Ber Borochov, *Ketavim nivharim*, (Selected writings), ed. Zalman Shazar (Rubashov) (Tel Aviv, 1944); *Ber Borochov: Geklibene Schriftn* (Yiddish: Selected writings), ed. Berl Locker (New York, 1928); also Ber Borochov, *Nationalism and the Class Struggle*.

69. The new world union was called Ha-ihud Ha-olami Poalei Zion-Tzeirei Zion (The World Union of Poalei Zion-Tzeirei Zion) and was known more simply as Ha-ihud Ha-olami.

70. Translated from the German as "Saron ha-ma'amadot ve-she'elat ha-yehudim" (1911), in Shlomo Kaplansky, *Hazon ve-hagshama* (Vision and realization) (Merhavia, 1950), pp. 33–50. The quotations that follow are from pp. 35–37.

71. Ibid., p. 37.

72. "Ha-tazkir ha-rishon le-misrad ha-internatzional ha-sotzialisti" (The first memorandum to the Office of the Socialist International) (1907) in Kaplansky, *Hazon ve-hagshama*, pp. 135, 136.

73. Kaplansky, "Saron ha-ma'amadot," pp. 33, 34, 38, 49.

74. Leon Chasanowitsch, "Ziele und Mittel des socialistischen Zionismus," *Socialistische Monatsheft* 20, no. 15 (July 30, 1914), pp. 965, 967.

75. Ibid., p. 962. The quotations that follow are from pp. 964, 965.

76. Hayim Fineman, *Poale Zionism: An Outline of Its Aims and Institutions* (New York, 1918). The quotations that follow are from pp. 7–10.

77. Yehuda Slutzky, ed., *Poalei Zion be-Eretz Israel, 1905–1919* (Tel Aviv, 1978), pp. 17, 18. The document is translated from the Yiddish original in *Der Proletarishe Gedank* (Proletarian thought), no. 3, 1907.

78. Aharon Gertz, ed., *Statistical Handbook of Jewish Palestine*, Jewish Agency for Palestine (Jerusalem, 1947), p. 37.

79. See the authoritative but unpublished work, Israel Kolatt, "Idiologia u-metziut be-tnuat ha-poalim ba-aliya ha-sheniya" (Ideology and reality in the workers' movement in the Second *Aliya*) (Ph.D. diss., The Hebrew University, Jerusalem, 1965).

80. On the Gedud Ha-avoda, see Anita Shapira, *Ha-halikha al kav ha-ofek* (Visions in conflict) (Tel Aviv, 1989), p. 157–207; also idem, "Gedud Ha-avoda—a Dream That Failed," *The Jerusalem Quarterly*, no. 30 (winter 1984), pp. 62–76.

81. In September 1919, Nahman Syrkin addressed the council of the World Confederation of Poalei Zion in Stockholm on the subject "Socialist Constructivism in Eretz Israel." See Yosef Gorny, *Ahdut ha-avoda, 1919–1930: Ha-yesodot ha-ra'ayoni'im ve-ha-shita ha-medinit* (The unity of Labor Party, 1919–1930: Its ideological foundations and political system) (Tel Aviv, 1973), p. 67. Gorny treats of the whole constructivist ideology and its organizational expressions such as Ahdut Ha-avoda and the Gedud Ha-avoda as an essentially utopian manifestation. However, his use of the term "utopian" is not in the sense of abstract literary cogitations depicting an ideal "no place" but rather in the sense of the nineteenth-century "utopian" socialism against which Karl Marx polemicized. In Gorny's words: "A socialist doctrine opposed to scientific Marxist socialism and posing as an alternative to it . . . an ideological attempt to create from the foundation upward, a society devoid of class contradictions . . . to plan the form of a [nationally] unitary society of the future and to fulfill this blueprint in the present."

82. Berl Katznelson, "Hatza'at ha-ihud" (Proposal for unity) (1919), in *Ketavim* (Writings), vol. 1 (Tel Aviv, 1946), p. 130. Also see the elegant and definitive biography Anita Shapira, *Berl: The Biography of a Socialist Zionist* (Cambridge, 1980), esp. pp. 82–116.

83. Katznelson, "Mekorot lo akhzav" (Inexhaustible sources) (1934), *Ketavim*, vol. 6, p. 388.

84. See Ze'ev Tzahor, *Ba-derekh le-hanhagat ha-yishuv: Ha-histadrut be-reishita* (On the road to *yishuv* leadership: The Histadrut's beginnings) (Jerusalem, 1982).

85. Ben-Gurion, "Likrat ha-ba'ot" (In anticipation of the future), speech to the Histadrut's sixth conference, January 1945, in David Ben-Gurion, *Mi-ma'amad le-am* (From class to nation) (Tel Aviv, 1955), p. 520.

86. See Shabtai Teveth, *Ben-Gurion: The Burning Ground, 1886–1948* (London, 1987), p. 28: "The thin patina of Marxism he acquired in Warsaw was to rub off very easily in later years, especially when he served as chairman of the Jewish Agency and prime minister of Israel." Cf. Israel Kolatt, "Ha-im haya Ben-Gurion sotzialist?" (Was Ben-Gurion a Socialist?), in *David Ben-Gurion: Dmuto shel manhig tnuat poalim* (David Ben-Gurion: Profile of a Labor Leader), ed. Shlomo Avineri (Tel Aviv, 1988), p. 153 and passim.

87. See, e.g., his statement in the course of negotiations with Ha-shomer Ha-tzair, March 1937, in which he said he did not in principle exclude a revolutionary stage. David Ben-Gurion, *Zihronot* (Memoirs), vol. 4 (Tel Aviv, 1974), p. 117.

88. Ben-Gurion, *Mi-ma'amad le-am*, p. 221.

89. Ibid., p. 42. The quotation is from a statement made in New York, January 1918.

90. Quoted in Gorny, *Ahdut ha-avoda*, p. 163.

91. Ben-Gurion, "Ha-yiud ha-leumi shel ma'amad ha-poalim" (The national mission of the working class) (1925) in *Mi-ma'amad le-am*, p. 244.

92. Ben-Gurion, "Shlihuteinu ba'am" (Our mission in the nation) in *Mi-ma'amad le-am*, p. 365, and see Yosef Gorny, *Ahdut ha-avoda*, p. 63. Also Yosef Gorny, "'Mi-ma'amad le-am': Mekorotav ha-histori'im u-mishnato ha-ra'ayonit" ('From class to nation': Its historical sources and its ideological significance) in *David Ben-Gurion: Dmuto shel manhig tnuat ha-poalim*, ed. Shlomo Avineri, pp. 73–90.

93. Ben-Gurion, "Ha-mashber ba-tzionut ve-tnuat ha-poalim" (The crisis in Zionism and in the labor movement), in *Mi-ma'amad le-am*, pp. 386, 398.

94. See Gorny, *Ahdut ha-avoda*, pp. 432–433; Yosef Shapira, *Ha-poel ha-tzair: Ha-ra'ayon ve-hama'ase* (Ha-poel-Ha-tzair: The idea and the practice) (Tel Aviv, 1967). A left wing of Tzeirei Zion groups formed for a time a separate world union in the Zionist Organization known as Ha-brit Ha-mizrahit Tzeirei Zion-ZS (The Eastern Union of Tzeirei Zion-ZS). Another section joined the World Union of Poalei Zion.

95. "Draft Program" 1906, reproduced in appendices to Shapira, *Ha-poel ha-tzair*, pp. 470, 471.

96. *Ha-olam* 1, no. 20 (May 22, 1907), reproduced in Shapira, *Ha-poel ha-tzair*, appendices, pp. 475–477.

97. Ibid., p. 478.

98. Quoted ibid., p. 92.

99. Quoted ibid., p. 371, and reproduced in appendices, pp. 481–482. The Hebrew term for socialism in vogue at this time and here used by Shohat was *sotzialiyut* rather than *sotzialism* as in contemporary usage.

100. *Ha-poel ha-tzair*, vol. 12 (1919–20), quoted in Baruch Ben-Avraham, *Miflagot u-zeramim politi'im be-tekufat ha-bayit ha-leumi, 1918–1948* (Parties and political movements in the period of the National Home, 1918–1948) (Jerusalem, 1978), p. 47.

101. "Letter from a group of workers, Ein Ganim, to Ahad Ha'am" (1911), in *Kitvei A. D. Gordon: Mikhtavim ve-reshimot*, (Writings of A. D. Gordon: Letters and notes), ed. S. H. Bergman and A. Shohat (Jerusalem, 1957), p. 44.

102. See the profound study, Eliezer Schweid, *Ha-yahid: Olamo shel A. D. Gordon* (The individual: The world of A. D. Gordon) (Tel Aviv, 1970).

103. Frances Burnce, trans., *A. D. Gordon: Selected Essays* (Boston, 1938), p. 194. This is a translation of *Kitzur kitvei A. D. Gordon* (Abbreviated writings of A. D. Gordon), ed. N. Taradyon and A. Shohat (Tel Aviv, 1943), p. 172.

104. Gordon, "Ha-adam ve-ha-teva" (Man and nature), in *Kitvei A. D. Gordon: Ha-adam ve-ha-teva* (Writings of A. D. Gordon: Man and Nature), ed. S. H. Bergman and L. Shohat (Jerusalem, 1951), p. 94.

105. Gordon, "Nationalism and Socialism," in *A. D. Gordon: Selected Essays*, pp. 31, 37.

106. Gordon, "Human-Nation" (*Am-adam*), in *A. D. Gordon: Selected Essays*, p. 14.

107. Gordon, "Man and Nature," in *A. D. Gordon: Selected Essays*, p. 241.

108. Ibid., p. 177, 178.

109. Ibid., p. 192.

110. Gordon, "Teshuvat poel" (A worker's reply) (1909), in *Kitvei A. D. Gordon* (Writings of A. D. Gordon), ed. Joseph Aharonowitz, vol. 1 (Tel Aviv, 1925), pp. 5, 6; see also p. 248.

111. Gordon, "Le-veirur emdateinu" (In clarification of our position), in *Kitvei: A. D. Gordon*, vol. 1, p. 255.

112. Gordon, "Nationalism and Socialism," *A. D. Gordon: Selected Essays*, p. 36.

113. Gordon, "Pitaron lo-ratzionali" (An irrational solution) (1909), in *Kitvei A. D. Gordon*, vol. 1, p. 32.

114. Gordon, "Nationalism and Socialism," in Burnce, *A. D. Gordon: Selected Essays*, pp. 37, 38.

115. Gordon, "Labor," in Burnce, *A. D. Gordon*, p. 52.

116. See the section on "The Work of Revival in the Diaspora," in the essay "Labor," in Burnce, *A. D. Gordon*, pp. 77–84.

117. Ibid., pp. 89, 90.

118. Gordon, "Nationalism and Socialism," in Burnce, *A. D. Gordon*, pp. 42, 43.

119. Gordon, "Avodateinu mi-ata" (Our work from now on), in *Kitvei A. D. Gordon: Ha-uma ve-ha-avoda* (Writings of A. D. Gordon: The nation and labor), ed. S. H. Bergman and L. Shohat (Jerusalem, 1954), p. 248.

120. Gordon, "Mi-kotzer ruah" (On account of impatience), in *Kitvei A. D. Gordon*, vol. 1, pp. 178, 179.

121. Gordon, "Me'at hitbonenut" (Some observations) (1911), in *Kitvei A. D. Gordon*, vol. 1, p. 88.

122. Martin Buber's *Drei Reden* were delivered as a series of talks to the Bar Kochba Verein, a Jewish students society in Prague whose participants included future Zionist intellectuals of distinction such as the philosopher Hugo Bergmann, the writer and editor Robert Weltsch, and the pioneering historian of nationalism Hans Kohn (who, however, became disillusioned after settling in Palestine and moved to the United States). Buber's talks were first published as *Drei Reden über das Judentum* (Frankfurt am Main, 1911). See Jehuda Reinharz, "Martin Buber's Impact on German Zionism before World War I," *Studies in Zionism* 6 (autumn 1982), pp. 171–184.

123. See particularly Martin Buber, *Paths in Utopia*, trans. R. F. Hull (London, 1958). Also see Eliezer Schweid, "Martin Buber and A. D. Gordon: A Comparison," in *Martin Buber: A Centenary Volume*, ed. Haim Gordon and Jochanan Bloch (New York, 1984), pp. 255–272; also idem, *Toldot ha-hagut ha-yehudit ba-mea ha-esrim* (A history of Jewish thought in the twentieth century) (Tel Aviv, 1990), pp. 171–178; Maurice S. Friedman, *Martin Buber: The Life of Dialogue* (Chicago, 1976), pp. 43–47.

124. See Gordon, "Man and Nature," in *A. D. Gordon: Selected Essays*, p. 207: "Why does man suffer from all things and all things suffer from man?"

125. Pinhas Lubianker, "Tnuat Gordonia" (The Gordonia Movement), in *Derekh ha-noar* (The way of youth), Anthology 1 (Tel Aviv, 1929/1930), pp. 58, 59. See also Yeshayahu Shapira, "Gordon and Gordonia," in *Gordonia: Tnuat noar amamit halutzit* (Gordonia: A people's pioneering youth movement) (Hulda, 1982), pp. 172–180.

126. Lubianker, "Tnuat Gordonia," pp. 57, 59.

127. Quoted in Elkana Margalit, *Tnuat ha-noar Gordonia: Ra'ayon ve-orah hayim* (The Gordonia youth movement: The idea and the way of life) (Tel Aviv, 1986), p. 136.

128. Ibid., p. 130.

129. See the brief but incisive study Shlomo Avineri, *Arlosoroff* (London, 1989), also Shlomo Avineri, "The Socialist Zionism of Chaim Arlosoroff," *Jerusalem Quarterly*, no. 34 (winter 1985), pp. 68–87. Cf. Miriam Getter, *Chaim Arlosoroff, biografia politit* (Chaim Arlosoroff: A political biography) (Tel Aviv, 1977); Yosef Shapira, *Chaim Arlosoroff* (Tel Aviv, 1975).

130. Chaim Arlosoroff, *Kitvei Chaim Arlosoroff* (The works of Chaim Arlosoroff), vol. 3 (Tel Aviv, 1934), p. 23. Also quoted in Avineri, "The Socialist Zionism of Chaim Arlosoroff," p. 70.

131. Arlosoroff, "Ha-sotzialism ha-amami" (People's socialism) (1919), in *Kitvei Chaim Arlosoroff*, vol. 1, pp. 36, 37.

132. Ibid., p. 56.

133. Ibid., pp. 26, 27.

134. Ibid., p. 51.

135. Arlosoroff, "Milhemet ha-ma'amadot ba-mitziut ha-Eretz Israelit" (The class struggle in the reality of Eretz Israel) (1926), in *Kitvei Chaim Arlosoroff*, vol. 3, pp. 121–132. The quotations that follow are from these pages.

136. See Arlosoroff, "Ha-taktziv ha-tzioni ve-atido" (The Zionist budget and its future) (1923), and his "Le-ha'arakhat ha-aliya ha-revi'it" (In evaluation of the Fourth *Aliya*) (1925), in *Kitvei Chaim Arlosoroff*, vol. 3, pp. 9–24, 107–120.

137. See Yosef Gorny, "Ha-poel ha-tzair ve-yahaso el ha-sozialism be-tekufat ha-aliya ha-sheniya" (Ha-poel Ha-tzair and its attitude toward socialism in the period of the Second *Aliya*), *Ba-derekh*, no. 1 (1971), pp. 74–83. Gorny notes that even in the Second *Aliya* period there was a range of differing attitudes to socialism in Ha-poel Ha-tzair. On the formation of Mapai, see Yaakov Goldstein, *Mapai: Gormim le-hakamata* (Mapai: The factors in its formation) (Tel Aviv, 1976).

138. See Israel Kolatt, "Poalei Zion bein tzionut le-kommunism," (Poalei Zion between Zionism and Communism), *Assufot* 2, no. 15 (November 1971), pp. 30–49. Also, Israel Kolatt, "Tnuat ha-avoda be-Eretz Israel bein ha-mizrah la-ma'arav" (The labor movement in Eretz Israel between East and West), *Divrei ha-kongress ha-olami ha-hamishi le-madaei ha-yahadut* (Proceedings of the Fifth World Congress of Jewish Studies), vol. 2 (Jerusalem, 1972), pp. 295–307.

139. "Memorandum of *Poalei Zion* to the Comintern," April 1921, and the reply from the executive of the Comintern, August 26, 1921, in *Yalkutei Poalei Zion: Ha-ma'avak ba-zira ha-proletarit ha-beinleumit* (Anthology of Poalei Zion: The struggle in the international proletarian arena), pp. 114, 133, 134, extracted in Ben-Avraham, ed., *Miflagot u-zeramim politi'im be-tekufat ha-bayit ha-leumi*, pp. 67, 68.

140. On Left Poalei Zion in Palestine, see Margalit, *Anatomia shel smol*, esp. pp. 395–411.

141. On the German *Wandervogel, Freideutsche* youth movements, and kindred phenomena, see Walter Laqueur, *Young Germany* (London, 1962). The genesis and development of Blau-Weiss and other Jewish youth movements has been researched in Haim Shatzker, *Tnuat ha-noar be-germaniya bein ha-shanim, 1900–1933* (The Jewish youth movement in Germany in the Years 1900–1933), (Ph.D. diss., The Hebrew University of Jerusalem, 1969).

142. See Elkana Margalit, "Social and Intellectual Origins of the *Ha-shomer Ha-tzair* Youth Movement, 1913–1920," *The Journal of Contemporary History* 4, no. 2 (April, 1969), pp. 25–46. The major work on Ha-shomer Ha-tzair is Elkana Margalit, *Ha-shomer ha-tzair: Mi-edat neurim le-marksism mahapkhani, 1913–1936* (Ha-shomer Ha-tzair: From youth community to revolutionary Marxism, 1913–1936) (Tel Aviv, 1985).

143. On the economic consequences of the Fourth *Aliya*, see Dan Giladi, *Ha-yishuv be-tekufat ha-aliya ha-revi'it 1926–1927* (The *yishuv* during the Fourth *Aliya*) (Tel Aviv, 1973).

144. See Margalit, *Ha-shomer ha-tzair*. Also, in briefer form: Elkana Margalit, "Bein Ha-shomer Ha-tzair le-Ahdut Ha-avoda ba-aretz" (Between Ha-shomer Ha-tzair and Ahdut Ha-avoda in Eretz Israel), *Assufot*, no. 13 (October 1969), pp. 29–50.

145. Quoted from Meir Ya'ari's address at the opening of the Third World Conference of Ha-shomer Ha-tzair, 1930, reproduced in *Sefer ha-shomer ha-tzair* (The Book of Ha-shomer Ha-tzair), vol. 1 (Tel Aviv, 1956), p. 188.

146. This quotation and those that follow are from "Hanahot ideologiyot shel ha-kibbutz ha-artzi mi-yesodo shel ha-shomer ha-tzair" (Ideological assumptions of the

Kibbutz Artzi of Ha-shomer Ha-tzair), accepted at the founding council, April 1–3, 1927, in Haifa (Sivan, 1927), reproduced in Ben-Avraham, ed., *Miflagot u-zeramim politi'im be-tekufat ha-bayit ha-leumi*, p. 72.

147. Anita Shapira has provided penetratingly perceptive analyses of this story of unrequited love in a number of works. See Anita Shapira, "The Dynamics of Zionist Leftist Trends," *Jewish History: Essays in Honour of Chimen Abramsky*, ed. Albert A. Rapoport and Steven J. Zipperstein (London, 1988), pp. 629–682; Anita Shapira, "Labor Zionism and the October Revolution," *Journal of Contemporary History* 24 (1989), pp. 623–656; Anita Shapira, "'Black Night–White Snow,': Attitudes of the Palestinian Labor Movement to the Russian Revolution 1917–1929," *Studies in Contemporary Jewry* vol. 4 (New York, 1988), pp. 144–171. On Berl Katznelson's special anxieties over the dangers of leftist defection from Zionism, see Anita Shapira, *Berl*, esp. pp. 105–109. Another perceptive analysis of this inner tension in mainstream labor Zionism is Meir Avizohar, *Be-rei saduk: Idealim hevrati'im ve-leumi'im ve-hishtakfutam be-olama shel Mapai* (In a cracked mirror: National and social ideals as reflected in Mapai) (Tel Aviv, 1990).

148. Yitzhak Tabenkin, *Devarim* (Collected speeches) (Tel Aviv, 1967), vol. 1, p. 54.

149. Quoted in Yehuda Harell, *Ha-sotzialism shel Yitzhak Tabenkin* (The socialism of Yitzhak Tabenkin) (Tel Aviv, 1972), p. 116. An abbreviated English version of this booklet is Yehuda Harell, *Tabenkin's View of Socialism* (Tel Aviv, 1988). The quotation is on pp. 69, 70.

150. Quoted in Harell, *Ha-sotzialism shel Yitzhak Tabenkin*, p. 48.

151. See ibid., pp. 53–57.

152. Yitzhak Tabenkin, "Le-or ha-tmurot" (In the light of changing times), *Le-ahdut ha-avoda* 1, no. 3/4 (September/October 1948), p. 148.

153. See Avizohar, *Be-rei saduk*, pp. 293–364.

154. Israel Otiker, *Tnuat he-halutz be-polin, 1932–1935* (The He-halutz movement in Poland, 1932–1935), pp. 24–30, and Yehuda Slutsky, "He-halutz," *Encyclopedia of Zionism and Israel*, ed. Raphael Patai (New York, 1971), p. 484.

155. See Henry Near, "Mi-hu halutz?" (Who is a *halutz*?), *Tura* 2 (1991), pp. 228–248.

156. Martin Buber, "He-halutz ve-olamo" (The *halutz* and his world) (1936), in Martin Buber, *Teuda ve-yeud* (Mission and destiny), vol. 2, 1960, pp. 255–257, also quoted in Near, "Mi-hu halutz?" p. 237.

157. "Memorandum of the World Organization of *He-halutz* to Delegates of the Nineteenth Zionist Congress, Lucerne, 1935" (Warsaw, 1935), reproduced in appendices of Otiker, *Tnuat he-halutz be-Polin*.

158. David Ben-Gurion, "Matan eretz" (The giving of a land) (1915), in his *Mi-ma'amad le-am*, p. 24.

159. Ze'ev Jabotinsky, *Ketavim* (Writings): *Autobiografia* (Autobiography) (Jerusalem, 1947), pp. 205, 206.

6. Revisionist Zionism

1. On the life of Jabotinsky, see Joseph B. Schechtman, *The Life and Times of Vladimir Jabotinsky: Vol. 1. Rebel and Statesman: The Early Years; Vol. 2. Fighter and Prophet: The Last Years*, Silver Spring, Md., 1986 (originally published as *The Life and Times of Jabotinsky* [New York, 1956–1961]). See also the recently published Shmuel Katz, *Jabo: Biografia shel Ze'ev Jabotinsky* (Jabo: A Biography), 2 vols. (Tel Aviv, 1993). By far the most comprehensive study of Jabotinsky's Revisionist Zionism is Yaacov Shavit, *Jabotinsky and the Revisionist Movement, 1925–1948* (London, 1988).

2. On Jabotinsky's role in the Helsingfors conference, see Joseph Goldstein, "Jabotinsky and Jewish Autonomy in the Diaspora," *Studies in Zionism* 7, no. 2 (1986), pp. 219–232.

3. The recognition of Jabotinsky's faction as a *Sonderverband,* the Separate Union of Zionist-Revisionists, was only formalized as late as 1933, not long before it seceded from the Zionist Organization. See *Report of the Executive of the Zionist Organisation Submitted to the 18th Zionist Congress at Prague,* August 21–29, 1933, Central office of the Zionist Organization, (London, 1933), p. 49.

4. On the formation of the Zionist Revisionist Organization (Ha-tzohar), see Benjamin Lubotsky, *Ha-tzohar u-Betar* (Ha-tzohar and Betar) (Jerusalem, 1946), pp. 1–7; Joseph B. Schechtman and Y. Benari, *History of the Revisionist Movement,* vol. 1 (Tel Aviv, 1970) (only vol. 1 has appeared to date).

5. It is estimated that the membership of Betar reached some 10,000 by 1929 and 70,000 to 80,000 by 1939. In elections to Zionist congresses Ha-tzohar gained the votes of 8,446 (out of 123,729) in 1927; 18,000 (out of 200,000) in 1929; 55,848 (out of 233,730) in 1931; 95,729 (out of 555,113) in 1933. See Shavit, *Jabotinsky and the Revisionist Movement,* p. 37.

6. See Meir Grossman's own account: Meir Grossman, "Reishit ha-tzionut ha-aktivistit" (The beginnings of activist Zionism), *Ha-uma* 9 (Tammuz, 1964), pp. 24–38.

7. In addition to various volumes of selected works of Jabotinsky, an eighteen-volume collected works was published between 1947 and 1959 by his son: Eri Jabotinsky, ed., *Ze'ev Jabotinsky, Ketavim* (Writings) (Tel Aviv, 1947–1959). *Each volume has its own title. In the endnotes that follow these will be cited as* Ketavim *followed by the title of the volume.* An analysis of his thought on the basis of these writings is Raphaella Bilski Ben-Hur, *Kol yahid hu melekh: Ha-mahshava ha-hevratit ve-ha-medinit shel Ze'ev Jabotinsky* (Every individual is a king: The social and political thought of Ze'ev Jabotinsky) (Tel Aviv, 1988). An annotated selection of extracts, reflecting the near canonization of Jabotinsky's thought characteristic of Revisionist Zionism, is Moshe Bella, *Olamo shel Jabotinsky: Mivhar devarav ve-ikarei torato* (The world of Jabotinsky: A selection of his works and the essentials of his teaching) (Tel Aviv, 1972).

8. This and the quotations that follow are from Ze'ev Jabotinsky, "Geza" (Race) (1913), in *Ketavim: Uma ve-hevra* (Nation and society), pp. 126, 127, 129, 130.

9. Jabotinsky, "Race and Nationality," (typescript, 1939), p. 5, in file 2509/10, JIA. In this English version of his essay on race he reiterated his opinion that

> someday science may achieve such refinement that it will become possible in the special analysis of the blood or, perhaps the secretion of the glands, to establish the "spectrum" or the "recipe" of the various racial types, showing all the ingredients that go to the making of a typical Italian or an average Pole. I venture to forecast that most "recipes" will be found to contain practically the same ingredients, only the proportions in which God and history have mixed them will prove different. What can, however, be quietly assumed even today apart from any forecasts, is that each race, however mixed, has a "spectrum" of its own: and in this sense the term "race" has a perfectly definite and scientifically legitimate meaning.

10. Ibid., p. 1.

11. Jabotinsky, "Hilufei mahmaot" (Exchange of compliments) (1911), in *Ketavim: Uma ve-hevra,* p. 147.

12. Vladimir Jabotinsky, "National Minority Rights" (manuscript, translated from the Russian by Jabotinsky himself [London, July 1938], pp. 11, 12, in file 2509/10, JIA. See also the discussion of Jabotinsky's dissertation on national minority rights in Oscar K. Rabinowicz, *Vladimir Jabotinsky's Conception of a Nation* (New York, 1946), p. 31.

13. For examples of his claim to be not only a liberal but indeed a believer in almost anarchic individualism, see Jabotinsky, "Sipur yamai" (The story of my life), in *Ketavim: Autobiografia* (Autobiography). "The messianic vision," he declares there, "is the garden of Eden of the individual, a brilliant anarchic polity."

14. Jabotinsky, "Mored or" (Rebel of light) (1912), in *Ketavim: Uma ve-hevra*, p. 110.

15. Jabotinsky, "Ra'ayon Betar" (The idea of Betar) (1934), in *Ketavim: Baderekh la-medina* (On the way to the state), p. 308.

16. Jabotinsky, "Sipur yamai," p. 38.

17. Ibid.

18. Ze'ev Jabotinsky, *Medina ivrit: Pitaron le-she'elat ha-yehudim* (A Jewish state: The solution to the Jewish Question) (Tel Aviv, 1937), p. 89.

19. Ze'ev Jabotinsky, "Ha-sakana ha-ahat" (The one danger), *Doar ha-yom*, October 9, 1930. The adjective "integral" is here used merely in a sense synonymous with "monistic." That is to say, it describes a nationalist ideology that tolerates no synthesis with other social political ideologies. It does not necessarily imply identity with particular European ideologies sometimes labeled "integral," such as that of Charles Maurras and the Action Française.

20. Jabotinsky, *Medina ivrit*, pp. 89, 90.

21. Schechtman, *Rebel and Statesman*, p. 54. Jabotinsky is quoted by Schechtman as telling one of his intimate friends: "I too [like Garibaldi] have been labelled 'a militarist and a warmonger;' yet, God is my witness, that I loathe war and the army; to me they are but cruel and revolting necessities." It is also noteworthy that in Jabotinsky's youth he wrote a play in verse, *Dam* (Blood), performed in autumn 1901 in an Odessa theater, that was distinctly pacifist in message.

22. Jabotinsky, "Wegen militarizm" (Yiddish: Concerning militarism), originally in *Haynt*, January 25, 1929; *Ketavim: Ba-derekh la-medina*, p. 45.

23. Jabotinsky, "Ha-banim shelo ve-shelanu" (His sons and ours), *Doar ha-yom*, October 12, 1930, quoted in Bella, *Olamo shel Jabotinsky*, p. 234.

24. Jabotinsky, "Ra'ayon Betar," pp. 307–336.

25. Ibid., pp. 321–323.

26. See Lubotsky, *Ha-tzohar ve-Betar*, pp. 14, 15.

27. Jabotinsky, "Ra'ayon Betar," p. 319.

28. Jabotinsky, "Majorizatsia" (Majoritarianism), *Doar ha-yom*, January 27, 1931.

29. Jabotinsky, "Hearot le-she'elat ha-federatzia" (Comments on the question of federation), *Hazit ha-am* (The People's Front), no. 137 (December 15, 1933), p. 2.

30. The evidence for this is clear. From the outset his preference had been for separatism and independence of action rather than for a strategy of attempting to "conquer" the Zionist Organization from within, as Meir Grossman and most members of the Revisionist Executive in London preferred. See especially Jabotinsky's letter to Lichtheim, March 20, 1931, in file A56/20 CZA; also Joseph B. Schechtman, *Fighter and Prophet*, pp. 139–183.

31. See Jabotinsky, "Be-drom Afrika—ha-kushim" (In South Africa—the blacks), in *Ketavim: Reshimot* (notes), p. 239; also "Ha-emet al ha-ie Tristan da-Runha" (The truth on the island of Tristan da Runha [*sic*]), *Ketavim: Uma ve-hevra*, pp. 281, 282, cited in Bilski Ben-Hur, *Kol yahid hu melekh*, pp. 49–59. Bilski Ben-Hur, whose overall thesis is that Jabotinsky was on balance a liberal, nevertheless judges this aspect of his thought to be incompatible with liberal-democratic principles.

32. Jabotinsky, "Al ha-shevitot be-Eretz Israel" (Concerning strikes in Eretz Israel) (1934), in *Ketavim: Reshimot*, p. 292.

33. Jabotinsky, "Mevo le-torat ha-meshek" (Introduction to economic theory) (1938), in *Ketavim: Uma ve-hevra*, p. 219.

34. Jabotinsky to Israel Anshelevitz, November 9, 1933, *Ketavim: Mikhtavim* (Letters), p. 286.

35. Jabotinsky, "Objektiva ba-trachtungen wegen iddishen parteileben" (Yiddish: Objective thoughts concerning Jewish party life), *Haynt*, September 29, 1932.

36. Jabotinsky, "Israel ve-ha-olam he-atid" (Israel and the world's future), *Ha-mashkif*, May 9, 1941.

37. The term "quasi-messianic" is used here in a value-free sense to describe the rhetorical use of messianic imagery on the part of persons who either were not necessarily halakhically observant or, even if they were personally of religious inclination (as was Avraham Stern, the founder of Lehi for example), did not base their messianism upon rabbinic authority and sources.

38. Both Abba Ahimeir and Uri Zvi Greenberg began to voice their opinions in the columns of labor Zionist organs such as *Kuntres* and *Davar*. Also Yehoshua Heschel Yevin had roots in the labor movement. See Shavit, *Jabotinsky and the Revisionist Movement*, p. 68.

39. See Joseph Nedava, ed., *Abba Ahimeir: Ketavim nivharim* (Selected writings), vol. 3: *Brit ha-biryonim* (Tel Aviv, 1972), pp. 217–229. The Sikarikin were a radical sect during the Judean war against the Romans, who used a short sword (*sika*) to assassinate their political enemies.

40. For Ahimeir's flaunting of these views, see in particular his articles "Mi-pinkaso shel fashistan" (From the notebook of a Fascist), in *Doar ha-yom*, October 8 and 10, 1928. A declaration of the "maximalist *Ha-tzohar*," in Abba Ahimeir's *Hazit ha-am*, August 9, 1932, called for "substitution of [democratic] opposition means by revolutionary means! Action in place of speech . . . to lift Revisionism out of the liberal swamp," and demanded, inter alia, "elevation of the leader's prestige to the level of dictator."

41. Abba Ahimeir, "Bamat ha-dror" (The stage of freedom), *Doar ha-yom*, September 26, 1928, p. 3. I owe this reference to Joseph Heller. See also Joseph Heller, "'Ha-monism shel ha-matara' o 'ha-monism shel ha-emtzaim'? Ha-mahloket ha-rayonit ve-ha-politit bein Ze'ev Jabotinsky le-vein Abba Ahimeir, 1928–1933," ('The monism of aims' or 'the monism of means'? The ideological and political dispute between Ze'ev Jabotinsky and Abba Ahimeir, 1928–1933), *Zion* 52, no. 3 (1987), pp. 315–369. Heller shows conclusively that partisan publications of Jabotinsky's and Ahimeir's writings have glossed over the latter's Fascist inclinations.

42. Jabotinsky, "Al aventurism" (on adventurism), *Hazit ha-am*, March 11, 1932, pp. 1, 2. Cf. the apologetic account in Schechtman, *Fighter and Prophet*, pp. 437–441.

43. Ahimeir found aspects worthy of emulation in the German Nazi model even when Hitler came to power in January 1933. Only with the anti-Jewish boycott and legislation of April 1933 did his Brit Ha-biryonim switch to condemnation of Hitler. It then engaged in some local anti-Nazi acts, such as burning the door of the German consulate in Jerusalem on May 13, 1933. See Heller, "Ha-monism shel ha-matara," p. 361.

44. Jabotinsky, "Germania" (Germany), *Hazit ha-am*, February 24, 1933; also "Lo ad ha-sof?" (Not until the end!), *Doar ha-yom*, May 3, 1933, reproduced in *Ketavim: Ba-sa'ar* (In the storm), p. 190; see also *Hazit ha-am*, May 19, 1933.

45. Jabotinsky to A. Weinshal, May 17, 1933, in letter collection A1/1/23/2. JIA; cf. Jabotinsky to the editors of *Hazit ha-am*, May 17, 1933, in Ze'ev Jabotinsky, *Ketavim: Mikhtavim*, p. 331.

46. On the political significance of Uri Zvi Greenberg, see Yaacov Shavit, "Uri Zvi

Greenberg: Conservative Revolutionarism and National Messianism," *The Jerusalem Quarterly* no. 48 (fall 1988), pp. 63–72. The quotation is from Greenberg's "Emet ahat ve-lo shtayim" (One truth and not two), in Uri Zvi Greenberg, *Sefer ha-kitrug ve-ha-emuna* (The book of indictment and faith) (Jerusalem, 1937), in which he censured Jewish self-restraint in the face of Arab atrocities.

47. See Yehoshu Heschel Yevin, *Uri Zvi Greenberg: Meshorer mehokek* (Uri Zvi Greenberg: Poet legislator) (Tel Aviv, 1938), p. 90.

48. *Ba-mahteret* (In the underground), no. 2 (1941), in *Lohamei Herut Israel: Ketavim* (Fighters for the freedom of Israel: Writings), vol. 2, cols. 27, 28. The "Eighteen Principles of the Revival" were formulated at a time when Stern's group called itself Ha-etzel be-Israel (The National Military Organization in Israel). It was called Lehi from the summer of 1943 onward. The document was first published in two parts, in October 1940 and February 1941. See the exhaustive study of Lehi's ideological development in Joseph Heller, *Lehi: Ideologia u-politika 1940–1949*, (Lehi: Ideology and politics), 2 vols. (Jerusalem, 1989).

49. Jabotinsky, "Anu ve-ha-poalim" (We and the workers), reproduced in translation from *Rasvyet*, September 10, 1929, in Ze'ev Jabotinsky, *Ha-revizionism ha-tzioni be-hitgabshuto: Kovetz ma'amarim be-Rasvyet, 1925–1929* (The crystallization of Revisionist Zionism: Anthology of articles in *Rasvyet*, 1925–1929) (Tel Aviv, 1985), pp. 328–334.

50. See Shavit, *Jabotinsky and the Revisionist Movement*, p. 273; also pp. 82–85. Shavit shows that the social carriers of Revisionist Zionism in Poland comprised a large stratum of the middle class plus an intelligentsia elite. Most Betar members were from middle-class families and were secondary school pupils. In Eretz Israel the members of Ha-tzohar were more heterogeneous. Of the party's 26,000 voters in 1935, some 5,000 were employees, 3,000 belonged to the oriental community and were mainly urban workers, and the remainder were lower middle class and some intelligentsia (journalists, writers, lawyers, and doctors).

51. Jabotinsky to Dr. von Weisel, August 11, 1926, in letter collection, A1/16/2, JIA.

52. Jabotinsky, "Malkhut khodinka" (The kingdom of Khodinka), *Doar ha-yom*, October 23, 1930. "Khodinka" was the name of field near Moscow where a calamity occurred during celebrations of Tsar Nicholas II's coronation.

53. Jabotinsky, "Ha-am'amad ve-ha-enoshiyut (Class and humanity), *Doar ha-yom*, December 8, 1930.

54. Jabotinsky, "Mashber ha-proletarion" (The crisis of the proletariat) (1932), in *Ketavim: Reshimot*, pp. 309–311.

55. Jabotinsky, "Anahnu ha-burganim" (We, the bourgeoisie), *Ha-tzafon*, May 8, 1927, quoted in Bella, *Olamo shel Jabotinsky*, p. 336.

56. See Shavit, *Jabotinsky and the Revisionist Movement*, pp. 278–290. Shavit quotes (p. 279) a letter from Jabotinsky to Oscar Gruzenberg, November 12, 1925, in which Jabotinsky acknowledged that "the pivotal class among the Jewish people and in Zionism . . . is the Jewish proletariat" but said that since it had been captured by the Socialists, "revisionism has to try and establish itself among the middle class." According to Shavit (p. 74), in the final analysis "it can be said that Revisionism set out to defend the economic and class interests of those who were not in need of such protection."

57. Ze'ev Jabotinsky, "Ken lishbor" (Yes, break!), *Hazit ha-am*, December 2, 1932, reproduced in *Ketavim: Ba-sa'ar*, p. 45.

58. Ze'ev Jabotinsky, "Al ha-NEP ha-tzioni: Pa'am sheniya" (On the Zionist new economic policy: For the second time), *Haynt*, April 23, 1928, reproduced in *Ketavim: Ba-derekh la-medina*, pp. 138, 139. On the implications of these proposals, see Shlomo

Avineri, *The Making of Modern Zionism: The Intellectual Origins of the Jewish State* (London, 1981), pp. 176, 177.

59. Vladimir Jabotinsky, "Der 'Untergang' fun Demokratia" (Yiddish: The 'decline' of democracy), *Der Morgen Journal*, July 24, 1926, pp. 4, 7. Similarly, idem, "Demokratia" *Ha-jarden*, October 26, 1934. On Jabotinsky's negative view of Mussolini's regime (albeit expressed with restraint), see his letters to Leone Carpi, the Italian Jew and Revisionist Zionist who was a supporter of Mussolini, June 24, 1931, and January 29, 1934, reproduced in *Ha-uma*, no. 11 (December 1964), pp. 495, 496. See also, much earlier, Vladimir Jabotinsky, "Zionist Fascism," *The Zionist*, June 6, 1926, pp. 38, 39. In this brief article he praised "the way called democracy, the way accepted in every civilized community," and repudiated the "Duce" concept, saying, "Buffaloes follow a leader. Civilized men have no 'leaders': civilized men and women elect stewards, executives, simple trustees who are entitled to act as long as their views coincide with those of the majority, and go when that ceases to be the case."

60. Letter (in English), Ze'ev Jabotinsky to S. Yaacobi, October 4, 1933, in letter collection, A1/2/23/2, JIA. See also Shavit, *Jabotinsky and the Revisionist Movement*, pp. 361, 362. Shavit there discusses the considerable interest evinced by contemporary Betar publications on the pros and cons of the Fascist corporative economic system and particularly by a book sympathetic to Mussolini, written by a Revisionist: Zvi Kolitz, *Mussolini, ishiyuto ve-torato* (Mussolini, his personality and teaching)(Tel Aviv, 1936).

61. Vladimir Jabotinsky, "Jews and Fascism," *Jewish Daily Bulletin*, April 11, 1935. At the same time Jabotinsky showed something of his ambivalence when he pointed out that Fascist Italy was one of the few countries where Jews enjoyed full equality and accordingly cautioned that it was "very unwise" to antagonize Italy "by turning to abuse a term and an idea which is so highly cherished both by its rulers and its youth."

62. David Ben-Gurion, *Tnuat ha-poalim ve-ha-revizionismus* (The labor movement and revisionism) (Tel Aviv, 1933). The first chapter was headed "Jabotinsky in the Footsteps of Hitler."

63. On the conflict, see Yaacov Goldstein, *Mapai: Gormim le-hakamata* (The Labor Party of Eretz Israel: The factors leading to its founding) (Tel Aviv, 1976), pp. 83–95; Yaacov Shavit, *Mi-rov le-medina: Ha-tnua he-revizionistit, ha-tokhniet ha-hityashvutit ve-ha-ra'ayon ha-hevrati* (From majority to statehood: The Revisionist movement, its settlement program and social ideas) (Tel Aviv, 1978), pp. 23–24, 236–255. Also Shavit, *Jabotinsky and the Revisionist Movement*, pp. 325–349.

64. On this intriguing chapter in the relationship between Revisionist Zionism and labor Zionism, see Yaacov Goldstein and Yaacov Shavit, *Le-lo pesharot: Heskem Ben-Gurion-Jabotinsky ve-kishlono, 1934–1935* (Without compromise: The Ben-Gurion–Jabotinsky agreement and its failure, 1934–1935) (Tel Aviv, 1979).

65. See Schechtman, *Fighter and Prophet*, pp. 158–183.

66. Jabotinsky, *Ketavim: Neumim* (Speeches), vol. 2, p. 226.

67. Evacuation was the term Jabotinsky preferred, likening his plan to the evacuation order given by a general to his troops, an order determined with dignity by the general himself in the interests of his troops' safety and in accord with military considerations. See his speech delivered in Warsaw, October 1936, in *Ketavim: Neumim*, vol. 2, pp. 201, 202.

68. See Yaacov Shavit, *Ha-mitologiyot shel ha-yamin* (The mythologies of the Right) (Tel Aviv, 1986), pp. 63–80.

69. Jabotinsky, "Ra'ayon Betar," p. 334.

70. Josef Popper-Lynkeus, *Die allgemeine Nährpflicht als Lösung der sozialen Frage*

(General subsistence right as a solution to the social question) (Dresden, 1912; 2nd ed, Rikola Verlag, Vienna, 1923). See Shavit, *Jabotinsky and the Revisionist Movement*, p. 305.

71. Jabotinsky, "Ha-geula ha-sozialit" (Social redemption), in *Ketavim: Reshimot*, pp. 297–298. The quotation is from an English version, "Social Redemption," in *Our Voice* (New York) 2, no. 1 (January 1935) in file 2509/10, JIA. See also "Prakim ba-filosofia ha-sozialit shel ha-tanakh" (Chapters in the social history of the Bible) (1932), in *Ketavim: Uma ve-hevra*, pp. 190, 191.

72. Jabotinsky, "Ma rotzim ha-tzionim ha-revisionistim?" (What do the Revisionist Zionists want?) (1928), in *Ketavim: Ba-derekh la-medina*, p. 285.

73. Ibid.

74. Ibid., p. 293.

75. Josiah Wedgwood (1872–1943), the British radical politician and member of the 1924 labor government, was a staunch supporter of Zionism. In 1928 he published the book *Palestine: The Seventh Dominion*, advocating that Palestine become a self-governing Jewish dominion as part of the British Empire.

76. In 1934 the Revisionists conducted a massive petition campaign addressed to various local governments and to the British Crown, urging freedom of immigration to Palestine. They claimed to have collected some 600,000 signatures. This independent initiative was branded as a breach of discipline by the majority in the Zionist Organization, and when sanctions were tightened this became a precipitatory factor in the secession of the Revisionists to form the New Zionist Organization in 1935.

77. See the perceptive comments of Shlomo Avineri on this contradiction in Jabotinsky's ideology: Avineri, *The Making of Modern Zionism*, p. 185.

78. Jabotinsky, "H. Slosberg" (1933), in *Ketavim: Zikhronot ben dori* (Contemporary recollections), p. 286.

79. See for example, Jabotinsky, "Ha-im ein breira?" (Is there no choice?), *Doar ha-yom*, August 6, 1930.

80. Ze'ev Jabotinsky, "Ma rotzim ha-tzionim ha-revisionistim," p. 283.

81. *Stenographisches Protokoll der Verhandlungen des 17 Zionisten-Kongresses, Basel, 30 June to 17 July 1931* (London, 1931), p. 386. The bracketed translation is as in the original text.

82. See Norman Rose, *Chaim Weizmann: A Biography* (London, 1986), pp. 290, 291.

83. See Shavit, *Jabotinsky and the Revisionist Movement*, esp. pp. 223–229; Joseph Heller, *Lehi, ideologia u-politika,* vol. 1, pp. 19–80. Even the fine two-volume biography of Jabotinsky by Joseph B. Schechtman, *The Life and Times of Vladimir Jabotinsky*, underplayed the gravity of the differences between Jabotinsky and the radical Right of Revisionist Zionism.

84. Jabotinsky was repeatedly on record, implicitly or explicitly endorsing the IZL's actions in Palestine, including the abortive attack on an Arab bus in the Galilee in April 1938 (unauthorized by the IZL command, as it happened) that led to the execution by hanging of Shlomo Ben-Yosef. See Schechtman, *Fighter and Prophet*, pp. 468–482. At the same time his correspondence reveals doubts and vacillation and, more particularly, disapproval of actions that endangered the lives of innocent men, women, and children. See Schechtman's personal testimony, p. 453. Cf. Joseph Heller, "Ze'ev Jabotinsky ve-she'elat ha-havlaga (1936–1939): Hashkafat olam be-mivhan ha-metziut" (Ze'ev Jabotinsky and the question of restraint (1939–1939): His world outlook put to the test of reality), in *Temurot ba-historia ha-yehudit he-hadasha* (Transformations in modern Jewish history), ed. Shmuel Almog et al. (Jerusalem, 1988), pp. 283–320.

85. See, e.g., Schechtman, *Fighter and Prophet*, p. 475. On the other hand, there is

some controversial evidence that, toward end of his life, Jabotinsky did fleetingly moot the notion of a military rebellion of sorts to be staged by the IZL. As outlined in secret letters he sent to the IZL's commanders, this was to involve an invasion by sea, bringing Jabotinsky himself to the shores of Palestine, and a simultaneous uprising aimed at taking control of the Mandatory's Government House for at least twenty four hours. During this time there would be the proclamation of a provisional government. The premise was that the uprising would certainly be suppressed but only after having left a demonstrative impression of proclaimed Jewish statehood and a government in exile. Hence, it is arguable that this fatuous plan still conformed to Jabotinsky's long-standing strategy. World War II broke out before the plan could even be considered. Thereafter Jabotinsky's policy immediately reverted to cooperation with Britian. See Shavit, *Ha-mitologiyot shel ha-yamin*, pp. 86–113.

86. See Schechtman, *Fighter and Prophet*, pp. 455–457.

87. In January 1941, Lehi approached Otto von Hentzig, a German diplomatic representative in Lebanon, then under Vichy French rule, with a proposal for "cooperation between the new Germany and a folk-national Hebraism" in the war against the British and in establishing a Jewish state allied to the German Reich. Describing itself as an organization "bearing an affinity to European totalitarian movements in regard to world-outlook and structure," Lehi suggested political as well as military cooperation. The offer was turned down by the Nazis. See David Yisraeli, *Ha-"reich" ha-germani ve-eretz Israel, 1889–1945* (The German Reich and Eretz Israel, 1889–1945) (Ramat Gan, 1974), pp. 227, 228. For a full analysis of the motives and significance of this step, see Heller, *Lehi, ideologia u-politika*, pp. 125–135.

88. "Din ve-heshbon shel ha-kinnus ha-olami ha-shlishi le-Betar," Warsaw, September 11–17, 1938 (Manuscript, report of the Third World Assembly of Betar) (Bucharest, 1940), 3/32/B2, JIA. esp. concerning Begin, pp. 29, 30, and Jabotinsky's response pp. 31, 33. Extracts are reproduced in H. Ben-Yeruham, *Sefer Betar: Korot u-mekorot* (The book of Betar: History and sources) (Jerusalem/Tel Aviv, 1975), vol. 2, part 2, pp. 862–864.

89. As noted above, Jabotinsky himself perhaps fleetingly switched to this notion. It is instructive that even the labor Zionist leader, Chaim Arlosoroff, whose basic strategic credo adhered closely to Chaim Weizmann's unswerving orientation on cooperation with Britain, experienced a momentary disillusionment and sense of desperation as early as 1932. In a letter to Weizmann he suddenly spelled out his conclusion that only by a couplike resort to force to grasp the reins of government in Palestine did the Zionists stand a chance of averting disaster and attaining their goal of Jewish statehood. See Arlosoroff to Chaim Weizmann, June 30, 1932, in Chaim Arlosoroff, *Yoman Yerushalayim* (Jerusalem diary) (Tel Aviv, 1953), pp. 333–342.

7. Zionism as Secular Jewish Identity

1. "Pirkei zikhronot" (Reminiscences), *Kol kitvei Ahad Ha'am*, (Collected writings of Ahad Ha'am) (Tel Aviv and Jerusalem, 1959), p. 481: "The truth is that I did not read, indeed I never saw *Ha-shahar* and Smolenskin's books until I took up residence in Odessa, when I was already more than thirty, with a certain well-defined outlook which I had derived from quite different sources." For a full discussion, see David Patterson, "Ahad Ha'am and Smolenskin," in *At the Crossroads: Essays on Ahad Ha-am*, ed. Jacques Kornberg (Albany, N.Y., 1983), pp. 36–45.

2. See Aryeh [Leon] Simon and Joseph Eliyahu Heller, *Ahad Ha'am: ha-ish, poalo*

ve-torato (Ahad Ha'am: The man, his work and his thought) (Jerusalem, 1955), pp. 139–148.

3. "Al parashat drakhim: Hakdama la-mahadura ha-sheniya" (At the crossroads: Preface to the Second Edition) (1902), reproduced in *Kol kitvei Ahad Ha'am*, p. 6.

4. "Shinui arakhin" (Transvaluation of values) (1898), in *Kol kitvei Ahad Ha'am*, p. 157.

5. "Avdut be-tokh herut" (Slavery in freedom) (1890), in *Kol kitvei Ahad Ha'am*, p. 69. For a fuller discussion of Ahad Ha'am's answer to the question "Why are we Jews?" see Simon and Heller, *Ahad Ha'am*, pp. 184ff.

6. "Shalosh madregot" (Three steps) (1898), in *Kol kitvei Ahad Ha'am*, p. 151. These are not Ahad Ha'am's own words but a quotation from an article by an unnamed Western rabbi whose views in this regard Ahad Ha'am wholeheartedly commended. The article, titled "Warum sind wir Juden?" appeared in *Brull's Monatshefte* 1 (1898).

7. See especially "Mukdam u-meuhar ba-haim" (Early and late in life) (1891), in *Kol kitvei Ahad Ha'am*, p. 79.

8. "Ha-musar ha-leumi" (The national morality) (1899), in *Kol kitvei Ahad Ha'am*, pp. 161, 162 (originally in *Ha-shiloah* 5, no. 1 (Tevet, 1899), under the name "Le-she'elot ha-yom" (Questions of the day).

9. Letter to Israel Abrahams (Cambridge), March 30, 1913, in Leon Simon ed., *Ahad Ha-am: Essays, Letters, Memoirs* (Oxford, 1946), p. 270. The letter was written in English.

10. Letter to Judah Magnes, September 18, 1910, in *Igrot Ahad Ha'am*, (Letters of Ahad Ha'am) (Jerusalem, Berlin, Tel Aviv, 1924), vol. 4, p. 149, as translated in Simon, *Ahad Ha-am: Essays, Letters, Memoirs*, pp. 268, 269.

11. Letter to a person designated M. K. B., written in Odessa, April 12, 1899, in *Igrot Ahad Ha'am*, vol. 2, p. 68.

12. "Ha-musar ha-leumi" in *Kol kitvei Ahad Ha'am*, pp. 159–164.

13. Ibid., p. 163.

14. "Al shtei ha-seipim" (lit., Between two outlooks [but rendered in Leon Simon's translation as "Judaism and the Gospels"]) (1911), in *Kol kitvei Ahad Ha'am*, pp. 370–377.

15. Ibid., p. 373.

16. Letter to Menahem Sheinkin, February 14, 1908, in *Igrot Ahad Ha'am*, vol. 4, p. 7.

17. "Divrei shalom" (Words of peace) (1895), in *Kol kitvei Ahad Ha'am*, p. 60; pp. 58, 59.

18. On changes in Ahad Ha'am's attitude to orthodoxy, see Joseph Goldstein, "Yahaso shel Ahad Ha'am la-dat be-aspeklariya historit" (Ahad Ha'am's attitude to religion as historically reflected), in *Temurot ba-historia ha-yehudit ha-hadasha: kovetz ma'amarim, shai le-Shmuel Ettinger* (Transition and change in modern Jewish history: Essays presented in honor of Shmuel Ettinger), ed. Shmuel Almog et al. (Jerusalem, 1987), pp. 159–168.

19. Letter to Menahem Sheinkin, London, February 14, 1908, in *Igrot Ahad Ha'am*, vol. 4, p. 7, as translated in Simon, *Ahad Ha-am: Essays, Letters, Memoirs*, p. 266.

20. Letter to Joseph Klausner, July 20, 1898, in *Igrot Ahad Ha'am*, vol. 1, p. 249, as translated in Simon, *Ahad Ha-am: Essays, Letters, Memoirs*, p. 262.

21. See the intellectual harangue directed at Ahad Ha'am by Baruch Kurtzweil: "Ha-yahadut ki-gilui ratzon ha-haim ha-leumi-biologi" (Judaism as manifestation of the national-biological will-to-life), in Baruch Kurtzweil, *Sifruteinu ha-hadasha: hemshekh o mahapekha?* (Our new literature: Continuity or revolution?) (Tel Aviv, 1959), pp. 190–224.

22. There is a considerable literature on the Bnei Moshe. An early work of permanent value is Shmuel Tschernowitz, *Bnei Moshe u-tekufatam* (Bnei Moshe and their times) (Warsaw, 1914). See especially Ehud Luz, *Parallels Meet: Religion and Nationalism in the Early Zionist Movement (1882–1904)* (Philadelphia, 1988), pp. 80ff; and Yosef Salmon, "Ahad Ha-Am and Bnei Moshe: An 'Unsuccessful Experiment?'" in *At the Crossroads,* ed. Jacques Kornberg, pp. 98–105. Ahad Ha'am was not the sole founder of Bnei Moshe. However, he had preeminent status throughout its brief history. At first that status was de jure, for in terms of the society's rules, which he himself drafted, its initial headquarters were in Odessa, the president of the Odessa lodge being also acknowledged as the head of the whole of Bnei Moshe. However, he relinquished titular headship when the headquarters was moved to Jaffa in 1892.

23. "Derekh ha-haim" (The way of life), in *Kol kitvei Ahad Ha'am*, pp. 438, 439, and "Miluim le-derekh ha-hayim" (Supplements to the way of life), in *Kol kitvei Ahad Ha'am*, pp. 440ff.

24. "Miluim le-derekh ha-haim" *Kol kitvei Ahad Ha'am*, p. 440. The phrase "the language of our forefathers, and its literature" was Ahad Ha'am's formulation. However, the version adopted by Bnei Moshe leaned more toward the religious tradition, replacing this with the phrase, "The Torah of Israel, its language and its wisdom."

25. Ibid.

26. See Tschernowitz, *Bnei Moshe u-tekufatam*, pp. 21, 23, 27, 42, 120, 121.

27. The secularists demanded a rabbinical dispensation since they held that refraining from agricultural work during every seventh year would be disastrous for the Jewish settlers. Some Hibbat Zion rabbis, including Rabbi Mohilewer, favored finding a rabbinical formula for such a dispensation, whereas others, including Pines, opposed it. See Luz, *Parallels Meet*, pp. 73–77.

28. See Yosef Salmon, "Yehiel Michael Pines: From the Vision of Zionism to the Reality," *Modern Judaism* 8, no. 1 (February 1988), pp. 78–79.

29. Yehiel Michel Pines, *Emet mi-eretz* (Truth from The Land) (Jerusalem, 1894), vol. 1, pp. 7, 9; vol. 2, pp. 4, 5.

30. Ibid., vol. 2, pp. 1–3, 16–18. Also reproduced in Getzel Kressel, ed., *Rabbi Yehiel Michel Pines: Mivhar ma'amarav* (Rabbi Yehiel Michel Pines: Selected articles) (Tel Aviv, 1946), pp. 101, 104.

31. "Nisayon she-lo hitzliah" (An experiment that did not succeed), in *Kol kitvei Ahad Ha'Am*, p. 437.

32. See Tschernowitz, *Bnei Moshe u-tekufatam*, p. 142.

33. See Dr. Israel Klausner, *Oppositzia le-Herzl* (The opposition to Herzl) (Jerusalem, 1960); Luz, *Parallels Meet*, pp. 182–190, 241–246.

34. *Stenographisches Protokoll der Verhandlungen des III Zionisten-Kongresses gehalten zu Basel, August 1899* (Vienna, 1899), p. 207; also *Stenographisches Protokoll der Verhandlungen des V Zionisten-Kongresses in Basel, Dezember 1901* (Vienna, 1901), p. 395. In modern Hebrew usage *kultura* has been replaced by the word *tarbut*. The course of the debate over the "question of culture" has been traced in detail in Moshe Rinott, "Religion and Education: The Cultural Question and the Zionist Movement, 1897–1913," *Studies in Zionism* 5, no. 1 (spring 1984), pp. 1–18, and in Yosef Goldstein, "Ha-ma'avak bein haredim le-hiloni'im al dmuta shel ha-tnu'a ha-tzionit, 1882–1922" (The struggle between Orthodox and secular Jews over the character of the Zionist Movement, 1882–1922), *Yahadut Zemaneinu*, vol. 2 (Jerusalem, 1984), pp. 237–260; also in Luz, *Parallels Meet*, pp. 137–256.

35. *Stenographisches Protokoll der Verhandlungen des I Zionisten-Kongresses in Basel,*

August 1987, 2nd ed. (Prague, 1911), p. 216. Also his statement in *Stenographisches Protokoll der Verhandlungen des III Zionisten-Kongresses in Basel, August 1899*, p. 78; also *Stenographisches Protokoll der Verhandlungen des V Zionisten-Kongresses in Basel, Dezember 1901*, p. 424. On Herzl's attitude to religion see Joseph Adler, "Religion and Herzl: Fact and Fable," in *Herzl Year Book*, vol. 4 (New York, 1961–2), pp. 271–303. See also David Vital, *Zionism: The Formative Years* (Oxford, 1982), pp. 207, 208.

36. Weizmann to Ahad Ha'am, June 9, 1901, in Chaim Weizmann, *The Letters and Papers of Chaim Weizmann*, ed. Meyer W. Weisgal et al. (London, 1968–1972), vol. 1: *Letters*, no. 86, p. 124; Ahad Ha'am to Weizmann, July 1, 1901, in *Igrot Ahad Ha'am*, vol. 3, p. 61.

37. See Israel Klausner, *Oppositzia le-Herzl*, p. 141.

38. *Stenographisches Protokoll der Verhandlungen des V Zionisten-Kongresses in Basel, Dezember, 1901*, pp. 389–392.

39. *Ha-tokhniet shel ha-fraktzia ha-tzionit-amamit* (The program of the Democratic Faction) (1902), in *Sefer Motzkin* (Motzkin Anthology), ed. Alex Bein (Jerusalem, 1939), pp. 55–62. This is a Hebrew translation of part of the original *Programm und Organisationsstatut der Demokratisch-zionistischen Fraktzion*, Heidelberg, June 22, 1902. It was published in Hebrew in *Ha-tzefira*, issues of September 3, 4, 7, 9, 1902.

40. This quotation and those that follow are from *Sefer Motzkin*, pp. 55, 56, 58, 59.

41. Nahman Syrkin formed an ephemeral Socialist group called Hessiana (after Moses Hess), whose activities paralleled those of the Democratic Faction. See Klausner, *Oppositzia le-Herzl*, pp. 97–102.

42. See Luz, *Parallels Meet*, pp. 146–149; Rinott, "Religion and Education," pp. 1–17.

43. Ahad Ha'am's lecture, as he revised it for publication in *Ha-shiloah* 1, nos. 5/6 (1903), is reproduced in *Kol kitvei Ahad Ha'am*, pp. 173–186. The quotations that follow are from the English translation: "The Spiritual Revival" (1902), in Leon Simon, *Selected Essays by Ahad Ha-am* (Philadelphia, 1912), pp. 253–305.

44. On these developments, see Yehuda Leib Ha-Cohen Fishman (Maimon), "Toldot ha-mizrahi ve-hitpathuto" (History and development of Mizrahi), in *Sefer ha-mizrahi: Kovetz le-zekher Rabbi Yitzhak Yaakov Reines* (The book of Mizrahi: In Memory of Rabbi Yitzhak Yaakov Reines), ed. Y. L. Ha-Cohen Fishman (Jerusalem, 1946), pp. 103–109. The quotation from the Lida Conference's resolution is on p. 109.

45. See Rinott, "Religion and Education," p. 9.

46. *Stenographisches Protokoll der Verhandlungen des IX Zionisten-Kongresses in Hamburg, Dezember 1909* (Cologne, 1910), pp. 206, 207.

47. See Yeshurun Keshet, *M. Y. Berdyczewski (Bin-Gorion): Hayav u-foalo* (M. Y. Berdyczewski: His life and work) (Jerusalem, 1958).

48. See Asher A. Rivlin, *Ahad Ha'am u-mitnagdav ve-hashkefoteihem al ha-sifrut ha-ivrit be-doram* (Ahad Ha'am and his opponents and their views on the Hebrew literature of their generation) (Tel Aviv, 1954).

49. See Joseph Oren, *Ahad Ha'am, M. Y. Berdyczewski, ve-havurat "tzeirim": Igrot u-pishran, 1891–1896* (Ahad Ha'am, M. Y. Berdyczewski and the "Tzeirim" group: Letters and their meaning) (Tel Aviv, 1985).

50. "Avdut be-tokh herut," in *Kol kitvei Ahad Ha'am*, p. 69.

51. "Harut ve-herut" (Prescription and freedom), in *Kitvei Micha Yosef Bin-Gorion [Berdyczewski]: Ma'amarim, ba-derekh: Part 2. Shinui arakhin* (Writings of Micha Yosef Bin-Gorion: Articles, on the way: Part 2. Transvaluation) (Lipsia, 1922), pp. 39, 40.

52. "Stira u-binyan" (Wrecking and building), in *Kitvei Micha Yosef Bin-Gorion*, pp. 19, 20.

53. "Du-partzufim" (Two faces), in *Kitvei Micha Yosef Bin-Gorion*, pp. 56, 57. First published in M. J. Berdyczewski, *Nemushot* (Epigones) (Warsaw, 1900), pp. 22, 23.

54. See, e.g., "Anu ve-hem" (We and they) and "Pesiot" (Steps), in *Kitvei Micha Yosef Bin-Gorion*, pp. 62–65, 58.

55. "Le-she'elat ha-tarbut" (On the question of culture), in *Kitvei Micha Yosef Bin-Gorion*, p. 46. Contrast this with "Avar ve-hove" (Past and Present), in *Kitvei Micha Yosef Bin-Gorion*, pp. 35, 36.

56. "Le-she'elat he-avar" (On the question of the past), in *Kitvei Micha Yosef Bin-Gorion*, p. 52.

57. Berdyczewski, *Nemushot,* pp. 95, 96.

58. Micha Yosef Berdyczewski, *Al em ha-derekh* (On the high road) (Warsaw, 1900), p. 49.

59. "Anu ve-hem," pp. 62, 63.

60. Micha Yosef Berdyczewski, *Al ha-perek* (On the agenda) (Warsaw, 1900), pp. 20, 21.

61. "Le-she'elat ha-tarbut," *Kitvei Micha Yosef Bin-Gorion*, p. 47.

62. To be sure, some ambivalences remained even in so thoroughly Socialist a thinker as Ber Borochov. See Eliezer Schweid, *Toldot ha-hagut ha-yehudit ba-mea ha-esrim* (A history of Jewish thought in the twentieth century) (Tel Aviv, 1990), pp. 292, 293.

63. "Ma nishtana proletari" (A proletarian innovation) (1912), in *Ber Borochov, Ketavim* (Writings), ed L. Levita and S. Rehav, vol. 3 (Tel Aviv, 1966), p. 323.

64. "Kol korei la-noar ha-yehudi" (1901), in *Kitvei Nahman Syrkin,* ed. Berl Katznelson and Yehudah Kaufman (Tel Aviv, 1939), pp. 68, 69. The phrase used by Syrkin, "dat yehudit ma'asit," translated here as "Jewish religion in practice," might alternatively be translated as "religious praxis."

65. "Ka-alot ha-shahar" (With the dawn) (1903), in *Kitvei Nahman Syrkin,* p. 104. That secular Zionists "desecrate the sancta of Israel" was a typical accusation made by orthodox rabbis. By quoting it thus, Syrkin was declaring provocatively that his policy was indeed to debunk certain orthodox religious beliefs.

66. Ibid., pp. 104.

67. "Min ha-hutza ha-ohala" (From the outside into the tent), in *Kitvei Nahman Syrkin,* pp. 168, 144–145.

68. See Yosef Gorny, "Changes in the Social and Political Structure of the Second *Aliya,* 1904–1940," *Zionism* 1 (1975), pp. 49–101. Gorny's analysis of an extant census, incorporating 957 members of the Second *Aliya* who were participants in the labor movement, provides an educational and social profile of this formative element's core of Zionist settlement in Eretz Israel. It shows that, before leaving the Diaspora, 47 percent of them had studied in a yeshiva and 11 percent received a traditional religious education at home. In all, 58 percent had a traditionalist religious background. Twenty-three percent had studied (but not necessarily completed such studies) in a secular secondary school, only 8 percent in a university and another 8 percent in a teachers seminary. Only 30 percent of the males (but 60 percent of the females) did not know Hebrew when they came to Palestine. As for the occupations of their parents, 55 percent were traders, as much as 13 percent were religious functionaries; 13 percent, artisans; and only 2 percent, laborers. Sixty-seven percent of them were from small townlets and 29 percent from large and medium-sized cities.

69. See Ittamar Even-Zohar, "Ha-tzemiha ve-ha-hitgabshut shel tarbut ivrit mekomit ve-yelidit be-Eretz Israel, 1882–1948" (The growth and consolidation of local and native Hebrew culture in Eretz Israel, 1882–1948), *Cathedra,* no. 16 (1980), pp. 165–189.

70. See David Kna'ani, *Ha-aliya ha-sheniya ha-ovedet ve-yahasa la-dat ve-la-masoret* (The Labor Second *Aliya* and its attitude toward religion and tradition) (Tel Aviv, 1976).

71. Yitzhak Volcani, "Ha-teologia ha-leumit" (The national theology), in *Kitvei Yitzhak Elazari-Volcani (A. Tzioni)* (The writings of Yitzhak Elazari-Volcani [A. Tzioni]), vol. 2: *Sfirot*, (Emanations) (Tel Aviv, 1950), pp. 13–70.

72. Ibid. This quotation and those that follow are, in sequence, from pp. 48, 34, 36, 37, 27, 26, 43.

73. "Ba-haim u-ba-sifrut" (In life and in literature), in *Kol kitvei Y. H. Brenner* (The complete writings of Y. H. Brenner), vol. 2 (Tel Aviv, 1960), pp. 59, 65; originally in *Ha-poel ha-tzair*, 1911, under Y. H. Brenner's pseudonym, Yosef Haver.

74. "Mi-kan u-mi-kan" (From here and from here), Second Notebook, in *Kol kitvei Y. H. Brenner*, vol. 1 (Tel Aviv, 1960), p. 326. Cf. "Ba-haim u-ba-sifrut: U-le-verur ha-inyan" (In life and literature: And in clarification of the matter), in *Kol kitvei Y. H. Brenner*, vol. 2, p. 60.

75. "Ba-haim u-ba-sifrut," p. 65.

76. Ibid., p. 61.

77. "Ha'arakhat atzmeinu be-shloshet ha-krakhim" (Evaluating ourselves in the three volumes), in *Kol kitvei Y. H. Brenner*, vol. 3 (1967), p. 78. This first appeared in 1914 and was an evaluation of the contribution of Mendele Mocher Seforim (Shalom Abromowitch) to modern Hebrew literature.

78. See the penetrating examination of the relation between the views of Brenner and Berdyczewski in Menahem Brinker, "Brenner's Jewishness," *Studies in Contemporary Jewry*, vol. 4 (New York, 1988), pp. 232–249.

79. "Stira u-binyan," in *Kitvei Micha Yosef Bin-Gorion*, p. 18.

80. Yosef Haver (pseudonym of Y. H. Brenner), "Ba-itonut u-ba-sifrut: Hearot ve-tziunim" (In the newspapers and literature: Comments and notes), *Ha-poel ha-tzair*, November 24, 1910; reproduced in *Kol kitvei Y. H. Brenner*, vol. 2, pp. 52–65. Extracts from this important essay by Brenner have already been cited above.

81. Ibid. (for this quotation and those following).

82. Brenner, "Hagigim" (Reflections), as reproduced in Nurit Govrin, *Meorat Brenner: Ha-ma'avak al hofesh ha-bitui* (The Brenner incident: The struggle for free speech) (Jerusalem, 1985), pp. 195–197; from handwritten notes titled "Shemad ve-natzrut: Od le-verur ha-inyan" (Apostasy and Christianity: In further clarification). These notes are deposited in the Labor Archives, Tel Aviv (sec. IV, 104 Brenner, File 30). My discussion of the controversy precipitated by Brenner's views is much indebted to Nurit Govrin's work.

83. "Kefira o hasata" (Heresy or incitement), *Ha-herut* (Freedom), November 2, 1910, p. 1, as reproduced in Govrin, *Meorat Brenner*, pp. 140, 141.

84. Ahad Ha'am (London) to B. Ledijinski (Odessa), December 14, 1910, in *Igrot Ahad Ha'am*, vol. 4, p. 181.

85. Ish Ivri [Joseph Klausner], "Herut ve-apikorsut" (Freedom and nonbelief), *Ha-shiloah* 25, no. 1 (February 1911), pp. 88–91.

86. The protocol of this meeting appeared as a report titled "Mi-asefat ha-sofrim" (From the Writers' Meeting), in *Ha-poel ha-tzair*, no. 9/10 (February 20, 1911), pp. 21–23.

87. David Ben-Gurion, "Ba-midron" (Downhill), *Ha-ahdut*, no. 17 (February 17, 1911), pp. 1–4. Ben-Gurion used the word *shehorim* (blacks) to describe the orthodox.

88. "Hofesh ha-deot; be-Eretz Israel" (Freedom of thought; in Eretz Israel), *Ha-olam*, March 16, 1911, pp. 2, 3, 16.

89. Ben-Zion Katz, "Ha-leumiyut, ha-yahadut ve-ha-dat" (Nationalism, Judaism and

religion), *Hed ha-zman*, March 3, 1911, no. 42 (morning ed.), pp. 1, 2; no. 43 (evening ed.), p. 2.

90. Simon Bernfeld, "Meora Brenner" (The Brenner incident), *Ha-tzefira*, March 16, 1911, pp. 1, 2, as reproduced in Govrin, *Meorat Brenner,* pp. 169–173.

91. *Ha-shiloah* 24, no. 4 (May 1911), pp. 360–366. Also reproduced in *Kol kitvei Ahad Ha'am*, pp. 406–409.

92. Aharon David Gordon, "Mikhtav galui le-haverai ha-poalim" (An open letter to my worker comrades), *Ha-poel ha-tzair* 4, no. 11 (March 13, 1911), p. 11.

93. Letter to Ahad Ha'am from "Ben-Moshe [A. D. Gordon], Workers' Group Ein Ganim-Petah Tikvah" (Heshvan, 1912), in *Kitvei A. D. Gordon: mikhtavim ve-reshimot* (Writings of A. D. Gordon: Letters and notes), ed. Samuel Hugo Bergmann and Eliezer Shohat (Jerusalem, 1957), pp. 44–50.

94. A. D. Gordon, "Man and Nature," in *A. D. Gordon: Selected Essays*, trans. Frances Burnce (New York, 1938), pp. 216–217. On Gordon's conception of religion as a cosmic rather than a historical phenomenon, see Nathan Rotenstreich, *Jewish Philosophy in Modern Times* (New York, 1968), pp. 239–252, esp. p. 240.

95. "Nationalism and Socialism," in Burnce, ed., *A. D. Gordon: Selected Essays*, pp. 45, 44, in that sequence.

96. *Kitvei A. D. Gordon: Mikhtavim ve-reshimot*, p. 89.

97. See "The Account We Must Settle with Ourselves," in *A. D. Gordon: Selected Esssays*, pp. 149, 153.

98. Ibid., p. 149.

99. A. D. Gordon, "Labor," in *A. D. Gordon: Selected Essays*, pp. 54, 55.

100. See Anita Shapira, *Berl: The Biography of a Socialist Zionist* (Cambridge, 1984), and more specifically in the context of the present discussion, Avraham Tsivion, *Diukano ha-yehudi shel Berl Katznelson* (The Jewish portrait of Berl Katznelson) (Tel Aviv, 1984).

101. See Tsivion, *Diukano ha-yehudi*, pp. 141–156.

102. Berl Katznelson, "Hurban u-telishut" (Destruction and detachment) (1934), in *Ketavim* (Writings), 12 vols (Tel Aviv, 1946–1950), vol. 6, pp. 365–367. See Tsivion, *Diukano ha-yehudi*, p. 256. The youth movement in question was Ha-mahanot Ha-olim (the Ascending Camps).

103. Katznelson, "Ba-mivhan" (The test) (1934), in *Ketavim*, vol. 6, p. 392.

104. See Tsivion, *Diukano ha-yehudi*, pp. 271–281.

105. See Katznelson, "Bifnei hayalim" (An address to soldiers) (1942), in *Ketavim*, vol. 5, pp. 364, 365.

106. Katznelson, "Le-ahar London" (After London) (1939), in *Ketavim*, vol. 9, p. 54.

107. Katznelson, "Hevlei ihud ve-shlavei ihud" (Pangs and stages of unity) (1938), in *Ketavim*, vol. 8, p. 149; and see Tsivion, *Diukano ha-yehudi*, pp. 148, 149.

108. Katznelson, "Ba-mivhan," in *Ketavim*, vol. 6, p. 390.

109. Ibid., p. 392.

110. See Tsivion, *Diukano ha-yehudi*, pp. 259, 260.

111. See Charles S. Liebman and Eliezer Don-Yehiya, *Civil Religion in Israel* (Berkeley, Calif., 1983).

112. See Tsivion, *Diukano ha-yehudi*, pp. 179–181.

113. See Yaacov Shavit, *Jabotinsky and the Revisionist Movement, 1925–1948* (London, 1988), p. 119. Cf. Isaac Remba, "Dat u-masoret be-hayav u-be-mahshavto" (Religion and tradition in his life and teaching), *Ha-uma* 3, no. 9 (June 1964), pp. 146–166.

114. Ze'ev Jabotinsky, "Tzionut ve-Eretz Israel" (Zionism and Eretz Israel) (1905), in

Ketavim: Ketavim tzioni'im rishonim, (Writings: Early Zionist writings) (Jerusalem, 1949) pp. 118, 119.

115. Ze'ev Jabotinsky, "Ra'ayon ha-yovel" (The jubilee idea), in *Ketavim: uma ve-hevra* (Writings: Nation and society) (Jerusalem, 1959), pp. 177–178.

116. Jabotinsky's speech at the founding conference of N.Z.O. (Vienna, September 9, 1935), in *Ketavim: Neumim* (Writings: Speeches), vol. 2 (Jerusalem, 1948), pp. 184–185.

117. Ze'ev Jabotinsky to his son Eri, September 14, 1935, in letter collection A1/2/38/2. JIA. See also Joseph B. Schechtman, *Fighter and Prophet: The Last Years* (Silver Spring, Md., 1986), p. 289.

118. Jabotinsky even noted further that his original proposal had been more far-reaching: it had been "to impose the sancta of the Torah in the life of the nation." This letter, originally written in Hebrew to Rabbi Levi Jungster, head of the Religious Section of the N.Z.O., was also published in Yiddish as Ze'ev Jabotinsky, "A Briv" (A letter), *Unser Welt* (Warsaw), May 21, 1937. It was retranslated into Hebrew in Moshe Bella, *Olamo shel Jabotinsky: Mivhar devarav ve-ikarei torato* (The world of Jabotinsky: A selection of his works and the essentials of his teaching) (Tel Aviv, 1972), pp. 169, 70.

119. Jabotinsky, "Hurdemu be-kloroform" (Anesthetized with chloroform), *Ha-mashkif,* June 16, 1939.

120. See, e.g., the criticism of Ahad Ha'am in "Ma zot tzionut ruhanit?" (What is spiritual Zionism?), in Yehoshua Yevin, *Ketavim* (Writings) (Tel Aviv, 1949), pp. 358–364; also Abba Ahimeir, "'Yavanut' be-yehuda ve-'vahadut' be-yavan" ("Hellenism" in Judah and "Judaism" in Hellas), in *Tzionut mahapkhanit* (Revolutionary Zionism) (Tel Aviv, 1966), pp. 235–239.

121. See Shavit, *Jabotinsky and the Revisionist Movement*, pp. 140–143.

122. See Even-Zohar, "The Emergence of a Native Hebrew Culture in Palestine: 1882–1948," *Studies in Zionism* 2, no. 4 (autumn 1981), pp. 167–184.

123. A number of scholarly studies have examined the works of Yonatan Ratosh and the phenomenon of Canaanism. A penetrating biographical study is Yehoshua Porath, *Shelah ve-et be-yado* (Shelah with pen in hand) (Tel Aviv, 1989). A thorough analysis of Canaanism to which this section is much indebted is Yaacov Shavit, *Mi-ivri ad kena'ani* (From Hebrew to Canaanite) (Tel Aviv, 1984). The revised English version is Yaacov Shavit, *The New Hebrew Nation: A Study in Israeli Heresy and Fantasy* (London, 1987). See also James S. Diamond, *Homeland or Holy Land? The "Canaanite" Critique of Israel* (Bloomington, Ind., 1986).

124. See Shavit, *The New Hebrew Nation*, pp. 31–35.

125. Quoted from the *Kongresszeitung der N.Z.O.*, in *Sefer Betar: Korot u-mekorot* (The book of Betar: History and sources), ed. Haim Ben-Yeruham, vol. 2, part 2 (Jerusalem, 1975), p. 516.

126. See Shavit, *The New Hebrew Nation*, pp. 26–30, 80–86.

127. Ibid., pp. 92–96. For a comparative survey of this phenomenon see Anthony D. Smith, *The Ethnic Origins of Nations* (Oxford, 1986), pp. 174–208.

128. "Ketav el ha-noar ha-ivri" (Epistle to the Hebrew youth), Ha-va'ad le-gibush ha-noar ha-ivri (The Committee for the Consolidation of the Hebrew Youth) (1943), reproduced in Yonatan Ratosh, *Reishit ha-yamim, petihot ivriyot* (The first days, Hebrew beginnings) (Tel Aviv, 1982), pp. 32–37. The translations are as given in Shavit, *The New Hebrew Nation*, pp. 59, 60.

129. An example, one of many, of Ratosh's contentions is Yonatan Ratosh, "The New Hebrew Nation (The Canaanite Outlook)," in *Unease in Zion*, ed. Ehud Ben-Ezer (New

York, 1974), pp. 201–234, esp. p. 208. (This documentation is an interview conducted by Ben-Ezer in July 1970.)

130. See Shavit, *The New Hebrew Nation*, p. 64.

131. Ibid., pp. 19, 20, and cf. the different emphasis in Boaz Evron's review of Shavit's *Mi-ivri ad kena'ani*: "Hama'ase u-bavuato ha-akademit" (The actuality and its academic reflection), *Yediot ahronot*, March 2, 1984, p. 20; also Boaz Evron, " 'Canaanism': Solutions and Problems," *The Jerusalem Quarterly*, no. 44 (fall 1987), pp. 51–72.

132. *Masa ha-petiha: Be-moshav ha-va'ad im shelihei ha-taim (moshav rishon)* (The opening discourse: In executive session with the agents of the cells, first meeting), Ha-va'ad le-gibush ha-noar ha-ivri (Tel Aviv, 1944), reproduced in Ratosh, *Reishit ha-yamim, petihot ivriyot*, pp. 152, 153. The translation is as given in Shavit, *The New Hebrew Nation*, p. 61.

133. Ibid., p. 63.

134. See Ben-Ezer, *Unease in Zion*, p. 212.

135. See *Ha-minshar ha-ivri: Ekronot ha-peula ha-shemit* (The Hebrew manifesto: Principles of Semitic action), Ha-merkaz le-peula shemit (The Center for Semitic Action) (Tel Aviv, September 1958), Clauses 1, 2, and 3, p. 8.

136. Examples of these post-Canaanite manifestations are the views of Uri Avneri and the weekly *Ha-olam ha-ze*, which he edited, and the Center for Semitic Action group formed in the late 1950s by Uri Avneri and former Lehi members such as Natan Yellin-Mor and Boaz Evron. As recently as 1988 there was published an eloquent exposition of this genre of post-Canaanism, constituting a scathing critique of the Zionist ideology underlying the State of Israel. See Boaz Evron, *Ha-heshbon ha-leumi* (The national reckoning) (Tel Aviv, 1988). Perhaps the most important transmutation of all was post-Canaanism's reorientation relative to the constellation of Israel's political parties. It underwent a paradoxical inversion: whereas Ratosh's pre-1948 circle had been a satellite of sorts of the Right, denying the existence of a distinctive Palestinian-Arab national entity, the post-Canaanites became satellites of the Left, ardently advocating coexistence of Israel with a Palestinian Arab state in a regional context.

137. See the introduction by Joseph Schechter in Jacob Klatzkin, *Yalkut masot* (Collected essays) (Tel Aviv, 1966), pp. 6–17.

138. See Jacob Klatzkin, *Shekiyat ha-haim* (The decline of life) (Berlin, 1925); Jacob Klatzkin, *Ketavim* (Writings), ed. Avraham Kariv (Tel Aviv, 1953). See also Shmuel Sheps, "Mishnato ha-filosofit shel Yaakov Klatzkin" (The philosophy of Jacob Klatzkin), in *Brit ivrit olamit, Kenes 2* (World Union of Hebrew, Conference 2) (Jerusalem, 1983), pp. 145–152.

139. Jacob Klatzkin, *Tehumim: Ma'amarim* (Spheres: Essays) (Berlin, 1925), p. 36. From the point of view of Zionist ideology, the two major articles in this volume are pp. 10–41, "Bokra shel tekufa" (The dawning of an age), which originally appeared as "Yahadut ha-ruah and ruah ha-yahadut" (Spiritual Judaism and the spirit of Judaism), in *Ha-shiloah*, vol. 26, (1912), pp. 40–107. Also "Galut ve-aretz" (Exile and land), which is a shorter version of the thesis developed in his work: Jacob Klatzkin, *Krisis und Entscheidung* (Crisis and Decision) (Berlin, 1921). A noteworthy critical examination of Klatzkin's nationalist ideology is Nathan Rotenstreich, "Galut ve-aretz le-Yaakov Klatzkin be-mivhan ha-zman" (Jacob Klatzkin's "exile and land" with the test of time), *Bitzaron*, no. 24/25 (1985), pp. 38–46.

140. Klatzkin, *Tehumim*, p. 36. The quotation that follows is from p. 22.

141. Ibid., p. 18.

142. Ibid. This quotation and those that follow are, in sequence, from pp. 25, 30, 26, 39, 36, 41.

143. Ibid., pp. 18, 19. The quotations that follow are, in sequence, from pp. 46; 76; 77; 64.

144. Ibid., pp. 76, 77.

145. Ibid., pp. 82, 81. The quotations that follow are from pp. 89, 90; 95, 96.

146. See Zalman Shazar, "Yehezkel Kaufmann u-foalo" (Yehezkel Kaufmann and his work), *Ha-doar*, 13 Kislev, 1963, pp. 59–61; also B. Mazar, E. Simon, and Y. Zeligman, *Al Professor Yehezkel Kaufmann* (Words in memory of Professor Yehezkel Kaufmann) (Jerusalem, 1964).

147. Yehezkel Kaufmann, "Yahaduto shel Ahad Ha'am" (The Judaism of Ahad Ha'am), *Ha-shiloah* (Tevet-Sivan, 1914), pp. 249–271.

148. Kaufmann added, however, that this did not mean that a Jew could not regard Jesus as a model from the aspect of his moral purity. It was the metaphysical aspect of Jesus—the pretension to messianic status—that was out of the bounds of the normative tradition.

149. According to Kaufmann, Ahad Ha'am was too rational to be able to appreciate the crucial importance of faith. He found this to be a defect even in Ahad Ha'am's understanding of the biblical period, in particular of Moses and the prophets. He had overlooked the deep religious faith with which they were imbued and saw only the realistic moral aspects of their teachings.

150. Yehezkel Kaufmann, "Hefetz ha-kiyum ha-leumi" (The national will to life), *Miklat* 4 (June–August 1920) pp. 175–194. The quotations are from p. 183. See also his critique of Simon Dubnow's national theory in Yehezkel Kaufmann, "Ha-leumiyut ha-demokratit" (Democratic nationalism), *Ha-shiloah* 31, (1914/1915), pp. 289–304; and his other essays that appeared in the period 1920–1921 and similarly anticipated the more elaborate exposition of his *Gola ve-nekhar* (Tel Aviv, 1954): Yehezkel Kaufmann, "Shelilat ha-galut u-shelilat hageula" (Negation of the exile and negation of redemption), *Miklat* 3 (1920), pp. 9–22; idem, "Hefetz ha-kiyum ha-leumi" (The national will to life), *Miklat* 4 (June–August 1920), pp. 175–194; "Le-she'elat ha-yahadut ha-modernit" (On the question of modern Judaism), *Ha-shiloah* 38 (1921), pp. 180–187.

151. Kaufmann, "Hefetz ha-kiyum ha-leumi," pp. 189–193.

152. Ibid. In Yehezkel Kaufmann, *Gola ve-nekhar*, vol. 2, p. 151, Kaufmann discussed the nature of religion more systematically, defining it as "the sphere of actual relationships between man and the ineffable in human experience." The emphasis is on "actual," i.e., what men do, such as prayer, precepts of behavior, and morals.

153. Later published by the Reali Hebrew Secondary School as Yehezkel Kaufmann, *Bein netivot* (Between pathways) (Haifa, 1952).

154. On the theoretical influences underlying Kaufmann's sociological history, see Lawrence J. Silberstein, "Historical Sociology and Ideology: A Prolegomenon to Yehezkel Kaufmann's Golah v'Nekhar," in *Essays in Modern Jewish History*, ed. Frances Malino and Phyllis Cohen Albert (East Brunswick, N.J., 1982), pp. 173–195; also Lawrence J. Silberstein, "Religion, Ethnicity and Jewish History: The Contribution of Yehezkel Kaufmann," *Journal of the American Academy of Religion* 42, no. 3 (September 1974), pp. 516–531.

155. Kaufmann, *Gola ve-nekhar*, vol. 2, p. 396. For Kaufmann's full critique of all the "spiritual Zionists," see ibid., sec. 9, pp. 348–424, and more concisely in Kaufmann, *Bein netivot*, pp. 134–208.

156. Kaufmann, *Gola ve-nekhar*, vol. 2, pp. 403, 404.

157. Kaufmann, "Hefetz ha-kiyum ha-leumi," p. 194. Also see Kaufmann's introduction to *Gola ve-nekhar*, where he declares his awareness that "[i]n what I have to say on the question of the future there are things that will be extremely hard on the ears of people in our generation. But what shall I do. I cannot say anything other than that which I have said."

8. The Right to The Land

1. The most comprehensive and thorough historical study of the field is Yosef Gorny, *Zionism and the Arabs 1882–1948: A Study of Ideology* (Oxford, 1987). The dilemmas associated with the use of the force are equally comprehensively analyzed in Anita Shapira, *Land and Power: The Zionist Resort to Force, 1881–1948* (New York 1992). For detailed examination of negotiation attempts, see Neil Caplan, *Futile Diplomacy: Vol. 1. Early Arab-Zionist Negotiation Attempts, 1913–1931* (London, 1983), and *Vol. 2. Arab-Zionist Negotiations and the End of the Mandate* (London, 1986).

2. See Martin Seliger, "Fundamental and Operative Ideology: The Two Principal Dimensions of Political Argumentation," *Policy Sciences* 1 (1970), pp. 325–338. Cf. the application of this distinction in Dan Horowitz and Moshe Lissak, *Origins of the Israeli Polity* (Chicago, 1978), pp. 120–156.

3. The passage cited is the fifth and last recapitulation of the divine promise to Abraham. The others are Gen. 12:7; 13:18–24; 15:18–21. The promise is reiterated to Isaac (Gen. 26:2–5) and to Jacob (Gen. 28:3–4, 13–15; 35:11–12).

4. See Rabbi Abraham Isaac Ha-Cohen Kook's citation of Rav Nahshon Gaon on this principle in his introduction to Reuven Gafni, *Zekhutenu ha-historit-mishpatit al Eretz Israel* (Our historical-legal right to Eretz Israel) (Jerusalem, 1933), p. 2. On the biblical texts relating to the divine promise, see Rabbi Yehezkel Abramsky, *Eretz Israel: nahlat am yisrael, be-aspeklaria shel ha-masoret* (The Land of Israel: Inheritance of the people of Israel, as reflected in the tradition) (Bnei Brak, 1959). (This work was first published in 1945.)

5. Owing to some geographical confusion this came to be popularly known as the Uganda Scheme, whereas the territory in question was in fact within the British East Africa Protectorate that today corresponds to a portion of Kenya. See Robert G. Weisbord, *Africa Zion* (Philadelphia, 1968). On the East African controversy at the sixth Zionist congress (1903) and its aftermath, see David Vital, *Zionism: The Formative Years* (Oxford, 1982), pp. 264–347.

6. The ideological ramifications of the Uganda controversy have been thoroughly examined in Shmuel Almog, *Zionism and History: The Rise of a New Jewish Consciousness* (New York and Jerusalem, 1987), pp. 238–304; Ehud Luz, *Parallels Meet: Religion and Nationalism in the Early Zionist Movement, 1882–1904* (Philadelphia, 1988), pp. 257–282.

7. Sporadic attempts to revive "territorialism" were made in the 1930s and 1940s. In 1931 a Jewish group in Berlin initiated negotiations to colonize a strip of territory in Angola. In 1935 the Freeland Movement for Jewish Territorial Colonization was founded in London. It explored settlement possibilities in a variety of countries, including South America, Africa, and Australia. In 1941 another group, Freeland League for Territorial Settlement, was founded in New York. All of these efforts proved futile. For an ideological and historical summary, see Isaak N. Steinberg, "Territorialism," in *Struggle for Tomorrow*, ed. Basil J. Vlavianos and Feliks Gross (New York, 1954), pp. 112–130. See also Eliahu Benjamini, *Medinot la-yehudim* (States for the Jews) (Tel Aviv, 1990).

8. *Stenographisches Protokoll der Verhandlungen des VI Zionisten-kongresses in Basel*

23–28 August 1903 (Vienna, 1903), pp. 9, 10. For a vivid eyewitness description of Herzl's closing speech, in which he declared "If I forget thee O Jerusalem, may my right hand forget its cunning," See Jacob de Haas, *Theodor Herzl: A Biographical Study* (New York, 1927), vol. 2, p. 179.

9. *Stenographisches Protokoll der Verhandlungen des VI Zionisten-kongresses*, pp. 71, 211.

10. See chap. 7.

11. For full analysis of Mizrahi's position in regard to the territorial controversy of 1903–1904, see Ehud Luz, "Zion and Judenstaat: The Significance of the 'Uganda' Controversy," in *Essays in Modern Jewish History: A Tribute to Ben Halpern*, ed. Frances Malino and Phyllis Cohen Albert (New York, 1982), pp. 217–239. Also, see Luz, *Parallels Meet*, pp. 257–269; Almog, *Zionism and History*, pp. 238–384. On the vote at the 1903 congress, cf. Israel Klausner, "Be-reishit yesod Mizrahi" (At the founding of Mizrahi), in *Sefer ha-tzionut ha-datit* (The book of religious Zionism), vol. 1 (Jerusalem, 1977), p. 362; David Vital, *Zionism: The Formative Years* (Oxford, 1982), p. 302. Also Mordecai Eliav, "Siat ha-mizrahi ba-hatzba'a al tokhniet Uganda ba-kongres ha-tzioni ha-shishi" (*Mizrahi* in the vote on the Uganda scheme at the sixth Zionist congress), in *Ha-tzionut* 12 (1987), pp. 85–98. According to the last mentioned, based on a careful reexamination of the voting cards in the Central Zionist Archives, 63 Mizrahi delegates voted in favor of the proposal (out of 292 or 295 ayes [there is a disparity between the official minutes and the extant voting cards]); 14 voted nay (out of 178), and 21 abstained (out of 99).

12. See Yitzhak Nissenbaum, *Alei heldi* (Pages from my life), 2nd ed. (Jerusalem, 1969), pp. 197, 198 (1st ed, Warsaw, 1929.)

13. See Klausner, "Be-reishit yesod mizrahi," pp. 361–366, citing Reines to Zangwill, 30 October 1905, A36/54, CZA. See also the letters of Rabbi Reines to Israel Zangwill reproduced in *Ba-mishor* (On the plane), year 1, no. 34 (September 13, 1940), pp. 11–12, and no. 35 (September 20, 1940), pp. 10–12.

14. Quoted from a statement by Rabbi Kook to the Palestine Commission on the Disturbances of August 1929, in Reuben Gafni, *Zekhuteinu ha-historit ha-mishpatit al Eretz Israel* (Our historical-legal right to Eretz Israel) (Jerusalem, 1933), p. 103.

15. Abraham Isaac Ha-Cohen Kook, "Mikhtav galui" (Open letter), (Jaffa, Adar, 1905), in *Igrot ha-ra'aya* (Letters of Rabbi Kook) (Jerusalem, 1962), vol. 1, p. 17.

16. Aharon Gertz, ed., *Statistical Handbook of Jewish Palestine 1947* (Jerusalem, 1947), p. 37. According to British mandate statistics, the Jewish population in Palestine at the end of 1935 was 355,157; at the end of 1936, 384,078; out of totals of 1,210,554 and 1,308,112, respectively. See Justin McCarthy, *The Population of Palestine* (New York, 1990), p. 65.

17. "Our Religious Rights to Eretz Israel: A Memorandum from the Chief Rabbinate and Mizrahi to the Royal Commission, 1936," 22 Kislev 5697, pp. 1, 2, S25/4664, CZA. Also *Din ve-heshbon shel ha-merkaz ha-olami shel ha-mizrahi la-veida ha-olamit ha-14* (Report of the World Center of Mizrahi to the 14th World Conference) (Geneva 1936), p. 62.

18. *Ha-kongress ha-tzioni ha-esrim, din ve-heshbon stenografi* (The Twentieth Zionist Congress, stenographic record), Executive of the Zionist Organization and the Jewish Agency (Jerusalem, n.d.), p. 50. Also Shmuel Dothan, *Pulmus ha-haluka be-tekufat ha-mandat* (The partition controversy in the mandate period) (Jerusalem, 1980), p. 172.

19. *Netiva*, year 12, no. 39 (June 25, 1937), p. 1.

20. See Shmuel Dothan, "Religious Polemics Surrounding the 1937 Partition Plan," *Jerusalem Cathedra*, vol. 2, (1982), p. 228–257; also Shulamit Eliash, "Ha-emda ha-datit, tzionit ve-lo tzionit, le-tokhniet halukat Eretz Israel (1937–1938)" (The religious Zionist and anti-Zionist attitudes regarding the partition plan), in *Iyunim be-tokhniyot ha-*

haluka, 1939–1947 (Studies in the Palestine partition plans, 1937–1947), ed. Meir Avizohar and Isaiah Friedman (Sde Boker, 1984), pp. 55–74.

21. Rabbi Moshe Avigdor Amiel, "Halukat ha-aretz mi-nekudat reut ha-torah" (The partition of Eretz Israel from the point of view of the Torah), *Ha-boker*, August 12, 1937, p. 2.

22. Erich Pinchas Rosenblueth, "Ha-ma'arakha ha-medinit" (The political struggle), *Ha-tzofe*, January 24, 1938, p. 2. An editorial note was appended to this article stating that it was published in the interests of free discussion.

23. Rabbi Dr. Yitzhak Unna, "Ha-medina ha-ivrit ve-dat ha-torah" (The Jewish state and the religion of the Torah), *Ha-hed*, year 12, no. 12 (1937) p. 12; also cited in Shmuel Dothan, *Pulmus ha-haluka be-tekufat ha-mandat*, p. 187.

24. See Eliash, "Ha-emda ha-datit," pp. 55–74, esp. p. 60.

25. The word *tehonem* has an ambiguous root. One possibility is the root *hanon*, meaning "show mercy" (i.e., *lo tehonem* could mean "show them no mercy"); another possibility is the root *hanon*, meaning "encampment" or "taking hold of land so as to encamp" (i.e. "you shall not allow them to hold land in Eretz Israel"). The subject is discussed in the talmudic tractate Avoda Zara (Idolatry), 20, 1, ff., and also in Maimonides' *Hilhot akum* (Laws relating to idolaters), 10, 3–6.

26. See Eliash, "Ha-emda ha-datit," pp. 57–59.

27. Gafni, *Zekhuteinu ha-histori*, passim.

28. "Brief Survey of Historical Legal Moral and Political Rights of the Jews to Palestine," submitted to the Anglo American Committee of Inquiry by Dr. Aaron Barth (Tel Aviv, March 1946), S25/8190, CZA. The author was an economist and assistant manager of the Anglo-Palestine Bank.

29. "Anglo-American Committee of Inquiry, Hearing in Jerusalem, March 26th 1946; Appearance of Chief Rabbi Dr. I. Hertzog," S25/6365, CZA.

30. "Memorandum of the *Mizrahi* World Organization to the Anglo-American Inquiry Commission," S25/6463, CZA.

31. See Gideon Aran, "From Religious Zionism to Zionist Religion: The Roots of Gush Emunim," *Studies in Contemporary Jewry*, vol. 2 (Bloomington, Ind., 1986), p. 138.

32. Zvi Yehuda Kook, "Torah Loyalty and The Land," in *Whose Homeland: Eretz Israel Roots of the Jewish Claim*, ed. Avner Tomaschoff (Jerusalem, n.d. [c. 1980]) p. 184.

33. "Our Religious Right to Eretz Israel: A Memorandum from the Chief Rabbinate and Mizrahi to the Royal Commission, 1936," 22 Kislev 5697, pp. 4, 5, S25/4664, CZA.

34. "Memorandum of the Mizrahi World Organization to the Anglo-American Inquiry Commission," S25/6463, CZA.

35. "Anglo-American Committee of Inquiry, Hearing in Jerusalem, March 26th 1946, Appearance of Chief Rabbi Dr. I. Hertzog," p. 4, S25/6365, CZA.

36. James Parkes, *Whose Land? A History of Palestine*, rev. ed. (London, 1970), pp. 135, 138, 168.

37. See Solomon Zeitlin, "Jewish Rights in Eretz Israel (Palestine)," *Jewish Quarterly Review* 52, no. 1 (July 1961), pp. 12–34. This article was part of a polemic with Arnold Toynbee, who was invited to present his contrary views in the same issue of this periodical. See Arnold J. Toynbee, "Jewish Rights in Palestine," pp. 1–11.

38. See Martin Buber and Judah Magnes, *Two Letters to Gandhi from Martin Buber and J. L. Magnes* (Jerusalem, 1939), p. 9. The quotations that follow are from this source.

39. Martin Buber, "The National Home and National Policy in Palestine" (speech to a Berlin chapter of Brit Shalom, October 1929), reproduced and translated in *A Land of*

Two Peoples: Martin Buber on Jews and Arabs, ed. Paul R. Mendes-Flohr (New York, 1983), p. 84.

40. This and the quotations that follow, unless otherwise stated, are from Buber and Magnes, *Two Letters to Gandhi*.

41. Buber, "The National Home," p. 84.

42. See, e.g., the profound debate on this very point between Martin Buber and the German Jewish philosopher Hermann Cohen in *Der Jude*, no. 5 (July 1916), pp. 281ff, and *K. C. Blaetter*, July–August 1916, pp. 683ff, partly translated in *The Jew in the Modern World*, ed. Paul Mendes-Flohr and Jehuda Reinharz (New York, 1980), pp. 448–452.

43. On Gandhi's views and pro-Moslem bias, see Gideon Shimoni, *Gandhi, Satyagraha and the Jews* (Jerusalem, 1977), esp. pp. 20–27.

44. Martin Buber, "And If Not Now, When?" (an address to a convention of Jewish youth, Antwerp, July 1932), reproduced and trans. in Mendes-Flohr, ed., *A Land of Two Peoples*, p. 105.

45. Ibid., Mendes-Flohr's introduction, pp. 22, 23. For an analysis of Buber's distinctive conception of politics, his "believing realism," and the line of demarcation he drew between absolute morality and political action, see Ernst A. Simon, *Kav ha-tihum: Leumiyut, tzionut, ve-ha-sikhsukh ha-yehudi-aravi* (The line of demarcation: Nationalism, Zionism and the Jewish-Arab conflict in the thought of Martin Buber) (Givat Haviva, 1973).

46. Buber, "The National Home," p. 86.

47. Buber and Magnes, *Two Letters to Gandhi*, p. 12.

48. See chap. 7.

49. Aharon David Gordon, "Mikhtavim mi-Eretz Israel: Mikhtav 5" (Letters from Eretz Israel: Letter 5), in *Kitvei A. D. Gordon* (Writings of A. D. Gordon), ed. Joseph Aharonowitz, vol. 2 (Tel Aviv, 1925), pp. 291, 292.

50. This and the above quotations are from Gordon, "Nation to Nation," *A. D. Gordon: Selected Essays*, trans. Frances Burnce (New York, 1938), pp. 23–28.

51. Aharon David Gordon, "Avodateinu me-ata" (Our work henceforth), *Kitvei A. D. Gordon: Ha-uma ve-ha-avoda* (Writings of A. D. Gordon: The nation and labor), ed. Hugo Bergmann and A. L. Shohat (Jerusalem, 1954), pp. 245, 246.

52. Shlomo Breiman, ed., *Moshe Leib Lilienblum: Al tehiat Israel al admat eretz avotav* (Moshe Leib Lilienblum: On the revival of Israel on the land of its forefathers) (Jerusalem, 1953), p. 70.

53. In most cases the Jewish "historical right" is taken for granted. It is left implicit or invoked only when alternative territories are contemplated. For example, in all of Ahad Ha'am's writings, historical right is barely mentioned, but he does invoke it in contesting Simon Dubnow's advocacy of diasporic minority rights as an alternative to Zionism. Ahad Ha'am there points out that "Eretz Israel is the only land for which our historical right is undoubted." "Shalosh madregot" (Three steps), in *Kol kitvei Ahad Ha'am* (Jerusalem and Tel Aviv 1959), p. 153.

54. Theodor Herzl, *The Congress Addresses of Theodor Herzl*, trans. Nellie Straus (New York, 1917), p. 13.

55. When, in July 1896, one of Herzl's associates, Professor A. S. Yahuda, warned of Arab hostility and urged that efforts be made to win their cooperation, Herzl maintained, according to Yahuda's evidence, "[t]hat the Palestine population would have no say in the matter; the Sultan was the decisive factor, and no one in Palestine would dare to oppose his orders once the country would be made open for Jewish mass immigration." A. S. Yahuda, "My Early Meetings with Herzl," *Zionews* (New York), vol. 4, nos. 29/30

(July–August 1943), p. 26; cited in Joseph Nedava, "Herzl and the Arab Problem," *Forum on the Jewish People, Zionism and Israel* no. 27 (1977), p. 66.

56. See Theodor Herzl, *Altneuland,* trans. Paula Arnold (Haifa, 1960), pp. 54, 94, 95.

57. See "Statement of the Zionist Organization to the Paris Peace Conference regarding Palestine, February 3, 1919," in *Reports of the Executive of the Zionist Organization to the XII Zionist Congress* (London, 1921), pp. 74–83.

58. Later published as *The Historical Connection of the Jewish People with Palestine* (Jerusalem, 1936). The quotations are from this version, pp. 39, 40, 42. This memorandum, in slightly amended form, was also included in the Jewish Agency's submissions to the Anglo-American Committee of Inquiry in 1946.

59. This quotation is from the introduction to *The Historical Connection of the Jewish People with Palestine* (Jerusalem, 1946). It does not appear in the 1936 version of the document.

60. Gafni, *Zekhuteinu ha-historit.* The quotations that follow are from pp. 79, 80, 96, 97, 104. Gafni was born in Poland, studied at the Slobotka yeshiva, and went to Eretz Israel in 1924, where he studied law at the Hebrew University and was active in Ha-poel Ha-mizrahi. He served as legal adviser to Chief Rabbi Kook when he appeared before the Palestine Commission on the Disturbances of 1929. He furthered his legal studies in New York, gaining a doctorate and at the same time continuing his religious Zionist activities. After returning to Israel in 1958 he was again prominent in Ha-poel Ha-mizrahi.

61. See Joseph Heller, *The Zionist Idea* (London, 1947), pp. 89–95.

62. Yehezkel Kaufmann, *Gola ve-nekhar* (Exile and alienness) (Tel Aviv, 1962), vol. 1, pp. 138, 139.

63. Ibid., vol. 1, p. 474; vol. 2, pp. 214–218.

64. Ibid., vol. 2, pp. 211, 212.

65. Ibid., vol. 2, pp. 467, 468.

66. Ibid., vol. 2, pp. 470.

67. Ibid.

68. Yehezkel Kaufmann, "Al derekh ha-shalom" (On the road to peace), in *Sheifotenu* (Our aspirations), vol. 3, no. 3 (Sivan 1932), pp. 76–84.

69. To be sure, the ideological position taken by the Arab opponents of Zionism denied even the fact of the Jewish historical connection. It deployed a variety of contentions, such as that the Jewish presence had been transient and the Arab presence was of longer duration, that the contemporary Jews were of European stock and not the racial descendants of the ancient Israelites at all, that the contemporary Arabs of Palestine were the descendants of the Canaanites and Philistines who preceded the Israelites in ancient times, and/or that they were in fact also the true racial descendants of the ancient Israelites themselves. See Henry Kattan, *Palestine and International Law* (London, 1973), pp. 3, 24; also idem, *Palestine, The Arabs and Israel* (London, 1969).

70. Nathan Feinberg, "The Recognition of the Jewish People in International Law," in *The Arab-Israeli Conflict: Vol. 1. Readings,* ed. John Norton Moore (Princeton, N.J., 1974), p. 66.

71. Ibid., p. 86. See also Nathan Feinberg, *Studies in International Law* (Jerusalem, 1979), pp. 274, 288ff, 448.

72. Nathan Feinberg, "The Question of Sovereignty over Palestine," in *The Arab-Israeli Conflict: Vol. 1. Readings,* ed. John Norton Moore, pp. 231–232; also Nathan Feinberg, *The Arab-Israeli Conflict in International Law* (Jerusalem, 1970), p. 50. On doubts concerning the binding legality of the principle of self-determination, see also

Alfred Cobban, *The Nation State and National Self-Determination* (London, 1969), pp. 104–106.

73. Julius Stone, *Israel and Palestine* (Baltimore, 1981), pp. 9, 16.

74. Feinberg, *The Arab-Israel Conflict in International Law*, p. 54; Feinberg, "The Recognition of the Jewish People in International Law," p. 66. Accordingly, Feinberg contended that, given the greater sufferings of the Jewish nation in the historical circumstances that applied during the First World War and its aftermath (and, indeed, applied, a fortiori, in the following decades), the satisfaction of Jewish national needs and aspirations merited priority.

75. Public Hearings before the Anglo-American Committee of Inquiry, Jerusalem (Palestine), March 8, 1946, p. 29, CZA.

76. Karl Kautsky, *Are the Jews a Race?* (London, 1926), p. 208.

77. Cited in Berl Locker, *The Jews and Palestine: Historical Connection and Historic Right*, trans. from the Yiddish by Joseph Leftwich, Palestine Labour Studies, no. 11 (London, 1938), p. 7. This first appeared in Yiddish during 1936 and 1937 in *Der Tag*, (New York).

78. *Dos Naye Leben* (London), no. 1 (March 1906), p. 30.

79. Chaim Zhitlowsky, "Unser menshlikhe recht tzu Eretz Yisroel" (Yiddish: Our human right to Eretz Israel), *Der Tag*, June 23, 1936, pp. 5, 6. The two quotations that follow are from the same source. Zhitlowsky began his political career in the Russian Social Revolutionary Party. In the 1890s he turned to advocacy of Jewish socialism and national minority rights in the Diaspora, with Yiddish as the national language. In 1908 he moved to New York, where he became active in the Jewish labor movement and continued to vacillate in his political orientation between Poalei Zion and cosmopolitan socialism.

80. Ber Borochov, "Le-she'elat tzion ve-territoria," (On the question of Zion and territory), in *Ketavim* (Writings), ed. L. Levita and D. Ben-Nahum, vol. 1 (Tel Aviv, 1955), p. 149.

81. Ibid., p. 148.

82. Borochov, "Ha-platforma shelanu" (Our platform), in *Ketavim*, vol. 1. This quotation and those that follow are from pp. 280, 283, 294, 295.

83. See Borochov, "Facing Reality" (1917), in *Nationalism and the Class Struggle: A Marxian Approach to the Class Struggle, Selected Writings by Ber Borochov*, ed. Abraham G. Duker (Westport, Conn. 1972), pp. 89–93; "Declaration to the Hollando-Scandinavian Socialist Committee Submitted by the Jewish Socialist Labor Confederation Poale Zion on August 6, 1917," in *Class Struggle and the Jewish Nation: Selected Essays in Marxist Zionism*, ed. Mitchell Cohen (New Brunswick, N.J., 1984), p. 209. See also Mitchell Cohen's introduction, p. 30.

84. Shlomo Kaplansky, *Hazon ve-hagshama* (Promise and realization) (Merhavia, 1950), pp. 14, 15.

85. Locker, *The Jews and Palestine*, pp. 27–30.

86. Haim Greenberg; *The Inner Eye: Selected Essays* (New York, 1953), vol. 1, pp. 235, 236.

87. Ze'ev Jabotinsky, "Ne'um ba-mo'etza ha-Eretz Israelit" (Speech to the Eretz Israel Council) (1919), in *Ketavim: Neumim* (Writings: Speeches) vol. 1 (Jerusalem, 1957), pp. 117, 118.

88. Ibid., pp. 115, 116.

89. Quoted from a letter in English to Leonard Stein, March 9, 1922, in Moshe Bella, ed., *Olamo shel Jabotinsky* (The world of Jabotinsky) (Tel Aviv, 1972), p. 220.

90. Jabotinsky, "Ha-musar shel kir ha-barzel" (The morality of the iron wall) (1925), in *Ketavim: Ba-derekh la-medina* (Writings: On the path to the state) (Jerusalem, 1950), pp. 263, 264.

91. Jabotinsky, "Neum ba-moetza he-Eretz Israelit" (1919), in *Ketavim: Neumim*, vol. 1, pp. 117, 118.

92. Vladimir Jabotinsky, *Evidence Submitted to the Palestine Royal Commission* (pamphlet) (London, 1937), pp. 10–29.

93. See Jabotinsky, "Al kir ha-barzel" (Concerning the iron wall) (1923), in *Ketavim: Ba-derekh la-medina*, p. 255. At the same time, it must be noted that Jabotinsky consistently held "the Arab East" in low esteem. See, e.g., a 1905 statement in *Ketavim: Ketavim tzioni'im rishonim* (Writings: Early Zionist writings) (Jerusalem, 1949), pp. 208–210, and a 1933 statement in *Ketavim: Ba-derekh la-medina*, p. 199.

94. Jabotinsky, "Al kir ha-barzel," pp. 258, 259.

95. Yehoshua Heschel Yevin, *Uri Zvi Greenberg: Meshorer mehokek* (Uri Zvi Greenberg: Poet legislator) (Tel Aviv, 1938), p. 90.

96. Reproduced in *Ba-mahteret* (In the underground), no. 2, 1941, in *Lohamei Herut Israel: Ketavim* (Fighters for the freedom of Israel: Writings) (Tel Aviv, 1960), vol. 2. The "Eighteen Principles of the Revival" were formulated at a time when Stern's group called itself Ha-etzel be-Israel (The National Military Organization in Israel). It was called Lehi from the summer of 1943 onward. The document was first published in two parts, October 1940 and February 1941. See Joseph Heller, *Lehi: Ideologia u-politika 1940–1949* (Lehi: Ideology and politics), 2 vols. (Jerusalem, 1989), pp. 117, 118.

97. See Heller, *Lehi*, for an exhaustive study of Lehi's ideological development. The interpretation of its ideological gyrations adopted here follows Heller's conclusions.

98. See chap. 6 above, n. 87.

99. Lehi's political orientation toward the Soviet bloc was quickened by the support lent to Zionism in Gromyko's celebrated U.N. speech of May 1947. It reached its apogee in the short-lived Lohamim Party (Fighter's Party) formed out of Lehi with the establishment of the State of Israel. See Heller, *Lehi*, pp. 501–528. Heller draws a parallel between this phase of Lehi's tactical ideological transmutations and the phenomenon of "national Bolshevism" in Weimar Germany.

100. The Hebrew version of Lehi's memorandum to UNSCOP is reproduced in *Lohamei Herut Israel: Ketavim*, vol. 2, pp. 535–586. It is noteworthy that the ideological and political character of this memorandum does not differ substantially from that of the IZL to UNSCOP. Cf. Irgun Tzvai Leumi be-Eretz Israel: Memorandum to UNSCOP, June 1947, typescript in JNUL, Jerusalem.

101. Hagit Lavsky, "Tzionei Germaniya ve-reishita shel 'Brit Shalom'" (The early days of Brit Shalom and the German Zionists), in *Yahadut Zemaneinu*, vol. 4 (Jerusalem, 1987), pp. 99–121.

102. "Takanot" (Statutes), May 1926, appended to *Sheifoteinu*, vol. 1, no. 2 (Jerusalem, 1927).

103. *Sheifoteinu*, 1, Jerusalem, 1927, trans. in Aharon Kedar, "Brith Shalom," *Jerusalem Quarterly*, no. 18 (winter 1981), p. 68.

104. First circular of Kedma Mizraha, S25/3111, CZA, and see Susan Lee Hattis, *The Bi-National Idea in Palestine during Mandatory Times* (Haifa, 1970), pp. 138–144.

105. Earlier, in 1939, Magnes had also formed a small, religiously inspired society that had only an ephemeral existence. Named *Ha-ol* (The Yoke, the reference being to the yoke of the Kingdom of Heaven) and in English "The Bond," it included Martin Buber, Hugo Bergmann, Ernst Simon, and Gershom Scholem. This small society was predicated

upon a sense of responsibility stemming from "faith in eternal values whose source is God," a faith "which carries a commitment to social action and practical political work." It was in the name of this society that Buber and Magnes tried to put the Zionist case before Mahatma Gandhi in their *Two Letters to Gandhi from Martin Buber and J. L. Magnes* (Jerusalem, 1939); see Arthur A. Goren, *Dissenter in Zion* (Cambridge, Mass., 1982), p. 50.

106. The reason given by Magnes for not joining Brit Shalom was his dissatisfaction with the approach of its founders, notably Ruppin, who (according to Magnes) sought peace with the Arabs not "as a logical deduction from the pacifist and Jewish position generally" but rather because it was "a tactical, practical necessity." Journal note, September 14, 1928, Magnes Papers, Central Archives for the History of the Jewish People, reproduced as document 62, in Goren, *Dissenter in Zion*, pp. 272–273.

107. Magnes to Weizmann, June 8, 1914, Magnes Papers, 838, reproduced in Goren, *Dissenter in Zion*, p. 12.

108. Magnes's pacifism owed much to his sympathy for the Yiddish-speaking immigrant Socialists whom he got to know in New York. See Zosa Szajkowski, "The Pacifism of Judah Magnes," *Conservative Judaism* 22 (spring 1968); see also Goren, *Dissenter in Zion*, pp. 23, 24.

109. Judah L. Magnes, "Evidences of Jewish Nationality," *The Emanuel Pulpit*, vol. 1 (New York, 1908), p. 2, quoted by Evyatar Friesel, "Magnes: Zionism in Judaism," in *Like All the Nations?* ed. William M. Brinner and Moses Rischin (New York, 1987), p. 75, n. 19, 20.

110. Judah L. Magnes, *Addresses by the Chancellor of the Hebrew University*, (Jerusalem, 1936), p. 62. Also Caplan, *Futile Diplomacy*, vol. 1, p. 42, quoting Magnes in a letter to Weizmann after the 1929 Arab riots: "A Jewish home in Palestine built up on bayonets and oppression [is] not worth having, even though it succeed, whereas the very attempt to build it up peacefully, cooperatively, with understanding, education and goodwill [is] worth a great deal, even though the attempt should fail."

111. Magnes repeated to Gandhi what he had said in an address delivered in New York in May 1919: "Palestine is, so they say, to be 'given' to the Jewish people. To my mind no peace conference has the right to give any land to any people even though it be the Land of Israel to the people of Israel." Buber and Magnes, *Two Letters to Gandhi*, p. 33.

112. Ibid., p. 34.

113. Journal entry, "The Arab Question," Jerusalem, July 4, 1928, Magnes Papers, 316, reproduced as document 61 in Goren, *Dissenter in Zion*, p. 271.

114. Magnes to Felix Warburg, September 13, 1929, Magnes Papers, 2396, reproduced as document 65 in Goren, *Dissenter in Zion*, p. 279.

115. Ernst Simon, "Neged ha-tzedukim" (Against the Sadducees), *Sheifoteinu* 3, nos. 5, 6 (1923), pp. 160, 162.

116. Ibid., p. 154. See also Ernst Simon, "Neum she-lo ne-emar ba-kongress" (A speech that was not given at the congress), *Sheifoteinu* 2, no. 5 (August 1931), pp. 164–169.

117. Simon, "Neged ha-tzedukim," p. 155.

118. See chap. 5 above and Elkana Margalit, *Ha-shomer ha-tzair: Mi-edat neurim le-marksism mahapkhani, 1913–1936* (Ha-shomer Ha-tzair: From youth community to revolutionary Marxism) (Tel Aviv, 1971).

119. See chap. 5 above.

120. *The Road to Bi-National Independence for Palestine* (Tel Aviv, 1947), pp. 31, 32. A

detailed analysis of Ha-shomer Ha-tzair's positions in regard to the Arabs is David Zait, *Tzionut be-darkei shalom* (Zionism and Peace) (Tel Aviv, 1985).

121. See Margalit, *Ha-shomer ha-tzair*, p. 206.

122. See Elkana Margalit, *Anatomia shel smol: Poalei zion smol be-Eretz Israel, 1919–1946* (The anatomy of the Left: Poalei Zion in Eretz Israel) (Tel Aviv, 1976), esp. pp. 205–232.

123. See especially Shabtai Teveth, *Ben-Gurion: The Burning Ground, 1886–1948* (London, 1987).

124. David Ben-Gurion, *Anahu u-shkheneinu* (We and our neighbors) (Tel Aviv, 1931), pp. 31–33. This originally appeared as an article in *Der Yiddisher Kempfer* (New York), in 1918. The translation is as given in David Ben-Gurion, *My Talks with Arab Leaders*, ed. Misha Louvish (Jerusalem, 1972), pp. 7–8.

125. Ben-Gurion, *Anahnu u-shkheneinu*, pp. 150, 151.

126. Testimony to the Anglo-American Committee of Inquiry, March 1946, reproduced in *The Jewish Case before the Anglo-American Committee of Inquiry on Palestine as Presented by the Jewish Agency for Palestine: Statements and Memoranda* (Westport, Conn., 1976), pp. 54, 55.

127. Ben-Gurion, *Anahnu u-shkheneinu*, Preface.

128. Ben-Gurion, "Mi-tokh ha-vikuah" (From the debate; the reference is to the debate with Brit Shalom in the fall of 1924) in Ben-Gurion, *Anahnu u-shkheneinu*, pp. 81, 82.

129. Shabtai Teveth, *Ben-Gurion and the Palestinian Arabs* (Oxford, 1985), p. 158, from a diary note of Ben-Gurion, March 11, 1936.

130. Ben-Gurion, "Mi-tokh ha-vikuah," in *Anahnu u-shkheneinu*, p. 184. The translation is an adaptation of that in David Hardan, ed., *Sources: Anthology of Contemporary Jewish Thought*, no. 5 (Jerusalem, 1975), pp. 97, 98.

131. Ben-Gurion, *My Talks with Arab Leaders*, p. 21. The quotations are from Ben-Gurion's own description of what he told Awni Abd al-Hadi. However, the available evidence from Arab sources indicates that Ben-Gurion's frank representation of Zionist aims was not only clearly heard but in fact had the effect of increasing their alarm and sense of injury at the impertinence of Ben-Gurion in actually expecting them to consent to minority status and the establishment of Palestine as a Jewish state. See Caplan, *Futile Diplomacy*, vol. 2, p. 8. Awni Abd al-Hadi (1889–1980), lawyer and politician, was a major spokesman of the Palestinian-Arab nationalist movement and served for a time on the Arab Executive. In 1932 he founded a Palestinian branch of the Istiqlal (Independence) Party, and as its head he joined the Arab Higher Committee that directed the Arab rebellion that broke out in 1936. He was arrested and lived in exile from 1937 to 1941. The Istiqlal, which fostered pan-Arab views, was a rather incohesive and inconsequential party in Palestine.

132. Ben-Gurion, *My Talks with Arab Leaders*, p. 33. The quotation is Ben-Gurion's version of the general lines of agreement he claimed to have reached with Mussa al-Alami at a meeting held on August 31, 1934. Mussa al-Alami was the son of a prominent landowning family. He held the senior position of government advocate in the Palestine mandatory government.

133. David Ben-Gurion, "Ha-mediniyut ha-tzionit me-ahar ha-meoraot" (Zionist policy after the riots), part 2, *Ha-poel ha-tzair*, no. 8 (December 5, 1930), pp. 7, 8.

134. David Ben-Gurion, "Mediniyut ha-hutz shel ha-am ha-yehudi" (The foreign policy of the Jewish nation), in David Ben-Gurion, *Mi-ma'amad le-am* (From class to nation) (Tel Aviv, 1955), p. 107.

135. For a thorough analysis of the relationship between Ben-Gurion's convictions and tactics, see Shabtai Teveth, *Ben-Gurion and the Palestinian Arabs*, passim. Teveth comments (p.viii) that "Ben-Gurion was a political man and was quite capable of pragmatic insincerity." See also Teveth, "Ideology, Naïveté, or Pragmatism," *David Ben-Gurion: Politics and Leadership in Israel*, ed. Ronald W. Zweig (London, 1991), pp. 69–84.

136. See Teveth, *Ben-Gurion and the Palestinian Arabs*, pp. 18, 19, 25, 26, 75–85.

137. "Tazkir la-internatzional ha-miktzoi be-shem ha-histadrut ve-ha-internatzional ha-sotzialisti, be-shem ha-miflaga, al ha-mehumot biglal ha-kotel ha-ma'aravi" (Labor Federation memorandum to the Trades International and party memorandum to the Socialist International concerning the riots at the Western Wall), in David Ben-Gurion, *Zikhronot* (Memoirs), vol. 1 (Tel Aviv, 1971), appendices, pp. 740–750.

138. Quoted by Teveth, *Ben-Gurion and the Palestinian Arabs*, p. 156, from Mapai Political Committee, April 7, 1936, in Labor Party Archives, Beit Berl.

139. In private, Ben-Gurion hinted at his conviction that whatever partition boundaries were to be agreed upon need not necessarily be regarded as final. He assumed that future stages of the Arab-Jewish national conflict might yet lead to changes to the further advantage of Jewish national interests. See, e.g., his letter to his son Amos, October 1937, in David Ben-Gurion, *Letters to Paula*, trans. Aubrey Hodes (Pittsburgh, Pa., 1968), p. 154.

140. Ben-Gurion, *Anahnu u-shkheneinu*, p. 188. This document, it should be noted, was initially rejected by his own Mapai party and only incrementally imposed upon it in practice. It was concerned primarily with Ben-Gurion's proposals for a new constitutional dispensation allowing for parity between Jews and Arabs under the mandatory regime. Building on the principle that neither people had the right to dominate the other, it envisaged three stages. The first was a stage of municipal national autonomy of the two groups, to last from ten to fifteen years. The second was the expansion of that municipal autonomy into regional spheres. Once the Jewish and Arab communities reached parity in numbers, the third stage would permit the ending of the mandate and its replacement by an independent Palestinian unit comprising two autonomous national cantons within a federal Palestinian commonwealth. Our concern here is not with the details of this constitutional program but with the explicit principles pertaining to Jewish and Arab rights set forth by Ben-Gurion as a preamble.

141. "Evidence of David Ben-Gurion," in *The Jewish Plan for Palestine: Memoranda and Statements Presented by the Jewish Agency for Palestine to the United Nations Special Committee on Palestine* (Jerusalem, 1947), pp. 324, 325.

142. There are differences of opinion in the historiographic literature on the degree to which Weizmann adopted views close to those of Brit Shalom in the early 1930s. See Susan Lee Hattis, *The Bi-National Idea in Palestine during Mandatory Times* (Haifa, 1970), pp. 82, 83. Cf. Gorny, *Zionism and the Arabs*, pp. 202–207; Norman Rose, *Chaim Weizmann: A Biography* (New York, 1986), pp. 239, 287–289.

143. The tensions between the two leaders became acute in the period between the Biltmore Conference (1942) and the 22nd Zionist congress at the end of 1946, at which Weizmann was deposed from the presidency. See Teveth, *Ben-Gurion: The Burning Ground*, pp. 747–750, 816–831.

144. "Testimony to the Anglo-American Committee, August 3rd 1946," in *The Letters and Papers of Chaim Weizmann*, ser. B: *Papers*, vol. 2, ed. Barnet Litvinoff (Jerusalem, 1984), pp. 594–595.

145. Our discussion here extrapolates the ideological representations of the Zionist

case. At the operative level the prospect of partition covertly underlay the policies of Ben-Gurion and Weizmann. The strategy adopted by the executive of the Zionist Organization was tactically to demand all of Eretz Israel for Jewish statehood (the resolution at the Biltmore Conference of 1942 in New York calling for "Eretz Israel as a Jewish Commonwealth") but with the intention of settling for a partition solution. At the same time, Ben-Gurion and Weizmann tried to avoid a repetition of the tumultuous internal controversy over partition that had taken place in 1937. They preferred an untrumpeted drift of Zionist policy toward partition. Without attempting to define exact boundaries, the Zionist Organization adopted the formula "viable state" at its 22nd Zionist congress, which took place in late 1946. On these developments see Joseph Heller, "Ha-mediniyut ha-tzionit be-tokhniyot ha-haluka shel Eretz Israel bi-shnot ha-arbaim" (Zionist policy and the partition plans for Eretz Israel in the 1940s), in *Iyunim be-tokhniyot ha-haluka, 1937–1947* (Studies in the partition plans, 1937–1947), ed. Meir Avizohar and Isaiah Friedman (Sde Boker, 1984), pp. 143–148.

146. "Evidence of Dr. Chaim Weizmann," in *The Jewish Plan for Palestine*, pp. 543, 544, 548.

Bibliography

Newspapers and Periodicals

Ba-mahteret (In the Underground). Lehi publication, 1940–1941.

Ba-mishor (On the Plain). Weekly of the Association of Religious Writers, Jerusalem, 1940–1946.

Doar ha-yom (Daily Post). Daily, Jerusalem, 1919–1931; a Revisionist Zionist organ between 1928 and 1931.

Ha-ahdut (Unity). Weekly of Poalei Zion in Palestine, 1910–1915.

Ha-boker (The Morning). Daily of General Zionists, Tel Aviv, 1935–1965.

Ha-hed (The Echo). Monthly, unofficial literary and religious organ of the Department of Religion of the Jewish National Fund, Jerusalem, 1926–1962.

Ha-kedem (The East). Quarterly, St. Petersburg, 1907–1909.

Ha-magid (The Narrator). Weekly, originally published in Lyck, East Prussia, later Berlin and Cracow, 1856–1903.

Ha-melitz (The Advocate). Varying frequency, from 1871 in St. Petersburg, daily from 1886 to 1903.

Ha-ohela (In the Tent). Irregular organ of Ha-poel Ha-mizrahi, Jerusalem, 1925–1926.

Ha-olam (The World). Weekly organ of the Zionist Organization, varying places of publication: Cologne, Vilna, Odessa, London, Berlin, 1897–1914; 1919–1949.

Ha-peles (The Level). Rabbinical publication, Berlin, 1900–1905.

Ha-poel ha-mizrahi (The Mizrahi Laborer). Monthly organ of Ha-poel Ha-mizrahi, Jerusalem, 1923–1925.

Ha-poel ha-tzair (The Young Laborer). Fortnightly and then weekly organ of Ha-poel Ha-tzair and in the 1930s, of Mapai, Jaffa–Tel Aviv, 1907–1916; 1918–1970.

Ha-shahar (The Dawn). Monthly, Vienna, 1868–1884.

Ha-shiloah (The Siloam). Monthly, Berlin, then Odessa and Jerusalem, 1896–1926.

Ha-tor (The Turtle Dove). Weekly organ of Mizrahi, Jerusalem, 1920–1934.

Ha-tzefira (The Clarion). Weekly, after 1886 daily, Warsaw, 1862–1906 (reappeared at various times until 1931).

Ha-tzioni ha-klali (The General Zionist). Weekly organ of General Zionists, Jerusalem, 1932–1935.

Ha-tzofe (The Observer). Daily of Mizrahi and Ha-poel Ha-mizrahi, Jerusalem–Tel Aviv, 1937–.

Ha-zman (The Age). Biweekly then daily, St. Petersburg, from 1905; Vilna, 1903–1915.

The Jewish Chronicle. Weekly, London, 1841–.

Jewish Daily Bulletin. New York, 1925–1935.

Der Jude (The Jew). Berlin, 1916–1928.

Kuntress. (Tract). Weekly of Ahdut Ha-avoda, 1919–1929.

Miklat (Sanctuary). Literary monthly, New York, 1919–1920.

Dos Naye Leben (The New Life). Organ of Socialist Territorialists, London, 1906–1916.

Netiva (Pathway). Organ of World Union of Tzeirei He-halutz Ve-ha-poel Ha-mizrahi, Jerusalem, biweekly since 1926; weekly, 1934–1954.

Sheifoteinu (Our Aspirations). Monthly (and irregular) organ of Brit Shalom, Jerusalem, 1927–1933.

Der Tag (The Day). Daily, New York, 1914–1953.

Der Yiddisher Kempfer (The Jewish Fighter). Weekly (and irregular) of the Poalei Zion party, Philadelphia, 1907–1927.

Works Cited in the Text or Notes
(Articles in the contemporary press are not included.)

Abramsky, Yehezkel. *Eretz Israel: nahlat am yisrael, be-aspeklaria shel ha-masoret* (The land of Israel: Inheritance of the people of Israel, as reflected in the tradition). Bnei Brak: Netzah, 1959.

Adler, Joseph. *The Herzl Paradox: Political Social and Economic Theories of a Realist.* New York: Hadrian Press and Herzl Press, 1962.

———. "Herzl's Philosophy of New Humanism." In *Herzl Yearbook*, vol. 3, edited by Raphael Patai, pp. 175–198. New York: Herzl Press, 1960.

———. "Religion and Herzl: Fact and Fable." In *Herzl Yearbook*, vol. 4, edited by Raphael Patai, pp. 271–303. New York, Herzl Press, 1961–1962.

Agus, Jacob B. *Banner of Jerusalem: The Life, Times and Thought of Abraham Isaac Kuk.* New York: Bloch, 1946.

[Ahad Ha'am]. *Ahad Ha-Am: Essays, Letters, Memoirs.* Edited by Leon Simon. Oxford: Phaidon Press, 1946.

———. *Igrot Ahad Ha'am* (Letters of Ahad Ha'am). 6 vols. Jerusalem-Berlin, Tel Aviv: Yavneh & Moriah, 1923–1924.

———. *Kol kitvei Ahad Ha'am* (The collected writings of Ahad Ha'am). Tel Aviv and Jerusalem: Dvir & Hotza'a Ivrit, 1959.

———. *Nationalism and the Jewish Ethic: Basic Writings of Ahad Ha'am.* Edited by Hans Kohn. New York: Schocken, 1962.

———. *Selected Essays by Ahad Ha'am.* Edited by Leon Simon. Philadelphia: Jewish Publication Society, 1912.

Ahimeir, Abba. *Tzionut mahapkhanit* (Revolutionary Zionism). Tel Aviv: Ha-va'ad le-hotza'at kitvei Abba Ahimeir, 1966.

[Alkalai, Yehuda]. *Kitvei ha-rav Yehuda Alkalai* (Writings of Rabbi Yehuda Alkalai). Edited by Yitzhak Raphael. 2 vols. Jerusalem: Mosad Harav Kook, 1974.

Almog, Shmuel. *Leumiyut, tzionut ve-antishemiyut: Masot u-mehkarim* (Nationalism, Zionism, antisemitism: Essays and studies). Jerusalem: Ha-Sifriya Ha-Tzionit, 1992.

———. *Zionism and History: The Rise of a New Jewish Consciousness.* New York: St. Martin's Press, 1987.

———, ed. *Lifne heyot ha-tzionut* (Before there was Zionism). Jerusalem: Merkaz Shazar, 1981.

Aminoah, Nehemia, and Yeshayahu Bernstein, eds. *Yalkut: Ma'amarim al ra'ayon torah ve-avoda* (Compendium: Articles on the idea of Torah Ve-avoda). Jerusalem: The Executive of the Torah Ve-Avoda Movement, 1931.

Anderson, Benedict. *Imagined Communities: Reflections on the Origin and Spread of Nationalism.* London: Verso, 1983.

Appel, Yehuda Leib. *Betokh reshit ha-tehiya* (At the beginning of the revival). Tel Aviv: Y. L. Goldberg, 1936.

Aran, Gideon. "From Religious Zionism to Zionist Religion: The Roots of Gush Emunim." In *Studies in Contemporary Jewry*, vol. 2, edited by Peter Y. Medding, pp. 116–143. New York: Oxford University Press, 1986.

———. "Mi-tzionut datit le-dat tzionit: shorshei gush emunim ve-tarbuto" (From religious Zionism to Zionist religion: The roots of Gush Emunim and its culture). Ph.D. diss., Hebrew University of Jerusalem, 1987.

[Arlosoroff, Chaim]. *Kitvei Chaim Arlosoroff* (The works of Chaim Arlosoroff). 7 vols. Tel Aviv: Stiebel, 1934.

Arlosoroff, Chaim. *Yoman Yerushalayim* (Jerusalem diary). Tel Aviv: Mapai, 1953.

Armstrong, John A. *Nations before Nationalism.* Chapel Hill: University of North Carolina Press, 1982.

Aronson, Michael I. "The Attitudes of Russian Officials in the 1880s toward Jewish Assimilation and Emigration." *The Slavic Review* 34, no. 1 (1975), pp. 1–18.

Aviad, Janet. "The Messianism of Gush Emunim." In *Studies in Contemporary Jewry*, vol. 7, edited by Jonathan Frankel, pp. 197–216. New York: Oxford University Press, 1991.

Avineri, Shlomo. *Arlosoroff.* London: Halban, 1989.

———. *The Making of Modern Zionism: The Intellectual Origins of the Jewish State.* London: Weidenfeld & Nicolson, 1981.

———. *Moses Hess: Prophet of Communism and Zionism.* New York: New York University Press, 1985.

———. "The Socialist Zionism of Chaim Arlosoroff." *Jerusalem Quarterly*, no. 34 (winter 1985), pp. 68–87.

———, ed. *David Ben-Gurion, demuto shel manhig tnuat poalim* (David Ben-Gurion, profile of a labor leader). Tel Aviv: Am Oved, 1988.

Avizohar, Meir. *Be-rei saduk: Idealim hevrati'im ve-leumi'im ve-hishtakfutam be-olama shel Mapai* (In a cracked mirror: National and social ideals as reflected in Mapai). Tel Aviv: Am Oved, 1990.

Avneri, Yossi. "Degel Jerusalem" (Banner of Jerusalem). In *Be-shvilei ha-tehiya: mehkarim ba-tziyonut ha-datit* (In the paths of renewal: Studies on religious Zionism), vol. 3, edited by Mordechai Eliav, pp. 39–58. Ramat Gan: Bar Ilan University, 1988.

Baldwin, P. M. "Liberalism, Nationalism and Degeneration: The Case of Max Nordau." *Central European History* 13, no. 2 (June 1980), pp. 99–120.

Bartal, Israel. "Messianic Expectations and Their Place in History." In *Vision and Conflict in the Holy Land*, edited by Richard I. Cohen, pp. 141–189. Jerusalem: Yad Yitzhak Ben-Zvi, 1985.

Barzilay, Isaac E. "National and Anti-National Trends in the Berlin Haskalah." *Jewish Social Studies* 21 (1959), pp. 165–192.

Bat-Yehuda, Geula. *Ha-rav Maimon be-dorotav* (Rabbi Maimon and his times). Jerusalem: Mosad Harav Kook, 1979.

———. *Ish ha-meorot: Rabbi Yitzhak Yaakov Reines* (The man of lights: Rabbi Yitzhak Yaakov Reines). Jerusalem: Mosad Harav Kook, 1985.

Bauer, Otto. *Die Nationalitätenfrage und die Sozialdemokratie*, 2nd ed. Vienna: Wiener Volksbuchhandlung, 1924.

Bein, Alex. "The Origin of the Term and Concept 'Zionism.'" *Herzl Yearbook*, vol. 2, edited by Raphael Patai, pp. 1–27. New York: Herzl Press, 1959.

———. *Theodor Herzl*. Philadelphia: Jewish Publication Society, 1941.

———, ed. *Sefer Motzkin* (Motzkin anthology). Jerusalem: The Zionist Executive & The World Jewish Congress Executive, 1939.

Bella, Moshe, ed. *Olamo shel Jabotinsky: Mivhar devarav ve-ikarei torato* (The world of Jabotinsky: A selection of his works and the essentials of his teaching). Tel Aviv: Defusim, 1972.

Beller, Steven. *Herzl*. London: Halban & Weidenfeld & Nicolson, 1991.

Ben-Avraham, Baruch. *Miflagot u-zeramim politi'im be-tekufat ha-bayit ha-leumi, 1918–1948* (Parties and political movements in the period of the National Home, 1918–1948). Jerusalem: Merkaz Shazar, 1978.

Benayahu, Meir. "Ha-'hevra kedosha' shel rabbi Yehuda Hasid ve-aliyato le-eretz Israel" (The 'Holy Society' of Rabbi Yehuda Hasid and its settlement in Jerusalem). *Sefunot* 3 & 4 (1960), pp. 133–182.

Ben-Gurion, David. *Anahnu u-shekheneinu* (We and our neighbors). Tel Aviv: Davar, 1931.

[Ben-Gurion, David]. "Evidence of David Ben-Gurion." In *The Jewish Plan for Palestine: Memoranda and Statements Presented by the Jewish Agency for Palestine to the United Nations Special Committee on Palestine*, pp. 295–386. Jerusalem: Jewish Agency for Palestine, 1947.

Ben-Gurion, David. *Letters to Paula*. Translated by Aubrey Hodes. Pittsburgh, Pa.: University of Pittsburgh Press, 1968.

———. *Mi-ma'amad le-am* (From class to nation). Tel Aviv: Ayanot, 1955.

———. *My Talks with Arab Leaders*, Jerusalem: Keter, 1972.

———. *Tnuat ha-poalim ve-ha-revizionismus* (The labor movement and revisionism). Tel Aviv: Minhelet Ha-Liga, 1933.

———. *Zikhronot* (Memoirs). 6 vols. Tel Aviv: Am Oved, 1971–1981.

Ben-Horin, Meir. *Max Nordau: Philosopher of Human Solidarity*. London: London Jewish Society, 1956.

———. "Reconsidering Max Nordau." In *Herzl Yearbook*, vol. 2, edited by Raphael Patai, pp. 153–170. New York: Herzl Press, 1959.

Ben-Israel, Hedva. "The Role of Religion in Nationalism: Some Comparative Remarks on Irish Nationalism and on Zionism." In *Religion, Ideology and Nationalism in Europe and America: Essays Presented in Honor of Yehoshua Arieli*, edited by H. Ben-Israel et al., pp. 331–340. Jerusalem: Merkaz Shazar, 1986.

Benjamini, Eliahu. *Medinot la-yehudim* (States for the Jews). Tel Aviv: Ha-Kibbutz Ha-Meuhad & Sifriyat Ha-Poalim, 1990.

Benvenisti, David, and Hayim Mizrahi. "Rabbi Yehuda Bibes ve-kehilat Corfu be-zemano" (Rabbi Yehuda Bibes and the contemporary Corfu community). *Sefunot* 2 (1958), pp. 303–330.

Ben-Yeruham, Haim, ed. *Sefer Betar: Korot u-mekorot* (The book of Betar: History and sources). 2 vols. Jerusalem: Ha-va'ad Le-Hotza'at Sefer Betar, 1975.

Berdyczewski, Micha Yosef. *Al em ha-derekh* (On the high road). Warsaw: Tzeirim, 1900.

———. *Al-ha-perek* (On the agenda). Warsaw: Tzeirim, 1900.

———. *Arakhin* (Values). Warsaw: Tzeirim, 1900.

[Berdyczewski, Micha Yosef]. *Kitvei M. J. Bin-Gorion (Berdyczewski): Ma'amarim, ba-derekh: Part 2. Shinui arakhin* (Articles, on the way: Transvaluation). Lipsia: Stiebel, 1922.

————. *Kol ma'amarei Micha Yosef Bin-Gorion* (*Berdyczewski*). Tel Aviv: Am Oved, 1952.

Berdyczewski, Micha Yosef. *Nemushot* (Epigones). Warsaw: Tzeirim, 1900.

Berlin, Isaiah. *The Life and Opinions of Moses Hess.* Cambridge: Heffer & Sons, 1959.

Berlin (Bar-Ilan), Meir. *Be-shvilei ha-tehiya* (In the paths of renewal). Tel Aviv: World Union of Torah Ve-Avoda, 1940.

[Berlin (Bar-Ilan), Meir]. *Kitvei Rabbi Meir Bar-Ilan* (Writings of Rabbi Meir Bar-Ilan), vol. 1. Jerusalem: Mosad Harav Kook, 1950.

Berlin (Bar-Ilan), Meir. *Mi-volozhin le-yerushalayim* (From Volozhin to Jerusalem). 2 vols. Jerusalem: Mosad Harav Kook, 1971.

[Bernstein, Peretz]. *Sefer Peretz Bernstein.* Edited by Joseph Nedava. Tel Aviv: Chechik, 1961.

Bernstein, Yeshayahu. *Yeud va-derekh* (Destiny and path). Tel Aviv: Moreshet, 1956.

Bilski Ben-Hur, Raphaella. *Kol yahid hu melekh: Ha-mahshava ha-hevratit ve-ha-medinit shel Ze'ev Jabotinsky* (Every individual is a king: The social political thought of Ze'ev Jabotinsky). Tel Aviv: Dvir, 1988.

Bloom, Solomon F. "Karl Marx and the Jews." *Jewish Social Studies* 4 (1942), pp. 3–16.

Bodenheimer, Max Isidor. *Prelude to Israel: The Memoirs of M. I. Bodenheimer.* Edited by Henriette Hannah Bodenheimer, translated by Israel Cohen. New York: Yoseloff, 1963.

Boehm, Adolf. *Die Zionistische Bewegung.* Berlin: Welt-Verlag, 1920, 1934.

[Borochov, Ber]. *Ber Borochov: Ketavim nivharim* (Ber Borochov: Selected writings). Edited by Zalman Shazar (Rubashev). Tel Aviv: Am Oved, 1944.

Borochov, Ber. *Class Struggle and the Jewish Nation: Selected Essays in Marxist Zionism.* Edited and with an introduction by Mitchell Cohen. New Brunswick, N.J.: Transaction Books, 1984.

[Borochov, Ber]. Ber Borochov. *Geklibene Schrifin* (Yiddish: Selected writings). Edited by Berl Locker. New York, 1928.

Borochov, Ber. *Ketavim* (Writings). 3 vols. Edited by L. Levita and D. Ben-Nahum. Tel Aviv: Ha-Kibbutz Ha-Meuhad & Sifriyat Ha-Poalim, 1951–1966.

Borochov, Ber. *Nationalism and the Class Struggle: A Marxian Approach to the Jewish Problem.* Edited by Abraham G. Duker. New York: Poale Zion-Zeire Zion of America and Young Poale Zion Alliance of America, 1937; Westport, Conn.: Greenwood Press, 1972.

Breiman. Shlomo. "Ha-pulmus bein Lilienblum le-vein Ahad Ha'am ve-Dubnov" (The controversy between Lilienblum, Ahad Ha'am and Dubnow). *Shivat Zion* 1 (1950), pp. 138–168.

[Brenner, Yosef Haim]. *Kol kitvei Y. H. Brenner.* 3 vols. Tel Aviv: Ha-Kibbutz Ha-Meuhad, 1955–1966.

Breuer, Mordechai. "Al ha-musag 'dati-leumi' ba-historiografia u-ba-hagut ha-yehudit" (On the concept "national-religious" in Jewish historiography and thought). In *Be-shvilei ha-tehiya* (In the paths of renewal), vol. 3, edited by Mordechai Eliav, pp. 11–24. Ramat Gan: Bar Ilan University, 1988.

————. "Ha-diyun be-shlosh ha-shvuot ba-dorot ha-ahronim" (The debate on the three oaths in recent generations). In *Geula u-medina* (Redemption and state), pp. 49–57. Jerusalem: Ministry of Education and Culture, 1979.

————. *Modernity within Tradition: The Social History of Orthodox Jewry in Imperial Germany.* New York: Columbia University Press, 1922.

Brinner, William M., and Moses Rishin, eds. *Like all the Nations? The Life and Legacy of Judah L. Magnes.* Albany: State University of New York Press, 1987.

Buber, Martin. *Paths in Utopia*. Translated by R. F. Hull. London: Routledge & Kegan Paul, 1958.

———. *Teuda ve-yeud* (Mission and destiny). 2 vols. Jerusalem: Ha-Sifriya Ha-Tzionit, 1960.

———. *Two letters to Gandhi from Martin Buber and J. L. Magnes*. Jerusalem: Mass, 1939.

Caplan, Neil. *Futile Diplomacy: Vol. 1. Early Arab-Zionist Negotiation Attempts, 1913–1931; Vol. 2. Arab-Zionist Negotations and the End of the Mandate*. London: Cass, 1983, 1986.

Carlebach. Julius I. *Karl Marx and the Radical Critique of Judaism*. London: Routledge & Kegan Paul, 1978.

Chasanowitch, Leon. "Ziele und Mittel des socialistischen Zionismus." *Socialistische Monatsheft* 20 (1914), pp. 962–973.

Cobban, Alfred. *The Nation State and National Self-Determination*. London: Collins, 1969.

Cohen, Israel. *Short History of Zionism*. London: F. Muller, 1951.

Cohen, Mitchell, ed. *Zion and State: Nation, Class and the Shaping of Modern Israel*. Oxford: Blackwell, 1987.

Cohen, Stuart A. *English Zionists and British Jews: The Communal Politics of Anglo-Jewry, 1895–1920*. Princeton, N.J.: Princeton University Press, 1982.

Confino, Michael. "On Intellectuals and Intellectual Traditions in Eighteenth- and Nineteenth-Century Russia." *Daedalus* 101 (1972), pp. 117–150.

De Haas, Jacob. *Theodor Herzl: A Biographical Study*. New York: Brentanos, 1927.

Diamond, James S. *Homeland or Holy Land? The "Canaanite" Critique of Israel*. Bloomington: Indiana University Press, 1986.

Din ve-heshbon shel ha-kinus ha-olami ha-shlishi le-Betar (Report of the Third World Assembly of Betar). Bucharest: Shilton Betar, 1940.

Din ve-heshbon shel ha-merkaz ha-olami shel ha-mizrahi la-veida ha-olamit ha-14 (ms.) (Report of the Third World Assembly of Mizrahi to the 14th Conference, Geneva). Zurich, 1936.

Dinur, Ben-Zion. *Be-mifne ha-dorot* (At the turn of the generations). Jerusalem: Mosad Bialik, 1955.

Dinur (Dinaburg), Ben-Zion. *Mevasrei ha-tzionut*. Tel Aviv: Mosad Bialik & Dvir, 1938.

Domb, I. *The Transformation: The Case of the Naturei Karta*. London: Ha-madpis, 1958.

Don-Yehiya, Eliezer. "Ideologia u-mediniyut ba-tzionut ha-datit—haguto ha-tzionit shel harav Reines u-mediniyut 'Ha-mizrahi' be-manhiguto" (Ideology and policy in religious Zionism: Rabbi Reines's conception of Zionism and the policy of Mizrahi under his leadership). *Ha-tzionut*, vol. 8, pp. 103–146. Tel Aviv: Tel Aviv University, 1983.

———. "Jewish Messianism, Religious Zionism and Israeli Politics: The Impact and Origins of Gush Emunim." *Middle Eastern Studies* 23, pp, 215–234. Tel Aviv: Tel Aviv University, 1987.

———. "Tefisot shel ha-tzionut ba-hagut ha-yehudit ha-ortodoksit" (Conceptions of Zionism in Orthodox Jewish thought). *Ha-tzionut*, vol. 9, pp. 55–94. Tel Aviv: Tel Aviv University, 1984.

Doron, Joachim. *Haguto ha-tzionit shel Nathan Birnbaum* (The Zionist thought of Nathan Birnbaum). Jerusalem: Ha-Sifriya Ha-Tzionit, 1988.

Dothan, Shmuel. *Adumim: Ha-miflaga ha-kommunistit be-Eretz Israel* (The Reds: The Communist Party in Eretz Israel). Kfar Sava: Shevna Ha-sofer, 1991.

———. *Pulmus ha-haluka be-tekufat ha-mandat* (The partition controversy in the mandate period). Jerusalem: Yad Yitzhak Ben-Zvi, 1980.

————. "Religious Polemics Surrounding the 1937 Partition Plan." *Jerusalem Cathedra* 2 (1982), pp. 228–257.

Drori, Yigal. *Bein yemin le-smol: Ha-hugim ha-ezrahi'im bi-shnot ha-esrim* (Between Left and Right: The civic circles in the 1920s). Tel Aviv: Mifalim Universitayim, 1990.

Druyanov, Alter, ed. *Ketavim le-toldot Hibbat Zion ve-yishuv Eretz Israel* (Documents on the history of Hibbat Zion and the settlement of Eretz Israel). 3 vols. Vol. 1. *Odessa: Palestine Settlement Committee, 1919.* Tel Aviv: Omanut, 1925–1932.

Elam, Yigal. *Ha-sokhnut ha-yehudit: Shanim rishonot, 1919–1931* (The Jewish Agency: Formative years, 1919–1931). Jerusalem: Ha-Sifriya Ha-Tzionit, 1990.

Eliash, Shulamit. "Ha-emda ha-datit, tzionit ve-lo tzionit, le-tokhniet halukat Eretz Israel (1937–1938)" (The religious Zionist and non-Zionist attitudes regarding the partition plan, 1937–1938). In *Iyunim be-tokhniyot ha-haluka, 1937–1947* (Studies in the Palestine partition plans, 1937–1947), edited by Meir Avizohar and Isaiah Friedman, pp. 55–74. Sde Boker: Ben-Gurion University, 1984.

Eliav, Mordechai. "Siat ha-mizrahi ba-hatzba'a al tokhniet Uganda ba-kongres ha-tzioni ha-shishi" (Mizrahi in the vote on the Uganda scheme at the sixth Zionist congress). *Ha-tzionut*, vol. 12, pp. 85–98. Tel Aviv: Tel Aviv University, 1987.

Elon, Amos. *Herzl.* New York: Schocken, 1986.

Encyclopedia of Zionism and Israel. 2 vols. Edited by Raphael Patai. New York: Herzl Press & McGraw-Hill, 1971.

Endelman, Todd M. "Comparative Perspectives on Modern Anti-Semitism in the West." In *History and Hate: The Dimensions of Antisemitism*, edited by David Berger, pp. 95–114. Philadelphia: Jewish Publication Society, 1986.

————. "Conversion as a Response to Antisemitism in Modern Jewish History." In *Living with Antisemitism: Modern Jewish Responses*, edited by Jehuda Reinharz, pp. 59–83. Hanover, N.H., and London: University Press of New England, 1987.

Ettinger, Shmuel. "Ben-Zion Dinur ha-ish u-poalo ha-histori" (Ben-Zion Dinur, the man and his historical work) Introduction to Ben-Zion Dinur, *Dorot u-reshumot* (Generations and records), pp. 7–18. Jerusalem: Mosad Bialik, 1978.

————. *Ha-antishemiyut ba-eit ha-hadasha* (Antisemitism in the modern period). Tel Aviv: Sifriyat Ha-Poalim, 1978.

————. "Ha-diyun ba-nitzul ha-yehudi be-da'at ha-kahal ha-rusit shel reishit shnot ha-shmonim la-mea ha-tsha-esrei" (The debate on Jewish exploitation in Russian public opinion at the beginning of the 1880s). In *Prakim be-toldot ha-hevra ha-yehudit bi-yemei ha-beinayim u-va-et ha-hadasha, mukdashim le-Yaakov Katz* (Chapters in the history of Jewish society in the Middle Ages and the Modern period, dedicated to Jacob Katz), edited by Imanuel Etkes and Yosef Salmon, pp. 287–307. Jerusalem: Magnes Press, 1980.

————. "The Modern Period." In *History of the Jewish People*, edited by Haim Hillel Ben-Sasson. London: Weidenfeld & Nicolson, 1976.

————. "The Origins of Modern Anti-Semitism." *Dispersion and Unity* 9 (1969), pp. 17–37.

Even-Zohar, Ittamar. "The Emergence of a Native Hebrew Culture in Palestine: 1882–1948." *Studies in Zionism*, no. 4 (vol. 2, no. 2, autumn 1981), pp. 167–184.

————. "Ha-tzmiha ve-ha-hitgabshut shel tarbut ivrit mekomit ve-yelidit be-Eretz Israel, 1882–1948" (The emergence and crystallization of local and native Hebrew culture in Eretz Israel. 1882–1948), *Cathedra*, no. 16 (1980), pp. 165–189.

Evron, Boaz. "'Canaanism': Solutions and Problems." *The Jerusalem Quarterly*, no. 44 (fall 1987), pp. 51–72.

———. "Ha-heshbon ha-leumi (The national reckoning). Tel Aviv: Dvir, 1988.

Feinberg, Nathan. *The Arab-Israeli Conflict in International Law*. Jerusalem: Magnes Press, 1970.

———. "The Recognition of the Jewish People in International Law." In *The Arab-Israeli Conflict: Vol. 1. Readings*, edited by John Norton Moore, pp. 59–87. Princeton, N.J.: Princeton University Press, 1974.

———. *Studies in International Law, with Special Reference to the Arab-Israel Conflict*. Jerusalem: Magnes Press, 1979.

Fineman, Hayim. *Poale Zionism: An Outline of Its Aims and Institutions*. New York: Central Committee of the Jewish Socialist Labor Party–Poale Zion of America, 1918.

Finlayson, Geoffrey B. A. M. *The Seventh Earl of Shaftesbury, 1801–1885*. London: Eyre Methuen, 1981.

Fishman, Aryei. *Judaism and Modernization on the Religious Kibbutz*. Cambridge: Cambridge University Press, 1992.

———. "Masoret ve-hidush be-havayat ha-tzionut ha-datit" (Tradition and innovation in the experience of religious Zionism). In *Be-shvilei ha-tehiya: Mehkarim ba-tzionut ha-datit*, vol. 1, edited by Avraham Rubinstein, pp. 127–148. Ramat Gan: Bar Ilan University, 1983.

———. "'Torah and Labor': The Radicalization of Religion within a National Framework," *Studies in Zionism*, no. 6 (vol. 3, no. 2, autumn 1982), pp. 255–272.

———, ed. *Ha-poel ha-mizrahi, 1921–1935: Teudot* (Ha-poel ha-mizrahi, 1921–1935: Documents). Tel Aviv: Tel Aviv University, 1979.

Fishman, Joshua A. *Ideology, Society and Language: The Odyssey of Nathan Birnbaum*. Ann Arbor, Mich.: Karoma, 1987.

Fishman (Maimon), Yehuda Leib Ha-Cohen. "Ha-tzionut ha-datit ve-hitpathuta" (Religious Zionism and its development). In *Azkara le-ha-rav A. Y. Kook* (Memorial for Rabbi A. Y. Kook), vol. 5, *Eretz Israel*, pp. 78–366. Jerusalem: Mosad Harav Kook, 1937.

———. *Hidush ha-sanhedrin be-medinateinu ha-mehudeshet* (The renewal of the Sanhedrin in our renewed state). Jerusalem: Mosad Harav Kook, 1951.

———. *Le-sha'a u-le-dor: Masot u-mehkarim* (For the present generation: Essays and researches). Jerusalem: Mosad Harav Kook, 1965.

———. *Zikhron le-nishmat Avraham Yitzhak Ha-Cohen Kook* (In memoriam, A. Y. Kook). 3 vols. Jerusalem: Mosad Harav Kook, 1945.

———, ed. *Sefer ha-mizrahi, kovetz le-zekher Rabbi Yitzhak Yaakov Reines* (The book of Mizrahi: An anthology in memory of Rabbi Y. Y. Reines). Jerusalem: Mosad Harav Kook, 1946.

———, ed. *Sefer Shmuel* (The book of Shmuel [Mohilewer]). Jerusalem: Mizrahi Organization, 1923.

Fraenkel, Josef. "Colonel Albert E. W. Goldsmid and Theodor Herzl." In *Herzl Year Book*, vol. 1, edited by Raphael Patai, pp. 145–153. New York: Herzl Press, 1958.

Frankel, Dov. *Reishit ha-tzionut ha-medinit ha-modernit: Josef Natonek, 1813–1892* (The beginning of modern political Zionism: Josef Natonek). Haifa: Omanut, 1956.

Frankel, Jonathan. "The Crisis of 1881–82 as a Turning Point in Modern Jewish History. In *The Legacy of Jewish Migration: 1881 and Its Impact*, edited by David Berger, pp. 9–22. New York: Columbia University Press, 1983.

———. *Prophecy and Politics: Socialism, Nationalism and the Russian Jews, 1862–1917*. Cambridge: Cambridge University Press, 1981.

Frankel, Mordecai. "Ha-rav Josef Natonek, hoge ha-tzionut ha-medinit le-or ketavav"

(Josef Natonek, political Zionist thinker, in the light of his writings). *Kivunim*, no. 24 (August 1984), pp. 123–143.

[Friedland, Natan]. *Kitvei harav Natan Friedland* (Writings of Rabbi Natan Friedland). 2 vols. Edited by Israel Klausner. Jerusalem: Mosad Harav Kook, 1980.

Friedman, Isaiah. *The Question of Palestine, 1914–1918*, 2nd ed., expanded. New Brunswick, N.J., and London: Transaction Books, 1992.

Friedman, Maurice S. *Martin Buber: The Life of Dialogue*. Chicago: University of Chicago Press, 1976.

Friedman, Menahem. *Ha-hevra ha-haredit: mekorot, megamot, ve-tahalikhim* (Haredi Society: Sources, trends and processes). Jerusalem: Makhon Yerushalayim Le-heker Yisrael, 1991.

Friedmann, Eliezer Eliyahu (Ben Ha-Rav). *El karyana de-igrata* (To the readers of the epistle). Warsaw: Schildberg's Press, 1899–1900.

Friedrich, Carl Joachim. *Man and His Government*. New York: McGraw-Hill, 1963.

Gafni, (Weinshenker) Reuben. *Zekhutenu ha-historit-ha-mishpatit al Eretz Israel* (Our historical-legal right to Eretz Israel). Jerusalem: Sifriyat Torah Ve-Avoda, 1933.

Gal, Allon. *Brandeis of Boston*. Cambridge, Mass.: Harvard University Press, 1980.

Gardiner, Patrick L. *The Nature of Historical Explanation*. Oxford: Oxford University Press, 1952.

Geertz, Clifford. "Ideology as a Cultural System." In *Ideology and Discontent*, edited by David Apter. New York: Free Press, 1963.

———. "The Integrative Revolution." In *Old Societies and New States: Primordial Sentiments and Civil Politics in the New States*, edited by Clifford Geertz, pp. 105–157. London: The Free Press of Glencoe, 1963.

Gelber, Nathan Michael. *Zur Vorgeschichte des Zionismus: Judenstaatprojekte in den Jahren 1695–1845*. Vienna: Phaidon Verlag, 1927.

Gellner, Ernest. *Nations and Nationalism*. Oxford: Blackwell, 1983.

Gertz, A., ed. *Statistical Handbook of Jewish Palestine*. Jerusalem: Jewish Agency for Palestine, 1947.

Getter, Miriam. *Chaim Arlosoroff, biografia politit* (Chaim Arlosoroff: A political biography). Tel Aviv: Ha-Kibbutz Ha-Meuhad, 1977.

Giladi, Dan. "Ha-baron, ha-pekidut ve-hamoshavot ha-rishonot be-Eretz Israel: Ha-arakha mi-hadash" (The baron, the officials and the first settlements in Eretz Israel: A Reevaluation). *Cathedra*, no. 2 (1976), pp. 59–68.

———. *Ha-yishuv be-tekufat ha-aliya ha-revi'it 1926–1927* (The Jewish community [of Palestine] during the Fourth *Aliya*). Tel Aviv: Am Oved & Tarbut Ve-Hinukh, 1973.

Glickson, Moshe. *Im hilufei mishmarot* (With the changing of the guard). 2 vols. Tel Aviv: World Ha-Noar Ha-Tzioni Organization, 1939.

Goldscheider, Calvin, and Alan S. Zuckerman. *The Transformation of the Jews*. Chicago: University of Chicago Press, 1984.

Goldstein, Joseph. *Ahad Ha'am: Biografia* (Ahad Ha'am: A biography). Jerusalem: Keter, 1992.

———. "Ahad Ha'am: A Political Failure?" *Jewish History* 4, no. 2 (fall 1990), pp. 33–48.

———. "The Attitude of the Jewish and the Russian Intelligentsia to Zionism in the Initial Period (1897–1904)." *The Slavonic and East European Review* 64 (1986), pp. 546–556.

———. *Bein tzionut medinit le-tzionut ma'asit: Ha-tnua ha-tzionit be-russia be-reishita* (Between political Zionism and practical Zionism: Russian Zionism, the formative years). Jerusalem: Magnes Press and Ha-Sifriya Ha-Tzionit, 1991.

————. "Jabotinsky and Jewish Autonomy in the Diaspora." *Studies in Zionism* 7 (1986), pp. 219–232.

————. "Ha-ma'avak bein haredim le-hiloni'im al demuta shel ha-tnua ha-tzionit, 1882–1922" (The struggle between Orthodox and secular Jews over the character of the Zionist movement, 1882–1922). *Yahadut Zemaneinu* (Contemporary Jewry) vol. 2, pp. 237–260. Jerusalem: Magnes Press, 1985.

————. "Some Sociological Aspects of the Russian Zionist Movement at Its Inception." *Jewish Social Studies* 47 (1985), pp. 167–178.

————. "Yahaso shel Ahad Ha'am la-dat be-aspeklariya historit" (Ahad Ha'am's attitude to religion as historically reflected). In *Temurot ba-historia ha-yehudit ha-hadasha: Kovetz ma'amarim, shai le-Shmuel Ettinger* (Transition and change in modern Jewish history: Essays presented in honor of Shmuel Ettinger), edited by Shmuel Almog et al., pp. 159–168. Jerusalem: Merkaz Shazar, 1987.

————. "Ha-tenua ha-tzionit be-russia, 1897–1904" (The Zionist movement in Russia, 1897–1904). Ph.D. diss., Hebrew University of Jerusalem, 1982.

Goldstein, Yaacov. *Mapai: Gormim le-hakamata* (The Labor Party of Eretz Israel: The factors in its formation). Tel Aviv: Am Oved, 1976.

Goldstein, Yaacov, and Yaacov Shavit. *Le-lo pesharot: Heskem Ben-Gurion-Jabotinsky ve-kishlono, 1934–1935* (Without compromise: The Ben-Gurion–Jabotinsky agreement and its failure, 1934–1935). Tel Aviv: Yariv-Hadar, 1979.

Gordis, Robert. "Mordecai Manuel Noah: A Centenary Evaluation." *Publications of the American Jewish Historical Society* [American Jewish History], vol. 41 (1951–1952), pp. 1–26.

[Gordon, Aharon David]. *A. D. Gordon: Selected Essays*. Translated by Frances Burnce. New York: League for Labor Palestine, 1938.

[Gordon Aharon David]. *Kitvei A. D. Gordon* (Writings of A. D. Gordon). 5 vols. Edited by Joseph Aharonowitz. Tel Aviv: Ha-poel Ha-tzair, 1925–1929.

[Gordon, Aharon David]. *Kitvei A. D. Gordon* (Writings of A. D. Gordon). Edited by S. H. Bergmann and A. Shohat. Vol. 1: *Ha-uma ve-ha-avoda* (The nation and labor), 1954; vol. 2: *Ha-adam ve-ha-teva (Man and nature)*, 1951; vol. 3: *Mikhtavim u-reshimot* (Letters and notes), 1957. Jerusalem: Ha-Sifriya Ha-Tzionit.

[Gordon Aharon David]. *Kitzur kitvei A. D. Gordon* (Abbreviated writings of A. D. Gordon). Edited by N. Taradyon and A. Shohat. Tel Aviv: Stiebel, 1943.

Goren, Arthur A. *Dissenter in Zion*. Cambridge, Mass.: Harvard University Press, 1982.

Gorny, Yosef. *Ahdut ha-avoda, 1919–1930: Ha-yesodot ha-ra'ayoni'im ve-ha-shita ha-medinit* (The unity of Labor Party, 1919–1930: Its ideological foundations and political system). Tel Aviv: Tel Aviv University & Ha-Kibbutz Ha-Meuhad, 1973.

————. "Changes in the Social and Political Structure of the Second Aliya in the Years 1904–1940." *Zionism* 1 (1975), pp. 49–101.

————. "Ha-poel ha-tzair ve-yahaso el ha-sozialism be-tekufat ha-aliya ha-sheniya" (Ha-poel ha-tzair and its attitude toward socialism in the period of the Second *Aliya*). *Ba-derekh*, no. 1 (1971), pp. 74–83.

————. *Zionism and the Arabs, 1882–1948: A Study in Ideology*. Oxford: Clarendon, 1987.

Govrin, Nurit. *Meora Brenner: Ha-ma'avak al hofesh ha-bitui* (The Brenner incident: The struggle for free speech). Jerusalem: Yad Yitzhak Ben-Zvi, 1985.

Graetz, Heinrich. *The Structure of Jewish History and Other Essays*. Translated, edited, and with an introduction by Ismar Schorsch. New York: Jewish Theological Seminary of America, 1975.

Graetz, Michael. "Ha-meshihiyut ha-hilonit ba-mea ha-tsha-esrei ke-derekh shiva la-yahadut" (Secular messianism in the nineteenth century as a way of return to Judaism). In *Meshihiyut ve-eskatologia: Kovetz ma'amarim* (Messianism and eschatology: A collection of essays), edited by Zvi Baras, pp. 401–418. Jerusalem: Merkaz Shazar, 1983.

————. "Le-'shivato' shel Moshe Hess la-yahadut: Ha-reka la-hibur 'Romi ve-Yerushalayim'" (On the "return" of Moses Hess to Judaism: The background to his "Rome and Jerusalem"). *Zion* 45, (1980), pp. 133–153.

————. "Mekomo shel Joseph Salvador be-gibush toda'at ha-yihud ha-yehudi" (Joseph Salvador's place in the crystallization of a consciousness of Jewish particularity). *Zion* 37 (1972), pp. 41–65.

Greenberg, Haim. *The Inner Eye: Selected Essays*, vol. 1. New York: Jewish Frontier Associations, 1953.

Greenberg, Uri Zvi. *Sefer ha-kitrug ve-ha-emuna* (The book of indictment and faith). Jerusalem: Sedan, 1937.

Gross, Walter. "The Zionist Students' Movement." *Leo Baeck Institute Yearbook*, vol. 4, pp. 143–164. London: Secker & Warburg, 1959.

Grossman, Meir. "Reishit ha-tzionut ha-aktivistit" (The beginnings of activist Zionism). *Ha-uma* 3 (1964), pp. 24–38.

Halevy, Moshe. "Darko shel Max Nordau el ha-tzionut" (Max Nordau's path to Zionism), *Ha-tzionut*, vol. 16, pp. 63–92. Tel Aviv: Tel Aviv University, 1991.

Halpern, Ben. "Herzl's Historic Gift: The Sense of Sovereignty." *Hertz Yearbook*, vol. 3, edited by Raphael Patai, pp. 27–36. New York: Herzl Press, 1960.

————. *The Idea of the Jewish State*. Cambridge, Mass.: Harvard University Press, 1969.

Ha-minshar ha-ivri: Ekronot ha-peula ha-shemit (The Hebrew manifesto: Principles of Semitic action). Tel Aviv: Ha-merkaz le-peula shemit (The Center for Semitic Action), 1958.

Handler, Andrew. *Dori: The Life and Times of Theodor Herzl in Budapest (1860–1878)*, University, Ala.: University of Alabama, 1983.

Hardan, David, ed. *Sources: Anthology of Contemporary Jewish Thought.* 5 vols. Jerusalem: World Zionist Organization, 1970–1975.

Harell, Yehuda. *Ha-sotzialism shel Yitzhak Tabenkin* (The socialism of Yitzhak Tabenkin). Efal: Yad Tabenkin, 1973.

Hattis, Susan Lee. *The Bi-National Idea in Palestine during Mandatory Times*. Haifa: Shikmona, 1970.

Heilman, Samuel C., and Menahem Friedman. "Religious Fundamentalism and Religious Jews: The Case of the *Haredim*." In *Fundamentalisms Observed*, edited by Martin E. Marty and R. Scott Appleby, pp. 197–264. Chicago: University of Chicago Press, 1991.

Heller, Joseph. "Ha-mediniyut ha-tzionit ba-zira ha-bein-leumit le-ahar milhemet ha-olam ha-sheniya: Parashat va'adat ha-hakira ha-anglo-amerikanit 1945/6" (Zionist policy in the international arena after World War II: The Anglo-American Committee of Inquiry 1945/46). *Shalem* 3 (1981), pp. 213–293.

————. "Ha-mediniyut ha-tzionit be-tokhniyot ha-haluka shel Eretz Israel bi-shnot ha-arbaim" (Zionist policy and the partition plans for Eretz Israel in the 1940s). In *Iyunim be-tokhniyot ha-haluka, 1937–1947* (Studies in the Palestine partition plans, 1937–1947), edited by Meir Avizohar and Isaiah Friedman, pp. 143–148. Sde Boker: Ben Gurion University, 1984.

————. "'Ha-monism shel ha-matara' o 'ha-monism shel ha-emtza'im'? Ha-mahloket ha-rayonit ve-ha-politit bein Ze'ev Jabotinsky le-vein Abba Ahimeir, 1928–1933" ("The monism of aims" or "the monism of means"? The ideological and political dispute between Ze'ev Jabotinsky and Abba Ahimeir, 1928–1933). *Zion* 52 (1987), pp. 315–369.

———. *Lehi: Ideologia u-politika, 1940–1949* (Lehi: Ideology and politics). 2 vols. Jerusalem: Merkaz Shazar & Keter, 1989.

———. "Ze'ev Jabotinsky ve-she'elat ha-'havlaga,' 1936–1939: Hashkafat olam be-mivhan ha-metziyut" (Ze'ev Jabotinsky and the question of restraint, 1936–1939: His world outlook put to the test of reality). In *Temurot ba-historia ha-yehudit he-hadasha: Kovetz ma'amarim, shai le-Shmuel Ettinger* (Transition and change in modern Jewish history: Essays presented in honor of Shmuel Ettinger), edited by Shmuel Almog et al., pp. 283–320. Jerusalem: Merkaz Shazar, 1987.

———. *The Zionist Idea*. London: Joint Zionist Publications Committee, 1947.

Heller, Otto. *Der Untergang des Judentums* (The downfall of Judaism). Vienna: Verlag für Literatur und Politik, 1931.

Hertzberg, Arthur. *The Zionist Idea*. New York: Atheneum, 1973.

Herzl, Theodor. *Altneuland*. Translated by Paula Arnold. Haifa: Haifa Publishing Company, 1960.

[Herzl, Theodor]. *The Complete Diaries of Theodor Herzl*. 5 vols. Edited by Raphael Patai, translated by Harry Zohn. New York: Herzl Press & Yoseloff, 1960.

———. *The Congress Addresses of Theodor Herzl*. Translated by Nellie Straus. New York: Federation of American Zionists, 1917.

Herzl, Theodor. *The Jewish State, (Der Judenstaat)*. Translated by Harry Zohn. New York: Herzl Press, 1970.

[Herzl, Theodor]. *Kitvei Herzl: Igrot mi-reishit ha-peula ha-tzionit ad ha-kongres ha-rishon* (The writings of Herzl: Letters from the beginning of Zionist activity until the First Congress). Edited by Alex Bein. Jerusalem: Ha-Sifriya Ha-Tzionit, 1945–1948.

Herzl, Theodor. *Old New Land* (Altneuland). Translated by Lotta Levensohn, with a new introduction by Jacques Kornberg. New York: Wiener & Herzl Press, 1960.

———. *Tagebücher* (Diaries). 3 vols. Berlin: Jüdische Verlag, 1922–1923.

———. *Zionist Writings: Essays and Addresses*. Translated by Harry Zohn. New York: Herzl Press, 1973.

[Hess, Moses]. *Moses Hess, Ausgewählter Schriften*. Edited by Horst Lademacher. Cologne: Melzer, 1962.

Hess, Moses. *Rome and Jerusalem: A Study in Jewish Nationalism*. Translated by Meyer Waxman. New York: Bloch, 1943.

Hirsch, Samson Raphael. *Horev: A Philosophy of Jewish Laws and Observances*. Translated by Isador Gronfeld. London: Soncino Press, 1962.

Hirschensohn, Haim. *Sefer malki ba-kodesh* (My king in holiness: Book of responsa). 6 parts. Hoboken, N.J. and Seini: Moinischter, 1919–1928.

The Historical Connection of the Jewish People with Palestine. Jerusalem: Jewish Agency for Palestine, 1946.

Hodder, Edwin. *The Life and Work of the Seventh Earl of Shaftesbury*. 3 vols. London: Cassel, 1886.

Horowitz, Dan, and Moshe Lissak. *Origins of the Israeli Polity*. Chicago: University of Chicago Press, 1978.

Horwitz, Rivka. *Zecharia Frankel ve-reishit ha-yahadut ha-positivit ha-historit* (Zecharias Frankel and the beginnings of positive-historical Judaism). Jerusalem: Merkaz Shazar, 1984.

Horwitz, Rivka, ed. *Yitzhak Breuer: Iyunim be-mishnato* (Yitzhak Breuer: Studies on his thought). Ramat Gan: Bar-Ilan University Press, 1988.

Hovannisian, Richard G. *Armenia: On the Road to Independence.* Berkeley: University of California Press, 1967.

Hutchinson, John. *The Dynamics of Cultural Nationalism: The Gaelic Revival and the Creation of the Irish Nation State.* London: Allen & Unwin, 1987.

Hyman, Paula E. "Joseph Salvador: Proto-Zionist or Apologist for Assimilation?" *Jewish Social Studies* 34, no. 1 (1972), pp. 1–21.

Ish-Shalom, Benjamin. *Ha-rav Kook: Bein ratzionalism le-mistika* (Rabbi Kook: Between rationalism and mysticism). Tel Aviv: Am Oved, 1990.

————. *Ketavim* (Writings). 18 vols. Jerusalem: Eri Jabotinsky Press, 1947–1959.

Jabotinsky, Ze'ev (Vladimir). *Evidence Submitted to the Palestine Royal Commission.* New Zionist Organization, London, 1937.

————. *Ha-revizionism ha-tzioni be-hitgabshuto: Kovetz ma'amarim be-Rasvyet, 1925–1929* (The crystallization of Revisionist Zionism: Collected essays from *Rasvyet*). Edited by Yosef Nedava. Tel Aviv: Makhon Jabotinsky, 1985.

————. *Ketavim* (Writings). 18 vols. Jerusalem: Eri Jabotinsky Press, 1947–1959.

————. *Medina ivrit: Pitaron le-she'elat ha-yehudim* (A Jewish state: The solution to the Jewish question). Tel Aviv: A. Kopp, 1937.

Jacobs, Jack. *On Socialists and "The Jewish Question" after Marx.* New York: New York University Press, 1991.

Janowsky, Oscar. *The Jews and Minority Rights, 1898–1919.* New York: Columbia University Press, 1933.

The Jewish Case before the Anglo-American Committee of Inquiry on Palestine as Presented by the Jewish Agency for Palestine: Statements and Memoranda. Westport, Conn.: Hyperion Press, 1976.

Kalischer, Zvi Hirsch. *Derishat Zion* (Seeking Zion). Lyck: Zvi Hirsch Fettzall, 1862.

[Kalischer, Zvi]. *Ha-ketavim ha-tzioni'im shel ha-rav Zvi Kalischer* (Zionist writings of Rabbi Zvi Kalischer). Edited by Israel Klausner. Jerusalem: Mosad Harav Kook, 1947.

Kaplansky, Shlomo. *Hazon ve-hagshama* (Vision and realization). Merhavia: Sifriyat Ha-Poalim, 1950.

Kattan, Henry. *Palestine, the Arabs and Israel.* London: Longmans, 1969.

————. *Palestine and International Law.* London: Longmans, 1973.

Katz, Jacob. "Demuto ha-historit shel ha-rav Zvi Hirsch Kalischer" (The historical image of Rabbi Zvi Hirsch Kalischer). *Shivat Zion* 2–3 (1951–1952), pp. 26–41.

————. *Exclusiveness and Tolerance.* New York: Oxford University Press, 1961.

————. *From Prejudice to Destruction.* Cambridge, Mass.: Harvard University Press, 1980.

————. *Jewish Emancipation and Self-Emancipation.* Philadelphia: Jewish Publishing Society, 1986.

————. *Leumiyut yehudit: Masot u-mehkarim* (Jewish nationalism: Essays and studies). Jerusalem: Ha-Sifriya Ha-Tzionit, 1979.

————. "Orthodoxy in Historical Perspective." In *Studies in Contemporary Jewry*, vol. 2, edited by Peter Medding, pp. 3–17. New York: Oxford University Press, 1986.

————, ed. *Towards Modernity: The European Jewish Model.* New Brunswick, N.J.: Transaction Books, 1987.

Katz, Shmuel. *Jabo: Biografia shel Ze'ev Jabotinsky* (Jabo: A biography). 2 vols. Tel Aviv: Dvir, 1993.

Katzburg, Netanel. "Ha-rav Meir Bar-Ilan u-mediniyuto ha-tzionit be-shnot ha-shloshim" (Rabbi Meir Bar-Ilan and his Zionist policies in the 1930s). *Niv Ha-Midrashiya* 8 (spring 1970), pp. 212–241.

[Katznelson, Berl]. *Igrot* (Letters). 6 vols. Edited by Yehuda Sharett. Tel Aviv: Am Oved, 1961.

———. *Ketavim* (Writings). 12 vols. Tel Aviv: Mifleget Poalei E. Y., 1946–1950.

Kaufmann, Yehezkel. *Be-hevlei ha-zman* (In the tribulations of our times). Tel Aviv: Dvir, 1936.

———. *Bein netivot: Prakim be-heker ha-mahshava ha-leumit* (Between pathways: Chapters of research into [our] nationalist thought), 2nd ed. Haifa: Reali Secondary School, Haifa, 1952.

———. *Gola ve-nekhar* (Exile and alienness). 2 vols. Tel Aviv: Dvir, 1954.

Kautsky, Karl. *Rasse und Judentum*, 2nd ed. Stuttgart: J. H. W. Dietz, 1921. Translated and revised as *Are Jews a Race?* London: Jonathan Cape, 1926.

Kedar, Aharon. "Brith Shalom" (Documents). *Jerusalem Quarterly*, no. 18 (winter 1981), pp. 55–85.

Kedourie, Elie. *Nationalism*, 3rd ed. London: Hutchinson, 1966.

Keshet, Yeshurun. *M. J. Berdyczewski: (Bin-Gorion) Hayav u-foalo* (His life and work). Jerusalem: Magnes Press, 1958.

Klatzkin, Jacob. *Ketavim* (Writings). Edited by Avraham Kariv. Tel Aviv: Am Oved, 1953.

———. *Krisis und Entscheidung*. Berlin: Jüdischer Verlag, 1921.

———. *Shekiyat ha-hayim* (The decline of life). Berlin: Dvir, 1925.

———. *Tehumim: Ma'amarim* (Spheres: Essays). Berlin: Dvir, 1925.

———. *Yalkut masot* (Collected essays). Compiled and with an introduction by Yosef Schechter. Tel Aviv: Yahdav, 1965.

Klausner, Israel. "Be-reishit yesod Mizrahi" (At the founding of Mizrahi). In *Sefer ha-tzionut ha-datit* (The book of religious Zionism), vol. 1, edited by Yitzhak Raphael and Shlomo Z. Shragai, pp. 361–366. Jerusalem: Mosad Harav Kook, 1977.

———. *Ha-tnua le-tzion be-russia* (The Zionist movement in Russia), part 1: *Be-hitorer am* (The national awakening). Jerusalem: Ha-Sifriya Ha-Tzionit, 1962.

———. *Oppositzia le-Herzl* (The opposition to Herzl). Jerusalem: Ahiever, 1960.

Kleinman, Moshe. *Ha-tzionim ha-klali'im* (The General Zionists). Jerusalem: Makhon Le-haskala Tzionit, 1945.

Kna'ani, David. *Ha-aliya ha-sheniya ha-ovedet ve-yahasa la-dat ve-la-masoret* (The Labor Second *Aliya* and its attitude toward religion and tradition). Tel Aviv: Sifriyat Ha-Poalim, 1976.

Kobler, Franz. "Charles Henry Churchill," *Herzl Yearbook*, vol. 4, edited by Raphael Patai, pp. 1–66. New York: Herzl Press, 1962.

———. *The Vision Was There: A History of the British Movement for the Restoration of the Jews to Palestine*. London: Lincolns-Praeger, 1956.

Kohn, Hans. *The Idea of Nationalism*. New York: Macmillan, 1944.

Kolatt, Israel. "Idiologia u-metziyut be-tnuat ha-poalim ba-aliya ha-sheniya" (Ideology and reality in the workers' movement in the Second *Aliya*). Ph.D. diss., Hebrew University of Jerusalem, 1965.

———. "Poalei Zion bein tzionut le-kommunism" (Poalei Zion between Zionism and Communism). *Assufot*, no. 2, New Series (no. 15) (November 1971), pp. 30–52.

———. "Tnuat ha-avoda be-Eretz Israel bein ha-mizrah la-ma'arav" (The labor movement in Eretz Israel between East and West). *Divrei ha-kongress ha-olami ha-hamishi le-madaei ha-yahadut* (Proceedings of the Fifth World Congress of Jewish Studies) 2 (1972), pp. 295–307.

Kolitz, Zvi. *Mussolini: Ishiyuto ve-torato* (Mussolini: His personality and teaching). Tel Aviv: Tevel, 1936.

Kook, Avraham Yitzhak Ha-Cohen. *Eder ha-yakar ve-ikvei ha-tzon* (A goodly price and the footsteps of the flock). Jerusalem: Mosad Harav Kook, 1967.

———. *Hazon ha-geula* (The vision of redemption). Jerusalem: Association for Publication of the Works of Rabbi Kook, 1941.

———. *Igrot ha-ra'aya* (Letters of Rabbi A. Y. Kook). 3 vols. Jerusalem: Mosad Harav Kook, 1943–1963.

———. *Orot* (Lights). Jerusalem: Mosad Harav Kook, 1961.

———. *Orot ha-kodesh* (The lights of holiness). 3 vols. Jerusalem: Mosad Harav Kook, 1963.

———. *Orot ha-teshuva* (The lights of repentance). Jerusalem: Yeshivat Or Etzion, 1979.

Kook, Zvi Yehuda. *Le-netivot Israel* (To the pathways of Israel). Jerusalem: Mosad Harav Kook, 1967.

Kornberg, Jacques. "Political Symbolism and Mass Mobilization in the Thought of Theodor Herzl." *Divrei ha-kongress ha-olami ha-shemini le-madaei ha-yahadut* (Proceedings of the Eighth World Congress of Jewish Studies) 2 (1982), pp. 157–160 (English section).

———. "Theodor Herzl: A Re-evaluation." *Journal of Modern History* 52, no. 2 (June 1980), pp. 226–252.

———. *Theodor Herzl: From Assimilation to Zionism.* Bloomington: Indiana University Press, 1993.

Kressel, Getzel. "Ha-hevra ha-rishona le-yishuv Eretz Israel" (The first society for settlement in Eretz Israel). *Zion* 7 (1941/2), pp. 197–205.

———, ed. *David Gordon: Mivhar ma'amarav* (David Gordon: Selected articles). Tel Aviv: Mitzpe, 1942.

———, ed. *Rabbi Yehuda Alkalai—Rabbi Zvi Hirsch Kalischer.* Tel Aviv: Mitzpe, 1942–43.

———, ed. *Rabbi Yehiel Michel Pines: Mivhar ma'amarav* (Selected articles). Tel Aviv: Sreberk, 1946.

Kurtzweil, Baruch. *Sifruteinu ha-hadasha: Hemshekh o mahapekha?* (Our new literature: Continuity or revolution?). Tel Aviv: Schocken, 1959.

Landa, Shlomo Zalman, and Joseph Rabinowitz, eds. *Sefer or la-yesharim* (The book of light for the righteous). Warsaw: M. Y. Halter Press, 1900.

[Landau, Shmuel Haim]. *Kitvei Shmuel Haim Landau* (Writings), vol. 1. Warsaw: Ha-Shomer Ha-Dati, 1935.

Laqueur, Walter. *A History of Zionism.* London: Weidenfeld & Nicolson, 1972.

———. *Young Germany.* London: Routledge & Kegan Paul, 1962.

Laskov, Shulamit. "The Biluim: Reality and Legend." *Zionism* 2, no. 1 (spring 1981), pp. 17–70.

———. *Ha-biluim* (The Biluim). Jerusalem: Ha-Sifriya Ha-tzionit, 1979.

Lavsky Hagit. "Tzionei Germaniya ve-reishita shel 'Brit Shalom,'" (The early days of Brit Shalom and the German Zionists). *Yahadut Zemaneinu* (Contemporary Jewry), vol. 4, pp. 99–121. Jerusalem: Magnes Press, 1987.

Lederhendler, Eli. *The Road to Modern Jewish Politics: Political Tradition and Political Reconstruction in the Jewish Community of Tsarist Russia.* New York: Oxford University Press, 1989.

Lehman-Wilzig, Sam N. "Proto-Zionism and Its Proto-Herzl: The Philosophy and

Efforts of Rabbi Zvi Hirsch Kalischer." *Tradition* 16, no. 1 (summer 1976), pp. 56–76.

Leon, Abraham. *The Jewish Question: A Marxist Interpretation.* New York: Pathfinder Press, 1970.

Levenberg, Schneier. *The Jews and Palestine: A Study in Labour Zionism.* London: Poale Zion, Jewish Socialist Labour Party, 1945.

Levine, Norman. "Lenin on Jewish Nationalism." *Wiener Library Bulletin* 33, no. 51/52 (1980), pp. 42–55.

Levitats, Isaac. *The Jewish Community in Russia, 1772–1844.* New York: Columbia University Press, 1943; New York: Octagon Books, 1970.

———. *The Jewish Community in Russia, 1844–1917.* Jerusalem: Posner & Sons, 1981.

Liebman, Charles S., and Eliezer Don-Yehiya. *Civil Religion in Israel.* Berkeley: University of California Press, 1983.

[Lilienblum, Moshe Leib]. *Kol kitvei Moshe Leib Lilienblum* (Collected writings of M. L. Lilienblum). 4 vols. Vols. 1–2: Cracow: Fischer Press; vols. 3–4: Odessa: Moriah Press, 1910–1913.

———. *Moshe Leib Lilienblum, al tehiat Israel al admat eretz avotav* (Moshe Leib Lilienblum, on the revival of Israel in the land of its forefathers). Edited by Shlomo Breiman. Jerusalem: Zionist Organization, 1953.

Locker, Berl. *The Jews and Palestine: Historical Connection and Historic Right.* Translated from the Yiddish by Joseph Leftwich. London: Palestine Labour Studies Group, 1938.

Lohamei Herut Israel: Ketavim (Fighters for the freedom of Israel: Writings). 2 vols. Tel Aviv: Committee for Publication of Lehi Writings, 1960 (2nd ed., 1982).

Lubianker (Lavon), Pinhas. "Tnuat Gordonia" (The Gordonia movement). In *Derekh ha-noar* (The way of the youth), Anthology no. 1, pp. 47–73. Tel Aviv: Eretz Israel Council for Gordonia, 1929/30.

Lubotsky, Benjamin. *Ha-tzohar u-Betar* (Ha-tzohar and Betar). Jerusalem: Makhon Le-haskala Tzionit, 1946.

Luz, Ehud. *Parallels Meet: Religion and Nationalism in the Early Zionist Movement, 1882–1904.* Philadelphia: Jewish Publication Society, 1988.

———. "Zion and Judenstaat: The Significance of the 'Uganda' Controversy." In *Essays in Modern Jewish History: A Tribute to Ben Halpern,* edited by Frances Malino and Phyllis Cohen Albert, pp, 217–239. East Brunswick, N.J.: Associated Universities Press, 1982.

McCarthy, Justin. *The Population of Palestine.* New York: Columbia University Press, 1990.

Magnes, Judah L. *Addresses by the Chancellor of the Hebrew University.* Jerusalem: Hebrew University of Jerusalem, 1936.

Margalit, Elkana. *Anatomia shel smol: Poalei zion smol be-Eretz Israel, 1919–1946* (The anatomy of the Left: Left Poalei Zion in Eretz Israel). Tel Aviv: Ha-Kibbutz Ha-Meuhad, 1976.

———. "Bein ha-shomer ha-tzair le-ahdut ha-avoda ba-aretz" (Between Ha-shomer Ha-tzair and Ahdut Ha-avoda in Eretz Israel). *Assufot,* no. 13 (October 1969), pp. 29–50.

———. *Ha-shomer ha-tzair: Mi-edat neurim le-marksism mahapkhani, 1913–1936* (Ha-shomer Ha-tzair from youth community to revolutionary Marxism, 1913–1936). Tel Aviv: Ha-Kibbutz Ha-Meuhad, 1971.

———. "Social and Intellectual Origins of the Ha-shomer Ha-tzair Youth Movement, 1913–1920." *The Journal of Contemporary History* 4, no. 2 (April 1969), pp. 25–46.

————. *Tnuat ha-noar Gordonia: Ra'ayon ve-orah hayim* (The Gordonia youth movement: The idea and the way of life). Tel Aviv: Ha-Kibbutz Ha-Meuhad, 1986.

Marx, Karl, and Friedrich Engels. *The Communist Manifesto*. Translated by Samuel Moore (1888). London: George Allen & Unwin, 1948.

Mazar, Benjamin, Ernest A. Simon, and Y. Zeligman. *Al Professor Yehezkel Kaufmann* (Words in memory of Professor Yehezkel Kaufmann). Jerusalem: Magnes Press, 1964.

Mendelsohn, Ezra. "The Jewish Socialist Movement and the Second International, 1889–1914: The Struggle for Recognition." *Jewish Social Studies* 26, no. 3 (1964), pp. 131–145.

————. *Zionism in Poland: The Formative Years, 1915–1926*. New Haven, Conn., and London: Yale University Press, 1981.

Mendes-Flohr, Paul R. *A Land of Two Peoples: Martin Buber on Jews and Arabs*. New York: Oxford University Press, 1983.

Mendes-Flohr, Paul, and Jehuda Reinharz. *The Jew in the Modern World*. New York: Oxford University Press, 1980.

Menes, Abraham. "The Am Oylam Movement." *YIVO Annual of Jewish Social Science*, vol. 4, pp. 9–33. New York: Yiddish Scientific Institute, 1949.

Meyer, Michael A. "The German Model of Religious Reform and Russian Jewry." *Danzig between East and West*. Edited by Isadore Twersky, pp. 67–91. Cambridge, Mass.: Harvard University Press, 1985.

————. *Ideas of Jewish History*. New York: Behrman House, 1974.

Mintz, Matityahu. "Ber Borochov." *Studies in Zionism* 3, no. 1 (spring 1982), pp. 33–53.

————. *Ber Borochov: Ha-ma'agal ha-rishon (1900–1906)* (Ber Borochov: Circle One, 1900–1906). Tel Aviv: Ha-Kibbutz Ha-Meuhad and University of Tel Aviv, 1976.

————. "Borochov ve-Bogdanov" (Borochov and Bogdanov). *Ba-derekh* (On the path) 1 (September 1967), pp. 96–122.

————. *Zemanim hadashim—zemirot hadashot: Ber Borochov, 1914–1917* (New times—new tunes: Ber Borochov, 1914–1917). Tel Aviv: Am Oved, 1988.

Mishkinsky, Moshe. "The Jewish Labor Movement and European Socialism." In *Jewish Society through the Ages*, edited by Haim Hillel Ben-Sasson and Shmuel Ettinger, pp. 284–296. New York. Schocken, 1971.

Morgenstern, Arie. *Meshikhiyut ve-yishuv eretz Israel ba-mahatzit ha-rishona shel ha-mea ha-yod tet* (Messianism and settlement of Eretz Israel in the first half of the nineteenth century). Jerusalem: Yad Yitzhak Ben-Zvi, 1985.

————. "Messianic Concepts and Settlement in the Land of Israel." In *Vision and Conflict in the Holy Land*, edited by Richard I. Cohen, pp. 141–162. Jerusalem: Yad Yitzhak Ben-Zvi, 1985.

Myers, Jody Elizabeth. "Attitudes Towards a Resumption of Sacrificial Worship in the Nineteenth Century." *Modern Judaism* 7, no. 1 (February 1987), pp. 29–49.

————. "The Messianic Idea and Zionist Ideologies." In *Studies in Contemporary Jewry*, vol. 7, edited by Jonathan Frankel, pp. 3–13. New York: Oxford University Press, 1991.

————. "Seeking Zion: The Messianic Ideology of Zevi Hirsch Kalischer, 1795–1874." Ph.D. diss., Los Angeles, University of California, 1985.

Naaman, Shlomo. *Emanzipation und Messianismus: Leben und Werk des Moses Hess*. Frankfurt: Campus Verlag, 1982.

Nahorai, Michael Zvi. "Le-mahuta shel ha-tzionut ha-datit: Iyun be-mishnoteihem shel ha-rav Reines ve-ha-rav Kook" (On the essence of religious Zionism: An examination of the thought of Rabbi Reines and Rabbi Kook). In *Be-shvilei ha-tehiya: mehkarim ba-tzionut ha-datit* (In the paths of renewal: Studies in religious Zionism), vol. 3, edited by Mordechai Eliav, pp. 25–38. Ramat Gan: Bar Ilan University, 1988.

Near, Henry. "Mihu halutz?" (Who is a *halutz?*). *Tura* 2 (1992), pp. 228–248.

Nedava, Joseph. "Herzl and the Arab Problem." *Forum on the Jewish People, Zionism and Israel,* no. 27 (1977), pp. 64–72.

———, ed. *Abba Ahimeir: Ketavim nivharim* (Abba Ahimeier: Selected writings), vol. 3: *Brit ha-biryonim.* Tel Aviv: Shamgar Press, 1972.

Netanyahu, Benzion. *Max Nordau to His People.* New York: Scopus, 1941.

———, ed. *Road to Freedom: Writings and Addresses by Leo Pinsker.* New York: Scopus, 1944.

Nissenbaum, Yitzhak. *Alei heldi* (Pages from my life), 2nd ed. Jerusalem: Mass, 1969.

———. *Imrei drosh* (Homiletical essays). Warsaw: Grafia, 1926.

[Nissenbaum, Yitzhak]. *Ketavim nivharim: ma'amarei yesod be-tzionut u-be-yahadut* (Selected writings: Basic articles on Zionism and Judaism). Edited by Eliyahu Moshe Genihowski. Jerusalem: Levin-Epstein, 1948.

Noah, Mordecai Manuel. "Discourse on the Restoration of the Jews, Delivered at the Tabernacle, October 28, and December 2, 1844," New York: Harper & Brothers, 1845; reprinted in *Call to America to Build Zion,* New York: Arno Press, 1977.

Nordau, Max. *The Conventional Lies of Our Civilization,* 6th ed., translated from the German. Chicago: Laird and Lee, 1895.

———. *Die conventionellen Lügen der Kulturmenschheit,* 12th ed. Leipzig: B. Elischer, 1886.

———. *Zionistische Schriften.* Berlin: Jüdischer Verlag, 1923.

Oliphant, Laurence. *The Land of Gilead.* New York: Appleton, 1881.

Oren, Joseph. *Ahad Ha'am, M. J. Berdyczewski, ve-havurat "tzeirim": Igrot u-pishran, 1891–1896* (Ahad Ha'am, M. J. Berdyczewski and the "Tzeirim" group: Letters and their meaning). Tel Aviv: Yahad, 1985.

Orlan, Hayim. "The Participants in the First Zionist Congress," *Herzl Yearbook,* vol. 6, edited by Raphael Patai, pp. 133–152. New York: Herzl Press, 1964–65.

Otiker, Israel. *Tnuat he-halutz be-polin, 1932–1935* (The He-halutz movement in Poland, 1932–1935). Tel Aviv: Ha-Kibbutz Ha-Meuhad, 1972.

Parkes, James. *Whose Land? A History of Palestine,* rev. ed. London: Penguin, 1970.

Patai, Joseph. "Herzl's School Years," *Herzl Yearbook,* vol. 3, edited by Raphael Patai, pp. 53–75. New York: Herzl Press, 1960.

Patterson, David. "Ahad Ha'am and Smolenskin." In *At the Crossroads: Essays on Ahad Ha-Am ,* edited by Jacques Kornberg, pp. 36–45. Albany: State University of New York Press, 1983.

Pawel, Ernst. *The Labyrinth of Exile: A Life of Theodor Herzl.* New York: Farrar, Straus & Giroux, 1989.

Pines, Yehiel Michel. *Emet mi-eretz titzmah* (Truth shall spring forth out of the land). 2 vols. Edited by Pinhas M. Grajewski. Jerusalem: Hevrat Megine Eretz, 1895.

Pinson, Koppel S. "Arkady Kremer, Vladimir Medem, and the Ideology of the Jewish Bund." *Jewish Social Studies* 7 (1945), pp. 233–264.

———, ed. *Simon Dubnow: Nationalism and History.* Philadelphia: Jewish Publication Society, 1958.

Porath, Yehoshua. *Shelah ve-et be-yado* (Shelah with pen in hand). Tel Aviv: Mahbarot Le-Sifrut, 1989.

Rabin, Haim. "The National Idea and the Revival of Hebrew." *Studies in Zionism*, no. 7 (vol. 4 no. 1, spring 1983), pp. 31–48.

Rabinowicz, Oscar K. *Vladimir Jabotinsky's Conception of a Nation.* New York: The Beechhurst Press, 1946.

Rabinowitz, Shmuel Yaakov (son of Shimon Meir). *Ha-dat ve-ha-leumiyut* (Religion and nationalism). Warsaw: M. Y. Halter, 1900.

Radler-Feldman, Yehoshua (Rabbi Benjamin), ed. *Sefer Ussishkin* (The book of Ussishkin). Jerusalem: Ha-Va'ad Le-Hotza'at Ha-Sefer, 1934.

Rafaeli (Zanziper), Arye L. "Veidot artziot shel tzionei russia" (National conferences of Russian Zionists). In *Katzir: kovetz le-korot ha-tnua ha-tzionit be-russia* (Harvest: Anthology on the History of the Zionist Movement in Russia), pp. 43–102. Tel Aviv: Masada, 1964.

Raisin, Jacob S. *The Haskala Movement in Russia.* Philadelphia: Jewish Publication Society, 1913.

Raphael, Yitzhak. "Mi-igrot Zion" (From Zion's letters). *Sinai* 17 (1944), pp. 324–337.

Raphael, Yitzhak, and Shlomo Z. Shragai, eds. *Sefer ha-tzionut ha-datit* (The book of religious Zionism), vol. 1. Jerusalem: Mosad Harav Kook, 1977.

Ratosh, Yonatan. "The New Hebrew Nation (The Canaanite Outlook)." In *Unease in Zion*, edited by Ehud Ben-Ezer, pp. 201–234. New York: Quadrangle, 1974.

———. *Reishit ha-yamim, petihot ivriyot* (The first days, Hebrew beginnings). Tel Aviv: Hadar, 1982.

Ravitzky, Aviezer. *Ha-ketz ha-megule u-medinat ha-yehudim: Meshihiyut, tzionut ve-radikalizm dati be-Yisrael* (Messianism, Zionism and Jewish religious radicalism). Tel Aviv: Am Oved, 1993.

Reines, Yitzhak Yaakov. *Or hadash al Zion* (New light on Zion). Vilna: Re'em Press, 1901/2.

———. "Orhot Israel" (The ways of Israel). In *Beit ha-midrash: Mikdash le-tora u-le-hokhmat Israel* (The house of study: Sanctuary of the Torah and the wisdom of Israel), edited by Micha Joseph Bardyczewskaya, pp. 60–70. Cracow: Verlag von E. Graeber, 1888.

———. *Sha'arei ora ve-simha* (The gates of light and joy). Vilna: Re'em Press, 1899.

———. *Shnei ha-meorot* (The two luminaries). Piatrakov: Belchatowski Press, 1913.

Reinharz, Jehuda. *Chaim Weizmann: The Making of a Zionist Leader.* New York: Oxford University Press, 1985.

———. "Ideology and Structure in German Zionism 1881–1933." *Jewish Social Studies* 42 (1980), pp. 119–146.

———. "Martin Buber's Impact on German Zionism before World War I." *Studies in Zionism*, no. 6, (vol. 3 no. 2, autumn 1982), pp. 171–184.

Reinholt (Rinot), Hanoch. "Joseph Salvador: Hayav ve-deotav" (Joseph Salvador, his life and opinions). *Zion* 9 (1944), pp. 109–141.

Remba, Isaac. "Dat u-masoret be-hayav u-be-mahshavto" (Religion and tradition in his [Jabotinsky's] life and teaching). *Ha-uma* 3 (1964), pp. 146–166.

Report of the Executive of the Zionist Organisation Submitted to the 18th Zionist Congress at Prague, August 21–29, 1933. London: Central Office of the Zionist Organisation, 1933.

Rinott, Moshe. "Religion and Education: The Cultural Question and the Zionist Movement, 1897–1913." *Studies in Zionism*, no. 9 (vol. 5, no. 1, spring 1984), pp. 1–18.

Rivlin, Asher A. *Ahad Ha'am u-mitnagdav ve-hashkafoteihem al ha-sifrut ha-ivrit be-doram*

478   *Bibliography*

(Ahad Ha'am and his opponents and their views on the Hebrew literature of their generation). Tel Aviv: Dvir, 1954.

The Road to Bi-National Independence for Palestine. Tel Aviv: The Executive Committee of the Ha-shomer Ha-tzair Workers' Party, 1947.

Rogger, Hans. *Jewish Policies and Right-Wing Politics in Imperial Russia.* Berkeley: University of California, 1986.

Rose, Norman. *Chaim Weizmann: A Biography.* London: Penguin, 1986.

Rotenstreich, Nathan. "Galut ve-eretz le-Yaakov Klatzkin be-mivhan ha-zeman" (Jacob Klatzkin's *Exile and Land* with the test of time). *Bitzaron,* no. 24/25, 1985, pp. 38–46.

———. *Jewish Philosophy in Modern Times.* New York: Holt Rinehart & Winston, 1968.

Rubinstein, Avraham. "Pa'amei mashiah ve-hevlei mashiah be-mishnato shel ha-rav Yitzhak Nissenbaum" (The heartbeat of the messiah and the travails of the messianic coming in the thought of Rabbi Yitzhak Nissenbaum). *(Sefer) Shragai* 1 (1981), pp. 118–126.

Salmon, Yosef. "Ahad Ha-Am and Bnei Moshe: An 'Unsuccessful Experiment?'" In *At the Crossroads: Essays on Ahad Ha-Am,* edited by Jacques Kornberg, pp. 98–105. Albany: State University of New York Press, 1983.

———. "Aliyata shel ha-leumiyut ha-yehudit be-merkaz Europa u-be-ma'arava" (The rise of Jewish nationalism in central and western Europe). *Ha-tzionut* 12 (1987), pp. 7–16.

———. *Dat ve-tzionut: Imutim rishonim* (Religion and Zionism: First encounters). Jerusalem: Ha-Sifriya Ha-Tzionit, 1990.

———. "Ha-rav Shmuel Mohilewer: Rabam shel Hovevei Zion" (Rabbi Shmuel Mohilewer, the rabbi of Hovevei Zion). *Zion* 56 (1991), pp. 47–78.

———. "Ha-tzionut ha-datit u-mitnagdeha: Masoret u-moderniyut, meshihiyut ve-romantika" (Religious Zionism and its opponents: Tradition and modernity, messianism and romanticism). *Zemanim,* no. 14 (1984), pp. 60–69.

———. "The Rise of Jewish Nationalism on the Border of Eastern and Western Europe." In *Danzig: Between East and West,* edited by Isadore Twersky, pp. 123–137. Cambridge, Mass.: Harvard University Press, 1985.

———. "Yehiel Michel Pines: From the Vision of Zionism to the Reality." *Modern Judaism* 8, no. 1 (February 1988), pp. 65–82.

Samet, Moshe. "The Beginnings of Orthodoxy." *Modern Judaism* 8, no. 3 (October 1988), pp. 249–270.

Sarna, Jonathan D. *Jacksonian Jew: The Two Worlds of Mordecai Noah.* New York: Holmes & Meier, 1981.

Schama, Simon. *Two Rothschilds and the Land of Israel.* New York: A. A. Knopf, 1978.

Schechter, S. Zvi. "Nimukeihem shel rabbanim bead shituf peula im ha-'maskilim' be-tnuat 'Hibbat Zion'" (Rabbinical reasons for cooperation with the "Enlightened" in Hibbat Zion). *Mehkarim be-toldot am yisrael ve-Eretz Israel* (Studies in the history of the Jewish people and Eretz Israel) 4 (1978), pp. 239–251.

Schechtman, Joseph B. *The Life and Times of Vladimir Jabotinsky.* Vol. 1. *Rebel and Statesman: The Early Years;* vol. 2. *Fighter and Prophet: The Last Years.* Silver Spring, Md.: Eshel Books, 1986.

———. *Ze-ev Jabotinsky: Parashat hayav* (Ze'ev Jabotinsky: The story of his life). 3 vols. Tel Aviv: Karni, 1956.

Schechtman, Joseph B., and Y. Benari. *History of the Revisionist Movement,* vol. 1. Tel Aviv: Hadar, 1970.

Schweid, Eliezer. *Demokratia ve-halakha: Pirkei iyun be-mishnato shel ha-rav Haim*

Hirschensohn (Democracy and *halakha*: Studies in the thought of Rabbi Haim Hirschensohn). Jerusalem: Magnes Press, 1978.

————. *Ha-yahadut ve-ha-tarbut ha-hilonit* (Judaism and secular culture). Tel Aviv: Ha-Kibbutz Ha-Meuhad, 1981.

————. *Ha-yahid: Olamo shel A. D. Gordon* (The individual: The world of A. D. Gordon). Tel Aviv: Am Oved, 1970.

————. "Martin Buber and A. D. Gordon: A Comparison." In *Martin Buber: A Centenary Volume*, edited by Haim Gordon and Jochanan Bloch, pp. 255–272. New York: Ketav, 1984.

————. *Toldot ha-hagut ha-yehudit ba-eit ha-hadasha* (A history of Jewish thought in the modern period). Tel Aviv and Jerusalem: Ha-Kibbutz Ha-Meuhad & Keter, 1977.

————. *Toldot ha-hagut ha-yehudit ba-mea ha-esrim* (A history of Jewish thought in the twentieth century). Tel Aviv: Dvir, 1990.

Sefer da'at ha-rabbanim (The book of rabbinic opinion). Warsaw: Yaakov Unterhendler Press, 1902.

Seliger, Martin. "Fundamental and Operative Ideology: The Two Principal Dimensions of Political Argumentation." *Policy Sciences* 1 (1970), pp. 325–338.

Seton-Watson, Hugh. *Nations and States: An Enquiry into the Origins of Nations and the Politics of Nationalism*. London: Methuen, 1977.

Shaari, David. *Mi-"stam tzionut" le-"tzionut klalit"* (From plain Zionism to General Zionism). Jerusalem: Mass, 1990.

Shaerf, Moshe. "Herzl's Social Thinking," *Herzl Yearbook*, vol. 3, edited by Raphael Patai, pp. 199–206. New York: Herzl Press, 1960.

Shapira, Anita. *Berl: The Biography of a Socialist Zionist*. Cambridge: Cambridge University Press, 1984.

————. "'Black Night–White Snow': Attitudes of the Palestinian Labor Movement to the Russian Revolution, 1917–1929." In *Studies in Contemporary Jewry*, vol. 4, edited by Jonathan Frankel, pp. 144–171. New York: Oxford University Press, 1988.

————. "The Dynamics of Zionist Leftist Trends." In *Jewish History: Essays in Honour of Chimen Abramsky*, edited by Ada Rapoport-Albert and Steven J. Zipperstein, pp. 629–682. London: P. Halban, 1988.

————. "Labor Zionism and the October Revolution." *Journal of Contemporary History* 24 (1989), pp. 623–656.

————. *Land and Power: The Zionist Resort to Force, 1881–1948*. New York: Oxford University Press, 1992.

Shapira, Yeshayahu. "Gordon and Gordonia." In *Gordonia: Tnuat noar amamit halutzit* (Gordonia: The people's pioneering youth movement: An anthology), pp. 172–180. Hulda: Pinhas Lavon Archives of Gordonia-Maccabi Ha-Tzair, 1982.

Shapira, Yosef. *Chaim Arlosoroff*. Tel Aviv: Am Oved, 1975.

————. *Ha-poel ha-tzair: ha-ra'ayon ve-hama'ase* (Ha-poel Ha-tzair: The idea and the practice). Tel Aviv: Ayanot, 1967.

Shatzker, Haim. "Tnuat ha-noar be-germaniya bein ha-shanim 1900–1933" (The Jewish youth movement in Germany in the years 1900–1933). Ph.D. diss., Hebrew University of Jerusalem, 1969.

Shavit, Yaacov. *Ha-mitologiot shel ha-yamin* (The mythologies of the Right). Tel Aviv: Emda Library, 1986.

————. *Jabotinsky and the Revisionist Movement, 1925–1948*. London: Cass, 1988.

————. *Mi-ivri ad kena'ani* (From Hebrew to Canaanite). Tel Aviv: Domino, 1984.

————. *Mi-rov le-medina: Ha-tnua he-revizionistit, ha-tokhniet ha-hityashvutit ve-ha-ra'ayon ha-hevrati* (From majority to statehood: the Revisionist movement, its settlement program and social ideas). Tel Aviv: Yariv-Hadar, 1978.

———. *The New Hebrew Nation: A Study in Israeli Heresy and Fantasy.* London: Cass, 1987.

———. "Uri Zvi Greenberg: Conservative Revolutionarism and National Messianism." *The Jerusalem Quarterly*, no. 48 (fall 1988), pp. 63–72.

Shazar, Zalman. "Yehezkel Kaufmann u-foalo" (Yehezkel Kaufmann and his work). *Ha-doar* 43 (13 Kislev 5724 [1963]), pp. 59–61.

Sheps, Shmuel. "Mishnato ha-filosofit shel Yaakov Klatzkin" (The philosophy of Jacob Klatzkin). *Brit ivrit olamit Kenes 2*, pp. 145–152. Jerusalem, 1983.

Shils, Edward. *The Intellectuals and the Powers and Other Essays.* Chicago and London: University of Chicago Press, 1972.

———. "Primordial, Personal, Sacred and Civil Ties." *British Journal of Sociology* 7 (1957), pp. 113–145.

Shimoni, Gideon. *Gandhi, Satyagraha and the Jews.* Jerusalem: Hebrew University, 1977.

Shneersohn, Shalom Dov Ber. *Kuntres u-ma'ayan mi-beit adonai* (A tract on: And a fount from the house of the Lord). Brooklyn, N.Y.: Otzar Ha-Hasidim, 1943.

Silber, Michael. "The Historical Experience of German Jewry and Its Impact on Haskalah and Reform in Hungary." In *Towards Modernity: The European Jewish Model,* edited by Jacob Katz, pp. 107–157. New Brunswick, N.J., and Oxford: Transaction Books, 1987.

Silberner, Edmund. "Austrian Social Democracy and the Jewish Problem." *Historia Judaica* 13, no. 2 (October 1951), pp. 121–140.

———. *Moses Hess: Geschichte seines Lebens.* Leiden: Brill, 1966.

Silberstein, Lawrence J. "Historical Sociology and Ideology: A Prolegomenon to Yehezkel Kaufmann's *Golah v'Nekhar.*" In *Essays in Modern Jewish History: A Tribute to Ben Halpern,* edited by Francis Malino and Phyllis Cohen Albert, pp. 173–195. East Brunswick, N.J.: Associated Universities Presses, 1982.

———. "Religion, Ethnicity and Jewish History: The Contribution of Yehezkel Kaufmann." *Journal of the American Academy of Religion* 42, no. 3 (September 1974), pp. 516–531.

Sills, David L., ed. *International Encyclopedia of the Social Sciences.* New York: Macmillan Co. & Free Press, 1968.

Simon, Ernst A. *Kav ha-tihum: Leumiyut, tzionut, ve-ha-sikhsukh ha-yehudi-aravi be-mishnat Martin Buber u-vi-feiluto* (The line of demarcation: Nationalism, Zionism and the Arab-Israeli conflict in the thought and deeds of Martin Buber). Givat Haviva: The Center for Arab Studies, 1973.

Simon, Leon. *Ahad Ha-am: A Biography.* London: East & West Library, 1960.

Simon, Aryeh (Leon), and Joseph Eliyahu Heller. *Ahad Ha'am, ha-ish, poalo ve-torato* (Ahad Ha'am, the man, his work and his theory). Jerusalem: Magnes Press, 1955.

Slutzki, Abraham Yaakov, ed. *Shivat Zion* (Return to Zion). Warsaw: M. Y. Halter, 1891–92.

Slutzky, Yehuda. *Ha-itonut ha-yehudit-russit ba-mea ha-tsha-esrei* (The Russian Jewish press in the nineteenth century). Jerusalem: Mosad Bialik, 1970.

———. *Mavo le-toldot tnuat ha-poalim ha-yisraelit* (An introduction to the history of the Israeli labor movement). Tel Aviv: Am Oved, 1973.

———. "Tzmihata shel ha-intelligentzia ha-yehudit-russit" (The growth of the Russian Jewish intelligentsia). *Zion* 25 (1960), pp. 212–237.

————, ed. *Poalei Zion be-Eretz Israel, 1905–1919* (Poalei Zion in Palestine, 1905–1919). Tel Aviv: University of Tel Aviv, 1978.

Smith, Anthony D. *The Ethnic Origins of Nations.* Oxford: Blackwell, 1986.

————. "The Myth of the 'Modern Nation' and the Myths of Nations." *Ethnic and Racial Studies* 11, no. 1 (January 1988), pp. 1–26.

————. "Nationalism and Religion: The Role of Religious Reform in the Genesis of Arab and Jewish Nationalism." *Archives de Sciences Sociales des Religions* 35 (1973), pp. 23–43.

————. *Theories of Nationalism,* 2nd ed. London: Duckworth, 1983.

————, ed. *Nationalism in the Twentieth Century.* London: Robertson, 1979.

————, ed. *Nationalist Movements.* London: Macmillan, 1976.

Smolenskin, Peretz. *Ma'amarim* (Articles). 4 vols. Jerusalem: Keren Smolenskin, 1925–1926.

Sokolow, Nahum. *History of Zionism, 1600–1918.* New York: Ketav, 1969.

Sorkin, David. *The Transformation of German Jewry, 1780–1840.* New York: Oxford University Press, 1987.

Stalin, Joseph. *Marxism and the National and Colonial Question,* 2nd ed. London: Lawrence, 1947.

Stanislawski, Michael. *Tsar Nicholas I and the Jews: The Transformation of Jewish Society in Russia, 1825–1855.* Philadelphia: Jewish Publication Society, 1983.

Stenographisches Protokoll der Verhandlungen des I Zionisten-Kongresses in Basel, August 1987, 2nd ed. Prague, 1911.

Stenographisches Protokoll der Verhandlungen des II Zionisten-Kongresses. Vienna, 1898.

Stenographisches Protokoll der Verhandlungen des III Zionisten-Kongresses gehalten zu Basel, August 1899. Vienna, 1899.

Stenographisches Protokoll der Verhandlungen des V Zionisten-Kongresses in Basel, Dezember 1901. Vienna, 1901.

Stenographisches Protokoll der Verhandlungen des VI Zionisten-Kongresses in Basel, 23–28 August 1903. Vienna, 1903.

Stenographisches Protokoll der Verhandlungen des IX Zionisten-Kongresses in Hamburg, December 1909. Cologne, 1910.

Stenographisches Protokoll der Verhandlungen des XII Zionisten-Kongresses in Karlsbad, 1–14 September 1921. Berlin, 1921.

Stenographisches Protokoll der Verhandlungen des 17 Zionististen-Kongresses, Basel, 30 June to 17 July 1931. London, 1931.

Stewart, Desmond. *Theodor Herzl: Artist and Politician: A Biography of the Father of Modern Israel.* New York: Doubleday, 1974.

Stone, Julius. *Israel and Palestine.* Baltimore: Johns Hopkins University Press, 1981.

Syrkin, Marie. *Nahman Syrkin Socialist Zionist: A Biographical Memoir, Selected Essays.* New York: Herzl Press & Sharon Books, 1961.

[Syrkin, Nahman]. *Kitvei Nahman Syrkin* (Writings of Nahman Syrkin). Edited by Berl Katznelson and Yehuda Kaufman. Tel Aviv: Dvir, 1939.

Szajkowski, Zosa. "The Pacifism of Judah Magnes." *Conservative Judaism* 22 (spring 1968), pp. 36–55.

Tabenkin, Yitzhak. *Devarim* (Writings). 7 vols. Tel Aviv: Ha-Kibbutz Ha-Meuhad, 1967–1972.

Taylor, Anne. *Laurence Oliphant, 1829–1888.* Oxford: Oxford University Press, 1982.

Teitelbaum, Yoel. *Sefer va-yoel Moshe* (The book of Va-Yoel Moshe). Brooklyn, N.Y.: Deitsch, 1961.

Teveth, Shabtai. *Ben-Gurion and the Palestinian Arabs*. Oxford: Oxford University Press, 1985.

―――. *Ben-Gurion: The Burning Ground, 1886–1948*. London: Robert Hale, 1987.

―――. "Ideology, Naivete, or Pragmatism." In *David Ben-Gurion: Politics and Leadership in Israel*, edited by Ronald W. Zweig, pp. 69–84. London: Cass, 1991.

Tirosh, Yosef, ed. *Religious Zionism: An Anthology*. Jerusalem: World Zionist Organization, 1975.

Tobias, Henry J. *The Jewish Bund in Russia: From Its Origins to 1905*. Stanford, Calif.: Stanford University Press, 1972.

Tomaschoff, Avner, ed. *Whose Homeland: Eretz Israel Roots of the Jewish Claim*. Jerusalem: Ha-Mishmeret Ha-Tzeira, Ha-Mizarahi & Ha-Poel Ha-Mizrahi, 1980.

Toynbee, Arnold. J. "Jewish Rights in Palestine." *Jewish Quarterly Review* 52 no. 1 (July 1961), pp. 1–11.

Tschernowitz, Shmuel. *Bnei Moshe u-tekufatam* (Bnei Moshe and their times). Warsaw: Ha-tzefira Press, 1914.

Tsivion, Avraham. *Diukano ha-yehudi shel Berl Katznelson* (The Jewish portrait of Berl Katznelson). Tel Aviv: Sifriyat Ha-Poalim, 1984.

Tuchman, Barbara W. *Bible and Sword*. New York: Macmillan, 1956.

Tzahor, Ze'ev. *Ba-derekh le-hanhagat ha-yishuv: Ha-histadrut be-reishita* (On the road to *yishuv* leadership: The Histadrut's beginnings). Jerusalem: Yad Yitzhak Ben-Zvi, 1982.

[Ussishkin, Menahem]. *Our Program: An Essay by M. Ussischkin [sic]*. Translated by D. S. Blondheim. New York: Federation of American Zionists, 1905.

Vital, David. *The Origins of Zionism*. Oxford: Clarendon Press, 1975.

―――. *Zionism: The Formative Years*. Oxford: Clarendon Press, 1982.

Vlavianos, Basil J., and Feliks Gross, eds. *Struggle for Tomorrow: Modern Political Ideologies of the Jewish People*. New York: Arts Inc., 1954.

Volcani, Yitzhak. *Kitvei Yitzhak Elazari-Volcani (A. Tzioni)*. Vol. 2: *Sefirot* (Emanations). Tel Aviv: Tverski, 1950.

Volkov, Shulamit. "Moses Hess: Problems of Religion and Faith." *Zionism*, no. 3 (vol. 2, no. 1, spring 1981), pp. 1–16.

Waxman, Mordecai, ed. *Tradition and Change: The Development of Conservative Judaism*. New York: Burning Bush Press, 1958.

Weinryb, Bernard Dov. "Noah's Ararat Jewish State in Its Historical Setting." *Publications of the American Jewish Historical Society (American Jewish History)* 43 (1953/4), pp. 170–190.

―――. "Tzionut etzel yehudei germaniya be-tekufat ha-haskala" (Zionism among Jews in Germany in the period of the *Haskala*). *Knesset le-zekher Bialik* 1 (1936), pp. 465–478.

―――. "Yesodot ha-tzionut ve-toldoteha" (The foundations of Zionism and its history). *Tarbiz* 8 (1937), pp. 69–113.

Weisbord, Robert G. *Africa Zion*. Philadelphia: Jewish Publication Society, 1968.

[Weizmann, Chaim]. "Evidence of Dr. Chaim Weizmann." In *The Jewish Plan for Palestine: Memoranda and Statements Presented by the Jewish Agency for Palestine to the United Nations Special Committee on Palestine*, pp. 525–555. Jerusalem, 1947.

[Weizmann, Chaim]. *The Letters and Papers of Chaim Weizmann*, 25 vols. Series A: *Letters*, vols. 1–23 (1968–1979), Meyer W. Weisgal, general editor. Series B: *Papers*, vols. 24–25 (1983–1984), Barnett Litvinoff, general editor. London, Jerusalem, New Brunswick, N.J.: Oxford University Press; Israel Universities Press; Transaction Books, 1968–1984.

Weltsch, Felix. *Allgemeiner Zionismus: Eine Ideologische Skizze (General Zionism: An ideological sketch)*. Prague: Studenska tiskarna, c. 1936.

———. *Das Wagnis der Mitte: Ein Beitrag zur Ethik und Politik der Zeit* (The daring of the middle way: A contribution to the ethics and politics of the times). Stuttgart: Kohlhammer, 1936.

Wistrich, Robert. "Eduard Bernstein and the Jewish Problem." *Jahrbuch des Instituts für deutsche Geschichte*, vol. 8, pp. 243–256. Tel Aviv: Tel Aviv University, 1979.

———. "Marxism and Jewish Nationalism: The Theoretical Roots of Confrontation." *The Jewish Journal of Sociology* 17, no. 1 (June 1975), pp. 34–54.

Wolfsberg (Aviad), Yeshayahu. *Ha-mizrahi, ha-poel ha-mizrahi*. Jerusalem: Ha-Makhon Le-Haskala Tzionit, 1946.

Yaron, Zvi. *The Philosophy of Rabbi Kook*. Translated by Avner Tomaschoff. Jerusalem: World Zionist Organization, 1991.

Yavnieli, Shmuel, ed. *Tekufat Hibbat Zion* (The Hibbat Zion period). 2 vols. Jerusalem: Mosad Bialik, 1961.

[Yevin, Yehoshua Heschel]. *Ketavim* (Writings). 2 vols. Tel Aviv: Ha-Va'ada Le-Hotza'at Kitvei Yevin, 1969.

Yevin, Yehoshua Heschel. *Uri Zvi Greenberg meshorer mehokek* (Uri Zvi Greenberg, poet legislator). Tel Aviv: Sedan, 1938.

Yisraeli, David. *Ha-"reich" ha-germani ve-eretz Israel, 1889–1945* (The German Reich and Eretz Israel, 1889–1945). Ramat Gan: Bar-Ilan University, 1974.

Zait, David. *Tzionut be-darkhei shalom* (Zionism and peace). Tel Aviv: Sifriyat Ha-Poalim, 1985.

Zeitlin, Solomon. "Jewish Rights in Eretz Israel (Palestine)." *Jewish Quarterly Review* 52, no. 1 (July 1961), pp. 12–34.

Zimmermann, Moshe. "Jewish Nationalism and Zionism in German Jewish Students' Organizations." *Leo Baeck Institute Yearbook*, vol. 27, pp. 129–153. London: Secker & Warburg, 1982.

———. "Mivne hevrati ve-tzipiyot hevratiyot ba-tzionut ha-germanit lifnei milhemet ha-olam ha-rishona" (Social structure and social prognosis in German Zionism before World War I). In *Uma ve-toldoteha* (The nation and its history; Compendium of articles arising from the Eighth World Congress of Jewish Studies). Part 2: *The Modern Period*, edited by Shmuel Ettinger, pp. 177–199. Jerusalem: Merkaz Shazar, 1984.

Zipperstein, Steven J. "Ahad Ha-'am's Politics." *Jewish History* 4, no. 2 (fall 1990), pp. 89–96.

———. *Elusive Prophet: Ahad Ha'am and the Origins of Zionism*. Berkeley: University of California Press, 1993.

———. "Haskala, Cultural Change, and Nineteenth-Century Russian Jewry: A Reassessment." *Journal of Jewish Studies* 34, no. 2 (autumn 1983), pp. 191–207.

Zlocisti, Theodor. *Moses Hess: Der Vorkämpfer des Sozialismus und Zionismus, 1812–1875*. Berlin: Welt Verlag, 1921.

———, ed. *Moshe Hess u-venei doro* (Moses Hess and his contemporaries). Translated by Getzel Kressel. Tel Aviv: Am Oved, 1947.

Zweig, Ronald W., ed. *David Ben-Gurion: Politics and Leadership in Israel*. London: Cass, 1991.

Index